Decolonization, Sovereignty, and Peacekeeping

Hanny Hilmy

Decolonization, Sovereignty, and Peacekeeping

The United Nations Emergency Force
(UNEF), 1956–1967

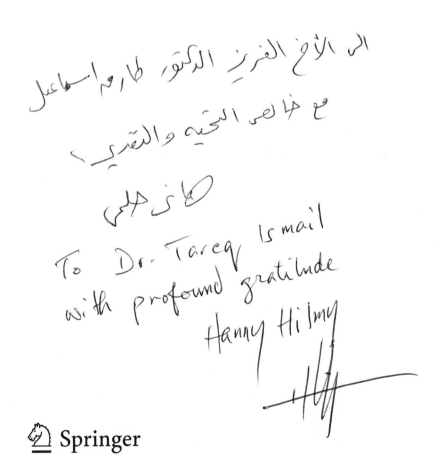

الى الاخ العزيز الدكتور طارق اسماعيل

مع خالص التحيه والتقدير

على كل المحبة

To Dr. Tareq Ismail
with profound gratitude
Hanny Hilmy

🐎 Springer

Hanny Hilmy
Centre for Global Studies
University of Victoria
Victoria, BC, Canada

ISBN 978-3-030-57623-3   ISBN 978-3-030-57624-0   (eBook)
https://doi.org/10.1007/978-3-030-57624-0

© Springer Nature Switzerland AG 2020
This work is subject to copyright. All rights are reserved by the Publisher, whether the whole or part of the material is concerned, specifically the rights of translation, reprinting, reuse of illustrations, recitation, broadcasting, reproduction on microfilms or in any other physical way, and transmission or information storage and retrieval, electronic adaptation, computer software, or by similar or dissimilar methodology now known or hereafter developed.
The use of general descriptive names, registered names, trademarks, service marks, etc. in this publication does not imply, even in the absence of a specific statement, that such names are exempt from the relevant protective laws and regulations and therefore free for general use.
The publisher, the authors and the editors are safe to assume that the advice and information in this book are believed to be true and accurate at the date of publication. Neither the publisher nor the authors or the editors give a warranty, expressed or implied, with respect to the material contained herein or for any errors or omissions that may have been made. The publisher remains neutral with regard to jurisdictional claims in published maps and institutional affiliations.

Copyediting: PD Dr. Hans Günter Brauch, AFES-PRESS e.V., Mosbach, Germany
Language editing: Dr. Vanessa Greatorex, Chester, UK

The external cover page photo. Credit: UN Photo, "U.N. Secretary-General Visits Brazilian Contingent of UNEF", Rafah, Gaza, December 1958. UN Photo # 117407. Authorized by: United Nations Photo Library Department of Global Communications UNHQ Secretariat New York, NY 10017. The internal title page photo depicting the battle for Al-Gamil Airport in November 1956 was taken by: Ashraf Fawzi and permission to use it here was given by: Public Domain, Port Said War Museum, Egypt. More on this book is at: http://afes-press-books.de/html/SA_06.htm

This Springer imprint is published by the registered company Springer Nature Switzerland AG
The registered company address is: Gewerbestrasse 11, 6330 Cham, Switzerland

To my wife

Marjukka (Välimaa) Hilmy

With Love and Respect

To my daughters

Nadine and Nora,

*With love that cannot be quantified
or surpassed*

To my late father

General and Ambassador Amin Hilmy II

With Eternal Love

Foreword

The matching of scholar and subject is not often as seamless as that exhibited by Hanny Hilmy's *Decolonization, Sovereignty, and Peacekeeping: The United Nations Emergency Force (UNEF), 1956–1967*. His examination of this underexplored era of the early Cold War in the Middle East provides both a robust empirical portrait of the events emerging from the 1956 attack on Suez by Britain, France and Israel and the conceptual and theoretical insights these events cast on our understandings of the international relations of the post-colonial era and the evolution of state autonomy within the emergent global system following the Second World War. Hilmy's work moves beyond the 1956 conflict itself and does not chase the personal politics of the era's larger-than-life figures such as Nasser and his clash with a retreating European hegemony that was transitioning to a Cold War between the United States and the Soviet Union. Rather, Hilmy's work crafts a basis by which the reader can look anew at regional explorations of Nasserism, other pan-Arab movements and more localized variants of Arab nationalism through their ability to mobilize Arabs in the numbers required to create new vistas for state sovereignty and citizenship across the newly independent states of the region. His focus remains on Egypt, with the lessons of its experience a touchstone for a re-examination of the period across the entire region. This period has not received the detailed examination it warrants in English and French scholarship, for while Arabic sources are richly informed by biography and memoirs, they lack much critical thought as well as synthetic works in the manner provided here.

Through his examination of the United Nations Emergency Force (UNEF) between 1956 and 1967, Hanny's work centres peacekeeping not as a palliative salve to the breakdown of international order as it is most often presented, but rather as an intervention that constitutes and asserts order through its challenge to the legitimate sovereign authority of the state in which it is operationalized. His examination of the relations between an Egypt still asserting its independence from foreign meddling on the one hand, and the United Nations and some of its most powerful member states on the other, queries the role of UNEF as a vehicle to insert these actors' authority into Egypt under the blue banner of the United Nations in a manner that would have been unacceptable were it flagged by the states animating the effort. Rather, in

Hilmy's telling, such a mission is shown to have been at the direction of the powerful challenged Egyptian sovereignty, especially when viewed from the perspective of Egypt's protracted struggle to secure freedom for its people and to safeguard its sovereignty and independence at the end of European imperial influence. By problematizing the peacekeeping variable, Hilmy's work provides contrasting views on sovereignty and the international responsibility for peace and security from a distinct position, challenging Anglo and American assumptions as well as characterizations of the UK, US and Israeli actions over the period of the study.

Hanny brings considerable credibility to an examination of these topics through the rigorous research conducted during his Ph.D. studies, but also through the decades of focus on these events informed by his diplomatic insight as well as his exposure to the period through his father's military experience in Egypt during Hanny's youth. The formative experience of first-hand exposure to senior Egyptian military officers and diplomats, exhibited through the service rendered to Egypt by his father, was then extended by his own extensive involvement in the diplomatic field, where the legacy of decisions made over this pivotal period in the Middle East seriously restrained the future possibilities for Egypt, and framed and informed this study. Hanny's ability to bring his own international experience and considerable analytic capabilities to the subject stand out in a unique exposé with an analytical approach informed by more than the archival documentary record.

My first encounter with Hanny came when he attended the Canadian-Arab Relations Conference in June 1981 at the University of Calgary. This gathering of academics and diplomats examined relations between the two regions as well as contemporary scholarship on the Middle East region by academics based at Canadian and US institutions. As a coordinating participant, Hanny was a consummate professional and his personal humility and open manner affected those in attendance and made positive contributions to the work of the Conference. In several capitals, Hilmy provided effective representation to the Arab League and to Egypt during the escalating Arab-Israeli conflict. Following his diplomatic career, and having earned an MA degree in international relations from the University of Pennsylvania in the USA, Hanny studied for a Ph.D. at the University of Victoria (Canada), where I was delighted to serve as his external examiner. He is to be commended for the rigour and depth of analysis provided in this richly empirical examination of the topic. While trained in many aspects of international affairs, Hilmy's project can be located within the traditions of both comparative politics and international relations theory, buttressed by outstanding archival and other empirical research, all anchored within a critical approach directed at the pivotal period of 1956–67 that he has developed over a lifetime.

While much historical scholarship has been stymied by a marked lack of access to original archival material on Egyptian and other Arab state responses to the growing Cold War tensions of the period, Hilmy brings insights from unearthed documents, his direct encounters with involved participants, and many important interviews as well as his own diplomatic service experience. In doing so he advances our field with an empirically rich analysis of the divergent political and diplomatic trajectories taken by Egypt in the pivotal first decade of the Cold War as it emerged as a fully independent state navigating its sovereignty within an emergent global order.

His work fills in several gaps in the historical record and sheds new light on a number of key issues and events, ultimately culminating in a sweeping explanation of why Egypt turned so decisively towards pan-Arabism, Third Worldism and the Non-Aligned Movement. Egypt's experience with UNEF was not the sole experience informing state posture towards foreign relations or state-society relations in a rapidly developing post-colonial nation, but Hilmy adroitly nods to its role in fortifying a policy of active or positive neutrality as well as that of pan-Arabism, thereby enabling it to remain independent of Western intervention. Tying these materials to an evaluation of Egyptian sovereignty and its connection to regional and foreign policy decision-making across the 1950s, Hilmy has extended our knowledge and provided a signpost to encourage further research on this important period for a greater understanding of Egypt and potentially that of other regional states attempting to construct a regional order.

Beyond the book's empirical contributions, Hilmy's problematization of peacekeeping in this manner provides a substantial theoretical reframing of the role of foreign intervention within the sovereign affairs of Egypt. Through his examination Hilmy highlights the bond between foreign policy and national discourse, a connection often unnoticed in contemporary political science examinations of Egypt in this period. The new regime's national legitimacy after 1952 was largely contingent on its success in garnering recognition in the international arena, which required the credible legitimacy arising from sovereign control over its territory. Egyptian policy after the 1952 Free Officers revolution clearly fits this mould, and therefore Hilmy's study is well positioned to provide the reader with a more clear-eyed examination of the regime's position and policy preferences as they were articulated over the decade that followed 1956. An understanding of Egyptian policy and action cannot be examined within the context of internal debates about national identity formation alone; it is also necessary to grasp the significance of the opportunities and constraints provided by UNEF intervention in an era of global transition between decolonization and the direct action of the two competing blocs of the Cold War superpowers.

Hilmy has provided a challenging and provocative comparative work that succeeds in casting new light on the policy behaviour of Egypt as it fulfilled its role as a key player in the 1950s Middle East. The book is deeply researched and exceedingly rich in its empirical contributions, allowing Hilmy to succeed in reconstructing a number of key events from the period with a great deal of nuance, deep understanding and clear correction that enable the reader to better comprehend the events that were to follow. Very few readers today can grasp the context and its meaning to the generation of Arabs who lived through independence from European imperialism, the hope that it brought to inform seemingly wide horizons of potential development and growth, and the challenges of forging a place within the bipolar environment of the 1950s. There are still some remnants of the optimism of that era, but there is a larger residue of the failed regional order that would follow, as well as dramatic declines in the hope for the future following 1967 and then 1990. Hanny's bold and brilliantly researched interpretation of the role played by UNEF during the early Cold War thus has a significance which extends well beyond Egypt and its influence over the Arab-Israeli conflict. Continued Western intervention across the region remains a critical dimension in the history of the modern international relations of the Middle East. A remarkable book, *Decolonization, Sovereignty, and Peacekeeping: The United Nations Emergency Force (UNEF), 1956–1967*, is thus both a major contribution to the history of modern Egypt and an inspiration for similar exciting and demanding research in other parts of the modern Arab world.

Tareq Y. Ismael
Secretary-General of the International
Association of Middle Eastern
Studies (IAMES)

Professor of Political Science
University of Calgary
Alberta, Canada

Preface

Readers will come to this volume with diverse interests and perspectives, but all who engage attentively with it will find it to be a unique, multifaceted study with original historical insights and pressing questions regarding international peace-keeping. In it, Hanny Hilmy focuses primarily on the establishment of the United Nations Emergency Force (commonly known as UNEF I) and on its evolution within the relationship between Nasserite Egypt and the United Nations Organization. Yet in the process of contextualizing that first instance of what would become a long string of the UN's armed peacekeeping operation, the author also unpicks several closely intertwined historical threads, including: the complex decades-long, late-colonial processes leading to the 1956 Israeli-British-French invasion of the Suez Canal Zone and other Egyptian territories; the ensuing Suez Crisis itself as an era-defining event in international relations generally and in Arab-Israeli relations in particular; and, throughout the period under examination, the shifting dynamics of upper-echelon Egyptian politics. This last topic the author approaches as one who in his youth observed those dynamics first-hand, from 1952, when the Free Officers' Movement assumed power, through to and beyond the Six Day War of June 1967. In addition, drawing on his later diplomatic experience with the Arab League and the Egyptian government and on his interdisciplinary academic formation, Dr. Hilmy presents a set of wide-ranging thematic reflections on the UN's peacekeeping record and on the conditions for the success of future peacekeeping operations.

The post-Second World War collapse of the European colonial empires, which provides the background to the developments under discussion in this work, was one of the most striking changes in power relations that unfolded during the twentieth century. Consider that, prior to the First World War, colonial rule and the ideologies of racial and religious superiority that supported it were taken for granted as accepted features of the 'civilized' world-order by the statesmen of the Great Powers as well as by most educated public opinion in the West. Yet, by the beginning of the twenty-first century, the institutions of direct colonialism had come to be largely abandoned in principle and were indeed often heartily reviled. This is not the place to rehearse in any detail the complex decades-long course of anti-colonial struggle, commencing effectively in the twentieth century's first decade and extending into the 1990s, but keeping the decolonization process in mind may be helpful as one approaches the story Hilmy tells and the perspectives he brings to it. In 1946, on the eve of the Cold War, the world featured four powers of global significance—the US and the USSR to be sure, but also the British Empire and the French Empire as reconstituted after the wartime occupations. Thirty years later, with the late dismantlement of Portugal's African empire, many people had come to consider colonial rule a relic of a bygone age. That the Suez Crisis of 1956 constituted a turning point in the process of twentieth-century decolonization and the demise of European colonial rule is something of a commonplace among historians, even if the exact role it played in that process remains a matter of debate. By the time the Crisis occurred, movements for independence and national liberation had already successfully ejected Britain, the Netherlands and France—the powers with the most populous empires—from nearly all their colonial territories in South and South-East Asia. Most dramatically, India and Pakistan had won independence from Britain in 1947, albeit tragically, via the bloody path of Partition; the Netherlands under American pressure had had to give up its attempts to continue ruling most of present-day Indonesia; and France, having waged a gruelling eight-year attempt to hold on to Indochina militarily, had finally surrendered its claims to Vietnam, Cambodia and Laos at the 1954 Geneva Conferences. In the Middle East, Syria and Lebanon had gained independence from France in 1946, and Britain's renunciation of authority over the Palestine Mandate was followed in 1948 by the establishment of the state of Israel, which was quickly recognized by both the USSR and the US, each inclined for its own reasons to weaken the British hold on the region. That change, and the searing tensions fed by the Arab-Israeli War of 1948–49, reverberated throughout the Middle East and remoulded both regional and global politics.

The 1952 overthrow of the Egyptian monarchy by the Free Officers' Movement emerged from that crucible, as did a heightened commitment to modernize Egypt's economy, most notably through construction of the Aswan High Dam. The Eisenhower administration's 1955 bid to use funding to lure Gamal Abdel Nasser into the pro-British, anti-communist Baghdad Pact failed when Nasser insisted on maintaining a neutral position between the American and Soviet camps and then set about acquiring Soviet-Bloc weapons for Egypt's ongoing confrontation with Israel. The immediate upshot was a tit-for-tat escalation of tensions between Egypt and the West, with Nasser establishing relations with the People's Republic of China, to Washington's great annoyance; the US putting the Aswan-funding offer on hold; and Nasser in turn nationalizing the Suez Canal Company in July 1956 as a way of enabling Egypt to raise the funds on its own. That move infuriated the governments of Britain and France, the latter already supplying Israel with advanced weaponry, incensed by Egypt's support for the Algerian *Front de libération nationale* (FLN). The stage was set for the coordinated Israeli-French-British invasions. The British Prime Minister, Anthony Eden, who had no compunction in labelling Nasser a new Hitler, assumed—wrongly, despite some equivocations by US Secretary of State John Foster Dulles—that the invasions and the toppling of Nasser would quickly garner American support: After all, US president Dwight Eisenhower had earlier joined with Britain in contributing to the overthrow of Iran's Mohammed Mossadeq in retaliation for the latter's nationalization of his country's oil sector. This time, however, Eisenhower was determined that he, not the British, would call the shots in dealing with Arab nationalism, and would do so if and when he chose. Amidst the drama of late October and early November 1956, with a popular uprising in Hungary and US elections imminent, American and Soviet positions once again briefly converged in condemning the tripartite attacks on Egypt. Moscow threatened to rain missiles on Paris and London, while Eisenhower effectively forced an end to the invasions by threatening to undermine the pound sterling. This turn of events not only heralded the eclipse of British and French imperial power in the Levant, North Africa, and soon enough Sub-Saharan Africa, but also initiated the high tide of secular pan-Arabism over the coming decade.

The proposal of the Canadian Foreign Minister, Lester Pearson, for a new kind of United Nations peacekeeping force—an initiative that led Canadian Tories to denounce him as a traitor to the British Empire, but that appealed to Dulles and to UN Secretary-General Dag Hammarskjöld—was born of that conjuncture. (Pearson would be awarded the Nobel Peace Prize for 1957.) Hanny Hilmy's discussion below reveals the negotiations around that proposal and the associated tensions over Egyptian sovereignty that haunted UNEF I throughout its institutional life. The fact that Israel refused to allow UN forces on its own side of the Armistice Demarcation Lines always stuck in the craw of Egypt's political and military leaders. For, while the outcome of the Crisis was indeed withdrawal of the invading forces, UNEF's placement seemed to contravene the principle that the victor in any conflict is spared encroachment on its own territory, as the shrewd French commentator Maxime Rodinson noted (1970: 80). Did that placement imply Egypt had lost? Subsequently, in 1967, the perceived affront to Egypt's freshly asserted sovereignty would lead to its government's demand, fraught with historic consequences, that the UN force be withdrawn. The UNEF sustained its first casualties in the process of being routed by a renewed Israeli strike on Egyptian territory at the outset of the Six Day War. But this is getting ahead of the story that Hanny Hilmy lays out in detail.

Here let us focus on a few of the multiple consequences of Egypt's success in withstanding the three-power assault in the autumn of 1956. One of the more unforeseeable outcomes lay in the way Egypt's success impacted the struggle for Algerian independence. An immediate response was an over-confidence among FNL leaders that set in motion the following year's urban guerrilla uprisings. In particular, the military leader in Algiers, Lardi Ben M'Hidi, imagined the situation could allow his city to become a Maghrebian *Diem Bien Fu*, i.e. the site of a decisive battle forcing a French withdrawal like that imposed by the Viet Minh three years earlier (Gallissot: 66). Far from that being the case, however, French para-commandos managed to brutally turn the Algerians' spectacular uprising into a painful defeat for the FLN. Nonetheless, as things turned out, the intense commitment of the Algerian revolutionaries to their cause, together with the ruthlessness of the French suppression, made a strong impression on international public opinion, including at the United Nations and in Washington (Connelly: 133–41). The growth of doubts regarding the French anti-revolutionary project—in some quarters about its legitimacy, in others about its feasibility—were not dissimilar to those that the Tet Offensive sparked eleven years later about the US war in Vietnam. When Charles de Gaulle returned to power in France in 1958, seeing the writing on the wall and stewing at what he bitterly took to be a lack of support from his Anglophone allies, he began re-defining France's priorities towards the European Economic Community, the first iteration of which had been formed in the year after Suez. As a key part of that process, he took the steps necessary to concede France's Sub-Saharan colonies self-government in 1958 and political independence in 1960 (apart from Guinea, which opted for it in 1958), followed by the independence of Algeria in 1962.

Meanwhile, a heavy blow to British power in the Middle East came in 1958 with the Iraqi revolution. As a key regional ally of Britain's at the time of the Suez Crisis, Iraq's Hashemite monarchy, nominally independent since 1932 but in fact still heavily reliant politically on the UK, had little choice but to back the Eden government's military adventure at Suez. Yet that position deepened the long-festering resentment felt towards British imperial power and the conservative monarchy among Iraq's general population and the country's officer corps. Nasser's calls for Arab solidarity, independence and modernization accordingly fell on fertile ground, and a coup reminiscent of that effected six years before in Egypt led to the establishment of an Iraqi republic that leaned towards the Soviet Union internationally in order to shore up its independence. In a flash, the Baghdad Pact, constructed by the UK and the US as an anti-USSR containment mechanism, was seriously weakened. Ironically, in the following years, the new Iraqi regime's friendly relations with Moscow served as a factor lessening the Soviet leadership's commitment to arming Egypt, even as Israel was becoming a key US regional ally, alongside Saudi Arabia, Iran and Turkey.

By the time of Iraq's revolution, Britain had been facing heightened calls for self-government and eventual independence from countries south of the Sahara as well. Faced with massive war debts and the loss of most of its dollar-earning colonies in Asia after the Second World War, the UK had resorted to increasing exports from its African colonies to shore up its international financial position. Yet, the mid-1950s brought a combination of falling post-Korean War commodity prices and a British desire to avoid spending more on colonial development. At the same time, independence movements continued to swell, including in export-orientated Nigeria and the Gold Coast (post-independence Ghana), both of which featured vigorous Gandhian-style mobilizations, and in Kenya, where the colonial administration had instituted emergency rule in 1952 to counter the anti-colonial Mau Mau insurgency (also supported by Nasser). Faced with these conditions, British planners even before Suez had found themselves looking to seriously scale back direct colonial rule on the continent (Hinds 2001: 170–71 & 185). The debacle (for the British) at Suez led UK politicians to accelerate that process, while simultaneously scrambling to build institutions and relationships that would enable them to retain effective control as much as possible through economic means. Led by the charismatic Kwame Nkrumah, Ghana moved from self-governance to full independence in 1957. Between then and 1965, when the Gambia won its independence, all but one of Britain's colonies on the African mainland rose to sovereign status, followed by admission to the United Nations. The technical exception was Southern Rhodesia (Zimbabwe after independence in 1980), whose white-supremacist government, aligned with that of apartheid South Africa, in 1965 made a unilateral declaration of independence that the international community rejected, leaving that country formally though not factually under British jurisdiction. In other words, in the nine years after the Suez Crisis, Britain and France had both given up formal colonial control of their African empires. In that sense, the inability of both powers to re-impose their will on Egypt in 1956 was a major turning point in the decolonization process.

One factor, admittedly among many, in that process was the emergence from 1947 onwards, originally under Indian stimulus, of the Afro-Asian solidarity movement, which underwent vigorous expansion during the 1950s. Egypt's revolutionary government took a notable strategic turn prior to the Suez Crisis when it associated itself with this movement, which was devoted not only to opposing colonialism and neo-colonialism, but also to promoting economic and cultural cooperation among newly independent states, and to non-alignment—*aka* 'neutralism', in the typical pejorative Western parlance—as between the US and the USSR. That movement's landmark 1955 conference hosted at Bandung by the Indonesian President Ahmed Sukarno and co-organized by the Indian Prime Minister Jawaharlal Nehru brought together delegates from thirty states representing markedly diverse regime-types, from Saudi Arabia to Japan to the People's Republic of China, spanning some sharp political-ideological divides (as e.g. between India and Pakistan; China and Japan; and North and South Vietnam). The meeting provided a forum geared towards stepping up support for anti-colonial struggles generally, but particularly in Africa. It was here that Nasser first emerged as a leading statesman on an international stage, taking the spotlight as one of the star personalities, along with the two co-organizers, plus the pan-Africanist Kwame Nkrumah and the Chinese premier, Zhou Enlai. Egypt's success in withstanding the three-power assault on its territory and sovereignty the following year was accordingly celebrated thereafter as a victory of the movement as a whole (see e.g. Chou 1964: 6–7).

Following Suez, Egypt's government doubled down on supporting national liberation movements across Africa. It allowed the Africa Executive of the Afro-Asian Solidarity movement to maintain its secretariat in Cairo as well as permitting the Algerian FLN's provisional government to reside in Cairo in its crucial early years of 1958–60. By that time, Nasser had also given his backing to the All-African Peoples' Conference, the first meeting of which—known as the Accra Conference—was hosted in 1958 by Nkrumah in the capital of the newly independent Ghana. That meeting brought together representatives of political parties, trade unions and other anti-colonial organizations from across the continent; and, while its effective political significance is contested by some, that it did have an impact is clear. Perhaps most famously, it put Patrice Lumumba, then involved in organizing and leading the first national, non-tribal political party in the resource-rich Belgian Congo, in touch with broader circles engaged in anti-colonial struggle across the continent, and in particular with the pan-African movement, with its opposition to colonialism, economic neo-colonialism and the imperial divide-and-rule political strategies Nkrumah called 'balkanization'. It is at this point that the story of the Suez Crisis segues into that of another dramatic, and tragic, early Cold War conflict, the Congo Crisis of 1960–65, during which the peace-keeping efforts of the *Organisation des Nations Unies au Congo* (ONUC, later *Opération des Nations Unies au Congo*) came to overlap in time and the-matically—in relation to concerns over sovereignty—with the mission of the United Nations Emergency Force in Egypt that Dr. Hilmy intimately details in the present volume.

Its vast size, tremendous resource-wealth and centrality within Africa made the Congo (aka Congo-Kinshasa, later Zaire, now the Democratic Republic of Congo) the single greatest object of international contention on the continent during the early Cold War. Accordingly, the Eisenhower administration also made it the site of the CIA's largest covert operation in the world, cultivating a slew of Congolese politi-cians and others via bribery and corruption. Ike was not about to let another piece of geopolitical real estate go down a 'neutral' path after Lumumba was sworn in as the country's first prime minister in June 1960. Ultimately, after five years of upheaval, one of the CIA's earliest 'assets' there, Joseph-Désirée Mobutu (later Mobutu Sese Seko), got the definitive nod and went on to rule kleptocratically for the next thirty-odd years. Until the Cold War ended, he did so with the backing of Western governments and corporations, and with impunity for his greed, even as stark poverty weighed down the general population. How the United Nations generally and the ONUF (1960–64) in particular played into the unfolding of the original Congo Crisis is a twisted tale that showed the world the limits of UN peacekeeping operations and gave such ventures a black eye internationally, including in Egypt. During its years in existence (1960–64), ONUC became by far the most contro-versial UN peacekeeping and peace-enforcement operation. At its height, it num-bered twenty thousand soldiers and large numbers of civilian administrators, and it put severe strain on the budget of the United Nations Organization as a whole (Weiss et al. 2001: 51–53). Despite the international composition of the force, the Eisenhower, Kennedy and Johnson administrations in Washington seem to have always held the reins in controlling the country's direction, while serving American, Belgian and other corporate interests (Weissman 2014).

ONUF's most dramatic period was its first year or so. When Lumumba attempted to deploy its troops to quash a Belgian-backed secession in the country's economically most profitable region, the southern province of Katanga, UN Secretary-General Hammarskjöld refused permission, arguing variously that ONUC's existing brief did not permit the use of force except in self-defence, that Katanga's relation to the centre was an internal Congolese matter in which the UN force could not interfere, and that a federal rather than centralized system of gov-ernment was more suited to the country's conditions. When Lumumba, in Nasser's footsteps, then requested Soviet trucks and aircraft to transport Congolese army troops to take Katanga, Hammarskjöld thought he was seeing the same kind of East-versus-West situation emerging as in Korea ten years earlier. In other words, he claimed to perceive a superpower clash in the making. To the chagrin of the Afro-Asian Solidarity movement, he moved to defuse the situation, in conjunction with the US, Belgium and Britain, by having Lumumba removed from office. As it happened, all three of those governments had already launched plans of their own to liquidate him. The Belgians, whose government had strongly supported the British and French attempt to topple Nasser five years earlier, got to him first. He was captured by Mobutu's troops, passed to his enemies under the secessionist regime of Moïse Tschombe in Katanga, and brutally executed in January 1961 (De Witte 2010). Eventually a contingent of Indian troops lent to ONUF by Nehru, and operating under peace-enforcing rules of engagement, succeeded in ending the by-then three-year Katangan secession. Tschombe took several months off in Franco's Spain before being called home to become Prime Minister of the very country from which he had previously seceded. To the satisfaction of his Western backers, and having evidently warmed to the notion of a centralized system of governance, he then employed Belgian, South African and other mercenaries to defeat the Lumumbist government that had operated since late 1960 in the country's northeast, under Lumumba's former deputy-premier Antoine Gizenga. This was the regime that the third meeting of the All-African Peoples' Conference, held in Cairo in March 1961, had recognized as the Congo's legitimate government.

For decades, ONUF was seen in the West, particularly in the US, as an example of a successful peacekeeping operation, on the grounds that it had kept the unified Congo out of communist hands. Nowadays academic and policy experts widely recognize that the perception of the non-aligned Lumumba as a communist or communist tool holds no water, and that the Congo Crisis's outcome and the US policies contributing to it needlessly antagonized African governments and liberation movements for decades (Weissman 2014: 23). Partly as a result of that alienation, no further UN peacekeeping operations took place in Africa until the end of the Cold War (when Namibia transitioned to independence from South Africa).

In light of such developments, it is hardly surprising that Egyptian political figures in the mid-1960s would have acute concerns about how foreign troops on a nation's soil might affect that nation's sovereignty. What became of those concerns, how they evolved and played out politically over a decade, is one of the key topics Hanny Hilmy addresses in his discussion below. At the same time, considering the issue of peacekeeping through a normative political-science lens, he draws our attention to the issue of what principles the international community might establish, in the light of historical experience, to duly respect the sovereignty of host nations while engaging in legitimate peacekeeping operations.

June 2020   Gregory Blue
                                                                                         Professor Emeritus
                                                                                    Department of History
                                                                                    University of Victoria
                                                                                     Victoria, BC, Canada

References

Chou En-lai [Zhou Enlai]. (1964): "Premier Chou En-Lai's Speech at the Reception Given by President Gamal Abdel Nasser (December 14, 1963)," in: *Afro-Asian Solidarity against Imperialism* (Peking [Beijing]: Foreign Languages Press).

Connelly, Matthew (2002): *A Diplomatic Revolution. Algeria's Fight for Independence and the Origin of the Post-Cold War Era* (Oxford: Oxford University Press).

De Witte, Ludo (2001): *The Assassination of Patrice Lumumba*, translated by Ann Wright and Renée Fenby (London: Verso).

Gallissot, René (2004): "La Décolonisation du Maghreb: De l'Afrique du Nord Française au Maghreb en Suspens," in: Mohammed Harbi and Benjamin Stora (eds). *La Guerre d'Algérie, 1954–2004: La Fin de l'Amnésie*, (Paris: Robert Laffont): 47–76.

Hinds, Allister (2001): *Britain's Sterling Colonial Policy and Decolonization, 1939-1958* (Westport CN and London: Greenwood).

Maxime Rodinson (1970): *Israel and the Arabs*, translated by Michael Perl (Harmondsworth: Penguin).

Weiss, Thomas G.; Forsythe, David P.; Coate, Roger A. (2001): *The United Nations and Changing World Politics* (Boulder CO: Westview).

Weissman, Stephen R. (2014): "What Really Happened in Congo: The CIA, the Murder of Lumumba, and the Rise of Mobutu," in: *Foreign Affairs*, 93,4 (July/August): 14–24.

Author's Preface

This book is based on my doctoral dissertation completed at the University of Victoria in British Columbia, Canada, as well as on my early exposure to the concept and application of peacekeeping deployment. The *basic research question* deals with the complex and contested relationship between the sovereign prerogatives of states and the international imperative of defusing world conflicts, and how this complex contestation played out during the mandate of the United Nations Emergency Force (UNEF) between 1956 and 1967. By its very nature, this multi-dimensional subject involves historical, political and international legal aspects. New theoretical considerations and policy options came to the fore following this unique peacekeeping experience. UNEF is undoubtedly responsible for a far-reaching—and perhaps unintended—change of directions aimed at strengthening the evolving UN ground rules for international crisis intervention and management and the evolution of the concept of sovereignty in international relations.

My father had a great influence on my life, as I was affected by his career in the military and later in the Foreign Service. I was forever asking questions about politics, and, as I grew older, was absorbed in long discussions surrounding the developments taking place in Egypt and the world. He never denied me time to explore the issues fully, despite the demands on his own time. As a young boy, I accompanied him on many of his inspection tours and field visits. While posted in the Suez Canal region, my father was involved in organizing resistance to the British presence there. As a reply, British agents tried to assassinate him by ambushing his car while I was with him. Luckily, the hail of bullets missed their target. I still remember him, moreover, in his army uniform in Alexandria, participating in the army take-over of the government of Egypt and forcing the abdication of King Farouq and his departure to his exile in Italy. I grew up in Egypt and I experienced at a young age the intensity of the bombing campaign unleashed by Britain and France with the help of Israel against Egypt during the Suez War. In the process, I received an early demonstration of the shameful application of conspiracy and deception in politics, also known as the real world and its *Realpolitik*.

Photo 1 The photo is showing the UNEF troops taking over from the French and British invasion forces as they evacuated their positions in Port Said on 22 December 1956. Photo credit: United Nations # 52457

Consequently, I developed a deep appreciation and critical evaluation of the principles underlying the role of peacekeeping. But, by necessity and belonging, I was also cognizant of the importance of the requirements of sovereignty and its attestation for Egypt in its protracted struggle to secure its freedom and to safeguard its sovereignty and independence during the end-of-empire struggle.

Photo 2 The author with General Hilmy at Abu Sweir airbase west of the Suez Canal during the arrival of the UNEF troops in November 1956. *Source* Author's personal photo collection

Many studies have dealt with the various aspects of the UNEF experience, and undoubtedly others will follow. I was fortunate enough to have a unique involvement with UNEF that accorded me special exposure from close quarters, where issues of sovereignty, consent, and decolonization occupied centre stage.

My research is based on the examination of relevant primary and secondary sources, including texts, articles, memoirs, and personal interviews, as well as direct observation. Publications of UN agencies and concerned international foundations have been consulted on various aspects of the subject.

'End of Empire' debates and the literature on Israel's role in the unfolding colonial-nationalist struggles in the post-World-War-II Middle East are analysed as a background to the main emphasis of the research. The deployment and termination of UNEF are evaluated from political and legal standpoints in a milieu of contrasting views on sovereignty and the international responsibility for peace and security.

The major approach of the work is to examine the theoretical, legal and political aspects of decolonization, sovereignty, consent, and peacekeeping, as well as the role played by the colonial powers and Israel, and to contrast that with the actual record and experience of UNEF in order to draw some conclusions pertaining to an 'optimal' peacekeeping regime, if such a thing is possible.

This volume includes theories, facts, and my opinions/reflections which I formulated as a result of my experience and research. The work is organized as follows:

Part I: Overview

Chapter 1: Introduction
This introductory chapter provides an overview of the issues of war and peace in relation to international peacekeeping, their global consequences as played out in the Middle East in the 1950s and 1960s, and their future consequences.

Part II: Theory

Chapter 2: Decolonization and the End of Empire
The theories underlying the struggle between Empire and national Liberation and the inevitable imperial retreat are analysed.

Chapter 3: Sovereignty: Westphalia and Beyond
The theoretical roots and evolution of sovereignty as it operates in the international system. The political and legal implications are paramount for the sovereign independent state in light of the application of peace operations.

Chapter 4: Peacekeeping: The Formative Years
The history and principles of traditional peacekeeping in the post-war period. Its success as well as failure will serve in developing a comprehensive modus operandi for renewed peace operations.

Part III: Evidence

Chapter 5: Anti-colonial Challenge in the Middle East
The final showdown between an energized national liberation movement and a weakened imperial structure as it played out in the Middle East. Israel's role in the struggle against the nationalist movement in the region played a prominent role.

Chapter 6: The Empire Strikes Back: The Suez War
The showdown between the crumbling imperial order in the Middle East and the growing nationalist liberation movement, which came to a head during the Suez War against Egypt. As planned, Israel was used to ignite the confrontation. The objectives of the old colonial powers and the plans of the new colonial-settler state in the Middle East converged to create the 'perfect conspiracy' designed to smother the rising national liberation tide.

Chapter 7: Imperial Rotation
The Suez War left no doubt as who was the new power in charge of Western interests in the pivotal Middle East region. The US was increasingly and firmly taking over from the exhausted British and French imperial order.

Chapter 8: UNEF (1956): Deployment
The introduction of UNEF to stop the Suez War in the midst of a raging war, political and legal equivocations, and dogged negotiations involving Egypt and the UN, led to a decade-long hiatus in the conflict but without meaningful conflict resolution.

Chapter 9: UNEF: Deployment Assessment
The pioneering UN peacekeeping experience set an example for future peace intervention. The deployment of UNEF is scrutinized, and its success and failure are highlighted.

Chapter 10: UNEF (1967): Demise and War
The unresolved Arab-Israeli political confrontation in the Middle East was rapidly coming to a boil. Eventually hostilities erupted again. The myth of an Israeli defensive war was fully exposed. The political struggle preceding the war also exposed the internal divisions within the Egyptian leadership, and highlighted the intra-Arab rivalry. The UNEF regime crumbled, and war swept the region, plunging the Middle East into deeper and protracted violent conflict prevailing until the present.

Part IV: Outcome

Chapter 11: UNEF: Legal and Political Battleground
The legal arguments engulfing the issue of national consent and the right of a sovereign nation to control the presence of foreign troops on its soil are fully aired and debated.

Chapter 12: Peacekeeping: The Assertive Years
The shortcomings of traditional-passive peacekeeping in resolving conflicts, as well as the need to protect human lives in areas of conflict, propelled the international community to rethink the peace intervention model in favour of a more active and robust involvement.

Chapter 13: Peace Operations in International Relations
Peace operations and their increasingly (neo)-liberal foundations have produced less than optimal outcomes for international conflict resolution.

Chapter 14: Epilogue

The result of the UNEF experience and the corresponding on-going influence on the purpose and modalities of peace intervention bring this book to a close.

Victoria, BC, Canada   Hanny Hilmy
June 2020

Acknowledgements

In addition to academic and archival sources, I have benefited from the contributions of many individuals (personal interviews and memoirs) who were directly involved in and contributed to the thorny contest between national sovereignty and international peacekeeping, in theory and in practice.

I was privileged to be present during the start and the termination of the UNEF project, observing events from a very close vantage point. As in many aspects in life, I also owe much to the circumstances which put me in places and situations—initially not of my choosing—which inspired me and provided the opportunity to develop a keen interest and involvement in the subject matter.

It was a unique and privileged opportunity to know the late General E. L. M. Burns, the first commander of UNEF, both in Palestine and later in the halls of academe (Carleton University in Ottawa, Canada) and to observe his unique contributions to the complex field of peace operations. My wife and I were very grateful for his hospitality when we first arrived in Canada.

I am indebted to Dr. Johan Galtung, a pioneer of peace research, for introducing me to this inspiring academic subject, giving me the opportunity to conduct research at the Oslo International Peace Research Institute in Norway, and being a mentor and a friend. The way he generously gave his time during my stay in Oslo, and the delightful conversation with his spouse, Fumiko, will always be in my memory.

I am also very fortunate to have known the Late General Indar Jit Rikhye, the last commander of UNEF, both in the field and as the President of the International Peace Academy (IPA) in New York, and to have exchanged endless views on issues of war and peace operations. My participation in the Helsinki IPA Project was a rich experience which opened the door and deepened my interaction with the various concepts underlying the complex field of peacekeeping.

The sharing of peacekeeping experience during conferences and seminars by the late General Freddie Carpenter of Canada, Major General Bjorn Egge of Norway, Professor Chadwick Alger of the US, and Brigadier General Michael Harbottle of the UK, brought the theoretical aspects of peacekeeping into a practical focus.

I was fortunate to encounter a world pioneer of international relations theory at the University of Pennsylvania, the late Prof. Robert Strausz-Hupé, who challenged my earlier assumptions of world politics. I am grateful to Professor Alvin Z. Rubinstein, also of the University of Pennsylvania, who guided my first encounters with political science and international politics.

I am indebted to Dr. M. S. Agwani, former Dean of the School of International Studies at Jawaharlal Nehru University in New Delhi, India for giving me the opportunity to conduct relevant research at the University. I owe Dr. John H. Sigler, former Director of the Norman Patterson School of International Affairs, Carleton University, Ottawa, Canada, gratitude for encouraging me to pursue further academic research.

I was also privileged to have the opportunity to engage in rewarding discussions with the late international law Prof. Roger Fisher of Harvard University, relating to peacekeeping and negotiations, and related issues of international security and conflict resolution. The late Ambassador Prof. Arthut Lall of India inspired me during many discussions about peacekeeping and international relations. I am grateful to Dr. Nabil Elaraby for his inspirational influence in the field of international law and peacekeeping.

I am grateful to the late Lt. General David Adamson (Ret), Royal Canadian Air Force (RCAF), for his hospitality and for sharing with me his experience with General Hilmy in the Gaza Strip in the early 1960s. I also gratefully acknowledge Major Charles Goodman (Ret), Canadian Army, for his account of the UNEF's Canadian casualties he witnessed during his deployment in the Gaza Strip.

I cannot neglect to acknowledge my great debt of gratitude to many individuals who inspired and influenced my work. I am truly grateful to Dr. Gregory Blue of the University of Victoria's History Department for his genuine support, insights, and friendship over many years. His encouragement has been very reassuring and much appreciated. I am indeed very thankful for the insights of Dr. Tareq Ismael, Professor of Political Science at Calgary University, and for his wealth of information and scholarly knowledge of the complex Middle East region.

I am also grateful to Dr. Oliver Schmidtke, Director of the Centre of Global Studies and Professor of Political Science at the University of Victoria, for his superb intellectual insights. I am truly thankful to Dr. Martin Bunton of the University of Victoria's History Department for his comprehensive review of an earlier version of this work and for his many helpful comments. I am also grateful to Dr. Perry Biddiscombe of the University of Victoria's History Department for his detailed and helpful comments.

To the late Dr. Andrew Rippin, former Dean of Humanities at the University of Victoria, I am grateful for championing the value of solid academic scholarship and critical thinking. My grateful thanks are also owed to the late Dr. Mohamed Selim, Professor of Political Science at Cairo University, for his incisive and valuable comments on my research ideas. And I would also like to thankfully acknowledge the late Dr. M. Jonas Sadek, Guelph University, Canada, for our numerous discussions on the developments in Egypt and the various peace prospects of the vexing Middle East quagmire.

I would like to acknowledge, as well, the help received from the Departments of History (particularly Karen Hickton and Heather Waterlander) and Political Science, the Faculty of Graduate Studies, and the MacPherson Library at the University of Victoria for their support and encouragement. To Jodie Walsh, Director of Operations and Research Coordinator, at the Centre for Global Studies (CFGS), University of Victoria, where I currently serve as an Associate Fellow, thank you for your genuine support and friendship.

My thanks are also due to the Al-Aram Centre for Political and Strategic Studies in Cairo, and to General Farid Hilmy, Egyptian Army (Ret.), for providing valuable research material.

Thanks are additionally due to Dr. Amr Mortagy of the American University in Cairo and Nile University in Egypt for facilitating my research in Cairo. Thanks are due to Ashnadelle Hilmy Mortagy for helping locate research material in Egypt. I cannot neglect to thank Dr. Shereef Hilmy, Marianne Thostrup Hilmy, and Dr. Ashraf Hilmy for helping me sift through General Hilmy's vast photograph collection in order to include some photos in this work. I also thank them for their continuous support and encouragement.

I also gratefully acknowledge the invaluable editorial help from Nora Hilmy and Ama Davies. Your painstaking efforts in deciphering my references made a huge difference. Thank you both. Certainly, no son can neglect to express heart-felt gratitude for the mother who provided unending love and support. Thank you Mother, the late Mrs. Horeya Mazhar Hilmy.

My father had a huge influence on me which must be acknowledged: The opportunity he provided for my involvement in international affairs, the pioneering role he played in peacekeeping, and the opportunity he gave me to witness first-hand the work of UNEF, helped to crystallize my interest in world affairs and peacekeeping. I sincerely hope that this work will contribute to the respect owed to his legacy.

I owe a great debt of gratitude to my wife, Marjukka (Välimaa) Hilmy, for her unflinching support and encouragement during the process of writing, despite the obstacles. Her Finnish 'Sisu' was a great inspiration for me to persevere. These words cannot really fully express the depth of my feeling. Thank you 'kulta'.

There are other individuals to whom I owe a lot of gratitude whose names do not appear here, but nevertheless, were very important for my work.

I also gratefully recognize Dr. Hans Günter Brauch for his superb guidance and infinite patience during the editorial process. I would like to thank Dr. Christian Witschel, Dr. Johanna Schwarz, Ms. Birke Dalia, and Ms. Marion Schneider, and Corina van der Giessen of Springer Publishers in Heidelberg (Germany) for their professional support. I am also grateful to Dr. Vanessa Greatorex of Chester, England, for her excellent language editing. Last, but not least, I am grateful to Ms. Jayanthi Krishnamoorthi and to Gowtham Chakravarthy and the team of book producers at Springer in Chennai, Tamil Nadu, India for their efficient work. The anonymous peer reviewers of the original script deserve a great thank you for their detailed comments and suggestions. They certainly helped in developing my arguments and structuring the contents of the book.

This work is the product of my own research and experience. I am truly grateful for all the help I have received; however, any shortcomings are mine alone.

Victoria, BC, Canada   Hanny Hilmy
June 2020

Contents

Abbreviations

AA	Armistice Agreement
ACPSS	Al-Ahram Centre for Political and Strategic Studies
AI	Amnesty International
AJAX	CIA plan for the overthrow of Iranian Prime Minister Mosadaq
Al-Ahram	Influential Egyptian Newspaper
ALPHA	British-US plan to resolve the Arab-Israeli Conflict
AMAN	Israeli Military Intelligence
AS	Anti-Semitism
AU	African Union
BC	Bandung Conference on Afro-Asian Solidarity
BP	Baghdad Pact
C-34	UN Special Committee on Peacekeeping Operations
CENTO	Central Treaty Organization
CIA	Central Intelligence Agency (USA)
CIVPOL	UN Civilian Police
CR	Conflict Resolution
CSCE	Conference on Security and Cooperation in Europe
CW	Cold War
DL	Demarcation Lines
DMZ	Demilitarized Zone
DPA	United Nations Department of Political Affairs
DPI	United Nations Department of Public Information
DPKO	United Nations Department of Peacekeeping Operations
ECOSOC	UN Economic and Social Council
ECOWAS	Economic Community of West African States
EIMAC	Egypt Israel Mixed Armistice Commission
EU	European Union
FC	Peacekeeping Force Commander
FRUS	Foreign Relations of the United States

FY	Former Yugoslavia
G-20	Group of 20 States
G-7	Group of 7 States
GATT	General Agreement on Tariffs and Trade
GFA	Good Faith Agreement
GLOB	Globalization
GNP	Gross National Product
GS	Gaza Strip
HAARETZ	A major Israeli newspaper
HAGANAH	The main Zionist military organization in Mandatory Palestine (1920–1948)
HAMILCAR	The three-country plan to attack Egypt in 1956
HC	High Commission
HDI	Human Development Index
HOLOCAUST	Nazi crimes against European Jews
HRC	Human Rights Council
HUMPROFOR	Humanitarian Protection Force
IAEA	UN International Atomic Energy Agency
IAF	Israeli Air Force
IBRD	International Bank for Reconstruction and Development (World Bank)
ICC	International Criminal Court
ICISS	International Commission on Intervention and State Sovereignty
ICJ	United Nations International Court of Justice
ICRC	International Committee of the Red Cross
IDF	Israel Defence Force
IDP	Internally Displaced Person
IFOR	Implementation Force
IMF	International Monetary Fund
IMTF	Integrated Mission Task Force
IPA	International Peace Academy
Irgun-Zvai-Leumi	A Violent Zionist organization in Palestine (1929–1949)
IS	Islamic Jihad
ISAF	International Security Assistance Force
ISIL	Islamic State in Iraq and the Levant
ISIS	Islamic State in Iraq and Syria
JMC	Joint Military Commission
Kadesh	Israel's plan for the invasion and annexation of Egyptian territories
Knesset	Israel's Parliament
LAS	League of Arab States (Arab League)
LEHI	A Zionist military group in Palestine (1940–1948), also known as the Stern Gang
LON	League of Nations

MAC	Mixed Armistice Commission
MEC	Middle East Command (US, UK, France, and Turkey)—Nov. 1951
MEDO	Middle East Defence Organization (during the 1950s)
MESC	Middle East Supply Centre (during WWII)
MFO	Multinational Force and Observers (Sinai deployment)
MI6	British Intelligence Service
MLO	Military Liaison Officer
MOSSAD	Israeli Intelligence Agency
MSC	Military Staff Committee
MUSKETER	(Originally Hamilcar). The plan for the invasion of Egypt in 1956
NAM	Non-Alignment Movement
NATO	North Atlantic Treaty Organization
NGO	Non-Governmental Organization
NIEO	New International Economic Order
NPT	Non-Proliferation Treaty
O(P)T	Occupied Palestinian Territories
OAS	Organization of American States
OCHA	UN Office for the Coordination of Humanitarian Assistance
ODA	Official Development Assistance
OECD	Organization for Economic Cooperation and Development
OIC	Organization of the Islamic Conference
OMEGA I, II	US-British plans to destabilize the Nasser Regime in Egypt
ONUC	United Nations Operations in Congo
OPEC	Organization of Petroleum Exporting Countries
Operation Atzom	Israeli plan to capture the Gaza Strip
Operation Cork	Blocking the Suez Canal
Operation Fajr	Aborted Egyptian plan to invade Israel in 1967
Operation Kardom	Israeli plan to capture Sinai and Gaza
Operation Leaven	Canadian naval deployment in the Mediterranean
Operation Moked	Israeli plans to destroy the Egyptian Air Force
Operation Rashid	Syrian plan to attack Israel
Operation Tarnegol	Plan to down General Amer's plane over the Mediterranean (1956)
P-5	Permanent Five Members of the UN Security Council
PA	Palestinian Administration
PALMACH	A Zionist elite fighting force of the Haganah in Palestine (1941–1948)
PKC	Peacekeeping Contingent
PKO	Peacekeeping Operation
PLA	Palestine Liberation Army
PLO	Palestine Liberation Organization
PN	Positive Neutrality
PRIO	Peace Research Institute in Oslo

PTSS	Post-Traumatic Stress Syndrome
R2P	Responsibility to Protect
RC	Red Cross
RCC	Revolution Command Council (Egypt 1952)
RDM	Rapid Deployment Mission
ROT	Right of Return
RSR	Red Sea Regatta (plan to storm the Strait of Tiran)
SA	Saudi Arabia
SC	United Nations Security Council
SCUA	Suez Canal Users Association
SD	Self-Determination
SFOR	Stabilization Force
SHIRBRIG	UN Standby High Readiness Brigade
SOFA	Status of Forces Agreement
SPA	UN Office for Special Political Affairs
SRSG	Special Representative of the Secretary-General
ST	Strait of Tiran
STERN Gang	Underground Jewish Terrorist Organization in Palestine (also known as LEHI)
UAR	United Arab Republic (Union between Egypt and Syria, 1958–1961)
UDHR	Universal Declaration of Human Rights
UN S-G	UN Secretary-General
UN	United Nations
UNAM	UN Assistance Mission
UNC	United Nations Charter
UNDOF	United Nations Disengagement and Observer Force
UNDP	United Nations Development Programme
UNDRO	UN Disaster Relief Office
UNEF	United Nations Emergency Force
UNESCO	UN Educational, Scientific, and Cultural Organization
UNFICYP	UN Peacekeeping Force in Cyprus
UNGA	United Nations General Assembly
UNHCR	UN High Commissioner for Refugees
UNIC	United Nations Information Centre
UNICEF	UN Children's Fund
UNIDIR	UN Institute for Disarmament Research
UNIFIL	UN Interim force in Lebanon
UNIM	UN Integrated Mission
UNITAF	Unified Task Force
UNITAR	UN Institute for Training and Research
UNMO	United Nations Military Observer
UNMOVIC	UN Monitoring, Verification, and Inspection Commission
UN-NGLS	UN Non-Governmental Liaison Service
UNO	United Nations Organization

UNPA	United Nations Protected Area
UNPREDEP	UN Preventive Deployment Force
UNPROFOR	United Nations Protection Force
UNRWA	UN Relief and Works Agency for Palestinian Refugees
UNRWA	United Nations Relief and Works Agency
UNSAS	United Nations Standby Arrangement System
UNSC	United Nations Security Council
UNSO	United Nations Staff Officer
UNTA	UN Transitional Authority/Administration
UNTAF	United Nations Task Force
UNTAG	UN Transition Assistance Group
UNTAT	UN Training Assistance Team
UNTEA	UN Temporary Executive Authority
UNTSO	United Nations Truce Supervision Organization
U-S-G	UN Under-Secretary-General
USSR	Union of the Soviet Socialist Republics
WHO	World Health Organization
WMD	Weapons of Mass Destruction
WP	Warsaw Pact
WP	White Paper
WSI	Wahhabi-Salafi Ideology
WTO	World Trade Organization
YISHUV	Jewish Community in British-Mandated Palestine

List of Figures

List of Photos

Part I
Overview

Chapter 1
Introduction

Abstract This introduction highlights the right of the sovereign nation to safeguard its independence and its right to provide or revoke consent for international
peacekeeping interventions. The post-World War II international system has
accorded the United Nations the prime responsibility for the protection of international peace and security as enshrined in the UN Charter. The 1956 Suez War
was the first serious test of non-enforcement international intervention in a military
conflict, and *The United Nations Emergency Force* (UNEF) became the pioneering
application of the post-War peacekeeping system. The issue of sovereignty versus
international intervention arose during the initial negotiations between Egypt and
the UN, and again during the termination of the force a decade later. The evaluation
of UNEF is also better framed in conjunction with the analysis of the end of empire,
decolonization, and national liberation struggles, as well as the role of Israel in its
unfolding. This introductory overview sets the stage for the complex political and
legal issues surrounding international peace intervention.

Keywords End of Empire · Israel · 1956 Suez War · United Nations Emergency
Force (UNEF) · The UNEF Generals · Peacekeeping · Capstone Doctrine ·
Sovereignty

1.1 Overview

Due to its historical setting following World War II, the national vs. international
staking of claims underlying the new concept of peacekeeping in the Middle East
was framed within the escalating imperial-nationalist confrontation and the
unfolding "end of empire" convulsions. Israel played a significant role in this saga
as a reliable outpost for Western interests in the heart of the pivotal Middle East
region. The 1956 Suez War, therefore, was not just a dispute over a vital waterway,
but a symptom of a collapsing imperial order and rising nationalist claims. The final
chapters in the history of the formal domination of the European colonial empires in

© Springer Nature Switzerland AG 2020   3
H. Hilmy, *Decolonization, Sovereignty, and Peacekeeping*,
https://doi.org/10.1007/978-3-030-57624-0_1

the Middle East, and the emergence of the United States as the new major Western power in the region, were written during this tumultuous period.

The leadership of Egypt in the anti-colonial struggle, and what became known as the era of decolonization, framed this historic confrontation. The 1956 Suez Crisis symbolized the escalating confrontation between anti-colonial nationalism and the attempts by the West to maintain control. By supporting the national liberation movements in the Middle East and Africa, Egypt's Nasser was the uncompromising bane of the struggling Western empires. A decisive confrontation was only a matter of time.

The introduction of UNEF in 1956 at this historical juncture in the Middle East, and the difficult negotiations to establish the ground rules for its deployment, must be understood in terms of the struggle to get rid of foreign military control in the region. The stationing of a foreign military force – although international in composition – was viewed by the national government in Egypt with suspicion as a possible continuation of unacceptable foreign intervention and an open-ended control. Protracted and contested negotiations also surrounded the termination of UNEF on Egyptian soil in 1967 over Egypt's decision to exercise its political-legal right to withdraw sovereign consent. Protecting national sovereignty, therefore, was the highest priority for Egypt during this unprecedented threat to its independence, and the demanding negotiations over the mandate of UNEF.

The birth of UNEF came about at a unique moment in international relations at the height of the Cold War. Disunity in the ranks of the Western allies over the Suez issue allowed the two superpowers to act together to advance a unified – albeit temporary and conditioned – objective. The dispute in the Western approach to revolutionary Egypt, however, was over methods, not objectives. There was an agreement among the Western powers that the revolutionary Egyptian leadership must be brought to heel. The Western disagreement was only over approach and timing. The two superpowers were able – with almost universal support and prodding – to push through the UNEF solution to the Suez War. Without this rare superpower rapport, the UNEF story would have been totally different or even non-existent.

The state of Israel was co-opted by the struggling colonial powers against the rising Arab nationalist tide, reinforcing World War I's Sykes-Picot betrayal, and fortified by the emergence of the United States as the undisputed Western arbiter in the pivotal Middle East region. Israel, moreover, has contributed in a significant way by thwarting the ability of the Arab world to develop real political and economic power, unshackled by never-ending confrontation and the haemorrhaging of resources. The increasing Soviet support for the national liberation movements, on the other hand, must be seen as fundamental to understanding the coalescing of events in autumn 1956 towards a major and dangerous world confrontation.

The Suez War triggered a fundamental assessment of the rights of sovereign states in the international arena. The war brought into stark relief the seemingly irreconcilable issues of national sovereignty rights and international responsibility for maintaining and protecting peace and security. Sovereignty, as a political and legal concept, and the international push-back to safeguard the new United Nations role, greatly influenced the course of events during the crisis (and shows every sign of continuing to influence them both now and in future). Egypt's insistence on upholding the country's sovereignty in the face of international force deployment (and withdrawal), and the high-stakes manoeuvering it took to come to a working compromise, largely contributed to the development and shaping of the original concept and the evolving ground rules underlying peacekeeping.

The 1956 war was also the historic landmark for the emergence of the concept of large-scale but "passive peacekeeping" in confronting international conflicts. The deployment of peacekeeping evolved out of the failure of the system of collective security during the League of Nations. Peacekeeping was also introduced because of the evident inadequacy of the system of peace observation used previously. This new phase was accomplished by deploying UN troops as a physical barrier, not just relying on "limited peacekeeping", such as observation and reporting. The new phase, however, was not entwined with a conflict resolution mechanism, a fundamental flaw in traditional peacekeeping. The *Capstone Doctrine* captured the essence of passive peacekeeping throughout its initial phase of operation. New rules and a broader consensus emerged later on as the global order was changing.

The fundamental *raison d'être* of UNEF, according to UN General Assembly Resolutions 997, 998, 999, 1000, 1001 and 1002 (1956), was to secure a ceasefire and the separation of combatants, and to supervise the withdrawal of the foreign invading and occupying forces of Britain, France and Israel from Egyptian (and Egyptian-controlled) territory.

The invaded territories ordered to be evacuated by the UN included the Suez Canal Zone, the Sinai (including Sharm El Sheikh and the strategic islands of Tiran and Sanafir at the entrance to the Gulf of Aqaba), and the Gaza Strip (under Egyptian trusteeship control since 1949, in accordance with the UN-mediated Armistice Agreement). This was an enormously important stand by the international community signalling that the old ways of invasion and territorial aggrandizement were no longer tolerated. The world majority was, in fact, putting to the test the efficacy of the new post-war world order. A decade later, the old ways resurfaced in June 1967. This time, the prevailing calculations of the Cold War prevented the international community from reasserting the primacy of the UN Charter.

By insisting on the total withdrawal of all foreign troops from all occupied areas under Egyptian control prior to 29 October 1956, Egypt was not only protecting its sovereignty and territorial integrity, but was also unwilling to concede to the invading powers the possibility of even a partial victory as a result of their aggression. Israel's annexation of the Sinai and the Gaza Strip, therefore, was eventually reversed following intense political and diplomatic pressures. (Israel, however, was able, with the help of the US, to quietly gain naval access through the Strait of Tiran – blocked by Egypt since the end of the Arab-Israeli war in 1949 – but not the Suez Canal, which had remained closed to Israeli shipping since 1949). The UN stand confirmed that the international community (the new vocal majority in the organization) was not going to tolerate territorial aggression in violation of the UN Charter. See Hammarskjold Reports at the height of the Crisis in 1956 (UN Reports A/3289 and A/3302).

The UN General Assembly also called on all parties to scrupulously observe the provisions of the Armistice Agreements, administered separately by a different body, the *United Nations Truce Supervisory Organization* (UNTSO), in existence since the end of the first Arab-Israeli War (1948–1949). UNEF was not allowed to influence the military balance prevailing at the time of its deployment. The duration of the deployment of the international force on Egyptian soil, moreover, was perceived to be temporary and dependant on the developments of the current conflict.

The successful deployment of UNEF for over a decade resulted in the absence of outright hostilities between Egypt and Israel during the deployment period. Yet, as events were to prove, the elements of conflict remained frozen in place and the prospect of a transition towards a conflict resolution phase was deliberately neglected, as both sides were satisfied by the convenient temporary absence of warfare. Overall, UNEF was thus a temporary success, and this crucial and ground-breaking effort amounted to a missed historic opportunity to develop a firm grounding in international peacekeeping principles to serve as a future template and guideline for successfully resolving international (and national) conflicts.

The Suez experience highlighted a stubborn contest between the defenders of the concept of national sovereign 'consent' and the advocates of "international intervention". Both the deployment of UNEF and its termination were surrounded by controversy and legal-political wrangling over the right of the 'host' country to maintain or withdraw its consent for the continuing deployment of foreign troops on its soil.

1.2   A New Global Institutional Framework

The new post-war *United Nations Organization* (UNO) enshrined the concepts of political independence and sovereign equality as foundational principles of legitimate international relations. It was inconceivable under the new international regime, therefore, to impose the deployment of UNEF on Egypt without its consent in the absence of Security Council Chapter VII (enforcement measure) authorization. It was equally difficult for the international community to shirk its responsibility to maintain peace and security by failing to act in the face of a fundamental breach of the UN Charter.

Contestation was inevitable as the ground rules for such international operation were not yet clearly established. Such an international intervention mission was based on unchartered territory, and the contested jurisdictional boundaries for both sides unfolded on an on-going basis, open to disputes and different political and legal interpretations. Both positions had a complex impact on the modus operandi of the peacekeeping force.

The possibility that the UNEF presence would be transformed into a permanent replacement for occupying enemy troops unanswerable to Egyptian sovereign control and consent was totally unacceptable to the Egyptian Government. An open-ended UNEF deployment was, therefore, out of the question. Having given its initial (sovereign) consent for deployment, Egypt insisted on having the right to exercise its sovereign prerogative to terminate without question the presence of foreign troops on its soil. The post-war international system – based on sovereign states – cannot function without the observance of the sovereign prerogatives of each state in the system.

The international peace force, on the other hand, sought freedom of action on Egyptian soil in order to carry out its mandate. The UNEF needed assurances from the host country that its work was not going to be obstructed, impeded or terminated prematurely before its mission was completed. The international force was deployed in Egypt and tasked with implementing the will of the international community under the guidance of the UN Charter, the relevant UN Resolutions, and the mentoring of the determined UN Secretary-General, Dag Hammarskjold, who strongly championed the deployment of the force against many obstacles. In fact, both Egypt and the UNEF were in need of clear operational guidelines based on a political-legal framework which was not yet available, and which came to be developed only through a shared – and sometimes contested and difficult – experience.

1.3 Sovereignty and Consent

Sovereignty and national 'consent' in relation to international intervention, there-fore, were essential arguments in the peacekeeping story of the 1950s and the 1960s under the shadow of the crumbling imperial order. However, it is difficult to make generalizations or extrapolate theories about the future of peacekeeping based solely on the UNEF experience. The concept of national sovereignty vis-à-vis international peacekeeping was later tested when the nature of conflict drastically changed, and the parameters of peace intervention consequently also underwent fundamental changes, with the concomitant result of challenging both the idea of sovereignty itself and the nature of the intervention required. The UNEF experi-ence, moreover, brought into sharp relief the need for conflict resolution as an integral component of any peace operation.

With the changing nature of global conflicts, the peacekeeping concept itself has undergone major transformations. The prerogatives of national sovereignty within international law have been increasingly challenged, forcing policy-makers and international legal experts to chart new territories in the *raison d'être* of peace-keeping and its legal foundations. The strict confines of sovereignty are being transformed to adapt to a new international legal environment, and a novel concept of collective human security has emerged. International human rights law – as distinct from international humanitarian law (marked by new concepts such as the *Agenda for Peace* and its *Supplement*, the *Brahimi Report*, the *Millennium Report*, the *Responsibility to Protect*, and the *HIPPO Report*) – is changing the peace-keeping landscape in favour of a more interventionist legal regime, at the expense of the traditional concerns for sovereignty and national consent.

Such fundamental change in the international political-legal environment owes its development and transformation to the experience gained during the pioneering creation and deployment of UNEF in Suez during the 1956 Crisis, and the changing profile of conflict. Inter-and-intra state conflict management and human rights protection are both, therefore, subject to increasing challenges and re-evaluation designed to produce a modified international intervention model and a commensurate conflict resolution paradigm. The conflicting concerns of 'national control' and 'international action' underlying the UNEF experience have undoubtedly had a lasting impact on the modus operandi and the future of peace operations. Peacekeeping intervention has indeed modified the principle of sovereignty, and vice versa.

In a nutshell, the UNEF experience highlights the extent and the degree of co-existence or inherent conflict between nationally-based sovereign consent and externally-sanctioned peacekeeping deployment. Are there unbridgeable theoretical and policy schisms between the two? Can we – at the end of the day fashion a workable rapprochement and an acceptable but modified modus operandi to bridge the gap, and produce, in the meantime, realistic policy applications based on a grounded theoretical approach?

In other words, can peacekeeping (in whatever form required) be fashioned not just to achieve a truce between international combatants or defuse internal conflicts, but also to provide a firm foundation for conflict resolution, while accommodating, in the meantime, the concept of national sovereignty? Finally, is the concept of peacekeeping a neutral policy tool for conflict management (but not necessarily resolution), or is it just an ideological tool utilized to serve certain agenda(s)?

The answer to that is governed by the ever-changing nature of international relations and the cold facts underlying world power configurations, as well as the growing concern over human rights violations. Hammarskjold's words were prophetic when he said in 1954 that the "United Nations was created not to bring humanity to heaven but to save it from hell". (Hammarskjold 1954; cited in Annan 2012: 156).

A final question must be asked: has the UNEF experience in 1956–1967 validated or repudiated the theoretical principles of passive peacekeeping and political-legal sovereignty? Hopefully, this volume will provide part of the answer.

A final *sobering thought*: in the wake of the expansion and increasing complexity of national and international conflicts, and the resulting difficulty of peace operations, Brian Urquhart, long time Under-Secretary-General of the United Nations responsible for UN peacekeeping operations, compared peacekeepers to "superintendents in a lunatic asylum" (Urquhart 1991, cited in Dombroski 2007: 105; Nelson 1985; and McDermott/Skjelsbeck 1991: 35).

1.4   The UNEF Generals

Three generals figured prominently in the creation of the United Nations Emergency Force (UNEF) and its termination, as will be seen in the pages ahead. Therefore, a brief biography of each general and the reasons why they were chosen for their respective tasks is presented here.

1.4.1 The Generals Answer the Call for Peace

The difficult birth and continued survival of the UNEF, which lasted close to eleven years in all, owed at the outset a great measure to two generals, one *Canadian* (General *Burns*) and the other *Egyptian* (General *Hilmy*). Both men were hard-working and tenacious in carrying out and defending their responsibilities. Both worked with integrity and dedication to ensure the success of UNEF and its international mandate, as well as to safeguard Egyptian sovereignty. Though they often butted heads and clashed fiercely over issues of jurisdiction and control, they never lost respect for each other, or lost sight of the overall objective of the mission with which they were entrusted. They genuinely tried to resolve the issues affecting the operations of UNEF.

Photo 1.1 The three Generals in the Gaza Strip in the late 1950s. Left to right: General Rikhye, General Hilmy and General Burns. *Source* General Hilmy's files

The contributions of Burns (the first Commander of the international force, UNEF) and Hilmy (the Chief Egyptian Liaison Officer with UNEF) towards laying the groundwork for the deployment and functioning of UNEF on Egyptian soil were indispensable for the success of the international force in the face of a dangerous military entanglement involving the armies of four countries, and then for fashioning a successful UNEF deployment despite many political and legal obstacles.

A third General from *India* (General *Rikhye*) was in charge of the UNEF during the last phase of its deployment. Under trying circumstances, he also oversaw the difficult and dangerous winding down of the international force with great professionalism, regardless of the tough conditions on the ground and complicated international political-legal pressures.

During their service in association with UNEF, the Generals developed a strong friendship and a warm sense of camaraderie which lasted for the rest of their lives. After UNEF, the three former colleagues went on to perform other distinguished duties for their countries and internationally.

1.4.2   General E.L.M. Burns (Nov. 1956–Dec. 1959)

Why did the UN and Canada choose General Burns to lead the UNEF? From Canada's point of view, Burns was an experienced field officer accustomed to leading large formations in battle during World War II. His removal from command during the War at the instigation of a higher-ranking British officer came as a shock and did not please the Canadian brass. His UNEF command was not exactly a rehabilitation – he was already involved with the UN – but certainly it represented a Canadian vote of confidence in the General. From the perspective of the UN, Burns was already familiar with its set-up in the Middle East, being in charge of the United Nations Truce Supervision Organization (UNTSO) formed after the Arab-Israeli War in 1948–49. He was also very involved in the Arab-Israeli conflict, supervising the implementation and the observance of the Armistice Agreements, as well as being an emissary between the involved capitals and familiar with the various political leaderships in the region. Moreover, choosing a Canadian general was a UN nod of recognition to Canada for Lester Pearson's efforts in sponsoring the UNEF resolution to end the military confrontation in Suez.

General Burns was a veteran of both world wars. He was appointed Chief of Staff of the *United Nations Truce Supervisory Organization in Palestine* (UNTSO), a post he held from 1954 until the end of 1956, when he was called upon to command the newly formed UNEF.

Burns received his officer training at the Royal Military College in Kingston, Ontario, where he graduated in 1914. He then joined the Royal Canadian Engineers, receiving a commission as a lieutenant in 1915. He served in Europe in both World Wars and in 1944 rose to command the 1st Canadian Corps. He was described as possessing "penetrating intellect and '*avant-garde*' thinking, in addition to his prolific writing. He was acknowledged as one of Canada's best intellectual generals" (Born/Wycznski 2001: 158). But he was also known for his lack of charisma and his constantly present serious demeanour. His personal nickname was Tommy, but he was also ironically called 'Smiling Burns' because of his no-nonsense, old-school mannerism.

By the end of the Second World War, Burns had become a rising star in the Canadian Forces. But due to his wife's illness, his career suffered. However, he recovered from the setback and resumed his upward progress. Burns was assessed as a "first class, damn good, excellent staff officer" (Vokes 1985: 184). Despite his success on the battlefield in Italy, he was removed from his command by the British for lacking sufficient 'field leadership'. He was also judged to be difficult, cold, and sarcastic (Ralston Papers 1943: 163).

Burns admitted that he did not possess the 'Montgomery technique' that let one jump on the hood of a jeep to address the troops. Moreover, Burns was not liked by his British colleagues or superiors during the war: there were complaints that he was not "British Army enough". His Canadian characteristics – diffidence, smarts, moderation, and an introverted nature – did not endear him to the British brass, so he was not accepted into the old boys' club. In this respect, he was like many other Canadian officers, who were referred to by their British peers as 'TGs', or Temporary Gentlemen, while serving with the British officers, before they reverted back to being 'Cs', or Colonials (Burns 1970: 9).

Burns may also have annoyed the British because "he was, as a nationalist, concerned about the British using Canadians as cannon fodder" (Maloney 2006: 83). The 'Empire' mentality was still alive and kicking during the war, although the Empire itself was soon to witness its final sunset.

Photo 1.2 GeneralBurns in Deir El-Balah, Gaza Strip, 1959. *Source* Photo by Hanny Hilmy

In a declassified report by the Directorate of History, at Canada's National Defence Headquarters, General Burns was described as the right man to command UNEF as he dealt with many "political booby-traps" in a volatile situation (Swettenham 1958).

History has proved that Burns was an exceptional officer and the right choice to lead UNEF at this critical stage. Despite having serious handicaps in the eyes of his contemporaries, Burns proved the critics' dismissive attitude wrong, as he employed his superior intellect and firm discipline to successfully accomplish the tasks awaiting him.

After leaving the UNEF, General Burns served as Canada's Principal Disarmament Negotiator from 1960 to 1968, and he did a stint as Deputy Minister of Veteran Affairs. From 1969 to 1975 he held the chair of Strategic Studies at the Norman Patterson School of International Affairs, at Carleton University in Ottawa. In 1975 he served as the President of the United Nations Association in Canada.

1.4.3   General M.A. Hilmy II (Nov. 1956–June 1961)

Why did President Nasser choose Hilmy to lead the Egyptian liaison responsibilities with the UN for the deployment of UNEF in Egypt? Nasser knew Hilmy very well from their officers' cadet college days. They also went through staff college training designation later on, and became instructors in the military academy at the same time. They became close friends and discussed the political situation in the country (Hilmy n.d.). While Nasser was busy building his *Free Officers* Movement inside the army, Hilmy was organizing resistance to the British presence in the Suez Canal Region, where he was stationed in Ismailia with the military intelligence branch. Hilmy's activities were noted and supported by Nasser.

The two officers were supportive of each other's role but were not organizationally connected, as Hilmy refused to join any political structure, whether Nasser's *Free Officers* or the King's *Iron Guard*. However, when called upon, Hilmy's support for the Army action against the *ancien régime* was crucial to the success of the Army take-over. By assuming command of Alexandria's artillery garrison, he was able, with the help of other officers and soldiers, to secure the city against the Monarchy's supporters in the Royal Guards and the Navy. The situation threatened to turn into a dangerous military confrontation with untold consequences. The Royal Palace was surrounded by troops loyal to the new army leadership, and Hilmy's intervention prevented the loyalist troops from blocking the advance of the rest of the rebellious units already marching on the city from Cairo. He also arrested the members of the Egyptian Cabinet residing in Alexandria (the summer capital of Egypt) and flew them under military guard to Cairo.[1] Hilmy's action was carried out at great risk to his life and career.

After the success of the military take-over, Hilmy remained in Alexandria in command of the anti-aircraft artillery units and training before being transferred to

---

[1]*Ibid* and conversations with the author.

Cairo and then back to Ismailia. During his command of the air defence system, Hilmy conferred with Nasser in Cairo over the agitation by some officers of the Artillery Branch and the Armoured Corps regarding the political direction of the new regime, following the forced resignation of the popular nominal President, General Mohamed Naguib, during what became known as the 'March/October 1954 Crisis'. Hilmy met Nasser at Army Headquarters, where Nasser was resting (on an army field bed) after an exhausting all-night discussions. Members of the *Revolution Command Council* (RCC) were engaged in heated discussions over the proper response to the officers. The Minister of War, General Amer, who was promoted from the rank of major, was extremely agitated. He regarded the action of the protesting officers as unacceptable disrespect and insubordination, and angrily removed his officers' shoulder rank insignia and threw them on the floor in protest. Nasser complained that the officers' action was threatening the stability of the whole regime. Jokingly, he said, "Amin, why don't you go and frighten the officers with your big moustache?" After the laughter subsided, Hilmy responded, as befitting friends and former colleagues, "Gamal, the army should relinquish power to a new elected civilian administration not tainted by the old politicians, and the soldiers should go back to their barracks, as the objective of overthrowing the old corrupt regime has been accomplished." Nasser replied that the 'revolution' needed time to implement the programme at the heart of the army action first. (After Nasser was elected President, Hilmy always addressed him as 'Mr. President'.)

Although the former army colleagues differed on the new regime's approach, they remained friends, with mutual respect and trust prevailing as future events would prove.

Photo 1.3 Cadet Hilmy in front of his platoon. Behind him, Cadet Nasser (front row, tenth from left), and Cadet Sadat (front row, 7th from left). Royal Military College, Cairo 1937. *Source* General Hilmy's files

After graduating from the Royal Military College in 1938, Hilmy was posted to the Artillery Corps. He also obtained a Master's degree in Military Science and went on to earn his staff designation. He participated in World War II (1939–1945), the Palestine War (1948–1949), and the Suez War (1956). During World War II he served as a liaison officer with the allied forces in Egypt. Later on, he held senior army positions in Cairo, Alexandria, and Ismailia. He was appointed Chief of Staff, Eastern Command, in charge of the implementation of the Anglo-Egyptian Treaty of 1954.

Photo 1.4 Colonel Hilmy with General Naguib in Alexandria during the army action against the monarchy, July 1952. *Source* General Hilmy's files

During the 1956 war, Hilmy was the mastermind behind the planning and implementation of the blocking of the Suez Canal against the British-French invasion. Hilmy refused repeated offers to get involved in the political process (including receiving government 'support' to get elected to Parliament), preferring to remain a professional soldier. His involvement with UNEF at the end of the Suez War, as President Nasser's choice for the task, shifted his focus more towards diplomatic-legal work.

After the Suez War and his work with UNEF, Hilmy joined the Egyptian diplomatic service in 1960 (while simultaneously retaining his UNEF Liaison position until 1961), again at the request of the President, where he served in the Foreign Ministry in Cairo, and then as Ambassador in New York, India, Nepal, and Vietnam until his retirement in 1979. After Hilmy finished his first posting in New York (he was posted there twice), he was transferred as Egypt's Ambassador to Canada. Hilmy was about to move to his new posting in Canada when Nasser had a meeting with Indira Gandhi, Prime Minister of India. The Indian leader informed Nasser that India sends its best diplomats to Egypt, and expects the same in return. Nasser promised to send her a new ambassador who would fit the bill. Nasser urgently instructed Hilmy to cancel his imminent transfer to Canada and move forthwith to India. It was a happy choice for both countries.

1.4.4 General I.J. Rikhye (January 1966–June 1967)

Born to a prominent Brahman family in Lahore in pre-Partition India, Indar Jit Rikhye joined the prestigious Indian Military Academy in Dehra Dun and graduated in 1939. During World War II he took an active part in the Allied campaigns in the Middle East and Europe between 1941 and 1945. Between 1947 and 1948 he saw action in Kashmir against Pakistan immediately following the Partition of India. After the 1956 Suez War, he commanded the Indian Contingent in the newly formed UNEF. He was then chosen as the Chief of Staff of UNEF (1958), and the Acting Commander of the international force.

After two years serving with UNEF, Rikhye returned to India, and, after a short deployment commanding an Infantry Brigade Group in Ladakh on India's border with China, in 1960 he was appointed to be the UN Secretary-General's Chief Military Adviser on the UN's troop intervention (ONUC) in the crisis in the Congo. He also assumed the post of Acting Head of the UN Mission in the Congo. With the death of Dag Hammarskjold in the Congo, Rikhye was appointed Military Adviser to the New UN Secretary-General, U Thant. (Rikhye 2002: 128–156).

Photo 1.5 The author with the late General Indar J. Rikhye during an International Peace Academy Conference in Helsinki, Finland. *Source* The author's photograph collection

His vast experience of peacekeeping assignments in the field and at the UN Headquarters made his choice as the Commander of UNEF in 1966 a natural progression. Moreover, Egypt lobbied for his appointment in view of the Indian-Egyptian friendship.

He proved to be the last Commander as the UNEF was dissolved with the onset of the 1967 Middle East War. His performance during the last turbulent days of UNEF could only be described as professional and disciplined in the face of tough challenges.

Fig. 1.1 Peacekeeping in a Dangerous World. *Source* Cartoon by Adrian Raeside, 8 April 1993, *Victoria Times Colonist*, British Columbia, Canada. With kind permission of the artist and the newspaper (Raeside 1993)

Rikhye went on to be involved in numerous peacekeeping activities, providing advice, research and lecturing for many years across the globe. He was instrumental in the establishment of the International Peace Academy in New York, dedicated to the advancement of the methods and practice of international peacekeeping. He served as its President and mentor for many years (Fig. 1.1).

References

Annan, Kofi (2012): *Interventions: A Life in War and Peace* (New York: The Penguin Press).
Born, B.; Wycznski, M. (2001): *Warrior Chiefs: Perspectives on Senior Canadian Leaders* (Toronto: Dundurn Press).
Burns, E.L.M. (1970): *General Mud: Memoirs of Two World Wars* (Toronto: Clarke Irwin).
Dombroski, Kenneth R. (2007): *Peacekeeping in the Middle East as an International Regime* (New York: Routledge).
Gordon, J. King (1985): "A Soldier for Peace", in: *The Citizen* (Ottawa, Canada): *A tribute in memory of General E.L.M. Burns* (24 September 1985).
Hammarskjold, Dag (1954): "Statement to the Press", cited in: Annan, Kofi (2012): *Interventions: A Life in War and Peace* (New York: The Penguin Press).

Hammarskjold, Dag (1956): *UN Secretary-General's First and Second Reports on UNEF*: A/3289 (4 November 1956), and A/3302 (6 November 1956), (New York: United Nations Public Information).

Hilmy II, Amin (n.d.): *Unpublished Memoirs.*

Maloney, Sean M. (2006): "The Forgotten: Lt Gen E.L.M. 'Tommy' Burns and UN Peacekeeping in the Middle East", in: *Canadian Army Journal*, 9, 2 (Summer).

McDermott, A.; Skjelsbeck, K. (Eds.) (1991): *The Multinational Force in Beirut, 1982–1984* (Miami: Florida International University Press).

Miller, Richard I. (1961): *Hammarskjold and Crisis Diplomacy* (New York: Oceana).

Nelson, Richard, W. (1985): "Multinational Peacekeeping in the Middle East and the United Nations Model", in: *International Affairs*, 61, 1 (Winter): 67–89.

Raeside, Adrian (1993): *Times Colonist*, 8 April 1993 (Victoria, BC, Canada).

Ralston Papers (1943): *Officer Assessment File,* 54 (Ottawa: IBID Report).

Rikhye, Indar Jit (2002): *Trumpets and Tumults: The Memoirs of a Peacekeeper* (New Delhi: Manohar Publishers).

Swettenham, J.A., Capt. (R.C.E) (1958/1959): "Some Impressions of the UNEF, 1957 to 1958", Report No. 78, Appendix A, Historical Section (G.S.), (Canadian Army Headquarters, Ottawa), Signed on 17 December 1958 and compiled on 2 January 1959.

United Nations Resolutions during the Suez Crisis, 1956:

UN General Assembly resolution A/RES/997 (ES-I) (1–2 November 1956);

UN General Assembly resolution A/RES/998 (ES-I) (4 November 1956);

UN General Assembly resolution A/RES/999 (ES-I) (4 November 1956);

UN General Assembly resolution A/RES/1000 (ES-I) (5 November 1956);

UN General Assembly resolution A/RES/1001 (ES-I) (7 November 1956);

UN General Assembly resolution A/RES/1002 (ES-I) (7 November 1956).

United Nations Reports:

UN General Assembly & Security Council Reports, *An Agenda for Peace: Preventive Diplomacy, Peacemaking and Peace-Keeping*, Report by Secretary-General Boutros Boutros-Ghali, A/47/277 - S/24111 (17 June 1992).

UN General Assembly & Security Council Reports, *Supplementary Report to the Agenda for Peace*, Position Paper by the Secretary-General Boutros Boutros-Ghali, A/50/60/-S/1995/1 (January 1995).

UN General Assembly Report, *We the People: The Role of the United Nations in the 21st Century (The Millennium Report),* by Secretary-General Kofi Annan, A/RES/55/2 (18 September 2000).

UN General Assembly & Security Council Reports, by the Panel on United Nations Peace Operations (*Brahimi Report*), A/55/305-S/2000/809 (30 November 2000).

United Nations: Accepted Report of the International Commission on Intervention and State Sovereignty (ICISS), (*Responsibility to Protect: Evans and Sahnoun – IDRC*) (December 2001).

UN General Assembly Reports, Restructuring the United Nations Peace and Security Pillar (*The HIPPO Report*), by Secretary-General Antonio Guterres, A/72/525 (13 October 2017) & A/72/L.33 (15 December 2017).

Urquhart, Brian (1987): A life in Peace and War (New York: Harper & Row).

Urquhart, Brian (1972): Hammarskjold (New York: Norton & Co.).

Urquhart, Brian (1991): "Superintendents in a Lunatic Asylum", in: Dombroski, Kenneth R. (2007): *Peacekeeping in the Middle East as an International Regime* (Routledge: New York): 105.

Vokes, Christopher (1985): *My Story* (Toronto: Gallery Publishing).

Part II
Theory

Chapter 2
Decolonization and the End of Empire

Abstract Both the British and French empires were facing their sunset as the anti-colonial movement was intensifying, on one hand, and the United States was emerging as the dominant Western power in the Middle East, on the other. These changes could only hasten the realization of the limitations of imperial staying power. A review of the theories of imperial retreat will bring the anti-colonial struggle in the Middle East and Egypt's leading role into focus.

Keywords Civilizing Mission · Theories of colonial collapse · Peripheral collaboration · Colonial nationalism · Cultural superiority · Hierarchy of domination · Accident of modernity · Invented imaginary nations · Territories, resources, and political control · Global domination

2.1 Imperial Farewell

The Suez War (1956–57) did not so much bring about the demise of the imperial order, as confirm it. The old empires were experiencing a serious decline because of a host of domestic and international reasons, as well as growing anti-colonial resistance. Internal and external contradictions in the assumptions and institutions of the imperial order doomed the colonial age as it had prevailed for decades or even centuries. World War II administered a body blow to all the European empires: the cost of rebuilding the ageing empires as going economic and military concerns was steadily rising and becoming increasingly prohibitive. With the collapsing economies and exhausted military capabilities of the battered European empires, the United States was poised to inherit Western imperial hegemony under a different banner. Intensifying and restive nationalist agitation and rebellion in the colonies marked the last chapter in the tale of formal imperial collapse.

Although 'Suez' and "the end of empire" are not interchangeable terms, clearly, the Suez debacle was a telling symptom of imperial decay and had a massive impact on the remaining chapters in the history of European imperialism. The Suez Crisis

© Springer Nature Switzerland AG 2020

H. Hilmy, *Decolonization, Sovereignty, and Peacekeeping*,

https://doi.org/10.1007/978-3-030-57624-0_2

exposed the failure of the British (and French) imperial enterprise, and encapsulated the drastic consequences for the entire imperial project in the post-World War II era:

> It split the British nation and brought down the prime minister; it revealed with startling clarity that Britain could no longer continue the pretense of being a great power; it was brought to a head by a conspiracy, or collusion, between France, Israel, and Britain to overthrow Colonel Gamal Abdel Nasser of Egypt; it complicated the intractable Arab-Israeli dispute and weakened the Western position in the Middle East; it was a test case for the United Nations; it exacerbated Cold War tensions and raised the specter of nuclear war (Kelly/Gorst 2000: 1).

Suez, in fact, was the symbol of the dramatic and inevitable consequences of the changing post-war world order, which all came to a head at this critical historical juncture. One of the principal participants in the Suez War, the French general André Beaufre, described the Suez conflict in the following terms:

> The Anglo-French expedition against Egypt, generally known as 'Suez', proved to be the turning-point of the post-war period. Before Suez, European prestige was still intact in the eyes of the Third World and the victor nations of 1945 had maintained their solidarity. After Suez both prestige and solidarity had vanished. This was the end of empire, the end of an epoch (Beaufre 1969: 14).

The Suez War demonstrated in concrete terms the inability of the old imperial order to maintain control or to prolong the colonial structure in the face of fundamental changes in the constituents of power locally and internationally.

2.2 Theoretical Perspectives

Since the Suez War was the epitome of the collapsing imperial order, a theoretical review of colonialism and imperialism is helpful to explain the forces that led to the storm in the Middle East in autumn 1956, and the resulting introduction of UN forces in the area.

The issue of colonialism can be seen as an expanding structure which developed from clusters of European settlers into fully fledged formal empires (Fieldhouse 1976). Colonialism can also be viewed as an elaborate complex of a "Hierarchy of Domination" (Blue et al. 2002: 3–22). Their definition is divided as follows:

(a) Formal empires, involving direct and indirect rule, relying on local allies and collaborators as tools of control,
(b) Informal colonialism, utilizing a system of diplomatic and economic domination tying the local centre to the metropolitan capitals,
(c) Protectorate status, a fuzzy system providing extra diplomatic flexibility to maintain control and dominance.

In 1956 the Middle East exhibited all the types of control and domination listed above.

The two wings of foreign domination are: *Colonialism*, described as the conquest and control of other people's land and goods; and *Imperialism*, defined as global strategic competition as well as the product of surplus capital looking for profits not available at home (Loomba 1998: 1–8). The physical (or political) control of the colonies and dependencies in terms of territories, resources, and political and cultural structures – i.e. Colonialism, in combination with a strategy for global domination, and Imperialism – were quite evident in the Middle East after the Second World War. Foreign occupation or the prevailing subservient domination, the control of oil resources, controlling the strategic transportation channels, the foreign military bases dotting the landscape, the large numbers of colonial officials and private settlers in the colonies, the abundance of investment with massive non-residual profits in many sectors, and the captive trade arrangements with the colonial powers provided the background for the decolonization struggle. The combination of enormous military, political, and economic powers globally renders the need for direct military and economic control superfluous.

Imperial control is defined by some, such as Duara (2004: 3), as simply a competition for control of global *resources and markets*. This is, however, an incomplete view of imperialism, as *political and strategic* rivalries have historically played a significant role in the expansion of the imperialist enterprise.

2.3 Colonial (Peripheral) Nationalism and Imperial Collapse

Hobson (1938) did not pull any punches earlier when he stated, "The *Pax Britannica*, always an impudent falsehood, has become a grotesque monster of hypocrisy" (Hobson 1978: 126). The break-down in the imperial order (Darwin 1991: 70–74) revolves around three major components:

First, the '*Metropolitan*' explanation centres on economic weakness at home, the declining economic benefit from the colonies, shrinking military power and its increased burden, as well as changing class interests resulting in the redefinition of the national interests in the metropolis away from overseas 'obligations'.

Second, the '*Peripheral*' explanation argues that colonial nationalism made the empire unworkable. This explanation is far from uniform, as the strength and components, as well as the *raison d'être*, of the anti-colonial movements varied from region to region and from one period to the next. However, the rising anti-colonial sentiments in the colonies, and the escalating calculus of maintaining control by the colonial powers figured prominently in the decision to seek an imperial exit.

Third, the '*International*' explanation is rooted in the emergence of the post-1945 two world superpowers, which left little room for middle-rank powers clinging hopelessly to the prerogatives of a bygone era. This reduced status of middle powers became obvious when the European 'Empire' became dependent on the US for economic and strategic survival. The 'Empires' were no longer able to survive as going concerns when the ingredients of their power, internally and externally, were falling apart and challenged by a new world reality.

The crystallization of colonial resistance was clearly an important factor – but not the only factor – in the imperial breakdown. Paradoxically, European influence helped the expansion of colonial nationalism, which became the ideology of the educated colonial elites and became necessary for the mobilization of mass anti-colonial movements. The accommodation reached between the British colonial power in Egypt and the colonial political, commercial, and landed elites for the operation of a system of informal imperialism and collaboration eventually failed in the face of increasingly strong anti-colonial pressure.

Darwin discusses decolonization in terms of Ronald Robinson's theory of 'Peripheral Collaboration' which implies that "colonial nationalism was more of a symptom than a cause of colonial breakdown" (Darwin 1999: 541–557). The imperial power at the centre had always relied on informal (later they often became formal) structures of collaboration in the periphery to maintain control. When, after World War I, the system of collaboration started to fail under nationalist pressures, Britain had the options of using coercive force to destroy the nationalist challenge, or of sweetening the deal for collaboration and installing a malleable regime in order to maintain its control. Suez may be seen as a case in which the first option was utilized after the second option failed after 1952. Darwin also describes what he terms the reliance of the colonial state and the structure of informal imperialism on carefully structured collaboration to maintain control.

Peripheral Collaboration and the support for malleable regimes in the colonies served colonial interests for a while, until colonial nationalism and resistance escalated. Suez may also be seen as a case in which beneficial colonial-nationalist collaboration collapsed and the use of force backfired, ending imperial control in an unceremonial maelstrom. In other words, the failure of the system of 'informal empire' due to increased nationalist pressures led to grudging acknowledgement of the inability to sustain the old imperial order at an acceptable cost. The only option left was to pull up the colonial-imperial stakes and terminate the 'formal empire'. The European empires were confronted not with a 'brave' new world, but rather with a bleak and uncertain future in a world slipping from their grip with the arrival of new power contenders on the world stage.

Moreover, Darwin argues elsewhere that 'the post-war international super-power rivalries enabled the newly independent colonies to maintain their independence' (Darwin 1988). Such a position begs the question: Was colonial freedom just coincidental? Was colonial political independence reliant and conditional only on superpower machinations and/or endorsement?

Indeed, Nasser exploited US-Soviet competition to further his nationalist agenda. But at no time was revolutionary Egypt willing to acquiesce to the demands of one or the other or to compromise on its independence – no matter how truncated or shackled it was – or to 'maintain' such independence at any cost. Suez was the proof that the periphery was willing to fight for its independence, regardless of the temporary alignment of the superpowers on Suez, each for its own advantage.

To complicate the narrative, Darwin (1991: 70–74) echoes Benedict Anderson's (and Immanuel Wallerstein's) view of the nationalist movements as invented imaginary nations (Anderson 2002; Wallerstein 1974).

According to Osterhammel (1977), reviewed by Callahan (1999), 'colonization' designates a *process* of territorial acquisition, 'colony' a particular type of sociopolitical *organization*, and 'colonialism' a *system* of domination. The basis of all three concepts is the notion of the expansion of society beyond its original habitat (Osterhammel 1977: 4). Post-colonial experience has shown – with some exceptions – that the new independent regimes have largely maintained previous political and commercial networks with the former colonial masters.

In a masterly survey of European decolonization, R.F. Holland (1985) posited the theory that the decolonization process affecting the declining European imperial control occurred because colonialism, as "a set of nationally orchestrated systems", ceased to possess the "self-sustaining virtue of internal equilibrium". External pressures on the imperial project, moreover, hastened the disintegration of the colonial edifice. The decolonization process itself lacked "any progressive, linear shape", as colonial dominance experienced "sharp declines and prolonged revivals". Multiple internal and external factors eventually brought the colonial structure to a torturous end. For the British, the challenge was how to find new conjunctions between local aspirations and imperial interests. The delicate structure of collaboration shattered, leading to "collaborative decomposition". Holland adds that colonization became a 'dysfunctional' project, ushering in a process of mutual 'dis-imperialism' in both the imperial core and the colonial periphery, reaching its zenith in the period 1964 to 1968. New world realities rendered the old collaborative system obsolete. The so-called 'civilizing mission' of colonialism was exposed as a self-serving tool, creating in the process a strong anti-Western reaction. Decolonization became a "process of voluntary disengagement" as the remaining colonies were "hustled rudely into independence".

Moreover, it is argued that although colonial independence was frequently seen as a sham, the colonies gained independence not because of their success in securing an advantage in the international arena, but because they had ceased to matter. Although decolonization began to assume a moral justification, it was, nevertheless, branded a 'mask' for "appropriating the resources of the Third World". European decolonization can thus be described as a "low-level equilibrium" between increasingly self-centred European powers and stagnating corrupt former colonies. The ambivalent and evolving US attitude towards the European colonial powers became clear when the post-war American government made it clear that it had no intention of sharing power with Britain in a reshaping of the international order. Britain's relations with the new emerging Third World was seen by the European powers as a necessary cushion against American dominance in world markets (Holland 1985: 1, 2, 15, 51, 205, 271, 270, 301).

Partha Chatterjee (1986) was blunt in his analysis of peripheral nationalism. Nationalist thought cannot constitute an autonomous discourse. Most of its elements were imported from Europe, and, despite its attempts to extricate itself from European dominance, it remains the prisoner of its European intellectual roots. The contradictory outcome was that colonial nationalism challenged Western political domination, but accepted the very intellectual premises of Western modernity.

Prasenjit Duara described anti-imperialist nationalism as mostly led by westernized leaders from modernized sectors (Duara 2004: 39). M. Mamdani (1996) chides the leaders of the newly independent colonial world for supporting the principles of the French Revolution to gain their independence, but denying the application of the same principles to their own people. In fact, 'post'-colonial leaders, especially in Africa, instituted a system of control relying on despotism and corruption.

In addressing the pattern of African colonization in *The Eye of the Leopard*, Mankell described the essence of colonial control and the resulting collapse as "an empire that rests upon the most precarious of all foundations…Oppression, alienation…Such an edifice must collapse before it's even completed". He asserts that the colonization of poor peoples by superpowers is just as great today as at any time before (Mankell 1990: 115).

Basil Davidson goes further by criticizing both the colonial system which destroyed the pre-existing structure, and the post-colonial nation state which failed miserably to transform and improve: "The colonial legacy…was not a blessing of benevolent paternalism but a coil of problems pregnant with serious crises of malfunction" (Davidson 1992: 190).

W.R. Louis and R. Robinson describe the post-war imperial system as essentially a bankrupt metropole trying to reconstruct the imperial system by relying on trade without formal rule where possible, and formal rule where necessary (Louis/Robinson 1994: 462–511). The resulting imperial ingredients were: relatively few resources for the imperial upkeep, utilizing few military forces, maintaining scattered military bases, and the cultivation of the old imperial prestige and grandeur. The choice for Britain was between a slide into permanent weakness and a futile effort to revive a terminally ill imperial position. The approach adopted in 1956 established once and for all that henceforth Britain had to work in concert with the US or suffer humiliating consequences.

In a study of post-colonialism, the notion that colonialism was described (Young 2001: 5) as an "unfortunate accident of modernity" and that the "West mistook technological advance" as "cultural superiority", is rejected as misleading and incomplete. Young differentiated colonialism from imperialism. But both "involved forms of subjugation of one people by another". The 'Empire' was controlled from the centre (metropolitan) and pursued 'ideological' and 'financial' objectives. Colonialism, on the other hand, operated locally (peripheral) for "commercial purposes". Imperialism was driven by 'ideology' as a strategic policy of state, while colonialism's motivator was largely economic (Young 2001: 16–17). In reality, the 'colony' acted as the agent for the 'empire', behaving as a franchised enterprise. However, in several situations the colony was at odds with the 'head office', insisting on pursuing an independent course. South Africa, Israel, and French Algeria are examples of anti-nationalist colonial rebellion. Although colonialism did indeed introduce some elements of modernity to the colonized world, sweeping "colonialism under the carpet of modernity" is problematic, as the effects of colonialism are still operating on the world stage, and the world economy is still shaped and operated by the leading colonial powers of the past and the neo-colonial powers of the present. In short, the new independent state, according to Young, remains economically, thus politically, directed from abroad.

Moreover, imperialism, first described in Britain as an "odious system of bluster and swagger", and "might against right", had its claims for upholding the "universal superiority of the Western culture" strongly rejected by Hobson. He also rejected the *civilizing mission* argument, as well as the "trade follows the flag" justification. Imperialism, in this reading, was unprofitable overall, but was very profitable for the privileged elite. Imperialism, therefore, operated as a "public guarantor of private financial investments abroad". British foreign policy was primarily a struggle for securing profitable markets for British investments (Hobson 1902): The controversial *mission civilisatrice* argument, justified as *dominer pour servir* (dominate to serve and civilize), was exposed as a phony excuse for *profit*. Adas (2004) posits that the 'civilizing mission' was how the "Europeans rationalized their colonial domination of the rest of mankind. This 'self-serving' rationale was the basis for 'uplifting' the 'backward' peoples they conquered." The colonial and neo-colonial masters would provide capital, and skills; while the dominated colonized (or formerly colonized) territories "would supply the primary products, cheap labour and abundant land" to ensure profitable investments in the colonies (Adas 2004: 78–82).

Indeed, many colonies ceased to have any strategic or economic significance to the imperial-colonial powers, but 'voluntary' disengagement, in Holland's reading, cannot be applied across the board. Many 'disengagement' outcomes were the result of protracted, and in many cases, violent confrontations. The British 'disengagement' from Egypt was anything but voluntary. Egypt was not "rudely hustled into independence" (Holland 1985: 271). Far from it, as the protracted anti-colonial resistance convinced, rather forced, the British to accede to the nationalist demands. And when Britain tried to reclaim its vanishing imperial control by force, the world by then was a different place, and the old empire was forced to disgorge its ill-attempted re-conquest.

2.3.1 A Benign View of Imperialism?

Raymond Betts brought India's late Prime Minister into the discussion by analysing his controversial view that the "shock value" of European imperialism was significant (Betts 1979: 193–204). Nehru believed that "European culture, with its scientific and technological base, aroused other cultures from their centuries-old complacency or traditionalism". The primary agency of change in the colonized world, according to this reading, was European imperialism. Nehru's argument, despite its painful connotation, has some merit, but only up to a point. No matter how the colonized world benefited from the colonial experience, colonialism was a brutal and dehumanizing chapter. There is no question that benefits accruing to the colonies were almost entirely bestowed on the colonial elites. Oxford-educated Nehru could be justified in acknowledging some benefits of the colonial experience, as he was a member of the privileged colonial elite himself, an experience denied to millions – indeed, to the vast majority – of people in the colonial world. Nevertheless, it is intellectually 'honest', at least, to acknowledge some benefits, even by osmosis, to society at large, regardless of the overall lopsided situation.

Colonialism helped maintain the pre-colonial social and class inequities and the prevailing structures of exploitation, mainly by solidifying the elites' hold on the existing – albeit skewed – social patterns. Accepting and supporting this form of native oppression was the prize offered by the metropoles to the colonial elites for cooperating with the colonial structure. Domination and exploitation continued in the colonies after they gained independence, albeit under a different flag, a different language, and a different skin colour.

Edward Said offered another interpretation, criticizing colonial leaders for mistakenly believing that cooperation with the imperial authority was the only way to move forward (Said 2003). He reasoned that the dialectic between the imperial perspective and the local one is inevitably adversarial and impermanent: at some later point the conflict between ruler and the ruled becomes uncontainable and breaks out into all-out colonial war.

Keith Oatley describes the central role played by London in the profitable colonial trade, sucking goods into London from all over the world:

> The ships worked in triangle. Clothes and firearms to West Africa. Slaves from there to America and the West Indies…Then back here, to the London docks, with cotton or sugar. A big profit at each point of the triangle (Oatley 2010: 126).

Undoubtedly, Said would have agreed more readily with the sentiments expressed by Oatley than with Nehru's shock-value argument.

Robert Holland notes in his study of the British Empire's Mediterranean role that after the Second World War the USA was determined to press its advantage and take the lead from the British, who were fiercely guarding their traditional command over the Mediterranean (Holland 2012). The changing world balance of power after the War played an important role in accelerating the process of decolonization. The British Prime Ministers Clement Atlee (1945–51) and Harold Macmillan (1957–63) were realistic enough to accelerate the process of colonial disengagement. Between their respective terms of office, however, Winston Churchill (1951–55) and Anthony Eden (1955–57), were consumed with the imperial idea and with preserving Britain's global role. Mistakenly, Eden believed that Washington (the new Western leader) had little option but to back up British actions during the Suez Crisis in order to defend 'mutual' Western interests. But the US was not prepared to follow the British script, or to share its newly acquired leadership role.

Moreover, the disastrous cultivation of Israel in the Suez debacle as a cover for the British and French strike against Egypt confirmed Israel's role in the eyes of the struggling Arab nationalists as an anti-liberation agent for the West. This *symbiotic relationship* has had a massive impact on the history and stability of the entire region.

The face of imperial control has changed. Imperial armies are not openly involved in direct territorial acquisition. The armies are there to lend authority to plans for control, sabotage, regime change, foreign resource security, and propping up co-opted governments. Under the direction of imperial and neo-imperial governments, their national security spy apparatuses and multi-national corporations – a ruthless two-way grand symbiotic relationship with local malleable regimes and commercial interests – ensure the required control, and the destruction of local resistance by disobedient governments or active opposition groups.

References

Adas, Michael (2004): "Contested Hegemony: The Great War and the Afro-Asian Assault on the Civilizing Mission", in: Duara, Prasenjit [Ed.] *Decolonization: Perspectives from Now and Then* (New York: Routledge).

Beaufre, Andre (1969): *The Suez Expedition* (London: Faber and Faber).

Bennett, Ronan (1997): *The Catastrophist* (New York: Simon & Schuster).

Betts, Raymond F. (1979): "The Retreat from Empire", in: *Europe in Retrospect: A Brief History of the Past Two Hundred Years* (London: Heath & Co.): 193–204.

Betts, Raymond F. (2004): *Decolonization: The Making of the Contemporary World* (New York: Routledge).

Betts, Raymond F. (2012): "Decolonization: A Brief History of the Word", in Bogaerts, E.; Raben, R. (Eds.) *Beyond Empire and Nation: The Decolonization of African and Asian Societies, 1930s–1970s* (Leiden: Brill Academic Publishers): 23–38.

Blue, G.; Bunton, M.; Crozier, R., (Eds.) (2002): *Colonialism and the Modern World: Selected Studies* (New York: M.E. Sharpe).

Callahan, Michael (1999): "Review of Jurgen Osterhammel", *Colonialism: A Theoretical Overview*, in: H-Diplo (April).

Chatterjee, Partha (1986): *Nationalist Thought and the Colonial World: Derivative Discourse?* (London: Zed Books).

Darwin, John (1988): *Britain and Decolonization: The Retreat from Empire in the Post-War World* (London: Macmillan).

Darwin, John (1991): *The End of the British Empire: The Historical Debate* (London: Blackwell).

Darwin, John (1999): "Decolonization and the End of Empire", in: Winks, R.W. (Ed.), *The Oxford History of the British Empire: Historiography*, Vol. V (Oxford: Oxford University Press).

Davidson, Basil (1992): *The Black Man's Burden: Africa and the Curse of the Nation-State* (New York: Random House).

Duara, Prasenjit (2004): *Decolonization: Perspectives from Now and Then* (New York: Routledge).

Elkins, Caroline (2005): *Imperial Reckoning: The Untold Story of Britain's Gulag in Kenya* (New York: Henry Holt & Co.).

Elkins, Caroline (2014): *Britain's Gulag: The Brutal End of Empire in Kenya* (New York: Vintage Publishing).

Fieldhouse, D.K. (1976): "Imperialism and the Periphery", in: Wright, H.M., (Ed.): *The New Imperialism: Analysis of Late-Nineteenth-Century Expansion* (Toronto: Heath Publications).

Hobson, John A. (1965): *Imperialism: A Study* (Ann Arbor: University of Michigan Press).

Hobson, John A. (1902 & 1978): *Imperialism* (London: Cosimo).

Holland, R.F. (1985): *European Decolonization 1918–1981: An Introductory Survey* (London: Macmillan).

Holland, Robert (2012): *Blue-Water Empire: The British in the Mediterranean since 1800* (London: Allen Lane-Penguin).

Kelly, Saul; Gorst, Anthony (Eds.) (2000): *Whitehall and the Suez Crisis* (London: Frank Cass).

Landes, David S. (1979): *Bankers and Pashas: International Finance and Economic Imperialism in Egypt* (Boston: Harvard University Press).

Loomba, Anita (1998): *Colonialism/Post-Colonialism* (London: Routledge).

Louis, W.R.; Robinson, R. (1994): "The Imperialism of Decolonization", in: *Journal of Imperial and Commonwealth History*, 22, 3.

Mamdani, Mahmood (1996): *Citizen and Subject: Contemporary Africa and the Legacy of Late Colonialism* (Princeton: Princeton University Press).

Mankell, Henning (1990): *The Eye of the Leopard* (London: Harvill Secker).

Mommsen, Wolfgang; Osterhammel, Jürgen (Eds.) (1986): *Imperialism and After: Continuities and Discontinuities* (London: Allen and Unwin).

Oatley, Keith (2010): *Therefore Choose* (Fredericton, N.B.: Goose Lane Editions).

Osterhammel, Jürgen (1977): *Colonialism: A Theoretical Overview* (Princeton: Markus Weiner Publishers).

Safi, Michael (2019): "Churchill's Policies Contributed to 1943 Bengal Famine", in: *The Guardian* (29 March).

Said, Edward W. (2001): "Imperial Perspectives", in: *Al-Ahram Weekly* (Opinion) (Cairo: 11 March).

Said, Edward W. (1979): *Orientalism* (New York: Vintage Books).

Urquhart, Brian (1989): *Decolonization and World Peace* (Houston: University of Texas Press).

Wallerstein, Immanuel (1974): *The Modern World-System* (Berkeley: University of California Press).

Young, Robert (2001): *Post-Colonialism: An Historical Introduction* (Oxford: Blackwell Publishing).

Chapter 3
Sovereignty: Westphalia and Beyond

Abstract The principles underlying the post-war concept of the sovereignty of the nation state are affected by the increasingly assertive right of the international community to intervene in order to protect global peace and security at the expense of the semi-sacrosanct sovereign prerogatives of states. The concept of sovereignty is locked into a serious fight against the increasing reach of internationalism. This is apparent in the battering of the concept of nationalism in the age of globalization. Sovereignty and the associated principle of sovereign consent played a major role in the UNEF deployment as well as the termination of the UNEF mission in Egypt. In this chapter the theoretical review of sovereignty, consent, and nationalism will be examined in terms of their effects on the evolving international system of states.

Keywords Westphalian Sovereignty · Sovereign Equality · Consent · Nationalism · Globalization · Autonomy · Liberation Sovereignty · Human Rights · Circumspection of Sovereignty

3.1 Sovereignty

State sovereignty, rooted in the original peace of *Westphalia* arrangements in the *seventeenth* century, was bolstered by the emerging concept of nationalism in the *nineteenth* century. The post-World-War-Two mantra of sovereign equality, along with the earlier 1933 *Montevideo* principle (Montevideo Convention 1933: 20–43) linking sovereignty to statehood, has predominantly governed the conduct of nations in the international arena for several centuries.

The principles of Westphalian sovereignty and the associated concept of nationalism were enshrined in the *United Nations Charter* in 1945 during the tumultuous *twentieth* century. Chapter I: *Article 2* (1) of the UN Charter enshrines the principle of sovereign equality. Chapter V: *Article 23* (1, 2) and *Article 27* (3) of the same Charter, however, undermines that very principle by awarding exclusive permanent Security Council membership to a few states and guaranteeing them the right of veto – a right not given to any other member state. This exclusive privilege has thwarted the development of the balanced and equitable conduct of international relations, reflecting the cold realities of power disparity and the enthroning of a new imperial distribution of power at the helm of the United Nations in what is supposedly an age of decolonization and equality (UN Charter 1945: Articles 2, 23, 27).

Sovereignty and nationalism underlined the idea that 'states', as independent entities, should correspond to identifiable boundaries of 'nations', forming in the process exclusive political, religious, cultural, and linguistic communities. The fact that many nations today do not correspond to the ideal homogenous purity aspired to by ardent nationalists is at the core of numerous sectarian divides and conflicts, many of which spread across 'national' boundaries. But sovereignty and nationalism, nevertheless, have become closely intertwined and mutually reinforcing. Moreover, the core meaning of sovereignty and its prerogatives have been mutually accepted by the community of nations as the undisputed 'supreme authority' of the national government within an exclusive territory.

The post-World-War-II international relations system is predicated on the acknowledgement of and respect for the requirements of sovereignty among states, as spelled out in the UN Charter and the various international treaties and resolutions that followed. The intersection of the principles of sovereignty and the requirements of the deployment of the pioneering United Nations Emergency Force (UNEF) during the 1956 Suez War created a contested jurisdictional dispute between the UN and Egypt from the outset which continued until the termination of the mandate of the international Force. It has also tested the validity of the existence of a sovereign 'national' entity within an 'international' system of states.

The distinction between inter-state and intra-state is crucial in situating the principle of sovereignty in relation to peace operations and international human rights law. Traditional peacekeeping concerns have shifted from initiating and maintaining ceasefires to a more interventionist response to internal conflicts, including the use of force for more than self-defence (moving from UN Charter Chapter VI to Chapter VII and any justification in between).

The theoretical overview explores the principles of national sovereignty in relation to the international peacekeeping regime, and the later development of 'robust' intervention. Fundamentally, the sovereign state is concerned with the protection of its sovereign prerogatives during international conflict intervention, when such prerogatives might come under pressure. Such national vs. international interaction was put to the test during the landmark case of the United Nations Emergency Force (UNEF) in the autumn of 1956. The obstacles encountered in fashioning a working formula for the UNEF deployment in Egypt, and the agreed basis for its modus operandi and termination, represent the launch of the UN peace operations following World War II. This new international engagement tested newer political and legal concepts involving sovereignty, consent, and international responsibility for preserving peace.

The UNEF experience in Egypt has highlighted the crucial role of the sovereignty of the nation state in international relations. Moreover, the failure of the UNEF model of 1956 to bring lasting peace to Egypt and Israel, and their eventual military confrontation in 1967, provided the impetus for the search for a better conflict resolution strategy. Additionally, the increasing complexity and type of conflicts, including not just international but also intra-national confrontations, has compelled the international community to search for an alternative modus operandi to deal with the changing parameters of conflicts and, in the process, engage in a re-evaluation of the principles and limits of sovereignty.

The debate over sovereignty after UNEF, however, has run into theoretical and practical difficulties. The concern over 'inter-state' conflicts, although real and present, has shifted over time towards concern with 'intra-state' conflicts. Sovereignty, although still important, has made room for human rights considerations as an overriding value parameter for the international community. International intervention to defuse conflicts, and increasingly to protect human lives, is becoming robust and less circumspect regarding the sovereign prerogatives of the national state.

The original concept of '*sovereignty*' and the resulting legal imperative of '*sovereign equality*' in international relations provided the backdrop for the decisions surrounding UNEF in the 1956–1967 period. However, an increasingly important concern, which was lacking during the UNEF presence, is the importance of a 'post-conflict resolution' phase, for both domestic and international conflicts, and how the increasing challenge of such intervention fundamentally affects the concept of sovereignty.

Consequently, other concepts and intervention mechanisms in relation to the requirements of sovereignty are being developed in response to the increasing magnitude of international and national conflicts, and the corresponding need for new and effective approaches to conflict resolution. Sovereignty as an important basic tenet of the international system is increasingly facing fundamental re-evaluation. 'International humanitarian law' (the protection of civilians during war) has been, therefore, reinforced by the developing doctrine of 'international human rights law' (the protection of human lives). Although the UNEF experience proved disappointing in the end, at least it partly provided the push for alternative models for peace operations to emerge in relation to the concept of sovereignty.

The examination of the principle of sovereign *consent* occupies a pivotal position in dealing with the UNEF experience during both the Suez War (the Tripartite Invasion) in 1956, and the Arab-Israeli War (the Israeli Invasion) in 1967. Newer concepts of international interventions and alternative enforcement mechanisms – in light of the Suez lessons and beyond – are analysed in relation to both International Humanitarian Law and International Human Rights Law. The ideological debate about the nature of peace itself in international relations is also examined.

There is a growing realization that the impact of the concept of sovereignty and its contested manifestations for the independent state in an international conflict situation must be part and parcel of the establishment of any peacekeeping regime.

Such an approach provides a political-legal reference point and helps in framing the interaction between a sovereign state and the legal (and political) basis for international intervention.

3.2 Evolution of the Concept of Sovereignty

The assertion of the ancient conception of sovereignty depended more on power and divine right than legality. Only military and territorial control settled the issue of sovereignty until a new challenge reversed it or created a new sovereign reality. Two interpretations of sovereignty have dominated and influenced the legal and political theories of Thomas Hobbes and John Locke. First, a 'Hobbesian' account, which "defines the nation state by its national borders and minimal obligations to its citizens". Sovereignty is defined as absolute "unlimited rule over territory and its people". Second, a Lockean account, which "extends the sovereign's obligations to protect its citizens' private property interests". Sovereignty is defined as a "limited constitutional state". "Sovereign authority, in Locke's interpretation, is limited by its obligation to respect the rights of its subjects" (Stacy 2003: 2,029–2,034).

Taylor (1983) distills the traditions in political philosophy to situate the concept of sovereignty and power in the international system of states. The three main traditions that dominated global politics are:

(1) the realist tradition espoused by Hobbes. International society, according to this interpretation, is governed by continuous competition, conflict, and war. The interests of each state in the system exclude the interests of other states. Morality and law are respected domestically, but they do not apply outside the borders of the state. In relation to each other, states must be prudent and expedient.

(2) the *internationalist* tradition championed by Grotius. States in the international system are not gladiators in a global arena. States are the principal actors in the system and are limited in their conflicts by common rules and global institutions. Socio-economic interaction between countries forms the main international activity predicated on coexistence and prudent cooperation.

(3) the *universalist* tradition as pronounced by Kant. The central focus in this tradition is the community of mankind and not the system of states. Higher morality and cosmopolitan attitudes are essential. Sovereignty in this tradition takes a back seat to the progressive replacement of the state system by a global society based on coexistence and cooperation (Taylor 1983: 405–406).

Sovereignty, nevertheless, is "one of the most misunderstood concepts in international relations, in part because its definition is changing, and the political and conflict resolution implications are significant", affecting the original concept itself. The earlier concept of sovereignty is no longer upheld or exercised as originally envisaged. The fundamental assumption of the 'fixity' of the concept no longer applies.

Variant forms of sovereignty existed over the centuries prior to Westphalia. It was fundamentally attached to the 'ruler' regardless of the differences in the basis of governance. Emperors, kings, nobility, and feudal lords vied and competed over the centuries to establish absolute and unchallenged sovereign authority. Eventually, the basis of sovereignty changed in alignment with the change in the basis of authority and the declining role of religious control. The sixteenth-century dogma, characterized by the ruler's unbounded authority, started to recede, and a new basis of governance and authority, grounded in the concept of nationalism, gradually began to develop. The essence of the present notion of national sovereignty was not known before the sixteenth century.

Bodin believed in a 'sovereign' wielding sovereignty that is 'absolute' and 'perpetual' and cannot be delegated. Sovereignty, according to him, is conferred by divine law, practised absolutely but without the past abuses of absolute power (Bodin 1992: 124–125). Hobbes supported the idea that people must submit to a 'Sovereign' authority – a 'Leviathan' which is an "abstract notion of the state". Such authority is able to force them to support the common good (Hobbes 1651). Both Bodin's Sovereign and Hobbes' Leviathan were above the law and are accountable only to God and to natural law.

The international legal scholar Lassa Oppenheim (1928: 103) believed that the meaning of the concept of sovereignty was never universally agreed upon. In its simplest formulation, sovereignty is "not originally or primarily an abstract idea" created by theorists or philosophers and applied to the real world. Rather, it is an "expedient idea" developed by rulers to repudiate and escape from the overarching papal authority. The rulers also asserted their sovereign authorities within their claimed jurisdictions against other rival rulers, establishing in the process the early foundations of the international system of states (Jackson 2007: xi).

Religious and civil wars in Europe opened the door to a new application of sovereignty. As divine and absolute sovereignty receded, ideas reflected in the works of Luther, Figgis, Hobbes, Locke, Hume, Rousseau, Montesquieu and others gradually introduced the notions of the social contract and popular sovereignty. Some sovereign authorities, however, undermine the essence of sovereignty as an 'ultimate power on behalf of a collectivity' by exercising absolute control as an an individual, a family, a tribe, or a party without observing any of the constitutional structures of a sovereign state or the existence of guarantees of the rights of citizens within the state.

State sovereignty began to assert its supremacy vis-à-vis the supremacy of the Church. The French Revolution emphatically transferred the provenance of sovereignty from the ruler to the nation, reflecting the will of the people. Political sovereignty is mirrored by territorial sovereignty, defining the extent and reach of the exclusive sovereignty of the state. Sovereignty, therefore, asserts a defined territorial control and authority which is recognized internationally on a mutual basis, as exclusive across national boundaries. The borders between sovereign states are thus inviolable.

J.N. Figgis believed that the removal (destruction) of the role of the 'Church' (and any 'extra-territorial authority') from the public space is essential for the unity and supremacy of the sovereign state. Figgis credited Martin Luther with the success of the concept of the 'sovereign territorial state' and the denial of any 'extra-territorial' authority (Figgis 1907: 72–91).

An important pioneering work published in 1957 describes the "transformation in the concept of political authority" over the centuries. Although rulers in the past wielded absolute authority, over time a gradual transformation began to take shape away from absolutism. Eventually, "Modern polity is known as the state, and the fundamental characteristic of authority within it, sovereignty. This examination of historical development shows that 'Sovereignty is the central organizing principle of the system of states". The nation state has emerged as the "primary unit of political organization". The sovereign entity has "supreme authority within a territory" or "absolute authority within a bounded territorial space". The sovereign government has a monopoly on the use of force internally, and enjoys the recognition of other sovereign states, which ensures the territorial integrity of the nation state, and its admission into the international arena on an equal footing with other states. The post-war international system has been operating on such sacrosanct foundations. The increasing scope and magnitude of international and national conflicts is challenging and putting to the test the essence of sovereignty (Kantorowicz 1957 1998: 1–4).

The state – as the supreme instrument of the nation – becomes the "political institution in which sovereignty is embodied". The holder of sovereignty derives *authority* to govern from a "mutually acknowledged source of legitimacy" (natural law, divine mandate, hereditary law, a constitution, and international law). Wolff elaborates this point, relying on J.J. Rousseau's contributions. In a majority rule system, autonomous citizens abide by the will of the majority "by giving up one's autonomy". By forfeiting autonomy, however, the right to govern, in this reading, means the right to command and the right to be obeyed regardless of the citizen's position on the issue. Such right confers legitimacy (Wolff 1970: 7–19).

J.J. Rousseau "challenged the traditional order of society" which kept freeborn men in 'chains'. Moreover, he saw sovereignty as the collectivity of "people within a state", ruling through their "general will". Sovereignty means that "the will of the people is supreme". For Rousseau, sovereignty is inalienable, indivisible, and infallible, but limited by the "common interest" as governed by laws (Rousseau 1762: 63).

The modern concept of sovereignty is rooted in the *Peace of Westphalia* arrangements, concluded on 15 May 1648 (Treaty of *Osnabrück*) and 24 October 1648 (Treaty of *Münster*). The series of Westphalian treaties were seen as the instruments which ended the European wars of religion. Westphalia initiated, consequently, a new political order in central Europe in the seventeenth century, and established the foundations of the modern international system of states dominating at present.

Key sacrosanct principles emanating from Westphalia, according to Osiander (2001: 251–287), Gross (1948: 20–41), and Jackson (2004: 53), and operating mutually at international level, include:

(a) The right of political self-determination and state sovereignty.
(b) Legal equality between sovereign states.
(c) Non-intervention in the internal affairs of other states.

Thus, the foundations for the system governing today's international relations were initiated several centuries ago in Europe. Westphalian sovereignty, nevertheless, is currently undergoing global modifications to hitherto sacrosanct principles in the face of accumulating challenges following World War II.

Sovereignty accords an inalienable right of legitimacy and authority to govern, and is understood to represent the ultimate pinnacle of national power (as overseen by a constitution), with the attached right to rule and legislate. The resulting sovereign state enjoys political independence and territorial integrity as mutually recognized by other sovereign states. Sovereignty, therefore, denotes a government in control of a country not answerable to any other authority outside its border, except international obligations freely entered into.

Sovereignty, which developed in Europe and spread to the rest of the world, is defined as "the basic constitutional doctrine of the law of nations" (Brownlie 1979: 287). It is also a "foundational idea of politics and law" (Jackson 2007: x). Any concept of sovereignty, however, which accords states "power above international law" is invalid. This view holds that the state is bound by the concept of the "equality of states", which implies that the "sovereign rights of each state are limited by the equally sovereign rights of others" (Dickinson 1920: 114–115).

In general, sovereignty is: absolute, perpetual, with exclusive supreme authority within a defined territory, and the legitimate right to govern. To be acknowledged, internally and externally, sovereignty must be both *de jure* and *de facto*. Both principles are required to validate the concept of sovereignty. "Sovereignty requires not only the 'legal' right to exercise power, but the 'actual' exercise of such power." Therefore, there can be "no *de jure* sovereignty without *de facto* sovereignty", as sovereignty requires both elements. In some cases, however, *de jure* sovereignty is claimed without having physical control, examples being voluntary or involuntarily imposed government in exile; declarations by national liberation organizations which are not in full control of the entire national territory; political sovereignty claims by competing groups inside or outside the national territory; or competing claims of sovereignty over a disputed territory by two national states (Dickinson 1920: 152).

The original concept of sovereignty is no longer upheld or exercised as originally envisaged. Currently, sovereignty is still the "constituent idea of the modern age" and the resulting "global system of authority". The system, however, is facing many challenges and contradictions. Moreover, sovereign statehood is not tied to any form of domestic governance, as sovereignty "does not entail a permanent fixed domestic arrangement of political life" (Jackson 2007: 19, 147). Domestic governance mode does not have to be tied to an idealized international image of politics, as such an image varies significantly according to ideologies and power profiles across the globe.

The changing conditions in the international system of states, including the increasing concerns for the protection of human rights, is behind "the gradual circumspection of the sovereign state" and has created clear and "increasing limits on the exercise of sovereign authority" within national borders. Contemporary developments since 1991 have affected the concept of traditional sovereignty in order to protect human rights and were driven by the horrors of World War II and the increasing abuse of fundamental rights by states in the post-war era. The emergence of overriding concern for human rights in international law and international relations has undoubtedly impacted the essence of sovereignty and the rules of international relations (Brahm 2004: 787–824).

Various political-strategic motivations – some dubious or at least suspect – have been used to justify the selective intervention in the internal affairs of some 'sovereign' states "without their acquiescence" (Wheeler 2000: 8–10). In many cases, crass political calculations have guided such intervention.

Moreover, since the end of the Cold War, the Security Council has increasingly reinterpreted the UN Charter by favouring human rights over state sovereignty. This increasing "legitimation of intervention" is based on the shift towards "humanitarian claims and justice" over the previous imperative of maintaining order based on the principle of "non-intervention" (Pugh 2005: 51). It should be acknowledged, however, that such limitations on state authority are not applicable across the board, as elements of human rights abuses in the US, Russia, China, and many other states across the globe demonstrate.

Although the "concept of sovereignty is under considerable pressure", "some aspects of sovereignty still exist and are honoured in most circumstances, but many inroads are being made into state authority by many actors in many different circumstances. Where this will lead has yet to be determined" (Nan 2005).

3.3 Legal Aspects of Sovereignty

A key to the concept of sovereignty, then, lies in the legal principle of the "*exclusivity of jurisdiction*", according to which a decision by a sovereign state cannot be overruled or interfered with by another authority (Oppenheim 1955: 163–267). The concept of sovereignty, however, has generated many critical debates over the years and garnered such descriptions as 'murky', 'emotional', and 'controversial' (Oppenheim 1905: 103). Some critical comments assert that the concept of sovereignty makes extensive claims, putting the state above the law, turning the concept into a "false doctrine" (Brierly 1963: 48–49).

Like the pre-war critics of sovereignty, several post-war political theorists, including de Jouvenel (1957) and Maritain (1951), criticized sovereignty as a dangerous idea concentrating power in the hands of the few and creating illegitimate authority contrary to natural law. Nevertheless, a high degree of agreement has been found for the proposition that in the modern world "sovereignty is an attribute of statehood", and "only states can be sovereign". The classic definition of a 'state' is found in the 1933 *Montevideo Convention on Rights and Duties of States* (Montevideo Convention 1933: 20–439).

Article I of the Convention states:

> The State as a person of international law should possess the following qualifications: (a) a permanent population; (b) a defined territory; (c) government; and (d) capacity to enter into relations with other states.

Sovereignty, accordingly, denotes both the "supreme authority of the state", and an exclusive territorially-defined "political and legal independence".

Sovereignty, however, raises the question of legitimacy. *Internally*, to what extent does the ruler exercise political authority over his subjects, and does the source of his authority issue from consent exercised through a social contract, oppressive control, or because it is thought to be ordained by divine right? *Externally*, sovereignty is basically concerned with the "relationship between a sovereign power and other states" as organized by international law, regardless of the existence of internal political legitimacy (Dickinson 1920: 114–159).

Spruyt (1994), indicated that Marx, Durkheim, Weber, Wallerstein and Anderson believed in an evolutionary process in state sovereignty based on the changes in the 'mode of production' associated with the functional shift from feudalism to capitalism, socialism, and beyond (a more efficient form of production displacing an older one). Spruyt rejects such a unilinear progression account of sovereignty, observing that evolution is not a unilinear process, but is "driven by fits and starts". He also rejects the notion, based on the world systems theory, that capitalism helped to forge the sovereign state system, contending that "States preceded the development of a capitalist world economy". In his views, nothing was "inevitable about the emergence of the sovereign territorial state". It emerged because of a "particular conjuncture of social and political interests" (Spruyt 1994: 18–21).

In a forthcoming publication in defence of territorial sovereignty in the age of globalization, Uta Kohl (2018: 1) posits that the state, based on territorial sovereignty, "provides the ideal mechanism for global capital and corporate activity to function and grow...The territorial nation state provides the legal framework" for the success of globalization.

A crucial element in the development of the concept of sovereignty was the demarcation of the lines of control between the various European powers in the European colonies in order to assert control over their colonized domains. Such artificially drawn lines were transformed into national boundaries after the independence of the colonies, regardless of the viability of such lines or the ethnic, cultural or historical affinity of the affected populations. Decolonization, in many instances, resulted in manufactured borders for the new sovereign states, with disparate domestic tribal, ethnic, cultural and religious allegiances.

In the wake of the colonial retreat, these post-colonial states "have lacked the internal dimensions of sovereignty" due to "general lack of capacity to govern". Moreover, sovereignty based on "arbitrarily drawn borders" (Brahm 2004: 2) created in the process divided populations, badly fractured societies, and a lack of cohesive nation-building ingredients. Additionally, the lack of trust in the central authority, and the absence of a viable and tested democratic tradition, rendered sovereignty incomplete and contested. Therefore, these new states are "not fully sovereign" (Krasner 1996: 472–96). The linkage between domestic and international attributes of sovereignty, in the wake of decolonization, has become a controversial legal-political issue. The assumption that attaining domestic capacity to govern must precede international recognition of sovereignty was not adhered to in many cases. The fear was that "rapid and hasty decolonization" would "produce disorder in international affairs" fundamentally because the new independent states "lacked any attributes of stateness" (Kay 1967: 786–811).

This opens the door to the discussion of 'homogeneity', on ethnic, religious, and cultural grounds, in relation to national sovereignty. The lack of perceived homogeneity and, consequently, challenged social and political harmony, has created massive fault lines and divisions in the political fabric of the nation state, with deadly outcomes.

Conflicts occurring domestically and spreading across contrived borders have, therefore, created instability, warfare, and undermined the basis of legitimacy of many sovereign states. Such a pattern took place in Latin America, Asia, the Middle East, and finally Africa, with the seeds of conflict firmly embedded in such sovereignties. A disputed and conflicted sense of belonging undermines the essence of sovereignty and creates the conditions for civil wars and genocide. Unlike older established mature democratic states where minority rights are established constitutionally and in practice, many of the new sovereign states, however, were only able to artificially consolidate the supremacy of the new independent structures without mature traditions and solid foundations of nationhood. The forces of division are lurking under the surface and could erupt at any juncture with devastating effects. There is no denying, however, that many of the artificially established states in the former colonies have managed over the years to create a semblence of legitimacy among the citizenry based on accrued benefits to the ruling elites, bureaucracy, force of habit, or just brute force, and, to borrow Anderson's famous phrase, as an imagined community, and finally, as a *fait acompli*.

The *Hobbesian* view of the absolute sovereign state based on protecting the national border and providing minimal obligations or protection to its citizens (limited constitutional state), and the *Lockean* account, which places greater emphasis on the protection of society (expanded constitutional state), are augmented by yet another view, labelled "*Relational Sovereignty*" (Stacy 2003: 2029–2059), based on a model of "responsible governance" rooted in a universal "broader notion of the state's responsibilities towards its citizens". This new interpretation rejects the idea that sovereignty stops at the border, as "states are no longer shielded from external intervention in internal actions". Such a radical departure from the Westphalian roots affects both the nation state and the international system as a whole.

The changing scene internationally tends to support the belief that sovereignty in the international system of states is no longer supreme (Petersmann 2006: 1) due to the emergence of *erga omnes* obligations to recognize inalienable human rights, and *jus cognes* limitations preventing the national state from renouncing human rights treaties. Clearly, the traditional concept of sovereignty is facing many challenges.

3.4   Sovereignty and Nationalism

The idea of sovereignty is a product of modern political thought, according to McIlwain, who stated that "conducive to a theory of sovereignty, is the idea of nationality, growing gradually into a sentiment of national unity" (McIlwain 1932: 392), as quoted in Jackson (2007: 6). Brian Urquhart agrees, however, with Vaclav Havel (the late President of the Czech Republic), who described the "concept of national sovereignty" as a "dangerous anachronism". This criticism was made, however, by a national leader who fought hard to rescue Czechoslovak national sovereignty from the control of the Soviet Union. Urquhart supports Havel's view by denouncing the "concept of national sovereignty, in the guise of extreme nationalism" as the cause of many wars (Urquhart 2000: 11). A distinction must be made, however, between peace intervention on human rights grounds, which is justified, and intervention to serve a political objective which may or may not be intended for neutral humanitarian protection.

One should tread carefully when condemning sovereignty and nationalism. Self-determination, freedom, national identity and grounded belonging, liberty in its widest sense, and other ethos of human dignity and self-fulfilment reside within the concept of national sovereignty. Condemnation should be reserved for the abuse of the concept, not the concept itself. "Extreme nationalism" and "dangerous anachronism" represent the abuse that could happen, but they do not represent the essence of national sovereignty. History is replete with evidence of such abuse, which sadly extends to the present in many jurisdictions. Totalitarian regimes have fought nationalism as a threat to their overarching unitary ideologies. Soviet brutal hegemony, Nazi horrific expansion, and Islamist genocidal oppression are some of the examples of ideologies battling and suppressing nationalist aspirations to impose their unwelcome views. A distinction must also be made between benign positive *patriotism* embodied in the love of country, its people and its ideals, and on the other hand, predatory *nationalism* and its destructive accompaniments.

The present international system and the UN Charter, however, are predicated on the principle of national sovereignty. The safeguards against abuse are tools available to the international community. The inability to properly utilize the tools available to deal with deviations, or to respect the principles of peaceful coexistence, is not the fault of the concept of sovereignty or nationalism. The competing ideologies and the realist school of international relations influencing the conduct of some states in the post-war era should shoulder some of the responsibility. Ideological interpretations and condemnation abound, but one must not throw out the baby with the bath water.

Over the years, the concept of '*nationalism*' has had its fair share of both support and criticism. Initially, nationalism was a cry for freedom and an escape from oppressive religious and dynastic structures. The 'nation', in the words of Renan (1882), a pioneer of the concept, is "a living soul, a moral conscience, a spiritual principle, a large-scale solidarity, a daily plebiscite, and a perpetual affirmation. The abdication of individuals for the common good of the community creates the legitimate right of a nation to exist.". But he also said that nationalism is not eternal, and that violence was a pre-requisite for unity and nationhood (Renan 1882: 1–18). And Weber (1991) believed that the nation is a "sentiment of solidarity" (Weber 1991: 172).

Anderson (2002), the proponent of the nation as an imagined community, stated that after World War I, "imperial uniforms were replaced by the national costume of the nation-state" (Anderson 2002: 113). Anderson's work is in the mould of Kohn's interpretation of nationalism as primarily a "state of mind" (Kohn 1944: 9). But Kohn warned of the conflict between nationalism as power and the degrading of individual liberty.

Gandhi championed non-violent nationalism as the ideal path to freedom. He viewed naionalism as assimilative and tolerant. Thus Gandhi (2015) stated that "It is not the nationalism that is evil, it is the narrowness, selfishness, exclusiveness which is the bane of modern nations which is evil" (Rai 2017: 1). For Steger (2000), Gandhi's insistence on *ahimsa* (non-violence) as a "conceptual source" and "political means" for independece set him apart from other nationalists (Steger 2010: 247). Patnaik (2019) summarized the traits of Gandhi's nationalism as inclusive, serving the people, and not imperialist. (Patnaik 2019:1).

More recently, *The Economist* (2016) wrote that 'civic nationalism' "appeals to universal values, such as freedom and equality". Ethnic nationalism', on the other hand, is "zero-sum, aggressive and nostalgic which draws on race or history to set the nation apart" (*The Economist* 2016: 9).

Einstein (1929) stated: "Nationalism is an infantile disease. It is the measles of mankind." He also said in 1933 that "Nationalism is an idealistic rationalization for militarism and aggression" (quoted in Smith 2014). Orwell (1945), moreover, stated that "Nationalism is power hunger tempered by self-deception." He warned, however, that nationalism should not be confused with patriotism. Orwell believes that patriotism signifies the defensive devotion to a place and a way of life without forcing it on other people, while nationalism is inseparable from the desire for power and prestige (Orwell 1945).

President Tito of the former Yugoslavia described nationalism as a "mixture of national egoism and national chauvinism" (Tito 1948). Moreover, academic literature is replete with analyses of the virtue or the vices of nationalism (*The Economist*, November 2016).

The Suez experience brought to the surface two types of competing sovereignties: an '*anti-colonial militant (Liberation) sovereignty*' focused on achieving political and socio-economic national independence, as exhibited by the anti-colonial struggle in the Middle East and Africa in the 1950s and the 1960s; and the Curzon/Milner '*rind sovereignty*' conjured in the 1920s to pacify Egyptian nationalist demands. This compromised sovereignty was offered by the colonial powers to absorb and deflect the rising anti-colonial resistance. This second sovereignty is devoid of any 'real' attributes of sovereignty, possessing only the trappings of artificial independence camouflaging a state of dependency and lack of genuine control. Variations of the 'rind' sovereignty dominated the decolonization process. Formal independence was granted but a complex 'network of dependency' was maintained through political and military alliances, co-opted elites, augmented through the incorporation in a subservient role into the world economy for investment, trade and profit extraction. This 'anaemic sovereignty' was further degraded through globalization, as the national state was undermined and robbed of its real independence.

3.5 Sovereignty and Peace Operations

The classic definition of *Westphalian* sovereignty as 'the exclusion of external authorities from the domestic decision-making processes considered the purview of a sovereign state' is being further categorized as *Domestic* sovereignty (the effective organization of authority within the territory of a state), *Interdependent* sovereignty (the ability of a state to regulate movements across its borders), and *International-Legal* sovereignty (the formal recognition of an entity as a state). According to Keohane, societies should develop on the basis of a "gradation of sovereignty" of their political authority, moving from 'limited' sovereignty to the full integration in a multilateral international framework. This view accepts, at least initially, 'conditioned' and 'incomplete' sovereignty which contradicts the principles enshrined in the UN Charter (Keohane 2003: 275–298).

The unbundled classical concept of sovereignty is proving problematic in relation to peacekeeping operations: "the classical, unitary conception of sovereignty as the exclusive right to determine policy within a defined territory is an *obstacle* to effective post-conflict reconstruction" (Krasner 2004: 85–120). The assumption that the sovereign state is an independent legal entity free to act without outside imposition (subject to freely-entered international obligations) is, in fact, being transformed in response to changes in the international political and legal environment. The assumed unrestricted freedom within national borders is being redefined, reduced, and compromised.

Needless to say, the move from strict sovereignty to multilateralism raises the ire of the 'purist' defenders of state independence. But as events over the last decades have proven, state leaders can no longer count on hiding behind the curtain of sovereignty while violating basic tenets of international relations, or committing human rights atrocities. The international community, in response, is sharpening all the legal tools available to override the barrier of sovereignty and intervene on the ground to save human lives. International intervention, however, is sometimes selective to serve political objectives, and is not resorted to only on a humanitarian grounds.

Morality aside, political considerations, therefore, largely underline the intervention operations of the international system even for humanitarian purposes. The consent of the sovereign state to international intervention affecting its sovereignty under certain conditions is no longer sacrosanct or unassailable. The changing international environment affecting sovereignty, however, is not applicable across the board. Power considerations still play an important role.

The distinction between 'inter-state' and 'intra-state' conflicts is crucial in situating the principle of sovereignty (and consent) in relation to peace operations, and to invocations of international human rights laws. The Suez War was an 'inter-state' conflict in which the principle of sovereignty was crucial in shaping the type of peace operation deployed. By contrast, the Rwanda tragedy was an 'intra-state' conflict requiring international intervention to uphold human rights law at the expense of the traditional concept of sovereignty. The example of East Timor blurs the distinction. The UN got involved there to secure independence for the persecuted population of East Timor from the Indonesian occupying power, which had claimed sovereign authority ever since Portugal's 1974 withdrawal from the territory. So, in reality, the UN was dragged into the business of national liberation whether the controlling authority was foreign in origin or part of the existing political structure.

Before the 1990s, traditional peacekeeping was concerned with maintaining ceasefires and separating combatants without changing the parameters of the conflict itself. Attaining final peaceful outcomes to conflicts was beyond the purview of traditional peacekeeping intervention. This reality was demonstrated in the Middle East in 1949–1956 and again in 1956–1967, as well as in Cyprus from 1964 to the present. Moreover, respect for the sovereignty of states and their right of consent were the ground rules for peace operations. With the end of the Cold War in the 1990s, and the demonstrated failure of existing peacekeeping methods to change ceasefires into situations of durable peace, and with the changing nature of conflicts, peacekeeping had to be transformed. It has become, in the process, more interventionist at the expense of the prevailing accepted notions of the sovereignty of the state system. Limiting the use of force by UN forces to self-defence is no longer the only option, as has been demonstrated by the increasingly interventionist UN (and other foreign powers) involvement in world conflicts.

In an important contribution to both the concept of sovereignty and the UN peacekeeping operations, Michael Barnett makes a distinction between 'Juridical Sovereignty' (external) and 'Empirical Sovereignty' (domestic) in relation to the international order as it impacts peacekeeping (Barnett 1995: 79–97). While sovereignty is manifested through both external independence and domestic control, the survival of the sovereign state in the international system (juridical) traditionally took precedence over considerations of the degree and extent of legitimacy internally (empirical). The participation in the international system of states overrides the type of governance and control internally. Peacekeeping was operating within such confines.

International relations and the international order of states, including the active decolonization movement, during the post-World-War-II period was premised on the dominance of 'juridical' sovereignty, with its emphasis on the universal and mutual recognition of the political independence of the states in the system (including the right of consent) and respect for territorial integrity. The international order – and its utilization of UN peacekeeping – was predicated on the upholding of such sacrosanct juridical sovereign national independence.

The post-Cold-War realignment of power on the international scene and the increasing domestic conflicts in the newly independent former colonies, however, shifted the emphasis to considerations of 'empirical' sovereignty (the degree of legitimacy and control *within* national borders). The international system, therefore, is incorporating and reflecting many elements of the domestic policies and practices of states in conflict situations, in deciding on the scope and type of deployment of peace operations. Juridical sovereignty is no longer the only criterion governing the international order; empirical sovereignty is equally taken into account. The international system of states is exhibiting a more interventionist profile at the expense of the requirements of political sovereignty. Consequently, peacekeeping mandates are less constrained in observing the requirements of the sovereignty of states.

Barnett goes as far as to posit that states can enjoy juridical sovereignty *only* after achieving empirical sovereignty (Barnett 1995: 79–97). What this argument forgets is that states, to become states, must obtain juridical sovereignty first, in one form or the other. Only then can the degree and legitimacy of empirical sovereignty come into play. But he is right in observing that peacekeeping operations embody the concern of the international community for the degree and quality of empirical sovereignty of many states in the international political system. 'Pure' sovereignty and the 'unrestricted' right of prior consent belong to a different era in the history of international law. However, sovereign consent cannot be written off completely without fundamentally affecting the post-war international system.

The '*Annan Doctrine*' (Annan 1999: 1–2) coined in the wake of UN intervention (or failure to intervene) in Kosovo, Rwanda, and East Timor, emphasized the "loss of traditional prerogatives of sovereignty in the face of crimes against humanity", according to H. Stacy (2003: 2035). UN intervention in confronting human rights abuses is, therefore, no longer bound by traditional sovereign barriers. Moreover, leaders who allow, condone, or participate in such abuses or prevent measures to bring the abuse to an end, risk international sanctions and legal prosecution.

Annan's position earned another comment by I. Arias (1999: 1004–1029), in which the author claims that the Secretary-General was modifying his position based on his target audience. In a statement in Geneva (April 1999), Annan said that the defence of human rights is at the heart of our work and our Charter. International intervention against violent repression must take precedence over concerns of state sovereignty, as no government has the right to hide behind national sovereignty or the existence of borders, implying support for NATO's intervention in Kosovo. No previous UN Secretary-General stated that "the sovereignty of state is not absolute".

As proponents of sovereignty were alarmed at the shift of the tone, Annan gave another speech in The Hague (May 1999) in which he seemed to have put a check on the right of unauthorized intervention outside the scope of the UN. Thus, the effectiveness and relevance of the Security Council must be the cornerstone for the promotion of international peace and security. To placate both sides of the argument, Annan was implying that the intervention in Kosovo was unavoidable, but it *should have been* conducted through the UN system.

Referring to the international disagreements on conflict resolution, Annan said that the Security Council must rise to the challenge. The choice must *not* be between Council unity and inaction in the face of genocide, as in the case of Rwanda, on the one hand; or Council division, and regional action, as in the case of Kosovo, on the other.

The conclusion: when the two principles – sovereignty and humanitarian intervention – collide, the necessary action taken should receive legal support (UN Security Council stamp).

3.6   Sovereign Equality

Samuel von Pufendorf relied on Hobbes and Grotius to build an analogy between the equality of individuals in the state of nature and the equality of states in international politics as presented in *Of the Law of Nature and Nations* and *On the Duty of Man and Citizen* written in the seventeenth century (Pufendorf 1672–1674). By the end of the seventeenth century, von Pufendorf's emphatic position on the principle of equality of rights and duties became the 'dominant view' in international law (Gaubatz 2012: 5).

The French delegate to the Hague Peace Conference in 1907 encapsulated an idealized notion of the sovereign equality of states in *The Inside story of the Peace Conference*, as quoted in Gaubatz (2012: 3):

> Each nation is a sovereign person, equal to others in moral dignity, and having, whether small or great, weak or powerful, an equal claim to respect for its rights, an equal obligation in the performance of its duties. (Emile Joseph Dillon 1920).

The Chief Justice of the United States Supreme Court stated as early as 1825 that "No principle of general law is more universally acknowledged, than the perfect equality of nations" (Marshall 1825: 219). Of course such sentiment prevailed before the US acquired its superpower status, and consequently its view on sovereign equality has somewhat diminished and diluted. The Soviet Union, now Russia (the somewhat curtailed other superpower), and increasingly China (another superpower contender) are not living up to the ideal of sovereign equality.

Westphalia provided a starting point for the establishment of the principles of equality between states, the right of self-determination, and the protection from foreign intervention in the internal affairs of the nation state. The original concept of 'Equality' in international law has had its share of controversy. Four rules were attached to this concept: first, every state is entitled to one vote in international bodies; second, legally, all votes have equal weight (the UN Security Council voting system is an obvious and anachronistic violation of this fundamental rule of sovereign equality); third, the *par in parem non habet imperium* rule emphatically means that 'no state can claim jurisdiction over another'; and fourth, equality means that the courts in one state cannot question the validity or legality of the official acts of another sovereign state (Oppenheim 1905 & 1955: 163–267).

US President Woodrow Wilson called for nothing less than a new international order when he declared to the world in 1919 in the last of his Fourteen Points Declaration that all nations should have "mutual guarantees of political independence and territorial integrity" in great and small states alike to be administered by a new world organization. The idealism of such a plan, however, did not stand the test of time, as the US itself refused to join the League of Nations, and the organization itself collapsed in the rubble of World War II (Wilson 1918: Statement to Congress).

Wilson's Secretary of State, Robert Lansing, was a strong supporter of complete sovereign equality during the Versailles negotiations. He believed that without such equality, "force rather than law" becomes the "fundamental principle" of international organization. Lansing was forced to resign because of his strong adherence to the equality principle (Lansing 1921: 44).

Many international legal scholars consider that the concept of equality signifies sovereign independence. All the rules of equality can thus be "attributed to the principle of independence rather than to that of equality", and therefore, the principle of equality is "redundant and unnecessary" (Westlake 1910: 321). Consequently, the notion that small states have equal weight in deciding international issues is criticized as "not only theoretically but practically indefensible and undemocratic" (Baker 1923: 19). Lord Robert Cecil, the British delegate to the Versailles Peace Conference, proposed that the "Great Powers must run the League" of Nations, and outright refused the notion of sovereign equality as "theoretically preposterous" and 'incompatible' with the conception of the League of Nations (Miller/Cecil 1924).

Although the principle of sovereign equality was tolerated during the nineteenth century, the more powerful states were functioning on the international stage around the notion of 'great power responsibility', reluctant to acquiesce to the principle of equality. The great powers were reluctant, however, to criticize the principle of sovereign equality in public. The British newspaper *The Times* harboured no such reluctance, labelling the principles of sovereign equality an "absurd fiction" (*The Times*, October 1907). Moreover, Hicks (1908) believed that "the convention that all states are equal is a fiction. Everybody knows that all sovereign states are not equal". Submission to such notion, he continued, "would involve the subjugation of the higher civilization by the lower, and would condemn the more advanced peoples to moral and intellectual retrogression" (Hicks 1908: 545). 1908 seems so far away indeed.

Regardless of the merits (or lack of) of this argument, the post-war international system does tend to function, in theory at least, on precisely the principle of 'equality' (The UN Security Council and limited number of international organizations, such as the International Monetary Fund, the World Bank, and UNESCO) are the notable exceptions. Understandably, Third World countries, emerging from a long period of colonial control, cherish the notion of equality as an insurance against violation of their sovereignty. But equally understandable is the frustration of great powers – with large capacities, including large economies, powerful militaries and other resources – at being expected to submit to this legal but unrealistic formality.

The concept of equality, however, has two important legal aspects:

First, 'equality before the law' is believed to be the *sine qua non* of any modern legal system, and the alternative to arbitrary control or universal anarchy (Dickinson 1920: 335).

Second, 'equality of rights and obligations' does enjoy similar consensus relating to its validity. This formulation, however, is rejected on the grounds that "If it is said that all states *ought* to have equal rights whether they actually do or not, then the doctrine ceases to be merely innocuous and becomes mischievous" (Brierly 1963: 132).

Nevertheless, the majority of opinions holds that equality of international rights and obligations is "a necessary consequence of the equality of states". Thus the consensus principle is that "the legal rights of the greatest and smallest states are identical" (Taylor 1901: 106). Similarly, "all states, whether great or small, have equal rights and duties in matters of international law" (Cobbett 1909: 50), and it is generally established that "among equals the laws should be equal and should be equally administered" (Jennings 1959: 291–292). But international law recognizes differences in status and allows for limitations on equality in certain situations, such as those relating to protected territories, neutral states, trusteeship, rules of supra-national organization, and limitations imposed freely by treaty or by customary usage.

The 1945 San Francisco Conference, responsible for drafting the UN Charter, resulted in an *expanded definition* of the 'equality' of nations. The report on Article 2(I) of the Charter stated that the term '*sovereign equality*' includes the following elements:

First, states are juridically equal; second, each state enjoys the rights inherent in full sovereignty; third, the personality, territorial integrity, and political indepen-dence of the state must be respected; and fourth, states are obliged to comply with their international duties and obligations (UNICO UN Conference 1945: 457).

3.6.1 Equality Challenged

Such a definition does not sit well with some legal experts, since the *UN structure* embodies *fundamental departures from the principle of equality* of states. Thus, "if the states are 'equal' in spite of the fact that some have privileges which others have not, the term 'equal' has lost its original sense" (Kelsen 1951: 51). The departure from the principles of 'equality before the law' and 'equality of rights' in the Charter represents a violation of 'juridical equality' between the states in the international arena. Similarly, if the United Nations is unable to take action against certain states because of their right of veto embedded in the Charter, then, in reality, there is no 'equality before the law', which is an essential quality in 'equal sovereignty'. The first principle of equality before the law, then, becomes nothing more than "an empty tautology" (Kelsen 1951: 51).

In the face of the debate over equality, the smaller countries feared for their independence and were pre-occupied with the notion of 'sovereign equality'. The principle of equality, a 'sacrosanct' artifact in inter-state relations, was viewed, in association with the principle of 'sovereignty', as an attempt to "curb the authority of the United Nations" in imposing policies or resolutions on weaker states, contrary to their interests. The small states wanted "equal rights and duties", and crucially, "equal capacity" to exercise those rights and duties (Kelsen 1951: 58).

An extension of the principle of sovereign equality in international relations is reflected in the norm of customary international law that has emerged since 1945 (embodied in the UN Charter), which places a "prohibition against the threat or use of armed force" by states against each other. Such a prohibition is partly intended to protect smaller and weaker nations from aggression by larger and stronger states, in the spirit of sovereign equality. Nevertheless, this prohibition has been violated with a vengeance over the years. The Suez War in 1956 was only one example of the sovereign inequality of states in practice (including the violation of the prohibition of the use of force), and this inequality has continued to taint the idealized international system since 1945.

A United Nations Special Committee to study the wider connotations of the term 'sovereign equality' was convened in 1964 in *Mexico* at the request of small UN member states, but achieved hardly any breakthrough. There was consensus, however, on the point that all states enjoy sovereign equality, and that under international law they have equal rights and duties. Furthermore, it was accepted that sovereign equality includes juridical equality; rights of full sovereignty; respect for other states; inviolability of political independence and territorial integrity; freedom to choose internal governance systems; and the duty to comply with international obligations and live in peace (UN Resolution 119, 1964). There was no intention, however, of redressing the inequality of the existing voting system in the UN structure, set in favour of the permanent members of the Security Council. Not surprisingly, the prevailing large powers *won the war* in 1945 and they *wrote the rules* for the international system (including the UN Charter). Again, the egalitarian legal formulations do not stand the scrutiny of application.

In view of the rigidity of the voting system in the UN Security Council, the UN General Assembly assumed greater importance to small and middle power countries which made up the majority of member states. The General Assembly was expected to pass only non-binding recommendations; in fact, it was originally only an assembly for powerless and helpless speech-making. However, that changed with the *Uniting for Peace Resolution* of 1950 (UN Resolution 377, 1950) adopted during the Korean conflict as the Security Council was bogged down in veto-paralysed inaction. This resolution was considered nothing short of a "*de facto* amendment of the Charter" (Anand 1967: 404).

As the General Assembly took active and increasing interest in international conflict resolution (UN Resolution A/520, 1970), the International Court of Justice agreed with the majority of the members of the Security Council regarding the legality of RES 377, Uniting for Peace Resolution. In their deliberations, the Court dealt a fundamental blow to those who wanted to minimize the role of the General Assembly. The Court ruled that the Security Council's traditional role in dealing with international peace and security is a 'primary' responsibility not an 'exclusive' one. The role of the General Assembly, traditionally limited to "discussing, considering, studying, and recommending", was thereby expanded to deal with issues of peace and security as well. Although the Security Council retained the exclusive power to order coercive action (enforcement measures under Chapter VII), the Court declared the General Assembly's responsibilities "not merely hortatory", or not just confined to exhortation (ICJ Reports 1962: 163).

This change in the responsibilities of the General Assembly eventually created a new environment for increased activism by the majority membership, particularly in its emphasis on anti-colonialism and self-determination, racial equality, economic development and national control over resources. The General Assembly thus became in the eyes of some detractors an "unwieldy body which bears no relationship to the realities of world power". US Senator W. Fulbright, known as a liberal internationalist, could not accept that smaller nations could have the "same voting power" as the United States or could "serve as a reliable instrument of peace enforcement" (Fulbright 1963: 787–803).

In a frontal attack on the UN General Assembly, I.L. Claude stated that "national-minded *sinners* are not transformed into world-minded *saints* by coalescing to form a majority voting bloc in the General Assembly" (Claude 1959: 138). Majority decisions in the 'equalitarian' General Assembly, in this view, were ineffectual and even dangerous because they were undemocratic, unrealistic (did not reflect the world's real power), and morally suspect. Another angry characterization described the majority decisions in the General Assembly as an expression of the "lowest common denominator" and 'unrealistic', as they did "not correspond to the actual distribution of population, wealth, power, or enlightenment", which made majority rule in the UN an "unmitigated vice" (Aspaturian 1958: 581).

In 1963, after the main waves of decolonization, US Senator Thomas Dodd boldly but ironically questioned the legitimacy of the voting system in the General Assembly on the grounds that "one African bushman becomes the equivalent of 100 Frenchmen or 400 Americans" (Dodd 1963: 93). He failed, however, to recognize the numerical disparity of a 10-to-1 ratio in favour of Indian citizens to UK subjects in the voting system, and the exclusion of hundreds of millions of Chinese from UN membership (at the time), proving a similarly perverse distribution of power on the world stage.

Yet it was precisely because of the fibre of the irresponsible, national-minded sinners inhabiting the halls of the General Assembly, however 'undemocratic', "morally suspect", 'dangerous', 'enlightenment-lacking', and bereft of an understanding of the realities of world power, that the United Nations was able to stop the aggression of two major powers (with the proper pedigree, of course) and their local accomplice (without pedigree), and to create the UNEF as the first serious international peacekeeping body in the history of the UN. And this majority General Assembly initiative successfully ended the Suez War. The underdogs in the halls of the UN were able to censure and end the renewed colonial invasion of Egypt with the help of the two post-war superpowers, each for its own particular interest.

Undoubtedly, moreover, large numbers in the UN membership are responsible for many 'sins' committed in total violation of democratic principles and values: totalitarianism, lack of democratic governance, the suppression of the fundamental rights of their citizens, corruption, lack of transparency, the creation of skewed socio-economic conditions in favour of a small ruling minority, religious intolerance, the maintenance of an intolerable status of women in many Muslim countries, and the wasting of national resources. But do all these infractions disqualify them from making decisions on war and peace at the UN? If this record disqualifies the 'troublesome' majority from participating in the decisions affecting the international arena, then the sordid record and history of some of the 'enlightened' minority must equally be subjected to scrutiny.

In comparison to the record of the 'sinners', the record of the 'saints' on the international stage speaks for itself, and it shows: a history of colonization, the destruction of aboriginal societies, the institutionalizing of the apartheid system and the practising of racial discrimination, the illegal waging of warfare against weaker countries, allowing the economic exploitation of the Third World, supporting brutal dictatorships around the globe, plotting the overthrow of reformist governments, supporting the unrestricted violation of the fundamental rights of people under settler apartheid regimes (in South Africa and Palestine), and monopolizing an unfair voting system in the international body. Yet nobody is questioning the right of these states to participate in the decisions of the UN on war and peace. Realities of power, perhaps, but not a superior entitlement.

The creation of the League of Nations after World War I, and especially the United Nations after World War II, however, have forced the principle of sovereign equality on the international stage as a concept that could not be ignored, regardless of the realities of world power distribution and the protestations of the privileged.

The deliberations and equivocations over 'sovereignty' and 'sovereign equality' in the international system have injected the associated consideration of '*sovereign democracy*' into the debate, and reflect the clear dichotomy between the non-democratic domestic structures of many sovereign states and the overriding mostly egalitarian international organizations system.

The contention was centred on the voting system in the United Nations. Proposals to create a truly equal voting system for all states (eliminating the veto privilege in the process) or to institute some form of proportional representation are not making any progress at international level. Reflecting on the discouraging domestic realities (an undemocratic political structure and the perceived lack of democratic governance in a large number of UN member states), and the non-implementable international ideal, opponents of voting reforms in the UN question the "wisdom of a democratic society [The UN] comprising of a [majority of] non-democratic states" (Suter 1991: 28).

The impasse centres around the insistence of the Third World countries on the adoption of the sovereign democracy model for any proposed UN democratic reforms, including the UN voting system, on the one hand, and on the other hand of opposing any attempt to link UN reforms to domestic democratic reforms, and hiding behind the principle of the non-interference in the domestic affairs of the member states. This argument is countered by the notion that the UN cannot push for democratization within its membership, while ignoring the same call for reforms of the management of the skewed international system, presided over by the UN, with its negative consequences for many members.

A United Nations affiliated research group, the South Centre, which speaks for the non-aligned states (a term which has ceased to reflect reality), opposed any scheme for weighted proportional representation (based on the attributes of power) at the UN, and declared that the "nonaligned states remain firmly attached to the sovereign democracy model" (Gaubatz 2012: 28). The group supports the call for democratic reforms within the United Nations but is firmly *opposed to any attempt to link UN reforms to domestic democratic reforms in the member states*. The view from the non-Western states is that the UN cannot push for democratization within its membership while ignoring the call for reforms of the UN structure and its management of global affairs.

In a proposal that must have riled the opponents of UN voting equality (Clark/Sohn 1966: xxi), it was suggested that the General Assembly should have 'population-weighted voting' to create a 'more equitable system', and in the process increase powers for the General Assembly, reflecting the world's majority opinion. Such a proposal would only be entertained under the heading of 'wishful thinking'. It would have carried the notion of egalitarian proportional democracy a step (or two) too far, given the world distribution of actual and real power. Legal niceties do not stand a chance in the face of large GDPs fortified by guns.

A speech during the 1995 UN General Assembly meeting tackled the fundamental disparity in the UN system, "The anachronistic privilege of veto and the abusive use of the Security Council by the powerful are *enthroning a new colonialism* within the United Nations itself" (Castro 1995: 19–20).

It follows, therefore, that "On the international stage, it is smaller and weaker states – irrespective of their adherence to democratic norms internally – who have been the strongest advocates of sovereign equality" (Gaubatz 2012: 31). This does not mean that states with domestic democratic governance modes have been exhibiting exemplary behaviour on the international stage. Such a binary view of the international system and the controversial equal sovereignty of states have and will continue to affect the international system.

Another US Senator (Jesse Helms), the former Chairman of the US Senate Foreign Relations Committee, stated that "the American people will not accept the authority of any super-national institution as being greater than the sovereignty of Americans to decide how to act in their own interest both at home and abroad" (Helms 2000: 9–10). Brian Urquhart, the former UN Under-Secretary-General, commented on Senator

Helms' statement, stating that "evidently some states are more sovereign than others". Urquhart added that the Senator's words "were a formidable reassertion of the paramountcy of national sovereignty" (Urquhart 2000: 10).

As in any other legal-political controversy, equality has had its share of ideological contestations. The norm underlying the concept was subject to a vigorous debate. States are expected to bring their internal values and their distinctive norms into the international system. Democratic states and totalitarian states have demonstrated different interpretations of the concept of equality as it applies in the international arena. Moreover, each type of polity does not always live up to the ideal it espouses internally and should be reflected in its international dealings.

The fundamental principle of sovereign equality, as stated in Article 2 (1) of the UN Charter ("The Organization is based on the principle of the sovereign equality of all its members"), was undoubtedly undermined by Article 23 of the same Charter that established permanent membership in the Security Council, exclusive to five members only. Moreover, Article 27 of the same 'egalitarian' Charter bestows on the select self-appointed permanent members the additional right of veto, not given to any other member state in the UN system.

As Kurt Gaubatz notes, the concept of sovereign equality has also reflected the contrast between an idealized view of politics and the more down-to-earth realities and exigencies of power. However, the "emerging moral authority of the equality principle" has influenced international relations since the 1907 Hague Conference. Moreover, democratic states championed – on the surface – equality norms based on the projection of internal democratic values on to the international system. In reality, the democratic states were not overly concerned with "organizing the international system" on a democratic basis. Moreover, these very democratic states sacrificed the essence of the "equality norms as a basis for international decision-making" (Gaubatz 2012: 7).

The principle of one-nation, one-'equal'-vote was jeopardized at the outset in the UN structure, despite all the lofty assurances of equality. In other words, the sovereign equality norm "has not shown a particular connection to democratic foreign policy", or egalitarian capacity in international decision-making. Despite the fact that the UN is based on the egalitarian principle of Article 2 (1) of the Charter, the harsh intersection between the legal foundation and the prevailing international distribution of power and practices "disturbs in no respect the force of the principle" of quality (de Martens 1920: 118). Nevertheless, it remains just a principle, with some laboured attempts at incorporation into the international system of states.

The principle of sovereign equality is challenged, moreover, by two different approaches (Walzer 1977: 87–91):

First, the *component norms* of such sovereignty, which assumes (a) non-intervention in the internal affairs of other states; (b) the equality of all states before the law in international legal procedures; and (c) that all states have equal voice internationally. Evidently, this approach is found wanting in the international system. The record does not demonstrate adherence to the fundamental equalitarian principle of sovereignty.

Second, the *alternative norms* applicable to sovereign states are based on ideological division. On the political *left*, 'liberal democracy', with its emphasis on the
individual rather than states as the focus of rights and legitimacy, translates into a
purportedly more egalitarian decision-making attitude and voting pattern, in fact
undermining the essence of 'state' sovereignty. On the political *right*, 'great power
responsibility' stresses collective security and stability, which translates into privileged and differentiated decision-making reflective of power status.

The legal theory of great power responsibility, therefore, asserts that international "decision-making authority should be proportionate to power" (Gaubatz
2012: 11). Permanent membership and veto power in the UN Security Council are
two obvious manifestations of this approach. The powerful states, in this reading,
reserve the right to intervene in the domestic affairs of other states under the cover
of security and stability.

The more powerful states, moreover, apportion legal rights to others – as well as
associated decision-making authority internationally – in direct correlation to their
power status. This division on the right and left in analysing sovereignty is
somewhat artificial, as many of the components cited intersect on the right and the
left of the political spectrum.

In an earlier reflection on the 'inequality' of states in a supposedly 'equal'
international system of sovereign states, Philip Brown wrote, "Statesmen are unable
to acknowledge the truth of the equality of states simply because that theory is in
patent antagonism with the actual facts of international life". (Brown 1915: 82).
Moreover, "there is no evidence that democratic states *per se* had a more democratic outlook on organizing the international system". It should not be forgotten,
however, that leaders with "little patience for democratic principles domestically
show no hesitation about drawing on democratic principles in their discussion of
United Nations procedures" (Gaubatz 2012: 29).

Despite all the arguments about the precise nature of sovereignty and its effects
on the international system, there is a realization that '*legal* sovereignty' is based on
the concept of absolute equality of states. '*political* sovereignty', on the other hand,
is conditioned by the relative attributes of military and economic assets and
capabilities among states, rendering the notion of absolute equality less absolute or
fixed.

In an early reflection on the issue of sovereign equality, Arthur Lall, the veteran
Indian diplomat and former professor of international relations at Columbia
University in New York (who was India's Ambassador to the United Nations),
wrote candidly – considering his diplomatic background – that: "theoretical
sovereignty" and "equality of states" as "affirmed in Article 2.1 of the UN Charter"
are "largely fictitious". He confessed that "the sovereignty of states has become
clouded with doubt". Increasingly, in a situation of international conflict, the issue
"is no longer determined exclusively by the parties" to the conflict. "Their sovereign right" to act on their own is "not recognized". In fact, the "right is repudiated
by the international system". He asserted that there is a "steady extension" of
international involvement into matters traditionally "regarded as falling within the
domestic jurisdiction of states". Sovereign independence during an international

conflict "is largely a phenomenon of the past". Finally, he observed that "there has never been any serious pretense" of "theoretical equality in international law" between weak and strong states (Lall 1971: 1–4).

A more recent view – similar and paradoxical at the same time – states that "The norm of sovereign equality in international law is so resolutely canonical"; however, such a view is disputed. "Whatever the general merits of the norm, its retention seems fairly open to question". This is due to the overwhelming power of one state in the international system in relation to the rest. "The value of the norm under this condition is particularly dubious". Finally, "The bedrock concept of sovereign equality neither fits nor suits the present world order" (Lee 2004: 147–167).

There is one redeeming feature of the UN system, however, that transcends fundamental differences between the ideologies and practices of the member states: it is the ability of the UN to *adopt fundamental declarations and principles* – despite differences between member states – which affect every aspect of life in the world and set optimal standards to be followed. It is worth noting that such measures represent the collective work and the consensus of all the member states, regardless of their divergent backgrounds. The issues involved include self-determination, human rights, support for anti-colonial movements, opposing racial discrimination, protection of women's and children's rights, promotion of socio-economic development, advancing labour laws, supporting democratization, and the fundamental mission to resolve disputes peacefully. The Geneva Conventions and their expanded Protocols have also lessened the sufferings during warfare. Naturally, not all states live up to these agreed standards, but their existence is the measure and the guarantee that the world will be continually judged on their level of attainment.

The issue of sovereignty was vital for Egypt during the Suez War as a guarantee to protect its independence and territorial integrity in the face of an external assault in total violation of the UN principles that were established at the end of World War II. After the Suez Crisis, the principle of sovereignty was also seriously tested in relation to the internationally-sanctioned peacekeeping operations that ensued. The original legal principle for allowing third-party intervention is found in the concept of *locus standi* (right to be heard in court), whereby peacekeepers' deployment rests on legal authority within the framework of the UN Charter. Only acting "in conformity with international law" will provide peacekeeping missions with the legality, trust, respect, and cooperation of the parties concerned.

Operations "not performed in accordance with international and national legal standards" cannot have legitimacy, credibility, or acceptability. Peacekeeping activity "is much less likely to raise objection if it rests on legal authority and is brought within the framework of the United Nations Charter." Moreover, a United Nations Force must adhere to the basic legal principles of the UN precepts and apply them in an "impartial, consistent, and reasoned fashion" (Schachter 1964: 1,098–1,110).

Egypt's struggle for the assertion of sovereignty during the whole UNEF experience, therefore, was a testament to the contradictions between the principles of the egalitarian international law on one hand, and the realities of the unequal distribution of power in the international system on the other. The inability to reconcile fundamental legal principles of sovereign equality with the prevailing facts of power will continue to undermine the international system of states.

3.7 Sovereignty and Consent

A sovereign state operating in the international system and equipped with the right of consent is akin to a mature individual interacting in general society. Both enjoy the freedom of action within their respective spheres according to the prevailing and applicable rules. And both have certain legal limitations imposed on their absolute freedom of action in accordance with domestic and international law. Their consent to such legal and moral limitations is immaterial. Violating such limitations could result, therefore, in associated negative consequences.

In general, independent states guard against real or perceived weakened sovereignty or violations of its prerogatives. Fundamental human rights norms, however, have "achieved the status of customary international law", affecting and limiting the "unfettered use of state power within a state's own territory." Human rights, therefore, cannot be considered any longer as simply "within the domestic jurisdiction" of the state (Hannum 1990: 19–22), and (Tolly Jr. 1987: 208). Sovereign states can, on the other hand, willingly impose some limits on their own sovereignty by accepting restrictions on their 'sphere of action' emanating from international regulations; or by signing an international treaty incorporating such limitations, without affecting their overall sovereignty.

State sovereignty can be "lost or ceded by agreement". It can also be lost through invasion or occupation, in which case sovereignty is "lost by force rather than consent". By the mere fact that a nation state has entered the membership of the United Nations and accepted the UN Charter, it explicitly and implicitly accepts the right of the Security Council to impose limits on its sovereign rights through enforcement measures authorized under Chapter VII of the Charter. Naturally, such measures would not be imposed on the permanent members of the Security Council, courtesy of the veto power they possess (Ciechanski 1996: 82–104).

The adherence to a treaty is considered an act of 'ultimate sovereignty' because it is normally accomplished on a voluntary basis without coercion through beneficial and reciprocal compromise. But, according to the principle of *pacta sunt servanda* (agreements in a contract must be adhered to), "states are not as free to denounce as they are to accede to treaties."

However, the 22 May 1969 Vienna Convention on Treaties, which came into force on 27 January 1980, "recognizes only two exceptions to the general rule against unilateral denunciation – Article 56": first, when the parties *intended* to allow denunciation or withdrawal; second, when that intention is "*implied* by the nature of the treaty" (Sinclair 1984: 185–202).

Egypt took the position that both intent and implication gave it the right to demand the withdrawal of UNEF in 1967 as their continued presence depended on the country's 'continuous consent', as clearly stated in the relevant documents governing the stationing of the Force in Egypt. The issue of unilateral denunciation or withdrawal lay at the heart of the controversy of the unilateral termination of UNEF's mandate in Egypt, just as it is at the foundation of any traditional peace operation.

The adherence to a freely-given consent is fundamental to any legal system. But giving, withholding, and withdrawing consent are considered prerogatives of the sovereign state. The issue of sovereign consent was a major bone of contention during the UNEF experience, from inception until termination. The dogged insistence by the host country on protecting the sovereign right of national consent was a reflection of the prevailing international order. The right of unilateral denunciation or withdrawal from international agreements lay at the heart of the controversy of the unilateral termination of UNEF's mandate in Egypt. The right of a host country to terminate consent must be taken into account in any Chapter VI peace operation. After the 1973 Arab-Israeli War, however, Egypt completely reversed its position under the new UNEF II mandate and gave up its cherished right of consent.

Respecting a freely-given consent is particularly crucial to the operations of the international legal system. But as conditions change, a new evaluation of the terms of consent becomes warranted. The developing international political-legal climate is amenable to the imposition of limits on the sovereign state's right of consent, as politicians and legal scholars contest the mantra that "consent plays an important foundational role in international law" and provides an important "legitimating device" in international relations. Lister argues that because the primary actors in the international system are states, "state consent is necessary for large parts of international law to be legitimate" (Lister 2011: 3).

This interpretation is based on the differentiation between provisions of domestic law, where consent is not a factor (subject to domestic regulations), and international law, where the primary subjects of the law are sovereign states entitled to give or withhold consent. In a challenge to the Lockean thesis that consent once given by states could not be withdrawn (withdrawing consent at will is similar to existing in the state of nature without controls or regulations), it is argued that states should be allowed to withdraw (terminate) consent due to the changed conditions surrounding the original given consent. Blind and strict adherence to such consent becomes irrational.

It is not suggested here that states toss out agreements they have consented to at will, but the context of the consent must be taken into account. Lister argues, moreover, that consent given in the past should not be binding on a new generation, as new governments reflecting generational change in priorities would refuse to be ruled by the "dead hand of the past". If states are not allowed such withdrawal, many would think twice before entering into a binding consensual obligation, or they would simply not comply with obligations already given. The legitimacy of international law would consequently be questioned (Lister 2011: 26).

In the case of UNEF, Egypt's consent was conditional on its ability to terminate the presence of the international troops on its soil unconditionally. The Egypt-UN agreement stated clearly that the continuation of the presence of the UNEF troops in Egypt was subject to Egypt's continued consent. Egypt's withdrawal of its consent, therefore, was not a violation of any international obligation.

According to a 1971 joint study by the UN and the International Peace Academy (IPA), there can be no peaceable intervention by a UN peace force (even under Chapter VI) without the request or consent of the concerned government(s). The required consent, however, becomes irrelevant as the UN Security Council has the power to impose such a force under Chapter VII. The intervention in this case is no longer 'peaceable' and is transformed into an enforcement action. Additionally, the same study noted that "It was agreed that there must be built-in provisions in any Force Agreement [regardless of the UN Charter Chapter used to authorise the deployment] to guard against abrupt withdrawal", as the consequences could be dire for any peace prospect (Rikhye 1971: 10).

Although it was stated earlier that the classical unitary unbundled concept of sovereignty as it relates to peacekeeping operations could act as an obstacle to effective post-conflict reconstruction, one must guard against the decimation of the concept itself, as this could open the door to external intervention by the powerful for political objectives not related to achieving peace. A fine balance must be struck between respect for the sovereign consent of states, and the need to intervene to realize genuine peace objectives.

3.8   The End of Sovereignty?

Not exactly! The "idea of sovereignty and the institutions associated with it will continue to evolve in ways that are not predictable". There "is no teleological terminus...no 'end of history' in the evolution of sovereignty...merely variations and stages" in its progression. Furthermore, predictions of a final demise of sovereignty are not warranted. The concept of sovereignty is fighting to stay alive, but there is no doubt that it has been wounded perhaps not fatally, but wounded nevertheless (Jackson 2007: 112).

The important work by J.M. Guéhenno about *The End of the Nation State* (Guéhenno 1995) was reviewed with the conclusion that, with the collapse of the Soviet Empire, the sense of the resulting popular triumph has nudged people around the world to "regard the democratic nation-state as the primary, even the only, goal and measure of civic and sovereign identity" (Schoenbaum 1966: 1). It is admitted, however, that "the democratic nation-state is out of reach" for a multitude of reasons. The world is now facing a whole new ball game. The bi-polar, then tri-polar, and now multi-polar world is grappling with new realities – not least of them the march of globalization – to arrive at a new rule book for national-international interaction.

With the need for 'Reimagining the Political' in the wake of the confused world political spectrum, R. Walker believes that "The nationalist rhetoric of the commentators and scholars may be difficult to ignore", but there is no denying the "historical shift from a world of more or less sovereign states to a world that is somehow global…Longstanding dynamics have been transformed" (Walker 1998: 2). Perhaps national sovereignty is in hospital in intensive care, but it is fighting back and far from being terminal.

Eric Brahm brilliantly sums up the current view of the concept of sovereignty, and questions the 'fixity' of the concept as the foundational principle of the international system of states due to: (a) sovereignty being a 'relatively recent innovation', and (b) more importantly, the "increasing limits on the exercise of sovereign authority" in response to changes in the international and national conflict profiles. Therefore, he believes that there is a "continual process of *renegotiating* the nature of sovereignty" to reflect the changing world conditions (Brahm 2004: 1).

Until the world arrives at a new formula for national prerogatives internationally, the concept of sovereignty, however, will always play a role as an identifying marker of independence, regardless of its shortcomings.

Conclusion: Theoretically, sovereignty is absolute and universal. Empirically, sovereignty is curtailed and selective.

References

Anand, R.P. (1967): "Sovereign Equality of States in International Law – II", in: *International Studies*, 8, 4 (April): 386–421.

Anderson, Benedict (2002): *Imagined Communities: Reflections on the Origin and Spread of Nationalism* (New York: Verso).

Annan, Kofi (1999): Speech to the General Assembly (New York: UN Press Release) (20 September).

Arias, Inocencio (1999): "Humanitarian Intervention: Could the Security Council Kill the United Nations?", in: *Fordham International Law Journal*, 23, 4 (Article 2): 1,004–1,014.

Aspaturian, Vernon V. (1958), cited in: Robinson, Jacob, 1958: *Metamorphosis of the United Nations*, in: *Recueil des Cours*, 94 (Collected courses of the Hague Academy of International Law), (Boston: Nijhoff, Leiden): 581.

Baker, P.J. (1923–1924): "The Doctrine of Legal Equality of States", in: *British Yearbook of International Law*, 4 (London): 1–19.

Barnaby, Frank (Ed.) (1991): *Building a More Democratic United Nations* (New York: Routledge).

Barnett, Michael (1995): "The New United Nations Politics of Peace: From Juridical Sovereignty to Empirical Sovereignty", in: *Global Governance*, 1, 1: 79–97.

Bodin, Jean (1576/1992): *On Sovereignty: Four Chapters from the Six Books of the Commonwealth*, edited and translated by Franklin, Julian (Cambridge: Cambridge University Press).

Brahm, Eric (2004): "Sovereignty", in: Burgess, G. and Burgess, H. (Eds.): *Beyond Intractability (Boulder: Conflict Information Consortium, University of Colorado)*, 52, 4: 787–824; at: http://www.beyondintractability.org/essay/sovereignty.

Brierly, James L. (1963): *The Law of Nations: An Introduction to the International Law of Peace* (Oxford: Clarendon Press): 48–49.

Brown, Philip (1915): "The Theory of the Independence and the Equality of States", in: *American Journal of International Law*, 9, 2: 305–335.

Brownlie, Ian (1979): *Principles of International Law* (Oxford: Clarendon Press): 287.

Burgess, Ed; Burgess, Heidi (Eds.) (2004): *Beyond Intractability* (Boulder: Conflict Research Consortium, University of Colorado). 52, 4: 787–824; at: http://www.beyondintractability.org/essay/sovereignty/.

Castro, Fidel Ruz (1995): Address to the UN General Assembly. A/50/PV.35 (22 October 1995).

Cecil, Lord Robert (1924/1928): Cited in: Miller, D., (1924): *My Diary at the Peace Conference of Paris* (New York: Appeal Printing): 337; and in: Miller, D., (1928): *The Drafting of the Covenant* (New York: Putnam): 64.

Ciechanski, Jerzy (1996): "Enforcement Measures under Chapter VII of the UN Charter: UN Practice after the Cold War", in: *International Peacekeeping*, 3, 4 (Winter): 82–104.

Clark, Grenville; Sohn, Louis B. (1966): *World Peace Through World Law: Two Alternative Plans*. 3rd Edn. (Cambridge: Harvard University Press).

Claude Jr, Inis L. (1959): *Swords into Plowshares: The Problems and Progress of International Organization* (New York: Random House).

Cobbett, Pitt (1909): *Cases and Opinions in International Law* (London), 1, 3: 50.

de Jouvenel, Bertrand (1957): *Sovereignty: An Inquiry into the Political Good* (Chicago: University of Chicago Press).

de Martens, Friedrich (1920), cited in: Dickinson, E. (1920): *The Equality of States in International Law* (Cambridge: Harvard University Press): 25.

Dickinson, Edwin DeWitt (1920): *The Equality of States in International Law* (Cambridge: Harvard University Press).

Dillon, Emile Joseph (1920): *The Inside Story of the Peace Conference* (New York: Harper).

Dodd, Thomas (1963): "Is the United Nations Worth Saving?", in: Moore Jr, Raymond, (Ed.): *The United Nations Reconsidered* (Columbia: University of South Carolina Press): 93.

Durkheim, Emile (1984): *The Division in Labour in Society* (New York: Free Press).

Figgis, John Neville (1907/1916): *Studies of Political Thought from Gerson to Grotius, 1414–1625* (Cambridge: Cambridge University Press).

Fulbright, J. William (1963): "A Concert of Free Nations", in: *International Organization*, 17, 3 (Summer): 787–803.

Gandhi, Mahatma (2015): *The Collected Works of Mahatma Gandhi* (New Delhi: Government of India Ministry of Information and Broadcasting).

Gaubatz, Kurt Taylor (2012): *Democratic States and the Sovereign Equality Norm* (Stanford: Stanford University Press): 1–36.

Gross, Leo (1948): "The Peace of Westphalia, 1648–1948", in: *The American Journal of International Law*, 42, 1 (January): 20–41.

Guéhenno, Jean-Marie (1995/2000): *The End of the Nation State* (Minneapolis: University of Minnesota Press).

Hannum, Hurst (1990): *Autonomy, Sovereignty, and Self-Determination: The Accommodation of Conflicting Rights* (Philadelphia: University of Pennsylvania Press): 19–22.

Helms, Jesse (2000): "A Statement to the UN Security Council", cited in: Urquhart, Brian (2000): *Between Sovereignty and Globalization: Where Does the United Nations Fit In?* (Uppsala, Sweden: Dag Hammarskjold Foundation).

Hicks, Frederick C. (1908): "The Equality of States and the Hague Conference", in: *The American Journal of International Law* 2, 3 (July): 530–561.

Hobbes, Thomas (1651/1981): *Leviathan* (London: Penguin, 1968; and New York: Penguin Classics, 1981).

Horowitz, Irving L. (1982): "Socializing Without Politicization: Emile Durkheim's Theory of the Modern State" in: *Political Theory* 10, 3 (August 1982): 353–377.

International Court of Justice (1962): *Reports* (The Hague: International Court of Justice).

Jackson, Robert H. (2004): "The Evolution of International Society", in: Baylis, J.; Smith, S. (Eds.): *The Globalization of World Politics: An Introduction to International Relations* (Oxford: Oxford University Press): 112.

Jackson, Robert (2007): *Sovereignty: Evolution of an Idea* (Cambridge: Polity Press).

Jennings, Ivor (1959): *The Law and the Constitution* (London: University of London Press).

Kantorowicz, Ernst H. (1957/1998): *The King's Two Bodies: A Study in Mediaeval Political Theology* (Princeton: Princeton University Press, 1998).

Kay, David (1967): "The Politics of Decolonization", in: *International Organization*, 21 (Autumn): 786–811.

Kelsen, Hans (1951): *The Law of the United Nations* (London: Institute of World Affairs): 51.

Keohane, Robert (2003): "Political Authority after Intervention: Gradations of Sovereignty", in: Holzgrefe, J.L.; Keohane, R. (Eds.), *Humanitarian Intervention: Ethical, Legal and Political Dilemmas* (Cambridge: Cambridge University Press): 275–298.

Kohn, Hans (1944): *The Idea of Nationalism: A Study of Its Origins and Background* (New York: Macmillan).

Kohl, Uta (2018): "Territoriality and Globalization", in: Allen, S., et al. (Eds.): *Oxford Handbook on Jurisdiction in International Law* (Oxford: Oxford University Press).

Krasner, Stephen D. (1996): "Compromising Westphalia", in: *International Security*, 20, 3: 472–496.

Krasner, Stephen D. (2004): "Sharing Sovereignty: New Institutions for Collapsed and Failing States", in: *International Security*, 29, 2 (Autumn): 85–120.

Lall, Arthur (1971): "Negotiating Theory", Paper for the International Peace Academy Conference, Helsinki, Finland.

Lansing, Robert (1921): *The Peace Negotiations: A Personal Narrative* (Boston: Houghton Mifflin).

League of Nations (1933/1936): *Montevideo Convention on the Right and Duties of States*, 1933 (Geneva: League of Nations Treaty Series, 165: 20–43. [Published on 8 January 1936]).

Lee, Thomas H. (2004): "International Law, International Relations Theory, and Preemptive War: The Vitality of Sovereign Equality Today", in: *Law and Contemporary Problems*, 67 (Autumn): 147–167.

Lister, Matthew (2011): "The Legitimating Role of Consent", in: *Chicago Journal if International Law*, 11, 2 (Winter): 1–29.

Maritain, Jacques (1951): *Man and the State* (Chicago: Chicago University Press).

Marshall, J., Chief Justice (1825): *Supreme Court of the United States*, 23 US 66 1825 US Lexis 219.

McIlwain, Charles Howard (1932): *The Growth of Political Thought in the West: From the Greeks to the End of the Middle Ages* (New York: The Macmillan Company).

Miller, David H. (1924): *My Diary of the Conference in Paris* (21 Volumes) (New York: Appeal Printing).

Miller, David H. (1928): *The Drafting of the Covenant* (New York: Putnam): 241–246.

Nan, Susan Allen (2005). "The Concept of Sovereignty", *CSS Forum* (22 August 2005); at: http://www.cssforum.com.pk/css-optional-subjects/group-i/international-relations/728-concept-sovereignty-print.html.

Oppenheim, Lasa (1905, 1912, 1955): *International Law: A Treatise* (London: Longmans).

Oppenheim, Lasa (1928): *International Law* (London: McNeir).

Orwell, George (1945): "Notes on Nationalism", in: *Polemic*, 1 (October 1945).

Orwell, George (1945): *As I Please: The Collected Essays, Journalism & Letters*, Volume 3 (Boston: Harcourt, Brace & World Inc.): 363.

Osiander, Andreas (2001): "Sovereignty, International Relations, and the Westphalian Myth", in: *International Organization*, 55, 2: 251–287.

Patnaik, Prabhat (2019): "Nationalism Without Other", in: *Indian Express* (5 October 2019): https://indianexpress.com/article/opinion/columns/mahatma-gandhi-nationalism-capitalism-marx-6054147/.

Petersmann, Ernst-Ulrich (2006): "Abstract", in: *State Sovereignty, Popular Sovereignty, and Individual Sovereignty: From Constitutional Nationalism to Multilevel Constitutionalism in International Economic Law* (Florence: European University Institute, Department of Law), Paper No. 2006/45 (December 2006).

Pufendorf, Samuel (1674): *On the Duties of Man and Citizen According to Natural Law,* edited by Tully, J. and translated by Silverthorne, M., 1992 (Cambridge: Cambridge University Press).

Pugh, Michael (2005): "Peacekeeping and Critical Theory", in: Bellamy, Alex J.; Williams, Paul (Eds.): *Peace Operations and Global Order* (New York: Routledge): 39–58.

Rai, Saurav Kumar (2017): "Nation and Nationalism: Revisiting Gandhi and Tagore", in: *Gandhi Marg,* 39, 2 and 3 (July–September and October–December): 205–216; at: https://www.academia.edu/36441992/Nation_and_Nationalism_Revisiting_Gandhi_and_Tagore.

Rikhye, Indar Jit (1971): *Consent, Good Offices and the future of Peacekeeping: Vienna Pilot Project* (New York: International Peace Academy).

Robinson, Jacob (1958): *Metamorphosis of the United Nations,* in: *Recueil des Cours,* 94 (Boston; Nijhoff, Leiden: The Hague Academy of International Law).

Rousseau, Jean-Jacques (1762/1968): *The Social Contract* (London: Penguin Classics, 1968).

Schachter, Oscar (1964): "The Use of Law in International Peace-Keeping", in: *Virginia Law Review,* 50, 6: (1,096–1,114).

Schoenbaum, David (1966): A "Review", in: Guéhenno, Jean-Marie, *The End of the Nation State* (1995) in: H-Diplo, H-Net Reviews (February); at: http://www.h-net.org/reviews/showrev.php?id=291.

Steger, Manfred B. (2000): "Mahatma Gandhi on Indian Self-Rule: A Nonviolent Nationalism?", in: *Strategies: Journal of Theory, Culture and Politics,* 13, 2: 247–263l; at: https://www.tandfonline.com/doi/abs/10.1080/104021300750022634?journalCode=cstj20.

Sinclair, Ian (1984): *The Vienna Convention on the Law of Treaties* (Manchester: Manchester University Press): 185–202.

Smith, Daniel (2014): *How to Think like Einstein* (London: O'Mara Books).

Spruyt, Hendrik (1994): *The Sovereign State and Its Competitors: An Analysis of Systems Change* (Princeton: Princeton University Press).

Stacy, Helen (2003): "Relational Sovereignty", in: *Stanford Law Review,* 55, 5 (May): 2,029–2,059.

Stanford Encyclopedia of Philosophy (2009): "Sovereignty: The Rise of the Sovereign State, Theory and Practice", in: *"The Social Contract"* (Book II, Chapter III).

Suter, Keith (1991): "The United Nations and Non-Governmental Organizations", in: Barnaby, Frank (Ed.): *Building a More Democratic United Nations* (New York: Routledge).

Taylor, Alastair M. (1983): "Peacekeeping: A Component of World Order", in: Wiseman, Henry (Ed.) *Peacekeeping: Appraisals and Proposals* (New York: Pergamon Press).

Taylor, Hannis (1901): *A Treatise on International Public Law* (Chicago: Callaghan & Co.): 106.

The Economist (2016): "The New Nationalism" (London: 17 November 2016).

The Times (1907): *"Editorial: The Hague Fiasco"* (London: October 1907).

Tolly Jr., Howard (1987): *The UN Commission on Human Rights* (Boulder: Westview Press): 208.

Tully, J. (Ed.), translated by Silverthorne, M. (1991/2000): *On the Duties of Man and Citizen According to Natural Law* (Cambridge: Cambridge University Press).

UN General Assembly Resolution (1950): *Uniting for Peace,* A/RES/377 (v) (3 November 1950).

UN General Assembly Resolution (1970): *Rules of Procedure of the General Assembly,* A/520/Rev.10 (9 November 1970).

UN General Assembly Resolution (1964): *Records of the General Conference* A/AcC, 119/SR, 30,7 (2 October 1964).

UN Conference on International Organizations: (1945): (UNICO), *Dumbarton Oaks Proposals* (San Francisco, USA) (25 April 1945).

United Nations (1945): *United Nations Charter,* Article 2 and Article 23 (San Francisco; New York: United Nations).

Urquhart, Brian (2000): *Between Sovereignty and Globalization: Where Does the United Nations Fit In?* (Uppsala, Sweden: Dag Hammarskjold Foundation): 1–23.

Walker, Robert B.J. (1998): *"Both Globalization and Sovereignty: Reimagining the Political",* lecture delivered at the Universities of Wales, Oslo, and Western Washington. A Policy Brief at the Centre for Global Studies (University of Victoria, Canada): 1–9.

Walzer, Michael (1977): *Just and Unjust Wars: A Moral Argument with Historical Illustrations*, 2nd Edn. (New York: Basic Books): 87–91.

Weber, Max (1948): "The Nation", cited in Gerth, H.; Mills, W. (Eds.) (1991): *From Max Weber: Essays in Sociology* (Oxford: Routledge).

Westlake, John (1910): *International Law*, 1 (Cambridge: Cambridge University Press): 321.

Wheeler, Nicholas J. (2000): *Saving Strangers: Humanitarian Intervention in International Society* (New York: Oxford University Press).

Wheeler, Nicholas J. (2001): "Humanitarian Intervention after Kosovo", in: *International Affairs*, 77, 1: 113–128.

Wilson, Woodrow (1918): *Fourteen Points Declaration* – War Aims and Peace Terms: speech to the US Congress, 8 January 1918 (Washington DC).

Wolff, Robert Paul (1970): *In Defence of Anarchism* (New York: Harper Row).

Chapter 4
Peacekeeping: The Formative Years

Abstract The principles underlying international peace intervention and the history and mechanism of deployment are examined. The still-evolving post-war concept of peacekeeping and the threat felt by the sovereign state facing internationally-sanctioned peace intervention are contrasted. Attempts to defuse international conflicts predated both the United Nations and the League of Nations. With the creation of the UN in 1945, the UN Security Council has the right – based on the UN Charter – to order the deployment of international troops in conflict zones with the consent (Chapter VI) or without the consent (Chapter VII) of the affected nation(s). The UN General Assembly also has the capacity – seldom exercised – as sanctioned by the International Court of Justice to dispatch peace-keeping troops with the consent of the parties involved. In the following pages, the development and principles of post-war traditional peacekeeping are presented and analysed.

Keywords Consent · Impartiality · Non-use of Force · Interposition · Absence of Conflict Resolution · Containment Regime · Passive Peacekeeping · Controlled Impasse · Truce Supervision · Observation · Sovereignty · UN Force

4.1 The Evolution of International Peace Operations: Concept and Practice

Traditional peacekeeping was not the first form of international intervention, as it was preceded by 'observation', 'supervision', 'fact-finding' and 'reporting' missions, under both the League of Nations and the United Nations. Later it was augmented by enforcement measures. Peace operations are, therefore, evolving to match the changing components of international and national conflicts.

UNEF was not the first operation to deal with an international conflict, and will not be the last. But UNEF was a pioneering post-war international intervention mechanism. What does peacekeeping consist of, what purpose can it serve, how does peacekeeping function in a world of sovereign states, and how has its mandate

© Springer Nature Switzerland AG 2020
H. Hilmy, *Decolonization, Sovereignty, and Peacekeeping*,
https://doi.org/10.1007/978-3-030-57624-0_4

changed over time? Also, can there be an overall international consensus on a theory of peacekeeping and corresponding application capable of providing theoretical and ideological grounding to guide peace operations? Can this theory apply across political structures, across different conflicts, and across time?

The simple answer is *not* in the affirmative! The nature of human beings and their political and ideological structures across the globe, as well as the nature and extent of conflicts preclude such unanimity.

The various international attempts to fashion a new peace operation regime have been immersed in a mixture of idealism, goodwill, naivety, and stubborn opposition. Nevertheless, efforts are continuing to fashion a modicum of operation capable of accommodating at least some of the ideals espoused by many involved in abetting international and national conflicts.

"The idea of an international force…to assist in the maintenance and/or restoration of international peace and security is much older than the United Nations, both in conception and in application" (Zeidan 1976: 1).

The ideal of preserving world peace was espoused by leading intellectuals, politicians, and scholars as early as the fourteenth century. It became the guiding force behind the concept of collective security protected by an international force, which developed – with varying degrees of success – over the centuries.

The first decades of the twentieth century, commonly referred to as the "Hague Period" (Zeidan 1976: 1–3; Rosner 1963: 208–209), saw several international conferences on the subject (including those held at the Hague in 1899 and 1907 and the dramatic one convened at Geneva which resulted in the Geneva Protocol in 1925), and statesmen and intellectuals articulated the need for a permanent military or police force to enhance collective security and for judicial mechanisms to settle international disputes. The principle of an international police force as an instrument of peace and the idea of peace enforcement thus gained momentum over the years.

The formulation of the Covenant of the League of Nations saw further proposals for peacekeeping and peace enforcement mechanisms aimed at avoiding a repeat of the horrors of World War I. Schemes for an international gendarmerie, a multi-national police force, and international military forces or military sanctions were made by governments, societies, associations and individuals. France made a substantial proposal for the establishment of a permanent "international force" controlled by the Council of the League (Miller 1928: 241–246). Although originally supportive of the idea of an international peace force, US President Wilson eventually rejected the plan, declaring that "the United States would never ratify any treaty which put the force of the United States at the disposal of an international body" (Possony 1946: 910–949). Clearly, the United States government exhibited an aversion to compromising its sovereignty or world status, or to placing its armed forces under international jurisdiction.

The League of Nations did eventually succeed in establishing the first international force through the provisions of its Council Resolutions 8 and 11 in December 1934. That force, comprised of troops from Britain, Italy, the Netherlands, and

Sweden, which became known as the Saar Force, was organized to ease the dispute between Germany and France.

It was entrusted with the supervision of a plebiscite which was to determine the future of the region. The Saar Force operated only upon the consent of the two countries concerned in the dispute. A truly international force in scope, composition, and mandate, moreover, the Saar Force enjoyed complete immunity from local jurisdiction, but the force had no coercive powers. Hence, the command structure of the force, its organs and members, were exempt from the "jurisdiction of the courts of the Saar" region.

The "League Council remained the ultimate source" of decisions and control (Rosner 1963: 213). Unlike the modus operandi of UNEF later on, the League Council decided independently on composition, deployment, command, and withdrawal. Due to this lack of similar central control, the problem of terminating the mandate of UNEF would become the Achilles heel of the post-war first generation deployment of international peacekeeping forces. But, similarly to the 1956 situation in Egypt, the League Council entrusted the governing authorities of the Saar territory with the charge of maintaining law and order. Egypt's sovereign control was respected. Also, as with UNEF, the Saar Force succeeded in fulfilling its task for a few years. UNEF was also successful in avoiding war, even for a longer period than the Saar Force was able to achieve in keeping apart France and Germany, but both interventions only delayed the onset of hostilities by ignoring fundamental issues at stake.

4.2 Post World-War-II Peace Environment

It was at the Dumbarton Oaks Conference in the USA in 1944 that the official negotiations between the victors of World War II for the formation of the United Nations Organization and its Charter took place. The resulting Charter established the primacy of peaceful settlement of international disputes. It also proposed remedies for international conflicts relying on peaceful non-enforceable measures. Finally, the new Charter established robust enforceable measures to counter threats to world peace and security. Chapter VI was designed to help in the peaceful resolution of conflicts. The more interventionist Chapter VII contained provisions for robust enforcement measures.

Article 42 of the Charter empowered the Security Council to "take such action by air, sea, or land forces as may be necessary to maintain or restore international peace and security". *Article 43* required member states to provide "armed forces, assistance, and facilities, including the rights of passage" for the purpose of maintaining international peace and security. After the wave of optimism following the Allied victory in the Second World War, *Article 47* was proposed, and it called for the establishment of a Military Staff Committee comprised of the Chiefs of Staff of the permanent members of the Security Council to oversee the military requirements of peacekeeping operations. However, the reluctance of both the

Soviet Union and the United States to place their armed forces under the command of an international authority rendered the relevant articles inoperative (UN Charter 1945).

The inability of the United Nations to invoke and implement Article 42 or Article 47 of the UN Charter (authorizing the use of force) during the Korean Crisis in the 1950s, due to the veto power of the permanent members of the Security Council, exposed the weakness of the UN peace enforcement mechanism. On 7 July 1950, the Security Council, which at the time was being boycotted by the Soviet Union, passed Resolution 84, which authorized intervention in Korea under US command but under the flag of the UN. Then, on 3 November 1950, and because of the impasse experienced during the Korean conflict debates, the UN General Assembly in effect bypassed the Security Council and passed the *"Uniting for Peace"* resolution. This resolution authorized the Security Council or the General Assembly to deploy military units from UN member states under the authority of the UN itself through the action of a Collective Measures Committee for use in international peace operations (UN Uniting for Peace Resolution 1950).

It was in accordance with the principle established by the Uniting for Peace resolution that the UNEF was formally constituted in 1956 by the authority of the UN General Assembly, a channel that avoided the veto power of Britain and France, who, though party to the dispute, were determined to block any Security Council resolution aimed at stopping their military operations in Egypt.

Although Articles 42 and 43 of Chapter VII of the Charter allowed the Security Council to authorize and impose enforcement measures, Article 38 of Chapter VI did not invoke similar steps, since the Security Council, according to the Article, could only "make recommendations to the parties with a view to a pacific settlement of the dispute". Significantly, Article 51 of Chapter VII of the UN Charter confirmed the right of any state to exercise the right of self-defence in the face of armed aggression until the Security Council authorized the necessary measures to protect international peace and security in accordance with the provisions of the Charter.

Peacekeeping forces can operate under the flag and control of the United Nations, a regional organization, or a military alliance. They can also be deployed independently of any groupings by a single country or a group of countries not belonging to a formal alliance. While peacekeeping can be utilized to serve a genuine conflict reduction purpose, it can also be manipulated to achieve political, military and economic objectives sought by one or more actors.

4.3 Early UN Peace Intervention

The responsibilities of UN early intervention prior to the introduction of the traditional peacekeeping operations were primarily limited in scope and mandate. Intervention was restricted to truce supervision, observation, and fact-finding missions in conflict spots in the Balkans (1946), Indonesia (1947), India-Pakistan

(1948), and Palestine (1948–49). Some of the missions are still active to date, betraying a fundamental failure in the conflict resolution aspect of peace intervention.

UN Supervision and Observation missions enjoyed the consent of the involved parties at the outset under Chapter VI of the UN Charter. It is important to note that the Security Council had the option of authorizing an enforcement measure under Chapter VII of the Charter, precluding the need for consent. Such a Security Council measure was indeed ordered during the Korean Crisis in 1950. Naturally, the Korean action was not a peacekeeping or observation mission, but rather an enforcement operation.

Although the UNEF is dubbed the 'maiden' post-war peacekeeping operation, it was the *United Nations Truce Supervisory Organization* (UNTSO), established during the 1948–49 Arab-Israeli War, that first introduced UN peace intervention in the Middle East (Boutros-Ghali 1993: 84–103). UNTSO was established by aUN Security Council Resolution number 50 on 29 May 1948, based on Article 40 of Chapter VI of the UN Charter, to deal with the war between the Arab states and the newly established state of Israel in British-Mandated Palestine. The Mixed Armistice Commissions (MAC) was set up between Israel and each of the states signatories to the Agreements to oversee the implementation and observance of the armistice agreements. Although UNTSO and UNEF performed different functions and had different mandates, UNTSO was nevertheless the first post-war effort by the international community to establish a measure of control over a conflict situation in the Middle East.

UN truce observation consisted of *supervision*, *observation*, and *reporting*, as well as the *investigation* of alleged violations by the parties to the truce agreement (s). The number of observers was too small to act as an interposition force. Truce supervision is a difficult task at the best of times. Resources are limited, the mandate is undefined, and the on-going conflict is unresolved. "The armistice regime might only serve to prolong the dispute by freezing the situation, thus relieving the pressures on the parties involved to find a solution to the conflict" (Dombroski 2007: 35–36).

Although an armistice agreement is preferable to continued warfare, in some situations maintaining the *status quo* of conflict is preferred by one or all the parties to the dispute:

> A temporary agreement can remain in effect for a limited period despite basic differences between the adversaries. However, it cannot overcome and resolve acute disparities. If such an agreement becomes permanent, the danger is that it will perpetuate and perhaps aggravate the disputes, until finally the agreement collapses under its own weight, and fighting resumes (Shalev 1993: 202–203).

According to one view, there were three reasons for the ineffectiveness of UNTSO in fulfilling its mandate:

> Lack of cooperation from the parties to the conflict; poorly marked demarcation lines; and UNTSO's structure of unarmed observer parties, which was inadequate to handle the types of problems in the demilitarized zones (Ghali 1993: 84–103).

The 'unarmed observers' part of the argument is not valid since this operation was an observation mission and not an enforcement action or even an interposition deployment requiring large number of troops, with military engagement mandate, if required. The limited number of dispersed observers available (even if armed) would not have been adequate at all in the face of several heavily equipped and manned armies operating in a war zone. The credibility of the UN as a peace-making influence, if observation was turned into confrontation, would have been harmed, given the limited nature of the observation mandate.

The advantages and disadvantages of UNTSO, according to El-Bouzaidi (2012: 1–6), are:

Advantages

(1) Voluntary contributions by Troop Contributing Countries (TCCs).
(2) Cost-effectiveness due to financing from the UN's regular budget.
(3) Non-use of force makes it easier to be supported by the host states, and to maintain national consent for deployment and international legitimacy.
(4) Impartial and objective reporting.
(5) It acts as a link between the Security Council and the 'facts on the ground' in the theatre of operations.
(6) The mandate is broad and flexible, with easier troop deployment and travel options to areas of crisis.
(7) Its mandate is open-ended (does not need renewal every six months), creating a stable presence in the region as the conflict continues.

Disadvantages

(1) The structure and composition of the observers group was initially Western-dominated and thus perceived as lacking balance and legitimacy.
(2) Lack of support from the participating states, and difficulty in enforcing agreements.
(3) Occasional lack of resources.
(4) Difficulties with the decentralized structure of the mission.

4.4 The Launch of the UN Peacekeeping Regime

In the views of the experienced international diplomat, Brian Urquhart, peace-keeping came into being essentially to facilitate the decolonization/sovereignty process and its aftermath:

> Peacekeeping, not mentioned in the United Nations Charter, was originally developed during the post-war decolonization period as a means of filling the power vacuums caused by decolonization, and of reducing the friction and temperature, so that an effort could be made to negotiate a permanent settlement of post-colonial conflict situation (Urquhart 1994: 91–94).

After World War II, a new international order emerged, based on the newly-adopted *UN Charter* (24 October 1945). The Charter put forth wide-ranging principles to encourage peaceful outcomes to international conflicts, and to counter threats to international peace and world security.

The relevant chapters of the United Nations' Charter (1945) are I, VI and VII.

Chapter I of the Charter emphasizes that the basic purpose of the United Nations is to maintain international peace and security and to take effective collective measures to achieve such objective.

Chapter VI highlights the requirement incumbent on all nations to seek peaceful solution to disputes by all peaceful means available. The Charter allows the UN to intervene peacefully to minimize or bring an end to non-military and military confrontations. The United Nations Emergency Force in 1956 was an example of such international intervention. This UN intervention was a non-enforcement action respecting the sovereignty and the required consent of the nation(s) involved.

Chapter VII outlines the mandate of the UN Security Council for the preservation of international peace and security, using all peaceful and *military* means to enforce the desired objective. This chapter also emphasizes the obligation of all the member states to comply with Security Council resolutions and directives.

The authors of the UN Charter in 1945 did not have a precise notion relating to the creation of a UN peacekeeping force planned when the Charter was written. But the principles embodied in the Charter undoubtedly were inspirational in forming UNEF as a response to a flagrant and dangerous violation of the Charter and to international peace and security. UN peace operations, moreover, have evolved over the years to meet the requirements of the changing international and national conflicts and threats to peace.

Sovereignty, political independence, and the inviolability of territorial integrity were conceptual and political foundational principles of the new post-World-War-II international order. No peacekeeping operation could have ignored such parameters, including the right of a sovereign independent state to consent to or to reject any international intervention in its territory, save for a UN Security Council resolution imposing a Chapter VII enforcement action.

There was no formal mechanism at this early stage for dealing with international military disputes, and even less for resolving domestic conflicts. Earlier UN intervention (1946–1949) took place on a small scale in a limited capacity as ceasefire, truce and armistice observers and monitors without the mandate or the resources to actively separate the combatants or to pursue conflict resolution options.

The first traditional 'peacekeeping' mission, the United Nations Emergency Force (UNEF) in Egypt (1956–1967) – during the height8.8 of the Cold War – significantly enhanced the ability of the UN to control the continuation and spread of the immediate conflict. The UN mission, however, was not mandated to pursue or engage in conflict resolution options. In reality, traditioanal peacekeeping provided the UN with a modest 'limited' peace which paled in comparison with the ambitious version in the UN Charter.

The whole mark – and acceptance – of traditional peacekeeping was that "The principle of non-violence sets peacekeeping forces above the conflict they are dealing with" (Urquhart 1992: 7).

4.5   The Traditional Passive Containment Peacekeeping Model: A + B + C

The Model's Basic Pillars are: (Fig. 4.1)

A. (1) Consent (2) Impartiality (3) Non-use of Force;
B. (4) Interposition;
C. (5) Absence of Conflict Resolution Mechanism.

A. This pioneering operation was based on the Westphalian sovereignty model known as the 'holy trinity' of peacekeeping, requiring (1) the 'consent' of the host independent nation for the stationing of foreign troops on its soil.
    The mission was also based on (2) the 'impartiality' of the UN troops between the antagonist, and on the principle of (3) the 'non-use of force' except in self-defence. UN troop deployment takes place following the acceptance of a ceasefire agreement.
B. This model was augmented by a fourth principle, which stipulated that Peacekeeping troops only act as a 'buffer' (4) *interposition* force without interfering in the military situation in favour of any side.
C. Finally, a fifth factor was evident because (5) 'no conflict resolution' or serious effort to resolve the continuing fundamental dispute was utilized. This classic inter-state conflict management model can be best described as a 'containment regime'. It is also described as 'passive peacekeeping' and 'controlled impasse'.

Fig. 4.1 Holy trinity: principles of peacekeeping. *Source* The author

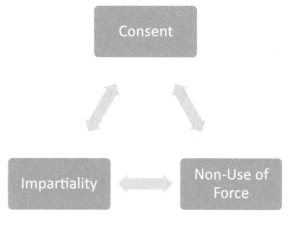

These fundamental principles for UNEF deployment guided the operation for over a decade (and influenced other future operations), namely: Consent – Impartiality – Non-use of Force. Interposition and lack of conflict resolution completed the model.

The conditions of the traditional peacekeeping passive-containment regime were fully observed during the deployment of UNEF in Egypt. The viability and credibility of effective UN peace intervention were at stake in this pioneering foray into large-scale deployment. By all accounts, UNEF was in full adherence to the model during its presence in the field, as all the requirements of the passive regime were observed.

The Achilles heel of the mission was the 'absence of conflict resolution' arrangements which led to the sudden and swift unravelling of the mission at the end and the resumption of warfare. The whole endeavour was a wasted opportunity for a genuine and credible settlement. At best, early peacekeeping intervention managed to freeze the military confrontation in place for a period without serious attempts at addressing the root causes of the conflict. In some cases (the Congo in the 1960s), the peacekeeping presence became embroiled in domestic violence (with international strings attached).

4.5.1   Interposition Deployment

Interposition deployment can take several forms (Fig. 4.2):

(1) Non-combat separation of forces.
(2) Establishing a physical buffer zone.
(3) Observing military movements.
(4) Monitoring any changes on the ground.
(5) Carrying out fact-finding missions.
(6) Reporting the general situation to UN HQ.

Fig. 4.2 Deployment: interposition force. *Source* The author

4.5.2   The Outcome: Absence of Conflict Resolution Commitment

Despite the absence of military engagement, disputes remain unresolved, opening the door for renewed military confrontation. It is not entirely accurate to define the purpose of peacekeeping as 'to restore and maintain peace', as real peace did not actually exist due to the factors which led to the prevailing conflict. What is being restored is a condition of dormant conflict: the conflict turned violent, and was then pacified through third-party intervention, but without a serious conflict resolution phase being activated. Without this crucial conflict resolution phase the possibility of returning to a situation of military confrontation is always present.

It is more factual, then, to state the purpose of the traditional peacekeeping intervention as efforts 'to end current hostilities' and 'to restore the *status quo ante*' i.e. prevailing prior to the beginning of hostilities. Such intervention presumably provides a breathing space, allowing, but not mandating, the parties to explore genuine conflict resolution options if they so choose or if other external factors permit.

Another fundamental characteristic of the early generation of peacekeeping intervention was its *ad hoc* (case by case) nature. There were no fixed guidelines or agreed trigger mechanisms established by the UN to launch an operation within an established framework.

4.6   Traditional Peacekeeping Definitions

An often-used definition of traditional peacekeeping is: the prevention, containment, moderation, and termination of hostilities between or within states, through the medium of a peaceful third-party intervention organized and directed internationally, using multinational forces of soldiers, police and civilians to restore and maintain peace (Rikhye 1984: 1–2).

This definition begins with the task of 'prevention', which was not the case with UNEF, as international intervention occurred only after hostilities had began and the UN ceasefire resolution had been accepted. Although the conflict was brewing for some time, the UN was powerless to intervene to 'prevent' the crisis from escalating into a full-blown armed confrontation. Clearly, prior prevention was not applicable to the peacekeeping philosophy. Prevention in this setting can only be understood as a tool to prevent *renewed* clashes from recurring *after* the peacekeeping force has been deployed following an agreed ceasefire.

The above definition also lacks any mention of *conflict resolution* as a formal end to international intervention. Peacekeeping then becomes a temporary first-aid measure, allowing the conflict to drag on without any incentive to reach a comprehensive settlement, as was the case with UNEF. A formal conditional requirement for entering into peace negotiation by the parties to the conflict should be considered in any peacekeeping mandate, if such a requirement did not precede the military clash. A mere absence of hostilities in an on-going conflict should not be equated with peace.

Traditional peacekeeping is seen as *ad hoc* and *reactive*: The United Nations "is *crisis driven*; peacekeeping operations are not often suggested, much less authorized, until lives have been lost and the prospects for war expansion are great" (Diehl 1994: 11).

Deployment, then, takes place after the crisis is in full swing, and the peacekeeping troops arrive after warfare has taken its course. Nevertheless, this was the pattern (and the model) of the early UN troop deployment.

Another definition emphasizes the *non-use of force* in peacekeeping intervention:

a military presence to impose restraints on the will of the parties to the dispute to resume fighting. United Nations peacekeeping forces accomplish their mission not by force at all but by the *persuasion of their presence* (Cassese 1978: 212).

A more candid definition, grounded in intervention experience, describes peacekeeping as a *"controlled impasse"* due to the inability to resolve conflicts. Such paralysis is due to (1) the complex political obstacles involved, and (2) military stalemate between the parties to the conflict. The frustrating outcome allows conflicts to become "objectively insoluble" (Sherry 1986: 753–771). This definition has haunted and is still haunting peacekeeping circles because it portrays peacekeeping as a "tool for the maintenance of the *status quo*", and also implies that "the role of peacekeeping is...*redundant*" in resolving deep-rooted and complex conflicts (Fetherston 1994: 25–26).

A more optimistic view of peacekeeping states that "Traditional UN peacekeeping was designed to provide the UN with a cautious role in constructing a *limited peace*" (Richmond 2008: 100).

In general, peacekeeping can be classified as:

(1) *Passive* (observation, supervision, monitoring, reporting, and fact-finding) deployed with sovereign consent.
(2) *Active/non-combatant* (interposition-buffer force) deployed with sovereign consent.
(3) *Robust* (enforcement) deployed with or without sovereign consent.

The UN Secretary-General established important principles governing the deployment of UN peace forces:

(a) The UN operation 'should not prejudge the solution' of the conflict;
(b) The UN action 'should not change the political balance' affecting negotiations; and
(c) The UN 'should not modify the prior status juris' (Hammarskjold 1957).

4.7 Peacekeeping Taxonomy

'Peacekeeping' is divided into two broad types:

The first is associated with conflicts arising *between* states (*inter*); the second confronts disputes occurring entirely *within* a single state or territory (*intra*).

The first type of peacekeeping is invoked to diffuse or terminate a state of belligerency existing between two (or more) sovereign states, with the aim of establishing a formal ceasefire and the separation of combatants. There is no requirement, however, to establish a conflict resolution mechanism as part of the mandate. The consent of the parties involved and the observance of their sovereign rights by the international community are important criteria in this type of inter-national peacekeeping. UN intervention is based on Chapter VI of the UN Charter. The deployment of UNEF during the Suez Crisis in 1956 is a prime and pioneering example of this type of consensual international peacekeeping operation.

The second type of peacekeeping is concerned with conflicts erupting within a single territory (and sometimes expanding across borders), such as a violent uprising, a secessionist movement, ethnic or religious strife. UN intervention can sometimes be mandated according to Chapter VII of the Charter, overriding, in the process, considerations of state sovereignty. In this type of operation the issue of consent and the requirements of sovereignty are more problematic, and usually contested. Moreover, the intervention mechanism is often dangerously unstable. The Rwanda and Bosnian conflicts during the 1990s represent this type of contested and complex conflict.

Peacekeeping has grown and expanded since the end of World War II to cover most of the world's crisis spots. Over the years, it has become "one of the most visible symbols of the UN role in international peace and security" (Thakur 2006: 37).

4.8 Authorization of UN Peacekeeping Operations

The initiation and control of a UN peace force were very important for the deployment of UNEF. The conditions for UN involvement in international conflict situations, however, are not fixed and they have changed over time.

Commenting on the first fifteen years of UN peace operations in *A Note on UN Peacekeeping Machinery* (1971: 1–3), Arthur Lall, formerly India's Ambassador to the United Nations, stated that "UN membership is still divided on the applicable legal sanction for and exact status of" current and future operations. He raised the point that clarity is needed because UN peace operations embark on a course "that was not foreseen by the law of the UN (the Charter)".

The modus operandi of UN peace forces follows two scenarios: (1) Authorization by the Security Council, or authorization by the General Assembly. Either authorization directs the Secretary-General to initiate and dispatch a UN force to the conflict zone. The Secretary-General must report back to the source of authorization periodically. (2) Only the Security Council can authorize the formation and dispatch of UN forces. Lall conceded that the first option constitutes a new approach to international conflict resolution not provided for in the Charter, but "not at variance with the Charter" either. The International Court of Justice found that it is not a violation of the Charter for the General Assembly to authorize UN peacekeeping operation.

In a follow-up discussion on the machinery of peacekeeping, Ambassador Lall and General Rikhye (Lall/Rikhye 1971: 1–2) discussed the issue of the authorization further. The Indian diplomat suggested that it would have been appropriate for the United Nations Truce Supervision Organization (UNTSO) to be "expanded to cover the Suez operation thus avoiding problems of cost and legality". This was not done, as Canada's proposal for the UNEF did not go through the Security Council approval mechanism, but it was adopted by the General Assembly. In response, General Rikhye, a veteran of UNEF, pointed out (1) that Britain and France agreed to end their operation in the Suez Canal "only if an international force was interposed"; and (2) that UNTSO was controlled by the Security Council, while UNEF was established by the General Assembly. Lall expressed the view that the likelihood in the future of the "General Assembly initiating peacekeeping action was very remote" because of the changing international environment.

The role and responsibilities of the UN Secretary-General in peace operations, moreover, were evaluated, reflecting the changing nature of the UN intervention profile. According to Lall, the visible involvement of the Secretary-General in the past "no longer exists". In the future, peacekeeping control would be in the hands of the Security Council. The "direct responsibility for peacekeeping operations" by the Secretary-General was "likely to be greatly reduced". The "general consensus" was that the Secretary-General should exercise some "control over the day-to-day operational management", but "only be a link between the Security Council and the [UN] Force Commander" (Lall 1971: 1–2).

4.9 Parameters of Peacekeeping

Peacekeeping forces can operate under the flag and control of the United Nations, a regional organization, or a military alliance. They can also be deployed independently of any groupings by a single country or group of countries not belonging to a formal alliance. While peacekeeping can be utilized to serve a genuine conflict reduction purpose, it can also be manipulated to achieve political, military and economic objectives sought by one or more actors.

Peacekeeping deployment could begin before a complete separation of combatants has been accomplished (as was the case with UNEF). But all parties to the conflict must accept the ceasefire arrangements *a priori*, allowing the peacekeepers to complete the separation of forces and the consolidation of their deployment.

Naturally, if the deployment is based on Chapter VII sanctions, not all parties (those targeted for sanctions) might be agreeable to the international deployment.

Some forces deployed under UN authorization, however, can be engaged in armed conflicts, as was the case in Korea, but such a situation falls outside the strict definition of 'peacekeeping'. The Korean intervention was an enforcement measure authorizing UN forces to engage in military operations. Such authority emanated from the provisions of Chapter VII of the Charter and was authorized by the UN Security Council.

4.10 Peacekeeping Mandate

UN peace operations mandates have expanded and may include some or all of the following:

- 'UN 'Representative' in the conflict area.
- Fact-finding and verification missions.
- 'Good Offices', mediation, and confidence-building missions.
- Border and foreign infiltration monitoring.
- Ceasefire observation and truce supervision.
- Transitional administration and electoral assistance.
- Peacekeeping interposition force.
- Civilian protection and security force.
- Disengagement and stabilization.

Regional organizations have increasingly become involved in peacekeeping operations, especially in Africa, and Central and South America.

Some of these missions do not fall within the scope of traditional peacekeeping. They have developed in response to changed conflict profiles. The continuous presence of peacekeeping deployment can be considered positive only if it eventually leads to its own termination following a successful political solution to the conflict. This last step in the peacekeeping chain, however, is not usually included in the mandate of the traditional (first-generation) peacekeeping deployment, and if it is included, it usually does not get acted upon.

Based on Henry Wiseman's (1983) pioneering work, Dombroski divided peacekeeping operations into several evolutionary phases: the *nascent* period, 1946–1956; the *assertive* period, 1956–1967; the *dormant* period, 1967–1973; the *resurgent* period, 1973–1978; and the *maintenance* period, 1978–1985. Another phase was added and identified as the *Renaissance* period, 1988–1994 (Dombroski 2007: 28).

It is difficult, however, to think of many of the missions taking place during and after this period as contributing to a 'renaissance' period, unless the term alludes only to the growth and expansion of peacekeeping missions themselves, and not their results. The nature of conflict has changed dramatically, and massive loss of life and brutal human rights abuses have become the norm. The capacity of the international system to cope has been tested, and new approaches to conflict control and resolution based on new human security ethos have emerged over the years. Since its inception, the UN has commissioned over seventy 'peacekeeping' missions. Many were successful, but others were – and still are – stymied by festering conflicts. The mandates for these missions reflect the difficult tasks facing the UN in establishing a grip over international and national conflicts.

More functions beyond the traditional role of a peacekeeping force have been added to the peacekeeping mandate over the years, such as local administration and maintaining law and order, in addition to facilitating humanitarian assistance. To emphasize the international nature of the intervention, the peacekeeping troops are placed under UN command, not the national headquarters of the participating countries.

As in the case of the League of Nations, there was also an attempt at the UN to create a permanent UN peacekeeping force, ready and able to respond to areas of conflict without delay. Although initially successful, the force, known as SHIRBRIG, lasted for a limited period, as it could not withstand the political and financial pressures to which the unit was subjected.

Ideally, peacekeeping also encourages confidence-building once the threat of military confrontation is contained. Peacekeeping deployment should be viewed as a temporary cooling-off period and breathing space, freeing the protagonists to pursue alternatives to war, with comprehensive peace settlement as the ultimate objective. The parties to the conflict must realize that peace intervention is not an open-ended licence to prolong the conflict (as in Suez in 1956 or Cypress in 1964), and the onus is on them (and the rest of the world) to move towards accommodation. This in turn promotes conciliation efforts by a third party, and ultimately leads to conflict resolution. But no resolution can be achieved without arriving at a fair, just, and equitable solution which answers the basic issues of all sides.

4.10.1 Expansion of the Peacekeeping Mandate

The increasing number and types of international peacekeeping interventions necessitated the development of wider classification criteria to identify the general types of peace operation within the global political structure. Bellamy et al. (2004) established five broad types:

(1) *Traditional Peacekeeping*: operations geared to the space needed for a political settlement.
(2) *Managing Transition*: operations designed to assist the implementation of a comprehensive political settlement.
(3) *Peace Enforcement*: operations to impose the will of the UN Security Council through military or economic means.

(4) *Wider Peacekeeping*: operations aiming to provide humanitarian help during on-going violence or unstable peace.
(5) *Peace Support*: operations to support the establishment of liberal democracy in war-torn socities.

The drive to establish what became known as 'Liberal Peace' in conflict-ridden Third World countries has faced a great deal of criticism. Critics contend that the imposition of a liberal-business ideology on weak societies tarnishes the whole idea of peacekeeping (see Chap. 13).

4.11   Conditions of Peacekeeping Success

Peacekeeping has been criticized because "its operations have beginnings but all too often no conclusion" (Taylor 1983). Taylor approaches the continuous reliance on inconclusive peacekeeping, or what he calls "resolution/perpetuation", as prevelant in other inernational groupings, such as NATO and NORAD. Although it does not lead to immediate conflict resolution, peace intervention "can quarantine an area [of conflict] until the infection [conflict] is removed [resolved]". Taylor believes that it is 'indispensable' to create a link or a 'nexus' between peacekeeping (concept of order) and peacemaking (concept of justice). This formula will, he asserts, help to strengthen world security and enhance universal economic benefits (Taylor 1983: 424–425).

The two *primary standards of success* (Diehl 1994: 33–40) in peacekeeping operations are:

(1) Limitation of Armed Conflict (deterrence against the continuation of violence). The physical and moral presence of peacekeepers block resumption of hostilities.
(2) Conflict Resolution (facilitating dispute resolution). Peacekeeping can provide the opportunity and context for reconciliation, but not the actual negotiating process.

Only with the fulfilment of these two standards can the peacekeeping operation be considered a success. An experienced hand in peacekeeping, General Romeo Dallaire, UN Commander in Rwanda, said:

> Clearly, peacekeeping cannot be an end in itself – it only buys time. In its goals and its design, it must always be a part of the larger continuum of peace-making, that is to say conflict avoidance, resolution, rehabilitation and development (Woodhouse 2000: 18).

Several UN resolutions reflected the developments surrounding the use of an international peace force in conflict situations. Chief among them was UN General Assembly Resolution A/290 (IV), *Essentials of Peace* (1 December 1949), calling upon every nation to refrain from threatening or using force contrary to the UN Charter. But it was UN General Assembly Resolution 377 (V), *Uniting for Peace*

(3 November 1950), adopted during the Korean Crisis, that had the dramatic impact on the Suez Crisis, as it set a precedent authorizing the UN General Assembly – if the UN Security Council failed to exercise its primary responsibility – to act immediately in the face of aggression in order to maintain or restore international peace and security.

The November 1950 Uniting for Peace Resolution was an enforcement act authorized by the assertive Chapter VII (in the absence of a Soviet Security Council veto), while the November 1956 resolution was authorized by the General Assembly under the non-enforcement provisions of Chapter VI. While the Uniting for Peace Resolution was the basis for the two resolutions on Korea and Suez, it was the Cold War rivalry which partly explains why the Soviet Union and the United States were on opposing sides with regard to Korea but were united on Suez. The agreement on Suez by the two superpowers during the Suez Crisis (unlike Korea) greatly facilitated the formation of UNEF.

The novel experience of forming and deploying the first peacekeeping force (UNEF) without an accepted and established formula was evident when the Soviet Union challenged the legality and legitimacy of UNEF. Although the USSR supported the international majority in demanding the end of the tripartite invasion of Egypt, it contended that it could not participate in sharing the cost of the peacekeeping operations, as required by all member states under Article 17 (2) of the UN Charter, because it was not established under Article 43 of the Charter. Moreover, the USSR believed that the nations committing the aggression should be responsible for the cost incurred by the international community. The International Court of Justice (ICJ) rejected the argument of the Soviet Union that UNEF was "illegally created" and instead held that Article 43 was only applicable in enforcement actions, and that UNEF was not established for such a purpose (ICJ 1962).

4.12 Peacekeeping-Related Concepts

Peacekeeping functions in the same orbit as two other associated concepts: preventive diplomacy and collective security. The three concepts influence each other but they are not identical. Preventive diplomacy, if successful, might render peacekeeping unnecessary. The utilization of preventive diplomacy and peacekeeping together go a long way towards enhancing – but not guaranteeing – collective security.

4.12.1 Preventive Diplomacy

"Prevention of conflicts is a moral imperative in today's world", according to Sweden's Jan Eliasson (1996: 318), former UN Under-Secretary-General.

What is preventive diplomacy? According to Mohammed Bedjaoui, former President of the International Court of Justice, using former UN Secretary-General Boutros-Ghali's definition, it "serves three purposes: (a) It aims to prevent disputes arising between the parties, (b) to prevent an existing dispute from being transformed into an open conflict, and (c) if conflict breaks out, to ensure that it spreads as little as possible" (Bedjaoui 1996: 36).

International and national leaders, as well as trusted persons of 'influence' and others, work openly or behind the scenes to prevent the initiation, the escalation, or the spread of conflicts. Such conflict defusion can prove crucial in some areas of disputes, and it can at least lead to lowering the temprature of the conflict, opening the door for future settlement. The success or failure of the efforts depend on the nature and complexity of the conflict, and on the importance and influence of the intermediaries in relation to the adversaries. The European Institute of Peace (EIP) considers preventive diplomacy to be "the most desirable and efficient employment of diplomacy". It is utilized "to ease tensions before they result in conflict". The idea "is to use different diplomatic tools to prevent disputes from arising – or to prevent existing disputes from escalating into violent conflicts" (Mullerleil 2016: 1). Diplomatic intervention is carried out in general by states, international organizations, NGOs, foundations and other non-state actors.

Article 33 of the UN Charter listed the methods to be utilized to avoid endangering world peace and security and to find a solution to conflict through: negotiation, inquiry, mediation, conciliation, arbitration, judicial settlement, involving regional organizations, or other peaceful means.

However, preventive diplomacy is not synonymous with *ad hoc* peacekeeping, as UN intervention on the ground typically occurs post-conflict. In other words, a peacekeeping force on its own cannot be considered an arm of preventive diplomacy. Similarly, preventive diplomacy cannot be equated with post-conflict peacekeeping intervention. In a different reading of the role of preventive diplomacy and peacekeeping in impacting the direction of conflicts, third-party or international engagement with the protagonists could halt the deterioration in the conflict before the point of no return. "The central concept underlying preventive diplomacy…is that…the United Nations may be able, through the employment of relatively modest forces [UN peacekeeping forces], to forestall the continued deterioration of a situation that might threaten the international peace" (Cassese 1978: 212).

In preventive diplomacy, the use, or the possibility of the use, of peacekeeping forces, in addition to intense political and diplomatic intervention, is intended to offer a breathing space in a conflict situation in the hope of avoiding an outbreak of hostilities. Such arrangements can also be utilized by regional blocks to defuse an escalating conflict that could otherwise lead to armed confrontation in their own regions.

At another level, preventive diplomacy is the application, as well as the result, of the projection of power by a regional or world power or set of powers intended to convince parties to a conflict to step back from military confrontation. Even after a conflict has already led to armed confrontation between states, the interjection of a UN peacekeeping presence can bring the fighting to a halt, pending negotiations.

Dag Hammarskjold, the late Secretary-General of the United Nations, who was considered the father of UN peace intervention, believed, however, that 'peace-keeping' is a form of 'preventive diplomacy'. His view was conditioned by the Cold War rivalry and his fear that local conflicts and wars supported by an entrenched ideological divide might drag the two superpowers into a devastating confrontation. Hence the need to contain local conflicts through the use of peace-keeping as a way of preventing a nuclear holocaust. In 1954, Hammarskjold said that "the United Nations was created not to bring humanity to heaven but to save it from hell" (Hammarskjold 1954).

Experience suggests that peacekeeping operations on their own, however, can never be a substitute for permanent peace or for tangible solutions to outstanding disputes between or within states. Peacekeeping can only help by defusing and containing conflicts until other options for peace are explored and acted upon. Similarly, preventive diplomacy can only attempt to help the parties resolve their differences in the hope of reaching a resolution before confrontation becomes inevitable. Without sincere commitment by the parties to the conflict or the existence of the right incentives for a solution, diplomatic efforts may not succeed.

4.12.2   Collective Security

Collective Security is a concept theoretically underpinning the post-World-War-II international security regime, ideally through the United Nations. The New United Nations Charter represents the blueprint and the guide book for ensuring world security and world peace. Ensuring security has become the interest of all nations. The pre-war ability to overrun neighbouring countries and communities for territorial and ideological aggrandizement is no longer tolerated. Each nation and country can now look at the UN for protection against aggression. Unfortunately, this new mantra is being put to the test at present.

The outbreak of the Second World War was a testament to the failure of the previous collective security regime overseen by the League of Nations. This newer security concept was nuanced by the developing Cold War and the emergence of two competing ideological camps outside and inside the UN. With the end of the Cold War, the Collective Security system is more complicated and is dependent on shifting alliances and more assertive middle powers. The notion that peacekeeping enhances collective security is only partially valid, since the eruption of a conflict, and the need for peacekeeping, somewhat discredits the international collective security system which is supposed to prevent conflicts from escalating into armed confrontation in the first place. Collective security can be arranged outside the jurisdiction of the UN whenever a group of nations enters into military-political pacts for collective defence purposes or to defend a shared ideological platform without violating or contradicting the UN Charter.

Article 36 of the UN Charter authorizes the Security Council to "investigate any dispute, or any situation which might lead to international friction or give rise to a dispute", and to "recommend procedures or methods of adjustment", and if the conflict continues unabated, the Council is authorized to "recommend such terms of settlement as it may consider appropriate" (UN Charter 1945, Article 36).

Based on the UN Charter, then, the Security Council may actually recommend terms of settlement for an intractable and persistent conflict. Due to the superpowers' rigid positions and veto power, however, the UN system is in reality paralysed and unable to affect comprehensive settlements – not just cessation of hostilities – in international disputes. Many UN peace intervention operations which were unthinkable during the Cold War, however, have been authorized when the interests of the dominant powers converged.

In addition to the moral presence of the United Nations as a beacon of peace and security in the world, scores of nations saw fit to enter into collective security pacts and alliances as extra insurance to guarantee their survival.

In a prescription for how to reduce threats and increase national and international security, M. Bedjaoui (1996: 55–56) suggests the following measures:

(1) Reduce your adversary's fear, and increase his confidence.
(2) Avoid making security an obsessive, unhealthy, and excessive political concern.
(3) The most secure boundaries are those separating friendly countries.
(4) Consider world peace as an indivisible whole.
(5) Cooperation is indispensable for security.

Lofty ideas indeed. But is anybody listening?

The lack of success of the traditional peacekeeping model and the international crisis management approach, despite partial success in containing – but not resolving – conflicts, forced the world to search for an alternative and dynamic model more concerned with outcomes and saving lives. It prompted the push over the years towards conflict resolution and peacebuilding reorientation of international intervention. The changing nature of conflict and of the international relations environment has changed the containment approach towards a more interventionist or 'robust' form of peacekeeping, and determined engagement with conflict resolution and human rights protection.

References

Bedjaoui, Mohammed (1996): "Preventive Diplomacy: Development, Education, and Human Rights", in: Cahill, Kevin M. (Ed.): *Preventive Diplomacy: Stopping Wars Before They Start* (New York: Basic Books): 35–60.

Bellamy, Alex J.; Williams, Paul; Griffin, Stuart (2004/2010): *Understanding Peacekeeping* (Cambridge: Polity).

Cassese, Antonio (Ed.) (1978): *United Nations Peace-Keeping: Legal Essays* (The Hague: Sijthoff & Noordhoff).

Diehl, Paul F. (1994): *International Peacekeeping* (Baltimore: Johns Hopkins University Press).

Dombroski, Kenneth R. (2007/2010): *Peacekeeping in the Middle East as an International Regime* (New York: Routledge).

El-Bouzaidi, Imane D. (2011/2012): "The United Nations Truce Supervision Organization (UNTSO): Does This Mark the End to the Observer Mission Model?", in: *Unmasking Illusions* (Online Publication – April 2012); at: http://bouzaidi.blogspot.com/2012/04/united-nations-truce-supervision.html.

Eliasson, Jan (1996): "Establishing Trust in the Healer: Preventive Diplomacy and the Future of the United Nations", in: Cahill, Kevin M. (Ed.): *Preventive Diplomacy: Stopping Wars Before They Start* (New York: Basic Books): 318–343.

Fetherston, A.B. (1994): *Towards a Theory of United Nations Peacekeeping* (London: MacMillan Press).

Ghali, Mona (1993): "United Nations Truce Supervision Organization", in: Durch, W.J. (Ed.): *The Evolution of UN Peacekeeping: Case Studies and Comparative Analysis* (New York: St. Martin's Press).

Hammarskjold, Dag (1954): "Statement to the Press*"*, cited in: Annan, Kofi (2012): *Interventions: A Life in War and Peace* (New York: The Penguin Press).

International Court of Justice (1962): *UNEF Expenses Opinion*. Advisory opinion (The Hague: International Court of Justice).

Lall, Arthur (1971): "A Note on UN Peacekeeping Machinery*"*. Paper for the International Peace Academy Conference (Helsinki, Finland).

Lall, Arthur; Rikhye, Indar (1971): "International Control of Violence: Machinery of Peacekeeping". Discussion at the International Peace Academy Conference (Helsinki, Finland).

Miller, D.H. (1928): *Drafting of the Covenant*. V. 2. (New York: Pullman): 241–246.

Mullerleile, Andreas (2016): *What is Preventive Diplomacy?* (Brussels: European Institute of Peace Publications, EIP).

Possony, Stefan T. (1946): "Peace Enforcement", in: *Yale Law Journal*, 55, 5 (August): 910–949.

Richmond, Oliver P. (2008): *Peace in International Relations* (New York: Routledge).

Rikhye, Indar Jit 1984: *The Theory and Practice of Peacekeeping* (London: Hurst & Co.).

Rosner, Gabriella (1963): *The United Nations Emergency Force* (New York: Columbia University Press).

Shalev, Aryeh (1993): *The Israeli-Syrian Armistice Regime: 1949–1955* (Boulder: Westview Press).

Sherry, George L. (1986): "The United Nations, International Conflict, and American Security", in: *Political Science Quarterly,* 101, 5: 753–771.

Taylor, Alastair M. (1983): "Peacekeeping: A Component of World Order, in: *Peacekeeping: Appraisals & Proposals* (New York: Pergamon Press).

Thakur, Ramesh Chandra (2006): *The United Nations, Peace, and Security: From Collective Security to the Responsibility to Protect* (Cambridge: Cambridge University Press).

Theobald, Andrew G. (2014): "The United Nations Truce Supervision Organization (UNTSO)", in: *The Oxford Handbook of United Nations Peacekeeping Operations* (OnlinePublication–October2014).

United Nations (1945): *United Nations Charter* (New York: UN Office of Public Information).

United Nations General Assembly Resolution A/290 (IV), *Essentials of Peace* (1 December 1949).

United Nations General Assembly Resolution A/377 (V), *Uniting for Peace* (3 November 1950).

Urquhart, Brian (1992): "Forward", in: Liu, F.T, *United Nations Peacekeeping and the Non-Use of Force* (Boulder: Lynne Rienner).

Urquhart, Brian (1994): "The UN and International Security After the Cold War", in: Roberts, A.; and Kingsbury, B. (Eds.): *United Nations, Divided World: The UN Role in International Relations* (New York: Clarendon Press).

Urquhart, Brian (1987): *A Life in Peace and War* (New York: Harper Collins).

Wiseman, Henry (Ed.) (1983): *Peace-Keeping: Appraisals and Proposals* (New York: Pergamon Press).

Woodhouse, Tom (2000): "Conflict Resolution and Peacekeeping: Critiques and Responses", in: Woodhouse, Tom; Ramsbotham, Oliver (Eds.): *Peacekeeping and Conflict Resolution* (London: Frank Cass).

Zeidan, A. M. (1976): *The United Nations Emergency Force, 1956–1967* (Stockholm: Almqvist and Wiksell International).

Part III
Evidence

Chapter 5
Anti-colonial Challenge in the Middle East

Abstract The Middle East was the theatre of an epic struggle in which old empires living beyond their shelf lives faced a determined national liberation revolt. A new world power was poised to take over as the leader of the Western world in a confrontation with the Soviet Union. The raging Cold War framed the international stage. Regional blocs in the West and the East were formed in confrontation and armed to the teeth. A new bloc of newly-independent countries was cautiously trying to assert its existence and independence. International politics was undergoing a major realignment.

Keywords National Liberation · Rind Sovereignty · 1936 Anglo-Egyptian Treaty · 1948 Creation of Israel · 1952 Egyptian Revolution · 1954 Anglo-Egyptian Treaty · Lavon Affair · Egyptian Anti-colonial Challenge · Cold War · Bandung Conference · Baghdad Pact · Operation Alpha · Omega I and Omega II Plans · Operation Gamma · Apartheid · BDS Movement · Zionism · AIPAC

5.1 Egyptian-Imperial Confrontation

The 1956 Suez clash was the culmination of a troubled history of control and resistance involving the two sides. For a long time, Britain's imperial strategy included the indispensable control of Egypt from the end of the nineteenth century onwards. Egypt's strategic location, its military importance for the British Empire, its vital transportation links, and its cultural and political weight and influence in the Middle East all convinced Britain to maintain its hold on the affairs of Egypt, despite the increasing cost of such contested control.

5.2   Egypt's Independence in 1922

The imperial project in colonial societies was facing serious obstacles due to the rise of nationalism and the inability to maintain or recruit collaborators. Thus, according to Darwin (1991), "the basis for cooperation between imperial rulers and colonial ruled had ceased to exist". It was, therefore, not feasible to "get away with an empire on the cheap". The traditional elites were, then, utilized to facilitate a "reluctant exit" (Darwin 1991: 92–97). The eventual handover of power, however, was complex and problematic as the new elites maintained oppressive control over their societies. Moreover, the cooperation of the newly independent governments with the former colonial masters continued previous patterns of dependency.

The 'temporary' British occupation of Egypt which began in 1882 morphed into a protectorate in 1914 and eventually changed to truncated and tainted *independence in 1922*. Nationalist demands were spearheaded by the *Wafd* party, led by educated and landed elite interests who were able to manipulate mass support. The resulting nationwide uprising of 1919 forced Britain to attempt to uncouple the alliance between the privileged elite and the downtrodden in the countryside and the urban centres. Consequently, the Milner Mission was dispatched to Egypt in 1919 to find a solution to the increasing nationalist pressures.

Protracted negotiations followed as the Egyptians demanded full independence, and Milner and his boss, Lord Curzon, the Foreign Secretary, insisted that in return for ending the protectorate status and granting nominal independence, Egypt must be tied to a treaty of alliance with Britain only. Moreover, Britain was to be in charge of Egypt's security and foreign relations under the direction of the British Resident General in Cairo. Egypt must also accept the continued stationing of British troops on Egyptian soil. In reality, Egypt was to graduate to the status of a satellite of Britain. Lord Milner found no difficulty in accepting the compatibility of nationalism and imperial control. A preliminary agreement was reached between Milner and Zaghloul, the leader of the Egyptian Wafd Party, in August 1920. Huge opposition to the agreement erupted among British politicians. (Darwin 1981: 112). Finally, the 1922 'February Declaration' was eventually made on 28 February, and the British Protectorate – imposed in 1914 during World War I – was abolished in favour of a nominal and tainted independence under the control of Britain. The new arrangements guaranteed Britain far-reaching rights and interests in the new 'independent' Kingdom of Egypt. The trappings of formal independence, including a royal family, parliament, diplomatic recognition and membership of international organizations, did not alter the fact that Egypt's sovereignty was a shell without substance.

Such illusory independence could only be charitably described as a 'Rind Sovereignty' as negotiated by Lord Milner, the British Colonial Administrator who engineered the agreement with the Egyptian elite. In defending the Milner-Zagloul Agreement, the Foreign Secretary, Lord Curzon infamously said "Why worry about the rind if we can obtain the fruit?" Egypt was left with the rind, while Britain enjoyed the fruit. Thus Curzon declared in triumph that "Egypt would remain inside rather than outside the British Imperial system" – in fact, a British satellite. Egyptian sovereignty after WWI was a sham (Darwin 1981: 115).

Holland (1985) stated that "the British Government had accepted the risks involved" in granting some concessions to "its key Middle Eastern satellite". The assumption – which was proven correct for thirty years – was that the Egyptian political landed elite and Britain "had a vested interest in constraining Egyptian life within the margins of the 1922 agreement". Thus, a tenuous "new equilibrium" was established between "imperial strategy and nationalist politics" in Egypt (Holland 1985: 18).

5.3   The 1936 Anglo-Egyptian Treaty

With continuous agitation against British presence, and the escalating challenge to the system of collaboration, Britain and Egypt signed the *1936 Anglo-Egyptian Treaty*. After fifteen years of independence, Egypt was negotiating to terminate the presence of the British occupying forces on its soil. The Treaty resulted in the redeployment of the British troops to the Suez Canal Region, securing for Britain its largest overseas military base consolidated in the strategic Suez Canal region. The British, moreover, used the terms of the Treaty to deploy their troops in the rest of Egypt during WWII, ignoring Egyptian 'independence'.

It has been argued that the 1936 Treaty reflected the "fundamental imbalance in the relationship between Egypt and Britain" (Gorst/Johnman 1997: 9) as British imperial objectives stubbornly overrode Egyptian nationalist requirements.

The British kept on meddling in Egyptian affairs to the extent of forcing a prime minister of their choice in 1942 on the king by threatening forced abdication if he did not comply, which he did. The humiliation of such blatant interference was felt for a long time, and was a contributing factor in the army take-over later. Also, by refusing to supply Egypt with badly needed weapons during the 1948 War with Israel, Britain did not live up to its treaty obligations.

Facing increased popular agitation, Egyptian politicians tried to achieve a more palatable accommodation with the British but without success. This continually-diminished Egyptian sovereignty, however, made the removal of the British forces from the country a fundamental Egyptian nationalist demand. The confirmation that the British imperial objectives indeed diminished the Egyptian nationalist requirements, consequently led the Egyptian Government to abrogate the 1936 Treaty on 8 October 1951.

In response, in November 1951 the British Prime Minister, Winston Churchill (the irrepressible defender of the British Empire), instructed his Foreign Secretary, Anthony Eden, to "Tell them [the Egyptians] if we have any more of their cheek we will set the Jews [the Israelis] on them and drive them into the gutter from which they should never have emerged" (Tvedt 2004: 201). Churchill's less than elegant threat clearly exemplified what the British government viewed the role of "the Jews" to be in relation to the Arab countries.

The escalating confrontation between the British and Egyptian Governments over the fate of the British Suez Canal Military Base following the Egyptian abrogation with no solution in sight, led the British Middle East Headquarters to suggest to London on 23 October 1951 an escalating multi-dimensional plan of economic and political siege, ending with a military invasion of the Egyptian Delta in order to bring about the collapse of the Egyptian Government and the installation of a friendly regime. General (Lt. Colonel at the time) Hilmy, who was head of the Egyptian military intelligence branch in the Suez Canal Region, was able to obtain a copy of the plans, code-named '*Bigot*', to occupy the Delta and send it to the Egyptian Government. Unknown agents (presumably working for the British) tried to assassinate him while his young son (the author) was with him in his car[1] The British operation (renamed Operation *Rodeo*) was expanded to include American troops landing in Tripoli and accompanying the British invasion force tasked with occupying Alexandria and Cairo (Heikal 1986: 20–21).

Amin Hewedy, a Nasser associate, confirmed the details of the *Bigot* Plan of 1951, renamed Rodeo Plan in 1953. "On 18 February 1953 [it was in 1951; please see footnote below],[2] Egyptian intelligence obtained a document from inside the Headquarters of the British High Command of the Canal Zone about a plan *Rodeo* prepared by the High Command to deal with agitation and disorder in the Canal or inside other parts of Egypt. The object of the plan was the occupation of the Delta, Cairo, and Alexandria" (Hewedy 1989: 163).

Operation *Rodeo* was evaluated by Anthony Eden, then Britain's Foreign Secretary, in a meeting with the heads of the British armed forces in January 1952:

> Discussion centred on the top-secret plans to take over the whole Nile Delta – from Alexandria in the west, to Port Said in the east, and down to Cairo in the south. Planning centred on two operations. The first – "Rodeo Bernard" – envisaged moving forces from the Canal zone to the Almaza airfield near Cairo…The second plan was called "Rodeo Flail" and focused on Alexandria. It involved the deployment of troops from Libya, along with naval and air support from Cyprus" (Thornhill 2002).

Apparently, the plan was judged to be too risky and explosive, with an unpredictable outcome, and was abandoned.

The position of the British forces in the Suez Canal region (the largest British overseas military establishment in the world after 1947) continued to be the source of increased conflict and confrontation. Acts of military resistance, including the

---

[1]Hilmy, A. (1986). Comments written on Heikal's Book (p. 20).

[2]The document was actually sent to Egyptian Army HQ in 1951 (as confirmed by Heikal above). Discovering the source of the leak, the British pressured the Egyptian government to order the transfer of Hilmy away from the Canal Zone. He was duly transferred to Alexandria without delay (to their regret, as he ended up playing a key role in the army action against the monarchy in 1952). In one of the leaflets issued by the Free Officers for distribution to the army officers' corps, Nasser attacked the government for its collaboration in removing Hilmy from his post in Ismailia. Ironically, General Hilmy returned to the Canal Zone to take charge of the British evacuation treaty from Egypt, and eventually succeeded in blocking the Suez Canal in the face of the Anglo-French and Israeli invasion in 1956.

assassinations of British personnel and sabotage, sometimes with the covert approval of the Egyptian Government, increased the degree of tension and confrontation between the two countries. After the 1952 army take-over in Egypt, an eventual agreement was reached with Britain on a final British withdrawal from Egypt.

5.4   The 1948 Arab-Israeli War and the 1950 Tripartite Declaration

The shock of the Arab defeat and the betrayal and suffocation of Palestinian rights by the new state of Israel in 1948, supported by a world still trying to come to grips with the horrors of WWII, was followed by the Western Tripartite pledge in 1950 to guarantee Israel's territory, including captured Palestinian territory assigned by the 1947 UN Partition Plan to the proposed Palestinian state. The establishment of the Arab League (League of Arab States) a few years earlier (1945) was a British attempt to create a friendly bloc to support British interests in the region. The involvement of the British government, and of the Foreign Secretary Anthony Eden in particular, in the move to create the Arab League was seen as an attempt to ensure a coordinated (and friendly) Arab-British policy by co-opting and controlling the Arab regimes, following the weakened position of Britain after WWII. The British position on Palestine in 1947 and 1950 shattered any illusion regarding Anglo-Arab solidarity.

The Western declaration was seen by the Arab countries as an attempt to impose a *fait accompli* in favour of Israel. The issuance of the Tripartite Declaration in London on 25 May 1950 (Slonim 1987: 135–149) by the Foreign Ministers of the US, Britain and France, guaranteeing the "Territorial Status Quo" between Israel and the Arab countries while totally ignoring the Palestinian issue, had cast renewed doubt about Western motives in the region. The Declaration also promised a freeze on arms shipment to Middle Eastern countries at a time when Israel was enjoying a clear military superiority over the Arabs and was still in violation of the applicable UN resolutions on territory and refugees. The Declaration was nothing short of an externally-imposed extension of a foreign-based neo-colonial scheme for the perpetuation of control. The fading imperial project found the perfect fit for the disruption of the Arab anti-colonial struggle.

In justifying the involvement of the US in the issuance of the Tripartite Declaration, US Secretary of State Dulles showed rare insightful recognition of the concerns of the Arab countries. If acted upon at the time, such insight would have changed the history of the Middle East. In June 1953 – after a fact-finding mission to the region – he declared that:

> Today the Arab peoples are afraid that the United States will back the new state of Israel in aggressive expansion. They are more fearful of Zionism than they are of Communism and

they fear the United States, lest we become the backer of expansionist Zionism (Dulles 1953: 831–835).

Dulles proceeded to attempt to balance his statement by expressing understanding over Israeli security concerns. In the end, however, support for Israel and opposition to the Arab nationalist anti-colonial aspirations became the cornerstone of Western policies towards the region.

Furthermore, in an attempt to close the file on the Palestinian refugees and end it as an issue threatening Israel's hold on the territories occupied during the 1948 war with the Arabs, the UNRWA and the US official Edward Clapp devised the UN-Clapp Plan to remove the Palestinian refugees from their camps and resettle them in the Egyptian Sinai Peninsula. Peretz (1993) reports that in 1953 and 1955 Egypt and the UN Agency UNRWA agreed to settle up to 200,000 Palestinian refugees in the Sinai Peninsula. Egypt also agreed to supply sufficent Nile water (siphoned under the Suez Canal) to irrigate huge tracts of land for agriculture and re-settlement for the benefit of the Palestinians (Peretz 1993: 96). The scheme was not intended as a political solution. It was suggested in order to alleviate the stark and dehumanizing conditions of the Palestinian refugees. The Egyptian agreement with the UNRWA (1955) stated:

> The Egyptian Government has long expressed deep and sympathetic concern on behalf of the refugees, and despite the fact that it is itself feeling the pressure of a growing Egyptian population, its co-operation with the United Nations Relief and Works Agency in alleviating the situation in Gaza resulted in an offer to furnish facilities for a refugee self-support project in the neighbouring Egyptian territory of the Sinai (Pruen/Selim 1955).

Hazboun (1994) emphasized, however, that any Israeli-supported schemes for resettlement of the Palestinian refugees in the Gaza Strip, Egypt, or any Arab country, "are part of a continuous policy to further disperse the Palestinian refugees. This policy has its roots in Herzel's early call to expel Palestinians from Palestine" (Hazboun 1994: i).

Paradoxically, in fact, this was a modified 'Transfer Plan' proposed earlier by the Zionist leadership in Europe before World War II to evict all the Palestinians (peacefully or by force) from Palestine and settle them in the neighbouring Arab countries (mainly Jordan and Iraq). Consequently, the December 1948 UN General Assembly-decreed 'Right of Return' resolution for the Palestinians would be fatally undermined.

5.5   The 1952 Egyptian Army Action

The massacre of Egyptian police officers in Ismailia in January 1952 during "Operation Eagle" by British troops stationed in the Suez Canal Base under the command of Brigadier General Kenneth Exham, which demanded the surrender and disarming of the Egyptian troops and their withdrawal from the Suez Canal Zone entirely (Thornhill 2002), was the last straw that led to the Fire of Cairo

(Black Saturday) by diverse political groups, creating serious instability in the country.

The increasing violence and the escalating turmoil in Egypt constituted the opening salvo in the army take-over in July 1952. The combination of instability in the political system, the serious socio-economic inequalities, the humiliation of the 1948 defeat, compounded by the refusal of the British to withdraw from Egyptian territory, led the clandestine Free Officers Group in the army under the leadership of Colonel Gamal Abdel Nasser to take over the army and eventually the government.

Although he was initially treated as yet another power-hungry, glory-seeking colonel by both camps of the Cold War, Nasser proved to be immune to pressures or even bribery. Indeed, he was not another run-of-the-mill coup leader, and eventually became the biggest thorn in the side of Western imperialism in the region. His ideas of governance and democracy did not fit the Western liberal mould. But he espoused an unshakable commitment to political independence and socio-economic reform and progress. Without a doubt, he earned the loyalty and support of large swathes of the people of Egypt and the Arab countries. There is no doubt, either, that a growing wave of widespread and grass-roots support for his leadership contributed to a sense of invincibility and carte blanche to pursue a challenging and confrontational decision-making style.

Photo 5.1 The casualties of Egyptian Police personnel after the British forces in the Suez Canal stormed Egyptian Police Headquarters in Ismailia on 25 January 1952. *Source* EgyptToday.Com

Photo 5.2 The Egyptian Revolution Command Council (RCC), 1952. *Source* en.ahram.org. eg.
Public Domain

The seismic change in Egypt in 1952 propelled the new regime to pursue its top
priority – after consolidating power: the termination of the British presence in Egypt.
Anti-British agitations in the Canal Zone intensified and the pressure against the British
became too great to ignore, or to continue past efforts of co-opting the political elite.
Moreover, Britain's imperial pretensions were humbled by the emergence of the new
hegemony in the area, the US. The American government was not opposed to the
continuation of a British role in the Suez Canal region as a part of the overall anti-Soviet
containment. The group of officers leading the Egyptian Government, however, were in
no mood to entertain any new collaborative arrangements with the British.

5.6   The 1954 Lavon Affair: Operation Susannah

Fearing the development of a close relationship between the new regime in Egypt
and the West, Israeli secret intelligence initiated a covert sabotage operation
(code-named Susannah) targeting US and British cultural and information centres,
and Egyptian post offices and cinemas in Cairo and Alexandria in the summer of
1954. Israeli Prime Minister Mosh Sharett was kept in the dark. A Mossad-con-
trolled cell of Egyptian Jews (code-named Unit 131), who were recruited and
trained by Israel, were caught and arrested by the Egyptian authorities and the
conspiracy was fully exposed.

One of the main objectives of the covert operation was the sabotage of
Egyptian-US relations. The second objective to convince Britain to abandon the
negotiations for the evacuation of the British military base in the Suez Canal region.

Teveth (1996: 81) stated that the operation was designed "to undermine Western confidence in the existing Egyptian regime". Shlaim wrote that the operation aimed to implicate Egyptians "in an effort to disrupt the Anglo-Egyptian base negotiations" (Shlaim 2001: 187). Fabricated accusations were levelled against Egyptian nationalists, Communists, and Muslim Brothers. The arrest of the Israeli agents, however, exposed the true identity of the planners behind the plot.

The erupting scandal in Israel forced the resignation of the Defence Minister, Pinhas Lavon. The Minister claimed that he had no knowledge of the operation and did not authorize it, but he ended up paying a political price for the in-fighting within the Israeli establishment. The Chief of Staff, Mosh Dayan, and the Director of Military Intelligence, Binyamin Gibli, both claimed that Lavon gave the order for the operation. A government commission of inquiry failed to reach a conclusion on his involvement. In 1958 an expanded cabinet committee found Lavon not responsible. The earlier evidence against him was a case of a political hot potato tossed around by people who were actually involved in the operation in order to absolve themselves of responsibility for the failure. As it turned out, both the civilian intelligence agency (Mossad), and the military intelligence arm (Aman) were involved.

Although, publicly, Israel denied any involvement in the sabotage operation, a stream of Israeli and foreign sources were used to plead for mercy after the trial in Egypt for those who were convicted by the court. Nasser's position was that the defendants were "mercenaries of a foreign intelligence service". Moreover, he could not politically show more leniency "toward Jewish than toward Muslim Terrorists" (Shlaim 2001: 120–121). Years later, however, the perpetrators of the failed scheme, which Israel denied any involvement in, were honoured by the Israeli state.

5.7   The 1954 Anglo-Egyptian Treaty

The two sides finally entered into negotiations, leading to the conclusion of the *1954 Anglo-Egyptian (Evacuation) Treaty* in October for the final withdrawal of the British troops from Egypt, to be completed by June 1956 (only for Britain to attempt a military re-invasion in October of the same year). Like the 1936 Treaty abrogated by the Egyptian Government in 1951, the 1954 Treaty was abrogated by Egypt after the 1956 tripartite invasion. After the war, Anglo-Egyptian relations entered into a deep freeze that lasted for several years. Britain's position in the Middle East became untenable, and within few short years the Empire experienced its final sunset in the region.

Photo 5.3 Egyptian General Ali A. Amer, Commander of the Eastern Command, seeing off the British Commander of the Suez Canal Base in June 1956. The British departure was short-lived, as Britain, France and Israel invaded Egypt in October 1956. *Source* General Hilmy's files

5.8 Egyptian Challenge

The period between 1954 and 1956 witnessed a steady escalation in the confrontation between the revolutionary regime in Egypt and the old empires, and increasingly with the US as well. The European capitals were busy trying to fashion new modes of maintaining their seriously threatened positions, while Cairo was leading and, indeed, fomenting the expanding anti-colonial resistance throughout the Middle East and Africa. Nasser's restoration of the dignity and pride of his people "triggered an outpouring of emotional mass support inside Egypt and throughout the Arab world" (Dessouki 1989: 32). Consequently, Egypt's Nasser became the voice of liberation for the entire Arab world. As Nasser consolidated his role as the undisputed leader of the new revolutionary tide in the area, he became the main target of Western chagrin.

Two events helped propel Egypt towards a more pronounced Arab identity but without complete identification with the Arab world. First, the establishment of the League of Arab States (the Arab League), seen initially as a British attempt to create a friendly bloc to support British interests in the region. Nasser's appearance on the political scene undermined the British objectives. Second, the Egyptian blood involvement in the 1948 'Palestine' war (Mayer 1986: 331–349), dragged Egypt further into the quagmire of Arab politics, notwithstanding growing Egyptian leadership aspirations in the area (Gerges 2001: 151–177).

One thing became clear during those transformational years: despite lingering strong support for an independent Egyptian sovereignty, a 'pure' version of Egyptian nationalism was giving way to a pan-Arab collective identity. Undoubtedly, 'Arab Nationalism' emerged in its heyday of the 1950s and the 1960s as a powerful unifying ideology, cutting across local and regional divisions and differences. While Egyptian nationalism had been struggling since the turn of the century to assert its viability, the Arab national movement had been brewing for years in Syria and Iraq. The two nationalist movements, in Egypt and in the Levant, were not in conflict or competition with each other (Choieiri 2000). Rather, they were two parallel, even complementary nationalist movements against colonialism. Egyptian nationalism was preoccupied with securing independence for Egypt, while the Arab nationalist movement had as its goal the unity of an independent Arab 'Homeland'. The two movements were indeed united by language and religion, but they had their own trajectories and objectives.

The 1967 Arab defeat at the hands of Israel, however, dealt a severe body-blow to the pan-Arab idea. Egypt's Arab leadership role was seen by some as a tool to serve Egyptian interests: "it was only as long as Pan-Arabism corresponded to elite views of Egypt's interests that Pan-Arab identity dominated" (Hinnebusch 2005). There is no doubt, however, that Nasser's leadership epitomized Egyptian and wider Arab anger against and challenge to foreign domination. Due to Egypt's long history prior to the arrival of the Arab conquest, a unique sense of Egyptian identity will nevertheless always be present in the national consciousness, sometimes in cooperation with an Arab identity, and other times in direct confrontation.

The old colonial empires considered the Egyptian revolutionary regime the main challenge to be contained. As the Western plans to co-opt Nasser followed by attempts to isolate and topple him failed, his popularity and appeal unsettled the West and endangered its changing position in the region. Egypt became the base and beacon of resistance and the engine of change in the entire area. The Egyptian threat was not only directed against the colonial powers, but also threatened Arab governments sympathetic to the West or deemed reactionary and conservative. In concrete terms, Egypt's propaganda machinery matched and even surpassed Western and local messages. The call for steadfastness and solidarity fell on receptive audiences in Egypt and the Arab world. Cairo became the magnet for many national liberation leaderships. Egypt provided them with political, financial, and military support.

Photo 5.4 Nasser addressing the crowds in Cairo, 1955. *Source* World History Archive/Alamy
ID: RJRN4F (with permission)

Cairo was also involved in efforts to unseat unfriendly Arab governments. The stage was set for an eventual showdown aimed at putting the Egyptian revolutionary upstart in his place. Crucially, Egypt was also resisting American overtures to join its circle of alliances in the intensifying confrontation with the Soviet bloc. Moreover, the USA was crafting its own plans for wresting control of Middle Eastern politics and resources. Such control was – at times – in direct competition with the old empires.

5.9   The Middle East and the Cold War

Prior to the Suez War, with the Cold War in full swing and the Western containment effort at its most robust, Western powers under the leadership of the United States were determined to involve the Middle East in a ring of steel around the Soviet Union. The aim was to prevent any Soviet penetration southwards that would pose a strategic threat to the West's vital oil supplies or military presence.

A *Middle East Command* (MEC) with eleven-point policy objectives was thus established in November 1951 by the US, the UK, France and Turkey to coordinate a defence strategy for the Middle East. The new collective security arrangement was not warmly received by Egypt or the Arab World, and consequently the whole project quickly collapsed. Nevertheless, Arab participation was deemed crucial in the global vision of American foreign policy at the time (Onozawa 2005: 117–148).

In 1952, the US did try to resurrect a collective defence mechanism again by proposing the establishment of a *Middle East Defence Organization* (MEDO). The United States lobbied hard in the Middle East for a joint anti-Communism crusade. The new Egyptian regime was firmly opposed to any Western-led security arrangement in the region.

The scope of behind-the-scene attempts by the Americans and the British to include Egypt in MEDO is revealed by declassified documents on US foreign relations in the Near and Middle East during the period 1952–1954. In a meeting in Washington, DC, on 10 November 1952, including representatives from the British Embassy and the US Department of State, Mr B.A.B. Burrows, Counsellor of the British Embassy, stated:

> We agree with the State Department that the Egyptian attitude is the key factor and that an approach to Egypt regarding MEDO is unlikely to produce any positive result unless it is accompanied by proposals for a settlement of the Suez Canal question. We welcome the United States' expression of interest in negotiations with Egypt with a view to facilitating an Anglo- Egyptian agreement and we will produce proposals for discussion with the Americans as soon as possible. As regards the suggestion of a programmme of military and economic assistance [to Egypt] we consider that such an offer should be linked with acceptance by Egypt of the principle of joint defence and preferably worked out through MEDO. It will be our main inducement to Egypt to co-operate in Middle East Defense (Burrows 1952).

The American response was delivered by Mr. Jernegan of the Near Eastern Affairs Bureau of the Department of State, who stated that:

> We made it clear [to the Egyptians] that US assistance to Egypt would be largely conditioned by the attitude of the Egyptian Government towards cooperating in the defense of the Middle East. (Jernegan 1952).

Clearly, Western policies toward Egypt in the early 1950s were a combination of inducement, threats and blackmail. Not waiting for Egyptian cooperation in the containment of the Soviet Union and the protection of the Western interests in the region, the Eisenhower Administration adopted in 1954 a policy thrust which contained two objectives:

(1) Reaching a settlement of the Arab-Israeli conflict…necessary…for a stable Middle East.
(2) Build the *northern tier* in the Middle East [Turkey and Iran] and connect it through security arrangements with the Arab world (NSC No. 5428, 1954).

Evidently, the US had bigger fish to fry than accommodating Nasser's anti-colonial plans. The US's concerns were articulated to ensure a commanding role in the Affairs of the Arab East regardless of the other players.

5.10   Operation Alpha (1955)

Nasser totally rejected the "perpetuation of Western regional hegemony" (Eveland 1980) and the associated Israeli threat. The Western powers finally tried to contain his opposition to a Western role in the region by offering him a mediated settlement of the Arab-Israeli conflict, thus removing one of the thorniest impediments to a regional peace. The Anglo-American "Operation Alpha" (Foreign Office 1955), authored by Evelyn Shuckburgh (Britain) and Francis Russell (USA), was thus proposed in 1955 to overcome Egyptian and Arab objections. The proposed plan aimed to achieve acceptable territorial and refugee outcomes to end the Arab-Israeli conflict.

Photo 5.5 Nasser and Eden In Cairo in 1955. *Source* Al-Ahram & mentalfloss.com

The principles of the Anglo-American plan for an Arab-Israeli settlement, according to Shamir (1989), evolved around the main underlying issues: "visible concessions by Israel (territory and refugees); guarantees of security by the major powers; an understanding worked out mainly with Egypt; and the definition of the objective as 'an overall settlement, not 'peace'." That broad outline of the Anglo-American initiative "was endorsed by Eden and Dulles…in January 1955" (Shamir 1989: 81).

The plan was initially expanded in February 1955 to include the ceding of two triangles in the Negev, one each for Jordan and Egypt, to allow a territorial connection between them without cutting Israel's link to Eilat. It also proposed the repatriation of a considerable number of Palestinian refugees and compensation for the rest with the help of international finance. Agreement was also sought for the distribution of the Jordan waters and on the final status of Jerusalem. Finally, the package included the termination of the Arab boycott of Israel, Western guarantees of the newly agreed frontiers, and general economic assistance to the region.

As an additional incentive, Egypt was offered help in financing the massive *High Dam* project, Egypt's cornerstone for a massive development drive. Of high importance to the outcome, the US was prepared to freeze the Baghdad Pact. Moreover, the US accepted Egypt's demand for an all-inclusive *Arab Defence Organization* free of any outside involvement, thus removing any possible Soviet inclusion in Arab affairs.

But without fundamental Egyptian-Israeli agreement on territory and refugees, no amount of incentives would have worked. The initial optimism about Alpha evaporated when Israel refused to make any concessions, matched by Egypt's persistence in opposing the original Western plans for the region.

Several additional factors contributed to the impasse in arriving at an acceptable agreement:

(1) The Israeli raid on Gaza in February 1955 and the exposure of the Egyptian military weakness vis-à-vis Israel heightened Egyptian fears of an increased Israeli threat.

(2) The birth of the Baghdad Pact in August 1955, alienating the anti-colonial leadership in Egypt.

(3) The return to office in August 1955 of the Prime Minister of Israel, the hard-liner David Ben-Gurion, who rejected any notion of compromise.

(4) The difficult position of Egyptian President Nasser and his fear of showing any betrayal of Arab rights.

(5) The US official position announced by Secretary Dulles in New York on 26 August 1955 for the foundations of an Arab-Israeli settlement. Dulles highlighted the main stumbling blocks in the face of an agreement: (a) the plight of the 900,000 Palestinian refugees; (b) the mutual distrust between the two sides; (c) the lack of accepted fixed borders. Dulles proposed the repatriation of some of the refugees to their ancestral homeland, and suggested offering them land for agriculture. He said the rest of the refugees should be compensated by Israel for their loss. He pledged to help the Israelis financially with the compensation scheme. Finally, he called for an acceptable territorial agreement guaranteed by international security guarantees (Secretary Dulles – Council on Foreign Relations, New York, 26 August 1955; Burns 1985: 52–53).

(6) The British position detailed by Prime Minister Anthony Eden during his Guildhall speech on 9 November 1955. Eden supported a negotiated settlement on the basis of the Anglo-American Alpha Plan. The main point regarding a territorial agreement was to have the border of Israel between the lines of the

status quo (since 1949) and the Partition Plan borders (1947) (Prime Minister Eden – Guildhall Speech – 9 November 1955).

In fairness to Eden and Dulles, such proposals would have gone a long way towards winning Nasser's (and the Arabs') support. At this period, the Egyptian President was seriously interested in a negotiated settlement with Israel. Addressing the refugee and borders problems were the two main sticking points preventing a reasonable and fair resolution of the impasse. The Alpha Plan's fundamental flaw was the bypassing of the issue of Palestinian self-determination and political sovereignty, indispensable for an overall achievable settlement.

The American proposal on refugees and the British proposal on borders created the impression in Israel, however, that the Western powers were ganging up to force a settlement not acceptable to Israel. In turn, the Israelis' adamant refusal of the Western compromise proposals led the Egyptians to conclude that an equitable settlement was out of reach.

History is replete with examples of rational junctures abandoned or logical roads not travelled. The 1955–1956 period in the Middle East was one of those turning points ignored at the peril of ensuring a continuous conflict. The admittedly imperfect Alpha Plan was one such missed opportunity. The US and Britain were unable (due to their own strategic and domestic considerations) to convince the Israelis that a compromise is better than a dragged-on deadly and unstable confrontation. The Israeli leadership chose ideology over rationality. The Alpha Plan would have provided Arab recognition and the end of the state of war; permanent and international guarantees of borders and security; a partial resolution of the refugees' problem; massive economic assistance; and the prospect of regional peace and cooperation. Military victors, however, tend to believe that their victories would last forever. History tells us otherwise.

5.11 Operation Gamma

The Alpha formula was running into trouble as both sides were making demands unacceptable to each other. An American mediator, Robert Anderson, a businessman and a friend of President Eisenhower, was dispatched in early 1956 by the President to take charge of the negotiations and was tasked with presenting the plan to two sides holding two entrenched and diametrically opposed positions. The Egyptian President and the Israeli Prime Minister were persuaded to write letters to President Eisenhower confirming their desire for a peaceful end to the conflict. Nasser wrote first, affirming "the desirability of seeking to eliminate the tensions between the Arab States and Israel…Egypt harbours no hostile intentions toward any other state and will never be party to an aggressive war", but adding: "Egypt must affirm its continuing desire to see the fundamental rights and aspirations of the Arab people respected" (Nichols 2011: 75). Ben-Gurion wrote next, affirming his government's "full and unqualified readiness…to explore possibilities of a settlement or of progress by stages towards an ultimate peace." In the same letter, the Israeli leader requested again, however, the sale of weapons to Israel (Nichols 2011: 75).

The Anderson Mission, dubbed Operation Gamma, failed to rescue the original Alpha Plan. Anderson was unable to earn the trust of either side: "both Egyptian and American participants agreed, the choice of mediator left much to be desired" (Shamir 1989: 98). The Egyptian leadership decided that it would restrict the negotiations to official professional diplomatic channels.

The principle author of the plan, Shuckburgh (1956), criticized Israel's negotiating position, claiming that Israel "is an obstruction…the greatest irritant of all" (Shamir 1989: 91–92). According to Almog (2003), "Evelyn Shuckburgh, the key figure behind Alpha, wanted to make it clear to the Israeli government that the plan was its great chance; if Israel rejected the proposal it would be responsible for the failure of the peace effort within the region" (Almog 2003: 44). Moreover, Caplan (1997) confirmed Schuckburgh's views: "It should be made very plain to the Israelis at this stage that this is their big chance and that, if they reject the proposed basis for discussion, the responsibility for failure of our effort will lie on them" (Caplan 1997: 93).

While the *British* saw Israel's refusal to entertain any compromise as the main reason for failure to reach an accommodation, they initially considered Nasser's willingness to recognize Israel as part of the proposed overall settlement as a fundamental change in the dynamics of the conflict, and a historical opportunity not to be wasted.

The *US* leadership, on the other hand, accepted the mediator's conclusion that "Nasser proved to be a complete stumbling block" (Doran 2016: 163). Eisenhower, however, wrote in his diary that making Nasser the villain bordered on crass electoral politics because "Israeli officials were hardly 'innocent bystanders'". He recalled that "the Israelis had been completely adamant in their attitude of making no concessions whatsoever in order to make peace". They would give up "not one inch of ground" and were "incessantly demanding arms" (Nichols 2011: 88).

Strangely, after the failure of the two principal sponsors of the plan to make a breakthrough in the face of the adamant refusal of Israel's Prime Minister, David Ben-Gurion, to accept any compromise (even a symbolic one), the US and Britain started to lay the blame for failure at Nasser's feet.

As the negotiations were nearing collapse, Nasser wrote to Eisenhower again. He told the US Ambassador to Egypt, Henry Byroad, that he assured President Eisenhower that "I will not start a war with Israel. I give to you and to him my word on that issue, not as a politician but as a soldier" (Nichols 2011: 88). Byroad wrote to Washington, counselling patience and raising the possibility that "Anderson had been impatient" and did not understand Nasser (Byroade 1956: 348–51).

Blaming Nasser for the failure of the Alpha peace plan was not surprising. Eisenhower must have been aware that Egypt's political influence in the Western capital was much weaker than Israel's, as the shadow of the Holocaust was looming in the background. He observed that "Egypt had no viable political constituency in the American electorate, whereas Israel had a very strong position in the heart and emotions of the Western world" (Nichols 2011: 88). Eisenhower's position was a repeat of Harry Truman's invocation of the 'Jewish vote' in 1947–48 to justify supporting the creation of the state of Israel in Palestine.

Secretary Dulles was pushing ahead with a new tough policy towards Nasser, trying to cut him down to size. Dulles wanted to diminish Nasser's leadership postion in the region, and, according to McNamara (2003), "In line with Omega, cutting Nasser down to size meant slowing, if not abandoning, Western support for the scheme" (McNamara 2003: 47). The Western short-sighted approach to Egypt, and the acquiescence to the Israeli position doomed the possibility of a balanced outcome to the conflict.

Eisenhower and Dulles did not have to wait long to experience the strength of the Israeli influence in the heart of the US political machinery. In the wake of the Suez War and Israel's refusal to withdraw from the conquered Egyptian territories, Secretary Dulles wrote in a memo for the record that Israel's position would "make it almost certain that virtually all of the Middle East Countries would feel that the United States policy toward the area was in the last analysis controlled by the Jewish influence in the United States" as the Israelis wielded "terrific Control" over the Media and the Congress (Dulles 1957: 142–144).

Nasser's willingness to engage in the (eventually inconclusive) Western attempts to engineer an Arab-Israeli solution was designed to earn some goodwill towards his leadership and tone down the degree of Western antagonism. However, when Western planners attempted to use their mediation attempts to perpetuate the Western strategic goals in the region, the contradictory objectives "could not be reconciled" (Caplan 1997: 93).

5.12   The 1955 Bandung Conference

The Western determination to maintain control of the Middle East in the face of the anti-colonial revolt, the insistence on including the region in an anti-Soviet encirclement, and finally, the twin weapon of supporting Israel and resisting Nasser's liberation goals led to new confrontational lines being drawn in the sand. It was an easy leap for Nasser to join the new Afro-Asian alliance in Bandung designed to resist the perpetuation of Western colonial control, and to steer an independent course.

Article 6a of the final Declaration of the Conference (April 1955) did not mince any words and was central in the Afro-Asian response to Western plans for the encirclement of the Soviet Union. It called on all signatory states to abstain "from the use of arrangements of collective defense to serve any particular interests of the big powers" (Bandung Conference 1955: Declaration).

Bandung laid the groundwork for the policy of "Positive Neutrality" pursued by the Third World, and became the basic push and inspiration later on for the "Non-Aligned Movement" that eventually emerged. Burke (2010: 13) observed that "The 1955 Asian-African Conference in Bandung, Indonesia was a landmark in the emergence of the non-aligned movement and the birth of the Third World". Not surprisingly, the Western powers were shocked and angered. The refrain that 'if you are not with me, you are against me' was exemplified by the attitude of the US Secretary of State, John F. Dulles, who believed "any form of neutralism to be immoral" (Heikal 1986: 117).

5.13   The Baghdad Pact (1955)

The failure to entice Egypt into a pro-Western Middle Eastern alliance, and to counteract Nasser's serious challenge, led the US and Britain to persuade their allies in the region (Turkey, Iraq, Iran, and Pakistan) to form a political and military alliance (*The Baghdad Pact*) established in 1955 to balance the Egyptian-led threat. Nasser viewed the new Western-backed group headquartered in Baghdad and formed under the leadership of Britain as a direct challenge to his leadership, and to the aspirations for national liberation in the volatile region. In 1958, the US joined the military wing of the alliance after the overthrow of the Iraqi monarchy and the seemingly unstoppable spread of Nasser's influence in the region. After the exit of Iraq from the Pact, the alliance was renamed the *Central Treaty Organization* and its headquarters were moved to Ankara, Turkey, demonstrating the difficulty of the Western powers in establishing reliable and willing allies in the area in the face of the anti-colonial tide orchestrated by Egypt.

5.14   Omega I and Omega II (1955–1956)

Nasser maintained his refusal of Western domination and became a principle player in the Afro-Asian liberation movement. The Egyptian regime and the Western powers were set on a collision course over Western plans for the entire Middle East. In 1955 the US and Britain framed Nasser as the 'target' for 'punitive' measures for refusing to yield. A joint plan was formulated and designed to eventually topple the Egyptian leader through a complex blend of pressure, blackmail and intimidation. In London in February 1956, the representative from the CIA, James Eichelberger, met his counterpart in SIS (MI6), John Young. The British intelligence officer spoke openly about the possibility of "assassinating Nasser" with the help of "suitable elements in Egypt" and the rest of the Arab world (Heikal 1986: 103–104).

At Eisenhower's request, new Middle East policy guidelines were included in a memorandum code-named *Omega* (28 March 1956) prepared by US Secretary of State Dulles.

The American leaders were angry at "the failure of bringing Egypt into a regional defence organization as the focal point of an anti-Soviet alliance" (Freiberger 1992: 148–150). The American plan (divided into two phases, I and II, depending on the degree of escalation required) envisaged several steps, among them: postponing the negotiation over financing the Aswan High Dam; indefinitely delaying Egyptian requests for wheat, grain and other aid items; visibly increasing greater support for the Baghdad Pact, as well as delaying the completion of British withdrawal from the Suez Canal Base; denying Western military supplies to Egypt; and building up King Saud as an alternative Arab leader in place of Nasser.

After the US turned down Egypt's repeated requests for arms to defend its territory against a better-armed Israel, Egypt reached an agreement with the Soviets for the supply of armaments. The CIA operative, Kermit Roosevelt, informed Henry Byroad, the US Ambassador to Egypt in a meeting in Cairo, that on hearing the news Secretary "Dulles was furious…and was behaving like an agitated ox… Dulles wanted Nasser to cancel the deal…[if not] the US would (1) stop all aid, (2) stop all trade, (3) break off diplomatic relations, (4) blockade Egypt." (Heikal 1073: 51–52). In his memo to the President of 26 May 1956, Dulles suggested even "more drastic action in the event that the above courses of action do not have the desired effect" (Dulles 1956: 419–421). In the official mind, the time had come to replace the "soft attitude" toward Nasser with "much stronger measures" (Rountree 1956: 658; 667). Accordingly, by the time of the NATO Council Ministerial Meeting in Paris in May 1956, Western policy had decidedly turned against Nasser, as the Western allies concluded "that the Aswan project should languish" (Freiberger 1992: 152–153). "In effect, a program [propagated by Dulles] to diminish Nasser's influence" was adopted by the Western alliance (Nichols 2011: 90).

Although in agreement on the need to confront Nasser, the Americans and the British had their own competing agendas to pursue. "Dulles pursued a policy with dual aims: to punish Nasser, and further to erode Britain's position in the Middle East" (Freiberger 1992: 157). The British, on the other hand, were stubbornly trying to maintain a privileged position in the region, but time was not on their side as the world was fundamentally changing around them. The old and the new empires were jockeying for a clear advantage in the muddy waters of a turbulent region.

Israel, for its part, was playing a double-edged role. First, it wanted to further its political entrenchment and territorial expansion. Second, it wanted to serve the colonial agenda in the region by helping to undermine and defeat the anti-colonial nationalist challenge. The imperial structure in the Middle East, which helped in the creation of Israel in the first place, was more than willing to induct the Zionist state into the fight for imperial survival. The harmonization of the imperial-Israel agendas would eventually produce one of the most sordid political-military episodes in the history of the Middle East in the 1950s (and later on in the 1960s and beyond).

The inevitable confrontation between the anti-colonial leadership of Egypt and the Western alliance was only a matter of time, as the situation was escalating without restraint. Each side was getting ready for a showdown.

5.15   Colonialism and the Israeli Project

The role of colonialism in the fate of the Middle East cannot be evaluated without considering the role played by Israel in this grand project. The old and the neo-colonial plans to control the Middle East for its geopolitical value and its resources have incorporated a Zionist-Israeli component almost from the very beginning. Undoubtedly, Israel played a major role in supporting and consolidating the colonial and neo-colonial agenda in the Middle East for its own advantage. A colonial-settler state itself, Israel did not find any difficulty in shoring up the old empires and becoming an extension of the new one.

Israel succeeded phenomenally in establishing a new exclusive state in Palestine coinciding with the colonial plans for the Middle East. The seasoned British diplomat, Evelyn Shuckburgh, was prophetic in assessing the role Israel would eventually play in the colonial story in the Middle East, and the "impact of the Arab-Israeli conflict on the British imperial project. The British association with Zionism, he believed, had from the very beginning been a tragic error, both moral and strategic. Palestine was the burial ground of our hopes for maintaining the British position in the Middle East. I suppose this was inevitable from the time of the Balfour Declaration" (Doran 2016: 100). The American diplomat, Henry Byroade, was equally scathing, describing "Truman's recognition of Israel as one of the greatest strategic blunders in American diplomatic history" (Doran 2016: 102).

Evidently, the *Sykes-Picot Agreement* to divide the Arab provinces of the collapsing Ottoman Empire between Britain and France became intertwined with the *Zionist project* to colonize Palestine. Both schemes worked to consolidate foreign control over the fate of the Middle East.

5.16   The Injurious Israeli Factor

Pro-Zionist Jews in Europe and the United States applied strong pressures on the British Foreign Secretary, Lord Balfour, to extract the Balfour Declaration in 1917 for the creation of a homeland for Jews in Palestine. Britain was desperate to bring the United States into the war against Germany in Europe.

In exchange, American Jews lobbied the American Government to support Britain in its war efforts. Political expediency eventually led to the creation of Israel in 1948, resulting in the destruction of Palestinian society and the expulsion of the Palestinians to neighbouring countries. Arendt (1973) stated that the Zionist strategy was based on the premise that "Palestinians should be transferred to the neighbouring Arab states or resettled elsewhere in order to liberate the land for Jewish nationalisation…The solution of the Jewish question merely produced a new category of refugees, the Arabs" (Arendt 1973: 290).

Numerous factors were involved, and the repercussions continue to this day:

Photo 5.6 Palestinian refugees being evicted from the Galilee in Palestine, October-November 1948. *Source* Wikipedia – Public Domain

- The pre-planned and deliberate scheme in the 1920s, 1930s, and 1940s by the Zionist organizations in Europe and North America for the 'transfer' of the Palestinians. The scheme revolved around the wholesale forcing of the Palestinians by all means possible to flee Palestine and settle in Jordan and Iraq, leaving British-Mandated Palestine free for mass colonization by European Jews. The historical record is replete with the numerous Zionist-Israeli claims that 'Palestine was a land without people ready for people without land'.

- Britain's acrobatic act in trying to balance its plan for a Jewish state in Palestine with its interests in the Arab world.
- Foreign support from the West, and initially from the Eastern Bloc as well.
- The pivotal role played by the US White House, and the Congress, under constant pressure from the American Jewish lobby.
- Efficient Israeli propaganda message well received in the West, and not matched by a professional Arab voice.
- Guilt over the Holocaust and anti-Semitism.
- The serious imbalance of power between Israel and the Arabs in favour of the Israelis, in terms of qualified numbers and quality of trained personnel, armaments, motivation, and planning. Despite the deliberately-defused wrong information, the Israelis were able to field more than double the fighting troops than the Arabs in 1948, while portraying themselves as the underdog.
- The establishment of an Israeli nuclear capability providing undeclared but real deterrence and acting as powerful intimidation and a permanent threat. (That threat was almost carried out during the 1973 War, and was ready to deploy in 1967 on a smaller scale.)

- The deliberate wave of terror unleashed during the British Mandate by the Jewish military units against the Palestinians. Moreover, the encroachment of the armed Jewish militias on the territories assigned to the Palestinian State under the UN 1947 Partition Plan occurring before the declaration of the state of Israel, and the indiscriminate acts of terror – such as the massacre of *Deir Yassin and the mass shootings and executions in Galilee* as well as the deliberate terror campaign throughout Palestine – forced the Palestinians to flee for their lives to neighbouring countries.
- Israel's inability to negotiate in good faith, as well as the violation of agreements already reached (the Oslo Accords, for one). Israel had already declared the Armistice Agreement it signed with Egypt dead and buried in order to annex the Israeli-Occupied Egyptian territories in the Sinai, and the Palestinian Gaza Strip in 1956.
- Israel's approach to the Arab-Israeli conflict is to create many *fait accompli(s)* and 'facts on the ground' in violation of international law, leaving the Palestinians and the Arabs stunned and unable to react.
- The control exerted by the pro-Israel lobby machinery in the USA over the White House and the Congress allows Israel to act with impunity. US politicians compete to declare their support for Israel. The former US Vice President, Joe Biden, was candid when he said that the existence of Israel saves the US the burden of stationing large number of US troops in the region.
- Persistent refusal to implement and abide by the UN Resolutions on Partition, Refugees, and the Occupied Territories.
- Israel's pathological inability to entertain a balanced settlement and a just solution for both sides. Sadly, there is no compromising bone in the Israeli body-politic.
- The Israeli sense of entitlement to act mercilessly as required regardless of the consequences, justified by the Jewish suffering encountered in Europe.
- It is a truly sad reflection on international politics and human nature that victims and decendants of the horrific Holocaust and the pogroms turn themselves into instruments of occupation, usurpation, oppression, and unspeakable brutal violations of human rights directed at people who were not connected in any way with the atrocities they themselves faced earlier.
- The trials and tribulations suffered by the European Jews entitle them to finally live in peace, dignity, and security. But they do not entitle them to inflict misplaced savage reprisals under mythical justifications against the people of Palestine.
- The pendulum of power in Palestine-Israel has gone too far in one direction. It is hoped that it will not swing back completely to the other direction, or that a colosal and historical confrontation will destabilize the Middle East beyond recognition.
- The child of the old empire and the tool of the new empire should consider stepping back from a reckless course hurtling the region toward an eventual melt-down. The position of almost unchallenged power can one day be

extinguished and overturned. The current turmoil in the region cannot be divorced from the Israeli policies in Palestine.

- The current US Administration's total identification with and encouragement of the aggressive Israeli-Zionist plans for illegal territorial aggrandizement and the continuous subjugation of the Palestinian people can only spell a renewed phase of increasing violence and dangerous instability for the region. The latest US ploy, "the Deal of the Century", developed over almost two years and revealed in 2020, proposed with the connivance of the Zionist establishment and designed to suffocate the legitimate Palestinian aspirations for freedom and sovereignty once and for all, can only spell the utter bankruptcy of an opportunistic American administration lacking any professional competence and a proper assessment of the disaster they are leading the Middle East towards. Several Arab regimes dependent on Washington for political and military survival have exhibited tacit support for the 'Deal'. In fairness to the American establishment, over the years professional diplomats, analysts in the State Department and the Pentagon counselled strongly against total support for Israel as very harmful to US interests and the interests of the Middle East. Political expediency trumped any such considerations.

- The American Israel Public Affairs Committee (AIPAC) has played an integral part in formulating US policy towards the Middle East for decades. To a lesser extent, the Canada Israel Committee (CIC) is trying to perform the same function in Canada. Other lobby groups advocating for Israel exist in several European countries. Although there is a large constituency of 'Christian Zionists' in the West which support Israel, there is larger and growing support for Palestinian rights. The 'Boycott, Divestment, Sanctions', known as the BDS movement, aimed at ending any international support for Israel, is just one aspect of the expanding realization of the scope of violation and oppression in Palestine by the Israeli authorities. The South African Apartheid movement suffered the same fate. In politics, there is always a trade-off between individuals, groups, and states to serve required objectives. In the United States such a trade-off has been elevated to an art form. In return for supporting Israel, American politicians at all levels expect – and rely on – the pro-Israel machinery in the US to help their electoral prospects.

- The inhumanity inflicted on Jews in Europe should not be repeated against others in the Middle East. Throughout history, the Jews have made enormous contributions in every field of human endeavour. It is disheartening, therefore, that the legacy of Israel in Palestine is unconscionably violent and oppressive. It stands in stark contrast to the genuine Jewish achievements, and to past Muslim-Jewish cooperative brilliance in Spain and elsewhere. The inability to be compassionate and magnanimus risks tarnishing and haunting succeeding generations of Jews. Their history of suffering cannot negate the atrocities and injustice committed in Palestine. Israel cannot continue to be aligned with foreign domination in the Middle East without eventually paying a price for such a strategic mistake. Moreover, the continuation of the Israeli brutal practices in Palestine stokes criminal anti-Semitic activities everywhere. Israel's irresponsible policies are short-sighted and self-defeating for Israel and for Jews everywhere.

- It is disingenuous for Israel to claim that it is engaged in self-defence when it is crystal clear that Israel is pursuing a policy of occupation and annexation. Self-deception is almost becoming a second nature in the Israeli narrative. One can only hope that some Israelis will see the peril of such a policy and modify and eventually overturn such an aggressive and uncompromising mindset.

It is customary to accuse critics of Israeli policies of anti-Semitism. Such tactics, however, cannot hide the truth or silence the critics. The crimes of anti-Semitism, which are real and undeniable, however, do not justify or excuse the Zionist crimes against the Palestinians in particular, and the Arabs in general. On the other hand, the unconscionable past pogroms and anti-Semitism in Europe constitute a stamp of shame on the entire human race. The heinous crime of the Holocaust was not just a crime committed against Jews, but against all of humanity, and must be condemned without any prevarication. Holocaust deniers, moreover, should be morally and legally exposed and confronted. It is sad that the Zionists did not fully appreciate the supreme moral act by the likes of Raoul Wallenberg, in German-Occupied Hungary, who defied the Nazi terror to save thousands of innocent Jews from certain death. Many others risked their lives in Europe and elsewhere to hide and protect Jews targeted by the Nazis. In the 1930s, many Egyptian groups were involved in efforts to provide financial assistance to German Jews to help them escape the Nazi regime. Such assistance was not connected to the Zionist plans for Palestine.

It should be remembered as well that huge numbers of Spanish Jews were escaping the brutal campaign of the 'Catholic Reconquest' (*Reconquista*) by taking refuge in the Arab countries in North Africa and the Levant (but not in Europe), where they resided, and many prospered, for hundreds of years. In Egypt, a vibrant Jewish community established a prominent presence in commerce and trade, and many were involved in the political system.

In 1994, when reviewing Benny Morris's book, *Israel's Border Wars* (1993), Avi Shlaim wrote: "What distinguishes the new Israeli historians most clearly from the traditionalist ones is a critical stance towards the claims made by Israeli governments, claims which were turned into national myths and as such continue to condition popular attitudes towards the Arabs down to the present day" (Shlaim 1994).

Ilan Pappe (2006, 2015), a prominent Israeli historian, is paying a heavy price for exposing Israel's colonial policies in Palestine. Professor Norman Finkelstein (1995, 2005), a Jewish-American political science professor, more than half of whose family perished in the Holocaust, bravely stood up for Palestinian rights and exposed Israeli atrocities, but paid a heavy price for his stand and was denied tenure despite his brilliant academic credentials and his illuminating Ph.D. thesis from Princeton University.

Another Israeli critic was professor Israel Shahak (1994, 2004) of the Hebrew University, who did not curtail his critical opinion of Israel's policies and Jewish fundamentalism. Shahak, who was the Chairman of the *Israeli League for Human and Civil Rights*, was subjected to severe criticism for his views, such as "There can be no longer any doubt that the most horrifying acts of oppression in the West Bank are motivated by Jewish religious fanaticism". His opinions were criticised in religious and political circles alike. He also criticized Israel's policy toward the Palestinian 'right of return'. He said that any converted Mexican to Judaism has the right to instant entry into Palestine-Israel, while a Palestinian refugee displaced by Israel who was born in Palestine cannot return to the land of his ancestors. American Rabbi Elmer Berger (1945, 1993) espoused his anti-Zionist views as early as 1945. He too was criticised and shunned in pro-Israel circles.

No one can doubt the service Miko Peled (2016) performed for Israel as a member of its elite Special Forces. He is the son of General Matti Peled, one of the heroes of the 1967 War with the Arab countries. General Peled eventually turned into a peace activist advocating Israeli-Palestinian accommodation. His son Miko gave up on Israel's deceptive commitment for a just peace, and is actively engaged in a campaign to expose Israel's colonial mentality.

Other prominent Jews, such as Noam Chomsky (1999) , and Maxime Rodinson (1973), also voiced their criticism of Israel's ideology and practices. Yehudi Menuhin 'Sees Nazi Illness in Israel' according to the *Chicago Tribune* (as reported in the French daily *Le Figaro*). He believed that the past Nazi illness in Germany is progressing now in Israel, as he compared the current atmosphere in the Jewish State with that of Nazi Germany (Menuhin 1998). Invariably, the critics were accused of being self-hating Jews, or even anti-Semitic.

The ruthless mentality of 'the winner takes all' has created massive injustice and suffering for the Palestinians, which I have witnessed first-hand. Jews have also suffered over the centuries in Europe due to endemic pogroms, anti-Semitism and the Holocaust. The Palestinians are paying a horrendous price as their land has been taken over, their history falsified, their culture denied or appropriated, and their very existence crushed. They are entitled – like every other nation on earth – to have their freedom and sovereign independence. The Israelis are burdened with the horrors of the past, and understandably they crave security. The Israelis, nevertheless, must divorce their colonial mindset if they wish for eventual coexistence and reconciliation with the Palestinians and consequently with the Arab World. The former UK Ambassador to the UN, Lord Hugh Caradon, reminded Israel that "A house built on injustice could not stand" (Caradon 1977). Perhaps Zionism was utilized brutally to establish the Israeli state, but the time has come for the adoption of a peaceful cooperative ideology instead. In today's world, there is no place – nor should there be – for apartheid or illegal territorial conquest and acquisition. Otherwise we would be condoning the repeat of previous historical atrocities and violations. Both sides need peace – not a winner's peace, but a just and fair peace.

5.17   Entanglement in the Middle East

With the end of the 1948, 1956 and 1967 Arab-Israeli Wars, the Arab world was under no illusion about the role of Israel as an extension of Western imperialism and domination in the Middle East. In fact, Israel's establishment in Palestine has become a convenient tool for the manipulations of Arab politics and the advancement of the Western designs in the region. Events in the Middle East since 1948 have confirmed such a conviction. Western imperialism was relying on Israel to maintain a choking control over the region. Additionally, the conflict was "fundamentally transformed...After Suez, it changed from a dispute primarily related to the question of the disposition of Palestine...into an inter-state conflict for regional hegemony" (Khalidi 1989: 377–392). The developing relationship between the US and Israel was re-asserted further with the conclusion of a US-Israel Strategic Cooperation Agreement during the presidency of Ronald Reagan in 1981. The special relationship between the two countries was now cemented into a formal agreement (camouflaged as cooperation against the Soviets), and removed any fig-leaf covering America's deepening dependence on Israel in the region, and Israel's role in the continuing strategy of preventing any strategic parity between Israel and the Arab world (Gwertzman 1981; International Legal Materials 1981: 1,420–1,423).

Increasingly, the West (old and new powers) was consolidating its military cooperation and political dependence on Israel. Between the 1956 Suez War and the 1967 Middle East War, France, followed by the US, began to supply Israel with the nuclear technology and the components which enabled Israel to develop its arsenal of nuclear weapons. The open secret of nuclear Israel is designed to blackmail and force the Arabs into submission with regard to its colonial-expansionist designs. Israel, moreover, is determined to keep nuclear technology from the hands of the Arab states (and Iran), as the attacks on the nuclear facilities in Iraq and Syria proved. Likewise, the assassinations of several Egyptian and Iraqi nuclear physicists have left no doubt about Israel's intention to maintain a monopoly over nuclear technology in the region. Warner D. Farr provides a detailed study of Israel's nuclear programme, developed with the help of France and then the United States (Farr 1999: 3–5). He notes that "nuclear Israel could be a counterforce against Egypt in France's fight in Algeria". France and Israel cooperated in nuclear science and technology and "remained closely linked throughout the early fifties", through Shimon Peres (the Israeli Minister of Defence), Ernst Bergmann (the chief Israeli nuclear scientist) and the officials of the French Atomic Energy Commission (CEA). Moreover, French experts secretly built the Israeli reactor underground at *Dimona* in the Negev desert, as a reward for agreeing to participate in the 1956 Suez War. The agreement to build the reactor was signed during the *Sèvres* meeting in October 1956 during the planning for the attack on Egypt. The United States, on the other hand, had already "furnished Israel heavy water, under the 'Atoms for Peace' program, for the small research reactor in *Soreq*" (Farr 1999: 1–24).

By 1956, Israel was the *agent provocateur* par excellence for the British and French empires in their confrontation with the anti-colonial tide. After 1967, Israel was fortified to become the West's extension in keeping control in the Middle East. The destructive effect of the Israeli role on the political stability and development, not to mention the squandered resources, in the Arab countries are felt until today. The political and military objectives of Britain, France, and Israel in 1956 coalesced to produce one of the most flagrant acts of aggression in the history of the post-war Middle East.

The post-Suez period saw the United States assuming the role of Israel's protector and supporter in deepening its illegal annexation of Palestinian and Arab territories, keeping the Arab world deeply mired in a never-ending conflict, and allowing the Islamist-Jihadist-Wahhabi wave to take hold.

Undoubtedly, the Arab-Israeli conflict has hindered – if not scuttled – the fragile reformist attempts in an Arab world suffocating under the excesses of an undemocratic and regressive governance model. The consequent failure of the secular attempts to reshape society, and the abdication of the promised social welfare function by corrupt regimes, have produced a challenging religious-based polity enjoying a measure of misguided popular support, but devoid of any democratic content.

The myth of the civilizing mission of colonialism, as well as the fiction that Israel is the only 'democracy' in the Middle East, are repeated *ad nauseam* to hide the painful truth of the consequences of occupation and exploitation. Democracy in Israel is the preserve of Israeli Jews (especially Jews of European origin), while a brutal apartheid system is ruthlessly enforced on the Palestinians. The Zionist-Israeli state has served the colonial-Western interests in the region and has been successful in preventing the emergence of a strong, modern, and independent Arab Middle East.

Currently, Israel – with the help of the US Trump Administration and co-opted Arab regimes – does not even try to mask its expansionist, aggressive, and destabilizing ideology, sabotaging in the process any prospects of a genuine peace in the volatile Middle East region.

Many have advocated mutual recognition between the Israelis and the Palestinians (Hilmy 1972), based on acceptance of full political sovereignty, a fairly-established territorial contiguity, and a balanced population distribution for both – in fact, a reasonable and fair two-state solution. Such an outcome – if achieved – should open the doors to a region-wide co-existence and real co-operation between a peaceful and neighbourly Israel, not tied to any imperial scheme, old or new, and a transformed and progressive Arab world willing to live in peace and friendship. Some still believe that the nature of the conflict and the ideological objectives involved would certainly undermine any possibility of a realizable, mutually acceptable outcome. The on-going developments on the ground sadly seem to validate such a belief. Evidently, the Zionist ideology precludes any hope of a fair historic accommodation. One thing is certain, though: this lopsided situation cannot go on indefinitely.

For further research sources on the various aspects of the role of Israel, please consult the additional references at the end of the list.

References

Almog, Orna (2003): *Britain, Israel and the United States, 1955–1958: Beyond Suez* (London: Frank Cass).

Bandung Conference Declaration (1955): *Ten-Point Official Declaration* (25 April 1955).

Burke, Roland (2010): *Decolonization and the Evolution of International Human Rights* (Philadelphia: University of Pennsylvania Press).

Burns, William (1985): *Economic Aid and American Policy Toward Egypt, 1955–1981* (New York: State University of New York): 52–53.

Burrows, Bernard A.B. (1952): "Memorandum of Conversation", in: *Foreign Relations of the United States, 1952–1954 (IX)* (Washington DC: US Government Printing Office).

Byroade, Henry, (1956): "Byroade Diplomatic Note to Dulles 14 March 1956", in: *Foreign Relations of the United States*, 1955–57 (XV) (Washington DC: US Government Printing Office): 191.

Caplan, Neil (1997): *Futile Diplomacy: The United Nations, the Great Powers, and the Middle East Peacemaking, 1948–1954* (London: Frank Cass).

Caplan, Neil (1997): *Futile Diplomacy: Operation Alpha and the Failure of Anglo-American Coercive Diplomacy in the Arab-Israeli Conflict 1954–1956, Vol. 4* (London: Frank Cass): 93.

Choueiri, Youssef M. (2000): *Arab Nationalism: A History, Nation and State in the Arab World* (Oxford: Blackwell).

Darwin, John (1981): *Britain, Egypt and the Middle East Imperial Policy in the Aftermath of War 1918–1922* (London: MacMillan).

Dessouki, Ali E.H. (1989): "Nasser and the Struggle for Independence", in: Louis, W.; Owen, R. (Eds.): *Suez 1956: The Crisis and Its Consequences* (Oxford: Clarendon Press).

Doran, Michael (2016): *Ike's Gamble: America's Rise to Dominance in the Middle East* (New York: Free Press).

Dulles, John F. (1957): "Memo by the Secretary of State", in: *Foreign Relations of the United States* (Washington DC: US Government Printing Office): 142–144.

Dulles, John F. (1956): "Memorandum from the Secretary of State to the President, 28 March 1956", in: *Foreign Relations of the United States, 1955–1957, XV* (Washington DC: US Government Printing Office, 28 March 1956).

Dulles, John F. (1955): Alpha Speech – Council of Foreign Relations, New York City, 26 August 1955 (1)-(4) [Dulles statement on an Arab-Israeli settlement (26 August 1955)]. Foreign Relations of the United States, 1955–1957, Arab-Israeli Dispute, 1955, Volume XIV.

Dulles, John F. (1953): "Statement by Secretary of State John F. Dulles", in: *Foreign Relations of the United States, 1952–1954, IX*: 831–835 (15 June 1953) (Washington DC: US Government Printing Office); also published in the *New York Times* (2 June 1953).

Eden, Anthony (1955): *Guildhall Speech on the Arab-Israeli Conflict* (the ALPHA Plan); at: https://ecf.org.il/issues/issue/4.

Eveland, Wilbur C. (1980): *Ropes of Sand: America's Failure in the Middle East* (New York: Norton & Co.).

Farr, Warner D. (1999): *The Third Temple's Holy of Holies: Israel's Nuclear Weapons* (Maxwell, Alabama: USAF).

Freiberger, Steven Z. (1992): *Dawn Over Suez: The Rise of American Power in the Middle East, 1953–1957* (Chicago: Ivan Dee).

Gerges, Fawaz A. (2001): "Egypt and the 1948 War: Internal Conflict and Regional Ambition", in: Rogan E.; Shlaim, A. (Eds.): *The War For Palestine: Rewriting the History of 1948* (Cambridge: Cambridge University Press).

Gorst, Anthony; Johnman, Lewis (1997): *The Suez Crisis* (London: Routledge).

Heikal, Mohamed H. (1986): *Cutting the Lion's Tail: Suez Through Egyptian Eyes* (London: Andre Deutch).

Hewedy, Amin, (1989): "Nasser and the Crisis of 1956", in: Louis, W.R.; Owen, R. (Eds.) *Suez 1956: The Crisis and its Consequences* (Oxford: Clarendon Press): 161–171.

Hinnebusch, Raymond (2005): "The Politics of Identity in Middle East International Relations", in: Fawcett, L. (Ed.): *International Relations of the Middle East* (Oxford: Oxford University Press).

Holland, R.F. (1985): *European Decolonization 1918–1981: An Introductory Survey* (London: MacMillan).

Jernegan, John D. (1952): "Memorandum of Conversation", in: US Department of State (1952), in: *Foreign Relations of the United States, 1952–1954,* IX (Washington DC: US Government Printing Office).

Khalidi, Rashid (1989): "Consequences of the Suez Crisis in the Arab World", in: Louis, W.R.; Owen, R. (Eds.): *Suez 1956: The Crisis and Its Consequences* (Oxford: Clarendon Press): 377–392.

Kingston, Paul W.T. (1996): *Britain and the Politics of Modernization in the Middle East 1945–1958* (Cambridge: Cambridge University Press).

Mayer, Thomas (1986): "Arab Unity of Action and the Palestine Question, 1945–48", in: *Journal of Middles Eastern Studies*, 22,3: 331–349.

McNamara, Robert (2003): *Britain, Nasser and the Balance of Power in the Middle East 1952–1967: From the Egyptian Revolution to the Six Day War* (London: Frank Cass).

Nichols, David A. (2011): *Eisenhower 1956* (New York: Simon & Schuster).

Onozawa, Toru (2005): "Formation of American Regional Policy for the Middle East, 1950–1953: The Middle East Command Concept and its Legacy", in: *Diplomatic History*, 29,1.

Rountree, William (1956): Memorandum from the Under-Secretary of State to Secretary Dulles (23 May 1956), *Eisenhower Library*, Memorandum Series, Box #4: 658–667.

Shamir, Shimon (1989): "The Collapse of Project Alpha", in: Louis, W.R.; Owen, R. (Eds.): *Suez 1956: The Crisis and Its Consequences* (Oxford: Clarendon Press).

Shlaim, Avi (2001): *The Iron Wall: Israel and the Arab World* (New York: Norton).

Shuckburgh, Evelyn (1987): *Descent to Suez: Foreign Office Diaries 1951–1956* (London: Norton & Co.).

Slonim, Shlomo (1987): "Origins of the Tripartite Declaration on the Middle East", in: *Middle Eastern Studies*, 23,2: 135–149.

Teveth, Shabtai (1996): *Ben-Gurion's Spy: The Story of the Political Scandal that Shaped Modern Israel* (New York: Columbia University Press).

Thornhill, Michael (2002): "Resistance at all Costs", in: *Al-Ahram Weekly* (25 January 2002).

Tvedt, Terje (2004): *The River Nile in the Age of the British: Political Ecology & the Quest for Economic Power* (London: Tauris).

UK Foreign Office (1955): "Detailed Alpha Plan", 371/115866 (February 1955).

United States Department of State (1954): US National Security Council: *Middle East Policy Paper No. 5428* (23 July 1954).

Additional References on the Role of Israel

Abu-Laban, Baha; Abu-Lughod, Ibrahim (Eds.) (1974): *Settler Regimes in Africa and the Arab World: The Illusion of Endurance* (Wilmette, Ill.: Medina University Press).

Abu-Lughod, Ibrahim (Ed.) (1971): *The Transformation of Palestine* (Evanston: Northwestern University Press).

Arendt, Hannah (1973): *The Origins of Totalitarianism* (New York: Harcourt Brace Javanovich).

Avineri, Shlomo (2013): *Herzel's Vision: Theodor Herzel and the Foundation of the Jewish State* (New York: BlueBridge).

Begin, Menachem (1951): *The Revolt* (New York: Bell Publishing Co.).

Bell, J. Bowyer (1977): *Terror Out of Zion: Irgun Zvai Leumi, LEHI, and the Palestine Underground, 1929–1949* (New York: St. Martin's Press).

Berger, Elmer (1945): *The Jewish Dilemma* (New York: Kessinger Publishing).

Berger, Elmer (1993): *Peace for Palestine* (Miami: University of Florida Press).

Black, Edwin (2001): *The Transfer Agreement: The Dramatic Story of the Pact Between the Third Reich and Jewish Palestine* (New York: Carroll & Graf Publishers).

Caradon, Lord Hugh (1977): "A Tragedy for Jew and Arab", in: *The Guardian* (6 Novemer 1977).

Cattan, Henry (1973): *Palestine and International Law: The Legal Aspects of the Arab-Israeli Conflict* (London: Longman Group).

Chomsky, Noam (1999): *Fateful Triangle: The United States, Israel, and the Palestinians* (Montreal: Black Rose Books).

Cockburn, Andrew; Cockburn, Leslie (1991): *Dangerous Liaison: The Inside Story of the US-Israeli Covert Relationship* (New York: Harper Collins Publishers).

Dershowitz, Alan (2003): *The Case For Israel* (New York: John Wiley).

Elmessiri, Abdel Wahab (1977): *The Land of Promise: A Critique of Political Zionism* (New Brunswick, N.J.: North American, Inc.).

Finkelstein, Norman G. (2005): *Beyond Chutzpah: On the Misuse of Anti-Semitism and the Abuse of History* (Berkley: University of California Press).

Finkelstein, Norman G. (2000): *The Holocaust Industry: Reflections on the Exploitation of Jewish Suffering* (London: Verso).

Finkelstein, Norman G. (1995): *Image and Reality of the Israel-Palestine Conflict* (London: Verso).

Galtung, Johan (2014): "Needed: Regime Change in Israel", in: *Palestine Israel Journal*, 19,3 (2014).

Ghilan, Maxim (1974): *How Israel Lost its Soul* (Middlesex: Penguin Books).

Gwertzman, Bernard (1981): "US and Israel Sign Strategic Accord to Counter Soviet", in: *New York Times* (1 December 1981); at: https://www.nytimes.com/1981/12/01/world/us-israel-sign-strategic-accord-counter-soviet-text-memorandum-page-a14.html.

Hazboun, Norma N.M. (1994): *The Resettlement of the Palestinian Refugees of the Gaza Strip* (Leeds: University of Leeds).

Halkin, Hillel (2014): *Jabotinsky: A Life* (New Haven: Yale University Press).

Herzel, Theodor (1896 & 1917): *A Jewish State: Proposal of a Modern Solution for the Jewish Question* (Leipzig – Vienna: Verlags-Buchhandlung).

Hilmy, Hanny (1972): "Re-Partition of Palestine: Toward a Peaceful Solution in the Middle East", in: *Journal of Peace Research*, 2 (Oslo, Norway).

Journal Article (1981): "Israel-United States: Memorandum of Understanding on Strategic Cooperation", in: *International Legal Materials,* Cambridge University, 20,6 (November): 1,420–1,423; at: https://www.jstor.org/stable/20692373?seq=1 (30 November 1981).

Khalidi, Rashid (2007): *The Iron Cage: The Story of the Palestinian Struggle for Statehood* (Boston: Beacon Press).

Khalidi, Rashid (1997): *Palestinian Identity: The Construction of Modern National Consciousness* (New York: Columbia University Press).

Khalidi, Walid (1988): "Plan Dalet: Master Plan for the Conquest of Palestine", in: *Journal of Palestine Studies,* 18,1 (Autumn): 4–33.

Khalidi, Walid (1971): *From Haven to Conquest: Readings in Zionism and the Palestine Problem until 1948* (Beirut: Institute for Palestine Studies).

Lesch, Ann Mosely (1979): *Arab Politics in Palestine, 1917–1939: The Frustration of a Nationalist Movement* (Ithaca: Cornell University Press).

Lilienthal, Alfred M. (1978 & 1983): *The Zionist Connection: What Price Peace?*, I & II. (Vancouver: Veritas Publishing).

Lilienthal, Alfred M. (1953): *What Price Israel?* (Washington DC: Henry Regency Company).

Lundstrom, Aage (1968): *Death of a Mediator* (Beirut: Newman Neame Ltd).

Mearsheimer, John J.; Walt, Stephen M. (2007): *The Israel Lobby and US Foreign Policy* (Toronto: Viking Canada).

Mendes-Flohr, Paul R. (1983): *A Land of Two Peoples: Martin Buber on Jews and Arabs* (Oxford: Oxford University Press).

Menuhin, Yehudi (1988): "Violinist Menuhin Sees Nazi Illness in Israel", in: *Chicago Tribune* (22 January 1998).

Menuhin, Yehudi (1997): *Unfinished Journey: Twenty Years Later* (New York: Fromm International).

Menuhin, Moshe (1969): *Not by Might, Nor by Power: The Zionist Betrayal of Judaism* (New York: Open Road).

Morris, Benny (2008): *1948: A History of the First Arab-Israeli War* (New Haven: Yale University Press).

Morris, Benny (2001): *Righteous Victims: A History of the Zionist-Arab Conflict, 1881–2001* (New York: Vintage Books).

Morris, Benny (1993): *Israel's Border Wars, 1949–1956: Arab Infiltration, Israeli Retaliation and the Countdown to the Suez* War (Oxford: Clarendon Press).

Pappe, Ilan (2015): *The Idea of Israel: A History of Power and Knowledge* (London – New York: Verso).

Pappe, Ilan (2006): *The Ethnic Cleaning of Palestine* (Oxford: Oneworld Publications).

Pappe, Ilan (2004): *A History of Modern Palestine: One Land, Two Peoples* (Cambridge: Cambridge University Press).

Peled, Miko (2016): *The General's Son: Journey of an Israeli in Palestine* (Charlottesville, Virginia: Just World Books).

Peretz, Don (1993): *Palestinians, Refugees, and the Middle East Peace Process* (Washington DC: United States Institute of Peace Press).

Pruen, John B.; Selim, Mohamed (1955): *Survey Report: Northwest Sinai Project: An Agreement between UNRWA and Egypt* (Cairo: Republic of Egypt).

Robinson, Shira (2013): *Citizen Strangers: Palestinians and the Birth of Israel's Liberal Settler State* (Stanford: Stanford University Press).

Rodinson, Maxime (1973): *Israel: A Colonial-Settler State?* (New York: Pathfinder).

Rogan, Eugene L.; Shlaim, Avi (Eds.) (2001): *The War for Palestine: Rewriting the History of 1948* (Cambridge: Cambridge University Press).

Sa'di, Ahmad H.; Abu-Lughod, Lila (2007): *NAKBA: Palestine, 1948, and the Claims of Memory* (New York: Columbia University Press).

Said, Edward W. (2001): *The End of the Peace Process: Oslo and After* (New York: Vintage Books).

Said, Edward W. (1980): *The Question of Palestine* (New York: Vintage Books).

Schoenman, Ralph (1988): *The Hidden History of Zionism* (Santa Barbara: Veritas Press).

Shahak, Israel (1994): *Jewish History, Jewish Religion: The Weight of Three Thousand Years* (London: Pluto Press).

Shahak, Israel; Mezvinski, Norton (2004): *Jewish Fundamentalism* (London: Pluto Press).

Shapira, Anita (2014): *Ben-Gurion: Father of Modern Israel* (New Haven: Yale University Press).

Shipler, David K. (1979): "Israel Bars Rabin From Relating '48 Eviction of Arabs", in: *The New York Times* (23 October 1979).

Shlaim, Avi (1994): "Israel's Dirty War", A Review of Benny Morris' Book (Oxford 1993) Israel's Border Wars: 1949–1956, in: *London Review of Books*, 16,16 (8 August 1994), at: https://www.lrb.co.uk/the-paper/v16/n16/avi-shlaim/israel-s-dirty-war and https://www.users.ox.ac.uk/-ssfc0005/IsraelsDirtyWar.html.

Smith, Gary V. (Ed.) (1974): *Zionism: The Dream and the Reality* (London: David & Charles).

Swedenburg, Ted (2003): *Memoirs of Revolt: The 1936–1939 Rebellion and the Palestinian National Past* (Fayetteville: University of Arkansaa Press).

Tyler, Patrick (2012): *Fortress Israel: The Inside Story of the Military Elite Who Run the Country – and Why They Can't Make Peace* (New York: Farrar, Straus and Giroux).

Waines, David (1977): *A Sentence in Exile: The Palestine/Israeli Conflict, 1897–1977* (Wilmett IL: The Medina Press).

Chapter 6
The Empire Strikes Back: The Suez War

Abstract Epic confrontation between the ageing empires and the vibrant anti-colonial surge under Egyptian leadership came to a head. The Sèvres Agreement between Britain, France, and Israel confirmed the coalescence between the attempts to rescue the threatened imperial position, and Israel's territorial expansionist plans. The war clearly demonstrated the inability of the European empires to stem the anti-colonial tide. A desperate military aggression involving the two European empires and their accomplice in the region was unleashed with disastrous consequences.

Keywords High Dam · World Bank · Humilation · Nationalization · Conspiracy · Egyptian White Paper · Diplomatic manoeuvres · Sèvres Protocol · Kadesh · Musketeer · Ultimatum · Israeli bait · Coordinated invasion · Blocking the Canal · Operation Cork · Strong UN and World reaction against the tripartite invasion

6.1 An Epic Confrontation

A variety of factors was involved in the developing impasse in Western-Egyptian accommodation in 1956, including Egypt's refusal to join in an anti-Soviet defence pact, the failure to arrive at an Arab-Israeli settlement and the continuous emergence of Israel as a serious military threat to Arab security and Egypt's anti-colonial leadership. The 1956 Suez War was not just a dispute over a vital waterway, but a symptom of a collapsing imperial order, and a colonial world refusing to accept subjugation any more. A serious confrontation between the Western powers and the Egyptian regime was set in motion as Egypt persisted in following an independent foreign policy and escalated its anti-colonial drive despite Western efforts at persuasion, then intimidation. Egypt was also determined to establish a strong economic and military structure, including an ambitious development programme anchored to the massive High Dam project. Finally, Egypt was bent on diversifying its sources of armaments. All these trends set the stage for a serious confrontation between the Western powers and the Egyptian revolutionary regime.

© Springer Nature Switzerland AG 2020   121
H. Hilmy, *Decolonization, Sovereignty, and Peacekeeping*,
https://doi.org/10.1007/978-3-030-57624-0_6

In a massive blow to the country and its leadership, the US and Britain withdrew their support for the World Bank's (IBRD) approved financing of the pivotal project. Relying on the involvement of the US in the growing confrontation, the mindset prevailing in London and Paris, as well as Israeli opportunism, precluded any peaceful end to the confrontation. The escalation and tightening of the political and economic screws against Nasser became irreversible. The Omega Plans (I and II) became fully operational. The old empires, however, decided to strike prematurely against Egypt on their own without the crucial blessing of the US.

6.2 Deliberate Humiliation

Reaching the end of his patience with Nasser's anti-colonial policies in the region, Prime Minister Eden went to Washington in January 1956 for a summit with President Eisenhower and Secretary Dulles. During the meeting, 'a possible hardening of policy was first discussed'. With the failure of all previous attempts to entice or to threaten Egypt, was the US abandoning its cautious position towards the Egyptian leader? Eden said that he "did not know how long we could go along with Nasser". Dulles replied "We might soon know whether our whole attitude towards Nasser would have to be changed". In effect, "Nasser and Egypt were placed on probation subject to good behavior". In the eyes of the Western powers, Nasser failed the test (Eden/Dulles in: Gorst/Johnman 1977: 43).

According to Bobal (2013), "racial identity assumptions" – for instance assertions "that Arab peoples were irrational and easily manipulated or deceived" – influenced the way that Nasser's behaviour was judged by the Americans. US policy-makers relied on "these beliefs to explain and contextualize Arab actions". Armed with such convictions, "Officials within the Eisenhower administration believed that Arab irrationality prompted Egyptian leaders to adopt a neutralist position in the cold war". Consequently, "These concerns made the Eisenhower administration's decision to contain Egypt, Gamal Abdel Nasser, and the Arab nationalist movement seem logical and necessary" (Bobal 2013: 943). This 'deep' psychological assessment was used in the second half of the twentieth century to guide state policy. Inaccurate, faulty, or incomplete perceptions played a significant role in exacerbating and damaging Western-Egyptian understanding during this crucial period.

A controversial analysis of the "Arab Mind" by the Israeli writer Raphael Patai (1973) has garnered both criticism and praise. It has been described as sensitive, an indispensable work, and a crucial masterpiece. The US Army has even used it in an effort to deal effectively with the local population during US deployment in the Middle East. Yet negative comments have accused it of being racist, reductionist, a classic case of orientalism, and the bible of neoconservatives. It seems that academic and psychological profiling – accurate or otherwise – forms an important part of the foreign policy conduct of many states.

Nasser's refusal to toe the line pushed the American and the British governments to abandon any hope of compliance by Nasser and to put into action the punitive plans, "Omega I and Omega II", to cripple and humiliate him. With the agreement to move towards a harder line with Nasser, The British and Americans "had agreed to 'drag out' negotiations over the dam", and "moved rapidly towards a withdrawal of the funding" (Gorst/Johnman 1977: 51).

The Egyptian Ambassador to the US met Secretary Dulles on 19 July 1956 and reiterated the Egyptian Government decision to accept the conditions attached to the financing of the dam. The Western alliance, however, was clearly bent on implementing one of the planks of the Omega plan: derailing the High Dam financing as a way to humiliate Nasser and what he stood for in the region. The US Secretary of State provided the Egyptian Ambassador with an *aide-mémoire* stating bluntly that under the prevailing atmosphere the American government was withdrawing its offer. The Ambassador countered by saying that this was a missed opportunity and Egypt would be obliged to look for other alternatives to complete the project. "Dulles retorted that they would have no objections if this happened" (Heikal 1986: 115). To add to the humiliation, the news of the official withdrawal of the offer was leaked to the press just before the arrival of the Egyptian representative for his meeting with the US Secretary of State. The American powerhouse was showing the new upstart in the Middle East that he could be cut down to size and easily put in his place. Nasser was not surprised at the message itself, but the way it was phrased and delivered did surprise him. The Indian Prime Minister, Jawaharlal Nehru, Nasser's ideological mentor, responded to the news by saying "There is no end to their arrogance! These people are arrogant! Arrogant!" (Heikal 1986: 115–116).

As early as 1953, both President Eisenhower and Secretary Dulles tried repeatedly to convince Egypt to be a "keystone in any structure which may be built for the defence of the Middle East" (Heikal 1986: 38). Nasser, however, refused to be dragged into a confrontation between superpowers. It soon became clear that the US was not only concerned about possible encroachment on the Middle East by the Soviet Union; oil played a huge part in its motivation, as can be seen from the official US objectives formulated as early as 1949 in a National Security Council NSC policy document (Heikal 1986: 38):

> United States policy is to keep the sources of oil in the Middle East in American hands and defend them at all costs, and deny them to the Soviet Union, even if this led to a confrontation or to the destruction of these resources by the Americans themselves (NSC 5401, 1949; FRUS 1954).

This aggressive approach regarding the strategic Middle East oil resources involved the participation of Britain. The policy was initiated during the Truman administration. A National Security Council directive (NSC 26/2) came to light in 1996 (Everly 1996: A1), and contained startling details. The plan was revised several times with new code numbers (26/2 – 176 – 5401 – 5714). US and British oil companies were enlisted to engage in an '*oil denial Policy Plan*' designed to "sabotage or completely destroy" oil facilities and equipment in Saudi Arabia, Iraq,

Iran, Kuwait, Qatar, and Bahrain. The CIA and various branches of the US military were involved in the planning, described as 'undercover' and involving "undercover operatives" recruited from the willing employees of the oil companies. The plan involved using a variety of weapons and methods to sabotage and destroy oil production. The methods ranged from using cement to plug or destroy the oil wells to dismantling or destroying the refineries and surface equipment. Explosive and cluster bomb stockpiles began to be buried in the desert in preparation for action. The plan also included the use of nuclear 'radiological measures' to poison the oil fields and render the areas concerned uninhabitable, creating the equivalent of an 'instant Chernobyl'. The air force representative in the planning deliberations suggested using aerial bombing operations against oil refineries. President Truman approved the 'oil denial plan' (NSC 26/2) in January 1949.

It almost defies logic and rationality to risk creating a nuclear wasteland in the heart of the Middle East in order to prevent an adversary from threatening an important resource used by the whole world, including the US and Britain. But logic does not always prevail in the corridors of power.

6.3 Nationalization

The public manner of the withdrawal of the finance deal for the High Dam was deliberately designed to humiliate Nasser and his anti-colonial agenda. The time of persuasion was over and the screws were firmly tightened. The slap triggered a deep emotional response not helpful to the Western objectives in the region. The withdrawal of finance was the final Western humiliation that Egypt could endure. When it was suggested to Nasser that Egypt should demand a fifty per cent share in the Suez Canal Company's profits as an alternative to the World Bank financing, Nasser replied "*But why fifty-fifty? Why not a hundred per cent?*" adding "Why not complete nationalization of the Suez Canal Company?" (Heikal 1986: xiv, 117). The intolerable insult created deep emotional response in the hearts of the Egyptian and broader Arab masses. Nasser believed that "Dulles had made the withdrawal of the offer to finance the High Dam a political act, not an economic one; Egypt must make its reply a political act also" (Heikal 1986: 124). The choice of the nationalization of the Suez Canal Company – a symbol of external control and exploitation – as the target of the Egyptian response was easy to understand.

Nasser's choice of an action involving the Suez Canal Company in response was almost instinctive. Thousands of Egyptians had died during the Canal construction, and Egypt had provided over fifty per cent of the original capital cost. The usurious European loans for the project constituted a financial blood-letting, which was then exploited by Disraeli in 1875 when he bought Egypt's entire shares in the Company for four million pounds, even though their original value was sixteen million. Erskine Childers (1962) noted that "until 1937 Egypt did not receive any income at all from the Canal shipping, and ships flying the Egyptian flag and passing through the Canal had to pay tolls to a foreign-owned Company in order to pass through

Egyptian territorial waters". Nasser's response represented an "irreversible watershed" which was "Egyptian to the core, rooted in the history of his country". Nasser's masterstroke had transformed the nation (and the region) instantly because of his "courage and audacity" (Childers 1962: 163–166). All Egyptians and Arabs held their heads higher in admiration of Nasser's determination.

There was irony in the fact that Americans scuttled the proposed High Dam financing. The United States had been the first power that the new Egyptian revolutionary regime turned to for support and help in getting the British to evacuate the military base they had established in the midst of Egyptian territory in the strategic Suez Canal region and also to provide Egypt with sufficient arms to defend its borders.

In a 1953 letter by the new US President, Eisenhower, to his Egyptian counterpart, General Naguib (the nominal first head of state in Nasser's revolutionary regime), the American President spoke of American support for "the natural aspirations of Egypt for full sovereignty over its own territory", with reference to Egypt's demand for the British evacuation of the Suez Canal Base. Significantly, however, Eisenhower proposed in return to make Egypt a "keystone in any structure which may be built for the defence of the Middle East". This was an idea Nasser resisted very strongly (Heikal 1986: 35–36).

During a meeting with US Secretary of State John F. Dulles in Cairo in May 1953, Nasser reiterated his objection to the American concept of Western-led defence arrangements for the Middle East, emphasizing instead the central role of the Arab League, as stated in the Arab Mutual Security Pact for defence against external aggression. The Arab League was seen by Nasser at this stage as a regional mechanism that could be controlled by the Arab states free from foreign intervention.

The United States, however, was more concerned with containing the Soviet Union and protecting Western (by now American) interests and oil resources in the Middle East (including the protection of the pivotal position of Israel as a Western foothold in the region) rather than allowing independent anti-colonial voices to emerge. The escalating confrontation with Nasser became the essence of Western policy in the region.

6.4 Emphatic Response

On 26 July 1956 at 7 p.m. Egyptian President Nasser gave a speech in Alexandria commemorating the 'Egyptian Revolution' and the abdication of King Farouq, which had taken place exactly four years earlier. A special committee had been formed earlier, under the overall direction of army engineer Mahmoud Younes, comprising Egyptian Army commanders, governors of the three Suez Canal Districts, and army and navy engineers. It met in absolute secrecy in the offices of the Eastern Command Headquarters in the *Al-Galaa* Barracks in Ismailia. Generals Ali Amer, Amin Hilmy, Foad El-Toudy, and a few others directly involved in the take-over plan were present. The Committee drew up plans to seize the Canal installations and take over operations. Troops and other personnel (all sworn to secrecy) deployed to their pre-assigned locations surrounding the Suez Canal Company's Headquarters and other offices and assets in the Suez Canal region and Cairo, and throughout Egypt, awaiting the orders to simultaneously take over.

Photo 6.1 President Nasser announcing the nationalization of the Suez Canal Company in Alexandria on 26 July 1956. *Source* Al-Ahram

Nasser's earth-shaking speech to the nation was full of anger at the Western attempts to maintain control in the region and at the West's refusal to accept Egypt's legitimate demands for socio-economic progress and military security against Israel's aggressive plans. He strongly criticized the World Bank and its manipulation by the West, describing the loan terms as "imperialism without soldiers". Nasser also assured his citizens and the Arab world at large that the struggle for liberation and national pride would never cease. This was his response to the Western snub – resolute, emphatic and challenging. Nasser threw down the gauntlet. In fact, the gloves were off on both sides.

The code word for the takeover of the Company's assets which the assigned group was waiting for was "de Lesseps", the name of the French engineer who had been the driving force behind the construction of the Suez Canal. Nasser repeated the code-word six times for emphasis. It was expected at around 10 p.m. but delayed by about fifteen minutes (Hilmy n.d.).

In a twist of fate, on the eve of its nationalization, the last Managing Director of the Suez Canal Company was none other than Jacques George-Picot, the grandson of François George-Picot of the infamous Sykes-Picot Agreement for the division of the Ottoman Middle East by the two imperial powers. Mr George-Picot boasted that the changes he had wrought in the structure of the old Suez Canal Company had expunged "the original Egyptian connection" of the firm and given it an "exclusively French" nature (Tignor 1998: 27–192). This 'colonial' attitude might explain the choice of the Suez Canal Company as the target of the Egyptian response, given its importance in the Egyptian anti-colonial challenge.

With immediate effect (Suez Canal Authority 1956: Law 285), Egypt took control of the Canal's installations and facilities and began to oversee its operation. In an attempt to demonstrate the failure of the new Egyptian authority to administer the operations of the Canal, Britain and France tried to obstruct navigation in the Canal by all methods. "Operation Pile-Up" to jam the Canal with large volumes of ships was followed by "Operation Convoy" to shepherd navigation through the Canal under British control. When these attempts failed to halt the navigation, the two imperial powers instructed their flag-carrier ships to refuse to pay the required passage tariff. The Egyptian Government instructed the new Suez Canal Authority to let the ships pass and to debit the ships' owners for the fees for later collection. Egyptian navy officers and a few volunteers from friendly countries worked around the clock to keep the Canal traffic moving. As a result, international navigation in the Suez Canal continued uninterrupted and unhindered until hostilities broke out in October-November 1956.

The British economic response to the nationalization act was swift and controversial. On 28 July Britain froze all Egyptian assets in Britain (as did the French government with regard to Egyptian assets in France). The claim that the nationalization act violated the Anglo-Egyptian Agreement of 1954, thus justifying freezing Egyptian assets, had no basis in law, and was used to vindicate the attack on Egypt. There was no Egyptian undertaking in the 1954 Anglo-Egyptian Agreement not to nationalize an Egyptian chartered company on its soil. The reference to the Suez Canal in the Agreement presented to the UK Parliament based on Article VIII of the Agreement stated that: "The agreement will recognise that the Suez Maritime Canal, which is an integral part of Egypt, is a waterway economically, commercially and strategically of international importance, and will express the determination of both parties to uphold the 1888 Convention guaranteeing the freedom of navigation of the Canal" (The Anglo-Egyptian Agreement, UK Parliament, July and October 1954). Clearly, the Agreement, signed on 19 October 1954, did not interfere with Egypt's sovereign right in relation to the ownership and administration of a commercial entity in Egypt. The nationalization act, furthermore, did not violate the 1888 Convention or threaten international navigation and commerce. Indeed, it was in Egypt's best interests to protect and maintain the operations of the Canal unhindered.

Britain also blocked repayment of the money owed to Egypt, which had accumulated during World War II in return for goods and services provided to the Allies during the war. The credit was worth 400 million pounds sterling. The repayment was restarted and regulated by the Anglo-Egyptian currency agreement finalized in 1955. Britain had already unilaterally stopped payment in 1947 due to international pressure on the pound. Egypt had suffered another loss in the value of its credit when Britain devalued the pound by 30 per cent in 1949 (Love 1969: 363). The Anglo-French move against Egypt's assets was more than economic in nature. It was a signal that the Egyptian challenge was going to be met at every level. It must be made clear that the nationalization of the Suez Canal Company by the Egyptian

Government was not equivalent to the "seizure of the Canal", as many writers claim. The Suez Canal Egyptian identity is not open to question. The 'seizure' of part of Egypt by Egypt is nonsensical. Sadly, Eden made the dispute with Nasser an existentialist confrontation far beyond the ownership of the Canal Company. Nasser, on his part, refused to accept the British Prime Minister's challenge to his policies. The ingredients of a Greek tragedy were put in motion, and the hopes for an Anglo-Egyptian *détente* were dashed.

Nasser considered the cancellation of the financing of the Aswan High Dam political in nature. "This is not a withdrawal [of the loan]…It is an attack on the regime and an invitation to the people of Egypt to bring it down" (Heikal 1973: 68). Egypt's response, therefore, had to be political. Likewise, Eden considered the nationalization of the Suez Canal Company a political act requiring a determined response. Eden, however, chose to make his response a military one, with far-reaching consequences for Britain and his own leadership.

Prime Minister Eden told Andrew Foster, the US *chargé d'affaires* in London, that "The Egyptian (Nasser) has his thumb on our windpipe. Tell Mr Dulles I cannot allow that," (Robertson 1964: 73). Eden was behaving "like an enraged elephant charging senselessly at invisible and imaginary enemies in the international jungle" (Nutting 1967: 34–35).

It seemed that "Eden's personal antipathy to Nasser had by now hardened into official policy". In a heated exchange between Eden and Anthony Nutting, the Minister of State for Foreign Affairs, the Prime Minister demanded, "I want him [Nasser] destroyed, can't you understand? I want him removed." In other versions of the conversation 'murdered' was used in place of 'destroyed' (Gorst/Johnman 1977: 46). The situation in the Middle East in the late summer and early autumn of 1956 was rapidly moving towards a major showdown. The details of the plans for confrontation were still being put together.

6.5   The Egyptian White Paper

In response to the continuous vociferous attacks by Britain, France and their supporters in the West, on 12 August 1956 the Egyptian Government issued an official document entitled *White Paper: On The Nationalization of the Suez Canal Maritime Canal Company* (White Paper 1956).

The White Paper stated that the Egyptian presidential *Nationalization Decree* stipulated that all the Suez Canal Company's shareholders would be paid the full value of their shares.

Article 1 of the decree states that:

> Shareholders and holders of constituent shares shall be compensated in accordance to the value of the shares on the Paris Stock Market on the day preceding the enforcement of this law. Payment of compensation shall take place immediately when the State receives all the assets and property of the nationalized company.

What was considered by the British and French governments to be the forced buy-out of the shareholders of the Company by the Egyptian Government was, in fact, similar to the act of the British Labour Government's nationalization of coal in 1948. As Anthony Gorst and Lewis Johnman point out, "this presented the British Government with a thorny dilemma" (Gorst/Johnman 1977: 549). The Egyptian Government made it clear that the nationalization of a private company operating on Egyptian soil was an act of sovereignty not open to challenge and not directed against any power.

The Government pledged to maintain the established freedom-of-navigation regime without change as well as full adherence to the 1888 Constantinople Convention governing the use of the Suez Canal. The pre-existing policy toward Israeli shipping was to be continued, as Egypt insisted that a state of war existed between the two countries, giving Egypt the right to continue denying enemy access to its territory. This position was asserted by Egypt despite a Security Council resolution (UN Resolution S-2322, 1951) calling for Israeli passage based on the existence of an Armistice Agreement between Egypt and Israel, regardless of Egypt's protestation.

The following explanatory notes highlighted the Egyptian position:

- The White Paper *condemned* the proposal by Britain, France and the United States to create an "international authority" to administer the operations of the Canal, describing the scheme as "collective colonialism", and a "pretext for interference in matters of Egyptian sovereignty".
- The White Paper *reaffirmed* that "The Suez Canal Company is an Egyptian company subject to Egyptian laws and customs", as stated in Article 16 of the agreement (known as the Concession) between the Egyptian Government and the Company in 1866.
- Moreover, the White Paper *quoted* the statement submitted in a memorandum by the British Government to the Mixed Court of Appeals in Alexandria in 1939, which declared: "The Suez Canal Company is a legal person in accordance with Egyptian law. Its nationality and character are solely Egyptian. It is, therefore, *subject to the Egyptian Laws*".
- Moreover, the White Paper was very *critical* of the tripartite communiqué for quoting Article 8 of the Anglo-Egyptian 1954 Treaty, recognizing the Suez Canal as "A waterway economically, commercially and strategically of international importance", but dropping the first part of the same Article which explicitly states that *"the Canal is an integral part of Egypt"*.
- In addition, according to Kennett Love (1969: 363), the Egyptian Government strongly *criticized* the Big Three for "deliberately confusing the *distinction* between the *1888 Convention* and the Company *Concession* in order to find pretexts for interference in Egypt".

6.6   The Pre-war Security Council Involvement

The political tug of war between Egypt and the Western powers reached the UN
Security Council in the autumn of 1956. The legal authority entitled to administer
the Canal, the freedom of navigation, and the right of Israel to use the Canal were
debated at the UN. Egypt was determined to prove that the Canal was open to
navigation in accordance with the *1888 Constantinople Convention* (Suez Canal
Authority – Treaties). The Convention regulating the use of the Suez Canal was
signed on 29 October 1888 by Britain, Germany, Austria-Hungary, Spain, France,
Italy, The Netherlands, Russia, and the Ottoman Empire. Egypt did not sign the
Convention but accepted its provisions when it gained its independence in 1922.
The Egyptian Government had every intention of keeping the Canal open to the
shipping of Britain and France and had every reason to prove that the Canal was
open to use as usual according to standard conventions.

Egypt contended, however, that Israel should be excluded because of the
existing state of war between the two sides. Israel's position was that the two states
had signed an Armistice Agreement, thus ending the state of war. Egypt's response
was that the Armistice Agreement achieved a cessation of hostilities, and only put
the conflict on hold without a final conflict resolution, and without ending the state
of war.

After a marathon of negotiation and counter proposals at the UN, the Security
Council Resolution of 13 October 1956 (Security Council Resolution 1956) agreed
that any settlement of the Suez question should meet the following requirements
among its operative principles:

- Free and open transit through the Canal without political or technical
  discrimination.
- Respect for the sovereignty of Egypt.
- No political interference in the operation of the Canal.
- Tolls to be fixed by agreement.
- Disputes involving the operations of the Canal to be settled by arbitration.
- A proportion of the Canal revenue to be set aside for development of the Canal.

The *International Suez Canal Board* established by the First London Conference
on 16 August 1956 was strongly opposed by Egypt; and the *Suez Canal Users
Association* established by the Second London Conference on 21 September 1956,
also against the position of Egypt, were left out of the final UN Resolution text by a
Soviet veto, despite the persistent attempts of Britain, France, and the USA to
include them.

Following the agreement in the UN Security Council on the Canal issue, the
conflict seemed to be on its way to a peaceful resolution. But others had a different
plan. The Empire had to strike back.

6.7   The Road to War

It became clear after the failure of the Western powers to seize control of the Suez Canal authority back from Egypt through the Security Council that 'other' methods would be employed. The tide of war was rising and the developing confrontation against Nasser by two desperate empires in association with their local ally to snuff out the anti-colonial revolutionary tide at its base was only a matter of time.

Operation Ajax, which restored the Shah to the throne and overthrew the nationalist Iranian Prime Minister Mossadeq in August 1953 for nationalizing Iranian oil production, was apparently not enough of a deterrent. *Ajax* was orchestrated by the CIA under the guidance of Kermit Roosevelt (the CIA Chief in the Middle East) and executed by Iranian General Fazlollah Zahdi.

Clearly a stronger response was needed for Egypt and Nasser's leadership. Plotting in the dark for a punishing strike proceeded apace. The planned Suez War involving Britain, France and Israel, therefore, had two objectives:

- First, to bring an end to the anti-colonial challenge to imperial domination.
- Second, to restore external colonial control over vital strategic national assets, and in the process dissuade other restive nationalist movements from challenging imperial domination.

The realization of these two objectives was a clear example of the role of Israel in the service of imperial objectives in the Middle East. The congruence of Israel's goals and the imperial counter-attack against the anti-colonial tide was a chilling reminder of the desperation of the co-conspirators. Since Britain and France thought that Nasser's challenge over the Suez Canal was unacceptable and had to be stopped, it was just a matter of time before there were more drastic measures to remove him. Israel, which had plans against Nasser of its own, was more than eager to cooperate in the *misadventure of Suez*. The conspiratorial nature of the plot against Nasser, the gross violation of post-World-War-II international legal principles, and the challenge to the authority of the new Western leader, the US, all doomed the Suez imperial project.

Conspiracy theories are generally scoffed at as a tool of analysis or explanation. But the British, French, and Israeli collusion in 1956 was a geopolitical conspiracy *par excellence*, and no theory was needed to predict it, only a proven and deadly fact.

The Western powers were in agreement on the need to end Nasser's anti-colonial challenge. Disagreement, however, centred on the best strategy needed to achieve the desired objective. The United States, moreover, was not prepared to allow the British and French to continue the ambitious assertion of imperial grandeur when real power was irrevocably being consolidated in the hands of a new supreme Western power.

British Prime Minister Anthony Eden had already enunciated British policy on the Middle East to his Cabinet on 6 March 1956. According to Howard Dooley (1989), this policy was to: (1) protect British oil interests in the region;

(2) counteract the growing influence of Egypt through the strengthening of the Baghdad Pact; (3) persuade the United States to support a policy of greater firmness toward Egypt; and (4) give up attempting Egyptian-Israeli settlement (UK Public Record Office 1956: 486–517).

J.C. Hurewitz noted that Eden should have listened to Bevin, who as early as 1949 had concluded that "there was no way of bringing Egypt into a British-managed regional [defence] organization" (Hurewitz 1989: 22). There was even less prospect of discouraging the anti-colonial struggle embarked upon under Nasser's leadership after the 1952 revolution.

The British, along with the French, opted to end the threat of Egyptian policy firmly and conclusively. The nationalization of the Suez Canal Company on 26 July 1956 reinforced the Egyptian danger to British interests beyond any shadow of a doubt. On 1 August 1956, shortly after the nationalization of the company, Eden instructed General Sir Hugh Stockwell, Chief of the Imperial Staff, to prepare a joint Anglo-French military plan for the invasion of Egypt. Previous contingency plans were dusted off, and a plan code-named *Hamilcar* was presented to the Prime Minister and approved on 10 August 1956.

Britain and France had, in fact, developed a strategy for a military assault on Egypt not only to regain control over the Canal (the jugular vein of the British Empire, according to British Labour politician, Ernest Bevin), now at risk of being severed by Nasser, but more crucially, to topple the regime of President Nasser (regime change in practice) and install a friendly and malleable pro-Western regime in its place. Nasser's stance convinced British and French policy-makers of the need to end the threat posed by President Nasser and to do so firmly and conclusively.

The United States was concerned about the possible repercussions of precipitate British action for the entire Middle East and the Third World. President Eisenhower and Secretary Dulles alternated in issuing warnings to the British about the danger of using force against Egypt. Dulles said on 30 July 1956 that "the United States Government would not be in sympathy with any attempt to make the Egyptian Government rescind their nationalization decrees...under the threat of force" (Dulles 30 July 1956). On 31 July 1956, President Eisenhower wrote to Prime Minister Eden, unambiguously criticizing his decision "to employ force without delay" without first attempting peaceful methods. The President warned him of "the unwisdom even of contemplating the use of military force *at this moment*" (Eisenhower 31 July 1956: 69–71). Next, Dulles warned Eden on 1 August 1956 against the use of force, but agreed that Nasser should not "get away with it", and that he had to be brought to 'disgorge' his booty (Dulles 1 August 1956: 98–99).

The plan involved landing in Alexandria again (the British first landed in Alexandria in 1882 at the start of their occupation of Egypt) and marching first to Cairo to dismantle Nasser's government and then to the Canal to seize control of the vital waterway (Sellers 1990: 17–53).

The US joined the chorus of anti-Nasser threats. On 1 August 1956, Secretary Dulles stressed in London the need to "make Nasser disgorge his theft". In other words, a sovereign government's nationalizing a private company operating on national soil and paying the shareholders the full value of their shares was treated initially as 'theft' by the top diplomat of the United States. However, after the initial harsh reaction, the American administration began to have sober second thoughts, mainly about moderating and eventually taking control of the developing crisis. President Eisenhower and Secretary Dulles began to formulate an independent US strategy "to distance the United States from the taint of colonialism". The US position was made clearer in August by President Eisenhower. "Nationalization of the Canal was not illegal…it was within Egypt's sovereign rights. Use of force could not be justified, legally or morally" (Bowie 1989: 200–201). Therefore:

(1) The US objective should be to assure the efficient and reliable operation of the Canal, not the discrediting or unseating of Nasser.
(2) Some form of international supervision should provide sufficient protection.
(3) The dispute must be resolved by peaceful means.

Although British Prime Minister Eden started to compare Nasser to a "Hitler on the Nile" or a "Mussolini in the desert", he also began to invoke the "Red menace". This characterization of the Egyptian leader was meant to enlist the support of the United States for his plans against Egypt.

France was bent on ending Nasser's leadership and his threat to French control in Algeria, in particular his political and military support for the revolt in Algeria and his sponsorship of the Afro-Asian resolution in the Bandung Conference calling for "support of the rights of the people of Algeria, Morocco, and Tunisia to self-determination and independence" (Bandung Conference 1955). Nasser's participation in the conference made him a priority target for France. French opposition to the role Nasser was performing in support of the Algerian rebellion against French occupation well before the Suez Crisis, led France to turn to Israel – as the enemy of Nasser – to bolster its military capabilities as a form of intimidation and direct threat to Nasser's anti-colonial drive.

Furthermore, since September 1956 France and Israel had been separately negotiating a French-Israeli plan for a joint military strike against Egypt without the British. On 22 September the French Cabinet approved the steps necessary for a joint action with Israel against Egypt. The date for the operation was set for 20 October. The two governments, however, wanted the British government to endorse their plan. The Israeli Prime Minister was worried that Britain might not authorize the use of British air bases in Cyprus for the attack. France, meanwhile, secretly delivered at least 75 French Mystère jet-fighters to Israel in early October 1956 for operations against Egypt. This was in complete violation of the Tripartite Declaration of May 1950, committing the USA, Britain, and France to refrain from providing offensive arms to Middle Eastern antagonists.

The French concern over Britain's slow-paced preparation for war increased as the time for the attack against Egypt drew nearer. As Terence Robertson notes, "The main obstacle was the British political objection to making any move before the Israeli attack began, so as to avoid later charges of collusion" (Robertson 1964: 132). In the autumn of 1956 Shimon Peres, Director-General of the Israeli Ministry of Defence, and Maurice Bourges-Maunoury, French Defence Minister, were involved in a secret scheme to oversee the arming of Israel in preparation for war, apparently with the full knowledge of the United States. The Secretary-General of the French Ministry of Defence, Abel Thomas, who was the principal liaison with Israel, commented on the accelerating military supplies to Israel:

> We could not supply everything ourselves, so asked the Americans for material supplies. In fact, the Americans were constantly informed of all we were doing on the military side (Robertson 1964: 132).

The above account also claims that the US was not only aware of the accelerated arms delivery to Israel, but was providing material supplies and allowing NATO supplies to go to Israel. It is difficult to differentiate in this case between 'conspiracy' and 'hypocrisy' on the part of the Americans. A realist, however, could simply describe it as 'politics' in the service of strategy, moral or otherwise.

Such an account does not square with President Eisenhower's own comments on the crisis and his assessment of the option of using military means to settle the dispute. According to Peter Hahn (1991: 218):

> Eisenhower and Dulles remained convinced that war would ruin Western prestige across the developing world and open the Middle East to Soviet influence, a view he conveyed to the British...this was not the issue upon which to try to downgrade Nasser.

Moreover, Hahn added, Eisenhower believed that the British and French were making "a mistake from which there was no recall". The progression of events in the period before Suez suggests that the US was playing a delicate balancing role, wishing to see Nasser finished politically, and by military means if necessary, but at the opportune time and on a convenient occasion (pretext) (Hahn 1991: 218).

In August 1956, following the nationalization of the Suez Canal Company, France and Israel entered into an additional agreement for accelerated arms delivery. Israel was already on the receiving end of French nuclear technology. It was becoming more and more evident that Nasser's nationalization of the Suez Canal Company "did not cause the decision that he must be overthrown. *That decision had been made already.*" Guy Mollet, the French Prime Minister in 1956–57, announced during a speech on 9 March 1960 that French arms were the weapons used by Israel in 1956 to deliver its strike against the Egyptians in Sinai. "I need hardly point out that it was with French material and French aeroplanes that the Egyptians were smashed" (Childers 1962: 174).

Although aware of the massive military supplies being sent to Israel from French and NATO stores, the Americans, still frustrated by Nasser and wanting him gone, were treading carefully. Eisenhower and Dulles remained convinced that war would ruin Western prestige across the developing world and open the Middle East to Soviet influence, a view he conveyed to the British..."this was not the issue upon which to try to downgrade Nasser". In the end, the US was not opposed to the removal of Nasser using a convenient pretext. Suez was not that pretext. Nevertheless, Nasser's challenge was too dangerous to be ignored or to appease.

Prior to the start of the Suez War, President Eisenhower had reluctantly been prepared to give Nasser some room to manoeuvre, despite a long-standing US desire to snuff out the revolutionary challenge of the Egyptian leader. Eisenhower, who was not as ideologically rigid as Dulles, took a more conciliatory approach to the conflict. On 9 August 1956, the official US position was announced by President Eisenhower when he informed the US National Security Council that:

> if Nasser were to prove (1) that Egypt could operate the Canal and (2) would indicate an intention to abide by the Treaty of 1888, then it would be nearly impossible for the United States ever to find real justification, legally or morally, for the use of force (Eisenhower, 9 August 1956: NSC).

He followed that observation by declaring on 5 September 1956 that "the United States is committed to a peaceful solution of the problem". To quell any doubt about US intentions and America's position on the conflict, on 11 September 1956 he answered a question about whether Britain and France would be justified in the use of force by saying, "We established the United Nations to abolish aggression, and I am not going to be a party to aggression if it is humanly possible." Eisenhower, moreover, rejected the Anglo-French claim that "Egypt had become an aggressor by grabbing the Canal" (Robertson 1964: 112).

President Eisenhower displayed alternating positions on Nasser's nationalization act. On the one hand, he was concerned about Nasser's threat to the position of the West in the region because of Nasser's anti-colonial drive. On the other hand, he held a grudging admiration for a strong and decisive leader, declaring, "No matter what you think of Nasser, at least he is a leader" (Heikal 1986: 132).

In all the American warnings about the use of military action against Nasser, there was a common thread. The Americans were opposed to Nasser's unilateral move and they wanted him out of the picture. US policy-makers, however, alternated between describing Nasser's nationalization act as a threat, and on the other hand, as a legal move by a sovereign country. Their vacillations coincided with the intensity of the British response and perceived plans against Nasser. Moreover, the United States was not prepared to allow the British and the French to continue in their ambition of asserting imperial grandeur when real power was irrevocably being consolidated in the hands of the new American Empire. The newest empire had its own designs for the region.

6.8   Tripartite War Planning

Israel had its own independent plan, code-named Kadesh, for military action against Egypt. The plan was based on an earlier Israeli attack in the Sinai in December 1948 (Operation *Horev*). Two more operational plans were added (*Safiah* and *Omer*) and revised to produce the final Kadesh Plan. The plan was created for the invasion and annexation of the entire Sinai Peninsula, the Gaza Strip, and the Gulf of Aqaba's strategic islands of Tiran and Sanafir close to Sharm El-Sheikh.

Since 1948, the General Staff of the Israeli army (IDF) had been preparing for another battle in Sinai based on the doctrine that "a war had to be shifted into the enemy heartland as soon as possible" through a pre-emptive strike. "In autumn of 1955, Israel and the IDF General Staff were rife with talk about the need for a pre-emptive war" (Bar-On 1990). According to Bar-on, the operational approach of the IDF since the appointment of General Moshe Dayan as Chief of Staff in 1953 was based on speed; air force and paratrooper deployment; rapid armour advancement; by-passing enemy positions; breaking through and capturing enemy territories. Such a strategy was in keeping with General Dayan's oft-repeated principles of "horses bursting ahead, galloping forward, speed and aggressiveness". The final pillar in the Israeli strategy was the utilization of external political and military support and cover (Bar-On 1990: 197–207).

Kadesh needed to be revised to accommodate the massive French weapons delivered to Israel. Kadesh also aimed to destroy the Egyptian army's supply of new Soviet weapons before Egypt absorbed the new weapon system. With planning afoot for a joint strike against Egypt, Israel revised its original Kadesh Plan to Kadesh-1 to accommodate possible Anglo-French direct military participation. Intense negotiations took place between the three countries on the best way to coordinate a joint strike to avoid implicating the British and French in an unprovoked attack against Egypt with the involvement of Israel. The French broke the logjam by suggesting an independent Israeli strike to be followed later by an Anglo-French intervention to "separate the warring parties" and "seize the Suez Canal" in order to 'save' the vital waterway (and rescue the imperial fortunes of the two ageing empires). This was the basis of the Tripartite Agreement at Sèvres in October 1956 (Bar-On 1990: 203).

The French were the first to come up with the plan to involve Israel in the assault on Egypt with Britain. "This plan was brought to Eden by General Challe, deputy to General Ely, the French Chief of Staff, on 14 October. Eden accepted the idea enthusiastically, but the French and Israelis still had their doubts about his resolution, so insisted that the deal should be signed and sealed at a clandestine meeting in a private villa at Sèvres near Paris. This took place in the evening of 22 October and was attended by Ben-Gurion, Dayan, and Peres for Israel; Pineau, Bourges-Maunoury, and Abel Thomas for France; Selwyn Lloyd and Patrick Dean for Britain. It was at this meeting that the terms of the ultimatums to be delivered to the two sides were drawn up" (Heikal 1986: 194–195).

Scott Lucas describes Nutting's characterization of the French proposal presented to Prime Minister Eden on 14 October as the "Challe-Glazier approach". In addition to French General Maurice Challe, Albert Glazier, the French Minister of

Labour, was at the Chequers meeting when the proposal to involve Israel in military action against Egypt was made, and so was Anthony Nutting, British Minister of State at the Foreign Office. Appalled at the scope of the scheme involving his government, Nutting resigned on 25 October following the signing of the Sèvres Agreement. His resignation was made public a week later. Another minister, Sir Edward Boyle of the Treasury, also resigned (Lucas 1990: 88–89).

The original Anglo-French Operation *Hamilcar*, devised to strike at Egypt, was modified after Sèvres to incorporate the separate French-Israeli joint military plan, which included Israel's *Kadesh* (now Kadesh-1). The unified Anglo-French-Israeli Hamilcar Plan was then renamed *Musketeer-I* to overcome the French inability to pronounce the initial H in Hamilcar. The plan's code-name was changed yet another time to *Musketeer-II* after the war plan was totally revised to replace Alexandria as the starting point for the invasion with Port Said at the northern entrance to the Suez Canal. Musketeer-II had a final amendment and became known as *Musketeer Revise*. This latest plan was adopted on 14 September 1956 by the Egypt Committee, comprised of British Ministers, civil servants and military commanders (Kyle 1989: 113–119). *Musketeer Revise* was the plan which was put into action on 29 October 1956.

6.9 The Sèvres Protocol – 1956

Representatives of the three governments met in secrecy in Sèvres near the French capital. Leading their respective delegations were Prime Minister David Ben-Gurion for Israel; Foreign Minister Christian Pineau for France; and Foreign Office Under-Secretary Patrick Dean for Britain. The British and French Prime Ministers did not attend in case the conspiracy was prematurely uncovered. At the insistence of Israel, a final agreement was signed by all the political leaders involved after difficult negotiations lasting from 22 to 24 October 1956, less than 10 days from the start of the war.

The text of the Agreement outlined in detail the role each country would play in the conspiratorial plot leading to the unseating of Egyptian President Nasser and the end of his challenge to the colonial powers and their regional ally. In a shocking pretext for intervention, the three countries descended to a new low in the conduct of international relations:

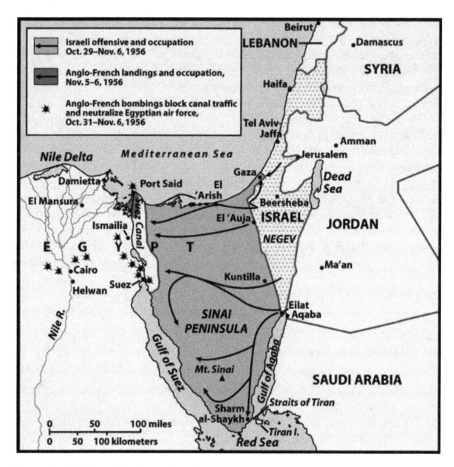

Photo 6.2 The Sèvres Plan for the Invasion of Egypt in October 1956. *Source* MSW, Weapons and warfare.com

(1) It was formally agreed that Israel would attack Egypt on 29 October 1956. The next day (30 October 1956) Britain and France, citing fears that the fighting following the Israeli attack and the Egyptian response would endanger the Suez Canal, would issue a joint ultimatum to Egypt and Israel.

(2) The Anglo-French ultimatum would demand the withdrawal of the Egyptian troops to ten miles west of the Canal. Israel would be requested to withdraw its forces to ten miles east of the Canal. Egypt was also asked to "accept the temporary occupation of key positions on the Canal by the Anglo-French forces".

(3) If Egypt refused to comply with the ultimatum, Anglo-French forces would "launch military operations against the Egyptian forces" on 31 October 1956.

(4) The three governments agreed that Israel would occupy the western shore of the Gulf of Aqaba and the Egyptian islands of Tiran and Sanafir, located at the entrance to the Gulf.

(5) Israel agreed not to attack Jordan during the joint military operations unless Jordan attacked Israel. The British government would then be absolved of its obligation to aid Jordan.

(6) The three contracting governments agreed that the protocol had to remain strictly secret.

(7) A related arrangement tied to Sèvres was the agreement between France and Israel to accelerate the development of Israel's nuclear power.

The *Sèvres Protocol* is a document that tarnished the integrity of the three governments involved and exposed their underhanded and illegal objectives. It also branded the imperial project in the region a bankrupt and broken enterprise destined to remain a historical failure.

Israel kept the original strategic objectives of Operation Kadesh intact and operational (outside the scope of *Musketeer Revise*). That is, Israel was willing to cooperate with the British and French to implement Musketeer Revise, but it had every intention of proceeding with the pre-planned territorial acquisitions of Operation Kadesh once the Anglo-French operations commenced.

At a meeting of the Israeli general staff on 25 October 1956 the revised Israeli war plan was made clear. First, "there would be a complete differentiation between what the IDF (Israel Defence Force) had promised the allies and what it had to do to achieve Israel's goals". Second, action to implement Israel's own objectives would be postponed until after the allies' military involvement had commenced, though "For the first 36 hours … the IDF will be acting alone". Third, after the allies' intervention, Israel was determined to pursue its own objectives on its own by quickly seizing all targets of interest, with the Strait of Tiran at the top of the list; in the process, Israel would have the opportunity to implement its plans without obstruction. Fourth, secrecy would be the most important consideration apart from victory itself (Bar-On 1990: 204–205).

The British and French agreed to Ben-Gurion's insistence that the allies' intervention, following Israel's thrust into Egypt, would not exceed 36 hours, instead of the 72 hours that the British favoured. He also insisted on the stationing of three French fighter squadrons in Israel to provide protection from Egyptian retaliatory air strikes, and on the deployment of French naval units for the protection of Israel's Mediterranean coast (Logan 1986: 97).

Israel's plan was based on initially waging a restrained campaign and creating the impression (diversionary tactic) that the Suez Canal was under threat, in order to ensure that Britain and France had a justification for joining the war.

Moreover, General Moshe Dayan, the military leader of the Israeli invasion, admitted in his memoirs that:

It is clear that the whole purpose of the [Anglo-French] ultimatum is to give the British and
the French Governments a pretext to capture the Canal Zone by military force (Dayan 1965:
979).

While Israel had strategic reasons for allowing itself to be used to facilitate an
Anglo-French invasion of Egypt, the British had their own post-invasion plans for
the future of Egypt. Dubbed the "post-war organization of Egypt and the Canal"
and overseen by the British cabinet ministers Harold Macmillan and Robert
Salisbury, the objective of the plan was to install an "acquiescent government" in
Egypt, presumably to do Britain's bidding and defuse the anti-colonial spark ignited
by Nasser (Brown 2001: *The Guardian*).

Additionally, France was aiming to extinguish the Algerian revolt, kept active
with Egyptian assistance.

6.10   Plan (KADESH)

Ever since December 1948, during the first Arab-Israeli war when Israel penetrated
deep into Sinai, the General Staff of the Israeli army (IDF) had been "preparing for
another battle in Sinai" (Bar-On 1990: 2020).

The resulting Operation, which was based on Operation Horev, Operation
Safiah, and Operation Omer and code-named 'Kadesh', had been ready for
implementation since 1953. Kadesh was temporarily abandoned for fear of outside
political backlash until its revival in the autumn of 1956 on account of
Anglo-French participation.

The Israelis had been spoiling to strike at Egypt before the Egyptian army was
able to absorb the new Soviet armaments and tactics that might enable it to pose a
serious threat to Israel's military plans. Although formulated independently of any
British or French involvement, Kadesh was quickly incorporated into the
Anglo-French final plans (*Musketeer Revise*) to attack Egypt in 1956.

The British, French and Israeli plans were brought together days before the start
of the war, combining the Kadesh, Kadesh I, Hamilcar, Musketeer I, Musketeer II,
and Musketeer Revise plans for the final combined assault on Egypt. According to
Keith Kyle (1989: 119), the final joint plan for the invasion incorporated three
phases: first, three days of bombing to neutralize the Egyptian Air Force; second,
seven to eleven days of air campaign to disrupt the Egyptian economy, impact
morale, and degrade the Egyptian armed forces, accompanied by intensive psychological warfare; and third, the move in to occupy the Suez Canal Zone with little
expected resistance remaining after the execution of the first two phases.

The French General, Andre Beaufre, stated that after the landing in Egypt and
securing of the Suez Canal Region, the invasion plan "had the advantage of placing
us within easier range of Cairo and, *provided it was not blocked*, the Canal could act
as our supply line". The General also emphasized the essential ingredient of the

tripartite operation "the Israeli attack ultimately came to constitute the *essential prerequisite* for the launching of the operation."

It is interesting to note that on the eve of the nationalization, Nasser's own assessment was that Israel would not get involved in the possible military action against Egypt. As documented by Heikal, "Participation of Israel in this operation ruled out. Eden would not accept. Israel may try but Eden will refuse. He will prefer to keep it European" (Heikal 1973: 889). Clearly, Nasser underestimated Israel's designs to impose a military and territorial outcome. However, Beaufre added that Israel "had become the detonator which set light to the powder barrel...her intervention was politically essential". But Beaufre admitted that including Israel in the Anglo-French assault on Egypt was a strategic mistake, handing Nasser a strong victory in Egypt and throughout the Arab World (Beaufre 1969: 139). Israel's role in the service of the Western empires could not have been better illustrated and proven.

Initially, the British were so obsessed with secrecy and keeping the role of Israel in the plan hidden that the British Cabinet Secretary, Sir Norman Brook, was "to round up any written evidence of collusion with the Israeli attack on Egypt and destroy it. There is therefore no direct account of Sèvres in the papers in the Public Record Office. However, in one copy only of Brook's minutes for 23 October is to be found a single reference to secret conversations which had been held in Paris with representatives of the Israeli government" (Kyle 2000: 74–75).

The British "Operational objectives were to destroy the Egyptian Army, to bring down the Nasser Government and to control the Suez Canal" (Kyle 2000: 70). The planning was supervised by cabinet ministers Harold Macmillan and Robert Salisbury with the purpose of installing an "acquiescent government" in the country. The political directive to the military command was to occupy Cairo and even Alexandria in order to install a "co-operative government", but under no account should the occupying forces accept "general responsibility" for "feeding the population" under the "new Geneva conventions dealing with military occupation". An "occupation army" of between three and four divisions would be required to maintain control, they indicated. The coalescing of the objectives of the three partners (each with a different objective) resulted in the doomed joint military action against Egypt (Kyle 1989: 120–121).

6.11   Operation Tarnegol

In a stroke of luck for the Israelis on the eve of the invasion, Israeli intelligence agents discovered that Egypt's Minister of War, Abdel Hakim Amer, and the entire Egyptian General Staff were travelling to Damascus and Amman for consultation. A hasty plan was put together to shoot down the minister's plane and thus paralyse the Egyptian Army's leadership at a crucial time. On 28 October 1956, the day before the war was to start, Amer's plane, Ilyushin Il-14, was intercepted in international air space over the Mediterranean and shot down by Israeli Major

Yoash Tsiddon and Navigator Elyashiv Brosh flying a Meteor 52 aircraft. Although the Egyptian General staff was decimated, Amer escaped because he had stayed behind in Damascus for further discussions. Top Egyptian staff officers perished before the war started, undoubtedly affecting Egyptian capabilities (Norton 2004; Tsiddon-Chatto 1995; Henkin 2015).

6.12   War and Invasion – October 1956

The realities of the colonial project in the Middle East and the Zionist onslaught were the ingredients driving the colonial war in the region, and provided the backdrop for the United Nations' intervention and the eventual deployment of UNEF. Weeks and months of high stakes international manoeuvres ended with three armies illegally attacking Egypt in an unholy collusion: two 'empires' living beyond their useful shelf-life and resorting to obsolete gun-boat diplomacy, and a colonial-settler regime trying to illegally annex additional territories with total disregard for international law and the UN Charter.

6.13   The Gathering Storm

International tensions ran sky high between the nationalization of the Canal in July and the start of the war in late October. Crucial stakes were involved. A resolute nationalist leader had challenged two of the mightiest empires in modern history. Nasser had been a thorn in the side of the British and French imperial powers and it was time to extinguish his anti-colonial crusade once and for all. His nationalization of the Suez Canal Company was both the last straw and a golden opportunity to administer a final blow to his nationalist aspirations and his radical leadership role of the international anti-colonial movement.

The threats, conspiracies, and gun-boat diplomacy that followed revealed the determination of the old imperial powers to assert some semblance of control and endurance. The crisis also involved the newly-independent/non-aligned nations and gave them a previously unheard voice in the international arena. The crisis, moreover, ushered in a unique and novel role for the United Nations in international crisis diplomacy and peace efforts.

In anticipation of an external attack involving the Suez Canal region, the Egyptian Army began to prepare for the defence of the country. Although the probability of war was considered unlikely by the Egyptian leadership, there was genuine concern about the obvious military advantage enjoyed by the British and French over Egypt.

The Nasser government was, therefore, relying on international diplomacy to avert a military confrontation. Egyptian units, nonetheless, were deployed near

Alexandria, around Cairo, and in the eastern Delta, close to the Canal Zone, in case an attack were to materialize.

The British and the French also began preparing for war in earnest almost from the beginning of the crisis in late July and early August 1956. British and French ports and bases in Algeria, Libya, Malta, Cyprus, Jordan, Iraq, Aden, and other military bases in the Middle East were used as mobilization and staging centres. The British Suez Canal Base's weapons storage facilities (left behind after the Anglo-Egyptian evacuation treaty from Egypt was completed in June 1956) were used to marshal the military resources needed to mount an attack on Egypt. Additionally, the French government sent a huge number of military supplies to Israel in preparation for the assault.

Until a few days, even a few hours, prior to the start of the war, Egyptian President Nasser refused to believe that Britain and France would collude with Israel against Egypt. He continued to hold on to that belief even when his military attaché in Paris, Colonel Tharwat Okasha, obtained information on 27 October 1956 confirming the tripartite plan for attack, information which was conveyed to Nasser by a personal messenger on the morning of the 29th (the day the war began).

"Surely it is impossible that both the French and the British would degrade themselves to such an extent", commented Nasser in disbelief (Hewedy 1989: 169). He based his position on the conviction that neither Britain nor France would risk exposing their 'friends' in the Arab world to disdain or destabilizing their position in the region by using military force against Egypt, and would especially not involve Israel. Additionally, Nasser did not think that Israel needed the British or the French to launch a military attack against Egypt, given the existing imbalance of military power between Egypt and Israel (Hewedy 1989: 169).

The Egyptian Military High Command, on the other hand, did have apprehensions about such collusion. In a report in September 1956 entitled *Military Situation in the Eastern Mediterranean*, the Command's assessment mirrored the exact development of the war with two exceptions: first, the enemy landing would begin in Alexandria and march on Cairo (correctly anticipating the original allied plan); second, the role of Israel would be confined to capturing the town of al-Arish in the Sinai in order to isolate and capture the Gaza Strip. The Egyptian High Command did not anticipate the major change of replacing Alexandria with Port Said before seizing the Canal and advancing on Cairo, nor did it factor in the ambitious Israeli plans for a massive territorial conquest (Hewedy 1989: 169).

6.14 Avoiding Provocation

Following the nationalization of the Canal Company, the Egyptian Government had an overriding preoccupation with maintaining navigation through the Canal without impediment. It was also determined to respect the provisions of the 1954 Anglo-Egyptian Treaty governing the British Suez Canal Military Base in order to avoid any pretext for military intervention. Respecting Egyptian obligations was strictly observed even though doing so threatened Egypt's military position. Egypt's cautious attitude became apparent on three occasions (Hilmy n.d.).

First, prior to the war, Britain requested the release of war material from its Canal base as per the Treaty. Despite the knowledge that such war material could be used against Egypt in the event of war, the Egyptian political authorities overrode their military's opposition to such a transfer. The Anglo-Egyptian Treaty of 1954 for the final evacuation of the British troops from the Suez Canal Base stipulated that Egypt was under a treaty obligation in times of war (excluding war against Egypt) to supply the British with war material left behind in storage in the Suez Canal region and guarded by Egyptian troops. Article 9 of the Treaty stated: "The United Kingdom is accorded the right to move any British equipment into or out of the base at its discretion" (Anglo-Egyptian Treaty 1954: 402–431).

The Egyptian General (Hilmy) in charge of the implementation of the treaty received hundreds of requests from the British prior to the war to release massive supplies of war materials kept in storage as per the 1945 Treaty. He wrote to the Egyptian Foreign Ministry about "the absurdity of the situation" as "It was clear that we were supplying the British with all the war material they would later use to attack us" (Hilmy n.d.). The British requests included aerial bombs, thousands of gallons of aviation fuel, military vehicles, small arms, concertina barbed wire, and tons of ammunition for all types of weapons. All the requested supplies were duly transported by Egyptian railway to Port Said, where Egyptian personnel carried them to waiting British ships bound for Cyprus and Malta, where the build-up of the Anglo-French forces was proceeding to attack Egypt.

Hilmy therefore requested authorization to delay responding to the British requests, using all the logistical excuses possible. The Ministry did not agree, replying, "Since we had signed a treaty with Britain we must honour it regardless of what they did. If we defaulted in carrying out our obligations, we would then furnish Britain with the excuse they were looking for to use force" (Hilmy n.d). Kenneth Love confirmed that the Egyptian Foreign Ministry replied to Hilmy, "No, don't give them [the British] any pretext...If they attack us, we will seize what is left in the base, but until then be scrupulous about complying with the agreement" (Love 1969: 457).

On the morning of 29 October 1956 (the day the war started in the Sinai), Sir Terence Garvey, the British Minister at the British Embassy in Cairo, was still negotiating on an urgent basis with General Hilmy, according to the provisions of the 1954 Treaty with Britain, over arrangements to remove the 800-plus British technicians manning the British installations in the Canal zone. General Hilmy was not in a cooperative mood. Having watched helplessly as the British successfully used legal measures to collect thousands of tons of war material destined for use against Egypt, he realized that the urgent request for evacuation meant that the war was imminent (Hilmy n.d.).

The early start of the war prevented the evacuation of the British personnel, who were taken into protective custody until the end of the conflict. Their families, however, had been airlifted from the Canal Zone earlier in August 1956 (*Operation Nursery*) with the deepening of the escalating crisis. Hilmy (n.d.) observed that the

British bombs dropped later "on our heads in Cairo, Port Said, Ismailia, and Suez were the same bombs that, obliged by the Treaty of Friendship, I helped send to the British bases in Malta and Cyprus for the Canberra and Valiant bombers".

Second, immediately following the Israeli attack on 29 October 1956, the Egyptian High Command gave "the absurd order" for Egyptian military troops crossing the Canal to reinforce the troops in Sinai "to give priority to Canal navigation over the movements of military units in a war situation", and to proceed only between ship convoys traversing the Canal in order not to disrupt normal ship traffic navigation. "While Israeli units were racing to reach the Mitla Pass in the Sinai, Egyptian units were waiting on the Western bank of the Canal for the normal ship traffic to pass first!"(Hilmy n.d.).

According to Kenneth Love:

> Nasser continued to try to avoid allowing any possible pretext to the British by giving ship traffic along the Canal priority over military movement across it. At 9 a.m. Radio Cairo reported that shipping continued normally and that the northbound convoy of twenty ships had reached Port Said (Love 1969: 515).

The Egyptian leadership did not have to wait long to realize the scope of the grave situation awaiting the Egyptian forces when these units finally crossed the Canal and began engaging the Israelis. On 30 October 1956, the Government of Egypt received the joint British-French ultimatum (appeal in the French version) (Anglo-French Ultimatum 1956) to cease fire and withdraw all Egyptian forces to a distance of ten miles west of the Canal, and to accept the 'temporary' occupation by Anglo-French forces of key positions at Port Said, Ismailia, Suez and along the entire length of the Canal, so as to ensure the safety of the waterway and protect freedom of navigation. Israel was asked to withdraw its forces the same distance but east of the Canal, even though the most forward position of the Israeli army was still at the Mitla pass, more than five times the distance from the Canal demanded by the ultimatum.

The ultimatum to Israel effectively invited the Israeli forces to advance further west inside Egyptian territory to positions they had not even approached at the time the joint ultimatum was issued. If Egypt refused, the joint British-French forces would occupy the entire Canal Zone in order to impose the terms of the ultimatum. The ultimatum was indeed officially rejected by Egypt, and accepted by Israel, as planned. Following Egypt's rejection, wide-scale Anglo-French bombing commenced, as scripted at Sèvres.

Third, as per the Egyptian military plans for the war, Hilmy, as the Chief of Staff of the Egyptian Eastern Command, requested permission for the Canal to be blocked after the war began. The Egyptian political leadership was initially reluctant to give permission during the early stage of the war. The impasse was resolved a few hours later as the military situation developed.

The Egyptian High Command prepared a list of 'Directives' to repel any invasion as follows:

First, Egyptian forces were to prevent the enemy from seizing the Canal Zone at any cost. Second, they were to guard the Red Sea shores to prevent enemy troops landing and advancing on Cairo. Third, any enemy troops landing in Port Said would have to be prevented from advancing south or seizing Ismailia. Fourth, the Canal would have to be blocked at the start of any enemy landings in the Canal Zone, as per the Hilmy Plan. Fifth, the National Guard troops were to be reinforced in the Delta. Sixth, detailed plans to defend Alexandria, Cairo, and Port Said were to be prepared (Hewedy 1989: 170).

In other words, the Egyptian High Command was clearly anticipating, or at least aware of, the possibility of enemy troops landing in Alexandria and of their projected march against Cairo and intention of toppling the regime, as part of the broader attack against the Suez Canal Zone. This awareness inadvertently achieved some of the Anglo-French objectives of diverting Egyptian troops away from the Canal Zone and diluting their concentrated strength. This was precisely the thinking of French General Beaufre, who foresaw on 12 August 1956 that "if threatened simultaneously from Alexandria, Port Said and Sinai (Israel), the enemy's forces would initially be dispersed" (Beaufre 1969: 32).

The British and French military leaders were agonizing over the choice of the landing site: Alexandria or Port Said. The initial inclusion of Alexandria in the planning was to move on Cairo for an ultimate regime change (considered a vital political-strategic objective). But the difficulties and danger in securing the city, and the high casualties anticipated, led to the abandonment of Alexandria, despite its strategic value in drawing Egyptian troops away from the Canal Zone (regardless of Beaufre's objection to the change). Marching towards Cairo from Alexandria, moreover, and securing the city, was deemed even more problematic. Crossing the Nile from Cairo towards the Suez Canal objective added another set of military and logistical problems. Having finalized Port Said as the initial landing target, "the entire success of the operation depended on a rapid break-out from Port-Said… along the narrow Canal embankments…The smallest demolition at any important point" could undermine the objective of seizing the entire Canal on the way to Cairo. Consequently, Beaufre advocated landing in Qantara on the Canal south of Port Said to avoid getting bogged down in securing the city (Beaufre 1969: 52–53).

Beaufre highlighted the two main obstacles in planning the invasion (besides Egyptian military and popular resistance) as (1) the blocking of the Canal and (2) the blowing up of its embankments.

6.15   Blocking the Suez Canal (Operation Cork)

One important part of the Egyptian Army's directives was the preparation of a detailed plan to block the Suez Canal in the event of an enemy attack. In August-September 1956 General Hilmy of the Eastern Command formulated the plan in order to prevent enemy forces from seizing the Canal and controlling the vital waterway. This plan, "*41/56*" (the Army Operations Order number), code-named *"Operation Cork"*, involved seizing Egyptian and foreign cargo ships, tug boats, dredges, cranes, barges, leisure boats, fishing boats, and even old decommissioned naval vessels.

Photo 6.3 General Hilmy, the mastermind behind the Suez Canal blocking in November 1956. *Source* General Hilmy's files

The Hilmy plan called for the military to seize all such ships and position them in the Canal's deep navigation channel at the entrance of the Canal in Port Said harbour in the north, at the entrance of the Canal in the Suez harbour in the south, and in the middle in Ismailia as well as along the entire length of the Canal. The vessels were to be sunk using a combination of explosives and large amounts of cement placed in the hulls. In the case of an attack on Hilmy's HQ or his absence, incapacitation, or death, the Egyptian Broadcasting Corporation was instructed to broadcast the code name for the plan repeatedly as a trigger to activate or complete its implementation by the waiting contingents along the length of the Canal (Hilmy n.d.).

Nasser was strongly advised by Hilmy that if blocking the Canal was not implemented at once, any further delay would result in an enemy take-over of the Suez Canal and the seizure of the entire Suez Canal region, and eventually the repeat of the events of the 1882 British invasion of Egypt (through Alexandria and the Suez Canal). Such an outcome would irrevocably achieve its military and political objectives. After further discussion, the President then gave his approval and the green light to Hilmy to commence the blocking of the Canal (Hilmy n.d.). Hilmy was able to speak forcefully with the President due to their friendship and shared history. Obviously, Nasser trusted Hilmy's judgement and his professional advice.

Within a few hours, and under heavy enemy fire, Port Said harbour in the north, and Suez harbour in the south, plus vital points along the entire length of the Canal, including Ismailia, were blocked by deliberately-sunk vessels. Both pre-assigned ships and other commandeered vessels of all types, that were found available at the time, were used to complete the blockade. The Egyptian navy destroyer *Abu Kir* was scuttled in the Suez harbour in such a way that its upper decks remained above surface so that its surviving guns could be used in an anti-aircraft role.

Kenneth Love (1969) reports that the Canal operation took place under heavy aerial bombardment. "Hilmy began a race with the British bombers to get the *Akka* [navy supply ship] into the Canal south of Lake Timsah (instead of the original location north of the Lake)." The change was made because the withdrawing Egyptian armoured units from Sinai were relying on a temporary pontoon bridge across the Canal in the location "where Akka was to have been scuttled". Once the armoured Egyptian withdrawal from Sinai was completed, the huge "ocean-going tug Edgar Bonnet was sunk at the spot originally designated for the Akka" (Love 1969: 527, 637–638).

Paul Johnson (1957) describes the confusion in London concerning the attempts to prevent the blockade of the Canal. Eden's advisors had told him:

> ...that if they were given men and machines in sufficient quantity they would seize the Canal before the Egyptians had time to block it. The Egyptians had block ships; but all their positions had been mapped out by aerial photography, and they could be destroyed before the Egyptians had time to manoeuvre them into position. [However], Eden had received the painful news that the Canal was now blocked from Port Said to Suez, and that the obstructions would take months to move (Johnson 1957: 105–106).

6.16   War and Deception

Following the Israeli invasion on 29 October 1956, the Anglo-French ultimatum was issued on 30 October, as agreed at Sèvres, and promptly rejected by Egypt. The British and French began around-the-clock bombardment of Egyptian strategic targets at one minute past midnight on 30–31 October 1956, and landed their troops in the northern Canal cities of Port Said and Port Foad on either side of the Mediterranean entrance of the Canal, but their advance southwards was blocked. The war continued in earnest with massive Anglo-French bombing of the main vital targets in Egypt. The Egyptian Eastern Command, however, successfully implemented the Hilmy Canal blocking plan by sinking tens of vessels along the length of the Canal starting in Port Said on the Mediterranean, thus preventing the invasion force from moving south.[1]

---

[1]Amin Hilmy II. As relayed to the author.

Photo 6.4 Entrance to the Suez Canal, November 1956. *Source* Imperial War Museum (public domain)

> The Egyptians had not stinted themselves at the task of wrecking. "Bridges, floating cranes, dredges, pilot boats, tugs, a frigate and a floating dock were willingly sent to the bottom of the Canal and its approaches. There were a total of fifty-one wrecks in all, of which twenty-two, varying in weight from 100 tons to 4,000 tons, were sunk in Port Said Harbour." (*Egyptian Chronicles* 1956: 7).

In response to the planned military trap to sandwich the Egyptian army between the Anglo-French forces advancing from the north and west on one side and the Israeli troops advancing from the east, Nasser ordered the immediate withdrawal of the army from the Sinai and its redeployment in the eastern Delta to oppose the Anglo-French landing in Port Said and block its further advance south. Nasser's decision led to a major clash with his Minister of War (Defence), General Amer, who wanted the army to move into the Negev to defeat Israel before turning back and attacking the Anglo-French invasion army.

Amer's ineptitude proved disastrous during the 1967 War when he, paradoxically, ordered the ill-advised and uncoordinated withdrawal of the army from the Sinai following the Israeli strike against the Egyptian Air Force. The Nasser-Amer confrontation led many in the Egyptian military and political leadership in 1956 to urge the immediate dismissal of the Major-turned-General from his post. But the President – displaying bad judgement himself – refused and stood by his friend. Nasser's reluctance to dismiss his Minister of War in 1956 would prove very costly in 1967.

Israel took advantage of the military situation and advanced into Sinai, which was beyond the agreed Sèvres Plan but in accordance with its own pre-war plan (Kadesh). Not waiting for the end of the hostilities to be confirmed, Israel made its territorial designs on the Sinai and Gaza very clear. Israel went to war on an opportunistic basis to achieve territorial conquest and political consolidation. Allying itself with the Anglo-French duo was a matter of extreme convenience and expedient precaution. That Israel had its own overriding objectives going beyond the Anglo-French plans became clear when the Israeli Prime Minister, David Ben-Gurion, declared in the Knesset on 7 November 1956 that "The Armistice Agreement with Egypt is dead and buried and will never be resurrected. Together with the armistice agreement, the armistice lines between us and Egypt are vanished and dead" (Love 1969: 638). And with the change in territorial control, Israel wanted to accomplish a *fait accompli* by changing the names of the physical landmarks: the Gulf of Suez was renamed the Gulf of Solomon, the Gulf of Aqaba was renamed the Gulf of Eilat, and Sharm El Sheikh at the southern tip of the Sinai was renamed Ophira.

Photo 6.5 Destruction in Port Said, November 1956. *Source* Al-Yaom al-Sabee, Cairo, 29 October 2017 (public domain)

Yossi Melman, an Israeli writer specializing in intelligence and strategic affairs, and a former Nieman Fellow at Harvard University, wrote a report about the Sinai Campaign based on files obtained from the archives of the Israeli army (Melman 2006). This report was published in the Israeli newspaper *Haaretz* on 8 August 2010. Melman suggests that initially Ben-Gurion was very concerned about Israelis projecting an image as mercenaries or collaborators with the French and the British. Later, with the call for a ceasefire gaining momentum at the United Nations, he was determined to find a way "to delay it to allow British and French forces to take control of the Suez Canal, as was decided at Sèvres" (Melman 2006).

The British Ambassador to Egypt, Sir Humphry Trevelyan "never disguised his opposition to the Anglo-French-Israeli invasion, describing it as a lamentable muddle", and recollecting that:

We commented that Nasser would fight if attacked and would block the Canal...The Egyptians would organize guerrilla warfare and it would be difficult for us to disengage without long and widespread operations. No government set up by the occupying Forces would last. Only a government untainted by collaboration with the British could hold its position (Trevelyan, cited by Thornhill 2000: 1, 17).

Moreover, Lord Mountbatten (1956), who was a member of the established ruling elite in Britain, and who opposed the Suez War strongly in writing and verbally, sent a letter on 2 November 1956 to Prime Minister Eden stating:

My dear Prime Minister, I know that you have been fully aware over these past few weeks of my great unhappiness at the prospect of our launching military operations against Egypt...I am writing to appeal to you to accept the resolution of the overwhelming majority of the United Nations to cease military operations, and to beg you to turn back the assault convoy before it is too late (Mountbatten, cited by Grove/Rohan 2000: 111).

Photo 6.6 Egyptian Stamp commemorating the Suez War, 1956. *Source* Egyptian Postal Authority

However, Sir Gerald Templer, the Chief of the Imperial General Staff, who supported the war, believed that Mountbatten's attitude toward the planned operation was "verging on cowardice...and he went so far as to call the First Sea Lord 'yellow' at a Chiefs of Staff meeting" (Grove/Rohan 2000: 104). On 4 November 1956, Mountbatten wrote to Lord Hailsham to report that:

"Eden spoke to me on the telephone to thank me for my letter; he said he fully understood my feelings but was not prepared to turn back the assault convoy...Eden added that I must make it clear that in my view such [expected civilian] casualties [collateral damage in today's parlance] cannot be avoided" (Grove/Rohan 2000: 112).

Smith (2013) said that Lord "Mountbatten believed his unique status as royal confidant and imperial consul...allowed him to buck constitutional convention". He offered his opinion to the "Chiefs of Staff Committee, and in advice to the cabinet, the First Sea Lord voiced his fears, querying what the exit strategy was" (Smith 2013: 105).

One of the most important Egyptian sources on the war is the account of Abd al-Latif al-Baghdadi (1990: 333–356), a founding member of the Free Officers Group that overthrew the Egyptian monarchy and later a vice president under President Nasser. Baghdadi describes in detail the tension, the emotional see-saw, and the political-military disputes between Nasser and Amer during the Suez War. Nasser, reports Baghdadi, complained to Amer "about [Nasser] being out of contact with the military command and being in the dark as to what was going on despite his responsibilities [as the President]." The pressures upon the Egyptian leadership almost brought it to breaking point.

Although Amer is usually considered an anti-Israeli hardliner, a somewhat different picture emerges from the al-Baghdadi memoirs. By Friday 2 November 1956 his bombastic and heroic position had clearly changed. On that date, in the midst of intensive air raids, as the British dropped flares to illuminate their targets on the ground (witnessed by the author during a night raid over the Heliopolis/Manchiet El-Bakry District, close to President Nasser's residence and the Almaza military airbase) there was fear that the flares were part of a landing attempt to seize Nasser and members of his government. Amer talked to Nasser first and then addressed a meeting of the assembled former members of the Revolution Command Council (RCC), stating: "The continuation of the war will bring about the destruction of the country and the death of numerous citizens. As a result of this the people will hate the regime and those who uphold it. [Amer] prefers, in order to prevent such devastation, to ask for a ceasefire."

Both al-Baghdadi and another future vice president, Zakariya Mohieldin, rejected any talk of ceasefire or even surrender, insisting on continuing the fight. But another member of the RCC, Salah Salem, betraying a sense of panic and shock, said "We must prevent further calamities and destruction in this country." He wanted Nasser, on behalf of the revolutionary regime, to address the nation and request approval of a ceasefire and a surrender.

According to al-Baghdadi, Salem proposed, "Let us rise and give ourselves up to Trevelyan, the English ambassador." He continued by saying, "It is you [Nasser] the British want. Go to the British Embassy and surrender yourself to Trevelyan before he leaves." Nasser replied that if it was only him the British were after "I would certainly go and give myself up. But is it not something bigger than that?" According to al-Baghdadi, Nasser put a stop to the talk of surrender by saying, "Far better for us to commit suicide here, before taking such a step." Nasser favoured going underground, if the military situation became untenable, and continuing the resistance. But vials of phosphate-cyanide were nonetheless duly ordered for each member of the RCC.

Undoubtedly, General Hilmy's pivotal intervention in securing the green light for his plan to block the Canal and, consequently, deprive the invaders of their prize objective of seizing the entire Canal region, would eventually prove to be a crucial military move in the otherwise bleak military catastrophe that befell Egypt. The General was also able to hastily construct defensive fortifications south of Port Said using the remnants of some of the retreating military units from Sinai, and some elements of the lightly trained National Guard troops to block the British from moving south toward Ismailia. Had the Anglo-French Allied Command accepted the recommendations of the French General Andre Beaufre for a speedy and direct assault on the Suez Canal itself by landing in Qanrara (North of Ismailia in the middle of the Canal region) instead of Port Said and seizing the entire length of the Canal "to prevent it being blocked" or its embankment blown up by the Egyptians (Beaufre 1969: 137), perhaps the history of the Suez War would have been different.

By the end of the war thousands of Egyptians (military and civilians) had been killed or wounded. The city of Port Said sustained widespread destruction and civilian casualties resulting from aerial and naval bombardment. All Egyptian air bases and civilian airports were destroyed or damaged. The bulk of Egypt's army was destroyed. Many infrastructure facilities were demolished or seriously damaged. The Sinai suffered massive and deliberate destruction and plunder.

When Israel was forced to give up control and withdraw its troops by March 1957, it carried out a systematic scorched-earth drive by destroying or pilfering the infrastructure components in the Sinai, removing all the Egyptian railway tracks, telephone and telegraph posts, and any salvageable machinery from the oilfields. The oil wells were blown up. Paved roads throughout the peninsula were ploughed and rendered unusable. Schools, hospitals, police stations, and any other useful asset were demolished. Notwithstanding the utter violation of international law, the human and economic cost to Egypt was staggering. Israel was never taken to task for its war crimes.

6.17 Clearing the Canal

The Egyptian concern for unobstructed navigation through the Canal was reversed after the war. Egypt's government insisted on keeping the Canal closed and refused offers to clear the damaged and sunken vessels blocking the waterway until all foreign troops had evacuated Egyptian territories and the Gaza Strip. Israel delayed the implementation of the UN resolution, which ordered the withdrawal of all the occupying forces, unless it was allowed access to the Suez Canal and the Gulf of Aqaba. Egypt held firm on the Suez Canal but quietly allowed Israeli shipping through the Gulf of Aqaba, an undertaking sponsored by the US. Israel obtained undeclared assurances from the US President for free access through the Straits of Tiran, at the entrance to the Gulf of Aqaba, with the tacit but unacknowledged approval of Egypt, as the price for completing the Israeli evacuation. However, no such arrangements were extended to Israeli passage through the Suez Canal. The Egyptian Government was not ready to compromise on this particular issue.

Eventually Israel was compelled to complete its withdrawal in the middle of March 1957. Only then was the Canal reopened for navigation (preliminary preparations for the clearing were already underway, headed by US army engineer

General Wheeler). Egypt refused the involvement of any British or French ships or technicians, even if they were placed under UN command. Navigation through the Canal resumed on 8 April 1957.

6.18   Israeli Post-war Reflection

Yitzhak Rabin, the late Prime Minister of Israel, commented on the Suez War and the "limits of power" in conflicts between nations (Rabin 1990: 238–242). He espoused the view that Israel could not impose its "political will" on unwilling Arabs by "military means". Rabin continued, "Peace cannot be imposed on our neighbours, nor can force of Israeli arms change their political systems or control them." He went on to say, "I do not believe that the superpowers would allow Israel to operate as a free agent or that they would stand aside if Israel attempted to achieve political goals by military means."

Rabin seemed to have forgotten that, with the active acquiescence of the United States, he was one of the main planners of the later 1967 War as Israel's Chief of Staff, which resulted in massive new territorial and political gains on the ground. His amnesia also extended to the fact that Israel did precisely what he declared about the limits of Israeli power to impose new political realities. This latter-day repentance does not change the fact that Israel has been using military means to achieve political ends ever since 1947 – before its formal independence until the present.

6.19   Canada's Position During the Suez War

Although the US's opposition to the Suez invasion – based on its own national interest – was vigorous and almost indignant, Canada's role in Suez was more subdued and circumspect. Canadian documents reveal that the Canadian government made its strong opposition to the British-led military action in Suez known in direct and confidential exchanges with the British government. Canada, as a member of the Commonwealth and NATO, as well as a close ally of the United States, had to play a delicate balancing act to stay in the good books of all its allies.

Canadian official documents reveal a nuanced position on the Suez Crisis. The Canadian government was greatly disturbed by the Anglo-French ultimatum issued to Egypt and Israel. Almost from the start of the crisis, on 27 July 1956, the Canadian High Commissioner to Britain, Norman Robertson, counselled patience and international cooperation through the United Nations. Robertson expressed his hope to the British government that "the United Kingdom would not be too quick to gather too many spears to its own bosom" (Canada: DEA Dispatch London to Ottawa: 27 July 1956).

With the commencement of hostilities, *Pearson* asked Canada's High Commissioner in London to convey to the UK government Canada's "grave anxieties" over the decision to issue the ultimatum. Moreover, the Canadian Secretary of State for External Affairs told the Canadian Ambassador to the United States that the Canadian government had the 'impression' that "the British and the French had been cooking this up". On the same day Pearson repeated his government's position on the ultimatum by calling Canada's high commissioner in the UK to ensure that he was able to express to the British government Canada's feeling of "bewilderment and dismay." Pearson also noted that the ultimatum "seems to be much more anti-Egyptian than anti-Israel" (Canada: DEA Pearson to Robertson: 30 Oct. 1956).

During the crisis the British and Canadian prime ministers exchanged several messages that revealed the deep disagreement between the two governments. The Prime Minister of the UK, Anthony Eden, wrote to Canada's Prime Minister, Louis St. Laurent, on 30 October 1956, saying that the UK "cannot allow a war between Israel and Egypt to block the Suez Canal". He then utilized the deception plan agreed to in the Sèvres Protocol by stating that "Israel has accused Egypt of aggression and is delivering a counter-attack" (Canada: DEA Eden to St. Laurent: 30 Oct. 1956). Eden knew full well when he wrote those words that there was no aggression committed by Egypt, and that the Israeli action was not a counter-attack but a premeditated invasion carried out to justify British and French intervention, as previously planned by the three countries.

St. Laurent replied by commenting on the "grave steps in Egypt" following the "action of Israel", saying that Canada "cannot come to the conclusion that [Israel's] penetration of its troops into Egypt was justified" nor could it accept that the situation "necessitated the decision of the UK and France to post forces in the Canal Zone". In this letter, St. Laurent also informed the British Prime Minister that Canada had "suspended all shipments of arms to Israel…in conformity with what we regard as our obligations under the Charter and our membership in the United Nations." St. Laurent, moreover, outlined three areas of anxiety caused by this "distressing situation": first, the "effect on the United Nations"; second, the "danger of a serious division within the Commonwealth"; and third, the "deplorable divergence of viewpoint and policy between the United Kingdom and the United States…which is a matter of deep and abiding interest to Canada" (Canada: DEA St. Laurent to Eden: 31 Oct. 1956).

Robertson, the Canadian High Commissioner in London, reported that the British Government was 'aghast' at the tone of St. Laurent's letter to Prime Minister Eden, and that it came as a "great surprise", According to the same report, the positions of St. Laurent and Pearson represent "the first occasion on which Canada had 'parted company' from the United Kingdom in public" (Canada: DEA Robertson to Pearson: 2 Nov. 1956).

A few days later, Eden wrote to St. Laurent, defending the Anglo-French intervention in Egypt and invoking moral pieties as the foundation for a futile cover-up by describing the 'operation' in Egypt as a "life-saving one." Eden informed the Canadian Prime Minister that the Arab countries, under Egypt's leadership, were about to "set about Israel", thus necessitating the life-saving intervention (Canada: DEA Eden to St. Laurent: 6 Nov. 1956).

It is worth noting that the St. Laurent Liberal Government was accused by the Canadian Conservative Opposition of betraying "Britain in its hour of need". John Diefenbaker, a Conservative Opposition party member and a future Prime Minister, said, "Canada should not be a mere tail on the American kite but should, as a senior member of the Commonwealth, give to the United Kingdom moral support and encouragement" (Robertson 1964: 83).

Pearson defended Canada's position by stating that his government pursued a policy of "bringing together the two pillars of the Western alliance – the United Kingdom and the United States – which would hold the Commonwealth together, including the three Asian members" (Carroll 2009: 39).

Canada was not incapable of employing some political-diplomatic gimmicks of its own. Shortly before the crisis came to a head, Canada had contracted with Israel for the sale of some F-86 Sabre jet aircrafts (having been requested to do by the United States). Canada had "reserved the right", however, to suspend the shipments of the fighter jets "if Israel committed aggression", according to a cabinet decision (Canada: Cabinet Conclusions: 18 Oct. 1956). After the hostilities had commenced with "the invasion of Egypt by Israel and the subsequent action of the United Kingdom and France", therefore, the Canadian Cabinet agreed that "all arms shipment to Israel be suspended". In an act of gamesmanship, the Cabinet also "suspended all arms shipments to the Arab countries". However, it was agreed that "the public statement on this subject [was] to refer only to the F-86 aircraft to Israel" (Canada: Cabinet Conclusions: 31 Oct. 1956).

Canada's Ambassador to the United States, Arnold Heeney, communicated to the government in Ottawa Eisenhower's message to the British and French Prime Ministers (before it became public) regarding the Franco-British ultimatum in which Eisenhower expressed dismay at "the 'great unwisdom' of taking the threatened 'drastic action' when the matter was still under consideration in the Security Council". The ambassador also conveyed the official feeling in Washington that "the failure of the UK and French Governments to consult or even to inform the USA Government in advance...has been a severe shock...and a very serious blow to the Western alliance" (Canada: DEA Heeney to Pearson: 31 Oct. 1956).

Furthermore, Canada's official position against the tripartite invasion of Egypt, and its eventual sponsorship of a UN peacekeeping force unleashed heated debates across Canada. The media and the opposition parties used UNEF "as a symbol of Canadian independence" or as a turning back on the "mother country". Thus, peacekeeping "became another symbolic battle for Canada's national identity" (McCullough 2016: 28–29).

Interestingly, Canada's lack of support for the British and French invasion of Egypt revealed two different approaches in the official government position.

Firstly, the Foreign Minister, Lester Pearson, was clearly sympathetic to the British. His immediate preoccupation was to help them save face and extricate themselves from the mess they had created. The *Calgary Herald* published an editorial on1 November 1956 lamenting Canada's failure to support Britain. The editorial, however, garnered the following comment, "Canada had finally severed her apron strings from Britain's imposed rule, and stayed out of a war that was not her business" (McCullough 2016: 115).

Secondly, the Prime Minister, Louis St. Laurent, was more forceful in his response. Affectionately nicknamed "Uncle Louis" in Canada, he had been scandalized by the larger powers of the world "who have all too frequently treated the Charter of the United Nations as an instrument with which to regiment smaller nations". He also said that "the era when the supermen of Europe could govern the whole world is coming pretty close to an end" (*Montreal Gazette* 1956: Editorial, quoted in: McCullough 2016: 29).

In short, Canada's strong position on the war in Suez combined criticism and concern, criticizing the "grave steps in Egypt", exhibiting "grave anxieties" at the "action of Israel" and rejecting the Anglo-French "justification" for intervention. Canada also expressed serious concern at the effects of the war on the United Nations, the Commonwealth, Anglo-American relations, and finally on NATO and the Western alliance in general.

References

al-Baghdadi, Abd al-Latif (1990): "Memoirs", in: Troen, Selwyn I.; Shemesh, Moshe (Eds.), *The Suez-Sinai Crisis 1956: Retrospective and Reappraisal* (London: Frank Cass): 333–356.

Anglo-Egyptian Treaty of Friendship and Alliance (1936): *League of Nations Treaty Series* (Geneva: League of Nations): 137, 6; (Article 9): 402–431.

Anglo-French *Ultimatum* to Egypt and Israel (30 October 1956).

Bandung Conference Declaration (1955): "*Ten-Point Official Declaration*" (25 April 1955).

Bar-On, Mordechai (1990): "The Influence of Political Considerations on Operational Planning in the Sinai", in: Troen, Selwyn I.; Shemesh, Moshe (Eds.): *The Suez-Sinai Crisis 1956: Retrospective and Reappraisal* (London: Frank Cass).

Beaufre, Andre (1969): *The Suez Expedition, 1956* (New York: Praeger).

Bobal, R. Thomas (2013): "A Puppet, Even Though He Probably Doesn't Know So: Racial Identity and the Eisenhower Administration's Encounter with Gamal Abdel Nasser and the Arab Nationalist Movement", in: *The International History Review*, 35, 5: 943–974; at: http://dx.doi.org/10.1080/07075332.2013.836117.

Bowie, Robert R. (1989): "Eisenhower, Dulles, and the Suez Crisis", in: Louis, W.R.; Owen, R. (Eds.): *Suez 1956: The Crisis and its Consequences* (Oxford: Clarendon Press): 200–201.

British Cabinet Document (1956): *Concealing the Anglo-French Connection with Israel* (CAB 134/1217, EC (56) 53 (25 September 1956).

British Political Directive to the Allied Commander-in-Chief (1956): CAB 134/1225, and CAB 134/815, D (T) C (56) 16th mtg (24 August 1956).

Brown, Derek (2001): "1956: Suez and the End of Empire", in: *The Guardian* (14 March 2001); at: https://www.theguardian.com/politics/2001/mar/14/past.education1.

Canada (1956): *Dispatch: London to Ottawa* (Norman Robertson), DCER (vol. 22, doc. 74) (27 July 1956).

Canada (1956): Department of External Affairs Correspondence (*Pearson to Robertson*), DEA-50134-40. Telegram M-1311 (30 October 1956).

Canada (1956): Department of External Affairs (*Eden to St. Laurent*), PCO-I-60-2 (a) (30 October 1956).

Canada (1956): Department of External Affairs (*St. Laurent to Eden*), PCO-1-60-2 (a) (31 October 1956).

Canada (1956): (Government) *Extract from Cabinet Conclusions*, PCO-105 (18 October 1956).

Canada (1956): Department of External Affairs (*Heeney to Pearson*), DEA-50134-40 (31 October 1956).

Canada (1956): Department of External Affairs (*Roberson to Pearson*), DEA-50134-40 (2 November 1956).

Canada (1956): Department of External Affairs (*Eden to St. Laurent*), PCO-I-60-2 (a) (6 November 1956).

Carroll, Michael K. (2009): *Pearson's Peacekeepers: Canada and the United Nations Emergency Force, 1956–67* (Vancouver: University of British Columbia Press).

Childers, Erskine B. (1962): *The Road to Suez: A Study of Western-Arab Relations* (London: MacGibbon & Kee).

Constantinople Convention (1888): *Convention Respecting the Free Navigation of the Suez Maritime Canal* (Constantinople: 29 October 1888).

Dayan, Moshe (1965): *Diary of the Sinai Campaign* (New York: Schocken Books).

Dooley, Howard J. (1989): "Great Britain's Last Battle in the Middle East: Notes on Cabinet Planning During the Suez Crisis of 1956", in: *The International Historical Review*, 11,3, (August): 486–517.

Dulles, John F. (1956): *Diplomatic Note to Sir Roger Makins*, PRO PREM 11/1018 (30 July 1956).

Eisenhower, Dwight (1956): "Letter to Prime Minister Anthony Eden", in: *Foreign Relations of the United States* (C), 1988, Eisenhower to Eden, document 35: 69–71 (31 July 1956).

Eisenhower, Dwight (1956): "Statement", in: US *National Security Council* (9 August 1956).

Everly, Steve (1996): "Truman OK'd Sabotage Plot", in: *The Kansas City Star* (Kansas City: 25 February 1996: A1).

Egyptian Chronicles Website (1956): "Jubilation as Anglo-French Troops Leave Port Said": (7); at: http://www.theegyptianchronicles.com/Article/1956Jubilation.html.

Eisenhower, Warner D. (1999): *The Third Temple's Holy of Holies: Israel's Nuclear Weapons* (Maxwell, Alabama: USAF).

Foreign Relations of the United States, 1952–1954, US National Security Council, The Near and Middle East, Statement of Policy, "Removal and Destruction of Oil Facilities, Equipment and Supplies in the Middle East", Volume IX, Part 1, Document 219 (Washington: Government Printing Office, 23 July 1954).

Foreign Relations of the United States, 1956, US Department of State, Memorandum of Conversation between Prime Minister Eden and Secretary of State Dulles in Washington, 31 January 1956, Document 54 (Washington: Government Printing Office, 1988).

Foreign Relations of the United States, 1956, US Department of State, Memorandum of Conversation between British Prime Minister Anthony Eden and US Secretary of State John Dulles, 10 Downing Street, London, 1 August 1956, 12:45 p.m., Document 42: 98–99. (Washington: Government Printing Office, 1988).

Gorst, Anthony; Johnman, Lewis (1977): *The Suez Crisis* (New York: Routledge).

Grove, Eric; Rohan, Sally (2000): "The Limits of Opposition: Admiral Earl Mountbatten of Burma, First Sea Lord and Chief of Naval Staff", in: Kelly, Saul; Gorst, Anthony (Eds.): *Whitehall and the Suez Crisis* (London: Frank Cass): 98–116.

Hahn, Peter L. (1991): *The United States, Great Britain, and Egypt, 1945–1956: Strategy and Diplomacy in the Early Cold War* (Chapel Hill, N.C.: University of North Carolina Press).

Haig, Alexander M. Jr (1966): *Military Intervention: A Case Study of Britain's Use of Force in the 1956 Suez Crisis* (Carlisle Barracks, PA: US Army War College).

Heikal, Mohamed H. (1986): *Cutting the Lion's Tail: Suez through Egyptian Eyes* (London: Andre Deutsch).

Heikal, Mohamed H. (1973): *The Cairo Documents* (New York: Doubleday).

Hilmy II, Amin (n.d.): *Unpublished Memoirs.*

Henkin, Yagil (2015): *The 1956 Suez War and the New World Order in the Middle East: Exodus in Reverse* (Lanham: Lexington Books).

Hewedy, Amin (1989): "Nasser and the Crisis of 1956", in: Louis, W.R.; Owen, R., (Eds.): *Suez 1956: The Crisis and its Consequences* (Oxford: Clarendon Press).

Hurewitz, J.C. (1989): "The Historical Context", in: Louis, W.R.; Owen, R. (Eds.): *Suez 1956: The Crisis and its Consequences* (Oxford: Clarendon Press): 22.

Johnson, Paul (1957): *The Suez War* (London: MacGibbon & Kee).

Kelly, Saul; Gorst, Anthony (Eds.) (2000): *Whitehall and the Suez Crisis* (London: Frank Cass).

Khalidi, Rashid (1989): "Consequences of the Suez Crisis in the Arab World", in: Louis, W.R.; Owen, R. (Eds.): *Suez 1956: The Crisis and its Consequences* (Oxford: Clarendon Press): 377–392.

Kyle, Keith (1989): "Britain and the Crisis, 1955–1956", in: Louis, W.R.; Owen, R. (Eds.): *Suez 1956: The Crisis and its Consequences* (Oxford: Clarendon Press): 120–121.

Kyle, Keith (2000): "The Mandarin's Mandarin: Sir Norman Brook, Secretary of the Cabinet", in: Kelly, Saul; Gorst, Anthony (Eds.): *Whitehall and the Suez Crisis* (London: Frank Cass): 70–75.

Logan, Donald (1986): "Narrative of Suez Meetings at Sèvres, 22–25 October 1956", Selwyn Lloyd Papers (SELO), Churchill College, Cambridge, 6/202, (24 October 1986), in: Gorst, Anthony; Johnman, Lewis (Eds.): *The Suez Crisis* (New York: Routledge).

Louis, W.R.; Owen, R. (Eds.) (1989): *Suez 1956: The Crisis and Its Consequences* (Oxford: Clarendon Press).

Love, Kennett (1969): *Suez: The Twice-Fought War* (New York: McGraw-Hill): 363.

Lucas, Scott (1990): "Redefining the Suez Collusion", in: *Middle Eastern Studies*, 26,1 (January): 88–89.

McCullough, Colin (2016): *Creating Canada's Peacekeeping Past* (Vancouver: Uinversity of British Columbia Press): 28–29.

Melman, Yossi (2006): "The IDF Archive Reveals Secret Files from Operation Kadesh", in: *Haaretz* (Israel) (8 October 2006).

Montreal Gazette (1956): "Editorial: Painful Departure" in: *Montreal Gazette* (28 November 1956): 8.

Mountbatten, Lord Louis (2013): *War History Facts* (27 February 2013).

Norton, William (2004): *Air War on the Edge – A History of the Israel Air Force and its Aircraft Since 1947* (London: Midland Publishing).

Nutting, Anthony (1967): *No End of a Lesson: The Story of Suez* (London: Constable): 34–35.

Patai, Raphael (1973): *The Arab Mind* (Tucson: Recovery Resources Press).

Rabin, Yitzhak; Avineri, Shlomo (1990): "The Sinai Campaign and the Limits of Power", in: Toren, S.I.; Shemesh, Moshe (Eds.): *The Suez-Sinai Crisis 1956: Retrospective and Reappraisal* (London: Frank Cass).

Republic of Egypt (1956): *White Paper: On the Nationalization of the Suez Canal Maritime Canal Company* (Cairo: Government Press, 12 August 1956).

Republic of Egypt (1954): *Anglo-Egyptian Agreement on the Suez Canal Base* (Cairo: State Information Service – 19 October 1954).

Robertson, Terence (1964): *Crisis: The Inside Story of the Suez Conspiracy* (Toronto: McClelland & Stewart): 73.

Sellers, J.A. (1990): "Military Lessons: The British Perspectives", in: Troen, S.; Shemesh, M. (Eds.), *The Suez-Sinai Crisis 1956: Prospective and Reappraisal* (London: Frank Cass): 17–53.

Smith, Adrian (2013): "Resignation of a First Sea Lord: Mountbatten and the 1956 Suez Crisis", in: *History*, 98, 329: 105–134.

Suez Canal Authority (1956): *The Suez Canal Company – Nationalization Law*, Government of Egypt, Decree Law No. 285 (July 1956).

Thornhill, Michael T. (2000): "Alternatives to Nasser: Humphrey Trevelyan, Ambassador to Egypt", in: Kelly, Saul and Gorst, Anthony (Eds.): *Whitehall and the Suez Crisis* (London: Frank Cass).

Tignor, Robert L. (1998): *Capitalism and Nationalism at the End of Empire: State and Business in Decolonizing Egypt, Nigeria, and Kenya, 1945–1962* (Princeton: Princeton University Press).

Tsiddon-Chatto, Yoash (1995): *By Day, By Night, Through Haze and Fog* (Tel Aviv: Ma'ariv Books).

UK Public Record Office (1956): *Conclusions: Cabinet Minutes* (19th), 128/30 (6 March 1956).

UK Parliament (1954): "Suez Canal Base (Anglo-Egyptian Agreement)", House of Commons debate (28 July 1954), in: *Hansard*, vol. 531, cc.495-7; at: https://api.parliament.uk/historic-hansard/commons/1954/jul/28/suez-canal-zone-base-anglo-egyptian-1.

UK Parliament (1954): Agreement Between the Government of the United Kingdom and Northern Island and the Egyptian Government Regarding the Suez Canal Case, Cmd. 9298 (19 October 1954).

UN Security Council Resolution (1951): *Freedom of Passage in the Suez Canal*, S/RES/2322 (1 Sept 1951).

UN Security Council Resolution (1956): *The Suez Question*, S/RES/118/3675 (13 October 1956).

US National Security Council Report (1948): "Removal and Demolition of Oil Facilities, Equipment and Supplies in the Middle East", NSC **26/1**, Top Secret (Washington: 19 August 1948).

US National Security Council Report (1948): "Removal and Demolition of Oil Facilities, Equipment and Supplies in the Middle East", NSC **26/2**, Top Secret (Washington: 30 December 1948).

Chapter 7
Imperial Rotation

Abstract The Suez conflict confirmed the ascendency of the US as the premier Western power in the Middle East. Britain was grappling with the inevitable realization that the sun would not continue to shine over the British imperial domain forever. Britain's special position in the Middle East was fading as the world was awakened to the new geopolitical realities in the region.

Keywords Imperial sunset · Limits of Empire · Perfidious Collusion · US ascendency · Eden's blunder · Delusions of Grandeur · End of Empire · Churchill's Dictum · Eisenhower Doctrine

7.1 The Old Guard: Suez and the End of Empire

The failure of the *Sèvres agreement* to achieve the intended objectives branded the imperial project in the region a historic failure. In his study of *The End of the British Empire*, John Darwin concludes that, contrary to the prevailing views at the time, definitive British decolonization, following the independence of India, was "already in train before the Suez Crisis" (Darwin 1991: 70–74). Similarly, in their introduction to *The Suez Crisis*, Gorst and Johnman contend that "while Suez may not have caused the major changes in Britain's status in the world, it both highlighted and accentuated developing trends. Suez on this reading is a catalyst rather than a harbinger of change" (Gorst/Johnman 1997: xi). Whether a catalyst or a harbinger, "There is little doubt that the end of the imperial era was greatly accelerated by the squalid little war in Egypt". (Brown 2001).

Photo 7.1 The Humiliation of the Old Empires following the 1956 Suez War. *Source* The Russian Kukryniksy Collective, 1958 (public domain)

Commenting on the fiftieth anniversary of the Suez War and Eden's role in it, the BBC World Affairs Correspondent, Paul Reynolds, noted in *The Times* that Eden "was the last prime minister to believe Britain was a great power and the first to confront a crisis which proved she was not" (Reynolds 2006). He added that Eden could not understand or accept that "the end of Empire was at hand". Earlier, Eden rejected and opposed Britain's membership of the continental European Common Market, claiming that "Our horizons are wider". Eden "did not understand that the world had changed". According to Reynolds, "Suez represented the end of a long phase of British imperial history" (Reynolds 2006).

Moshe Shemesh notes that the impact of Suez on the Middle East and the Western powers represented a turning point in the history of the region:

The West, and in particular Britain, did not grasp the significance to Egypt and to the Arab world of the decision to nationalize the Suez Canal...They neither appreciated nor understood the new political process taking place in the Arab world as a result of the revolution in Egypt and the emergence of Nasser...On the other hand, Nasser did not understand that he had very seriously wounded British Imperial pride...The gap between Eden and Nasser was historical. In this situation, armed confrontation was inevitable (Shemesh 1990: 159).

Shemesh creates a symmetry between Nasser and Eden where symmetry does not exist. The armed confrontation was perhaps inevitable. But it should be labelled for what it was, a premeditated aggression by one side against the other. There is no symmetry in aggression, particularly when the victim had no aggressive intent and was operating legally, peacefully and entirely within universally-acknowledged sovereign rights.

7.2   The Fishbone in the Gullet

There is no doubt that Suez evoked many responses among Britons. Recording the views of many leading British politicians and public figures, Russell Braddon notes that "the majority of Britons today are certain that Suez 1956 sounded the death knell of their country's imperial greatness". Braddon quotes British politician Enoch Powell lamenting the agreement for the withdrawal of British troops from the Suez Canal in 1954: "the Suez Canal, with its British garrison, was the keystone in the Imperial arch." By removing the keystone Powell believed "that arch was one day bound to collapse" (Braddon 1973: 172).

Lady Gaitskell was quoted as saying "Suez…did infinite harm." Lord Boothby offered "Suez was only the final shock in the disintegration of the Empire that began with World War II." Braddon captures Anthony Nutting's views, saying that Suez was both "the complete end of an era", and "the beginning of the end…it drained us of both cash and stamina". (Braddon 1973: 173). Braddon offered his own summing up comment on the fate of empire:

> No matter how they differ as to the event that precipitated the decline of imperialism they all agree that Suez caused its death. Whether Suez was a crisis, an adventure, a war, a turning point, a milestone or a non-event, it seems to have stuck like a *fishbone in the gullet of Britain's self-esteem.* (Braddon 1973: 175).

The renowned British historian, Corelli Barnett affirmed in 2007 that the Suez War "was the last thrash of empire…A last attempt by a British government to do the old imperial thing…It was a complete folly". Barnett also observed that Britain's Government at the time was suffering from "Delusions of Grandeur" (*folie de grandeur*). Britain's contraction of its overseas commitments after Suez is "the lasting legacy of our transient world hegemony". Barnett added that "Britain's economic standing did not and does not justify its claim to be a major power" (Barnett 26 October 2007).

In his 1990 assessment of the European imperial position in the Middle East following the Suez debacle, Julian Amery, one of the staunchest supporters of the imperial idea and among the main leaders of the "Suez Group" (British politicians who opposed the 1954 Anglo-Egyptian Treaty for abandoning control over the Suez Canal Base), highlighted two points, according to Amery. The first related to the imperial position in general:

> The failure of the British and French to succeed in what should have been a relatively minor effort of gunboat diplomacy was psychologically disastrous for their prestige in the rest of the Middle East and Africa...After Suez, both (Britain and France) felt themselves cut down to size (Amery 1990: 123).

The second point concerned France in particular. Amery asserted that the "failure at Suez led directly to the collapse of French policy in Algeria" (Amery 1990: 123).

7.3   British Leadership and the Suez War

Kelly and Gorst present an important examination of the decision-making and the various positions adopted along the road to Suez. Sir Norman Brook, the Cabinet Secretary and the Head of the Civil Service, thought that Anglo-French intervention in Egypt was 'folly'. Brook was also aware, they report, that Prime Minister Eden knowingly "lied to Parliament about Suez": Brook was convinced that Eden was determined to topple Nasser without declaring this as an aim of British policy. But the British cabinet was very sensitive to not having its own position as seen completely allied with Israel's (Kelly/Gorst 2000: 3)

The 'real' official "operational objectives" of the British Government for the Suez expedition were summed up by Sir Norman Brook as "to destroy the Egyptian Army, to bring down the Nasser Government and to control the Suez Canal". The objectives were to be followed by the formation and installation of a new "co-operative...successor Egyptian Government" which will disavow Nasser's policies" (Kyle 2000: 70).

The political directive issued to the Allied Commander, Sir Charles F. Keightley, was more precise with the aim of bringing about a new Egyptian Government that will "undertake the pacification of the country, order co-operation with Allied forces and be ready to negotiate an international regime for the Suez Canal" (British Cabinet 24 August 1956).

The British Cabinet's political directive to the British Commander for the Suez operation, Sir Charles F. Keightley, containing the "incriminating documentary evidence of collusion" concerning the anticipated role of Israel in the plan, stated that "...It is politically most important that...there should be no association or appearance of association between your forces and Israeli forces..." (British Cabinet, 25 September 1956). This directive was issued by the same cabinet which signed the Sèvres Agreement plotting collusion with Israel. Although "it fell to Brook to undertake the unpleasant task of destroying any incriminating documentary evidence of collusion", the sordid details eventually found their way into the public domain. The public 'official' reason for the Anglo-French intervention stated in the ultimatum to Egypt was a massive political miscalculation, an outright deception, and a colossal moral failure.

The by-now famous, or infamous, instruction issued by Prime Minister Eden to his junior Foreign Office Minister, Anthony Nutting, prior to the start of the Suez War, to destroy Nasser and his anti-colonial threat to the British Empire came after Nutting proposed a scheme simply to isolate and neutralize the Egyptian President.

Nutting's earlier 'enraged elephant' description of Eden's rising anger against Nasser betrayed Eden's furious state of mind. Moreover, Eden had a big pair of shoes to fill by replacing the Churchill war time leadership. Eden's desire to 'destroy' Nasser following his nationalization act became obvious in the exchange between Eden and his Foreign Minister. Eden revealed the extent to which he was prepared to go to end Nasser's leadership and the challenge the Egyptian president represented. Nasser became equally antagonistic towards Eden. The earlier genuine and 'warm' encounter between the two leaders in Cairo in 1955 evaporated after Eden feared Nasser's national liberation influence in the region. Clearly, the burden of defending a challenged imperial domain was a huge responsibility for any leader to bear. After the war, Nasser said in a reference to Eden that, "I can deal with someone I hate but not with someone I despise" (Heikal 1973).

Eden would have benefited from the advice given by the Labour leader, Hugh Gaitskell, who told the British Prime Minister in a letter on 10 August 1956:

Lest there should be any doubt in your mind about my personal attitude, let me say that I could not regard an armed attack on Egypt by ourselves and the French as justified by anything which Nasser has done so far or as consistent with the Charter of the United Nations. Nor, in my opinion, would such an attack be justified in order to impose a system of international control over the Canal – desirable though this is (Turner 2006: 231–232).

7.4   The New Masters: The American Ascendency

The new post-war reality as played out in the Middle East, was accurately captured by Simon Smith: "The events of 1956 are widely interpreted as marking a watershed in both Anglo-American relations and Britain's status as an imperial Power" (Smith 2010: 17).

Suez also confirmed that Britain's customary "special relationship with the USA" had lapsed. With a run on the British pound as the invasion failed, Britain needed a US-backed IMF loan. But the Americans refused to back the IMF loan to stave off the pressure on British currency. Eventually, the British pound was devalued. The British Empire had to toe the American line. It agreed to a ceasefire and eventual withdrawal from the Suez, which turned into a "complete fiasco" (Barnett/BBC, 24 July 2006).

Britain's closest ally "pulled the plug". Eisenhower's response was pointed and unequivocal, "no ceasefire, no loan". In a study of Eden's quandary, Stone-Lee stated: "The Suez invasion may have been a folly, but it was the pressure from the US Treasury on the pound which forced him to accept a ceasefire and proved the ultimate humiliation" (Stone-Lee/BBC, 21 July 2006).

With the US rebuking Britain for its "act of aggression" in Suez, the painful conclusion for Britain was that Suez "marked a turning point in Britain's retreat from empire and ensured that London would never again attempt global military action without first securing the acquiescence of Washington", according to Ian Gilmour, a future Conservative Cabinet Minister. In other words, there should be "no solo flying" by post-imperial Britain. The Anglo-American "special relationship" which had existed until the middle of the 1950s was apparently over. Future events would modify that dictum. Labour's Attlee "foresaw Britain's retreat from the Middle East in the 1940s". Even Churchill, the ultimate imperialist, conceded that "it was someone else's turn – America's – to do the heavy lifting" in the Middle East. Churchill, moreover, learned the lessons of the past concerning Britain's world role. He coined the dictum: "We must never get out of step with the Americans – never". For the British Empire, "Suez remains the moment of truth" (White, 12 July 2006).

When the British struck in October 1956, the Americans were furious and vociferous in their opposition to the British because the British did not toe the American line. The USA, the non-imperial/neo-imperial superpower, however, did not exhibit a principled position in defence of Egypt; rather, its position reflected American priorities in the evolving and volatile Middle East.

It is remarkable that as early as 1897, long before the US aspired to world supremacy, Theodore Roosevelt, then the Assistant Secretary of the US Navy, declared that the British Empire was showing definite signs of waning. He concluded that the US must strive to replace it and become the world's premier power (Roosevelt 1897).

The effects of the Suez War on the Western position in the Middle East was put succinctly: "The events of 1956 are widely interpreted as marking a watershed in both Anglo-American relations and Britain's status as an imperial power. Nevertheless, the aftermath of the crisis by no means led to Britain's subservience to Washington, nor a wholesale collapse of British imperial status...despite the reverse, Britain resolutely defended its dominant position" (Smith 2010: 17–18). Such an assessment is clearly contrary to the actual position of the British in the Middle East after Suez in relation to the new grounds established by the US.

While Britain's role in the Middle East until Suez constituted an asset to the US in the region, the British had their doubts about the suitability of the Americans to inherit the imperial mantle in the Middle East. The Head of the Eastern Department in the Foreign Office, D.H.M. Riches, rejected the notion that in the aftermath of Suez Britain should consult America over Middle East issues. In a non-diplomatic and somewhat patronizing tone, Riches wrote:

> The Americans are ignorant and impossible in colonial and semi-colonial situations in the Middle East...We should enlighten their ignorance but not give them responsibility until we are quite sure they will shoulder it (Riches 1957a).

Riches continued his criticism of the American role by writing to Britain's political resident in the Gulf, Bernard Burrows, stressing that:

> we should certainly not wish it to appear that we are being ousted in any respect by the Americans (Riches 1957b).

The indisputable rise of the US to a position of absolute Western dominance in the region was not late to follow.

For a while, Britain resisted US engagement in the Middle East, especially in the Gulf, Aden and Yemen, but eventually realities on the ground resulted in assertions of US leadership regardless of British reservations. America signalled its intent of getting engaged in the Middle East on a grand scale, despite some old imperial protestations. However, Nasser's antagonism towards the West had added a new American face to the older powers he was facing. The golden opportunity for Egyptian and Arab cooperation with the West, and primarily with the US, especially after Eisenhower's role during the Suez War, floundered on the rocks of the West's anti-Communist crusade, as well as its antipathy towards anti-colonial nationalist movements.

The Foreign Office wanted to avoid giving the impression that Britain was surrendering its Middle East position and influence to America. Fortified by this position, the new British Prime Minister, Harold Macmillan, announced during a summit meeting with US President Eisenhower in Bermuda in March 1957 that "despite recent events [the Suez War!]...the United Kingdom still has an important role to play in the Middle East" (Smith 2010: 9–40).

Dulles shocked the British in October 1956 with his questionable and self-serving dictum that "the US had no intention of complicity in colonialism" (Holland 1985: 197). Dulles added that "the British, together with the French, still possessed a nineteenth-century mentality", and that "the colonial regimes should be dismantled". Dulles saw the role of the US primarily as "to facilitate the shift from colonialism...in a constructive evolutionary way, and not through violent processes" (Louis 2006: 656).

The changing British and US roles on the world scene was captured by R.F. Holland (1985: 52–56). The post-war desire of the US to play a leading international role and to have access to British-controlled colonial regions and markets caused a potential clash between US and British interests. The British were prepared to accept a subordinate role during the War, but resented American designs to accord them a permanently inferior status.

Undoubtedly, Suez forced British politicians to rethink the limits of their imperial pretensions and to undercut unrealistic aspirations to continue a world role larger than their capacities could handle. For a time it seemed that the London-Washington axis was teetering and there was for a brief period in the second half of the 1950s a "congruency of aims between American strategy and anti-colonial nationalism", promising "limitless possibilities for the moulding of world affairs" (Holland 1985: 52). But that illusion was shattered quickly when the US realized that the colonial nationalists were not in the mood for a change of colonial lords. US hunger for resources and its desire to lay siege to the growing Soviet influence ensured the continuation of an anti-Western mood in the emerging Afro-Asian world.

In opposing the Suez war, the US was emphatically signalling to the embattled European empires that world power configurations were changing, and that the change must be in accordance with US priorities. "The United States cannot be expected to identify itself 100 per cent with the colonial powers", or to endorse obstacles in the face of Third World desires for "getting independence as rapidly and as fully as possible" (Robertson 1964: 139). British resistance to US ascendancy softened, however, when Soviet containment on one hand, and the protection of imperial interests on the other, converged.

The increasing ascendency of the USA in the Middle East resulted in the assertion of US Western leadership in the region regardless of British reservations. The US was signalling the intent of its serious engagement in the Middle East on a grand scale, despite old imperial protestations. A new, and more energetic face, flush with power, openly took charge of the Western interests in the region.

Contrary to the post-war changing realities, and as early as 1945, Britain was seriously occupied with maintaining a commanding position in the Middle East. British concerns centred on securing "oil resources", "sea and air communications", "an Imperial Strategic Reserve in a main administrative base", "defence commitments of dependent territories and states", and containing "Soviet ambitions in the region". For Britain, it was essential to "obtain general recognition of our predominant interest in the Middle East and of our right to play the leading role in the area" (Gorst/Johnman 1997: 10–11). In 1947, the Imperial Chiefs of Staff again reported to the British Cabinet that it was essential to have a "firm hold in the Middle East" (Gorst/Johnman 1997: 20–21). It is not a coincidence that Britain's realization of its weakened post-war position made support for the creation of an Israeli state in Palestine indispensable for the maintenance of the British colonial-imperial interests in the region.

Much has been said about the role played by the US in opposing the tripartite invasion of Egypt. The Eisenhower administration was widely believed to be furious at being deceived and not consulted, despite the common wish among the Western powers to see the end of the regime of President Nasser in Egypt. Was the anger a case of an emerging superpower no longer tolerating its junior partners' challenge to its own plans for the region? Or did its fury flow from a sense of its own prerogative to pull the strings financially, politically, and militarily for the entire Western alliance, including the old empires? In objecting to Suez, the USA was signalling that the fading empires should not to ignore the new power realities. The irony is that the US also had its own plans, utilizing Israel, to topple the regime of President Nasser and end his revolutionary challenge to Western colonial interests.

While the US was in the process of unofficially inheriting the colonial privileges in the Middle East, Secretary Dulles admitted on 2 October 1956 that, regarding the Suez dispute, there were "differences of approach" between the British and the American strategies arising from different "fundamental concepts" (Robertson 1964: 139). The dilemma was palpable when Eisenhower exclaimed, in defining the US position over the Suez War, "How could we possibly support Britain and France if in doing so we lose the whole Arab world?" (Hahn 1991: 232).

Nevertheless, according to Smith (2010), the United States' attempts to mould British policy in accordance with Cold War imperatives frequently foundered on British determination to pursue its own imperial interests. Cooperation occurred only when containment and imperial concerns converged. Even the post-Suez attempts of British Prime Minister Macmillan to "forge Anglo-American interdependence", based on the ideology of a "special relationship", became bogged down in the face of America's ascendency and Britain's imperial limitations (Smith 2010: 9–40).

The British lion, showing unmistakable signs of deterioration and decline, was giving way to the soaring American eagle, young, inexperienced but brash and self-confident.

Regardless of the increasingly controversial and competitive US and British positions in the Middle East after the Second World War, both countries were part of a larger Western front, even if they were temporarily at odds with each other. The US dispute with the ageing empires was simply about means not ends. Both wanted Nasser and the anti-colonial movement defeated. The US President told his Secretary of State that "we regard Nasser as an evil influence. While we share in general the British and French opinion of Nasser, we insisted that they chose a bad time and incident on which to launch corrective measures" (Speigel 1985: 86).

Based on the assessment of Sir Roger Makins, Britain's Ambassador to Washington, Saul Kelly concluded that if Eden had waited until after the US presidential election, the Americans would have helped him to bring Nasser down (Kelly 2000: 157–177). Certainly, years after the Suez Crisis ended, President Eisenhower admitted that "not supporting Eden over Suez had been his greatest foreign policy mistake" (Roberts 30 October 2006).

Eisenhower, though not in favour of Nasser's nationalization of the Canal Company, was able to correctly assess the legal and moral issues involved. But more importantly, he manoeuvered to allow the United States to exploit the crisis to its advantage. Staking America's position clearly against military intervention must have rubbed salt in the British and French wounds because it implied that, despite the conflict with the West, Nasser was viewed by Eisenhower as a true leader with whom he could do business. International Communism was not about to take hold in the sands of the Middle East; the only future threat to Egypt and the Arabs seemed to be coming from Israeli expansionist designs. It was Israel that had formally announced the annexation of the Sinai after its invasion in 1956. The Soviets were not seen by Nasser as a threat to Egypt, having helped condemn the invasion of Egypt.

The US Administration tried very forcefully to dissuade the British from resorting to military action against Egypt very early after the nationalization of the Canal Company. America was concerned about the possible repercussions of a precipitate British action for the entire Middle East and the Third World. Almost immediately after Nasser's nationalization act, the British government, at the behest of Prime Minister Eden, made a decision to go to war to reverse the Egyptian step. The US leadership reacted decisively, regardless of the consequences to US-British relations. Secretary Dulles informed the British Ambassador in Washington, Sir Roger Makins, on 30 July 1956 that "the United States Government would not be in sympathy with any attempt to make the Egyptian

Government rescind their nationalization decrees, or to regard them as inoperative, under the threat of force" (Dulles 30 July 1956).

In all the American warnings about the use of military action against Nasser, there was a common thread. The Americans were opposed to Nasser's unilateral move and they wanted him out of the picture. US policy-makers, however, alternated between describing Nasser's nationalization act as a threat and, on the other hand, as a legal move by a sovereign country. Their vacillation was in contrast to the intensity of the British response. Finally, when the British struck in October 1956, the Americans were furious and vociferous in their opposition to the British.

What is clear from the examination of Eden's position before the Suez War, as revealed from the Minutes of the British Cabinet, was that he did not subscribe to Churchill's position on the changed role of Britain, and he rejected the primacy of keeping in step with the Americans. Eden was operating under a different sort of preconceived notion when, on 4 October 1955 (almost a year before the war started), he said in Cabinet that:

> The British should not allow themselves to be restricted overmuch by reluctance to act without full American concurrence and support. We should frame our own policy in the light of our interests and get the Americans to support it to the extent we could induce them to do so. (Eden, 4 October 1955).

However, on 16 January 1957, a few months after the war ended, in a revealing and candid admission to his Cabinet Secretary, Sir Norman Brook, Eden wrote:

> I was wrong...in understanding the American – or rather the Ike-Dulles – hostility. I suppose they had always wanted us out of the Middle East, or at least Dulles did. I was warned of this years ago when the Republicans came in, but I did not believe it. Now I do (Eden 16 January 1957: 76).

The Suez war exposed the magnitude of the conspiracy to violate international law, as well as the colossal political-military blunder committed by the three countries. The stage was set for the new post-war international organization's involvement in the conflict between seriously weakened empires and a rebellious anti-colonial challenge, as well as the emergence of a new and powerful player in the affairs of the Middle East. The ensuing consequences changed the Middle East and the imperial powers irrevocably, and began a new chapter in UN involvement which prevented the military confrontation from escalating, but froze in place for over a decade the underlying causes of the conflict.

The competing interests and plans over the previous decade changed many pre-existing power assumptions and moved international conflict management to a new international platform in the autumn of 1956. The whole world became involved in untangling the epoch-changing Suez War. With the acceptance of the ceasefire following the high drama in New York and the resulting UN General Assembly resolutions, in November 1956 the Middle East entered a new phase in politics and a new experiment in peacekeeping with far-reaching effects for the Middle East and for the nature of international conflict management, pitting the prerogatives of national sovereignty and consent in direct contestation with the need for international intervention to control conflicts.

7.5   The Eisenhower Doctrine (January 1957)

The United States' involvement in, and impact on, the Middle East had begun long before Suez. After World War I, the US ignored the pleas of the Arabs for independence at Versailles. The recommendations of the King-Crane Commission on Palestine were concealed and ignored. The US played a vital role in ensuring the passage of the UN Palestine Partition Resolution in 1947. In 1948–49 many US battle-hardened demobilized servicemen were allowed to participate in the Arab-Israeli war on the side of the new Israeli state.

The US intervened to ensure Israel's control of the Negev in 1949. In 1950, the US was one of the powers behind the Tripartite Declaration, which, in effect, froze the military situation in the Middle East in favour of Israel. For years, following World War II, Egypt was subjected to a relentless campaign to join a Western-led Middle East alliance. For years, the British secured American support for their position on maintaining control over the Suez Canal Base, despite Egyptian attempts to dislodge them.

The US (with British help) intervened to overthrow Prime Minister Mohammad Mosaddegh of Iran in 1953 because he had nationalized his country's foreign-owned oil industry. From 1952 until 1955 the US turned down Egypt's repeated requests for arms to defend itself against continued Israeli aggression. The Baghdad Pact was set up with American backing to counter Nasser's nationalist anti-colonial appeal. Financing for the High Dam project in Egypt was sabotaged and then cancelled by the US and Britain in 1956. Western pressures against Nasser's Egypt in 1955–56 aimed at overthrowing the Egyptian leader (Operations Omega I and II).

The US Administration had been (and still is) providing massive political, economic, and military support to Israel, maintaining in the process decided superiority against the combined Arab countries. In the spring of 1956, the US approved "Operation Stockpile" to store weapons in the Mediterranean and Europe for use against any aggressor in the Arab-Israeli dispute. The American plan was not implemented when Israel attacked Egypt later the same year. Enunciation of the Eisenhower Doctrine in 1957 marked the latest attempt by the US to gain some measure of control in the Middle East in the face of a militant anti-colonial and anti-Western tide. The post-Suez US position has to be viewed in light of the history of American engagement in the Middle East.

The USA, the non-imperial/new-imperial superpower, did not exhibit a principled position in defence of Egypt, a country under attack and facing treacherous aggression; rather, its position reflected American priorities, not the lofty principles of international law or the UN Charter. In the aftermath of the disastrous Suez failure, the US unilaterally moved to assert its design for the Middle East. Barely a few days after the British and the French withdrew their forces from Egypt on 22 December 1956, the US President addressed a joint session of the US Congress on 5 January 1957 to announce what became known as the *Eisenhower Doctrine* (actually authored by Secretary Dulles):

Just recently there have been hostilities involving Western European nations that once exercised much influence in the area. Also the relatively large attack by Israel in October has intensified the basic differences between that nation and its Arab neighbors. All this instability has been heightened and, at times, manipulated by International Communism (Eisenhower January 1957).

This document announcing the new American Doctrine for US involvement in the Middle East could be considered the first misstep by the Eisenhower Administration in dealing with the post-Suez Arab world. Instead of cultivating its role in opposing the 'Tripartite Aggression', *the US went back to the anti-Communist crusade* pursued without let-up. American policy-makers could not comprehend that the Arabs were not about to adopt the Marxist Manifesto and join the Communist International. Repeatedly, the Arabs' avowed objectives were the end of colonialism and the confrontation with Israel. The US move amounted to a colossal missed opportunity to establish positive lines of communication and a more cooperative approach involving the Arab world.

The US was serving notice that it was formally taking over from the European empires the responsibility for defending Western strategic interests in the vital geostrategic region of the Middle East. The doctrine's main thrust was aimed at the Soviet Union. It stated that at the President's discretion the USA could "use armed forces" on behalf of any Middle Eastern state being threatened by armed aggression, in order "to secure and protect the territorial integrity and political independence of such nations, requesting such aid against armed aggression from any nation controlled by international communism".

The wording of the Doctrine made it clear that the target was not just the Communist Eastern Bloc, but countries and leaderships in the Middle East 'controlled' by Communism. The unmistakable inference was that the Doctrine was targeting Nasser's leadership and Egypt's role in the anti-colonial agitation (Eisenhower January 1957). The dust had barely settled over the Suez War when the US Administration trained its guns on Nasser's leadership, taking over the mantle of confronting the anti-colonial movement in the Middle East. The Eisenhower Doctrine immediately became the new flash-point in Middle Eastern politics as Nasser strongly opposed the new Western thrust. Nasser was not prepared to replace the British and French occupiers with a new American hegemony.

This newly proclaimed Eisenhower Doctrine (also known as "Filling the Vacuum") was explained and defended by Secretary Dulles when he said:

There is a highly dangerous situation in the Middle East, and there is today a [vacuum of power] as a result of the recent British-French action, so that if we do not find some way in which to put our support back of the free nations of the area to reassure them and give them strength, then that critical area will almost certainly be taken over by Soviet Communism (Dulles: Statement to Congress 1957).

In Schulzinger's evaluation, by 1957 the Eisenhower Government was attempting to apply what it believed were the three principal lessons of Suez: first, the United States had greater influence in the Middle East than any other outside power; second, Communism was the major problem of the Arab Middle East; third,

Gamal Abdel Nasser of Egypt was an agent of the Soviet Union. The results failed to confirm these propositions (Schulzinger 1990: 251).

The Egyptian leadership was incensed at the unveiling of the Eisenhower/ Vacuum Doctrine, ostensibly proclaimed to repel Communist-supported invasion, when the only invaders were British, French, and Israeli. In fact, since the late 1940s and early 1950s Britain and then the US tried to create an anti-Communist bloc in the Middle East. Ignoring the danger of the Israeli presence to the Arabs, their efforts failed in the face of the surging anti-colonial tide.

Nasser led the charge against the new Western attempt to gain traction in the region following the disastrous Suez War. He remained steadfast, as he had done against the previous overt and covert Western attempts to co-opt him, and failing that to bring about his downfall. American foreign-policy-makers – like their previous European imperial cousins – had consistently misread the Arab mood and had undermined Arab aspirations since World War I. The drive for Arab independence was viewed as purely anti-Western in nature instead of being correctly assessed as anti-colonial.

The Americans wasted a golden opportunity to develop a new partnership with the Arabs, but their Cold War phobia with its strategic calculations prevailed, and their own imperial ambitions took hold. The Americans were also subjected to a domestic pro-Israel lobby directed against the Egyptian leadership (Mearsheimer/ Walt 2007). Israel was increasingly viewed by the Arab countries as the West's proxy. In this reading, Israel was not just a country engaged in territorial disputes, but it had another function to perform as the West's willing and able ally.

Israel was deliberately utilized by the Western powers to keep the restive and rising Arab world at bay. The new American Doctrine, which totally ignored Arab concerns about the Israeli threat, led Richard Miller to conclude that "the Doctrine was not worth the price it cost the United States in goodwill among Middle East countries" (Miller 1961: 117).

In the face of the emergence of Nasser as a major player threatening the established order, the Eisenhower Doctrine also sought, in Schulzinger's view, "to project the United States as the savior of conservative Arabs from Nasserism". However, US military intervention in Lebanon in 1958 "placed the United States in the eyes of the Arabs in a position hardly distinguishable from that which the British had just been forced to relinquish" (Schulzinger 1990: 251–265). The US dual objective of confronting perceived growing Soviet influence in the region and defending the old monarchical Middle Eastern regimes against an invigorated and anti-colonial Nasserist republican tide created a major flash point in US-Arab relations. The earlier attempts before Suez to include the Middle East in a string of defence pacts against the Soviet Union "had been replaced by a doctrine which projected the international hunt for communists into Arab politics" (Spiegel 1985: 86).

The overriding concern of the Arab countries at that time was the role played by Israel in advancing the colonial agenda, and not the fear of Soviet penetration. Alfred Atherton, a veteran American diplomat of the Middle East, affirmed years after the Suez debacle that the Eisenhower Administration "failed to understand" the depth of the resurgent Arab nationalist movement, the wounded Arab rejection of Israel, and the sense of deep Arab humiliation and resentment at their military and political weakness, all of which Nasser was able to articulate. After the Suez Crisis the US emerged in the eyes of the Arabs as a power that intended to continue the British colonial policy of domination, albeit with an American face and accent. The Eisenhower Doctrine was viewed in much of the Middle East as "an effort to ensnare the Arabs in a neo-colonialist embrace". The United States' popularity in the region in the immediate aftermath of the war tumbled and almost evaporated in Arab eyes (Atherton 1990: 266–273).

Israel's reaction to the Eisenhower Doctrine was non-committal. Some Israeli officials saw value in it if Israel was included in the policy objectives of the doctrine. Israeli diplomat Abba Eban mockingly called it the "Doctrine of the Immaculate Assumption" (Spiegel 1985: 65), based on the unlikely idea that the Arab States would be willing to adopt anti-Communism in place of anti-Zionism.

References

Amery, Julian (1990): "The Suez Group: A Retrospective on Suez", in: Troen, S.; Shemesh, M. (Eds.): *The Suez-Sinai Crisis 1956: Retrospective and Reappraisal* (London: Frank Cass): 110–126.

Atherton, Alfred (1990): "The United States and the Suez Crisis: The Uses and Limits of Diplomacy", in: Troen, S. and Shemesh, M. (Eds.): *The Suez-Sinai Crisis 1956: Retrospective and Reappraisal* (London: Frank Cass): 266–273.

Barnett, Corelli (2006): As quoted in Reynolds, Paul "*Suez: End of Empire*", (London: BBC News Website (24 July 2006); at: http://news.bbc.co.uk/2/hi/middle_east/5199392.stm.

Barnett, Corelli (2007): *Britain's Delusions of Grandeur*. Seminar at Churchill College, Cambridge, quoted in: Reynolds, Paul "Britain's Delusions of Grandeur" (London: BBC News Website (26 October 2007); at: http://news.bbc.co.uk/2/hi/americas/7063374.stm.

Braddon, Russell (1973): *Suez: Splitting of a Nation* (London: Collins).

British Cabinet Document (1956a): *Concealing the Anglo-French Connection with Israel,* (CAB 134/1217, EC (56) 53 (25 September 1956).

British Cabinet Document (1956b): *Political Directive to the Allied Commander-in-Chief,* (CAB 134/1225, and CAB 134/815, D (T) C (56) 16th mtg (24 August 1956).

Brown, Derek (2001): "1956: Suez and the End of Empire", in: *The Guardian* (14 March 2001); at: https://www.theguardian.com/politics/2001/mar/14/past.education1.

Darwin, John (1991): *The End of the British Empire: The Historical Debate* (London: Blackwell).

Dulles, John F. (1956): *Diplomatic Note to Sir Roger Makins*, in: PRO PREM 11/1018 (30 July 1956).

Dulles, John F. (1957): *Statement*. US Senate Committee on Foreign Relations, Vol. IX, 85th Congress, 1st Sess., 1957.

Eden, Anthony (1955): *British Cabinet Minutes*, 34, (55) 8 (4 October 1955).

Eden, Anthony (1957): "Brook Papers: Eden to Brook, 16 January 1957", cited in: Kyle, Keith, "The Mandarins' Mandarin: Sir Norman Brook, Secretary of the Cabinet", in; Kelly, S.; Gorst, A.: *Whitehall and the Suez Crisis* (London: Frank Cass): 76.

Eisenhower, Dwight (1957): *Address to a Joint Session of Congress*, United States Department of State, *United States Policy in the Middle East*. Washington, DC. (5 January 1957).

Gorst, Anthony; Johnman, Lewis (1997): "Introduction", in: *The Suez Crisis* (London: Routledge).

Hahn, Peter L. (1991): *The United States, Great Britain, and Egypt, 1945–1956: Strategy and Diplomacy in the Early Cold War* (Chapel Hill, N.C.: University of North Carolina Press).

Heikal, Mohamed H. (1973): *The Cairo Documents* (New York: Doubleday).

Holland, R.F. (1985): *European Decolonization 1918–1981: An Introductory Survey* (London: McMillan).

Kelly, Saul (2000): "Transatlantic Diplomat: Sir Roger Makins, Ambassador to Washington and Joint Permanent Secretary to the Treasury", in: Kelly, Saul; Gorst, Anthony (Eds.): *Whitehall and the Suez Crisis* (Portland: Frank Cass): 157–177.

Kyle, Keith (2000): "The Mandarin's Mandarin: Sir Norman Brook, Secretary of the Cabinet", in: Kelly, S.; Gorst, A. (Eds.): *Whitehall and the Suez Crisis* (London: Frank Cass): 64–71.

Louis, W. Roger (2006): *The End of British Imperialism: The Scramble for Empire, Suez and Decolonization* (London: MacMillan).

Mearsheimer, John J.; Walt, Stephen M. (2007): *The Israel Lobby and US Foreign Policy* (Toronto: Viking Canada).

Miller, Richard I. (1961): *Dag Hammarskjold and Crisis Diplomacy* (Washington DC: Oceana Publications).

Nutting, Anthony (1967): *No End of a Lesson: The Story of Suez* (London: Constable): 34–35.

Petersen, Tore T. (Ed.) (2010): *Challenging Retrenchment: The United States, Great Brutan and the Middle East, 1950–1980* (Trondheim, Norway: Tapir Academic Press).

Reynolds, Paul (2006): "Suez: End of Empire", in: *BBC News* and *The Times* (24 July 2006); at: http://news.bbc.co.uk/2/hi/middleeast/5199392.stm.

Riches, D.H.M. (1957a): *Minutes*, in: "TNA, FO 371/126910/EA 10345/1", UK Foreign Office, (London: 25 January 1957), in: Smith, Simon C. "Anglo-American Relations and the End of Empire in the Far East the Persian Gulf", published in: Petersen, Tore T. (Ed.): *Challenging Retrenchment: The United States, Great Britain and the Middle East, 1950–1980* (Trondheim, Norway: Tapir Academic Press) (2010).

Riches, D.H.M. (1957b): *Letter from Riches to Burrows*, in: "TNA, FO 371/126910/EA 10345/1", UK Foreign Office, (London: 8 February 1957), in: Smith, Simon C. "Anglo-American Relations and the End of Empire in the Far East the Persian Gulf", published in: Petersen, Tore T. (Ed.): *Challenging Retrenchment: The United States, Great Britain and the Middle East, 1950–1980* (Trondheim, Norway: Tapir Academic Press) (2010).

Roberts, Andrew (2006): "Suez: The Betrayal of Eden", in: *BBC News Website* (30 October 2006); at: http://news.bbc.co.uk/2/hi/middle_east/6085264.stm.

Robertson, Terence (1964): *Crisis: The Inside Story of the Suez Conspiracy* (Toronto: McClelland & Stewart).

Roosevelt, Theodore (2014): "1897 Address to the Naval War College", in: *"The Roosevelts"*, a *PBS Documentary,* aired (14 September 2014).

Schulzinger, Robert D. (1990): "The Impact of Suez on United States Middle East Policy, 1957–1958", in: Troen, S. and M. Shemesh, M. (Eds.): *The Suez-Sinai Crisis 1956: Retrospective and Reappraisal* (London: Frank Cass): 251–265.

Shemesh, Moshe (1990): "Egypt: From Military Defeat to Political Victory", in: Troen, S. and Shemesh, M. (Eds.): *The Suez-Sinai Crisis 1956: Prospective and Reappraisal* (London: Frank Cass): 159.

Smith, Simon C. (2010): "Anglo-American Relations and the End of Empire in the Far East the Persian Gulf, 1848–1971", in: Petersen, Tore T. (Ed.): *Challenging Retrenchment: The United States, Great Britain and the Middle East, 1950–1980* (Trondheim, Norway: Tapir Academic Press): 9–40.

Spiegel, Steven L. (1985): *The Other Arab-Israeli Conflict: Making America's Mideast Policy from Truman to Reagan* (Chicago: University of Chicago Press).

Stone-Lee, Ollie. (2006): "Eden: A Man Under Strain", in: *BBC News Website* (21 July 2006); at: http://news.bbc.co.uk/2/hi/uk_news/politics/5193202.stm, US Liberty also available: https://www.rallypoint.com/deployments/israel/shared-links/uss-liberty-dead-in-the-water-bbc-documentary-2002–4?loc=similar_main&pos=4&type=qrc.

Turner, Barry (2006): *Suez 1956, The World's First War for Oil* (London: Hodder & Stoughton): 231–232.

White, Michael (2006): "How Suez Debacle Proved the Tipping Point in Final Retreat From Empire", in: *The Guardian* (12 July 2006).

Chapter 8
UNEF (1956): Deployment

Abstract The Suez War rallied most nations against gun-boat diplomacy and military aggression, and ushered in a new expanding role for the UN in resolving international disputes. The confrontation in Suez in October and November 1956 was about to enter a new phase with the involvement of the United Nations, and in the process a new international intervention regime would be established for conflict control. The crucial role played by the UN in this crisis set in motion a new willingness to censure international aggression, and a new approach to defusing a serious conflict endangering international peace and security. In this new uncharted territory a majority vote in the UN General assembly let the international community impose its will without the adoption of Security Council Chapter VII enforcement measures, while at the same time upholding the principles of the UN Charter against aggression and the violation of international law. Sovereign consent played a major part in the negotiation to establish UNEF, and later on in its termination. The success and failure of UNEF became a template for peace intervention in the post-war period. The UNEF experience helped to shape future peace operations with a more comprehensive approach to conflict resolution.

Keywords Gun-Boat Diplomacy · UN Reaction · Hammarskjold's Declaration of Conscience · Security Council paralysis · General Assembly in charge · Uniting for Peace · Chapter VI · Cold War · Eisenhower · Lester Pearson · Good Faith Agreement · Status of Forces Agreement · UNEF born · Egyptian Declaration

8.1 A New International Phase for the Suez

The situation in Suez was about to enter a new phase with the involvement of the United Nations, and in the process a new international intervention regime would be established for conflict resolution. The crucial role played by the UN in this crisis set in motion a new willingness to censure international aggression, and a new approach to defusing a serious conflict endangering international peace and security. In this new uncharted territory a majority vote in the UN General assembly let

H. Hilmy, *Decolonization, Sovereignty, and Peacekeeping*,
https://doi.org/10.1007/978-3-030-57624-0_8

the international community impose its will without resorting to the Chapter VII Security Council enforcement measures, while at the same time upholding the principles of the UN Charter against aggression and the violation of international law.

The agreement to establish the United Nations Emergency Force (UNEF) and its eventual birth was a problematic and very complex process. A stillbirth was not far from reality at many stages of the tortured negotiation process. Multiple disputes revolved around almost every aspect of the formation of this new international force. The international political struggle around the concept of creating a UN force to replace the occupying forces in Egypt and the Gaza Strip was challenging. Its mandate, composition, name, uniform, and legal status, as well as the sovereign consent of the host country or countries (Israel refused consent), were all sources of serious wrangling and contestation.

Undoubtedly, Egypt needed international intervention to help it redress the illegal tripartite invasion and its aftermath. But Egypt was equally concerned that such international/UN help should not occur at the price of diminishing Egypt's sovereignty or territorial integrity, or of creating new conditions or privileges not previously enjoyed by the aggressors in violation of or undermining the status quo ante.

The birth of UNEF occurred when the Egyptian armed forces – after suffering grievous harm in the Sinai and battered military infrastructure elsewhere – were trying to regroup, contain the Anglo-French presence in Port Said, and bring about Israeli withdrawal to the Armistice Demarcation Lines in place on 29 October 1956. Egypt's limited military capacity, the overwhelming superiority of the forces arrayed against it, and the intricate pressures of the raging Cold War all combined to limit Egypt's options.

On the other side of the ledger, Egyptian resistance was resolute (i.e. the anticipated collapse of the popular will hoped for by the invaders did not materialize), and there was overwhelming support in the UN General Assembly and among most of the developing and non-aligned countries, not to mention outraged world public opinion (even in Britain).

After securing the 'final' evacuation of the British troops in the Suez Canal base on 18 June 1956 (only a few months before the start of the Suez War), Egypt was not prepared to compromise on having new forces of occupation returning to the country, or on seeing its control over its territory violated, and certainly not on having its sovereign rights handed over to an international regime.

The situation facing the world and its global organization in the autumn of 1956 was without precedent. The UN-sponsored action in Korea was considered a collective military intervention relying on unity in the Western ranks, and it was made possible only by Soviet abstention in the Security Council. In the Middle East, Western armies other than the British and French were not getting ready to intervene, the NATO alliance itself was fractured, and the two superpowers were on the same side of the conflict.

The possibilities considered by the United Nations in dealing with the crisis in the Middle East included: first, collective sanctions and the use of collective military forces; second, conciliation through negotiation and mediation; and third, some combination of the two. Yet these three options could not be relied upon to bring about a resolution to the conflict in a timely fashion consistent with the principles of the UN Charter.

8.2   The Miraculous Birth

Egypt was reeling under relentless bombardment across the country, but just before the adoption of the ceasefire resolution at the UN in November 1956, General Hilmy (n.d.) relates in his memoirs that he was contacted at his advance post south of Port Said, preparing for an attack on forward British positions, with an urgent request to go to Cairo for an immediate meeting with the President:

> Upon arrival in Cairo, I was ushered into Nasser's office with my clothes and army boots still covered with dry mud. After initially listening to my assessment of the military situation, Nasser suddenly said: "The war is over. There will be no attacks. There is a ceasefire. Forces from the United Nations will be sent to the area. I called you because I want you to be responsible for them – you will see the cables between Dr Fawzi [Egypt's Foreign Minister] and Dag Hammarskjold [UN Secretary-General] in this respect. Dr Fawzi is on his way here now. You will meet him with me also."

The undeclared power struggle between Nasser and Amer was again confirmed by the fact that Egypt's War Minister was not aware of the details of the impending ceasefire given to Hilmy by Nasser. "Before meeting Nasser," Hilmy stated, "Amer had told me to report to him what it was the President wanted me for." Later on, with the beginning of the arrival of the UNEF contingents, Nasser telephoned Hilmy in Abu Sweir to enquire about the weaponry brought by the UN forces. He ended the call by saying, "Call me direct by phone or come to my office or house anytime you feel it is important." Hilmy observed that, "Once again I felt strange that though I was a general in the Armed Forces, and as such under the command of General H. Amer, yet I was given free access to the President, bypassing Amer."

At the international level, charged accusations and counter-accusations filled the halls of the United Nations with the realization of the scope of the military operation against Egypt. The Security Council was paralysed because of the Anglo-French veto. There was no clear alternative except to involve the General Assembly in taking charge of the situation. The crisis was a test for the UN in its ability to deal with international crisis management. As expected, the Third World supported Egypt, and so did the Soviet bloc. The real surprise was the position of the United States and the leadership of President Eisenhower. The agreement of the US and USSR to take a firm stand against the invasion of Egypt was a huge factor in stopping the aggression in its tracks. The Secretary-General of the United Nations, Dag Hammarskjold, had a major influence on the events by placing his job on the line and demanding that all member states, regardless of their status, must respect the UN Charter and refrain from violating its principles.

In a nutshell, during this incendiary conflict, the many possibilities considered by the United Nations in dealing with the crisis in the Middle East included: sanctions, military force, conciliation. Yet these three options could not be relied upon to bring about an immediate resolution to the conflict.

8.3   The Role of Dag Hammarskjold, UN Secretary-General

Hammarskjold was shaken by the brazen attack against Egypt undertaken in flagrant violation of the UN Charter, despite the agreed six-point Council resolution that had been reached on 13 October 1956. He urgently addressed the UN Security Council on 31 October 1956. In his address he emphasized that the duty of the Secretary-General of the UN is to uphold the principles of the UN Charter, which all member nations are pledged to respect. Therefore, he said he would exercise the right to censure any violation of the Charter. If the member states did not agree with his interpretation of his duties as the Secretary-General, he was ready to resign.

Photo 8.1   UN Secretary-General Dag Hammarskjold. *Source* The UN.org

In the address, entitled "*Declaration of Conscience*", Hammarskjold (31 October 1956) outlined the principles under which he could continue to serve as the UN Secretary-General:

The Principles of the Charter are, by far, greater than the Organization in which they are embodied, and the aims which they are to safeguard are holier than the policies of any single nation or people. As a servant of the Organization, the Secretary-General has the duty to maintain his usefulness by avoiding public stands on conflicts between Member Nations unless and until such an action might help to resolve the conflict. However, the discretion and impartiality required of the Secretary-General may not degenerate into a policy of expedience. He must also be a servant of the principles of the Charter, and its aims must ultimately determine what for him is right and wrong. For that he must stand. A Secretary-General cannot serve on any other assumption than that within the necessary limits of human frailty and honest differences of opinion – all Member Nations honour their pledge to observe all Articles of the Charter. Were the Members to consider that another view of the duties of the Secretary-General than the one here stated would better serve the interests of the Organization, it is their right to act accordingly. (Hammarskjold, 31 October 1956)

Although Hammarskjold thought the Secretary-General had to be impartial and had to retain the confidence and trust of the member nations, he nevertheless held that he had a "political role" to play in international affairs and that Article 99 of the UN Charter provided a 'legal basis' for such a capacity. Hammarskjold actively developed this role during the Suez Crisis while defending UN principles. His foray into high stakes political negotiations is a clear testimony to his activist-internationalist approach.

Brian Urquhart, a former Under-Secretary-General of the United Nations, described Hammarskjold's post-1957 period as even more 'preventive' than 'corrective', as became clear in Lebanon, Jordan and Tunisia (Urquhart 1972). In a memorial lecture at Uppsala University, Urquhart stated that Hammarskjold hoped that the United Nations "would gradually be transformed from an *institutional* mechanism into a *constitutional* instrument recognized and respected by all nations". Urquhart, who worked closely with Hammarskjold, considered the Secretary-General a visionary and a pioneer in his own right (Urquhart 1987: 7). As Harry Kreisler notes, "Hammarskjold was the person who made the UN an active peace organization rather than the diplomatic, bureaucratic outfit it had started as. He was the person who developed peacekeeping, and he became the world's chief negotiator of really difficult problems" (Kreisler 1996: 5).

Undoubtedly, the role played by the Secretary-General in the crisis was pivotal in moving the events in the direction they took. His integrity and the force of his personality, coupled with his impeccable neutral pedigree, ensured that he was capable of confronting all sides (as he did) with the need to respect the UN Charter and international legality. His skills as an international and diplomatic negotiator who knew when to compromise and when to apply pressure were indispensable in defusing the crisis and in reaching an agreement to speedily interpose UN troops between the warring parties, leading to the successful withdrawal of the invading troops from Egyptian soil.

Despite Hammarskjold's unmatched qualities and dedication, his formula for deploying UNEF in the Middle East eventually foundered in the face of determined contestation of the concept of sovereign consent. Moreover, the Arab-Israeli conflict was left to fester without serious attempts to bring the parties to a just and equitable settlement, despite the opportunity offered by the presence of UNEF. The

Secretary-General had to shoulder some of the blame for not persisting in pushing the parties – under international supervision – towards an accommodation. In fairness, however, other factors were present to prevent an Arab-Israeli rapprochement.

But the question must be asked: what was the role of UNEF and why did this international force stay in place after accomplishing its initial responsibilities of bringing about a ceasefire and ensuring withdrawal of the invasion forces in accordance with UN resolutions? UNEF could have been withdrawn in March 1957 without changing the profile of the Arab-Israeli confrontation at all. There is no doubt that the presence of UNEF was instrumental, at least psychologically and politically, in preventing continued hostilities. But the fact also remains that, without any existing mechanism to prevent a return to armed confrontation, hostilities could be and were renewed almost immediately when political circumstances changed. Was UNEF's prolonged deployment, then, a waste of time, resources and the opportunity to achieve a lasting peace? Although the deployment bought a decade of 'non-war', unfortunately the qualified answer must be, on balance, in the affirmative.

Photo 8.2 Lester Pearson of Canada during the 1956 Suez Crisis. *Source* UN Photo # 101490

The West would not contemplate using military force against prominent members of NATO, and the Third World could not tolerate the continuation of old-style colonialism. In this situation, Canada's Lester Pearson advocated a course, through diplomatic channels, to bring about a cessation of hostilities on terms acceptable to all parties through the immediate involvement of the UN in the process. Remarkably, Pearson proposed the creation of a UN Force "large enough to keep those borders at peace while a political settlement is being worked out – a truly international peace and police force" (Pearson/UN, November 1956). Such a proposal assumed that the invading forces would withdraw to the borders, and that a peace mechanism would be implemented to bring the *original conflict* to a close. This was indeed a visionary position, which, unfortunately, was only partially implemented, for a resolution to the original conflict was deemed unrealizable at the time and ignored.

Pearson almost disqualified himself as a serious peacemaker by abstaining from voting against the tripartite invasion, condemned by most of the world, betraying an unspoken support for the aggressors. However, in justification of this decision he said, "By abstaining we keep our freedom to put forward our own proposal for a United Nations force" (Robertson 1964: 189). In fact, however, Pearson's vision almost floundered before it even began. The Canadian statesman envisioned a plan whereby the British and French invading forces in Egypt would be allowed to remain in place but be designated within the United Nations framework as an intervention force performing "police action" on behalf of the UN, a plan mirroring the Anglo-French declaration. Pearson's intent was undoubtedly, as Terrence Robertson concludes, "to extricate Britain and France from their difficult situation, to save their face, and to cement the crack in their relations with the United States" (Zeidan 1976: 32). Terrence Robertson also confirmed Pearson's interest in "helping Britain and France … to make it possible for them to withdraw with as little loss of face as possible". But the UN General Assembly "was in a mood to punish … flagrant aggression" (Robertson 1964: 188).

Pearson's proposal was a non-starter as far as Egypt was concerned. To reward the invading armies by allowing them to remain at 'the scene of the crime' and then appoint them to function as a police force entrusted with upholding international law was an incredible insult to the victim and completely out of the question.

"Mr. Pearson abandoned this idea very soon after reaching the United Nations headquarters and sampling the mood of anger, alarm, and fright which, while strongest among the Afro-Asian delegations, was not confined to them" (Zeidan 1976: 22–32).

The majority mood at the UN was to brand Britain and France (as well as Israel) as aggressors under the Charter and to apply the appropriate sanctions. To propose instead that the first two countries perform police enforcement on behalf of the world community defied logic and political realities, not to mention the majority of an enraged world public opinion.

Facing such an indignant reaction in the UN General Assembly, Pearson submitted a draft "Canadian resolution" (actually drafted by the *US State Department*) (McCullough 2016: 28), requesting the Secretary-General of the United Nations,

Dag Hammarskjold, to propose a plan "with the *consent* of the nations concerned" to set up an "emergency international force" to "secure and supervise the cessation of hostilities" and the withdrawal of the invading forces. From that point onward, Pearson's plan became increasingly the responsibility of the UN Secretary-General, who shepherded it until UNEF became a reality. Hammarskjold thereby fashioned UNEF into a "sword for peace" for the United Nations (Heikal 1973: 163).

Not surprisingly, the British Prime Minister, Anthony Eden, tried to take credit in his memoirs in 1960 for the creation of UNEF by declaring that "The action we took has been an essential condition for…a United Nations force to come into the Canal Zone itself" (Eayrs 1964: 407). Eden, however, had insisted during the British House of Commons debates on 1 November 1956 that the United Nations Organization did not have the capability to intervene in small wars (he was referring to the invasion of Egypt by Israel, with the full support of the British and French as a small war). This alleged lack of capacity by the UN gave Britain and France the right to act. If the UN, he continued disingenuously, "were then willing to take over the physical task of maintaining peace in that area, no one would be better pleased than we" (Eden 1960: 535–6).

Anthony Eden did not mention that the Anglo-French action was not an innocent foray to separate combatants, but part of a conspiracy to invade Egypt in order to achieve military and political objectives. The Good Samaritan camouflage wore very thin and was indeed insulting to the intelligence of most UN members, i.e. those who did not wear blinkers.

The Labour Party responded to Mr. Eden's claims when Mr. Aneurin Bevan said that it was "exactly the same claim which might have been made by Mussolini and Hitler, that they made war on the world in order to call the United Nations into being." Less charitably, Bevan continued, "If it were possible for bacteria to argue, they would say that their chief justification was the advancement of medical science" (Bevan, 5 December 1965).

8.4   The Suez Crisis: UN Resolutions

In the autumn of 1956 the UN faced a fundamental test of its *raison d'être* as the pre-eminent world organization charged with maintaining peace and preventing aggression. The Suez Crisis occurred at a historical juncture when the international system was undergoing new challenges related to the post-war weakening of the European imperial domains and the geopolitical complications associated with the Cold War. The United States was poised to inherit Western imperial dominance at a time when the colonial world was striving for independence and freedom.

The UN vetoed the U.S. SC Resolution (S/3710, 30 October 1956). US leadership was challenged by Britain and France, which launched the Suez War without any prior coordination. In response to the challenge, the US submitted a *draft resolution* (S/3710) to the UN Security Council calling upon Israel to immediately withdraw its armed forces behind the armistice lines established in 1948–49. Britain and France again challenged the US by exercising their Security Council veto rights and blocked the resolution on 30 October 1956. The US was not prepared to be ignored, and it supported moving the centre of opposition to the invasion to the UN General Assembly, thus bypassing the Security Council veto barrier.

The provisions of the UN General Assembly Resolution, "*Essentials of Peace*", adopted on 1 December 1949 (Resolution 1949: A/290), which called upon every nation to "refrain from threatening or using force contrary to the Charter", as well as the provisions of the UN General Assembly Resolution, "*Uniting for Peace*", adopted on 3 November 1950, (Resolution 1950: A/377), which stated that the "failure of the Security Council to discharge its responsibilities on behalf of all the member states…does not relieve Member States of their obligations or the United Nations of its responsibility under the Charter to maintain international peace and security", were recalled as the basis for the collective action taken in the face of the violation of the provisions of the UN Charter by the three conspiring countries.

A series of Suez Crisis Emergency Resolutions were adopted by the United Nations in the face of the urgent and escalating crisis:

UN General Assembly Resolution 997 (2 November 1956) called for immediate ceasefire, and the withdrawal of all forces behind the armistice lines.

UN General Assembly Resolution 998 (4 November 1956) requested the Secretary-General to submit a plan for the setting up, with the consent of the nations concerned, an emergency international United Nations Force to supervise cessation of hostilities.

UN General Assembly Resolution 999 (4 November 1956) called on all parties to comply with the ceasefire, and requested the Secretary-General to obtain and report compliance with the ceasefire and the withdrawal of the troops.

UN General Assembly Resolution 1000 (5 November 1956) authorized the establishment of a United Nations Command for the Emergency Internation Force (later renamed the United Nations Emergency Force – UNEF) to secure and supervise the cessation of hostilities, and appointed Canadian Major-General E.L. M. Burns to command the Force.

UN General Assembly Resolution 1001 (7 November 1956) approved the guiding principles of the Force, approved the rules for its financing, and established an Advisory Committee to undertake the planning for the functioning of the Force.

UN General Assembly Resolution 1002 (7 November 1956) called on Israel to withdraw all its forces behind the armistice lines, and once again called on Britain and France to immediately withdraw all their forces from Egyptian territory.

UN General Assembly Resolution 1124 (2 February 1957) deplored the non-compliance of Israel in withdrawing its forces behind the armistice lines despite repeated requests by the UN General Assembly, and called upon Israel to complete its withdrawal without further delay.

UN General Assembly Resolution 1125 (2 February 1957) called upon the Governments of Egypt and Israel to scrupulously observe the provisions of the Armistice Agreement signed by both on 24 February 1949.

Meanwhile, as requested by the UN General Assembly, the Secretary-General, Dag Hammarskjold, submitted two *Reports* outlining his efforts to bring about the implementation of the UN resolutions:

First Report of the Secretary-General (A/3289), adopted on 4 November 1956.

The Report recommended the immediate establishment of a UN Command for the UN Force, and the appointment of the Canadian Major-General E.L.M. Burns to "secure and supervise the cessation of hostilities" with a view to securing the withdrawal of foreign forces from Egyptian territory, in accordance with the relevant General Assembly resolutions.

Second Report of the Secretary-General (A/3302), adopted on 6 November 1956.

The Report defined the concept of the new Force, its basic rules, and the guiding principles of its organization and functioning. In this important Report, Hammarskjold outlined the three possible bases for establishing the Force. The General Assembly agreed that the Force should be UN-controlled and answerable only to the UN. It was agreed that recruitment for the Force should be from member states other than the permanent members of the Security Council. The 'emergency' basis of the Force was emphasized with clearly defined terms of reference "to secure and supervise the cessation of hostilities". The General Assembly indicated that the Force should be of "temporary nature", and its length of assignment should be determined by the needs arising out of the 'present' conflict. The Force was not established to influence the military balance and, thereby, the political balance. A fundamental point in the Report was the UN acceptance of the principle of 'consent' by the Government of the sovereign host state to approve the request for the stationing and operation of the Force on its territory. The international Force was not deployed as a part of an enforcement measure as it was "not a force with military objective".

The international Force was, therefore, primarily intended to "secure and supervise the cessation of hostilities", and to implement an "immediate ceasefire", as well as to ensure the prompt 'withdrawal' of all forces involved in the invasion.

The Secretary-General wrote several additional reports covering the various aspects of the deployment and operation of UNEF (see below).

Despite British attempts to take credit for the creation of UNEF, the UN moved ahead with its resolutions to force the foreign troops in Egypt out with the help of a truly neutral international force. The UN resolutions secured a shaky and tenuous ceasefire, allowing the UN troops to start arriving in the theatre of operations and begin separating the various armies involved in the fighting. It took major efforts by the UN with the cooperation of Egypt to see a successful deployment of UNEF and its functioning in accordance with its UN mandate.

It cannot be overstated that the legal-political pressures surrounding the creation of the UN Force were daunting and involved considerable negotiations and manoeuvres. The principle of *sovereign consent* was a key issue in shaping the deployment of the international Force, as well as the foundation of its mandate.

What became clear during this period was that Egypt and Israel were both very reluctant to accept the presence of UNEF for different reasons.

Egypt was not prepared to accept an exchange of one set of occupiers for another. Nasser demanded iron-clad guarantees about its precise role, its mandate, its proposed functions and responsibilities, its length of deployment, and binding assurances that Egypt's consent and control over the continued presence of the international force on its territory was indisputable. Israel, on the other hand, did not want any control or impediments in the face of its territorial expansionist ambitions.

Because of the sovereign equality of nations under the UN Charter, Chapter I, Article 2 (7), which prohibits the UN from intervening in the domestic affairs of member states, peacekeeping operations could not commence without the consent of the host nation. Chapter 27, Article 2 (7) states, "Nothing…shall authorize the United Nations to intervene in matters which are essentially within the domestic jurisdiction of any state". In other words, according to Davis Brown (New York University School of Law), "U.N. peacekeeping operations cannot violate a state's sovereignty" (Brown 1994: 561).

The single exception allowed to Chapter I, Article 2 (7) is provided by Chapter VII, which authorizes the Security Council to act regardless of the requirements of national sovereignty if a threat to international peace and security exists. However, UNEF was not authorized as a Chapter VII resolution. As events in the UN had clearly demonstrated during the early phase of the crisis, the UN Security Council was not involved in its creation at all, due to veto power paralysis. It was merely informed by the Secretary-General of the General Assembly's Resolutions to create UNEF. Indeed, it was a UN General Assembly Resolution which activated the international Force (in defiance of the Security Council veto power). Due to the jurisdictional stipulations within the UN Charter, however, the issue of national sovereignty became an integral matter in the negotiations for the establishment of UNEF.

Due to the urgency of the situation, the UN Secretary-General communicated to the Government of Egypt his interpretation of the General Assembly Resolutions for "a plan for the setting up, *with the consent of the nations concerned*, of an emergency international United Nations Force". Such interpretations and recommendations in his *First Report* and *Second Report* crucially confirmed the *principle of consent* by stating clearly that the General Assembly "could not request the Force to be stationed or operate on the territory of a given country without the consent of the Government of that country."

On the same day (7 November 1956), in the Israeli *Knesset* (Parliament) Israel's Prime Minister, David Ben-Gurion, not only declared the abolition of the Armistice Agreement with Egypt and the consequent annexation of the invaded Egyptian territories, but also stated Israel's position on the acceptability of UNEF:

> Israel will not consent under any circumstances that a foreign force called whatever it may take up positions whether on Israeli soil or in any area held by Israel (Ben-Gurion 1956): Israeli records.

A different wording for his statement was:

On no account will Israel agree to the stationing of a foreign force, no matter how called, in her territory, or in any of the areas occupied by her (Ben-Gurion, 7 November 1956): UN records.

"On hearing of this statement, the Secretary-General immediately wrote the Minister for Foreign Affairs of Israel, Mrs. Golda Meir, to inform her that this position was in violation of the resolutions of the General Assembly and, if maintained, would seriously complicate the task of giving effect to those resolutions" (Hammarskjold 1956): UNEF Background: 12.

Taking advantage of the issue of required consent, the Israeli representative in the UN, Abba Eban, immediately staked Israel's position. He stated that "the stationing of any force in a territory under Israel's jurisdiction or control is not possible in law without the Israel Government's sovereign consent". Israel, taking a leaf out of Egypt's reservations about consent, rejected the placement of UNEF on its side of the armistice lines (Eban UN 1956). It would have been possible, or perhaps probable, that the 1967 War could have been prevented if UNEF had been placed on the Israeli side as well. But as the American news analyst, Eric Sevareid, stated: "History does not reveal its alternatives" (Sevareid CBS 1968).

UN General Assembly Resolutions 998 and 1001 not only constituted the basis for the establishment of the international force, but also established the principle that UNEF could only "enter Egyptian territory with the consent of the Egyptian Government", as the international action was not authorized as an enforcement action under Chapter VII of the UN Charter. Having satisfied the consent issue, and Egypt's acceptance of the force (by accepting General Assembly Resolution 1000), the Secretary-General pushed for an immediate dispatch of the advance elements of the force to begin implementing the relevant UN Resolutions. His provisional message to the Egyptian Government (which was approved by the Advisory Committee set up according to Resolution 1001) was that the UN would not infringe Egyptian sovereignty, and that *UNEF would continue its presence in Egypt only with Egypt's consent*.

8.5   Important Precedent

Another important legal precedent was established when Israel demanded on 14 January 1957 changes to the political and territorial status quo ante (annexation) in the Sharm-el-Sheik area (including the strategic islands of Tiran and Sanafir) at the entrance to the Gulf of Aqaba, as well as the status of the Gaza Strip. Following extensive discussions with the Israeli Government, the UN General Assembly adopted Resolution A/1123 on 19 January 1957, rejecting Israel's position and requesting the Secretary-General "to continue his efforts for securing the complete withdrawal of Israel". Furthermore, the Secretary-General stated in his Report A/3512 on 24 January 1957 that "UNEF should not be used to prejudice the solution" to the conflict. He also added that the "United Nations could not recognize a change of the de facto situation [of Israeli territorial expansion] unless the change is brought about through settlement between the parties". Any change in *the status quo ante*, he continued, "would require the consent of Egypt".

Egypt's consent to the entry and deployment of UNEF in principle was based on its acceptance of Resolution 1000 (ES-I), but equally important was Egypt's approval of the 'clarification and interpretation' of the relevant UN resolutions on the basis of the stationing of UNEF in Egypt provided by the UN Secretary-General himself to the Government of Egypt (Zeidan 1976). Clearly, Egypt did not accept any limit on its sovereign consent right, as the Secretary-General's clarification indicated, otherwise the fate of the Good Faith Agreement would have been in serious doubt.

It is not surprising that at the end of the hostilities in Egypt in 1956, and with the deployment of the United Nations troops in the Canal region to oversee the final Anglo-French withdrawal from Port Said on 22 December 1956, the Commander of the United Nations Forces, General E.L.M. Burns, observed that this event marked "the last time that an Empire (here two Empires in association) would seek to impose its will by force on a weaker nation. It marked the end of an epoch" (Burns 1962).

Accurately predicting the eventual realignment of the great powers, the General continued by calling the moment "perhaps only the end of an epoch for Britain and France, for they were really withdrawing under the pressure of greater Powers than themselves".

Of course, historically speaking, empires come and go, depending on the global distribution of power and the interests at play at any given historical junction. Other empire(s) or power concentration(s) in one form or another will appear on the world scene when domestic and world factors allow.

8.6 The UNEF Generals

The difficult birth, continued survival, and difficult winding down of the UNEF, which lasted close to eleven years in all, owed a great deal to three Generals, one *Canadian* (General *Burns*), one *Egyptian* (General *Hilmy*), and one *Indian* (General *Rikhye*) . The first two men on the ground were particularly instrumental in guiding the force from its initial uncharted course to a fairly cooperative phase of operations. The third had the unenviable task of dismantling the force with as little loss or damage as possible.

The three Generals discharged their respective responsibilities in a professional and exemplary manner. After UNEF, the three former colleagues went on to perform other distinguished duties at national and international scenes (see Chap. 1 for details).

8.7   Critical Negotiations

Photo 8.3 General Hilmy receiving Secretary-General Hammarskjold in Cairo, November 1956. *Source* General Hilmy's personal files

The complexities of the UNEF mission were tackled at a meeting in Nasser's office with Foreign Minister Fawzi and General Hilmy. First, Nasser said that the most important issue in the cable exchange between Hammarskjold and Fawzi was the phrase "the continuous approval of the Egyptian Government". Hilmy (n.d.) recounts that Nasser referred to the phrase and told him, "Remember this phrase, it is most important" for the continuous operations of UNEF "on Egyptian soil or on territories under Egyptian control".

This emphasis by Nasser was due to his paramount concern to ensure Egyptian control over the continued presence of UNEF, and to prevent the Force's status from being transformed from temporary to permanent with an open-ended presence without Egyptian consent. When Egyptian fears were allayed by assurances that the international force would not operate without Egyptian consent, Egypt gave its consent for the arrival of the United Nations Forces on 14 November 1956. The first contingents flew from the staging area at Capodichino Airport in Naples, Italy, to the Egyptian airbase in Abu Sweir near the Canal Zone on 16 November 1956, a mere nine days after the UN General Assembly endorsed the Secretary-General's *Second Report*. Initially the UN Force was airlifted using the 'neutral' airline

Swissair. Subsequently, the airlift was continued by the Royal Canadian Air Force and the Italian Air Force.

Photo 8.4 Dr. Mahmoud Fawzi, Egypt's Foreign Minister during the 1956 Suez War. *Source* eBay

The operation intended to deploy UNEF in Egypt as early as was practically possible almost came to an abrupt halt because of the dispute over its precise mandate. Both Egypt and the Secretary-General, however, sought a stand-alone document spelling out clearly and unambiguously the legal status of both parties. A decade later, this insistence on safeguarding Egyptian sovereignty would paradoxically prove detrimental to the very sovereignty Egypt was trying to protect. The decision to exercise this right of sovereignty by ordering the UNEF out in 1967 opened the door to Israel's "Operation Kadesh II", which aimed at occupying the Sinai Peninsula.

8.8   The Good Faith Agreement

Because of the complexity and sensitivity of the issues involved, Hammarskjold
went to Cairo on 15 November 1956, accompanied by his UN Secretariat advisors,
in order to confer with Nasser directly in an attempt to arrive at a workable
arrangement acceptable to all sides. The first item raised by Hammarskjold was his
interpretation that the UNEF could only be withdrawn from Egypt with the
approval of the UN. Nasser would have none of that: Egypt must retain the right to
make the ultimate decision. But Hammarskjold was careful to assure Nasser that
"the UNEF can be temporarily stationed on your territory only with your consent"
(Urquhart 1972).

The Secretary-General tried to dispel Nasser's misgivings about the expected
role of UNEF, but he warned the President about "the danger Egypt would run of
alienating general sympathy if she created difficulties in establishing the UN force
in the theatre". The President was also told that "The presence of the force would
help rectify the situation produced by the aggression and would symbolize the
solidarity of the majority of the General Assembly with Egypt" (Burns 1962).

Photo 8.5 President Nasser and Secretary-General Hammarskjold negotiating in Cairo,
November 1956. *Source* AP Wire Service and Amazon

Hammarskjold also wanted to provide UNEF with diplomatic immunity in Egypt. Nasser countered by offering certain guarantees for the operations of the forces but insisted that foreign personnel operating on Egyptian soil would have to be subject to Egyptian law. A compromise comprehensive agreement on the status of UNEF personnel in Egypt was eventually arrived at in February 1957.

In marathon political-legal negotiations between 15 and 18 November, the Egyptian authorities and the UN personnel, headed by Hammarskjold, tackled the terms of the deployment of UNEF on Egyptian soil. President Nasser was most insistent on clarifying the consent issue; the UNEF's length of stay; the areas of deployment of the international force (the ADL and the Canal Zone); the composition of the contributing countries to the force and their positions toward the conflict; and finally, the overall operational terms of reference of the force.

Hammarskjold's personal preference to resolve the dispute over consent and withdrawal was to create an "agreement on withdrawal" between Egypt and the UN in which it would be declared that "withdrawal should take place only if so decided by the General Assembly". Nasser was most insistent on maintaining the decision entirely in Egyptian hands. For Egypt, placing the decision to maintain foreign troops on its soil in outside hands was anathema to its sovereignty and national dignity.

Finally, a "workable compromise" formula was reached, in which a "dual statement" included mutual promises of performance by both sides in *good faith*. The agreement reaffirmed UN respect for Egypt's sovereign rights, and Egypt's acceptance of the need to fully implement the applicable UN resolutions. The draft of the formula was negotiated and amended until it took its final form as a mutual double-sided pledge.

The talks were an exercise in high stake gamesmanship, during which Nasser threatened not to approve the agreement, and Hammarskjold threatened to walk out and pull UNEF out of Egypt. Successive amendments proposed by both sides averted a diplomatic catastrophe, as the two sides finally accepted the terms of the Agreement submitted to, and later approved by, the UN General Assembly.

Initially, a confidential "Fourteen Points Agreement" was in the hands of the Egyptian officials involved in the negotiations with the UN. "The confidential parts of the Agreement [which] governed the relations between the UN and Egyptian forces: airfields to be used, joint patrols, etc." were not made public. Other parts of the Agreement "relating to customs, immunities, privileges, ports of entry" were released (Hilmy n.d.). It is not clear whether or not this 'confidential' agreement was, in fact, a working draft which was incorporated into and became the final Status of Forces Agreement.

The accord hammered out in Cairo became known as the Good Faith Agreement. The principles of the agreement were included in an "Aide-memoire on the basis of the presence and functioning of the United Nations Emergency Force in Egypt" (Urquhart 1987: 7). The aide-memoire was submitted to the UN General Assembly on 20 November 1956 as document (A/3375). The General Assembly approved the document in Resolution 1121 (XI) on 24 November 1956.

The operational principles in the *Good Faith Agreement* document include the following stipulations:

1 The Government of Egypt declares that, when exercising its sovereign rights on any matter concerning the presence and functioning of UNEF, it will be guided, in good faith, by its acceptance of General Assembly Resolution 1000 (ES-I) of 5 November 1956.
2 The United Nations takes note of this declaration of the Government of Egypt and declares that the activities of UNEF will be guided, in good faith, by the task established for the Force in the aforementioned resolutions; in particular, the United Nations, understanding this to correspond to wishes of the Government of Egypt, reaffirms its willingness to maintain UNEF until its task is completed.

Undoubtedly, this agreement was a brilliant feat of international diplomacy and legal astuteness. In the face of a determined Egyptian position on sovereign consent, Secretary-General Hammarskjold managed the impossible: an agreement that neutralized the reservations of both Egypt and the United Nations Organization. For Egypt, the UN accepted Egypt's sovereign rights in relation to UNEF. For the UN, Egypt accepted the presence of the UNEF until its task, as accepted by the Egyptian Government, was completed.

Both sides were under an obligation to act in good faith, a novel concept in international relations. Despite the diplomatic triumph of crafting the Agreement, the ambiguity embedded in it would prove detrimental to the status of UNEF a decade later. The obvious lack of an acceptable, clearly enunciated mechanism to terminate the presence of the force would shatter ten years' worth of quiet on the front lines.

One explanation for the urgency of the agreement could be that it was made to assuage Nasser's fears about encroachment on Egyptian sovereignty. Hammarskjold was eager for agreement on the basis of UNEF operations in Egypt, as he judged the situation critical and the agreement was absolutely necessary to save the UNEF project. The UN Secretary-General was certainly most anxious about the chances of UNEF actually coming into being if an agreement with Egypt addressing fears about sovereignty was not dealt with immediately.

Undoubtedly, however, Hammarskjold had great leeway in negotiating on behalf of the UN, given his interventionist-activist bent; and the obvious need by Egypt for international help against the foreign invasion of its territory. But to sign a secret agreement with the government of a member state was unorthodox, unless, of course, he judged the situation critical and the agreement absolutely necessary to save the UNEF project. Hilmy did not elaborate on the agreement further, as he considered it a confidential undertaking entrusted only to him and a few others in the government. The Agreement, therefore, is a testament to Hammarskjold's diplomatic skills.

Another difficult issue which arose during the negotiation concerned navigation in the Suez Canal. This matter too was handled between the Egyptian President and the UN Secretary-General. Nasser was adamant that Israel could not gain any political rewards from its illegal invasion of Egyptian territory. The parties were still in a state of war and only the provisions of the armistice agreement of 1949 between them could be enforced. Nasser was not prepared to make Israel's withdrawal from Egyptian territory conditional on Israel gaining the right to use the Canal, thus changing the status quo ante in favour of one of the aggressive belligerent parties and conferring a political advantage in the process.

In their meeting in Cairo following the tripartite invasion, President Nasser said, "Dr. Hammarskjold, I am going to speak to you completely frankly. As long as I am in this country no Israeli ship is going to pass through the Canal. The idea is totally unacceptable." The Secretary-General still tried to persuade Nasser by saying that Israel expected Hammarskjold to resign if he failed to let Israeli ships through the Canal. Nasser replied by saying, "And if they go through the Canal I shall have to resign" (Heikal 1986: 207). Clearly, neither of these two gentlemen was seriously contemplating resignation. Their declarations were nothing more than negotiating tactics.

On the Canal issue, Nasser's argument won, and the agreement with the UN was concluded without Israeli right of passage through the Canal. The passage through the Strait of Tiran, however, was a different story, thanks to pressure from the US to convince Israel to complete its withdrawal from Egyptian territory in return for passage through Tiran, which had previously been blocked.

8.9   Status of Forces Agreement

The Status of Forces Agreement followed the Good Faith Agreement and was finalized on 8 February 1957. It was made retroactive to the date of the arrival of the first UNEF units in November 1956. The Agreement was the result of detailed discussions between the UN Secretariat (the Secretary-General and the Advisory Committee established according to Resolution 1001-ES-I) and the Egyptian Government which comprehensively covered the various aspects of the operational status of UNEF in Egypt.

In addition to accepting the principle of sovereign 'consent', and the separation of the issue of the reopening of the Suez Canal from the operational responsibilities of UNEF, it was agreed that the area to be occupied by UNEF after Israel's withdrawal would be subject to an agreement between the two sides, and that UNEF would have no function or presence in the Port Said or the Suez Canal region following the withdrawal of the Anglo-French forces.

The Agreement was formalized through an exchange of letters between the Secretary-General of the United Nations and Egypt's Foreign Minister on 8 February 1957 (A/3526 – I & II), which was endorsed by UN General Assembly Resolution 1126 (XI) on 22 February 1957. Finally, UNEF was established as a "subsidiary organ of the UN General Assembly" on the basis of Article 22 (regulation # 6) of the UN Charter. This legal structure was chosen to offer the UN protection on the ground for the Force in the theatre of operation, and to structure a chain of command under the General Assembly (which created UNEF in the first place), thus removing UNEF from the Security Council squabbling and interference (UN 1957: Status of Forces Agreement, A/3526 & A/1126).

8.10   The Experience Derived From UNEF

The UN Secretary-General wrote another Report (A/3943: 9 October 1958): "This report presents a summary analysis of the organization and operation of the Force". The emphasis of the Report "is on those principles and conclusions which emerge from a study of the operation as a whole and which might afford useful guidance for any future efforts looking towards the establishment or use of international United Nations instruments" serving peacekeeping purposes.

8.11   The Legal-Political Principles of the UNEF Deployment

According to Hamilton Armstrong, the *raison d'être* of UNEF and its mandate as viewed in international law can be described as follows: "*Its main task was to help bring about the status juris existing before the Anglo-French-Israeli invasion of Egypt*" (Armstrong 1957: 606–609). In essence, according to this legal view, UNEF was created for a specific purpose which was spectacularly achieved. The fact that the architects of UNEF did not include an internationally-supervised binding mechanism for conflict resolution based on numerous existing UN resolutions was not the fault of the international force. Rather, it lay with the planners of the post-Suez UN intervention, as well as the complicated international balance of power.

Despite many attempts of re-writing the history and the rationale of UNEF, it must be made unambiguously clear that the *raison d'être* for the deployment of UNEF in Egypt – a victim of conspiratorial-colonial aggression in utter violation of the UN Charter – was to secure the unconditional withdrawal of the foreign invading forces from Egyptian sovereign territory. The deployment was based on several UN General Assembly resolutions, and several reports by the UN Secretary-General based on the negotiations with the Egyptian Government, as well as the foundations of international law. The principle of Egypt's absolute right of sovereign consent over the deployment of the international force on its territory was clearly and firmly established.

Several principles underlined the formation and deployment of UNEF based on legal interpretations and UN General Assembly deliberations:

First, the cardinal rule agreed to by the UN, as stated by Secretary-General Hammarskjold, was that UNEF cannot "be stationed or operate on the territory of a given country without the consent of the government of that country", and UNEF would "enter Egyptian territory with the consent of the Egyptian Government" (Hammarskjold 1956: Report A/3302: 4–5).

Public international law, according to Herbert W. Briggs, confirms that:

> The obligation imposed by international law upon a State not to exercise its power, in the absence of a permissive rule to the contrary within the territory of another State is the counterpart of the right of the State to maintain the inviolability of its territory. States are entitled to regard as violations of international law breaches of their territory committed by foreign military or naval authorities (Briggs 1952: 312).

Second, sovereignty prohibits the "entry of foreign forces, without *consent*, into territory of a State unless such forces were dispatched by the Security Council according to Chapter VII of the UN Charter". According to Hammarskjold, the main function of UNEF, after securing a ceasefire and the withdrawal of the invading forces, was to maintain quiet and secure compliance with all relevant UN resolutions (Hammarskjold 1958: Report A/3943).

Third, it is assumed in international law that practically, politically, and legally "the *consent* of the host State to a UN peacekeeping force on her territory must be a *continued* one" (Hammarskjold 1958: Report A/3943).

Moreover, as the succeeding Secretary-General, U Thant, reflected in his own Report (18 May 1967), it is:

> very doubtful that member States would agree to the establishment of a precedent that might empower the General Assembly...to decide to station such force on the territory of a sovereign state without her consent, or not to withdraw it when the host State demanded withdrawal of the force (U Thant 1967: Report A/6669).

Fourth, each UN peacekeeping operation is by definition a "*temporary opera-tion*" established on an "emergency basis" to help restore or bring about a cessation of hostilities in a crisis situation. The model for this principle was laid down with UNEF. The "length of assignment" of UNEF was uncertain and could not be predicted at the outset, except to delineate a set of objectives to be realized at the earliest practicable opportunity as a result of the deployment of the international force. In the interpretation of Article 22 of the Charter, the "temporary nature" and the "length of assignment" in relation to UNEF were "being determined by the needs arising of the present conflict" (UN 1956, Report A/3302, Report A/3512, and Resolution A/1125). Clearly, the General Assembly saw the purpose of UNEF as 'temporary' and tied to ending the crisis at hand, namely the tripartite invasion, and as nothing more that might require the stationing of UNEF indefinitely. The use of the description 'emergency' in the name of the international force could only confirm the transient nature of the mission.

Fifth, the creation of UNEF was not intended to *influence or change* the military and political balance in the conflict except to secure a ceasefire and withdrawal of invading troops, or a return to the *status quo ante bellum*. Peacekeeping must be a neutral operation except when UN Charter Chapter VII is involved. It was hoped, nevertheless, that, during the cessation of hostilities, the injection of an international third-party buffer would help the two sides work on a political accommodation to resolve the underlying conflict. Clearly, the deployment of UNEF did not result in any form of political agreement or a fundamental resolution of the overall impasse. The invaders had political and territorial objectives in total contradiction to Egyptian sovereignty and international law. In fairness, no reasonable accommodation was possible under such conditions without a major realignment in the international rules to ensure respect for all the relevant international resolutions and principles.

Sixth, the host country had the right to ask for and obtain at any time the *removal* of the international force from its territory without objection or obstacles, unless there was an unambiguous agreement in place to organize the withdrawal on a different basis. In the agreement reached between Egypt and the UN on the stationing of UNEF in Egypt, the host country's sovereign consent for the continuous presence of the Force was clearly acknowledged.

Seventh, UNEF was a creation and a *subsidiary organ* of the UN General Assembly, as provided in Article 22 of the UN Charter. The Force was, therefore, answerable only to the General Assembly. As an international body, UNEF's chief responsible officer was to be appointed by and answerable to the United Nations and its General Assembly. The role of the head of UNEF was assumed to be neutral and independent of the policies of any nation, including his own. Moreover, UNEF itself was not to be subject to interference by any country. The political neutrality of the international force was to be grounded in its international loyalties as the collective creation of the international community through the United Nations.

Eighth, UNEF was not deployed to bring about a military objective by force. UNEF was instead tasked with *securing* a ceasefire and withdrawal of foreign troops, and not *enforcing* such an objective militarily. In other words, the UNEF was not a *belligerent force*. Moreover, it was not in any sense to be a successor to the invading forces. Its purpose was to separate the combatants – thus achieving a ceasefire – and to bring about a withdrawal as required by the UN. UNEF acted as a shield between armies and created a buffer zone and a safety cordon to help achieve its UN-mandated objectives.

8.12   Regulations of the UNEF Operations

After consultation with the Advisory Committee on UNEF, the participating states, and the Commander of the Force, the Secretary-General issued the *Regulations of UNEF* governing all the administrative and executive functions of the Force established under the authority of the UN General Assembly. The Regulations were proclaimed on 21 February 1957 (Zeidan 1976: 118–120).

8.12.1   Naming the International Force

The name proposed for the international force was not free of controversy, either. This time it was Egyptian Foreign Minister, Dr. Mahmoud Fawzi, who objected to the earlier proposed name "*International Police Force*", citing British Prime Minister Eden's description of the war as a "police action". The UN Secretariat suggested the names "Emergency International United Nations Force" for the Force, and "Chief of Command" for the leader of the troops. The 'emergency' description was deliberately used to indicate that the force was deployed to deal with a *temporary situation* and was *not a permanent occupation force*. It was the Force's first commander who suggested the name change to "*United Nations Emergency Force*", and also proposed to change his own title from the proposed "Chief of Command" to 'Commander'. Both suggestions were adopted by the UN on 8 November 1956.

8.12.2   Consent by Participating UNEF Countries

The sovereign consent of Egypt was not the only instance of state consent required to formalize UNEF's operations. The consent of the member states contributing national contingents to UNEF was also "a fundamental pre-requisite." On 21 June 1957, the UN and particular member states entered into a formal agreement based on the issuing of a letter by the UN Secretary-General and the acceptance of the letter by the countries concerned. Enclosed with the UN Letter to the participating countries were copies of the Status of Forces Agreement and the UNEF Regulations. The UN letter and the accompanying agreement and regulations, along with the individual replies, formed the combined legal basis for the participating states' consent to their participation in UNEF. With the exchange of the documents a legally binding agreement was formalized.

The Secretary-General's letter emphasized that "It is the intention that this letter together with your reply accepting the proposals set forth herein shall constitute an agreement...It is also intended that it shall remain in force until such time as your national contingent may be withdrawn from the Force" (Zeidan 1976: 194–201). The UNEF Regulations and the members' consent, as well as "the UN 1946 General Convention on Privileges and Immunities" formed the basis for operations by UNEF on Egyptian soil.

8.12.3   Dual Allegiance of Participants

Contractually, members of the participating countries in UNEF "although remaining in their national service", were designated, "during the period of their assignment with UNEF, international personnel under the authority of the United Nations and subject to the instructions only of the Commander and his chain of command".

The accepted legal modus operandi for the presence of UNEF in Egypt rested on the United Nations acknowledging "the obligation of its personnel and the members of the Force to respect the laws and regulations of Egypt and to refrain from actions incompatible with their international status." On the other side of the ledger, the participating troops in UNEF enjoyed qualified legal immunity from criminal prosecution by the Egyptian legal authorities, because members of the Force were "under the exclusive jurisdiction of their respective national states." However, the Agreement between Egypt and the UN stipulated that "immunity from the jurisdiction of Egypt is based on the understanding that the authorities of the participating States would exercise such jurisdiction as might be necessary with respect to crimes or offences committed in Egypt."

The Secretary-General, therefore, sought assurances from each participating government that it would be prepared to exercise this jurisdiction as to any crime or offence which might be committed by a member of its contingent. As far as civil jurisdiction was concerned, members of the Force enjoyed legal immunity "in any matter relating to their official duties". On the other hand, in other civil cases involving the troops, "where jurisdiction…might be exercised in Egypt, there are agreed measures to prevent the proceedings from interfering with the performance of…official duties" (UN Secretary-General 1958: Report A/3943).

8.12.4 Contributing Countries to UNEF Troops

At this early stage of the UNEF's birth, not just the mandate of the force but the choice of the countries contributing to the force became an issue of major contention. Egypt was not expecting any participation from the Security Council permanent member states, as Britain and France were party to the conflict. The participation of the Soviet Union and the United States was avoided because of their Cold War rivalry. The Guomindang regime in Taiwan, which held China's place in the UN and thus on the Security Council, was in no position to send troops.

No member states in NATO were acceptable to Egypt because of their treaty alliance with the aggressors, Britain and France. This added another element of complication to the situation, as two of the countries proposed for the international force, Denmark and Norway, were members of the NATO alliance.

8.12.5   UNEF Final Composition and Deployment

Ten participating countries formed the combined strength of UNEF, totalling over 6,000 troops. The contributing countries to UNEF were: Brazil, Canada, Columbia, Denmark, Finland, India, Indonesia, Norway, Sweden, and Yugoslavia.

UNEF had six Commanders from four countries: Canada (General E.L.M. Burns), India (General P.S. Gyani and General Indar J. Rikhye), Brazil (General Carlos F. Paiva and General Syseno Sarmento), and Yugoslavia (Col. Lazar Musicki).

The deployment of UNEF began in association with the withdrawal of the invading troops in the Suez Canal area first, then moved into Sinai, and into the Gaza Strip, followed by Sharm El Sheikh, and finally the length of the Armistice Demarcation line. The first of the invaders to leave were the British and the French, who left from Port Said on 23 December 1956. The Israelis, however, used every excuse to avoid and delay withdrawal from the areas they occupied. Finally, on March 1957, the last Israeli soldier left Egyptian territories.

8.13   Canada's Participation

Canada, the author of the resolution offer to send peacekeepers, was not an acceptable UNEF participant because, as President Nasser and Foreign Minister Dr. Fawzi both reasoned, Canadian soldiers owed ultimate allegiance to the British Queen as the Head of the Canadian state as well as of the UK. How could Egypt accept Her Majesty's soldiers to help supervise the evacuation of Her Majesty's soldiers? The British and Canadian uniforms, moreover, were virtually identical, which could lead to confusion or unforeseen confrontations with the Egyptians.

General Burns had to deal with the Egyptian objections to Canada's participation in UNEF. In a meeting in Cairo with Egyptian Foreign Minister Fawzi on 8 November 1956, Burns was told that Canada's inclusion presented a host of problems for Egypt. Burns informed Fawzi that if Canada was excluded he would not be able to serve as the Commander of UNEF. Fawzi assured him that the Egyptian Government "had confidence in my impartiality as a servant of the United Nations, etc." (Burns 1962: 197–198). On 12 November 1956, Nasser raised the same issue with Burns in the presence of General Hilmy. Nasser asked Burns, "How do you expect me to accept Her Majesty's Forces from Canada (The Queen's Own Rifles) to come to Port Said to kick out Her Majesty's Forces from Britain?" To this question Burns answered appropriately, "Sir, this is a political matter. I shall raise it with the Secretary-General since I was told to go to New York for briefing" (Hilmy n.d.).

The British Prime Minister did not make it easier for Egypt to accept Canadian participation when he declared to the British House of Commons, justifying withdrawal, that, "while one lot of Her Majesty's troops were moving out, another lot (Canadians) were moving in" (Heikal 1986: 206). And to add to the quandary facing both the UN and Egypt, the Canadian unit chosen to participate in the UNEF structure was indeed none other than the "Queen's Own Rifles", a name evoking a lot of discomfort and mistrust among the Egyptian leadership. This choice even prompted the Canadian General designated to lead UNEF to question why "out of Canada's six regular infantry regiments this one had been selected" (Burns 1962: 209).

Two more contentious Canadian positions contributed to the Egyptian reluctance to accept Canada's participation in the proposed international force. The first was Prime Minister Louis St. Laurent's declaration that the Canadian troops' "presence in Egypt did not depend on the will of the Egyptian government" (Heikal 1986: 206). Also, Lester Pearson, Canada's Minister of External Affairs and the force behind the proposal for the creation of an international peacekeeping force, amplified his Prime Minister's position by asserting that "once Egypt had accepted their (UNEF) entry she could not insist on their withdrawal" (Armstrong 1957: 608).

This Canadian stance was in direct contradiction to the need for a "continued sovereign consent" which Egypt adamantly insisted on. The second obstacle complicating the issue of Canada's participation in the force was Pearson's proposal at the UN for placing the Gaza Strip (occupied by Israel during the tripartite invasion) "under UN control" (Heikal 1986: 205). The Canadian approach raised serious suspicions among the Egyptian leadership. Egypt, moreover, had not forgotten that Canada only abstained and did not vote for the UN General Assembly Resolution 997 calling for the immediate withdrawal of foreign troops from Egyptian soil.

8.13.1   Canada's Quandary

After difficult negotiations involving India, the United States, and the Secretary-General, the Canadians, as well as the Danes and the Norwegians, were accepted as participants in UNEF. Canada's contribution, however, was confined to administration, logistics, signals and air transport duties, and it was allowed no combat role. Although many quarters intervened to resolve this impasse over participation, it was a personal appeal by Lester Pearson to President Nasser for an apparent face-saving outcome to avoid national humiliation for Canada, as well as personal embarrassment for Pearson, that produced the compromise.

In his memoirs, General Hilmy sheds some light on the efforts made by Canada to secure its participation in UNEF. He says:

> Nasser called me again to his office in Cairo and enquired why I had prevented the Canadians from coming to Port Said. I answered that I was carrying out his orders. I reminded him about what he said to me earlier about "Her Majesty's forces coming in to kick out Her Majesty's forces", upon which he opened a drawer in his desk and produced a letter and asked me to read it. The letter was signed by Mr Lester Pearson (Hilmy n.d.).

Photo 8.6 Canada's Ambassador to Egypt, E. Herbert Norman, presenting his Official Letter of Accreditation to President Nasser in Cairo in 1956. *Source* Egyptian Presidency, and University of British Columbia, Rare Books and Special Collections (BC2-124-246 – September 1956)

The letter mentioned British Prime Minister Eden's criticism of Pearson for threatening "to pull out of the British Commonwealth because of Egypt". Eden had reminded Pearson, that the Egyptians were refusing "to accept the Canadian forces" in UNEF. Pearson admitted to Nasser in the letter that "it had been a bad – but unintended – mistake to choose a Canadian unit with the name the Queen's Own Rifles". He assured Nasser that the unit was 'excluded'. Nasser felt that "reading between the lines…the letter was an appeal to save Pearson's face" (Hilmy n.d.)

Pearson's appeal had been delivered directly to Nasser by E. (Egerton) Herbert Norman, Canada's newly appointed Ambassador to Egypt. The Ambassador told Nasser that he could not understand Egypt's position in light of Canada's record in the Middle Eastern conflict (this was, in fact, a huge diplomatic stretch, given Canada's behind-the-scene proxy military support as well as its public political stance in favour of Israel). Apparently, Nasser was partially swayed by the Ambassador's pleading to allow the entry of at least non-combatant reconnaissance troops. Norman stressed to Nasser that opposition to Canada's participation "was unreasonable". Nasser was clearly under pressure to allow Canada's inclusion in light of its leading role in proposing the international force.

Hilmy continues:

> Nasser asked for my opinion about the letter. I replied that Pearson's criticism of the British
> attack and his threats to break with the Commonwealth were courageous, and his efforts in
> the United Nations were very positive. Nasser agreed and gave me the green light to receive
> the Canadians, preferably administrative and not combat units. The Canadian troops had
> been kept in Naples and denied permission to come to Port Said on my orders. After
> meeting the President, arrangements were made to receive the ship…I personally welcomed
> the Canadians in Port Said on board the Canadian carrier *Magnificent*. General Burns and
> the Canadian Ambassador to Egypt, Herbert Norman, were also on hand to meet the
> Canadian troops (Hilmy n.d.).

However, the Ambassador's role in convincing Nasser was more than saving the
reputation of Canada and the United Nations. Carroll (2009) stated that the idea that
the Canadian Liberal Government "had betrayed Britain in its hour of need ran deep
in parts of Canada." In 1956, "The *Calgary Herald* vehemently denounced
Canadian policy…as a day of shock and shame…On that day the Government of
Canada chose to run out on Britain. Canada limply hitched its wagon to the irresponsible shooting star of United States foreign policy." Moreover, *Macleans*
magazine lamented that "we do not yet understand the meaning and chief obligations of loyalty" (Carroll 2009: 38–39). The Conservative opposition "condemned
the Liberal Government as the United States chore boy", and Canada's position as
representing "The most disgraceful period for Canada in the history of this nation"
(Suez Crisis 2014: 2). In the Canadian context, "colonial chore boy" was used to
describe Canadians who did not rush to condemn Britain and France for their
military action in Egypt (Igartua 2005: 60). Clearly, imperial sentiments ran high
among some Canadians. Pearson and his government had to take that into account.

   That is why a successful Canadian move at the international level was essential
for the government of the day. For Pearson, "success in Suez was necessary to
saving his boss's political skin" (*Canadian Mysteries* 1957a). Pearson was being
severely attacked at home, and Canada's successful inclusion in UNEF would have
weakened the accusations that he was not loyal to the Commonwealth and the
Western Alliance. Yet, what was at stake here was not just local Canadian politics;
Pearson's efforts were, in fact, a face-saving means offered to Britain, France and
Israel to disengage from the awful mess they had mired themselves in without
incurring further condemnation from the rest of the world. Pearson informed
Secretary Dulles during the UN emergency meeting over Suez in November 1956
that "We're interested in helping Britain and France. I would like to make it
possible for them to withdraw with as little loss of face as possible, and bring them
back into realignment with the United States" (Robertson 1964: 188).

   Raafat (1997) reported that the resurfacing of the US's damaging but unsub-
stantiated accusations about Norman's alleged connection to the Soviets was linked
to Norman's "support for Egypt's position during the July Suez Canal Crisis and his
subsequent condemnation of the October 1956 Tripartite Aggression". Raafat
credited the "sympathetic voice from the West" with "winning the confidence of
President Nasser and using it to assist in the establishment of UNEF", in the words

of Professor Peyton Lyon's Report to the Canadian Government (Raafat 1997: 4–5).

Stevenson (1957) highlighted the role of Washington in sidelining Ambassador Norman and his transfer earlier to New Zealand away from policy-making circles:

Western diplomats, who had high regard for Norman's integrity and talent, regarded this as temporary banishment from more useful spheres and it was generally considered that Ottawa was shelving one of its best foreign service men in response to US pressure (Stevenson 1957).

Norman had a humanist inclination to support the underdog, hence his open-minded attitude: "Canada has a responsibility in the Middle East to hear both sides" (Stevenson 1957).

Brayley (1957) claimed that, "E. Herbert Norman personally cleared the way for the use of Canadian reconnaissance troops in UNEF by convincing Egyptian President Nasser that Egyptian opposition to them was unreasonable". Nasser "promised the Ambassador that the Canadians would not be hindered." (Brayley 1957).

Photo 8.7 General E.L.M. Burns, Ambassador E. Herbert Norman, Captain A.B. Fraser, and General Amin Hilmy II aboard the Canadian carrier *HMCS Magnificent* receiving the Canadian contingent in UNEF at Port Said, Egypt, on 19 January 1957. *Source* General Hilmy's files and University of British Columbia, Rare Books and Special Collections (BC2-124-145, January 1957)

A closer look at the ambassador's mindset at the time of the Suez Crisis might explain his success with Nasser at such a crucial time. Norman was accused by the CIA of being a Communist agent. In a letter to his brother and sister-in-law, dated 24 November 1956 and written in Cairo during the Crisis, he denounced the Suez conspiracy, saying "This whole episode will go down in history as one of the sorriest bits of tragic fiasco." His disenchantment shows in the statement "It is amazing what a favourable press Israel enjoys through the West" (The Estate of Herbert Norman 1957).

Finally, he showed an inner understanding of the dilemma facing the Arabs, writing: "I can see why the Arab nations around Israel have good cause for worry and concern with this *tough, intransigent and aggressive neighbor planted down in their midst.*" Perhaps faced with such an attitude on the Ambassador's part, it was not difficult for Nasser to be receptive to the Canadian diplomat's interjection. Ambassador Norman committed suicide in Cairo on 4 April 1957 after the renewal of the CIA's accusation that he was a pro-Soviet Communist (The Estate of Herbert Norman 1957).

It was General Burns' practical compromise solution of excluding Canadian ground troops in favour of non-combat troops, as he suggested to the Canadian Government, which convinced the Canadians that participation without ground troops was better than no participation at all. The Canadian support troops blocked from entering Egypt were thus finally allowed to proceed to their destination based on the agreement reached with the Egyptian Government on 17 November 1956. In a meeting between Nasser and Burns, the Egyptian leader elaborated his earlier opposition to a more prominent role for Canada in the international force, saying that he "hoped that Mr. Pearson would understand his [Nasser's] position, and that there was no prejudice against Canada" (Burns 1962: 204).

Photo 8.8 UNEF Troops in the Middle East, October 1962. *Source* UNEF HQ, Gaza: *The Sand Dune*, vol. VI, no. 43

8.14   Uncharted Course

The arrival of UNEF troops on Egyptian soil marked the beginning of a decade-long interaction characterized by initial tension and uncertainty, and the subsequent easing into routine cooperation that was marred by occasional bouts of friction. Despite the ups and downs, the overall experience before 1967 could only be described as positive. The first units of UNEF arrived on Egyptian soil in November 1956. The last contingent left Egypt in June 1967, following the 1967 Six-Day War earlier that month.

Photo 8.9 General Burns and General Hilmy discussing the exchange of POWs in the buffer zone in El-Cap, Suez Canal Region, Egypt, 21 December 1956. *Source* General Hilmy's files; authorized by the United Nations/DPI

8.15 The Egyptian Declaration on the Suez Canal

After the withdrawal of the invasion forces from Egypt, the dust had begun to settle following the full deployment of UNEF, and Egypt issued a *Declaration (S/3818)* on 24 April 1957 to record its legal position on the Suez Canal (Egyptian Declaration 1957). *Legally, the Declaration constituted an international instrument concerning the Suez Canal and its operations*, in accordance with the accepted obligations under the six principles of the earlier Security Council resolution (S/3675, 13 October 1956). The Declaration was intended by Egypt to be *complementary to the Constantinople Suez Canal Convention of 1888* and the UN Charter, and to enter into record Egypt's understanding of the Security Council resolution of 13 October 1956 governing the operations of the Suez Canal.

In the Declaration, Egypt: (1) reaffirmed its adherence to the "terms and spirit of the Constantinople Convention of 1888 and the rights and obligations arising therefrom"; and committed itself to: (2) respecting the freedom of navigation [Egypt still excluded Israel for being in a state of war]; (3) the maintenance of tolls in accordance with existing agreements; (4) the progressive maintenance and development of the Canal; (5) the autonomous management of the Canal by the Suez Canal Authority; (6) the establishment of a Suez Canal Capital and Development Fund into which 25 per cent of all gross receipts would be paid to meet development needs and capital expenditure; (7) proclaiming a Canal Code embodying the regulations governing the operation of the Canal; (8) the equal treatment of all Canal users; and (9) submitting any complaints or violation of the Canal Code to international arbitration under the direction of the International Court of Justice.

The Declaration was registered with the United Nations Secretariat. The Secretary-General of the UN, in response, sent a letter (Document S/3819) to the Foreign Minister of Egypt stating his understanding that "the government of Egypt considered the Declaration an engagement of an international character coming within the scope of (Article 102) of the (UN) Charter" (Hammarskjold 1957). In another follow-up Declaration, Egypt confirmed its intention of accepting the compulsory *ipso facto* jurisdiction of the International Court of Justice, in accordance with Article 102 of the UN Charter, by signing its accession to the jurisdiction of the Court under Article 36, Para. 2 on 18 July 1957 (Fawzi 1957). Egypt linked its accession to the jurisdiction of the Court to its earlier Declaration on the Suez Canal Operations. It was feared earlier by some members of the Security Council that Egypt could revoke its Declaration any time prior to its irrevocable accession to the provisions of the International Court of Justice. But such fears evaporated after Egypt's accession.

References

Armstrong, Hamilton F. (1957): "The UN Experience in Gaza", in: *Foreign Affairs*, 35,4 (July): 606–609.

Ben-Gurion, David (1956): "Statement to the Knesset by the Prime Minister", 1–2, 1947–1974, in: *Israeli Ministry of Foreign Affairs* (7 November 1956).

Ben-Gurion, David (1956): "Statement to the Knesset", in: "*Background: Middle East – UNEF 1*".

Bevan, Aneurin (1956): *Commentary in the British Parliament (House of Commons)* London (5 December 1956).

Brayley, Jack (1957): "Norman Swayed Nasser's Decision", in: *Montreal Gazette* (29 April 1957); at: https://www.canadianmysteries.ca/sites/norman/coldwarhotwars/suezcrisis/5575en.html.

Briggs, Herbert W. (1952): *The Law of Nations: Cases, Documents, and Notes* (New York: Appleton-Century-Crofts).

Brown, Davis (1994): "The Role of the United Nations in Peacekeeping and Truce-Monitoring: What are the Applicable Norms", in: *Revue Belge de Droit International* (Bruxelles: Bruylant) 2: 559–602.

Burns, E.L.M. (1962): *Between Arab and Israeli* (Toronto: Clark, Irwin & Co).

Canadian Mysteries (1957a): "Suez Crisis"; at: https://www.canadianmysteries.ca/sites/norman/coldwarhotwars/suezcrisis/indexen.html.

Canadian Mysteries (1957b): "Norman on the Suez Crisis and Israel"; at: https://www.canadianmysteries.ca/sites/norman/coldwarhotwars/suezcrisis/5579en.html.

Canadian Mysteries (1957c): Death of a Diplomat: "Murder by Slander?"; at: https://www.canadianmysteries.ca/sites/norman/archives/newspaperormagazinearticle/indexen.html.

Carroll, Michael K. (2009): *Pearson's Peacekeepers: Canada and the United Nations Emergency Force, 1956–67* (Vancouver: UBC).

Eayrs, James (1964): *The Commonwealth and Suez: A Documentary Survey* (London: Oxford University Press).

Eban, Aba (1956): *Statement*, UN General Assembly, Plenary Meeting 565 (4 November 1956).

Eden, Anthony (1960): *Full Circle: The Memoirs of Anthony Eden* (London: Houghton Miffin).

Fawzi, Mahmoud (1957): *Egypt's Letter of Accession* (to the Jurisdiction of the International Court of Justice Relating to the Suez Canal Operations) (The Hague: ICJ Article 36, Para 2) (18 July 1957).

Frye, William R. (1957): *A United Nations Peace Force* (New York: Oceana).

Hammarskjold, Dag (1956): *Declaration of Conscience*, Address to the UN Security Council, 11th year, 751st Meeting, (31 October 1956) (New York: UN Official Records).

Hammarskjold, Dag (1956): *First Report of the Secretary-General* A/3289 (4 November 1956).

Hammarskjold, Dag (1956): *Second Report of the Secretary-General* A/3302 (6 November 1956).

Hammarskjold, Dag (1956): *Report of the Secretary-General on the Presence and Functioning in Egypt of the United Nations Emergency Force*, A/3375 (20 November 1956).

Hammarskjold, Dag (1956): "Response by the UN Secretary-General to Israel" (Refusal of Israel to Station UNEF on its Side of the Lines), in: "*Background: Middle East – UNEF 1*": 12.

Hammarskjold, Dag (1957): *Report of the Secretary-General on the Status of the United Nations Emergency Force in Egypt (Status of Forces)*, A/3526 (8 February 1957).

Hammarskjold, Dag (1957): *Report of the Secretary-General* (Demanding Israeli Withdrawal), A/3512 (GA XI, Annexes, Vol. II, a.i. 66).

Hammarskjold, Dag (1957): *UN Response to the Egyptian Declaration* on the Suez Canal (S/3819).

Hammarskjold, Dag (1958): *Report of the Secretary-General*. (Summary of the UNEF Experience (A/3943, para 128)) (9 October 1958).

Heikal, Mohamed H. (1973): *The Cairo Documents* (New York: Doubleday).

Heikal, Mohamed H. (1986): *Cutting the Lion's Tail: Suez through Egyptian Eyes* (London: Andre Deutsch).

Hilmy II, Amin (n.d.): *Unpublished Memoirs.*

Igartua, Jose E. (2005): "Ready, Aye, Ready No More? Canada, Britain and the Suez Crisis in the Canadian Press", in: Buckber, Phillip (Ed.): *Canada and the End of Empire* (Vancouver: UBC): 60.

Kreisler, Harry (1996): "A Life in Peace and War: Conversation with Sir Brian Urquhart", in: *Critical Currents*, 5 (19 March 1996).

McCullough, Colin (2016): *Creating Canada's Peacekeeping Past* (Vancouver: UBC Press).

Norman, Estate of E. Herbert (1956/1957): "Private Papers", in *Special Collections* Box 1, File 1-2, (BC2-124-246, September 1956) and (BC2-124-145, January 1957) (Vancouver: University of British Columbia, Canada).

Pearson, Lester B. (1957): "Address to the UN General Assembly", in: *The Crisis in the Middle East: January–March 1957*, Parliament of Canada (Ottawa: The Queen's Printer).

Raafat, Samir (1997): "Death in Dokki", in: *The Egyptian Mail*, Cairo (31 May 1997); at: http://www.egy.com/people/97-05-31.php.

Republic of Egypt (1956): *Declaration on the Suez Canal* (S/3818) (24 April 1957).

Robertson, Terence (1964): *Crisis: The Inside Story of the Suez Conspiracy* (Toronto: McClelland and Stewart).

Rogers, C.M. Ann (1988): *Murder By Slander? A Re-Examination of the E.H. Norman Case*, (MA thesis, University of British Columbia, Vancouver, Canada).

Sevareid, Eric (1968): *Commentary*. CBS, USA, News, n. d. (*circa* 1968–69).

Stevenson, William (1957): "Norman Seen Victim of US Witch Hunters", in: *Toronto Daily Star* (4 April); at: https://www.canadianmysteries.ca/sites/norman/murderbyslander/5560en.html.

Thant, U. (1967): *Report of the UN Secretary-General*, A/6669 (18 May 1967).

United Nations General Assembly (1949): *Essentials of Peace Resolution* A/290 (IV) (1 December 1949).

United Nations General Assembly (1950): *Uniting for Peace Resolution* A/377 (V) (3 November 1950).

United Nations General Assembly (1956): *Suez Crisis Resolutions I*. A/997 (2 November 1956), A/998 (4 November 1956), A/ 999 (4 November 1956), A/1000 (5 November 1956), A/1001 (7 November 1956), A/1002 (7 November 1956).

United Nations General Assembly (1956): *Approval of the Secretary-General's Aide-Memoire on the Presence of UNEF in Egypt*, A/1121 (XI) (24 November 1956).

United Nations General Assembly (1957): *Suez Crisis Resolutions II*: A/1123 (19 January 1957), A/1124 (2 February 1957), A/1125 (2 February 1957), A/1126 (22 February 1957).

United Nations General Assembly (1957): *Approval of the Secretary-General's Status of Forces Agreement with Egypt*, A/1126 (22 February 1957).

United Nations Security Council (1956): *US Vetoed Draft Resolution* S/3710 (30 October 1956).

University of British Columbia, Rare Books and Special Collections (BC2-124-145, January 1957).

University of British Columbia, Rare Books and Special Collections (BC2-124-246, September 1956).

Urquhart, Brian (1972): *Hammarskjold* (New York: Alfred Knopf).

Urquhart, Brian (1987): "International Leadership: The Legacy of Dag Hammarskjold" (lecture delivered on 18 September 1986), in: *Development Dialogue*. 1, (Uppsala: Dag Hammarskjold Foundation).

United Nations (n.d.): "Background: Middle East-UNEF1"; at: https://peacekeeping.un.org/en/mission/past/unef1backgr2.html.

Zeidan, Abdel-Latif M. (1976): *The United Nations Emergency Force* (Stockholm: Almqvist & Wiksell).

Chapter 9
UNEF: Deployment Assessment

Abstract UNEF came into being as the world's pioneering peacekeeping operation stemming directly from the post-war decolonization struggle. The deployment
of the international troops faced both success and setbacks. It is not a surprise that
the deployment of this novice uncharted large-scale international effort aimed at
defusing a dangerous conflict threatening world peace and security would face a
complex deployment experience. The mammoth task of assembling and deploying
multiple foreign troops in a conflict zone was a remarkable achievement for all
involved. Naturally, the deployment was not a smooth or trouble-free undertaking.
Many political and administrative factors were involved and were capable of
undermining the whole project at any moment. It took almost a super-human effort
to keep this peacekeeping ship on an even keel. The cooperation and friction
between the international force (and its UN H.Q.) and the Egyptian authorities offer
an experience to be learnt from.

Keywords Difficult deployment · Sovereignty Contested · Consent · Cooperation
and Friction · Gaza Strip · UNEF and Local Population

9.1 Egyptian-UNEF Cooperation

The success of UNEF in defusing the Suez conflict and its endurance for over a
decade can be attributed to the efforts and dedication of many, internationally and in
the field.

The first test was met during the initial encounter between the UNEF's leadership and the representatives of the Egyptian Government. The first UNEF
Commander, General Burns, describes his first encounter with General Hilmy, the
Egyptian Chief Liaison Officer, and his overall assessment of his Egyptian
counterpart:

> Having been informed that President Nasser would see me on the 12th, I flew to Cairo that
> day with the UNEF headquarters nucleus staff…At this meeting the President introduced to
> me Brigadier (later Major General) Amin Hilmy, the officer he had designated chief liaison

© Springer Nature Switzerland AG 2020   211
H. Hilmy, *Decolonization, Sovereignty, and Peacekeeping*,
https://doi.org/10.1007/978-3-030-57624-0_9

officer to the UNEF…The President made a very fortunate selection of Brigadier Hilmy as the force's chief liaison officer – that is to say, the officer through whom we would work in our dealings with the Egyptian Army and Air Force, and in most of our dealings with the Egyptian Government and local authorities. Brigadier Hilmy had extensive experience in staff appointments and also in dealing with other departments of the Egyptian Government.

His previous appointment as Chief of Staff of the Eastern Command carried over authority which enabled him to get action which otherwise might have been slow and difficult. However, it was his personal character which made him particularly suitable. Courteous, friendly, and good-humoured, he was also quick in action and showed an ability to get results, to produce the co-operation UNEF needed. He appeared to take very seriously the orders to give UNEF every co-operation, which he told me he had received personally from the President (they had been instructors at the Egyptian Staff College together). Of course, from time to time there were arguments and difficulties, but one felt in dealing with him there was always goodwill, and a sincere intention to treat UNEF as one would treat an ally in wartime, at the least. His help to the UNEF was invaluable, and one does not like to think of the difficulties we might have met had an officer of another type been appointed (Burns 1962: 204–205).

Photo 9.1 President Nasser meeting with General Hilmy in Cairo after the 1956 war. *Source* General Hilmy's files

The genial relations that quickly developed between General Burns and General Hilmy seem to have been an integral component of UNEF's successful functioning. A few examples may help to illustrate the tone of that relationship.

The following account of their settling into the temporary front lines head-quarters relies on General Hilmy's memoirs (Hilmy n.d.). Early in their relationship, the two Generals flew together over the Canal region to reconnoitre a suitable temporary headquarters for UNEF. El-Ballah, thirty miles north-east of Abu Suweir on the Canal (north of Ismailia and south of Port Said), was chosen. A school was selected to house General Burns and his staff. General Hilmy arranged for office furniture and supplies to be brought to the new HQ. He also ordered a field bed, a table and a few chairs for Burns' sleeping quarters. To show their hospitality, Egyptian Army HQ ordered – on a top priority basis – the items needed from one of Egypt's best furniture manufacturers, located in the city of Damietta. Twenty-four hours later the furniture was delivered.

General Burns entered his new sleeping quarters to be greeted by a four-poster double bed raised like a throne, with the most elaborate bed covers and golden and red draperies hanging around it. There were also a matching chaise longue, a table with triple mirrors, an elaborate chest of drawers, two bedside tables, a large mirrored closet, and a dressing table. In fact, Burns had been gifted a bridal suite.

The following morning Burns went to Hilmy's office, which had a regular military field bed folded into one corner. Unaware of the furniture overkill for Burns, Hilmy asked Burns about the sleeping accommodation. Without batting an eye Burns replied: "Where is the bride?" Although Burns was not known for his easy sense of humour, after explaining the new exquisite accommodation to Hilmy, the two generals were heard howling with laughter.

Later, during a meeting Hilmy had with President Nasser, who was enquiring about the status of the UNEF forces and their accommodation, he told Nasser about Burns' bridal suite story. "When I told him about what had been sent to General Burns in his field headquarters and Burns' comment, he almost choked with laughter…One of the President's aides observed that he had never before heard so much laughter from the President, ever."

Other Egypt-UNEF encounters illustrate the goodwill that Egypt accorded to UNEF members, considered guests on Egyptian soil. With the arrival of the UNEF troops, catering had to be arranged in a hurry. General Hilmy contacted the General in charge of the army's Logistics Branch, suggesting the catering be provided by the Swiss-owned establishment, Groppi's, the most famous restaurant and pastry shop in Egypt, hailed as the premier watering hole for the Egyptian elite, the British establishment in Egypt, and Allied troops during World War II. There was genuine disappointment among the UNEF troops when the catering responsibilities were turned over to their HQ and their own participating governments, and the superb Groppi cuisine was cut off. Additionally, the Egyptian army assigned a Rolls Royce limousine for the use of General Burns in Egypt. Unfortunately, the car was involved in a serious accident near UNEF's temporary base at Abu Sweir. Sportingly, General Hilmy lent Burns his own staff car until a replacement car was provided for the UNEF commander.

Once the essential political issues between the United Nations and Egypt were settled, and despite various thorny issues related to the UNEF adjustments and the establishment of an effective relationship with its Egyptian host, the two sides were able to establish a smooth working relationship. Before long, Egypt and the UN Forces were able to reach practical accommodations and strike agreements on many jurisdictional and routine issues in keeping with the letter, intent, and spirit of the Status of Forces Agreement between the UN and Egypt (Hilmy n.d.).

Photo 9.2 Nasser returning to Port Said after the War. *Source* Al-Ahram, Cairo and English.ahram. org.eg

9.1.1 Canada Invites Hilmy

In 1960, in appreciation of his work with UNEF, General Hilmy was officially invited to Canada to visit several Canadian military installations, particularly those of units participating in UNEF. In a dispatch from Abdel-Hamid Saoud, the Egyptian Ambassador to Canada, to the Foreign Ministry in Cairo, the Ambassador confirmed that the General's visit was very successful and that the Canadian authorities went out of their way to welcome him (Saoud 1960).

Several functions were arranged for him by the Department of National Defence and the Department of External Affairs, where he met several high-ranking Canadian officials. Some of the Canadian officials informed the ambassador that they were honouring Hilmy as repayment for his hospitality to the members of the Canadian contingent during their service with UNEF.

Photo 9.3 General Hilmy arriving in Canada on an official visit, June 1960. Behind him is Air Vice-Marshal Fred Carpenter. *Source* Canadian DND and General Hilmy's files

General Hilmy was invited to attend Canadian military manoeuvres. Afterwards the Egyptian General held talks with the Canadian Chief of Staff and the Canadian Air Force Commander, followed by an extensive round of meetings with Canadian officials. The main topic discussed during his meetings with military and civilian officials was the Canadian role in peacekeeping operations in the Middle East. The Ambassador took this genuine Canadian hospitality as an indication that Canada was keen to improve Canadian-Egyptian relations, which had positive implications for the status of UNEF in Egypt (Saoud 1960). Such positive interaction from both sides can be seen as steps in the building of amicable relations between UNEF and its host country. One should not think, however, that relations were always rosy. Years later, Hilmy was appointed Egypt's Ambassador to Canada. Because of an intervention by India, however, at practically the last minute Nasser switched Hilmy's appointment to India.

9.2   Meeting an Old Enemy-Friend

En route to Canada (1960) from Al-Arish, the Canadian Air Force North Star plane carrying General Hilmy stopped at Gibraltar to refuel. The then Governor-General of the British colony was none other than General Sir Charles Frederic Keightley, the overall military Commander of the doomed Suez Expedition.

The Canadian government informed the colony's government, as a matter of protocol, that General Hilmy was en route as a guest of Canada. General (by then Sir Charles Frederic) Keightley arranged an official reception for General Hilmy, although diplomatic relations were still severed between the two countries, and the two men had faced each other in battle in the Suez War not too long earlier. During the reception, Keightley said to his guest, "The best time I had in my life was the time I spent in the Canal Zone." Since Keightley was in the Canal Zone for two different assignments, the first as the Commander of the British Forces in the Middle East, and the second as the Commander of the 1956 Suez invasion force, Hilmy asked tongue-in-cheek, "Which of the two times do you refer to Sir Charles?"

Keightley answered, "You know well the time I refer to." Then he added, "I am sorry about the whole Suez Affair. It was a controversial issue in England. But you and I were both soldiers doing our duty." Keightley was very diplomatic in his response, not openly criticizing the Suez Affair (only a hint) but not endorsing it either. It was generous on his part to receive his old enemy and treat him as a guest, given the fact that he was principally involved in the invasion planning and was, unlike Lord Mountbatten, a strong supporter of the tripartite action (Hilmy n.d.). One can only speculate whether the Keightley-Hilmy encounter was, like Hilmy's reception in Canada, intended as a sign that Britain too had decided to mend fences with Egypt.

9.3   Egyptian-UNEF Friction

Although the UN and Egypt were able to reach an understanding governing the deployment of the international force on Egyptian soil, several issues proved difficult to settle and threatened the overall deployment of UNEF.

9.3.1   UNEF Presence in the Canal Zone

A huge point of contention for the Egyptian Government, as confirmed by General Burns, was that "the Egyptians suspected that the UN Emergency Force might remain in Port Said and elsewhere along the Canal after the British and French had left, and would constitute the international control which the British and French, and to some extent the other 'users' of the Canal, had been demanding since the Canal Company had been nationalized" (Burns 1962: 199). The main fear of the Egyptian Government was the possibility of a plot to force the internationalization of the Suez Canal using UNEF as a cover for this objective. "In the circumstances, the suspicions of President Nasser and his colleagues were not surprising", wrote Burns. The Force Commander thus assured President Nasser that "the UN General Assembly...would never permit the force to be used to compel the internationalization of the Canal". However, "President Nasser wanted specific assurance on this from the Secretary-General" (Burns 1962: 199–200). In this way the Egyptian President sought to remove any doubt about the actual mandate of UNEF vis-à-vis the status of the Canal in the wake of the Anglo-French withdrawal. Egypt would not accept any role for UNEF that would threaten or reduce its sovereignty or control.

Although Israel denounced the 1949 Armistice Agreement with Egypt and annexed the Sinai Peninsula during the 1956 war, as documented above, the US ambassador to the UN, Henry Cabot Lodge, sought to confer on the proposed UNEF force a function that Egypt considered political and not in accord with its proposed mandate. The US representative stated that the role of UNEF would be "as a restraint against any attempt to exercise belligerent rights or to engage in hostile actions contrary to the armistice agreement, the decisions of the Security Council or the resolutions of the General Assembly". Such an interpretation for the mandate of the UNEF was clearly designed to meet some of Israel's demands for political engagement by the force and did not involve its immediate purpose of securing disengagement and withdrawal of the occupying forces. To underscore Egypt's position regarding the expected role of UNEF in the conflict, the Egyptian Foreign Minister, Dr. Fawzi, firmly and unambiguously informed the UN General Assembly that the UNEF "is not in Egypt as an occupation force, not as a replacement for the invaders, not to resolve any question or settle any problem, be that in relation to the Suez Canal, to Palestine or to the freedom of navigation in territorial waters" (Armstrong 1957: 609). Naturally, if a political role had been assigned as part of an overall approach dealing with all the issues of the conflict, the future trajectory of the conflict may have looked very different indeed.

9.3.2 Control of the Gaza Strip

One of the most contentious issues concerning the invasion and the complex withdrawal negotiations centred on who would end up in control of the Gaza Strip and under what conditions. Both the Afro-Asian bloc, spearheaded by India and its colourful defence minister, Krishna Menon, and the Soviet bloc were behind the principle that there should be no 'reward' for the aggressor. This meant unconditional withdrawal of the invading troops without any change in the status quo ante. Moreover, as the victim of aggression, Egypt was not prepared in the least to concede any change in the status quo prevailing prior to the start of the invasion, precisely because such a change would be a 'reward' resulting from an illegal, unprovoked act of war based on a conspiracy. The 1949 Armistice Agreement in place between Egypt and Israel until the start of the Suez War recognized Egypt as the power in control of the Gaza Strip.

Having failed in its attempt to annex Egypt's Sinai Peninsula because of threats of international sanctions (including US sanctions), Israel was determined to prevent Egypt from regaining full control of the Gaza Strip (as well as Sharm El Sheikh, which controls the Straits of Tiran, at the entrance to the Gulf of Aqaba, and thus access to the Israeli port of Eilat). Initially, Israel was planning to keep the Strip under its permanent control and promising to absorb the Palestinian residents, numbering approximately 350,000. General Burns, based on his prior experience in the region, wrote that any suggestion of letting Israel keep the Gaza Strip would have to come with a proviso by the UN that Palestinian refugees expelled by Israel who resided in the Strip should be settled in their former homes inside what had become Israel. General Burns was sceptical of this proposal, however. He wrote:

> But Israelis had a record of getting rid of Arabs whose land they desired…I have been credibly informed that what the Israeli authorities really had in mind, if they had been able to keep the Strip, was to absorb only about 80,000 of the strip's population. The remainder would have been 'persuaded' to settle elsewhere (Burns 1962: 191).

In other words, Burns foresaw that they would be expelled. Burns came to the conclusion that allowing Israel to keep the Strip "was not politically realistic". It subsequently did not take place (until the renewed Occupation in 1967).

When outright annexation failed, Israel proposed to hand over control of the Gaza Strip to UN administration and not to the Egyptian authorities, who had held the legal governing status in the territory until then. Israel was, in the process, resisting any return to the status quo ante. The internationalization of the Gaza Strip and the termination of Egyptian control over the territory would have been considered a partial triumph for the aggressors and a 'reward' for aggression. A final outcome and a fair resolution of the Palestinian problem would also have been prejudiced by such a move. Most of the UN General Assembly member states – through their voting during the conflict – believed that Israel should not create territorial changes on the ground through aggression and without a balanced and comprehensive political settlement to the overall Arab-Israeli conflict. Any such settlement, they held, must include the legitimate grievances of both parties, not just the claims of Israel alone.

Complicating the situation further, Canada's Lester Pearson formally introduced a resolution in the UN General Assembly on 26 February 1957 to place the Gaza Strip under UN control. The Pearson Plan included the appointment of a "United Nations Commissioner for Gaza" working with the "Commander of UNEF" and the "Director of UNRWA" (United Nations Refugee and Work Agency) for Palestinian refugees to replace the Israeli occupation and administer the Strip. Pearson also added that any final agreement on the status of the Gaza Strip should be the responsibility of the United Nations (Pearson 1957: 27–29). Mr. Pearson's position was one of the accumulated reasons Egypt viewed Canada's role with suspicion and distrust from the beginning.

The Gaza population was not prepared to accept any notion of internationalization. With the arrival of advance UNEF troops in Gaza in the wake of the Israeli withdrawal on the night of 6–7 March 1957, "wild demonstration for Nasser broke out in the Strip" (Love 1996: 668), confirming the popular feelings. A race developed between the UN machinery and the Egyptian authorities to wrest control of the Gaza Strip in the wake of Israel's withdrawal. General Burns laboured under the notion that it was UNEF's responsibility to take possession of the Strip from the Israelis. General Hilmy was acting in the belief that Egypt was entitled to regain control over the Strip in order to reinstate its legitimate control according to the 1949 Armistice Agreement and to restore the status quo prior to the illegal invasion. General Burns and UN senior official Ralph Bunche, who had negotiated the 1949 Armistice Agreements, concluded that the popular agitation "could get out of hand if Egypt were not restored to at least nominal authority in the Strip" (Love 1996: 668). Meanwhile, the Egyptian Government announced separately the immediate appointment of an Administrative Governor for the Strip, an announcement that "came as a shock" (Love 1996: 668).

General Burns confirmed the same sentiments prevailing among the Egyptian authorities regarding the volatile situation in Gaza by expressing the belief that "an Arab Government" must be restored to Gaza, and that "the Egyptians must at least have nominal authority". Burns continued that not to "re-enter the Strip" would be "politically impossible" for the Egyptian Government, as "[i]t would have amounted to an abandonment of Egypt's rights in the Strip, set forth in the armistice agreement" (Burns 1962: 266–269).

Acting on behalf of the Egyptian Government, Hilmy had already installed an Egyptian Governor for the Strip to take over all administrative and security functions. To inject a sense of humour camouflaging a *fait accompli* in this saga of international gamesmanship, Hilmy arranged for Burns to be met upon his arrival in the Strip with an Egyptian guard of honour for the 'visiting' dignitary. When Burns complained about the turn of events and the prevention of UNEF from securing the territory under UN control, Hilmy responded "General, you are not here to strip us from the Strip".[1]

It is generally accepted that the final cause of an Israeli withdrawal from the Gaza Strip (and Straits of Tiran), despite previous stubborn Israeli refusals, was US pressure, as well as an overwhelming push in the United Nations to impose sanctions against Israel for its continued refusal to implement repeated UN resolutions demanding compliance. On 11 February 1957, US Secretary of State Dulles delivered an aide-memoire to Israel stating: "Israeli withdrawal from Gaza should be prompt and unconditional". To this, Israel's Ben-Gurion responded in his own aide-memoire on 15 February 1957 "there is no basis for the restoration of the status quo ante in Gaza" (Ben-Gurion 1957).

---

[1]Hilmy, A. *Comments* written on M.H. Heikel's book, *Cutting the Lion's Tail*, p. 205.

In response, Eisenhower seriously considered joining the UN majority in imposing sanctions against Israel. Countering Israel's efforts to apply pressure on the US government through pro-Israel domestic US support, including influential elements of the Congressional leadership, Eisenhower sought to refute the notion that United States policy was "controlled by Jewish influence in the United States", a view which he thought could "drive the Arabs to see Russia as their only hope" (Love 1969: 664). He instead advocated "a resolution which would call on all United Nations members to suspend not just governmental but private assistance to Israel". In the case of the US, such assistance amounted to hundreds of millions of dollars annually.

Eisenhower followed his threat by sending a warning cable to Ben-Gurion and made a televised speech to the American people in which he said:

> Should a nation which attacks and occupies foreign territory in the face of United Nations disapproval be allowed to impose conditions on its own withdrawal? If we agree that armed attack can properly achieve the purpose of the assailant, then I fear we will have turned back the clock of international order (Love 1964: 666).

Israel, in its determination to hold on to conquered Egyptian and Palestinian territories, communicated its intentions through its Ministry of Foreign Affairs to General Burns on 4 November 1956 – at a point when he was still the Chief of Staff of the United Nations Truce Supervision Organization. Based on this contact, the Secretary-General issued on the same day the following notice:

> The Secretary-General was informed by General E.L.M. Burns, Chief of Staff of the United Nations Truce Supervision Organization, that the Ministry of Foreign Affairs of Israel, in a communication of 2 November said 'Israel representative stated in the Assembly last night the Government's position that the General Armistice Agreement had become a *fiction* and no longer had validity. The Government did not intend to return to the General Armistice Agreement with Egypt. United Nations Truce Supervision Organization personnel had no function to perform in Gaza or Beersheba and I was asked to give orders for their withdrawal.

The UN General Assembly Emergency Session (2 November 1956) documented the exchange between the Israeli Ministry of Foreign Affairs and General Burns, according to UN Secretary-General Hammarskjold's Report, A/3267 (2 November 1956). In the Report, the Secretary-General confirmed that the personnel of the UN *Truce Supervision Organization* (UNTSO), (para 7) as well as the members of UN *Relief and Work Agency* (UNRWA), (para 6), were instructed to remain in their posts and to carry on their normal assigned duties.

Additionally, General Burns' reply to the Israeli Government stated:

> That in view of his instructions he was unable to accede to the demand for withdrawal. Moreover, General Burns added that if the Government of Israel disagreed with his decision, their representative might be instructed to take up the matter with the Secretary-General [UN Secretary-General's Report, A/3284, (Annex), para 3 (4 November 1956)].

A few days after the Israeli Foreign Ministry declared the Armistice Agreement a fiction with no validity, the Israeli Prime Minister, in support of such a position, announced in the Knesset on 7 November 1956 that both the 1949 Armistice Agreement and the armistice lines with Egypt were dead and vanished. Using the *fait accompli* of the military occupation, Israel wanted to turn the conquest into a permanent annexation by unilaterally cancelling the demarcation lines with Egypt in total violation of the UN Charter and the signed international agreements.

Israel had the experience of the fate of the UN 1947 Palestine Partition Plan as a guide, as Israel (including Jewish forces in Palestine before 1947) conquered and annexed large areas of the UN-designated Palestinian State in total violation of the Plan. The illegal conquest began even before Israel was declared a state through the military operations of the Jewish paramilitary units in Palestine, while the British Mandate authority was helpless (by design or inability) to stop the conquest and the expulsion of hundreds of thousands of Palestinians. Egypt was not willing to see the violations of 1947, 1948, and 1949 repeated again in 1956 and 1957, in the Egyptian territory of Sinai, and in the Palestinian territory (Gaza Strip) under its Trusteeship.

Secretary-General Hammarskjold believed that any negotiations over the Middle East conflict had to be based on the 1949 Armistice Agreements and that the rapid withdrawal of the occupying troops and the re-establishment of the agreed demarcation lines had to have top priority. Based on his Report to the UN to that effect, Hammarskjold, reflecting the views of many governments, could not but concede Egypt's right to re-establish control over the Gaza Strip despite massive efforts to deny Egypt's return to the territory (Hammarskjold 1957: UN Report A/ 3512 (24 January 1957: 47).

Formulating a general rule concerning territorial acquisition by force as the result of an armed conflict, the Secretary-General stated in his Report that effective UN measures for conflict resolution must be anchored within the following *limitations*:

> The United Nations cannot condone a change of the status juris resulting from military action contrary to the provisions of the Charter. The Organization must, therefore, maintain that the status juris existing prior to such military action be reestablished by a withdrawal of troops, and by the relinquishment or nullification of rights asserted in territories covered by the military action and depending upon it.

Applying the interpretation of this fundamental principle to the issue of the deployment of UNEF in Gaza, the Secretary-General made it clear that "any broader function for UNEF" or "a widening of United Nations administrative responsibilities", as demanded by Israel and proposed by Canada in the UN, "in view of the terms of the General Armistice Agreement and recognized principle of international law, would require the consent of Egypt."

The Secretary-General continued that even if the UN General Assembly were to recommend such changes, "it would lack authority" to force compliance from Egypt.

The Secretary-General made it very clear that Egypt had given its consent for UNEF operations for the objectives of "withdrawal of foreign forces from the territory of Egypt, including territory covered by the General Armistice Agreement between Egypt and Israel [Gaza and al-Auja]...Activities beyond this required additional consent". Clearly, Israel, and other interested parties, failed at this juncture to achieve the objective of annexing the Gaza Strip and, failing that, to place the territory under UN Administration, thus illegally affecting the Armistice Agreement with Egypt and undermining the principles of international law.

9.3.3   UNEF-Israel Spy-Sex Incident

One episode that represented an important test of the *Status of Forces Agreement* between Egypt and the UN was a 1959 spying scandal. Clearly, the arrest of Israeli citizens inside the Gaza Strip, who had been smuggled across the Armistice Demarcation Lines by Canadian members of UNEF, constituted a breach of UNEF neutrality, particularly if the Israelis involved had been engaged in more than 'recreational' activities and thus were endangering Egypt's national security. As members of the Force were immune to the criminal jurisdiction of the host state because they were under the exclusive jurisdiction of their respective national states, the Status of Forces Agreement (para 11) dealt with this *jurisdictional vacuum* for alleged crimes committed on Egyptian or Egyptian-controlled territories. The Agreement stated that "immunity from the jurisdiction of Egypt is based on the understanding that the authorities of the participating states would exercise such jurisdiction as might be necessary with respect to [alleged] crimes or offences committed in Egypt" (Status of Forces Agreement 1957, Report A/3526, 22 February 1957).

These arrangements were agreed to because some participating states might have standards of justice different from the Egyptian justice system. What is considered a crime and its corresponding punishment, if required, can differ greatly from society to society. Not only could sentences differ widely, but conditions of incarceration, in cases of conviction, could be unacceptable to the participating states who were concerned with the welfare of their citizens in legal trouble. As part of the Agreement with Egypt, the UN Secretary-General sought contractual assurances from the contributing states that they were prepared to exercise such jurisdiction in place of Egypt in return for the host country's waiving its right to criminal jurisdiction on its soil.

The Gaza incident witnessed the implementation of the Agreement between Egypt and the UN without a hitch. Undoubtedly, however, the involvement of some members of UNEF, particularly "Her Majesty's troops" from Canada, in potential spying activities against Egypt (on top of the obvious purpose of the liaison between the Canadian soldiers and the Israeli women), could only inflame public feelings and increase suspicions of the UN, and especially Canada.

In January 1959, Sergeant Harold Carter, a member of the Canadian contingent in UNEF, was on holiday in Israel, where he met three Israeli citizens named Janet Rachel Ahovadi (aged 22), Marcel Dalia Shouan (aged 21), and Rachel Zaltes (aged 25). Carter drove the Israeli women in his UNEF military vehicle across the ADL from Israel into Gaza, where he 'hosted' them in the UNEF guest house for a couple of weeks. Three other Canadian military personnel participated in offering 'hospitality' to the Israeli women.

Upon discovery of the women by Egyptian security and police forces, all those involved were arrested. The three Israeli women were charged with crossing the borders without authorization for the purpose of spying. They were tried by an Egyptian court and sentenced to five years in prison and five hundred pounds penalty each. Sergeant Carter was ordered to be deported from Gaza immediately and turned over to the UNEF Headquarters for appropriate procedures in accordance with the Agreement between Egypt and the UN.

The UNEF legal branch then proceeded to court-martial four Canadian military personnel. They were found guilty of providing shelter to Israeli citizens in Gaza, contrary to the neutrality expected from a United Nations authorized operation. They were sentenced to prison terms ranging from 60 to 90 days and were ordered to be immediately deported to their country of origin, as required by the Egypt-UNEF agreement on immunity and criminal charges.[2] All sentences of UNEF personnel were to be served in their country of origin. According to Carroll (2009), there was no "malicious intent behind the affair", rather a case "fuelled by excessive amounts of alcohol and testosterone". The Canadians involved "were demoted and returned to Canada to serve out their ninety-day detention" (Carroll 2009: 152–153).

Surprisingly, the reporting on the case by the authoritative newspaper, *Al-Ahram*, was subdued and factual. The verdict of the trial was reported without inflammatory comments. Perhaps the Egyptian authorities did not wish to escalate the situation by turning the incident into a full-fledged confrontation with the UN. Firstly, Egypt would not have gained any advantage by stirring the pot with the UN. Secondly, the Egyptian Government must have realized that there was not a serious breach of national security resulting from the infiltration of the three Israelis (spies or otherwise) with the help of the Canadian soldier.

If this operation was a serious espionage attempt, it amounted to a flimsy effort, because without giving the agents credible credentials for operating behind enemy lines, they were bound to be discovered and apprehended, as actually did happen. On the other hand, it is very doubtful that this apparent sex escapade would have taken place without the prior knowledge, planning and sanction of the Israeli authorities. The Israel spy agency, MOSSAD, was known for mounting many espionage operations using professionally trained female agents who could infiltrate Arab territory and entrap important Arab officials. To target Canadian members of UNEF would have been a change in tactics, perhaps not well-thought-out or organized, unless, of course, the Canadians were only used to gain access, receiving sexual services in exchange for their assistance in breaching Egyptian lines.

---

[2]Al-Ahram. Information provided by the *al-Ahram Centre for Political and Strategic Studies* in Cairo, Egypt. The information was documented from issues of al-Ahram on 16, 17, and 19 February 1959. I am grateful to both the Centre and to General Farid Hilmy II, Egyptian Army (Ret.), for their efforts in locating the information in the middle of unsettled conditions in Egypt after the 2011 uprising.

One can conclude that the Gaza escapade was probably no more than an attempt to get some information on the UNEF presence and its interaction with the local authorities and inhabitants, and to do so by seducing few unsuspecting Canadian soldiers. The relative speed with which the infiltrators were discovered and arrested demonstrated the surprising lack of thought given to the operation by the Israeli handlers. The *Globe and Mail* (Toronto, Canada) reported on 21 January 1959 that the Egyptian authorities had placed the Canadian soldier suspected of organizing the affair under surveillance for two months. A report by the same newspaper over a year and a half earlier (11 April 1957) had revealed that Egyptian Army officers (not specified) had complained that UNEF soldiers in the Gaza Strip "are falling for pretty Israeli girl soldiers across the demarcation line". The *Globe* also reported that the Egyptian weekly paper *Akhir Saa* (n.d.) "published photographs of girls in Israeli Army uniforms dancing with UNEF soldiers to accordion music provided by Israeli soldiers". The Egyptian officers, continued the paper, emphasized their trust in the UNEF soldiers but wanted "to make sure Israeli girls don't talk military secrets out of UNEF soldiers".

This UNEF-Israeli fraternization had occurred less than a month after Israel finally completed its withdrawal from Egypt and Gaza. It is remarkable in light of the fact that UNEF was supposed to provide a buffer presence between Egypt and Israel in complete neutrality, and its deployment was confined to the Egyptian side of the ADL (due to Israel's refusal to accept UNEF troops on its side of the line) that such neutrality was breached by the Israelis. The early UNEF fraternization with Israeli troops was, therefore, ill-advised and was bound to create problems for the Force in Egypt.

9.3.4   UNEF Casualties

The UN Force suffered several casualties over the course of its deployment in Egypt and Gaza. UNEF suffered 110 fatalities in all; 31 of them were Canadians (Chase 2008). The casualties occurred as a result of landmines, mistaken exchange of fire with Egyptian or Israeli units, road accidents, and the fighting during the 1967 War. Major Charles Goodman (2014) of the Canadian Army confirmed that, upon his deployment in Rafah (Gaza Strip) in March 1957 (where the Canadian contingent to UNEF was based), he was tasked by the commanding officer, Colonel Ross Heuchan, to arrange the funeral of four members of the Canadian Reconnaissance Squadron.

The Canadians came under fire while on patrol along the Demarcation Line. Both the Egyptians and the Israelis accused the other side of opening fire on the Canadians. General Hilmy offered Egypt's official condolences to the Canadian contingent in person. The Canadian soldiers were buried with full military honours in the Commonwealth Cemetery in Gaza.

9.4 Egyptian Military Deployment in the Sinai

Disputes over the extent of Egypt's sovereign rights in relation to UNEF's rights of operations began early in the mandate of the international force:

In autumn 1958, when General Rikhye was UNEF Chief of Staff (and temporary Acting Commander), the issue of Egypt's sovereign rights in the Sinai became a subject of contention with the UN. In response to Soviet warnings about Israeli military training and increased troop levels in the Negev, Egypt increased its own deployment of fighter jets at Al-Arish airport, as well as deploying additional troops in the Rafah-Al Arish-al-Auja triangle. Rikhye explained to the Egyptian Commander in Al-Arish that such an increase in troop numbers was considered a violation of the General Armistice Agreement (GAA) with Israel.

The Egyptian Commander responded by saying that Israel was the first to violate the GAA by occupying the entire Al-Auja demilitarized zone and refusing to withdraw despite Security Council demands. Therefore, Egypt would maintain its troop levels according to the requirements of the military situation. The Egyptian Commander also added that "by permitting UNEF on its soil, Egypt had not abrogated its sovereign right to move its troops freely in order to defend its territory" (Rikhye 2002: 124).

Another point which was not raised – at least according to Rikhye's account – was the Israeli declaration the year before that the Armistice Agreement with Egypt was dead and buried. In fact, Israel – and the UN – expected Egypt to live up to the Armistice Agreement requirements when Israel unilaterally abrogated the Agreement and absolved itself from any obligations under its provisions.

After intense negotiations between Egypt and the UN, an agreement was reached, however, reaffirming UNEF's exclusive patrol zone (5 km by day, and 2 km by night) along the frontier. "The Egyptian sovereign right to deploy its forces in the Sinai was at least tacitly reaffirmed", and it was made clear that the UNEF was there with Egyptian consent; "recognition of Egypt's sovereignty was the key to our negotiations". According to Rikhye, Egypt maintained that it "had established a precedent for its sovereign right to defend its territory and deploy its troops for such a task regardless of the limits imposed by the GAA. Egypt further maintained that the United Nations had accepted this interpretation of arrangements between Egypt and UNEF" (Rikhye 2002: 123–127).

Another related friction over Egyptian military deployment in the Sinai arose in late 1958 when "a series of overflights into United Arab Republic (UAR) territory by the Israeli Air Force led UAR officials to station two squadrons of MIG fighters at El Arish airport alongside UNEF [planes]" (Carroll 2009). According to Carroll, "An informal agreement between the UN and the UAR on the use of the airfield was arrived at in January 1959." Canadian and UN officials were very concerned about the possibility of an international military accident. Afterwards, "Problems were generally few and far between while Brigadier Hilmy was the Egyptian liaison officer to UNEF. Any problems that did occur were usually rectified with one phone call, or threat of a phone call, to the Egyptian liaison officer" (Carroll 2009: 138) (Please see Sect. 9.6 below: 'High-Level Meeting'.).

In 1960, another Egyptian troop surge in the Sinai occurred in response to Israeli clashes with Syria, and a similar dangerous situation had arisen that put the existence of UNEF at risk and threatened a region-wide war. Egypt mobilized its forces and deployed them in the Sinai ready for battle if the situation in Syria escalated. However, and more crucially, Egypt did not request the withdrawal of UNEF, which could have dramatically changed the outcome if the request had been made. Eventually, the crisis subsided. But crucially, Egypt's right of deployment was not challenged. Behind-the-scene efforts to contain the situation were made, and the region moved on, avoiding a serious military confrontation.

As in 1958, the Egyptian move in 1960 in support of Syria had earned Nasser and the Egyptian leadership huge popularity. But Nasser was wise enough, or lucky enough, not to have requested the withdrawal of UNEF, whose presence did undoubtedly prevent a possible large-scale military confrontation with untold consequences.

A Canadian scholar, Janice Stein (1985: 615–620), claimed in 1985 that there was in existence, during UNEF's deployment, the "rudiments of a security regime" based on informally shared expectations between Egypt and Israel of security requirements in the Sinai, including a *"tacit agreement"* between Egypt and the UN to allow Egypt only "limited forces" in Western Sinai (and implying no troop existence in Eastern Sinai). There is no record, however, of the existence of any such agreement. The only formal agreement in existence at that time was that of the General Armistice Agreement (GAA) covering troop levels in the border regions of BOTH countries. Moreover, Egypt saw no need to confine its troop level to the mutual requirements of the Agreement during the military emergencies in 1958 and 1960, when Israel had declared time and again that the Armistice Agreement with Egypt was dead and buried, removing any restrictions on its own troop levels. Any Egyptian decision to restrict troop levels in the Sinai was independently and solely based on Egyptian calculations and strategic requirements.

Stein (1985) advances the notion that Egypt and Israel shared what she described as a "common aversion" to an accidental war between them. The basis of such an understanding was repudiated due to miscalculation, she added; both countries immediately recognized that "a war which neither sought directly was now inevitable". The problem with this analysis is that it ignores the well-established fact that Israel had for a long time planned to invade and annex the Sinai in accordance with Plan Kadesh. This depiction of the situation based on the assumption that the two sides innocently stumbled into war in 1967 is utterly ahistorical.

Stein's take on Egypt's right to legally withdraw its consent to the stationing of UNEF on Egyptian soil is based on an interpretation which was not the basis of the official Good Faith Agreement signed in 1956 by the UN and Egypt. Stein uses

Hammarskjold's 1957 post-agreement *private* wish list (revealed only in 1967) for the withdrawal mechanism, which requires the General Assembly, the Advisory Committee on UNEF and the Secretary-General himself to decide on withdrawal. Egypt had already rejected such a proposal during the negotiations, refusing any restrictions on its right of consent. Officially, Hammarskjold had accepted the principle that UNEF could remain in Egypt only with Egypt's continued sovereign consent.

After the end of the1956 War and the stationing of UNEF as a buffer with Israel, there was no pressing need for Egypt to enlarge its military deployment in Sinai. As in 1958 and 1960, only when the possibility of a confrontation with Israel arose did Egypt reinforce its troops. UNEF Commanders pressed for de-escalation, but Egypt held firm, invoking sovereignty. Apart from the agreed 5 km stretch along the border with Israel, reserved for UNEF patrolling, Egypt controlled the level of its troop deployment in the rest of Sinai in accordance with its political calculations. Clearly such calculations failed miserably in 1967, but at no time was Egypt's right to deploy its army within its national territory open to debate.

It is important to realize that such dogged protection of Egyptian sovereignty following the 1956 war received a body blow after the 1973 war with the deployment of UNEF II. The concept of 'consent' was downgraded to the lesser right of 'cooperation' (i.e. non-binding consultation). Decisions on the withdrawal of the international force were taken out of Egypt's hands and transferred to the Security Council. Egypt lost its right to withdraw its sovereign consent for the continued deployment of foreign troops on its soil. Unlike the freedom of the Secretary-General to decide on a request for the withdrawal of UN peacekeeping troops, as U Thant did in 1967, the right of the Secretary-General was terminated. The Egyptian decision-maker was so eager to reach an agreement under the auspices of the US that he forfeited a hard-fought right of sovereignty. The Egyptian Government's acceptance of such a fundamental violation of its own sovereignty constitutes a stain on the country's previous fight to protect its sovereign independence, and an insult to those who fought hard to preserve it.

Egypt's downgrading of its sovereignty continued in 1979 after the signing of the 'peace' treaty with Israel, mediated by the US. A *permanent* structure of foreign observers, the Multinational Force and Observers (MFO) outside the control of the UN, was installed to ensure that the Sinai was practically demilitarized, with only a small symbolic number of Egyptian troops allowed in strictly controlled zones. Movement and deployment of Egyptian troops in the Sinai are now subject to Israeli approval. No such right is given to Egypt over the movement and deployment of Israeli troops in the Negev. Clearly, Egypt's sovereign control of its national territory has been severely compromised. Now, the Sinai is practically outside the sovereign control of Egypt. Many regard this outcome as a shameful capitulation and a threat to Egypt's national independence and security.

9.5   The 'UNEF-Local Population' Encounter: An Assessment

In a landmark study undertaken in February 1964 on the effects of the deployment of United Nations Forces, a "Pilot Project" was carried out in the Gaza Strip by Norwegian social scientist Johan Galtung (1964: 1–25).[3] This study was meant to gauge the interaction between UNEF and the local population. The aim of the research was to define and study the "factors that facilitate or impede the acceptance of such forces". It was "concerned with patterns of attitudes and interactions between civilians...and the UN forces". Previous studies of the history of UN peacekeeping in Gaza, Congo, and Cyprus had focused mainly on the reaction of the main antagonists (governments or civil war factions), and the role played by UN forces as the only issue that mattered. Such studies were weakened by not taking into account the importance of the reaction of the civilian environment in which the forces are embedded.

The Gaza Strip, a sliver of the former British-Mandated Palestine, remained under Egyptian temporary trust-control following the Arab-Israel 1948–49 War. In total, the Strip housed three UN bodies interacting on a daily basis.

Galtung's study was concerned with the third UN organizational presence in Gaza, UNEF, which invariably influenced and was influenced by the other two (UNRWA and UNTSO). This report examined how UNEF's presence and its interaction with the population was affected by politics, culture, customs, and varied expectations. The study presented several notable findings.

Although UNEF was basically considered by Palestinian refugees in Gaza to be an internationally-imposed barrier between them and the return to their homes in what was – in their view – an Israeli-occupied Palestine, only very low-level incidents occurred that required the attention of UNEF (individual crossings or shootings across the Armistice Demarcation Lines). The study likened the refugees in Gaza to a "population in a prison" condemned to an undetermined period of incarceration with a typically high degree of frustration (as based on observed prison studies). Such an attitude was demonstrated when it was publicly announced that the UNRWA mandate had expired on 30 June 1963 (though it was immediately renewed). Riots took place not because of anger against UNRWA but because of the "symbolic significance" of the fact of renewal. It represented an indefinite extension of the population's confinement to the refugee camps without hope of ever returning to their homes.

---

[3]All the following quotations in this section are taken from the Pilot Project study.

Photo 9.4 Professor Johan Galtung, pioneer of peace research. *Source* Wikipedia (public domain)

Galtung's study was supportive, therefore, of setting no "time-limit" for the UNEF operations, thus raising (or lowering) hope among Palestinians for the end of their ordeal. Based on my own personal observations, however, during four years spent in Gaza in the late 1950s and early 1960s and interacting with Palestinians in school, in refugee camps, and in the broader society, there was an overwhelming desire among Palestinians to retain their refugee status and not to be settled on a permanent basis, lest their status and political demands for repatriation be compromised. Collectively, the refugees resisted perceived attempts by others, which they saw as "buying the Arabs off and tying them to the Gaza Strip". As a matter of fact, any refugee who wanted to lead a semblance of a normal life, or to support a Palestinian political entity (al-Kayan al-Falastini) carved out of Gaza and the West Bank alone (as proposed in some Arab circles as a solution to the problem), was fearful of being labelled a traitor to the cause of freedom for the whole of Palestine. This was confirmed by the study, which stated that "to improve [local conditions] was to settle and to settle was treason".

Cultural sensitivity played an important role in affecting UNEF's relations with the Palestinian environment in Gaza, where they were deployed. According to Galtung, UNEF was generally successful in hiding the huge disparities between the relatively high living standard of the international Force and the miserable conditions of the Palestinian refugees. Also, the less-than-puritanical behaviour of members of the force was "successfully concealed from the eyes of the local population" behind closed doors or in the various UNEF clubs in the area. Arab taboos and local customs related to sex and alcohol were reinforced by "military orders" prohibiting UNEF members from associating with local women. Cairo and Beirut were used for recreational activities by UNEF members on leave, and these were the places where they spent most of their cash, not locally in Gaza. In general, "behaviour defying" customs was "well checked", according to the Galtung report.

The study suggests, however, that such "conspicuous puritanism" should not be taken for granted as a requirement for acceptance, because of the high degree of "trained tolerance" by the Arabs for less puritanical habits expected from members of foreign cultures. In other words, in Galtung's opinion, puritanism "should not be deduced" as an "infallible key" required for acceptance wherever an international force comes in contact with local populations. The local population also held views of the national characteristics of the participating national contingents in UNEF in line with widely held stereotypes. The study warned that negative stereotypes of participating nations (Nordic liberal attitudes towards sex and alcohol) could adversely affect relations with the international force in general. Such attitudes should be taken into consideration, Galtung argued, when deciding on the composition of an international force proposed for any region of conflict.

Building trust between the local population and members of UNEF was crucial in ensuring a cooperative co-existence. Many contingents in the UNEF engaged in goodwill activities among the Palestinian residents of the Strip. These activities ranged from collecting donations and organizing activities for the children to building a hospital (Canada), providing medical care (Sweden and Norway), and providing scholarships for education and vocational training (Educational rates among the Palestinian refugees in Gaza under the Egyptian administration and financing were among the highest in the Arab world, with 100% attendance for school-age children, independent of modest UNEF contributions.). Other trust-building activities included adopting a refugee child for special educational purposes, providing drinking water and medical care to the Bedouin tribes, and even helping the monks in the remote St Catherine Monastery in the Sinai (which was far away from UNEF deployment positions). Galtung suggested that the extra activities undertaken by UNEF were similar to the activities of American Peace Corps volunteers. The value of such goodwill creating engagements, moreover, was that they were not expected at all. The good deeds were not conceived as part of the activities of military units poised on the highly-charged confrontation lines between two bitter enemies – hence their positive impact.

Maintaining a general perception of symmetry in the Arab-Israeli confrontation helped to ease tensions in the region. One of the most difficult situations facing UNEF concerned perceptions of its even-handedness, or lack thereof, vis-à-vis the Israelis. As a third-party observer of the conflict, UNEF was expected to act as an honest intermediary, with a basic responsibility for keeping the antagonists apart. Any uneven contact with the Israelis (suggesting asymmetry of commitment) was therefore viewed with extreme suspicion. Fraternizing with the Israeli forces on the "other side of the ADL", such as "throwing gifts to Israeli women soldiers" on patrol, was seen as a violation of neutrality. (It is interesting that UNEF's charitable work with the Palestinians was not considered a violation of neutrality.)

Since UNEF was stationed, however, on the Arab side of the Armistice Demarcation Lines (and had no presence on the Israeli side), its greater interaction with the local Palestinian Arab population was inevitable. Many Palestinians believed that UNEF was deployed "only to watch the Arabs [and their misdeeds] and not the Israelis." This was reinforced initially due to the refusal of Israel to allow UNEF on the other side of the ADL, strongly emphasizing the lack of 'symmetry' in the situation. The impression created among the Palestinians, therefore, was that the international community was concerned only with problems expected to occur from the Palestinian side.

In fact, day-to-day contact between UNEF and the local Palestinian population (both refugees expelled by Israel and the original residents of Gaza) was limited and confined to normal commercial activities in the markets and shops, or transportation when off-duty. Contact with families was rare, as some neighbours viewed any hospitality offered to UNEF members with suspicion. The Galtung study was not definitive on the policy that should be adopted in relation to contact between an international force and the local population in the theatre of its deployment and operation. "It is very difficult to know where the line should be drawn", Galtung wrote. Too much contact would create "empathy and identification", while, on the other hand, restricted contact would reinforce the sense of distance required for the use of force or threats of force by the international troops.

The generally ambiguous attitude towards UNEF in Gaza was influenced by the international nature of the force. On the one hand, the UN was an ally that had "helped Egypt beat the joint assault of France, Britain and Israel". On the other, the UN had never succeeded in implementing several of its own resolutions against Israel or in defence of violated Palestinian rights. The UN (and the UNEF by extension), therefore, was seen as "at least partly responsible" for the "miserable situation" of the Palestinians. However, in line with the saying, "misery loves company" or, as the study put it, "the enemy of my enemy is my friend", a certain affinity developed between the Palestinians and the UN due to the fact that the Israelis were violating UN principles "by not obeying its recommendations and resolutions". The refugees and the UN were seen, therefore, tied together as "victims of Israeli disrespect, arrogance and non-cooperation".

The success of UNEF was dependent on the perception that the international force was not an 'occupation' force (following the initial attempts to change the legal status of the Gaza Strip by Israeli annexation or internationalization by the UN). Compared to the 'horror stories' associated with the Israeli occupation of the Gaza Strip from November 1956 to March 1957, the return of the Egyptian administration and the deployment of UNEF were seen in a positive light. This contrasted with the atmosphere of "permanent fear and danger" prior to the arrival of UNEF. The local Palestinians were also aware of the instructions issued to UNEF of "not to fire except in self-defence", which removed any sense of danger associated with the international force.

Moreover, UNEF's primary function was the creation of a buffer or "neutral zone" separating the Arabs and the Israelis. Within that limited function, UNEF itself could not punish violators of the Armistice Demarcation Lines. UNEF was also not allowed to "maintain law and order" in the Gaza Strip, nor was its responsibility "to interfere in case of a declared or undeclared war". The only argument against the continuous presence of UNEF was the fear that it would "freeze the status quo", precluding any satisfactory solution to the Palestinian predicament.

Galtung's study was a very important contribution to the pioneering field of peacekeeping. It highlighted many of the problems and issues surrounding the interaction resulting from the introduction of an international peace force into a conflict zone and into the midst of a population with major grievances and demands. The fact that UNEF managed for a decade to navigate its presence with only minor friction was a testament to the success of the experience. Similar studies could be very helpful if carried out in relation to interactions between UN (or regional organizations) and local populations in other conflict zones.

The overall UNEF experience in Egypt can be evaluated as positive. Inevitable adjustments and friction at the initial deployment, during operations, and on termination cannot obscure or downgrade the genuine cooperation by both sides to ensure the success of the mission and the prevention of armed hostilities for over a ten-year period (Galtung 1964: 1–25).

9.5.1 Other Local Population-Peacekeeping Encounters Studies

Echoing Galtung's pioneering work, other studies confirm the need for the presence of several factors, in addition to interaction with the local population, necessary for peacekeeping deployment to be successful (Fetherston 1994: 40–42).

More studies found that essential local support for UN peacekeeping missions can be jeopardized when soldiers are culturally different from local communities. When the peacekeepers, however, are perceived as sufficiently distant or unbiased, the cooperation between the two sides is more successful (Bove/Ruggeri 2019: 1,630–1,655).

The importance of the local population in relation to international peacekeepers was highlighted by Heiberg's conclusion that "a relationship to local civilians built on communications and confidence is a necessary factor for success". She also concluded that "a relationship characterized by mounting hostility, suspicion and lack of communication is a sufficient cause for failure". Therefore, the relationship of peacekeepers with the local civilians (positive or negative) is crucial for the outcome of the deployment (Heiberg 1991: 147–169).

General I.J. Rikhye, the last Commander of UNEF, confirmed that "the members of UNEF enjoyed excellent relations with the local inhabitants and contributed to the local economy in many ways" (Rikhye 2002: 116).

In conclusion and based on empirical evidence, the successful deployment of an international peace force relies to a great degree on positive interaction with the local population and the ability to gain their trust and cooperation. Similarly, a negative experience engulfing the interaction could only complicate and hinder the peacekeeping mission.

Finally, in addition to the above factors, the most important factor, in my view, is the ability of the peacekeeping mission to facilitate a constructive conflict resolution path.

9.6   Operational Fine-Tuning: A Revealing High-Level UN-Egyptian Meeting in Cairo (January 1959)

A meeting between Egyptian and UN officials in January 1959 clearly illustrates the struggle of the two sides (despite ample goodwill) to defend and maintain their respective understandings and control of the mandate governing the operations of the international force on Egyptian soil. There were arguments over many contested issues, such as the Egyptian claim to have a right to patrol the border zone with Israel, against UNEF's insistence on its having exclusive rights to operate in the zone. Egypt's repaving of the Sinai roads next to the borders was also disputed. Control and access to Egyptian air space was the subject of a heated exchange. The role of Palestinian police in patrolling the border was a further area of disagreement. Egypt's right to fight border smuggling was another issue of debate. The UN officials advanced the position that UNEF needed freedom of action without Egyptian restrictions or interference. Clearly, the two parties were at odds on many issues: their differences put into focus some of the difficulties an international operation faces while functioning within a sovereign domain.

The minutes of the meeting give a rare inside look at the original and unpublished record of the interaction between Egyptian and UN officials. They throw light on how the two sides grappled both with sensitive issues and with their different interpretations, and how they did so at the highest level with intensity, but equally with respect. There was a desire on both sides to facilitate the operations of UNEF, and equally to take into account Egyptian sovereign requirements.

9.6.1   Minutes of the Unpublished: Egyptian-UN Officials' Meeting, Cairo (6 January 1959)

Top Secret

(High-Level Meeting 1959)

Minutes of the Meeting Between
Dr. Mahmoud Fawzi, Egypt's Minister of Foreign Affairs
and
Mr. Dag Hammarskjold, Secretary-General, United Nations
Attended by
Egyptian and UN Officials

Participants:
Dr. Dag Hammarskjold, United Nations Secretary-General
Dr. Mahmoud Fawzi, Foreign Minister of Egypt
Mr. Hussein Zul-Fiqar Sabri, Deputy Minister of Foreign Affairs of Egypt

General Edison Burns, Commander, UNEF
General Amin Hilmy II, Chief, Egyptian Liaison Officer with UNEF
Mr. Fathi Radwan, Director of the Arab Affairs Dept., Egyptian Ministry of Foreign Affairs
Mr. Hernando Sampir, Political Assistant to Mr. Hammarskjold
Major Adly El-Sherif, Dept. of Palestine Affairs, Egyptian Ministry of Foreign Affairs
The Meeting was held at the Ministry of Foreign Affairs in Cairo at 11:30 AM,
6 January 1959.

Introduction:

Prior to the meeting Dr. Fawzi conferred with General Hilmy over the issues concerning Al-Arish Airport, and Al-Auga Road project, and other issues raised during the previous meeting between Dr. Fawzi and Mr. Hammarskjold. The Minister asked General Hilmy to explain in detail all the issues involved during the current meeting.

The Meeting:
   (Names without titles or ranks)

Fawzi: Welcomed Mr. Hammarskjold and General Burns and turned over the floor to General Burns to present his issues.

Burns: I would like to discuss the following subjects:

A. The Al-Auga Road project which has reached point 267 near the international lines.

B. The situation in Al-Arish Airport in light of the presence of UAR jet fighters next to the UN planes.

C. The withdrawal of the Columbian Contingent.

D. The presence of the Palestinian Police inside the 500-metre zone along the Armistice Line.

A. *Al-Auga Road Construction*:

Hammarskjold: I would like to mention that as far as the road project is concerned you have every right to build any road within your borders, and that the issue of sovereignty is not under discussion here as it is fully accepted.

Burns: The work on the road project has now reached the vicinity of the international borders. I have already written to General Hilmy

	concerning that, and he has informed Dr. Fawzi. I fear that a military clash might occur between the Egyptian troops, advancing ahead of the road project work crew, and the Israeli troops. I prefer, and the Secretary-General agrees with me, that the road project stops without further progress in order to avoid any incidents.
Fawzi:	When will the road project conclude?
Hilmy:	It will conclude in a few weeks. I would like to comment on what General Burns said. The road under discussion is being built as part of a road network planned for the whole country. What General Burns described as advancing Egyptian troops are in fact few members of the Border Police Guard entrusted with the security of the equipment of the builder who is under contractual obligations with the Government to complete the project. I also explained to General Burns that there is nothing in the Agreement [Status of the Force Agreement], from a legal or political standpoint, to prevent us from building the road. That is why the General's request was rejected when it was first made.
Fawzi:	Although I am not a military man, I can say that the remaining short distance for the completion of the project, which is about three kilometres, will not change the military situation at all.
Sabri:	There is an existing United Nations Truce Supervision Commission (UNTSO) as well as UNEF troops in the area. They could be informed and take responsibility for preventing any incidents, and make determination of culpability.
Burns:	There is no need to wait until a dozen of your men are killed before the Truce Commission makes a decision.
Sabri:	Israel only observes the provisions of UNTSO with Jordan which are to its liking, such as Section 8 of the Agreement, but does not recognize the UNTSO Agreement with the UAR. For instance, Israel has completely violated the provisions for the Al-Auga demilitarized zone. What is required now is to demand that Israel recognizes and respects the application of UNTSO on the Egyptian Border.
Hammarskjold:	We are heading now towards more serious problems. Each problem has its time and its occasion. This is not a weakness or a compromise on our part, as we have already secured some privileges from the UAR government. The benefits of further extending the road currently under construction are extremely limited. The problem that appears small at present, in the light of the involvement of the UN Forces, could become a large problem. And if other small problems are added then in the end we will be facing a truly large problem indeed with a widening circle of

conflict. I can anticipate tying these problems with other problems in other areas.

The lesson I have learnt from this region is that if we press on one finger the pain will be felt in another finger. That is why I connect these incidents with other incidents in the Northern Region of the UAR (Syria), such as the Hula area. We are concentrating our efforts there now as there is a strong correlation between the two problem areas (Al-Auga, Egyptian Region; and Hula, Syrian Region). I, therefore, confess that I have some serious concerns. I would like to enquire if you have any objections to the presence of the Yugoslav contingent alongside the road construction crew to help prevent any incident.

Hilmy: We not only welcome that, but we had already asked the Yugoslav forces which patrol the border area to be close to the road construction crew to avoid any problem but General Burns refused our request.

Burns: What are the reasons for building the road anyway?

Hilmy: My dear General, progress could be one of the reasons.

Sabri: Yes, that is very possible.

Hilmy: Why is this subject being taken as an aggressive act? Why not consider it a development effort in the Sinai Desert, and an effort to facilitate the lives of the Bedouins, as well as a means to combat smuggling? Why don't we consider the fact that the road did exist already and was destroyed by the Israeli forces during the last aggression (1956–57)? Finally, why don't we remember that Israel builds whatever roads it wants in the Negev?

Fawzi: Such a question [by Burns] should not be addressed to a sovereign state, and General Burns knows that very well. I can refuse to discuss the subject altogether.

Hammarskjold: I hope it is taken as a suggestion to avoid confrontation, and not for any other motive.

Fawzi: Let us move to other subjects in the agenda.

Hammarskjold: Yes, but I have to confess that the road issue is still worrisome.

B. *Al-Arish Airport*:

Burns: According to the March Agreement [between the UN and Egypt], we have the freedom of passage and flight over Sinai. The UAR government has, consequently, allowed us the use of Al-Arish airport. We have spent large sums on the airport, and General Hilmy has provided valuable assistance associated with our preparations. Lately, an Egyptian squadron of fighter jets arrived at the airport, causing our pilots a great deal of anxiety. The UN pilots were informed by Egyptian officers, not even posted at the airport, that if their planes were delayed by even two minutes from their E.T.A. [Estimated Time of Arrival] they would be fired upon. Because the airport is surrounded by Egyptian troops and anti-aircraft artillery units, the pilots were concerned for their safety and the safety of their passengers of UNEF troops. Consequently, I was forced to order the suspension of all internal and external flights. I confirmed my order with our Flight base in Pisa in Italy.

The other issue associated with the airport is the theft of the electric cables and the landing lights of the runway and many other items by Egyptian military personnel. The situation has considerably improved, though, due to the efforts of General Hilmy. However, the situation at the airport is fraught with a great deal of uncertainty, and I require an urgent solution as we cannot continue operating under such circumstances.

Fawazi: I believe General Hilmy has something to say.

Hilmy: I heard from General Burns around midnight about his decision to suspend all flights. By six o'clock the next morning I had completed my investigations and informed the General that all his flights could resume normally as I am in a position to guarantee their safety. I explained to the General the circumstances of the air battle which took place over the airport, and that the request not to delay and to adhere to the E.T.A. of the UN planes was to guarantee the safety of the UN flights in the midst of military clashes. [Editor's note: A week earlier Egyptian jet fighters intercepted Israeli jet fighters inside Egyptian airspace. The ensuing air battle between the two air forces took place in the vicinity of Al-Arish airport, the largest Egyptian air base in the Sinai as well as the base for UNEF air transport operations].

When General Burns flew to New York, I wrote to the Chief of Staff of UNEF, candidly informing him that we authorize UNEF to use Al-Arish airport, but we do not authorize them to own it. The airport belongs to Egypt and will be used in accordance with Egyptian needs. I have repeatedly informed General Burns that our radar stations have repeatedly recorded the infiltration of Israeli planes of our airspace. The UN forces at the General's disposal are completely unable to prevent such aerial infiltration unlike their ability to confront ground infiltration. We have the right, therefore, to defend our national territory, which includes scrambling our fighter jets to meet the intruders. It is imperative, consequently, to account for all friendly UN planes in the air in order to separate them from enemy aircraft.

It is an international practice for all planes to identify their locations so they can be tracked and, in case of an emergency, be found. Such practice is not considered an imposition of limitations on the freedom of flights, as claimed by General Burns.

As for the incidents of theft, I can confirm that a soldier in one of the communications units was laying a cable for his unit along the UN cable. Later on when he retrieved the cable belonging to his unit he also retrieved the UN cable, mistakenly believing it to be part of a joint network. I ordered the UN cable to be returned to UNEF immediately.

Hammarskjold: This is what I call "Joint Operations". (Laughter)

Sabri: Al-Arish airport is very important for our air defences and for tracking aircraft in the air in order to avoid unintended clashes. General Burns has just acknowledged the extensive assistance provided by General Hilmy; it is not clear, therefore, the reasons for the complaints.

Hammarskjold: The defence around Al-Arish airport is the responsibility of the UAR government alone. But this situation has caused some problems due to the presence of the international forces at the same airport. Such a problem should not continue. Our Generals have expressed their respective views on the issue.

Fawzi: I ask General Burns to comment on General Hilmy's reply.

Burns: When the international force is operating in an area, there should not be other armed forces operating next to it in the same area.

Fawzi: This is not a "joint operation", but a case of one force receiving assistance from another force.

Hilmy: The principle being invoked by General Burns has very serious adverse consequences. The UNEF has a logistical unit in Port Said. Should the UAR forces be withdrawn from this area in order not to be in the same area as UNEF? Moreover, the UNEF uses many transportation routes. Does that mean that we should withdraw all our forces from the routes used by the UN? Is it reasonable to accept that? The UN force is authorized to be stationed along the armistice lines and the international borders as its theatre of operations. Other areas are considered logistical bases and transportation routes only.

Hammarskjold: I accept what General Hilmy has said. However, the occurrence of an air battle over Al-Arish and the presence of UAR fighter jets in the same airport where UN planes are stationed will turn the airport into a military target for the Israeli fighter jets. We require a ruling in accordance with international law, because our presence in Al-Arish is very problematic.

Fawzi: I suggest that General Burns and General Hilmy hold a meeting this afternoon to study the Al-Arish airport issue, and we can then

	reconvene tomorrow at 4:00 in the afternoon to study the result of their discussions.
Burns:	I held numerous meetings with General Hilmy, and we exchanged many letters concerning this issue. I want to state as a matter of principle that the presence of UAR forces alongside the neutral international force and to use the same airport under UAR control and commanded by a UAR officer renders the international force not strictly neutral.
Fawzi:	What does General Hilmy think about coordinating the airport operations?
Hilmy:	The UNEF is a neutral force. As far as we are concerned, they are not belligerent but guests in our country and we always treat them as such, and we offer all the facilities they require.
Hammarskjold:	I do not believe that our Generals will be able to resolve this issue.
Fawzi:	I doubt that within twenty-four hours we will be able to discover new approaches.
Hammarskjold:	Clearly, the two Generals are holding fast to their positions.
Burns:	I prefer to postpone dealing with this issue until a guiding principle is established. I will then study the new interpretation with General Hilmy.
Fawzi:	Let us then deal with another Item.

C. *The Withdrawal of the Columbian Contingent*:

Burns:	Since the withdrawal of the Columbians from participation in UNEF, the Indian and Brazilian units have been working overtime and are overextended to fill the gap. The peaceful conditions prevailing in the (Gaza) Strip at present – unlike the past – compel me to request the re-evaluation of this situation.
Fawzi:	This is a purely political issue and is being evaluated between now and tomorrow.
Hammarskjold:	Of course General Burns was reviewing the situation of the Brazilian and Indian forces from a technical perspective.
Fawzi:	We move on then to the next item.

D. *The Palestinian Police*:

Burns:	General Hilmy has requested the cancellation of the previous agreement to maintain the 500-metre zone along the armistice line for the exclusive use by UNEF. He now considers this agreement

already cancelled. General Hilmy has also requested the entry of the Palestinian Police to the zone. If the Palestinian Police is allowed into the zone, I fear that clashes might occur between the Palestinians and the Israelis. In the past, when the UN forces were using the zone alone, peaceful conditions prevailed to the benefit of the Strip, so why change the arrangements now?

I do not agree that the Palestinian Police should be present in the border zone, and I have communicated my position to the Secretary-General. I was supposed to discuss that with General Hilmy after meeting Dr. Fawazi, but unfortunately Hilmy's illness prevented me from completing the discussions.

Hammarskjold: Of course this issue has nothing to do with your sovereignty in the Strip.

Hilmy: The Palestinian Police was supposed to enter the zone from the beginning. General Burns was asking me to expedite the entry of the Police to participate with the UN forces in overseeing the Armistice Line area. General Burns suddenly changed his mind and the resulting exclusion of the Palestinian Police has continued until now. The Egyptian Administration has noticed that the Police do not have the freedom of action to maintain security in this area along the Armistice Line. Based on past experience, we have found that asking permission from UNEF for the Police to enter the area is impractical, insulting and violates our sovereignty, and we cannot accept it.

Burns: What kind of police is the General talking about, regular soldiers or guerillas?

Hilmy: Do the guerillas have an identifiable badge known to General Burns?

Burns: I see them myself armed with machine guns.

Hilmy: Any police force in any country has regular soldiers and plain-clothes elements. I had explained that in detail in a meeting with the UNEF Chief of Staff, and a record of the meeting was sent to New York, and there is no reason to repeat all that here. Unfortunately, my illness at the time prevented me from reaching an agreement with General Burns until now.

Fawzi: This is a lesson that General Hilmy does not get ill again.

Hilmy: I would like to present some practical examples. Sometimes, the Narcotics Bureau requests, based on their information about drug smuggling from Israel across the Armistice Line, assistance in allowing a tracker to identify the route of the smugglers. This happens sometimes around midnight or at dawn. It is not practical to ask the General's permission to enter the zone, and in turn he

	gives permission to the battalion commander, who then passes the order to the platoon commander, etc. This is totally impractical as we found out from past experience.
Sabri:	It is known that Israel encourages such smuggling, and even participates in the operations.
Hammarskjold:	Why does Israel participate in narcotics smuggling? I am not aware of the reasons for that.
Hilmy:	As Japan did in encouraging opium use in China.
Hammarskjold:	I appreciate what General Hilmy has said and understand the resulting problems because of such situation.
Burns:	I can discuss this issue with General Hilmy. We can then submit a report to you about the results of our discussions.

The Meeting Adjourned

(Minutes Ended)

References

Armstrong, Hamilton F. (1957): "The UN Experience in Gaza", in: *Foreign Affairs*, 35,4 (July 1957): 600–619.

Bove, Vincenzo; Ruggeri, Andrea (2019): "Peacekeeping Effectiveness and Blue Helmets' Distance from Locals", in: *Journal of Conflict Resolution*, 63,7: 1,630–1,655.

Burns, E.L.M. (1962): *Between Arab and Israeli* (Toronto: Clark, Irwin & Co).

Carroll, Michael K. (2009): *Pearson's Peacekeepers: Canada and the United Nations Emergency Force, 1956–67* (Vancouver: University of British Columbia Press).

Chase, Sean (2008): "Ambush in the Desert", in: *Pembroke Daily Observer*, Canada (Thursday, 27 November 2008).

Fetherston, A.B. (1994): *Towards a Theory of United Nations Peacekeeping* (New York: St. Martin's Press).

Galtung, Johan; Galtung, Ingrid (1964): *Some Factors Affecting Local Acceptance of a UN Force: A Pilot Project Report from Gaza* (Oslo: International Peace Research Institute): 1–25.

Goodman, Major Charles (2014): A conversation between Major Goodman (Canadian Army, retired) and the author (28 December 2014).

Hammarskjold, Dag (1956): *First Report of the Secretary-General*, A/3289 (2 November 1956).

Hammarskjold, Dag (1956): Annex to the *First Report of the Secretary-General*, A/3267 (2 November 1956).

Hammarskjold, Dag (1956): *Second Report of the Secretary-General*, A/3302 (6 November 1956).

Hammarskjold, Dag (1956): Annex to the *Second Report of the Secretary-General*, A/3284 (4 November 1956).

Hammarskjold, Dag (1957): *Report of the Secretary-General*, A/3512 (XI), Annexes, Vol. II, a. i. 66 (24 January 1957).

Hammarskjold, Dag (1957): *Report of the Secretary-General*, A/3943 (October 1957).

Heiberg, Marianne (1991): "Peacekeepers and Local Populations: Some Comments on UNIFIL", in: Rikhye, I.J.; Skjelsbaek, K. (Eds.), in: *The United Nations and Peacekeeping: Results, Limitations and Prospects* (New York: International Peace Academy and Palgrave Macmillan): 147–169.

High-Level Meeting (1959): *Between UN and Egyptian Officials* in Cairo, Egypt (Unpublished Document) (January 1959).

Hilmy II, Amin (n.d.): *Unpublished Memoirs.*

Love, Kenneth (1969): *Suez: The Twice-Fought War* (New York: McGraw-Hill).

Pearson, Lester B. (1957): "Address to the UN General Assembly" on (26 February 1957), as printed, in: *The Crisis in the Middle East: January-March 1957*, Parliament of Canada (Ottawa: The Queen's Printer).

Rikhye, Indar Jit (2002): *Trumpets and Tumults: The Memoirs of A Peacekeeper* (New Delhi: Manohar Publishers).

Saoud, Abdel-Hamid (1960): *Confidential Dispatch from the Egyptian Ambassador to Canada* to the Egyptian Ministry of Foreign Affairs in *Cairo*, Egypt (13 July 1960).

Stein, Janice G. (1985): "Detection and Defection: Security 'Regimes' and the Management of International Conflict", in: *International Journal*, 40 (Autumn): 615–620.

UN First Emergency Session (1956): *Plenary Meeting* 565, Item 5 (4 November 1956).

UN General Assembly (1956): *The Good Faith Agreement*, A/3375 [1121 (XI)] (24 November 1956).

UN General Assembly (1957): *The Status of Forces Agreement*, A/3526 - I & II [1126 (XI)] (22 February 1957).

United Nations (n.d.): "Background:MiddleEast–UNEF1"; at: https://peacekeeping.un.org/en/mission/past/unef1backgr2.html.

Chapter 10
UNEF (1967): Demise and War

Abstract The first post-war large-scale pioneering international peace operation floundered for two fundamental reasons. The first was the absence of a built-in conflict resolution component designed to address the core of the dispute. The second, was the changed Cold War profile, pitting – unlike Suez – the two superpowers on opposite sides of the conflict. The deceptive charade of an Israeli war waged for self-defence was soon unmasked to show the West's collusion in this project of defeating and dismantling the anti-colonial tide in the Middle East. Israel was allowed – against all notions of the post-war international legal regime – to illegally occupy and annex Arab territories. The resulting 1967 War demonstrated the internal divisions within the Egyptian leadership. It also showed the confusion over the Egyptian decision to ask for the termination of UNEF's presence in Egypt. Nasser wanted partial redeployment, while the military leadership was determined to force a total withdrawal. In accepting the request for UNEF's withdrawal, Secretary-General U Thant was acting correctly – if not wisely – by respecting the principle of sovereign consent. The war achieved the West's objectives, while Israel reaped (with the help of the US, and the disarray and collusion of some of the Arabs) a much larger booty than was believed possible. Both the consent issue and Israel's conquest are still affecting the international system.

Keywords Old Israeli war plans activated · Egyptian leadership division · Strategic blunder · Withdrawal of UNEF · Gulf of Aqaba · Arab divisions · General Rikhye · U Thant · Foreign involvement · Edifice of Peace crumbled

10.1 The Dismantling of the Edifice of Peace

The UNEF peacekeeping Operations began and developed almost on an *ad hoc* basis. The international force was hastily deployed before a final agreement (the Good Faith Agreement) on the political-legal basis of its operation was attained. And it was several months after its deployment that a Status of Forces Agreement

© Springer Nature Switzerland AG 2020

H. Hilmy, *Decolonization, Sovereignty, and Peacekeeping*,

https://doi.org/10.1007/978-3-030-57624-0_10

was reached. There was no prior agreement, however, on the modality of the withdrawal of the force at the end of its mandate.

The Good Faith Agreement was deliberately left vague for convenient interpretation by each side. Two fundamental points were agreed to by Egypt and the UN: first, Egypt's sovereign consent in accepting the force was paramount; second, the UNEF would remain in Egypt until its task was completed. The contradiction built into this agreement is apparent when pitting the UN right of maintaining the force in place until the job was done (without defining the completion target) against Egypt's uncontested right to pull its consent plug, as entitled by its sovereign prerogatives.

Who had the right to declare whether the UNEF task was completed or not – the UN or Egypt? The 1956 military encounter was terminated, invaders withdrawn, and the border pacified. The task, in fact, was done. Indeed, well done. Logically, Egypt could even have asked for a termination and withdrawal much earlier than 1967 (in fact in 1957). Regardless of who had the right of consent and termination, the fact was that a painstaking project for peace was destroyed or dismantled. in the words of General Rikhye (1980: 45), without achieving a peaceful outcome.

The UNEF was temporarily deployed to end the 1956 Suez War, not to remain in place on an open-ended basis. Egypt was not prepared to accept the presence of an international force within its territory indefinitely. The international community as a whole, including the involved parties, shoulder the responsibility for the failure to reach an accommodation which rendered the need for international intervention unnecessary. The success of UNEF in overseeing the withdrawal of the invading forces from Egypt and Gaza in 1956–57, and its role as a barrier between the warring parties for many years, important though they were, ultimately ended in failure; the lack of conflict resolution or a formal peace agreement meant that there was no obstacle to the resumption of war by any party to the unresolved conflict.

The complex efforts expended over a decade to prevent war crumbled in just a few weeks in June 1967, leaving the international community with a profound sense of failure and betrayal, and the Middle East in a more dangerous and unstable situation than ever. The UN's greatest pioneering peacekeeping success turned into the organization's abysmal failure and a colossal wasted opportunity to lay the foundations for a permanent Arab-Israeli peace as a model for conflict resolution for other conflict regions.

Paradoxically and tragically, the presence of UNEF on the borders between Egypt and Israel from 1956 to 1967 offered a false sense of security and relative calm that was deceptive and in the end counterproductive. UNEF "lulled the international community into slackening its pursuit of a resolution to the basic Arab-Israeli conflict" (Rikhye 1980: 157).

The withdrawal of UNEF and the resulting massive Arab defeat was described euphemistically in official Arab circles as the 'setback', when in fact, it was a catastrophic defeat not just for the Arab armies, but for the entire Arab anti-colonial nationalist-secular front. The failure of the international peacekeeping efforts between the Arabs and Israel had the unintended and unforeseen consequence of the emergence of other ideological-radical alternatives exploring other identity markers, and destroying in the process the seeds of eventual progressive social transformation. The Middle East has yet to recover from the 'setback'.

10.2   The Mayhem: The 1967 Arab-Israeli War

There are several fundamental facts about the failure of the peacekeeping regime in May 1967 and the rush to war in that fateful late spring:

10.2.1   The Egyptian Account

Egypt and its leadership walked into the biggest trap in its modern history in May 1967, and manufactured in the process its largest military defeat in the Arab-Israeli confrontation. It was a self-made catastrophe committed by the leadership in biting the Israeli bait. Israel's designs to defeat Egypt and annex more territories should have been known and anticipated, judging by the 1956 experience. The rush to dance to the Israeli tune was an inexcusable – some say criminal – lapse in rational behaviour. In May 1967 Egypt received intelligence reports from the Soviet Union suggesting that Israel threatened to invade Syria and occupy Damascus as retaliation for Syria's endorsement of the rights of the Palestinians to engage in armed struggle against Israel. The Syrian-Israeli border region was already tense because of competing claims over the control of the water sources of the Jordan River and the Sea of Galilee.

Because of Israel's increasingly public threats against Syria in April and May 1967, Egypt invoked in May 1967 its Mutual Defence Agreement (signed in 1966) with the Syrians by declaring a military alert and requesting the withdrawal of UNEF from the Rafah-Taba Sinai border area (Armistice Lines) only, as requested by the Egyptian military. Nasser would have lost all credibility and leadership status in the Arab world if he had not come to the aid of threatened Syria, whether the threat was real, manufactured or imagined. Undoubtedly, fractured Arab politics contributed to the gathering storm in May 1967.

Following the rapid withdrawal of UNEF from all its positions, including the islands of Tiran and Sanafir at the entrance to the Gulf of Aqaba (contrary to the initial Egyptian request), Egypt had no option but to close the Straits of Tiran to Israeli shipping and restore the status quo ante before the 1956 war – breaching an unpublicized right acquired by Israel after the 1956 Suez War with the help of the US government. The new right of naval passage enjoyed by Israel through Tiran between 1957 and 1967 was an embarrassing open secret.

The Egyptian domestic leadership squabble between Nasser and his Vice President and Army Commander Amer meant that decisions affecting foreign policy and the army were practically removed from Nasser's control. The struggle between Nasser and Amer (who were very close friends for many years) became extremely dangerous as early as 1961 and 1962 when Amer refused to allow Nasser's requests for senior staff appointments in the army. Amer, in fact, staged a white coup excluding Nasser from military affairs while maintaining a deceptive façade of unity and loyalty to the President.

Tragically, when Nasser had confronted Amer over his challenge, Amer had left his post in anger and retired to his home base. In hindsight, it is unfortunate that Nasser felt compelled to appeal to his old friend to return to his post, setting in motion the disastrous consequences of Amer's later inept military leadership during the 1967 crisis.

The Egyptian army became the personal power base of Amer, who excluded Nasser from any leadership role. Due to Nasser's mass appeal and popularity, Amer was satisfied with using Nasser as an icon and hiding behind his status as the leader of the regime when in fact he was kept as a figurehead. Moreover, the leadership of the Egyptian armed forces were split in 1962, with all the branches of the army siding with Amer except the Air Force, which threw its support behind Nasser.

During the 1962 confrontation General Ali Shafiq, Amer's assistant, communicated to Nasser the threat that if any air force plane took off, Nasser's house would be bombarded with artillery fire. Nasser then decided to avoid a confrontation, as pitting branches of the army against each other would threaten the entire regime and the stability of the country as a whole (Ghaleb 2001). Amer held the upper hand in deciding military matters, including the fate of UNEF in Egypt. Nasser had real concern about a deteriorating and explosive situation getting out of hand. But he was the President and he had the support of the overwhelming majority of the people. It was his duty to act to regain control. His failure to take charge led directly to the withdrawal of UNEF and the calamitous 1967 war.

Amer and his faction had wanted to get rid of UNEF for some time. He instructed his chief of staff to order the withdrawal of the international Force from the Egyptian border only (excluding the Gaza Strip and the Gulf of Aqaba) as a deterrent against a possible Israeli attack against Syria.

Still, Nasser felt obligated to make a show of force by sending Egyptian troops into Sinai and demanding that some of the UN peacekeepers be removed from their posts. Despite the bellicose speeches that followed, Nasser seemed to be bluffing. He didn't expect all of the UN troops to be withdrawn.

The UN said, "Withdraw all or keep all." Instead of giving diplomacy a chance, as Nasser was doing (or at least hoping to), Amer rushed Egyptian troops to occupy the entrance to the Gulf of Aqaba and created in the process a *fait accompli* for Nasser.

The closure of the Strait of Tiran would be one of the initially unscripted developments (by the political leadership) in the gathering conflict. It was the spark (justification) that ignited a war that Israel had been planning and preparing for over many years. Israel wanted to make good on its aborted plans to annex Arab territories in 1956. The Israelis had their modified Kadesh plan on the shelf, ready to be dusted off and activated at the opportune time. The crisis over UNEF was the perfect scenario for the activation of the Israeli designs. The irresponsible ineptitude of the Egyptian political-military leadership during the 1967 crisis thus allowed Israel to deliver on its plan in a way not even Israel was capable of envisioning.

Once the closure of the Straits was ordered, as strongly recommended by his military, Nasser had no choice but to take ownership of the decision, especially when he had been constantly attacked by other Arab leaders over Israel's free use of the Straits. Nasser was accused in many Arab circles of "hiding behind the skirts of UNEF" (Rikhye 1980: 158). Undoubtedly, intra-Arab conflicts and rivalries contributed in a significant way to escalating the conflict and cornering the Egyptians into a confrontation they had no hope of winning. This was a catastrophic failure in leadership. Nasser allowed his constitutional prerogatives to be usurped and consequently allowed others (in Egypt and outside) to dictate the scenario of the conflict. The closure of the Strait of Tiran gave Israel the *casus belli* to launch a war which had been planned long before the Aqaba justification.

10.2.2   Helping Syria?

An obvious question is: why did the Egyptian leadership invoke its mutual Defence Pact with Syria and declare military mobilization in response to a non-confirmed military threat, relying only on verbal Israeli threats? The most likely answer is that Egyptian and intra-Arab politics played a major role in the move to confront Israel. Officially, the Egyptian leadership could hardly have ignored the threats made publicly and repeatedly by Israel to use military force against Syria. But the same leadership was not given iron-clad proof that Israel was about to strike, which would have justified an Egyptian reaction (not necessarily kicking out UNEF). With posturing an essential part of conducting public policy in the Arab World, Egypt, to its peril, succumbed to the temptation to play the hero of the moment.

The better part of Egypt's fighting forces were mired in the war in Yemen, fighting on the Republican side. By all accounts, Egypt's involvement in the Yemen War of 1962–1970, which ostensibly marked a Nasserite victory, actually weakened the capabilities of the Egyptian military vis-à-vis Israel. To ignore such a fact was extremely irresponsible.

In his book, *Nasser's Gamble*, Jesse Ferris advances the argument that the Egyptian involvement in Yemen overburdened Egyptian resources, coalesced internal and external opposition to Nasser, and caused a general decline in Egyptian power in the region. The resulting "six-day war ended a decade and a half of Egyptian ascendancy…Not since Muhammad Ali's defeat at the hands of Great Britain in 1840 had a rising local power suffered such an imperial contraction… Egypt's misfortune was more than the shattering of an imperial dream. It was the end of an era" (Ferris 2012: 295–312).

Not coming to Syria's aid would have been a shameful failure. Personal glory for Nasser's leadership, moreover, in the quick sands of Arab politics, was a risk worth taking. After all, confronting Israel over its threats to Syria in 1958 and again in

1960 paid rich political dividends without triggering a deadly military confrontation.

The two-headed Nasser-Amer leadership team and the competition it involved could only have contributed to decision-making confusion, miscalculation, and incalculable disaster. Nasser, the undisputed popular and mythical leader, and Amer, the affable but strategically and tactically ineffective military leader, sang fundamentally different tunes. Nasser wanted political triumph without significant military risk, while Amer opted for military challenge (and potential glory) without due regard for the possible dangerous consequences. It was Amer who forced Nasser on a course he was not planning to follow in 1966–67. Nasser wanted to come to the aid of Syria and win politically, but Amer wanted to up the ante militarily.

10.2.3   The Strait of Tiran and the Gulf of Aqaba: A Self-inflicted Trap

Nasser wanted to exploit the deteriorating Israeli-Syrian situation and score a big political win without actually going to war, while Amer was applying intense pressure to secure the right to strike militarily against Israel first and early before Israel completed its mobilization (a possibility feasible only in the absence of the US commitment to Israel). Nasser did not understand or realize the magnitude of the risk his government was taking, while Amer was totally unprepared for a full-scale war. The combination of divided leadership, bravado and ineptitude doomed the Egyptian position from the start. Israel, meanwhile, was happy to play along and exploit a manufactured and unnecessary confrontation. The termination of the role of UNEF in maintaining "the absence of war" and the resulting closure of the Straits of Tiran in this rapidly and uncontrollably escalating crisis was the trigger for the tragedy of 1967. Thousands died, huge resources were wasted, and the Arab-Israeli conflict deepened. The presence of the UNEF was the biggest lost opportunity in a generation for a comprehensive peace in the history of the modern Middle East.

Many Arab states exerted enormous pressure on Nasser to confront Israel. Indeed, many of the Arab leaders who were opposed to Nasser were hoping that the Egyptian President would either shy away from the confrontation and therefore lose credibility, or else get involved and suffer a humiliating defeat. Nasser was on the horns of a dilemma, as he related to his confidant, Mohamed Heikal. Letting Syria face Israel alone and thereby suffer a massive defeat would result in Egypt's status in the region being "vastly diminished" (Heikal 1990: 448–451). Nasser concluded, therefore, that he "could no longer sit aside and watch". But it was Vice President Amer who wanted the UNEF out of the way. While on a visit to Pakistan in December 1966, Amer cabled Nasser "with a proposal for ordering UNEF off

Egyptian soil, concentrating Egypt's army in Sinai and reinstating the blockade in the Straits of Tiran" (Oren 2002: 39).

The intra-Arab rivalries that contributed to the flare up in 1967 led Nasser to feel that he had no choice. As Rikhye notes, "To assert his leadership, he chose to re-militarize the Sinai but not to go to war" (Rikhye 1980: 172). In fact, Nasser had a choice but, goaded by hawkish elements in his government and military, he overplayed his hand. Reluctantly at first, he eventually overstepped the bounds of responsible prudence, especially when Israel was long waiting for such an opportunity. Nasser wanted a grand political victory, and Israel wanted a decisive military victory. Nasser was doomed from the moment he responded to Israel's threat of invading Syria. While Nasser clearly did not want war, the last UNEF Commander observed that the Israeli threats against Syria and Egypt's counter threats placed the UNEF into an untenable position. In fact, he added that the Arabs created a "false euphoria to a level from which there was no retreat" (Rikhye 1980: 172).

Undoubtedly, Nasser did not anticipate the UN's all-or-nothing response to his request for partial UNEF withdrawal. Consequently, Egypt lost the ability to manoeuvre politically and war became inevitable. The strategic mistake in the problematic initial Egyptian request was to view the partial withdrawal of UNEF as an acceptable risk, potentially allowing Egypt to reap a political victory without actually going to war. The UN response was not a possibility the Egyptian leadership properly calculated or anticipated. The Egyptian position in May-June 1967 demonstrated a political failure of policy planning of gigantic proportions, leading to an equally disastrous military collapse.

Tragically for Egypt, Nasser was not contemplating an attack on Israel during the May crisis in 1967. Israel was not on his radar as an imminent target of confrontation. For instance, Marianne Rostgaard and Martin Jorgensen note that "Egypt…long had Israel lower on its list of priorities than the destruction of Anglo-American regional influence in its struggle for regional hegemony" (Rostgaard/Jorgensen 2012: 33). Further confirmation of Nasser's lack of interest in a military confrontation with Israel was documented by international law scholar John Quigley. According to Quigley's research, the US Ambassador to Israel, Walworth Barbour, informed Israeli officials that the UNEF withdrawal would not affect the "fundamental military situation" and that there was "every reason for Nasser" not to attack Israel (Quigley 2012: 495–497).

Despite the bravado of Vice President Amer, even he informed the Soviet Ambassador to Egypt, Dmitri Pozhidaev, that if Israel was worried about an Egyptian invasion it "could accept UNEF on its own side of the Armistice Line". Israel "can make its own territory available", he said. Moreover, UN Secretary-General U Thant proposed to Israel's Ambassador to the UN, Gideon Rafael, the same suggestion for the transfer of UNEF to the Israeli side as a "protection against possible invasion". The Israeli Ambassador replied that such a proposal was "entirely unacceptable to his Government" (Quigley 2012: 495–497). One can conclude that Israel's apprehension about a possible Egyptian invasion was a ruse. Placing UNEF on the Israeli side would have hindered, if not stopped,

Israel's own plans for the invasion of Egypt. The Egyptians thus placed themselves in a corner with no escape route.

The split in the Egyptian Cabinet due to the desire of the hawkish elements to strike the first blow against Israel, as well as Nasser's concerns about his armed forces' limited capabilities and his more realistic reading of the international scene, led the President to approve the movement of the army into the Sinai but to prevent it from initiating military action. General Rikhye's own observation of the political situation and the actual military deployment of the Egyptian army led him to believe that "there clearly was a difference in views between the armed forces and President Nasser". As he observed, "The troops had been sent forward, readied for attack, but Nasser stopped them from attacking". Moreover, Nasser was apprehensive about possible military intervention by the US in case of war with Israel. The UN Secretary-General conveyed to Nasser a warning by the US Ambassador to the UN, Arthur Goldberg, that the previous understanding between President Eisenhower and Israel – namely, that the US would help to defend Israel if attacked – was still in place (Rikhye 1980: 166–167).

With the realization of the possible disastrous military-political outcome for Egypt, however, the Egyptian president was desperately trying to de-escalate the situation by agreeing to UN Secretary-General U Thant's proposal for a moratorium on implementing the blockade in the Gulf of Aqaba. Nasser also agreed to receive US Vice President Hubert Humphrey for talks in Cairo (on 3 June 1967) and to send Vice President Zakaria Mohieddin to Washington (on 5 June 1967) for talks with President Johnson, the purpose of which would be to find a way out of the crisis. "The United States was holding direct talks with Nasser, and hoped to buy time by inviting his vice president, Zakaria Mohieddin, to Washington, and sending Vice President Humphrey to Cairo" (Segev 2007: 302)

Egypt's former Foreign Minister, Dr. Morad Ghaleb (2001), also confirmed in his memoirs that the negotiations in Cairo and in Washington, DC were scheduled to take place involving the two Vice Presidents. However, Dr. Ghaleb stated that the purpose of the proposed negotiations was in reality to keep Egypt in the dark. The minister believed that the contrived push for a peaceful outcome was a strategic deception by the United States, which knew in advance of Israel's plan to administer a crushing blow to Egypt. "Such strategic deception" was also confirmed by General Rikhye when he stated that a peace initiative:

> appeared a possibility with the announcement that Zachria Mohieddin, the Vice-President, and Mahmoud Fawzi were to visit Washington to meet President Johnson and members of his administration. But the initiative came too late and the inexorable progress of events never allowed the visit to take place (Rikhye 1980: 95).

The Egyptian Ambassador to Washington, Mustafa Kamel, assured the American administration that Nasser was committed to keeping the confrontation with Israel "in the icebox". Moreover, the US National Security Advisor, Walt Rostow, confirmed this reading of Nasser's intention by writing a memo to President Johnson, stating "Nasser...has restrained wilder Arabs who have pushed for a disastrous Arab-Israeli showdown" (Rostow 1967). However, according to

Oren, there was "a countervailing force in the Egyptian military, one that assidu-ously pressed for war," but was unknown to the Americans (Oren 2002: 56). This "countervailing force" was more than matched, Oren might have added, by the assiduous forces existing in the Israeli Army and the political class which aimed to vanquish Egypt's military capabilities, as very well known by Washington.

Incredibly, Amer informed Nasser in May 1967 that "Our armed forces are not only capable of repulsing Israel but moving eastward...Egypt can establish a position from which to impose its own political conditions and to force Israel to respect Arab and Palestinian rights" (Mutawi 1987: 96). To be fair to this inter-pretation, had Egypt struck first and moved its mobilized troops into the Negev, the Israeli attack would have been blunted and the military outcome would have been perhaps less bleak for Egypt. The unknown factor in this scenario is the extent of a possible US intervention, and the role of the Soviets in such an eventuality.

Although built on wishful thinking, intrigue, and split leadership, popular trust in Nasser's views had made Egypt's position in the eyes of the Egyptian people and the rest of the Arab world absolutely legitimate and unassailable. The state infor-mation apparatus, which took its cues from the country's leadership, spared no time in glorifying the official stand without the benefit of a free debate. Any attempt by Nasser, at this juncture of the crisis, to remove Amer from his entrenched position would have turned the leadership problem into an open confrontation involving the military, threatening the survival of the regime itself. Moreover, opposing Amer's aggressive stand against Israel would have portrayed Nasser as a weakling who had lost his justification for holding the leadership.

In the face of the escalating tension, Nasser tried to pacify Amer by offering to "appoint him Prime Minister" in return for relinquishing control over the army. Amer not only refused Nasser's offer, but ordered the mobilization of key army units and called up the army reserves for active duty (Oren 2002: 57). According to Oren, nothing seemed left for Nasser but to go along with a disastrous decision with earth-shaking results (which as President he had the duty and the opportunity to avoid).

Although Nasser was content to have UNEF withdrawn only from the armistice lines with Israel from Rafah to Taba, his hand was forced when Vice President Amer engineered UNEF's total withdrawal (from not only the armistice lines with Egypt, but also from the Gaza Strip, and the all-important Straits of Tiran in the Gulf of Aqaba as well). Such total withdrawal from all UNEF deployment posts was the inevitable outcome of the formal request Egypt made to the UN for partial withdrawal only (Rafah to Taba), as the international organization had refused to carry out a partial withdrawal (offering all or nothing).

With the Straits back under Egyptian control, the inevitable (and yet reluctant, at least for Nasser), next step was to blockade Israeli naval access to the Gulf, returning to the pre-1956 status. Tragically, for Egypt, Nasser, "never wanted or even approved complete withdrawal of UNEF", according to the UNEF Commander. The UN General believed that "the Egyptians were willing to nego-tiate for a continued UNEF presence as long as Egyptian forces could move suf-ficiently close to the International Frontier for Nasser to satisfy his critics" (Rikhye 1980: 169).

10.2.4   Egypt's International Borders

As an *explanatory* note on the definition of the border area between Egypt and Israel: before 1948, the lines between Egypt and British-Mandated Palestine (Rafah to Taba) were the international border between Egypt and Britain (as the Mandatory power) on the one hand, and the Ottoman Empire on the other. The Rafah-Taba line was formalized in a treaty in 1906 between Britain (on behalf of Egypt) and the Ottoman Empire, which controlled Palestine at that time. With the creation of Israel and the end of the 1948–49 War, the lines between Egypt and Palestine were transformed into Armistice Lines between Egypt and Israel, as well as Gaza (under Egyptian Trusteeship) and Israel, in accordance with the Armistice Agreement between the two sides. The Armistice Lines became the demarcation lines between Egypt and Gaza, on one side, and between Egypt and Israel on the other.

There was always a distinction between the Lines between Egypt and Israel, and the Lines between Gaza and Israel. This was to emphasize that Gaza was under Egyptian control only as a Trustee Power following the war with Israel, and was not part of Egyptian territories. The Lines between Israel and both Egypt and Gaza were not regarded as recognized international borders because the conflict was far from resolved. Moreover, Israel was claiming additional Palestinian and Egyptian territories and did not want to accept a final formal limit on its territorial acquisitions in line with the 1947 UN Partition Plan.

When Egypt requested the withdrawal of UNEF in 1967, it made a distinction between Egyptian and Palestinian territories. The request was for a withdrawal from Rafah to Taba; there was no request for the withdrawal of UNEF from the borders with Gaza. Moreover, the UNEF positions at the entrance of the Gulf of Aqaba also bypassed the withdrawal request.

The rationale for choosing Rafah to Taba only was to emphasize that Egypt's request was covering the immediate border positions between Egypt and British-Mandated Palestine (now Israel), and not Gaza or Tiran. This deliberate choice was also to show intent of Egyptian action and a desire to save the UNEF from getting embroiled in a military confrontation, in case Syria came under Israeli attack. However, the UN chose an all-or-nothing response, enabling Israel to start the hostilities without the complication of a UNEF presence.

As it turned out, not only did Israel have offensive plans to strike at Egypt, but, unknown to Nasser, Vice President Amer had his own offensive plan, code-named *Fajr* (Dawn), which called for strategic air strikes and the capture of the entire Eilat salient; he later expanded this goal to include the entire Negev.

To avoid Nasser's opposition, Amer directed the preparations for *Fajr* from his own fortified house. "Amer's Dawn clearly violated Nasser's strategy of drawing Israel into starting the war" with Egypt (Oren 2002: 92). Nasser did not want Egypt to shoulder the blame for initiating the hostilities. "Amer, alone, devised the operation in blatant opposition to Nasser's will". Since Amer's intention of penetrating the Negev would "almost certainly be frustrated by UNEF...Amer wanted the force disbanded completely, and not merely removed from the border, as Nasser preferred". The Amer plans for UNEF, the Negev and Tiran were recipes for certain Israeli strike already in train. Amer was warned by the senior Egyptian military leadership, "but Amer ignored their advice". When eventually Nasser discovered Amer's plans, he "lacked the political strength to override" the scheme (Oren 2002: 92). Clearly, this was a massive failure in leadership, the consequences of which would be fatal for his regime, the army and his country's position in the region.

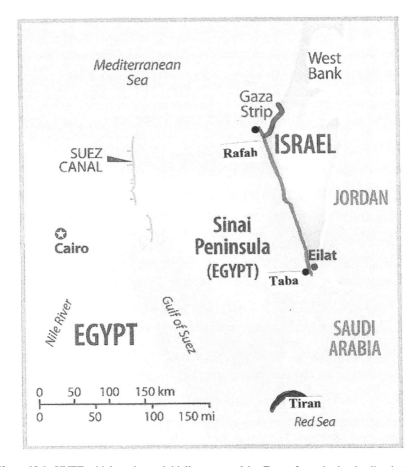

Photo 10.1 UNEF withdrawal was initially requested by Egypt from the border line between Egypt and Israel, i.e., from Rafah (on the Mediterranean) to Taba (on the Gulf of Aqaba) (Red Line). UNEF positions in the Gaza Strip and Tiran at the entrance to the Gulf of Aqaba (Blue Lines) were excluded. *Source* The author

The miscalculation ('blunder' in Rikhye's terminology) associated with the withdrawal of UNEF was painfully evident later on, when the senior Egyptian diplomat, Mohamed Riad, later the Minister of State for Foreign Affairs, sadly asked General Rikhye during the UN General Assembly Special Session in July 1967, "Why did you withdraw UNEF? We didn't want you to pull out." Rikhye answered: "But you did ask us to withdraw from the Sinai…We could not pull out from part of our responsibilities and continue with the rest…You left us no option." Riad then indicated that the UN reply of all or nothing to Egypt's partial withdrawal request also left Egypt no option but to ask for a total withdrawal since the partial withdrawal was not feasible. The Egyptian diplomat insisted that "The UN therefore invited us to tell UNEF to go" (Rikhye 1980: 163–164). Riad believed that the Secretary-General should not have responded the way he did, in fact closing the door to a 'face-saving' compromise.

The veteran Egyptian diplomat, Nabil Elaraby, later a judge in the International Court of Justice, echoed Riad's sentiments when he pointed out that "Egypt did not want the force completely withdrawn, but only deployed for political ends" in order to deflect criticism that Egypt was "hiding behind the shield of the UNEF" (Elaraby 1968: 148–149).

As it turned out, the letter requesting the UNEF withdrawal written by Egyptian Chief of Staff Mohamed Fawzi at the instigation of his boss, Vice President and overall Commander, Marshal Amer, was not even reviewed or approved by the Egyptian ministry of foreign affairs prior to its delivery to the UNEF commander! This fact precluded any possibility of wiser and more professional feedback and advice as to the ramifications of such a fateful request. The privileged role of the army in Egyptian politics and the lack of a national democratic oversight mechanism allowed the military to initiate steps with profound implications for Egypt. Moreover, the Egyptian Ambassador to the UN, Mohamed El Kony, a respected official highly trusted by the Nasser government, advised the UN Secretary-General not to appeal the original withdrawal request directly with President Nasser, as U Thant first proposed.

El Kony, who genuinely supported Egypt's right to ask for the withdrawal of UNEF, was afraid that U Thant's appeal would have been considered a challenge to the Egyptian President. At the same time, in Rikhye's opinion, the "United Nations had misread all the signals from Egypt" (Rikhye 1980: 165–166) due to the lack of resident UN representation on the ground in Egypt. Thus they were in no position to properly assess the political situation and advise the UN Headquarters about the political factors at play in the country and about the complex situation surrounding its leadership. This lack of representation and engagement with the Egyptian regime was allowed to continue despite the crucial role of UNEF in preventing military confrontation in a pivotal region and despite the dire consequences of unwisely terminating such a role.

Nasser was directly implicated in the request for the *partial* UNEF withdrawal, but not for *full* withdrawal. In order to deal with Amer's insistent demand for the withdrawal of the international Force, Nasser consulted with his trusted foreign affairs advisor and the former foreign minister during the 1956 Suez Crisis, Dr.

Mahmoud Fawzi (who became a presidential advisor on foreign affairs). The President indicated that he was not in agreement with Amer's insistence on complete withdrawal and kept insisting on retaining UNEF in Gaza and the Strait of Tiran. Dr. Fawzi prepared a briefing file confirming Egypt's sovereign right to evict UNEF, but he recommended the course favoured by Nasser for withdrawing UNEF from the international border only, not from Gaza or Tiran. Dr. Fawzi also recommended that instructions to this effect be "given to General Rikhye rather than U Thant, thus emphasizing their practical, as opposed to legal, nature". Naturally, making such a request to the Commanding General and not to the Secretary-General had huge political and legal implications. It should have been evident to the Egyptian leadership that it was not feasible for the UNEF Commander to agree to the Egyptian request without consulting the political brass at the UN (another part of the 'blunder' in the Sinai). Nasser approved Dr. Fawzi's strategy and the decision was made to proceed on this basis. By so doing, Nasser was hoping to send a "double message to Israel: Egypt had no aggressive designs, but neither would it suffer any Israeli aggression against Syria" (Oren 2002: 52).

According to Heikal, after reviewing the draft letter, Nasser ordered the replacement of the word 'withdraw' with 'redeploy', and crossed out the word 'all' before 'these troops'. This change was intended to "prevent any misunderstanding regarding the continued presence of UNEF in Gaza and in Sharm al-Sheikh [Tiran]". Nasser then asked General Amer to insert the changes into the final version, "only to be told that the letter was already being delivered". Moreover, the last line and a half in the Egyptian note was added to the original copy that the President had already approved, without his knowledge (Heikal 1990: 457–459).

10.2.5   Initial Withdrawal Request

The text of the Egyptian withdrawal request reads as follows: (Fawzi 1967, UN Doc. S/0316)

COMMANDER UNEF (GAZA)

For your information, I gave my instructions to all UAR armed forces to be ready for action against Israel, the moment it might carry out any aggressive action against any Arab country. Due to these instructions our troops are already concentrated in Sinai on our eastern border.

For the sake of complete security of all UN troops which install OP's [Observation Posts] along our border[s], I request that you issue your orders to withdraw all these troops immediately. I have given my instructions to our commander of the Eastern Zone concerning this subject. Inform back the fulfillment of this request.

Yours,

General Mohamed Fawzi

Chief of Staff of the UAR. [16 May 1967]

The Egyptian note spoke only of UNEF withdrawal from the '*borders*' (with Israel). Nothing was mentioned about the UNEF positions in the "Gaza Strip" or "Sharm El Sheikh". Clearly, the Egyptian domestic strife was creating a disastrous outcome for the country.

In fairness to Nasser and to historical accuracy, when it became all but certain that war was imminent, military commanders requested permission to commence operations quickly to at least blunt Israel's expected assault. Permission was denied by Nasser because of his pledges to US President Johnson and UN Secretary-General U Thant that Egypt would not initiate hostilities against Israel. The US President, however, had other expectations for the conflict and was fully aware of Israel's impending military strike. Paradoxically, Amer's *Fajr* Plan, if deployed, would have changed the outcome of the war drastically. The French stance, on the other hand, was clearly against the country initiating the first strike. Nasser was later blamed for this principled but disastrous stand.

10.3   The Withdrawal of UNEF

With the escalating rhetoric on both sides, and the real or rumoured Israeli mobilization on the Syrian front, some elements in Egypt's leadership upped the anti and mobilized the army.

The controversial decisions surrounding Egypt's precipitous request to the UN to pull its UNEF troops out of Egypt set the stage for the start of the 1967 Arab-Israeli War. As a consequence, Egypt and the entire Middle East suffered a body blow from which they have not recovered. The region's geopolitical balance shifted irrevocably. New facts on the ground – relying on external support – were changing the face of the Middle East. Resources and efforts were diverted from nation-building plans to a futile military confrontation with foregone conclusions.

On 16 May 1967, General Rikhye, was asked to attend an urgent meeting in the office of General Ibrahim Sharkawy, Egyptian chief liaison officer to UNEF, and another Egyptian General, Eiz E. Mokhtar, representing the Egyptian High Command. General Rikhye was handed a brief communiqué signed by General Mohamed Fawzi, the Egyptian Chief of Staff, that would begin a chain of events changing the history of the Middle East and fundamentally impacting the mandate and principles of all future UN peacekeeping operations.

The Egyptian note requested the immediate withdrawal of UN troops deployed along the Egyptian border. The request may have left open the possibility that the reference to the 'border' meant only the line between Rafah on the Mediterranean (south of the Gaza Strip) and Taba on the Gulf of Aqaba (south of Eilat). But in fairness to the UN decision-makers, the request could have meant the total withdrawal of UNEF, regardless of where they were deployed. The restricted interpretation of the request was the intent of President Nasser, although the execution was flawed.

According to General Rikhye, Egyptian General Mokhtar requested immediate compliance with the request of the Egyptian High Command. Unfortunately, the Egyptian General also seemed to have taken it upon himself to *verbally* request UNEF's withdrawal from Sharm el Sheikh (and not just from the international borders with British-Mandated Palestine), a request which was not included in the *written* note. "For the second time I re-read General Fawzi's letter, but found no specific reference to El Sabha and Sharm el Sheikh" (Rikhye 1980: 19).

Sharm el Sheikh is not located on Egypt's international border with Israel (being hundreds of miles south of the border), and therefore could not have been targeted in the Egyptian note which only specified the request for withdrawal from the 'border[s]'. A withdrawal of UNEF from the Egyptian border with Israel alone, without involving the Gaza Strip or Sharm el Sheikh (Tiran), could have avoided escalation of the conflict over the freedom of navigation through the Strait of Tiran (adjacent to Sharm el Sheikh), and hence could have avoided providing Israel with the pretext for launching the war.

Whether the Egyptian General was acting on his own and improvising, or whether the additional verbal requests were intended by army HQ but deliberately not included in the written note, would require further examination of the historical record. Of course, a third explanation could be that the army Headquarters did not want to include the additional requests but that the power struggle in Egypt allowed General Mokhtar to enlarge the request, reflecting the views of some in the leadership who wanted to get rid of UNEF once and for all. Considering the open leadership conflict after the war, one can credibly conclude that the power struggle in Egypt may have contributed to the mixed signals communicated by the Egyptian General to the UNEF Commander.

In the face of insistent requests by the Egyptian General for immediate compliance, the UNEF Commander replied that he had no authority to order the withdrawal of the UN troops without the authorization of the Secretary-General of the UN. However, the UN Commander promised to send an immediate request to the UN Headquarters in New York for instructions, which he did around midnight. In response, the Egyptian General advised General Rikhye that in order to avoid any unintended confrontation between the UN troops and the Egyptian troops then being deployed in Sinai, Rikhye should order the UN troops to be confined to their camps (Rikhye 1980: 20).

As the tension in this encounter subsided somewhat, General Rikhye confirmed Egypt's right to ask for the withdrawal of UNEF, but he cautioned General Mokhtar about the consequences of such a withdrawal. According to General Rikhye's memoir, it was General Sharkawy who replied this time, saying that if war erupted, "we shall meet in Tel Aviv". In fact, General Rikhye later informed the writer, during a meeting in 2001, that General Sharkawy actually told him that if war erupted, "I will invite you to lunch in Tel Aviv".[1]

---

[1] Hanny Hilmy, discussion with General Indar Jit Rikhye, Victoria, Canada, 2001.

I believe General Rikhye did not want to include the Egyptian General's exact words in order to avoid highlighting the obviously misinformed and misplaced bravado about the Israeli trap (a bait for Kadesh) Egypt was about to walk into without its leaders realizing (or realizing too late) the scope or the magnitude of the disaster around the corner. Such an attitude was symptomatic on the part of many in the Egyptian leadership and it filtered down to some segments of the general public in both Egypt and the rest of the Arab World. Others had a feeling of foreboding, or at least an apprehension that 'this is too good to be true'. The billions of dollars spent on armaments following the 1956 war, fortified by the regime's glorification of Egypt's military prowess, managed to instil a sense of unfounded invincibility (the same sense of invincibility Israel was exhibiting on the eve of the 1973 War).

The Israeli policy-makers exploited this delusion by playing the underdog role, thus giving the Egyptians unfounded confidence in their military ability, and biding their time for the opportunity to strike (it took several years of preparation and the 1973 War to restore some confidence by the Egyptians in their armed forces). The misguided attitude in 1967 explains the feelings of utter shock – following weeks of giddy euphoria – which swept across Egypt and led to Nasser's resignation on 9 June 1967, later retracted in the face of a genuine popular demand that he should stay on to fight another day.

On 17 May 1967 a Cairo Radio broadcast stated: "The UAR (Egypt) has made it clear by all means and without any doubt that it is prepared to enter into operations against Israel if Syria is subjected to any kind of Israeli aggression as referred to by the Israeli Prime Minister, Chief of Staff, and other officials all during last week, which also included a warning to invade Syria." The broadcast continued the warning that the UAR authorities had also received reports [from the Soviet Union] that Israeli armed forces commanders had decided to use force against Syria. Therefore, the UAR had no alternative but to enforce the mutual defence agreement concluded with Syria (Rikhye 1980: 25).

The charged situation was escalating by the hour. On 12 May 1967 the Israeli Chief of Staff, Yitzhak Rabin, made a public threat to overthrow the Syrian Government. In an address to his Mapai party on 11 May 1967, the Israeli Prime Minister Levi Eshkol had already threatened to escalate the military confrontation to teach Syria a sharp lesson. It was also widely reported in the Egyptian media, notes Michael Carroll (2009), that the Soviet leadership warned Anwar Sadat (then the Speaker of the Egyptian Parliament) during a visit to Moscow on 13 May 1967 that "Israel had mobilized at least eleven brigades along the Syrian border and was poised for invasion". This information was relayed to the Egyptian leadership and was undoubtedly partially responsible for the Egyptian moves in support of Syria (including the request for the withdrawal of UNEF). Nasser's hand was forced; moreover, the League of Arab States, in accord with prevailing intra-Arab dynamics, officially called on Egypt in April 1967 to seek the withdrawal of UNEF from Egypt. However, according to Carroll, "It is doubtful that Nasser intended to provoke a war with Israel, but the alternative – losing prestige and influence throughout the Arab world – was deemed less palatable than war" (Carroll 2009: 163).

The same day, Cairo Radio, an arm of the official Egyptian Broadcasting Corporation, also reported that "Field Marshal Hakim Amer had ordered that the UNEF commander be instructed to withdraw UNEF troops stationed on the International Frontier and to collect them in the Gaza Strip for the purpose of the safety of the UNEF troops in case military operations became necessary" (Rikhye 1980: 24–25). This broadcast reveals who was in charge of the UNEF file and was orchestrating events on the ground, and it was not the President. Nasser only took ownership of the issue when events were moving fast and were beyond recall. Undoubtedly, however, he was not averse to basking in the groundswell of popular support he garnered in Egypt and all over the Arab World as a result of this unexpected, and at first sight seemingly opportune – albeit risky – development.

It eventually backfired disastrously and practically brought an end to Nasser's leadership and his ambitious plans for the region. Another unforeseen outcome was the eventual defeat of the secular drive in the Arab world, which eventually opened the door to the regressive Wahhabi-Salafi-Jihadi interpretation of Islam, with devastating consequences for the region and, ultimately, the whole world.

10.4 The UN Response

Secretary-General U Thant's response to UNEF Commander General Rikhye's request for instructions in response to Egypt's request for immediate termination of UNEF presence on Egyptian soil made it clear that the Egyptian move "*could leave him with no other option but to withdraw UNEF*". His rationale was that Egypt's consent for the presence of UNEF had become "so qualified and restricted" that it rendered it impossible to function according to its mandate. The Secretary-General reminded the UNEF Commander that the Force was on Egyptian soil and "could remain there only" with Egypt's continued consent. There was a flurry of deliberations and communications that involved the Egyptian authorities, the Egyptian diplomatic delegation to the UN, and the UN Secretary-General and his staff trying to clarify the initial Egyptian note from General Fawzi. U Thant wanted to clarify whether the nature of the Egyptian request was for 'partial' and 'temporary' withdrawal. The Secretary-General informed the Egyptian ambassador that such a blunt request for partial withdrawal could only be considered as "tantamount to a request for the complete withdrawal of UNEF" (Rikhye 1980: 52–53). The UNEF entered Egypt as a unified force performing a primary task of separating the Egyptians and the Israelis. Compromising the geographical deployment undermined the essence of the whole mission.

In response to the Egyptian request, the Secretary-General presented an *aide-memoire* to the Egyptian Ambassador to the UN on 17 May 1967 stating that if the consent of Egypt were withdrawn "or so qualified as to make it impossible for the Force to function effectively, the Force, of course, will be withdrawn". In this way, U Thant indicated that he felt he had no option but to accede unconditionally to the host country's evident request for withdrawal under the existing UN-Egypt agreement (U Thant 1967: UN/6730).

10.5   Egypt's Formal Withdrawal Request

Events were progressing very rapidly as the UN concluded it had to refuse a partial withdrawal by UNEF from the international frontier, which would have left the international troops only in Gaza and Sharm el Sheikh, and this all-or-nothing position of the UN left Egypt's leaders feeling cornered into requesting the withdrawal of the entire force from all locations. Gaza and Tiran were, therefore, included in the fateful request. On 18 May 1967 the foreign minister of Egypt accordingly sent the following message to the Secretary-General of the UN:

> Dear U Thant,
>
> The Government of the United Arab Republic [Egypt] has the honour to inform your Excellency that it has decided to terminate the presence of the United Nations Emergency Forces from the territory of the United Arab Republic and Gaza Strip. Therefore, I request that the necessary steps be taken for the withdrawal of the Force as soon as possible. I avail myself…etc.
>
> Mahmoud Riad,
>
> Minister of Foreign Affairs
>
> (Riad 1967, UN Doc. S-464-373, 18 May 1967).

Although the Minister mentioned the territory of the UAR (Egypt), which includes Sharm El Sheikh/Tiran, he did not specify that separately, as he did with the deployment in the Gaza Strip. History is 20/20 in hindsight, of course, but the UN Secretary-General could have seized upon this omission to maintain UNEF troops at the entrance of the Gulf of Aqaba, saving Egypt from the folly of blocking the Gulf and thereby inviting the Israelis to launch their pre-planned attack.

10.6   U Thant's Initial Response

A few hours later, the Secretary-General, believing that Egypt's consent for the presence of UNEF had been officially rescinded, instructed General Rikhye, the Force commander, to begin the process of withdrawing the Force from Egypt and Egyptian-controlled territory (the Gaza Strip) in what became a highly controversial move. Having already informed the Egyptian Government of his acceptance of the withdrawal request, U Thant also told the UN General Assembly of his decision. After consulting with the Advisory Committee on UNEF, the Secretary-General promptly responded to the Egyptian note as follows:

Dear Mr. Minister,

Your message informing me that your Government no longer consents to the presence of the United Nations Emergency Force on the territory of the United Arab Republic [Egypt], that is to say in Sinai, and in the Gaza Strip, and requesting that the necessary steps be taken for its withdrawal as soon as possible, was delivered to me by the Permanent Representative of the United Arab Republic at noon on 18 May.

As I have indicated to your Permanent Representative on 16 May, the United Nations Emergency Force entered Egyptian territory with the consent of your Government and in fact can remain there only so long as that consent continues. In view of the message now received from you, therefore, your Government's request will be complied with and I am proceeding to issue instructions for the necessary arrangements to be put in train without delay for the orderly withdrawal of the force, its vehicles and equipment and for the disposal of all properties pertaining to it. I am, of course, also bringing this development and my actions and intentions to the attention of the UNEF Advisory Committee and to all Governments providing contingents for the force. A full report covering this development will be submitted promptly by me to the General Assembly. And I consider it necessary to report to the Security Council about some aspects of the current situation in the area.

Irrespective of the reasons for the action you have taken, in all frankness, may I advise you that I have serious misgivings about it for, as I have said each year in my annual reports to the General Assembly on UNEF, I believe that this force has been an important factor in maintaining relative quiet in the area of its deployment during the past 10 years and that its withdrawal may have grave implications for peace.

U Thant, UN Secretary-General (18 May 1967).

The last paragraph of U Thant's letter contained prophetic words. Egypt would have done well to heed the Secretary-General's warning, but the die was cast, and history-changing events were set in motion.

The Secretary-General's request to the Egyptian Ambassador to the UN (Mohamed El-Kony) to review or re-evaluate the Egyptian military request for UNEF's withdrawal before taking any action, and thus giving the government a breathing space, was turned down by the Egyptian Government. Many faulted U Thant for accepting the response relayed to him by El-Kony without insisting on communicating directly with the Egyptian leadership, a step which could have provided a face-saving alternative for both sides. However, U Thant believed not only that the Egyptian request should not have been addressed to the Force commander procedurally, but also that the request itself needed clarification.

The Secretary-General's position was that any withdrawal of UNEF from Egypt's "eastern border" only, as requested by the Egyptian Chief of Staff, could not be accepted by the UN. This Egyptian request meant in reality that the UN troops would be withdrawn from the international border area only (not Gaza or Sharm El Sheikh), leaving the two countries free to initiate hostilities across their unguarded borders while the remaining UNEF detachments in the north (Gaza) and the south (Sharm El Sheikh) would be left on the sidelines, ineffectively watching hostilities develop but without the ability to stop them in accordance with the United Nations' original mandate.

U Thant was thus put in a very awkward position as he could not agree to a temporary or partial withdrawal without raising a host of international legal arguments and wading into a diplomatic minefield. U Thant knew very well that refusal to go along with the initial qualified Egyptian request would lead to total UNEF withdrawal and certain war. But his hands were tied by the UN-Egyptian sovereign consent agreement.

10.7   Sovereignty and Consent

The issue of national sovereign consent by an independent country for the initial stationing and *continued presence* of foreign troops on its soil proved to be the Achilles heel encumbering the UNEF's operations.

There is no doubt that the style of successful posturing against Israel in 1958 and 1960 was repeated in 1967. Unlike 1958 and 1960, however, in 1967 Egypt exercised its right to withdraw consent and demand termination of the deployment of UNEF. The resulting UNEF withdrawal in 1967, a major miscalculation – a blunder in fact – led to totally different and unintended disastrous consequences. Egypt's rush to help Syria – and presumably to earn political acclaim in the process – blew up in the faces of the Egyptian policy-makers in 1967. From being the hero of the Arab World, Nasser was reduced overnight to being a defeated and wounded leader, the fragility of whose leadership and tenuous hold on power were both starkly exposed. The secular-progressive brand of politics he espoused also suffered a devastating body-blow. The region is still grappling with the search for an alternative ideological system.

It is worth noting that U Thant's reading of the diplomatic/political situation of UNEF in 1967 was not the only possible interpretation. Since General Fawzi's letter to General Rikhye requested the withdrawal of UN troops from the "eastern border" only and not from all territories under Egyptian control, the Canadian ambassador to the UN, George Ignatieff, considered the Egyptian note as a request for 'redeployment' and not for total withdrawal (as Nasser wanted the Egyptian note to Rikhye to read instead of the term used, 'withdrawal'). The Canadian ambassador commented on the request, however, saying that the host country could not ask for partial redeployment to enable its army to take battle positions along parts of the borders, leaving other sectors under UN observation. On 18 May 1967 Israel formally and strongly objected to Egypt's unilateral request for the withdrawal of UNEF, although that request also seems to have suited Israel's plans for the invasion of Egypt, unimpeded by the presence of international troops in its path. (Such an Israeli position can be seen as part of the strategic deception adopted in June 1967 to avoid international censure for starting the war. Moreover, Israel sounded air-raid sirens in Israeli cities, claiming fictitious Egyptian air raids at precisely the time when Israeli jets were pounding Egyptian airfields all over Egypt). Amidst these fast-moving political-military developments, the United States and the United Kingdom – according to General Rikhye – worked together in trying to "reactivate UNEF" by redeploying international troops "on both sides of the Armistice Demarcation Line along the Gaza Strip and the Egyptian-Israeli frontier", but this plan "was rejected by Israel" (Rikhye 1980: 61). If Israel had been sincere about its declared desire to avoid war and pre-empt the Arab 'onslaught', the UNEF redeployment could have reduced the probability of war by a large margin. But there was no such desire in Israel, as the Israeli mobilization and the countdown to war were already underway. Israel, in fact, was eager to have the UN troops removed as a barrier in order to carry out its long-awaited strike against Egypt.

Israel's refusal to accept the redeployment of UNEF on its side of the Egyptian-Israeli lines in 1967 was based on a long-standing legal argument eloquently stated by its veteran diplomat, Abba Eban, in early November 1956. Addressing the UN General Assembly, Eban stated: "It would seem to my delegation to be axiomatic under the law of the Charter that the stationing of any force in a territory under Israel's jurisdiction or control is not possible in law without the Israel Government's sovereign consent" (Eban 1956: UN A/PV.565). However, if Israel had been serious about preventing the outbreak of hostilities in 1967, it could have given its sovereign consent for the stationing of UNEF on the Israeli side. If Egypt had then moved to start a war it would have earned instant worldwide condemnation. Israel, which started the war, escaped such condemnation.

But it is clear that Israel had other plans, and rejecting UNEF's role as a ready and capable buffer preserved Israel's freedom to deliver a long-sought military strike against Egypt, and so was convenient, if not an absolute necessity, for Israel's plans. Ironically, while Israel was rejecting the UNEF's presence on its territory, citing the prerogative of sovereign consent, it opposed Egypt's right – under the same principle – to withdraw such consent and request the withdrawal of UNEF from its territory. In reality, Israel was making a public stand in favour of the principle of sovereign consent for its own convenience, while Egypt's insistence on applying the same principle tremendously aided Israel's plans to violate Egypt's sovereignty and territorial integrity.

With the inevitable closure of the Strait of Tiran by Egypt following the withdrawal of UNEF from Sharm El Sheikh, the USA reiterated its support for the freedom of navigation through the Straits of Tiran for all nations. It was the former US Secretary of State, John F. Dulles, who had presented Israel with an *aide-mémoire* on 11 March 1957 to confirm that the United States considered the Gulf of Aqaba and the Straits of Tiran to be "international waters", and to declare that "no nation has the right to prevent free and innocent passage in the Gulf and through the Straits" (Dulles 1957: 392–393). The American assurance to Israel was the price the USA (and Egypt) had paid to secure final Israeli withdrawal from Egyptian territories in 1957.

On 22 May 1967, US President Johnson, a strong supporter of Israel, reiterated previous American positions on the Gulf of Aqaba/Straits of Tiran by issuing the following statement:

> The purported closing of the Gulf of Aqaba to Israeli shipping has brought a new and very grave dimension to the crisis. The United States considers the gulf to be an international waterway and feels that a blockade of Israeli shipping is illegal and potentially disastrous to

the cause of peace. The right of free, innocent passage of the international waterway is a vital interest of the entire international community (Johnson 2009: 170).

In an opinion contrary to the official American position on Tiran, the noted Harvard professor of international law, Roger Fisher, wrote the following in the NY Times on 9 June 1967:

The United Arab Republic [Egypt] had a good legal case for restricting traffic through the Strait of Tiran. First it is debatable whether international law confers any right of innocent passage through such a waterway [in light of the state of war existing between Egypt and Israel at the time]...Secondly a right of innocent passage is not a right of free passage for any cargo at any time. In the words of the Convention on the Territorial Sea: Passage is innocent so long as it is not prejudicial to the peace, good order, or security of the coastal state...taking the facts as they were I, as an international lawyer, would rather defend before the International Court of Justice the legality of the UAR's action in closing the Strait of Tiran than to argue the other side of the case (Fisher 1967, *NY Times* Editorial).

Meanwhile, the US Ambassador to Egypt, Richard Nolte, asked the Egyptian authorities in late May – shortly after his arrival in the Egyptian capital to present his letter of diplomatic credentials – to agree to keep the UN troops in Gaza and Sharm El Sheikh "until a consensus would emerge" in the United Nations regarding an acceptable outcome to the crisis. It is interesting to note that this latest American request mirrored the initial Egyptian request for partial withdrawal, which the UN Secretary-General had already rejected. Evidently, Egypt was prepared to leave UNEF stationed in Sharm El Sheikh, clearly indicating that the Egyptian Government was not contemplating at that stage of the crisis blocking the Straits of Tiran against Israeli shipping. That move was only undertaken when the Secretary-General refused Egypt's request for partial UNEF withdrawal.

General Rikhye's first-hand account of the termination of UNEF is an authoritative record, well-informed and professional. General Rikhye's intimate knowledge of Egypt and Egyptian officials over many years during his service with the international Force in many capacities gave him an accurate reading of the Egyptian mood and position towards UNEF and its role. He sensed that the Egyptians were really never keen on having an international force stationed on their soil. This perceived foreign imposition was less palatable once Egyptians became aware that Israel had rejected the UN demand to station UNEF on its side of the border as well. The UNEF, moreover, was a constant reminder of the 1956 tripartite invasion. The departure of UNEF, regardless of the consequences, was viewed as an opportunity for Egypt to return to its condition of independence before October 1956 and was seen as a necessary step for regaining the nation's honour. In Rikhye's words, the people of Egypt "were overjoyed at the elimination of the last scars left by the 1956 invasion by Israel, Britain and France". The Commander of the UN Force believed, however, that "Israel need not have gone to war at that time and should have allowed diplomacy to prevail. Nevertheless, Israel chose war over diplomacy as they were confident that in one blow they could eliminate the Arab threat for years to come. They also hoped to reduce Nasser's influence, if not cause his downfall."

Tragically, for Egypt, Nasser, "never wanted or even approved complete withdrawal of UNEF", according to General Rikhye. The UNEF commander believed that the Egyptians were convinced, based on previous precedents, that the "UNEF would have few grounds to object to the removal of some of its posts in the Sinai". Rikhye was also convinced that "the Egyptians were willing to negotiate for a continued UNEF presence as long as Egyptian forces could move sufficiently close to the International Frontier for Nasser to satisfy his critics", and to prevent Israel "from taking any offensive action against Syria" (Rikhye 1980). Had Egypt sent its army into the Sinai in a show of force without the accompanying request for partial UNEF withdrawal, as happened before in 1958 and 1960, would the history of the Middle East have been totally different?

10.8   U Thant–Nasser Last Ditch Attempt to Avoid War

In Rikhye's account of Secretary-General U Thant's negotiations on May 24 1967 in Cairo with the Egyptian President, Nasser, and the Egyptian Foreign Minister, Mahmoud Riad, the Egyptian leaders elaborated on the reasons for the request to terminate UNEF's presence on Egyptian soil. In addition to the declared reason of deterring any Israeli invasion of Syria, the Egyptians specified that they wished to bring down "the last curtain on the Israeli aggression of 1956".

Mr. Riad insisted on the hope that "Israel would no longer profit from its previous aggression". President Nasser, moreover, said that by blocking the Gulf of Aqaba as a result of the termination of UNEF, Egypt "fully restored the situation as it prevailed before the 1956 war" and thus vindicated its honour.

The Egyptian Foreign Minister also revealed that on 15 May 1967 he had had a meeting with the US Chargé d'Affaires, David Ness, in Egypt to discuss the reports of Israeli troop concentrations on the Syrian front, but that the American diplomat would not give "any guarantees for the prevention of the outbreak of hostilities." The minister added that the American attitude was a throwback to the "situation which existed in 1956 when the United States Ambassador in Cairo assured his government then that there were no Israeli concentrations, and yet Egypt had been invaded".

Finally, the Minister added that Israel was refusing to respect the terms of the General Armistice Agreement between the two countries, including the illegal occupation of the Al-Auja demilitarized zone and the eviction of the UN observers from that area.

For his part, the UN Secretary-General warned his Egyptian hosts that Israel had informed him that it would be "prepared to go to war" over the closure of the Straits of Tiran, and that the US had also restated to him "its commitments to assist Israel" in the case of war. The Foreign Minister replied that his government was prepared to submit "matters relating to the Gulf of Aqaba" to "legal and constitutional" international adjudication. The Secretary-General then enquired whether Egypt was prepared to reactivate the *Egyptian Israeli Mixed Armistice Commission* (EIMAC), which was established as part of the 1949 Armistice Agreement, and permit new UN observers from it to patrol and establish Observation Posts "in the areas vacated by UNEF". The Minister replied that his government would not object to EIMAC operations but would not permit the UN "military observers to enter the Sinai as long as Israel would not permit them to do the same on its side" of the Armistice lines. The Secretary-General proposed a three-point approach to deal with the crisis: first, establish a limited moratorium (two to three weeks) to allow for discussions; second, persuade Israel to reactivate the terms of the General Armistice Agreement; and third, appoint a UN special representative to the area.

Photo 10.2 U Thant, UN Secretary-General during the 1967 Middle East War. *Source* UN.org

Nasser surprised U Thant by immediately accepting a two-week moratorium to ease tensions and to allow for negotiations. He further surprised him by promising not to enforce the Straits of Tiran blockade, provided that Israel did not challenge it. Finally, the President indicated his acceptance of the reactivation of EIMAC as long as "it was on a parallel basis" for both Egypt and Israel. Nasser also shared with U Thant the situation in the Egyptian cabinet, which was determined to "undo the consequences of events of 1956" but was divided on whether to initiate hostilities against Israel. Powerful ministers, including Defence Minister Shams Badran, the majority of the military leadership and the entrenched Vice President, Amer, wanted to take advantage of the mobilization underway and strike first. The President, however, indicated to U Thant that he did not consent to the initiation of hostilities. According to Rikhye, he had been able to secure a decision to "only fight if attacked by Israel". Nasser had given the same assurances, explains Rikhye, to the Soviet Ambassador and the US Chargé d'Affaires in Cairo: "I told them that we will not attack; we have no intention of attacking unless we are attacked first, and then we will defend ourselves." Nasser then addressed U Thant directly, saying, "We give you the same assurance. We will not attack first" (Rikhye 1980).

Many in Egypt and the Arab World blamed Nasser for his reluctance to start the war, accusing him of causing the worst Arab defeat since 1948. The US Administration received a direct pledge from President Nasser that Egypt would not initiate hostilities, but the Americans were fully aware of Israel's plans to deliver a massive military strike against Egypt. Nevertheless, the US chose to look the other way when Israel invaded Egypt and the other Arab territories. The sense of betrayal was pervasive in the entire Arab world.

Upon his return to the UN Headquarters, Secretary-General U Thant addressed the UN Security Council to report on his discussions with the Egyptian leadership. He informed the Council that he had received assurances that Egypt "would not initiate offensive action against Israel". He also indicated that the Egyptian position was in favour of "a return to the conditions prevailing prior to 1956 and to full observance by both parties of the provisions of the General Armistice Agreement between Egypt and Israel". U Thant indicated that he hoped that the Government of Israel would "reconsider its position and resume its participation in EIMAC". He then "appealed to the parties concerned to exercise special restraints" and to avoid belligerent acts (U Thant 1967: S/7906, 26 May 1967).

The US Ambassador to the UN, Arthur Goldberg, called upon the Security Council "to endorse the Secretary-General's appeal" without delay in order to give the parties a "breathing spell" to allow the explosive tensions a chance to subside. He also called on the Council to address the major underlying issues contributing to the conflict. The US Representative asserted his country's belief that the Gulf of Aqaba constituted an international waterway, a position the US still holds now. The Egyptian Ambassador, Mohamed El-Kony, responded by saying that Egypt's request for the withdrawal of UNEF was motivated, among other considerations, by concern for the safety of the international Force in case of the eruption of hostilities. As for the Gulf of Aqaba, he believed that Egypt considered it, as it still does, to be an inland waterway passing through internationally recognized Egyptian territorial water. Moreover, Egypt had, in its opinion, the sovereign right, according to accepted provisions of international law, to bar enemy vessels in a state of war from violating its territorial integrity. In excluding Israeli shipping, Egypt was simply returning the situation back to what it was prior to the 1956 Israeli invasion.

The Egyptian Ambassador cited the Report submitted by UN Secretary-General Hammarskjold to the UN General Assembly on 8 February 1957 and approved on 22 February 1957 in which he stated that "the stationing of UNEF *could not be used to impose a solution for political or legal questions that were controversial*, since UNEF's only function was to prevent hostilities". The Secretary-General added that UNEF could not be "used to prejudice the solution of the controversial questions involved" (Hammarskjold 1957: A/3526; A/1126). The Egyptian position laid out by El-Kony centred on resisting Israel's attempts to formalize a situation (in which it had unimpeded access to the Gulf of Aqaba) that did not exist prior to 1956, a situation that had been allowed *de facto* due to the presence of UNEF. With the UNEF presence now terminated, Egypt was anxious to restore the status quo ante and prevent Israel from acquiring a new legalized advantage when the core issues of the Arab-Israeli conflict remained unresolved.

The Israeli Ambassador, Gideon Rafael, strongly denied that Israel had any intention of launching a military attack against Syria (the reason for Egypt's demand for the withdrawal of UNEF). He then added that "it was not too late for reason to prevail". The reality was that it was too late to stop Israel's countdown to a major attack on Egypt based on the original Kadesh Plan, which had been modified in 1956 and incorporated into the Anglo-French invasion of Egypt. The ultimate failure of the invasion in 1956 had frozen Israel's plans for the destruction of the Egyptian Army and the annexation of Egyptian territory, at least temporarily. In 1967 Israel was ready to implement Kadesh alone (with the tacit approval of the United States, which later opposed any call from the UN to force Israeli withdrawal unilaterally from the captured territories).

In his intervention in the debate, the Soviet Ambassador to the UN, Nikolai Fedorenko, supported the Egyptian position and demanded strong Security Council condemnation of the "Israeli provocations and threats against the Arab States" (Rikhye 1980).

The precedent was the 1954 Israeli occupation of El-Auja demilitarized zone in the Negev on the border with Sinai, which occurred in violation of the 1949 Armistice Agreement after the Israelis forced out UNTSO (United Nations Truce Supervisory Organization) observers. This fact of recent history was on the minds of the Egyptian policy-makers when they sought to deploy their own armed forces in the border areas with Israel in conjunction with a partial UNEF withdrawal.

If Israel could kick out UN observers from a UN-administered demilitarized zone without detrimental consequences, so too could Egypt demand the withdrawal of UNEF without negative consequences. The difference, however, was that during the occupation of El-Auja by Israel in 1954, Egypt had no plans to attack Israel, while the withdrawal of UNEF in 1967 allowed Israel to carry out a plan already in place for the invasion of Egypt.

10.9   UNEF: The Dangerous Winding Down

The early withdrawal of the Canadian contingent created a huge dent in the UNEF logistical support, including air transport, necessary for the efficient functioning of UNEF operations. Air service was crucial for the completion of the withdrawal of UNEF as well. The Egyptian Government, therefore, provided two transport planes dedicated to helping UNEF fill the gap created by the departure of Canadian logistical support. Not only did the withdrawal of UNEF face logistical problems, but the outbreak of the war on 5 June 1967 (with the Israeli invasion of the Sinai and the Gaza Strip) considerably further complicated the entire withdrawal process.

UNEF was caught – as feared earlier – in a shooting war with grave consequences. UNEF sustained serious casualties as a result of Israeli shelling of its headquarters and camps. Tens of officers and members of other ranks in the Indian contingent were killed and wounded, and their bases were surrounded. Upon the initiation of the Israeli air and ground attacks on UNEF positions, causing serious casualties, General Rikhye sent a cable to the Israeli Chief of Staff, Itzhak Rabin, via the UN office in Jerusalem, asking him to "order your forces, especially your aircraft, to take special care to avoid inflicting further unnecessary casualties on UNEF personnel". Other UN personnel (field service staff) were arrested by the advancing Israeli troops, roughed up and left without food or water. It took a Norwegian military doctor, Colonel Lutzov-Holm, to provide blankets from the UNEF hospital to the detainees. Eventually, all UNEF personnel were successfully evacuated.

The Israeli invasion was so successful that UNEF was not able to withdraw in an organized fashion, and thus suffered serious losses. The Israeli Air Force chief, Mordechai Motti Hod, said after the war that his forces had been training for the implementation of the air campaign against Egypt for many years. Without going into detail, Rabin admitted to General Rikhye in Tel Aviv on 17 June 1967 that Israel had planned the land offensive against Egypt 'meticulously'. Moreover, General Moshe Dayan, the newly appointed Defence Minister, in confirmation of intentions expressed by the Prime Minister, David Ben-Gurion, in 1956, informed Colonel van Huevan, Chairman of the Egypt-Israel Mixed Armistice Commission (EIMAC), on 10 June 1967 that "the General Armistice Agreement was dead" (Rikhye 1980).

Inevitably, UNEF was destined to be caught in a military confrontation due to the lack of any attempt to resolve the underlying conflict. On 26 June 1967, not long after the start of the war, the recriminations began at the UN Headquarters in New York over the circumstances of the withdrawal of UNEF. "There were many who felt that the rapid withdrawal of UNEF troops had unnecessarily precipitated a tragic war" (Rikhye 1980), which occasioned serious casualties among the UN troops themselves. General Rikhye, as the last UNEF commander, placed the blame for failure to anticipate the tragic events surrounding the withdrawal of UNEF squarely on the shoulders of the "United Nations High Command" and himself as the Commander in the field. Although fighting had been anticipated following the rapidly developing political and military situation, he said "it never crossed our minds that it would be that soon and that we would be caught so badly" (Rikhye 1980).

General Rikhye concluded that the "Force [UNEF] would no longer be able to carry out its functions as a buffer", but he insisted that it "would not cease to exist or to lose its status or any of its entitlements, privileges, and immunities until all of its elements, had departed from the area of its operation". He also made it clear that the Force was to remain under his 'exclusive command', taking no orders from any other authorities, be they Egyptian or the commanders of the national contingents. The Secretary-General did, however, instruct the Force Commander to proceed on the assumption that the Egyptian authorities would provide "full cooperation...on all aspects of evacuation", having requested that from the Egyptian Government through their diplomatic mission to the UN in New York.

General Rikhye's insistence on maintaining "exclusive command" of UNEF, rejecting any intervention by the Egyptian authorities or the national HQs of the participating countries in the affairs of the international Force during the stand-down and termination period, was justified due to the critical phase in the life of UNEF, and the fast-moving developments in the political situation, as well as the very possibility of unintended confrontations with the armed forces of the host government. Egyptian units had already begun their deployment along the inter-national border alongside some UNEF units. In some locations, Egyptian troops took up positions in the "immediate vicinity" (Rikhye 1980) of the Observation Posts of the Yugoslav troops or near UNEF deployment camps, in El-Sabha, El-Amr and El-Qusaima, causing some friction and uncertainty. Rikhye's imme-diate intervention to persuade the Egyptian troops to keep their distance from the UNEF detachments (which they did), and Egypt's close friendship with Yugoslavia kept a potentially dangerous situation from leading to a possible military confrontation.

As a result of the rapid deployment of the Egyptian troops to the Sinai, UNEF aircraft were denied air clearance during the surge of troop movements to the frontier area. This meant, however, that some UNEF posts would run out of sup-plies. The Egyptian authorities tried to avoid any military clash with UNEF aircraft due to mistaken identification in a time of heightened tension and massive troop movements. It took several attempts by General Rikhye to contact the Egyptian operational command and air defence system to finally lift the restrictions and provide the needed clearance. UNEF aircraft not only faced some difficulties from the Egyptian authorities during this critical period, but Israel also did its share in complicating UNEF air operations. According to the UNEF Commander, General Rikhye's UN aircraft was intercepted by Israeli jets and was ordered to land in Israel "while on a legitimate operational flight [between Al-Arish and Gaza] along an authorized air route". This was not a simple error but "a blatant attempt to hijack our plane" because the aircraft was flying "more than one kilometre west of the Armistice Demarcation Line and the International Frontier which were well defined" (Rikhye 1980).

The Israeli pilots, asserted the UNEF Commander, "would have had to be blind not to recognize the distinctive United Nations colours and markings" on the UN plane. The Israeli air force nonetheless fired on the UN plane after making several close intimidating passes to force it to land in Israel. Had the Israeli jets succeeded in forcing down the UN plane inside Israel, it would have had "grave consequences for the United Nations", as accusations of deliberately violation of Israeli airspace would have been plausible, Israel having attempted to make such claims six months earlier. Moreover, Israel could have claimed that the UN was conducting unau-thorized reconnaissance activities against its national security. The General summed the situation up by stating that "It was obvious to me and my staff that the Israeli allegations on this and on a number of other occasions in the past were completely unfounded". The UNEF Commander described the Israeli action as "banditry in the air", and the Secretary-General of the UN lodged a "strong protest" with the Israeli Government. Based on his "knowledge of their general attitude towards UNEF since it had first been deployed in the area" the UN commander believed that Israel "had something to conceal" with regard to its own troop mobilization. He felt that the UN plane, even though flying well inside Egyptian territory, "could perhaps pick it up in their innocent passage". The Israelis, the General observed, were "highly sensitive to anyone observing their activities", to the extent that they risked dangerous interference with the UNEF Commander's aircraft and came very close to creating an international incident with major ramifications. This incident suggests that Israel was well on its way to completing its military mobilization for the invasion of Egypt and did not want anybody (especially the UN) to confirm the unfolding of its plans, which were already in progress. The UNEF Commander still believed (now vindicated by events) that his recommendation for "the immediate withdrawal of the entire Force" should have been accepted following the early withdrawal of the Canadian contingent. He was convinced that once "fighting broke out UNEF would be the first casualty".

There had been efforts underway at the UN Headquarters in New York and elsewhere to enable UNEF to remain in place until a diplomatic breakthrough could be achieved, with the idea that its presence lessened the probability of hostilities commencing. However, once Egypt requested the immediate removal of the Canadian contingent, he had advised removing the rest of the entire Force without delay, wise counsel as events proved. Eventually, the entire UNEF force was withdrawn, and the war that followed demonstrated that engaging in peacekeeping in a vacuum is counterproductive without fairly resolving the fundamental elements of the conflict (Rikhye 1980).

10.10   UNEF: The Complicated Withdrawal

The Egyptian request caused a tense political and logistical situation. The Commander of UNEF, sensitive to the cohesion and morale of his Force, requested, in the wake of the Egyptian request, the speedy and total withdrawal of the entire UNEF, not just the Canadian contingent. He was immediately overruled by UN Headquarters. Ralph Bunche, the UN Under-Secretary-General, replied to the Commander's request by stating, "While UNEF is an international force, it is composed of national contingents [facing] hard realities…political considerations have always been involved in connection with the UNEF operation." The UN was committed to maintaining the original withdrawal timetable agreed earlier with the Egyptian authorities for all of the UNEF contingents. Apparently, there were moves by the Security Council to de-escalate the spiralling crisis and somehow avert a looming showdown in the region, and the continued presence of UNEF was deemed important at this critical stage (Rikhye 1980: 91).

The possibility of conflicting positions held by different factions in the Egyptian hierarchy was raised at the time by General Rikhye. On 4 June 1967 the newly appointed Egyptian Commander of the Sinai Front, General Mohsen Mortagy, issued what was described by General Rikhye as a "clarion call" to war addressed to his troops facing Israel. In a fiery speech reflecting the hard line taken by the military leadership, the Egyptian General promised his men a sacred battle to restore Arab rights, a battle in which he pledged victory would be theirs. The UNEF commander observed that "The spirit of this message was in total contradiction to the assurances" given to Secretary-General U Thant during his visit to Cairo by President Nasser and Foreign Minister Riad.

Moreover, Rikhye observed on 4 June 1967, during his journey between El-Arish in the Sinai and the Gaza Strip, that the deployment of the Egyptian troops near the international frontier could not be considered defensive as it was more suited to the kind of offensive action "usually resorted to for a last-ditch stand". Rikhye's conclusion was that the Egyptian armed forces "were anxious for a showdown with Israel, whereas their political masters...looked forward to an easing of tensions." The deployment of the Egyptian army in the Sinai in early June 1967 was, according to the UNEF commander, an indication of the "opposing trends" that divided Egyptian policy-makers (Rikhye 1980: 97).

Internal disagreement became very clear and, following the start of the hostilities, it had tragic consequences for Egypt. On the evening of 6 June 1967, barely two days after the beginning of the war, Field Marshal Amer's bravado turned into pathetic panic when at 6 p.m. he ordered – without consultation with the supreme commander of the Army, President Nasser – the immediate and total withdrawal of 180,000 troops to the west side of the Canal. General Fawzi, the Army Chief of Staff, contacted the President, who rushed to the Army Headquarters.

A tense confrontation took place between the President and his Vice President, and the order to withdraw was rescinded. However, the new order came too late to stem the westward march or to ease the added panic due to the lack of air cover. With casualties mounting by the hour, the President ordered the elite Fourth Armoured division to cross back into the Sinai and stem the Israeli advance. The new plan was to establish a 100 km-wide defensive front extending from the Suez Canal to the Sinai passes region. Israeli war-plans had anticipated Egyptian defensive deployment facing the Israeli thrust, as happened in 1956. But this time there was no opportunity to establish the Egyptian defensive fortifications, as the order came for immediate total withdrawal. The outcome was more deadly in its consequences (Heikal 2009–2010).

10.11 Egyptian Society in Turmoil

Not surprisingly, the devastating defeat affected Egyptian society to its core. The conflicted relationship between, on the one hand, the admiration, even adoration, for Nasser as a strong national leader embodying the nation's goals and aspirations, and, on the other, repugnance at the strong and ruthless tactics of the regime came to the fore in *The Return of Conciousness*, a book by one of Egypt's greatest writers. It was written in 1972 by Tawfiq Al-Hakim and published in 1974 (an English translation appeared in 1985). Before 1952, Al-Hakim had written many books exposing the ills of Egyptian society. After 1952, he continued his candid treatment of many social and political issues.

Al-Hakim was considered one of the many intellectual and writers who greatly admired Nasser for his dedicated and non-corrupt governance, and his struggle for Egypt's liberation and renaissance. Nasser threw in his lot with the crushed majority of his people, antagonizing in the process the privileged minority. Al-Hakim supported Nasser's policy, and described his 1952 revolutionary overthrow of the *ancien regime* as the "Blessed Movement".

Nasser bestowed on Al-Hakim the state's highest literary awards. Nasser also approved many of Al-Hakim's critical writings, despite the opposition of many leading figures of the regime.

That is why it came as a shock when Al-Hakim executed an about-face and unleashed stinging criticism of Nasser after his death in 1970. Al-Hakim accused Nasser of undermining Egypt's progress which was underway because of the war with Israel. He also accused Nasser of mesmerizing the Egyptian people and the Arab world by accepting a non-democratic rule with catastrophic consequences.

Al-Hakim was entitled to react strongly to the humiliating defeat of 1967. He was also correct in exposing the failure of the regime. But he could not excuse himself then for showing strong support for Nasser during his life. He also could not ignore the tangible results of the regime – despite the failures. Such spectacular transformational reform results in every field were what Al-hakim himself was calling for before Nasser appeared on the scene.

Internationally, the old colonial powers and the new Western leader – along with Israel – had vilified and subjected Nasser to a sustained attack for his anti-colonial secular leadership. To the peril of these critics, the defeat of Nasser's secular reformist agenda – despite its shortcomings – has opened the door to a tidal wave of regressive, malignant, destructive, and anti-modern religious-based polity, dragging the Arab and Muslim worlds back to the dark ages of Wahhabism and Salafism.

10.12   The Israeli Account of the War

One of the most outrageous deceptive claims in the history of the twentieth century was Israel's 'defensive' war against an imminent Arab attack. For a long time, Israel was portrayed as the small peaceful country which fended off the aggression of its neighbours. Western media, echoing Israeli claims, magnified the Israeli narrative of standing up to the Arabs, and implanted this fabrication in the minds of the public across the globe.

Fearing that success in the international diplomatic moves underway would mean a missed Israeli opportunity to realize its long-sought goal of destroying Egypt's military capabilities and annexing its territory, Israel struck in the morning of the first scheduled negotiations in Washington. The history of the Middle East took a decidedly different course after the first bombs exploded on the Egyptian runways in the Sinai and elsewhere in Egypt.

The reality was that Israel wanted desperately to make good on its aborted plans to annex Arab territories in 1956. The Israeli Generals ended up laughing all the way to their newly acquired territorial conquests. Their decade-old plan finally worked to perfection. Getting rid of UNEF was a blessing in disguise. First, the withdrawal request was portrayed as an Egyptian aggressive intent. Second, it opened the way for Israel to invade Egyptian territory without an international obstacle in the way.

The well-informed study *Six Days of War* by the Israeli diplomat and official Michael Oren offers a detailed look – *from an Israeli perspective* – at the circumstances leading up to the withdrawal of UNEF and the beginning of the 1967 War (Oren 2002: 80).

The Israeli Air Force (IAF) had a plan code-named Focus (*Moked*) for a "massive attack to destroy Egypt's air force. For years, the IAF had been perfecting such a plan". Brigadier Mordechai Hod, the Commander of the Israeli Air Force, admitted after the war in the London *Sunday Times* on 16 July 1967 (barely over a month after the hostilities began) that Israel had been perfecting its attack plan for sixteen years in preparation for an invasion of Egypt:

> Sixteen years' planning had gone into those initial 80 minutes. We lived with the plan, we slept on the plan, we ate the plan. Constantly we perfected it (Hod 1967: 7).

It did not take long for the masks to fall off, as the narrative that Israel was defending itself went out the window in a huff.

Other Israeli military commanders had their own plans for the invasion of Egypt. Itzhak Rabin's plan, code-named *Atzmon*, was designed to capture the Gaza Strip and use it as a political bargaining chip. Israeli Air Force General Etzer Wiseman (later Minister of Defence), provided the plan code-named *Kardon*, designed to attack Egypt's land forces in the Sinai. Chief of Staff Moshe Dayan (soon to be appointed Minister of Defence in the national unity cabinet formed just before the war) "recommended mounting an all-out air and ground attack against Egypt", thus in effect resurrecting Operation Kadesh (Oren 2002: 90).

Success in this confrontation, the Israeli Prime Minister Levi Eshkol told his cabinet on 21 May 1967, would depend on "who will attack the other's airfields first". Eshkol, however, was inclined to listen to American advice, which was not to start the war until Nasser went too far and Israel was in a position to strike without the kind of international condemnation it had faced in 1956. The Israeli generals, however, forced Eshkol's hand by deciding to mount a strike without delay.

Former Prime Minister David Ben-Gurion, an old hand at dealing with Nasser, was more cautious. He said, "I very much doubt whether Nasser wanted to go to war...while Israel remained utterly isolated." Without great power support for Israel against Egypt, Ben-Gurion opined, Israel's security would be jeopardized.

The Israeli military, however, had a strong belief that given the right approach, Israel could prevail militarily. But it was Foreign Minister Abba Eban who emphasized the absolute necessity of Israeli 'deterrence'. He cautioned, "unless a stand was made here, nobody in the Arab world...would ever again believe in Israel's power to resist" (Oren 2002: 89).

The elaborate hoax perpetrated by Israel to get rid of UNEF and start the war with Egypt followed a deceptive pattern. Syrian-based infiltration against Israel had been described by Israeli Chief of Operations, Itzhak Rabin, in a report to the Knesset: "There is no major wave of infiltration...Israel does not have to get caught up in a frenzy of escalation" (Rabin 1996: 73–75). The Syrian-Israeli border region was already tense for years because of claims over the control of the water sources of the Jordan River and the Sea of Galilee, but there was a need for new military escalation or confrontation to justify Israeli threats against Syria.

The manufactured threats to Israel on the Golan Heights as the trigger for Egypt's involvement were put into context by General Moshe Dayan in 1976, when he admitted that Israel's deliberate policy between 1949 and 1967 was "to seize some territory and hold it until the enemy despairs". Dayan further admitted that Israel had provoked more than 80 per cent of the border clashes with Syria in the lead-up to the 1967 war (Zisser 2002: 168–194; Schmemann 1997).

The Commanders of UNTSO, Odd Bull (Norway) and Carl Von Horn (Sweden), both confirmed that the Israelis gradually took over positions in the demilitarized zone established between Syria and Israel since 1949, in the process evicting Arab villagers and demolishing their homes, despite repeated protests from the UN Security Council (Finkelstein 2003: 131–132).

Israel also violated the Armistice with Egypt by seizing the demilitarized zone of Al-Auja and refusing to relinquish it. Syria's claim that the escalating conflict was a result of Israel's plan to increase tension in order to justify a large-scale operation against Syria proved accurate (Lesch 2012: 81–82). Moreover, Israeli General Moshe Dayan candidly admitted that Israel must invent dangers, and to do this it must adopt the strategy of provocation and revenge.

10.13   US Involvement

Unlike 1956, the US was more than determined to break Nasser's leadership role in the Arab world once and for all. Clearly, the anti-colonial battles of the 1950s were about to reach a crucial climax, putting an end to the challenge to Western dominance in the Middle East. The US made more than a promise of defence to Israel. It actively engaged in helping the Israelis launch their attack against Egypt in June 1967.

First, American air force pilots landed in Israel in April and May 1967 and flew unmarked advanced reconnaissance flights (some markings were changed from US to Israeli symbols) over Egyptian air bases and conveyed the results to the Israelis. The 2002 BBC documentary *Dead in the Water* (BBC 2002), confirmed – through interviews with some of the American pilots who took part in the operation – the US involvement in helping Israel launch its war against Egypt.

Second, the BBC documentary portrays a picture of a "daring ploy by Israel to fake an Egyptian attack on the American spy ship, and thereby provide America with a reason to officially enter the war against Egypt". Deliberately unmarked, Israel's air force jets attacked a clearly identified US ship (USS *Liberty*) in the Mediterranean close to the Egyptian city of el-Arish on 8 June 1967 with the intention of sinking the ship and destroying all the intelligence data collected. The attack resulted in the death of thirty-four US servicemen and the injury of 171. What is more disturbing and a script for a doomsday scenario is the documentary's revelation of "how the *Liberty* incident provoked the launch of nuclear-armed planes targeted against Cairo from a US aircraft carrier in the Mediterranean. They were recalled only just in time, when it was clear the *Liberty* had not sunk with all hands, and that Israel was responsible". When the Americans thought it was an Egyptian attack, they almost obliterated Cairo. When the attack, however, was confirmed to be Israeli, a deliberate cover-up was immediately activated.

The BBC documentary, furthermore, "offers evidence of a secret collaboration between America and Israel before and during the war" (BBC 2002). In the documentary, the former US diplomat, Richard Parker, who had served in many Middle Eastern countries, said that if it were known that America was involved against Egypt, causing the eventual demise of the anti-colonial Arab regimes led by Egypt, "it would have finished our relations with the Arab World for a long time to come." US foreign policy-makers have myopically and consistently misread the pulse of the Arab world, with disastrous consequences. Even the co-opting of Egypt after the 1973 War has not pacified the region as the pro-Western Arab corrupt and totalitarian regimes have only managed to stoke the fires of instability and extremism. Ambassador Parker's prediction is currently manifesting itself in a worse scenario than he ever feared. The drama and intrigue of the Israeli attack on a US naval ship was also documented in great detail in Anthony Pearson's study, *Conspiracy of Silence* (Pearson 1978).

In an investigative article by Arieh O'Sullivan in the *Jerusalem Post* (June 2004; O'Sullivan 2004: 20) and confirmed by Ralph Lopez in 2014 (Lopez 2014, 6

November). The record confirms that "Israeli forces knew the USS *Liberty* was an American ship". The report was based on the recorded Hebrew "transcript of the raw audio" of the communications amongst "Israeli military personnel" in the air force and the navy at the time of the attack. The report goes on to say that "American sailors were ruthlessly, deliberately attacked in order to draw the US into war with Egypt".

Third, in his account of the US involvement in the 1967 War, Stephen Green confirms that the US naval intelligence ship *Liberty* was cruising along the Egyptian coast during the war, gathering information with its sophisticated equipment. The ship was attacked by Israeli jets because the US was gaining intelligence that Israel was about to invade the West Bank. Also, the ship was able to record evidence about the execution of a large number of unarmed Egyptian POWs. According to Green's account, the US operation helped the Israelis achieve "certain territorial objectives within a very finite, limited time". Green wrote that "President Lyndon B. Johnson and his national security advisor, Walt Rostow, were most probably aware of the operations [as] such operations would have required approval by the highest authorities" (Green 1984: 215, 239).

Fourth, as revealed by Daniel Southerland, US Air Force pilots stationed in Upper Heyford, outside Oxford in England, were flown to Moron in the Negev in Israel (on 4 June 1967). They were issued with civilian passports and disguised as civilian workers contracted by Israel. Their RF-4C jets (a modified version of the F-4 Phantom jet fighters) were painted with Israeli markings. The pilots were deployed before the start of the war to provide reconnaissance flights over the coming battlefield. With the start of the war, the pilots "began flying reconnaissance missions over bombed and burning air bases in Egypt, Syria, and Jordan". Thus, "With US help, the Israelis gained strategic ground at a blinding rate" (Southerland 1984, 15 March), due to the sophisticated US equipment and radar capabilities.

Fifth, Michael Oren (2003) documents in great detail the extensive involvement and prior knowledge of the US of the Israeli war plans for the June 1967 attack against Egypt. Tom Segev (2007), moreover, provided an account of the detailed negotiations between the Israeli and US officials over the justification and the timing of the start of the Israeli attack. Both writers highlighted the massive scope of Israel's pressure to secure an American green light for the start of the war. Israeli officials involved in the efforts were Prime Minister Levi Eshkol, Foreign Minister Abba Eban, Head of Mossad Meir Amit, Head of Military Intelligence Aharon Yariv, Israeli Ambassador to the US Avraham Harman, Israeli diplomat Efraim Evron and many others. On the American side were President Lyndon B. Johnson, Secretary of State Dean Rusk, Secretary of Defence Robert McNamara, CIA Director Richard Helms, and US Ambassador to the UN Arthur Goldberg. The Israelis were planning to strike on 25 May 1967, but the Americans pressured them to delay in order to exhaust all the diplomatic efforts and prolong strategic patience. Meanwhile, Israeli Generals almost staged a rebellion against Prime Minister Eshkol, demanding immediate action. Israeli politicians were involved in tortuous debates about when – not if – should Israel start the war without losing American support if they acted prematurely. Meanwhile, the Head of Mossad, Meir Amit, travelled to Washington using a fake passport to meet US Defence Secretary Robert McNamara on the eve of the war and secured support for Israel's war plan. Meir emphasized that Israel must strike first. To that McNamara responded that he heard him loud and clear. The Head of Military Intelligence, Aharon Yariv, returned from Washington with the following assessment: "The Americans view a pre-emptive strike on our part as reasonable, as long as they themselves are not required to take action. They will act only in the case of a defeat of our side" (Segev 2007: 276). There is no doubt that the US was fully aware of Israel's war plans and complicit in its support.

The US started moving large naval units (sixty-five in total) to the Eastern Mediterranean (far enough from the Egyptian coast, but near enough to be deployed when needed). The aircraft carrier *Intrepid,* returning from Vietnam, joined the two other carriers, *America* and *Saratoga,* to form a formidable strike force, ready for any eventuality (Oren 2002: 142).

Sixth, Israel mounted an intense political and media campaign to secure American support for an Israeli first-strike against Egypt. In a meeting with Israel's Foreign Minister, Abba Eban, on 26 May 1967, US President Johnson is said to have informed him that "America's intelligence" conclusions confirmed that "there is no Egyptian intention to … attack", and that if Israel attacked first "Israel will not be alone unless it decides to go it alone". Secretary of State, Dean Rusk, was blunter, saying that "if Israel fires first, it'll have to forget the US" (Oren 2002: 113). It is difficult to reconcile Oren's account of US warnings against an Isreali impending strike against Egypt with President Johnson's own intelligence about the lack of Egyptian intention to attack Israel. Despite such alleged warnings, Israel struck first and the United States acted counter to its own forged warning. Unlike his American counterpart, French President Charles de Gaulle warned that France would condemn the party starting the war, and he was true to his word.

Seventh, some Israeli jet fighters engaged in the first waves of attack against Egypt were permitted to fly out of the US Wheelus Air Base in Libya to strike Egypt simultaneously from the West, as reported to the Egyptian military attaché in Libya by Libyan air force officers who witnessed the departing Israeli flights (Heikal 2009–2010). Nasser's fear of American involvement thus proved accurate.

10.14   Other Foreign Involvement

The Americans were not the only power involved in the efforts to defeat Nasser. Saudi Arabia and its head, King Faisal, considered Nasser and Egypt the main enemy of the Saudi throne and the Saudi 'Royal' family. When he was still a prince, King Faisal had been considered pro-Egypt and supporter of Nasser; but Egyptian support for the Republican overthrow of the Yemeni monarchy changed the calculations for the by then King Faisal. The Egyptian involvement in Yemen in the early 1960s posed an immediate threat to the Saudi establishment. Egypt also represented a threat to the British presence in Aden.

The following is an account of the official Saudi move against Nasser, as reproduced and documented (No. 342) and stamped with the Saudi Council of Minister Official Seal (Qarqout 2006: 505–506 [in Arabic]). King Faisal requested the convening of a high-powered committee to present recommendations to counter Nasser's threat. The committee included the following:

Prince Fahd, Minister of the Interior (Police and Security).
Prince Sultan, Minister of Defence and Aviation (Air Force).
Prince Salman, Governor of Riyad.
Mr. Kamal Adham, Head of Saudi Intelligence and Special Counsellor to the King.
Mr. Kim Roosevelt, CIA Operative and Consultant to the Saudi establishment.
Other military and civilian officials and advisors from Saudi Arabia and the USA.

The meeting was held on 16 December 1966, and issued recommendations to confront the Egyptian 'enemy' in Yemen, and suggestions to remove the threat. A report was forwarded to the King with the following points:

(1) The recommendations to get rid of the enemy and all other opponents are to be viewed by the King for comments or deletion or addition, before sending the report to President Lyndon Johnson of the USA.
(2) It is evident without a doubt that the Egyptian aggressors would not withdraw from Yemen without being forced by an overwhelming power capable of administering a crushing blow to neutralize them forever. If our great friend, the USA, does not move to help Israel deter the Egyptians, we will face 1970 with an existential threat from Egypt to our throne and to our interests. All the resources we spent along with our American friends, and the oil company ARAMCO to provide weapons, munitions, medicine, paper money, silver and golden currencies exceeding 1 billion dollars (to the Royalists in Yemen), will have been wasted. We will end up paying more than double the resources to achieve victory over the Egyptians and their revolutionary allies in Yemen. All the money and resources will achieve nothing as long as our American friends do not move to help uproot the common enemy entirely. We are greatly gratified, however, that the USA is now in agreement with our views more than any time in the past. This change was confirmed to us by Mr. Kim Roosevelt and senior US Generals, and other US experts. We confirm our support for the recommendations of the American experts.

Based on Saudi support, the US advisors forwarded the recommendations to President Johnson in Washington.

In reply, the US President requested through his advisors that King Faisal, in his capacity as the King of Saudi Arabia, should take the initiative and communicate his position directly by writing officially to President Johnson, who was dealing first-hand with this problem. President Johnson added:

> Although Israel had previously requested support and permission to wage a decisive battle against the Egyptians and the Syrians in order to paralyze their support for something called 'Arab Nationalism'…we did not wish that the United States support Israel in such a pivotal

battle in a region with a majority of Arab states surrounding Israel without consulting our most important Arab friends in the area, and particularly, the approval of King Faisal and his royal Saudi family, as well as taking into account the opinion of King Hussein of Jordan. When such consultation is accomplished, we will then begin our support for Israel to execute the final paralysis of Egypt and Syria, as we will throw all our weight behind Israel to guarantee the success of the battle.

In 2006 Sami Sharaf, Nasser's close assistant, also published the exact Saudi document, which he obtained in 1995 personally from the Syrian President Hafez al-Assad. The document was smuggled from the Royal Palace in Riyadh to the Syrian President's office in Damascus (Sharaf 2006: First Volume [in Arabic]).

According to the Sharaf-obtained documents, in response to President Johnson's suggestion, on 27 December 1966 King Faisal wrote the following letter to the American leader: (Hamdan 2006: 489–491 [in Arabic]).

Based on the report of our Committee sent to you already, it is evident that Egypt is the largest threat and enemy to all of us. If this enemy is left to foment trouble and support our enemies militarily and through media campaigns, then by 1970 our very existence will be doubtful, as supported by Mr. Kim Roosevelt. Therefore, I propose the following "Salvation Plan":

(1) The USA supports Israel in launching a lightning attack against Egypt to seize the most important and vital points in the country. Not only will this force Egypt to withdraw its army from Yemen, but the result will keep Egypt preoccupied with Israel for a long time. No Egyptian will be able to raise his head again beyond the Suez Canal in an attempt to re-establish the Mohamed Ali's conquest and Nasser's plans for Arab unity. By achieving that we would give ourselves a long period necessary to destroy such destructive principles, not only in our kingdom, but in the rest of the Arab world. Following that, we will not mind giving some aid to Egypt and other affected Arab countries in their hour of humiliation in order to avoid their vicious propaganda messages against us.

(2) Syria also cannot escape the attack. By occupying parts of its territory, it will not be able to replace the position of Egypt, when the latter falls.

(3) The West Bank and the Gaza Strip must be occupied to remove any ability for the Palestinians to agitate, and also to prevent their exploitation by any Arab country under the guise of liberating Palestine. The hope of Palestinian Refugees' repatriation will be smothered, and their settlement in the surrounding Arab countries will be much easier to implement.

(4) We believe that 'Mola' Mostafa Barazani in Northern Iraq must be supported in order to establish a Kurdish Government capable of keeping any government in Baghdad occupied, and unable to pursue the cause of Arab unity based in the north of our kingdom, at present or in the future. You should know that we have already started since last year (1965) to supply Barazani with money and weapons through infiltration from within Iraq or through Turkey and Iran.

(5) Your Excellency, this is a joint fight and a joint cause. Our survival depends on the implementation of our recommendations. Meanwhile, please allow me to renew my wishes for continuous victory, and to wish the continuation of our excellent relations.

Michael Oren (2003) documented the Saudi involvement and support for the strike against Egypt. In a meeting between the British Ambassador to Saudi Arabia and King Faisal in June 1967 following the Arab-Israeli war, the King said: "Nasser is an arch intriguer and a bogus leader...If I'd been in the Jews' place, I'd have done exactly the same thing to him" (Oren 2003a: 318). Despite Faisal's opinion of Nasser, he attended the Khartoum Arab Summit (July 1967) with Nasser and pledged to help Egypt and Syria defeat the Israeli 'aggression'. Intra-Arab politics have always been steeped in deceit, betrayal, and disputes.

Mohamed H. Heikal, the well-informed influential journalist and a key advisor to President Nasser, wrote in a book published in Arabic that:

> after all the plans to strike Egypt were finalized, President Lyndon Johnson decided in May 1967 to gauge the possibilities of anger of the Arab street and the effects on the Arab thrones following the Israeli attack on Egypt. Johnson decided to consult the two kings (King Faisal and King Hussein) in the region whose survival is of paramount importance to the national security of the US (Heikal 2006).

Johnson dispatched Richard Helms, Head of the US Central Intelligence Agency (CIA) to London to meet King Faisal, who was on an official visit to the UK. The meeting took place on 29 May 1967. At the time, Faisal was concerned about the fate of Aden (in light of the Egyptian threat). Faisal sought the help of the British government in establishing a regional group comprising all the Arab countries of the Arabian Peninsula and the Persian Gulf, under the leadership of Saudi Arabia, to pose a counter balance to the League of Arab States (Arab League) in Cairo amenable to Egyptian influence.

Heikal met Kamal Adham in London in the spring of 1985 and asked him what had transpired during the meeting between Faisal and Helms in May 1967. Heikal also asked whether King Faisal was aware of the Israeli and American plans against Egypt and Nasser. Adham did not provide a direct answer to the direct questions. Instead:

> Adham answered that Nasser was in an open and violent confrontation against the Kingdom of Saudi Arabia. The confrontation or the battle was political and psychological and then it became a military confrontation in Yemen. You have to know that King Faisal was responsible for the welfare of his kingdom, his (royal) family, his brothers and his sons, as he must discharge his responsibilities to them. His duty was to the throne and to the Saud family, and he had to act to protect their interests regardless of any other considerations. Adham added that "The greatest danger facing Saudi Arabia was Nasser. In the end, Faisal won over the threat of Nasser. We do not care how. Faisal won."

The plan for the defeat of Egypt and its anti-colonial policies scripted by Saudi Arabia, the USA, and Israel worked like a charm, with unbelievable level of success beyond the wildest belief of the co-conspirators. The destructive outcome, however, of crippling the reformist-secular content of the modern Arab nationalist movement, has plagued the region ever since, and the carnage is still percolating until the present time. The door was opened wide for the emergence of the Wahhabi-Salafi radical Islamic ideology and its violent and destructive manifestations. Moreover, Israel's role in the service of the imperial-colonial plans was confirmed once again for all to see (at least, those not wearing blinkers).

10.15   Canada's *faux pas*

On 27 May 1967 General Mohamed Fawzi, Egypt's military Chief of Staff, sent the following message to General Rikhye, Commander of UNEF, regarding the Canadian contingent under his command:

> Major-General Rikhye,
>
> Owing to the biased attitude of the Canadian Government towards Israel, the general feeling among the masses of the people and the armed forces became mobilised against Canadian policy, and being aware for the safety of the Canadian troops and for the reputation of the United Nations Emergency Force, which have done their best in carrying out their task, we demand the immediate withdrawal of the Canadian troops from the UAR (Egypt) territory within 48 hours, and we are ready to give all facilities if required for their transport by air or any other means.
>
> General Mohamed Fawzi, UAR Chief of Staff (Rikhye 1980: 88).

The first impression on reading this communiqué is that it was written in a hurry, without proper care to language in terms of what was expected from an official government document. Although the communiqué was purportedly drafted by the Egyptian Ministry of Foreign Affairs, it obviously lacked the polish displayed during previous communications regarding UNEF. The fact that the note was signed by General Fawzi, the Chief of Staff, might suggest the influence of Vice President Amer and the military in forcing a more confrontational stance. However, the Foreign Minister, Mahmoud Riad, an ex-military man himself and an associate trusted by the President, also communicated with the UN Secretary-General in the same vein, requesting an early withdrawal of the Canadian contingent in UNEF.

The Minister too cited fears of negative reaction in Egypt against the Canadian policy that could affect or harm the Canadian forces and, by extension, the whole UNEF presence. It was an irony of fate that the country that had first proposed the establishment of UNEF to help Egypt face the consequences of armed aggression was now asked to remove its troops, ahead of all other national contingents in the UNEF, as a sign of Egyptian displeasure at a perceived Canadian bias in the brewing conflict.

This dramatic escalation in the process of terminating the presence of UNEF in Egypt, targeting the Canadian contingent, came about as a result of Canada's active opposition at the UN in New York to the withdrawal of UNEF. The Egyptian Government became incensed when it was revealed that two Canadian naval units and a supply frigate (in an initiative code-named *Operation Leaven*) had sailed through the Straits of Gibraltar heading towards the eastern Mediterranean.

This Canadian move came on the heels of news of increased US and British naval deployment in the Mediterranean and the Red Sea near the Gulf of Aqaba. In this heightened atmosphere, Egypt feared a concerted Western plot either to break the blockade of Israeli shipping in the Straits of Tiran or to challenge Egypt's mobilization in the Sinai. Egypt feared the formation of a US-British-Canadian 'Red Sea Regatta' to open by force the Straits of Tiran to Israeli shipping. These fears seemed confirmed when Canada's Prime Minister, Lester Pearson, suggested that "international control over the Gulf of Aqaba might be a viable option to keep peace in the Middle East" (Carroll 2005: 12).

It is interesting that Canada, which had strongly opposed the withdrawal of UNEF, began to change its position when, on 26 May 1967, the Canadian "decided to seek a hastened withdrawal of the Canadian contingent from UNEF" (Canada 1967; DEA, 20 May), *even before* Egypt officially requested the Canadian withdrawal on 27 May 1967.

A meeting, however, which took place on 20 May 1967 involving the Canadian Minister for External Affairs, Paul Martin Sr, and Egypt's UN Ambassador might shed some light on Canada's changed position. In this meeting, Egypt's El Kony assured Martin that Egypt's respect for Canada remained high. But there was concern in Egypt and elsewhere in the Arab world that there was "a sort of conspiracy" to challenge Egypt's "sovereign right to ask for the withdrawal of UNEF" (Rikhye 1980: 87). Following that meeting, Canadian officials at the Department of External Affairs began to question the wisdom of opposing UNEF's withdrawal "while Canadian troops were still on the ground" (Rikhye 1980: 92). Acceptance of the developing political realities on the ground, and compliance with the Egyptian demand, led to the Canadian contingent's evacuation earlier than other UNEF contingents. The Canadian troops departed from El-Arish airport in the Sinai before the start of the war.

Missing in the reporting on all the frantic diplomatic moves to avert a military confrontation and defuse the crisis, however, was the very wise Canadian proposal (floated at the time) to accede to Egypt's demand for the withdrawal of UNEF, but to redeploy the international force immediately on the Israel side. Earlier, the USA and the UK proposed the reactivation of UNEF by redeploying the international force on "both sides of the Armistice Demarcation Line" but this "was rejected by Israel". As established already, Israel had rejected such a proposal when it was made by the Secretary-General in 1956 (Rikhye 1980: 61). Undoubtedly, the redeployment on both sides of the Lines, or on the Israeli side alone, would have blocked any possible alleged Egyptian attempt to strike at Israel. But more importantly, it would have prevented Israel from carrying out its carefully planned attack. Clearly, Israel had consistently ejected any deployment of UNEF on its side of the borders precisely to preserve its freedom of operation when the timing was opportune.

With the War over and UNEF history, a political-legal post-mortem of the UNEF saga was due. The issue of sovereign consent occupied centre stage in this drama.

References

Al-Hakim, Tawfiq (1972/1974/1985): *The Return of Conciousness* [in Arabic and English] (Basingstoke: Macmillan).

BBC Documentary (2002): *Dead in the Water* (London: BBC); at: https://www.bbc.co.uk/programmes/b0074n0x, and http://www.informationclearinghouse.info/article5073.ht.

BBC News (2002): "New evidence for American cover-up of Israeli attack on US warship, 2002-06-08".

Canada (1967): *Department of External Affairs*, vol. 21596 (20 May 1967).

Carroll, Michael K. (2005): "From Peace (Keeping) to War: The United Nations and the Withdrawal of UNEF", in: *The Middle East Review of International Affairs*, 9,2, Article 5 (June): 1–24.

Carroll, Michael K. (2009): *Pearson's Peacekeepers: Canada and the United Nations Emergency Force, 1956–67* (Vancouver: UBC Press): 163.

Cristol, A. Jay (2002): *The Liberty Incident: The 1967 Israeli Attack on the US Navy Spy Ship* (Ann Arbor: The University of Michigan & Brassey's Inc.).

Dulles, John F. (1957): United States, *Department of State Bulletin* (11 March 1957): 392–93.

Eban, Abba (1956): *Statement to the UN General Assembly*, A/PV.565 (4 November 1956).

Elaraby, Nabil A. (1968): "United Nations Peacekeeping by Consent: A Case Study of the Withdrawal of the United Nations Emergency Force", in: *Journal of International Law and Politics* 1,2: 148–149.

Fawzi, General Mohamed (1967): "*Fawzi – Letter to Rikhye*", S/0316, box 9, file 2, UN-UAR Letters (17 May 1967).

Ferris, Jesse (2012): *Nasser's Gamble: How Intervention in Yemen Caused the Six-Day War and the Decline of Egyptian Power* (Princeton: Princeton University Press): 295–312.

Finkelstein, Norman (2003): *Image and Reality of the Israeli-Palestine Conflict* (New York: Verso): 131–132.

Fisher, Roger (1967): "Editorial Letter", in: *The New York Times* (9 June 1967).

Ghaleb, Morad (2001): "Pages from the *Memoires of Dr Morad Ghaleb*", in: Al-Ahram, Cairo [in Arabic] (11 January 2001).

Green, Stephen J. (1984): *Taking Sides: America's Secret Relations with Militant Israel* (New York: William Morrow & Co.): 215 & 239.

Hamdan, H. (2006): *Decades of Failures* [in Arabic]) (Cairo: Bisan Publishers).

Hammarskjold, Dag (1957): *Report to the UN General Assembly*, A/3512 (24 January 1957), and *Resolution* A/1125 (2 February 1957).

Heikal, Mohamed H. (1990): *1967: Al-Infijar* [*The Explosion*], [in Arabic] (Cairo: Markaz al-Ahram).

Heikal, Mohamed H. (2006): *Discourse in Politics: The Year of Crises* [in Arabic] (Cairo: Al-Shorouq).

Heikal, Mohamed H. (2009–2010): "Tagrobat Hayat" [A Life's Experience]. Various interviews [in Arabic], Al-Jazira Network.

Hod, Mordechai (1967): "Interview", in: *The Sunday Times* (London) (16 July 1967): 7.

Johnson, Lyndon B. (1967): "Remarks on the Near East Situation", in: LBJ, NSF, NSC, *History, Middle East Crisis*, vol. 1, tabs 11–20 (23 May 1967).

Lesch, David W. (2012): "Syria: Playing with Fire", in: Shlaim, A.; Roger, W.: *The 1967 Arab-Israeli War: Origins and Consequences* (Cambridge: Cambridge University Press): 81–82.

Lopez, Ralph (2014): *Jerusalem Post confirms Israel knew USS Liberty was American*; at: http://www.digitaljournal.com/news/world/Jerusalem-post-confirms-israel-knew-ussliberty-was-american/article/413296#ixzz5b6WZ68H0 (6 November 2014).

Mutawi, Samir (1987): *Jordan in the 1967 War* (Cambridge: Cambridge University Press): 96.

Oren, Michael B. (2002): *Six Days of War: June 1967 and the Making of the Modern Middle East* (New York: Oxford University Press): 39.

Oren, Michael B. (2003a): *Six Days of War: June 1967 and the Making of the Modern Middle East* (New York: Ballantine Books).

Oren, Michael B. (2003b): "Levi Eshkol, Forgotten Hero", in: *Azure*, 14 (Winter): 5,763; at: http://azure.org.il/article.php?id=248.

O'Sullivan, Arieh (2004): "Liberty Revisited: The Attack", in: *Jerusalem Post* (4 June 2004): 20.

Pearson, Anthony (1978): *Conspiracy of Silence: The Attack on the USS Liberty* (London: Quartet Books).

Qarqout, Z. (2006): *The Modern History of the Arab Nation: The Incomplete National Project* [in Arabic] (Cairo: Madbouli Publishers).

Quigley, John (2012): *The Six-Day War and Israeli Self-Defence: Questioning the Legal Basis for Preventive War* (Cambridge: Cambridge University Press): 495–497.

Rabin, Itzhak (1996): "A Report to the Israeli Knesset", based on: *The Rabin Memoirs* (Berkley: University of California Press): 73–75.

Riad, Mahmoud (1967): "Riad Letter to U Thant", S-464-373, file 3017, UN-UAR Letters (18 May 1967).

Rikhye, Indar Jit (1980): *The Sinai Blunder: Withdrawal of the United Nations Emergency Force leading to the Six-Day War of June 1967* (London: Frank Cass).

Rostgaard, Marianne; Jorgensen, Martin Ottovay (2012): "Academic History and the Future of the Past", *Academic Minutes,* 33.

Rostow, Walt (1967): *Memo to the President,* in: LBJ, National Security File, Country File, Middle East – UAR (Box 16) (14 February 1967).

Schmemann, Serge (1997): "General's Words Shed Light on the Golan", in: *The New York Times* (11 May 1997).

Scott, James (2009): *The Attack on the Liberty: The Untold Story of Israel's deadly 1967 Assult on a US Spy Ship* (New York: Simon & Schuster).

Segev, Tom (2007): *1967: Israel, the War, and the Year that Transformed the Middle East* (New York: Metropolitan/Henry Holt): 302.

Sharaf, Sami (2006): *Days and Years: Witness to Nasser* [in Arabic] (Cairo: the Egyptian Bureau of Publications).

Southerland, Daniel (1984): "Ex-Pilot Says US Jets Spied for Israel in 67", in: *The Christian Science Monitor* (15 March 1984).

Thant, U. (1967): "Aide Mémoire" by the UN Secretary-General, A/6730, para 7 (17 May 1967).

Thant, U. (1967): "Letter to Riad", A/6730, from the Report to the UN General Assembly) (18 May 1967).

Thant, U. (1967): *Report to the UN Security Council,* S/7906 (26 May 1967).

Zisser, Eyal (2002): "June 1967: Israel's Capture of the Golan Heights", *Israel Studies,* 7: 168–194.

Part IV
Outcome

Chapter 11
UNEF: Legal and Political Battleground

Abstract From its very inception, UNEF was mired in the fundamental dispute of a sovereign state's right to provide or withdraw its sovereign consent. Egypt insisted on retaining the right of consent for acceptance and termination of the deployment of foreign forces on its territory, claiming the right of sovereignty and the principles of the UN Charter. A major political and legal storm erupted in May 1967 when the Egyptian authorities invoked its sovereign privileges in demanding the redeployment of UNEF on its borders but this ended in a total withdrawal. Egypt's action was deemed in compliance with its Good Faith Agreement with the UN. A 'secret' private note written by the UN Secretary-General at the time, Dag Hammarskjold, commented on the Agreement with Egypt, and cast doubt on Egypt's automatic right to withdraw its national consent for the stationing of UNEF in its territory. The following highlights the political-legal arguments surrounding the issue. Such a debate affects the legal grounds for deploying international troops in conflict areas currently and in the future.

Keywords Conflicting legal reasoning · Hammarskjold secret *aide memoire* · U Thant response · Sovereign Consent challenged

11.1 The UN Secretary-General's Unavoidable Dilemma

Huge controversy followed Egypt's request to the UN to withdraw UNEF troops from Egyptian soil. Many blamed Secretary-General U Thant for agreeing to the Egyptian request without any discussions on the request or a vote by the UN General Assembly, the body which had authorized the formation of UNEF. Hammarskjold's Good Faith Agreement was cited by U Thant in support of his position that the UN was bound to respect Egypt's sovereignty and its right of consent for the continuing deployment of UNEF on Egyptian territory. The principle of consent was not in dispute by any side. The requirement to complete the task given to UNEF, on the other hand, was the main problem. Egypt was honour-bound not to request withdrawal before the task assigned to UNEF was

© Springer Nature Switzerland AG 2020   289
H. Hilmy, *Decolonization, Sovereignty, and Peacekeeping*,
https://doi.org/10.1007/978-3-030-57624-0_11

completed. Egypt, however, believed that apart from securing and maintaining a ceasefire and ensuring troop withdrawal, there were no other tasks that UNEF had left unfinished.

It was not part of the UNEF mandate to remain in place until a permanent peace agreement was in place, which was a failure both for the UN and for Egypt. That this marked an irresponsible lack of foresight did not enter into the discussion then taking place within Egypt. Nor was it considered seriously enough by the international community. This stipulation was never a condition for the deployment of UNEF. Hence, Egypt's request was not prematurely interrupting any agreement with the UN or violating the Good Faith Agreement in any sense. As far as Egypt was concerned, there was no violation of UNEF's mandate and it was perfectly within its right to demand UNEF's withdrawal unconditionally, as per the provisions of the battered Good Faith Agreement.

The lack of clarity, however, on what constituted the completion of UNEF's task (s) and on how to come to an acceptable agreement between the UN and the host country was the main shortcoming of the Agreement. It was this lack of clarity that killed the UNEF mandate, and with it peace in the Middle East even for a long time to follow. The continuous reference to Egypt as the host country presented a difficulty of its own, as no 'host' is obligated to accept the continued presence of the 'guests' against his will; otherwise the 'visit' is transformed from a temporary arrangement into an unwelcome 'intrusion', with serious consequences.

Sir Brian Urquhart, an experienced UN diplomat who participated in the negotiations with Egypt in 1956 and in 1967, "recalled that when Hammarskjold negotiated the 'good faith agreement', Egyptian sovereignty was not compromised in any way. Thus Nasser's decision to remove UNEF was within his rights". Urquhart continued, "Nasser had a perfect sovereign right to do what he did. It was an extremely stupid thing to do, as we told him at the time, but he had a perfect right to do it, under the agreement that got UNEF in" (Urquhart/Gordenker 1984).

Nabil Elaraby, Egypt's veteran international legal expert, stated that Nasser's request for the withdrawal of UNEF was "certainly a natural corollary stemming directly from its [Egypt's] sovereignty as a state, acknowledged by the General Assembly in its resolutions regarding the establishment of UNEF" (Elaraby 1968: 149–177).

11.2   U Thant's Explanation

In the face of severe criticism of the decision to accept Egypt's request for UNEF's withdrawal, U Thant published an explanation in July 1967 (Thant 1967: A/6672) of the factors behind the decision in May 1967 to agree to the withdrawal and reiterating the obligation of the UN under the Good Faith Agreement to respect Egypt's sovereign right of consent. But U Thant's explanation fell on deaf ears as the sound of war engulfed the Middle East. The Secretary-General stated in his report on 12 July 1967 that the *most crucial lesson* to be drawn from the UNEF experience was "the desirability of having *all conditions* relating to the presence *and* the withdrawal of a peacekeeping operation *clearly defined* in advance of its entry onto the territory of a host country" (Thant 1967).

Undoubtedly, the controversy over the Good Faith Agreement informed his conclusion. However, the Secretary-General also acknowledged the difficulty of this proposition due to the emergency nature of the original conflict situation, which required speedy deployment of the international Force. He also noted that any host country would not "be inclined to accept formal limitations on its sovereignty with regard to the exercise of its consent for the presence of an international force". The report stated further that "when a United Nations peacekeeping operation...is no longer welcome in a country...it cannot hope to continue to perform any useful function". A fundamental principle arrived at in the report was that "the full consent of the host country...is the indispensable precondition for the stationing of the Force". It is very significant to note, moreover, that "At no time was the Secretary-General's position officially challenged by any member state, and no attempt to convene the General Assembly was made" (Carroll 1976: 14). It is reasonable to state that the Secretary-General's report reflects fairly and accurately the dilemma of maintaining an international peacekeeping operation on the territory of a sovereign country outside the scope of a UN Security Council enforcement action.

With the withdrawal of Egypt's consent, U Thant believed that UNEF's "usefulness as a buffer between Egypt and Israel had ceased". U Thant also stated that once UNEF became a *persona non grata*, its continuation on Egyptian soil would have been "humiliating and untenable". U Thant was convinced that with the withdrawal of consent to UNEF's presence on Egyptian territory, the "force was no longer viable" (Brown 1994: 563). Allan James suggested that the future of (non-enforcement) peacekeeping operations depended on UNEF "not overstaying its welcome in Egypt" (James 1990: 563).

11.3   The Good Faith Agreement Revisited: Hammarskjold 1957 Unofficial Second Thoughts

It is one of the mysteries of the Suez War why Secretary-General Dag Hammarskjold, having in November 1956 concluded the Good Faith Agreement with the Egyptian Government, wrote an unofficial aide-memoire on 5 August 1957 to express reservations about Egypt's absolute right of consent. Hammarskjold's note, however, was not an official document, or the result of an agreement with the Egyptian Government, and was never entered into the UN's official record.

The eruption of the military hostilities in June 1967, and the resulting tragic consequences for peace and security following the withdrawal of UNEF, also ignited a war of words concerning the ultimate responsibility for terminating the presence of UNEF, the step seen as one leading to the break-out of hostilities. U

Thant's futile attempts to explain away the withdrawal of UNEF by employing the sovereign consent card, and the resulting disastrous consequences for the credibility of the UN in conflict management, compelled a former US diplomat and a confidant of the late Dag Hammarskjold, Ernest Gross, to reveal the existence of the unofficial memorandum written by the late secretary-general.

It seems to have been Hammarskjold's habit to compose such documents when faced with a vexing issue. Due to the sensitivity of the contents, he kept this memorandum a secret but provided a copy to his US friend and legal adviser. Gross, however, contended that by handing him a copy of the document, Hammarskjold intended it to be part of the public domain. The question is: if that was indeed the true intent of the Secretary-General, why did he not make the memorandum public himself when it was written or during his time in office? In response to the controversy accompanying U Thant's decision to agree to the withdrawal of UNEF unconditionally, Gross decided to leak the private document as a rebuttal to U Thant's position. Hammarskjold's note, accordingly, was leaked to the American Society of International Law and published in the *New York Times* on 25 May 1967 (Hammarskjold 1967).

The Secretary-General knew very well – based on his negotiations with the Egyptian authorities – that Egypt would not have accepted any limitations on its sovereign right to unconditionally terminate the presence of foreign troops on its soil. And on that basis he had concluded his negotiations with the Egyptian Government for the original deployment of UNEF. The resulting Agreement was submitted to the UN General Assembly without qualifications and was accepted without modifications. Amazingly, Hammarskjold described the Agreement to the Advisory Committee on UNEF as "a combination of one-sided but interlocking declarations".

This suggests a feat of obfuscation in international law, and it is one reason why the secret memorandum composed after the fact and contradicting the accepted, UN-approved interpretation of the understanding between Egypt and the UN is both intriguing and legally assailable.

Despite apparent accord on the primacy of the principle of sovereign consent in the operations of UNEF, a behind-the-scenes legal battle was brewing in November-December 1956 and threatening the stationing of UNEF on Egyptian soil. This diplomatic-political row, with far-reaching legal implications and consequences, that was escalating was between the Egyptian Government and the Secretary-General of the United Nations. The exchanges, quotations, and analysis discussed below are based on the secret memorandum.

In his secret memorandum, Hammarskjold affirmed that the establishment of UNEF by a UN resolution "did in no way limit the sovereignty of the host state" because it was based on Chapter IV of the UN Charter. But he then moved to qualify this right of sovereignty; according to him, "Egypt had the right" of consent, but there remained a question of "whether that right in this context should and could in some way be limited". Clearly, Egypt believed very strongly that there could be no limit on its right of consent. The Secretary-General, however, was willing to countenance limitations on Egypt's sovereign right that would be "in the interest of political balance and stability in the UNEF operation".

In fact no reference to any limitations on Egypt's sovereign right was ever included in the Agreement, but in his secret memorandum Dag Hammarskjold held that by accepting the UN General Assembly resolution, Egypt "had consented to the presence of UNEF" to perform "certain tasks". Egypt, therefore, could not ask for the withdrawal of UNEF "before the completion of the tasks" without contradicting its "own acceptance of the resolution". On the surface, this may have sounded logical, but the actual text of the Agreement clearly stated not only that the UN "reaffirms its willingness to maintain the UNEF until its task is completed" but also that the completion of the task was "to correspond to the wishes of the Government of Egypt" (Article 2 of the Good Faith Agreement).

What did it mean for the Secretary-General to accept a confirmed absolute right on the one hand, and then provide a later interpretation undermining such a right, on the other? The Secretary-General had some reservations about Egypt's right of consent, and the Egyptian President was determined to protect this right. Thus the Good Faith compromise agreement was concluded. Hammarskjold's leaked memorandum – unknown until its release a decade after the original Agreement – surprisingly made those reservations public on the eve of the June 1967 War. The leak, therefore, represented an injection into the controversy over Egypt's right to unilaterally withdraw its consent in order to deliberately cast doubt on Egypt's entitlement to exercise such right.

The difficult nature of the UN-Egypt negotiations to set up UNEF is revealed by Hammarskjold's position, according to his memorandum. On 9 November 1956, Dr. Fawzi, Egypt's Foreign Minister, requested clarification from General Burns, the designated commander of UNEF, as to the length of time the Force "would stay in the demarcation line area". Burns in turn sought clarification from Hammarskjold, who replied the same day that "A definite reply is at present impossible".

But the Secretary-General seemed to have linked the "emergency character" of UNEF to the "immediate crisis" (the invasion of Egypt). He then, however, added that if there were to be a difference of opinions "as to when the crisis does not any longer warrant the presence of the troops, the matter will have to be negotiated with the parties". To soften his interpretation affecting Egypt's presumed unquestioned right of consent, he added that "as the United Nations force would come with Egypt's consent, they cannot stay nor operate unless Egypt continues to consent". If that was the case, one wonders why he expressed his reservations in the first place.

Hammarskjold's 9 November 1956 proviso regarding the need for negotiations in case of a difference of opinions upset the Egyptian Government. As a response, Omar Loutfi, Egypt's Ambassador to the United Nations, met Hammarskjold on 11 November 1956 and stated that "It must be agreed that when the Egyptian consent is no more valid, the UN force should withdraw". The Secretary-General records in his memorandum that he replied, "I did not find that a withdrawal of consent could be made before the tasks which had justified the entry had been completed". He then reiterated that if "different views on the degree of completion" developed, the "matter should be negotiated".

This reply must have riled the Egyptians further. Loutfi then submitted an official memorandum on 11 November 1956 to the Secretary-General, stating, "It being agreed that consent of Egypt is indispensable for entry and presence of the UN forces in any part of its territory, if such consent no longer persists, these forces shall withdraw." Hammarskjold's reply on 12 November 1956 challenged this interpretation by stating that Egypt's withdrawal of its consent "before completion of the task would run counter to the acceptance of Egypt of the decision of the General Assembly". Again, the Secretary-General tried to finesse his interpretation, saying that the "conditions which motivate the consent" were tied to the "tasks established for the force in the General Assembly resolution". Based on this interpretation, his memorandum then concludes that "as long as the task, thus prescribed, is not completed, the reasons for the consent of the government remain valid".

The Secretary-General's position forced Egypt's Foreign Minister to reply on behalf of the Egyptian Government on 13 November 1956. Fawzi informed the Secretary-General that Egypt "could not subscribe" to *his interpretation* of consent and withdrawal and that the announced agreement on dispatching the UNEF troops to Egypt, therefore, "*should remain inoperative*".

Again, Fawzi insisted that "if consent no longer persisted, the UNEF should withdraw". Hammarskjold admitted that his stand involved taking a gamble, and that the risk of further delays over interpretations "might cause Egypt to change its mind…and throw our approaches overboard". This legal tussle delayed the arrival of the first UNEF contingents by more than twenty-four hours.

Fearing further delays and complications, Hammarskjold replied to Fawzi the same day, stating that his stand on Egypt's withdrawal of consent being tied to the interpretation of 'the completion of the task of the international force' represented his '*personal opinion*'. In other words, the idea that the original consent by Egypt would remain valid as long as the task of UNEF was not completed was the Secretary-General's personal interpretation, and not the official UN position.

He added that his "reference to negotiation" (in the case of a divergence of views between Egypt and the UN) "was intended to indicate *only* that the question of withdrawal should be a matter of discussion" as to whether the task of UNEF was fulfilled or not. The Secretary-General became very concerned that the stalemate over consent was jeopardizing the UNEF mission altogether. He felt strongly that the troops must arrive in Egypt immediately – "it now was a must to get the troops in" – and that he would go to personally negotiate the impasse with President Nasser in order to save "the face of Egypt while protecting the UN stand".

In addition to Hammarskjold's official reply to Fawzi, his memorandum tells us that he sent him a special personal message, pleading for understanding of the Secretary-General's stand on consent and withdrawal. He made it clear that both sides had to limit their "freedom of action", but that the UNEF deployment should nonetheless "go ahead" according to the accepted UN Resolutions, in the hope that "*a controversial situation would not arise*". This suggested an amazing trust in providence not normally seen in international relations. And, inevitably, the feared controversy did arise, with devastating consequences, a decade later.

But Hammarskjold also issued a *subtle warning*, or threat, that if negotiations did "break down on this issue" – referring to the "conflict which had developed between us on this question of principle" – he "could not avoid going to the *General Assembly*", *either to support his position or even to scuttle the UNEF mission altogether*. This implicit threat that the Secretary-General might get the UN General Assembly to endorse his own interpretation of the legal dispute raised the spectre that Egypt might be placed in the very tight spot of needing the UNEF to get the invaders out of the country and having to compromise on its fiercely protected sovereign right of consent.

Hammarskjold declared himself in the memorandum very anxious to avoid "most embarrassing…political repercussions", but he warned that few would support Egypt's position in asking UNEF "to withdraw at a time when the very reasons" which had prompted acceptance of the Force "were still obviously valid". Of course, Hammarskjold's stand was expressed within the context of the early stages of the conflict, when UNEF was needed to complete the 'tasks' of ceasefire and withdrawal outlined by the UN General Assembly resolutions. Certainly, the 'tasks' were not completed at this early stage, and the Secretary-General could be justified in November 1956 in threatening to involve the General Assembly. Such reasoning could not be extended to the long term of the deployment when the tasks of the Force would have been indeed completed.

The Secretary-General believed that his position made it clear that if Egypt did not accept his stand on withdrawal, "the matter would be raised in the Assembly". Yet Egypt's concern was already focused on the long term consequences of accepting UNEF presence on its soil without guarantees of withdrawal if demanded by Egypt.

With the beginning of the arrival of the international Force in Egypt in November 1956, Hammarskjold became – wrongly – convinced, based on the *mistaken interpretation* of the exchange of letters in his memorandum, that – according to his recorded conclusion – Egypt had "finally tacitly accepted" his position. Despite the Secretary-General's erroneous conclusion, Egypt could not have been clearer on its position of sovereign consent.

While his preference was still that withdrawal would be explicitly "decided by the General Assembly", thus taking the decision completely out of Egypt's hands, he admitted that "in this *naked form*…the problem could never have been settled". Moreover, the Secretary-General showed an understanding of Nasser's potential difficulties if he accepted limitations on "Egypt's political freedom of action". His (Nasser's) concerns, in Hammarskjold's opinion, were "not without justification", for Nasser, admitted the Secretary-General, would be accepting "a far-reaching and unpredictable restriction" due to the "possible consequences of differences of views" associated with a rigid "legal construction".

In addition, Hammarskjold's threat "to propose the immediate withdrawal of the troops" if an agreement between the UN and Egypt were not reached, could not change the formula arrived at for the basis of the Good Faith Agreement, which did not require withdrawal to be based on an agreement approved by the UN General Assembly. Hammarskjold was a great man and a superb international diplomat, and Egypt owed a lot to him for his principled intervention against aggression and the invasion of its territory. But trying to change the basis of the agreement with the Egyptian Government unilaterally and in a secret *aide-mémoire*, when he could not achieve the results he was after in direct negotiations, was not his finest moment.

It was the stalemate over the conditions of withdrawal of UNEF troops that prompted Hammarskjold to come up with the Good Faith Agreement's *"dual statement"* formula developed after hours of high-wire negotiations with Nasser and his officials. The two stipulations were: first, Egypt would assure the UN that its exercise of sovereign rights would be "on the basis of a good faith interpretation of the tasks" of UNEF; and second, similarly, the UN would reciprocally assure Egypt that UNEF would only remain "as long as the task was not completed". The respect for Egypt's sovereign consent was the fundamental basis for the agreement.

11.4   Competing Legal Interpretations

In a superb instance of legal reasoning, Hammarskjold maintained that instead of an explicit agreement, the UN and Egypt had created a mutual obligation to reach an interpretation of the terms of withdrawal *in good faith*. Hammarskjold's brilliant negotiating logic was in full display when he accepted that "Egypt constitutionally had an undisputed right to request withdrawal of the troops, even if initial consent had been given". However, his secret memorandum went on to say that "it should be possible on the basis of my own stand as finally tacitly accepted (by allowing the UN troops to enter Egypt), to force them into an agreement in which they limit their freedom of action" by "making a request for withdrawal dependent on the completion of the task".

Such a request, in turn, would have to be submitted to "interpretation by the General Assembly", thus placing in reality a clear international control over Egypt's sovereign independence. While this interpretation was never agreed to or stated in the final agreement between Egypt and the UN, Hammarskjold's ability to speak from both sides of the mouth nonetheless helped float the Good Faith Agreement. Eventually, however, the Agreement was doomed because of the inherent contradictions embedded in it and the problems associated with one-sided interpretations. In the end, it was too good to be true.

It is interesting that Hammarskjold ended his memorandum by reiterating his interpretation of the UN's agreement with Egypt to mean that there was an implied obligation to ensure the completion of the tasks prior to withdrawal. His argument was, in fact, qualified by Egypt's consistent refusal to sign a commitment to reach a negotiated agreement on withdrawal first. His assertions in the private document that his interpretation of the understanding with Egypt was the only valid one, discounting any previously stated objections by Egypt against violating its sovereign right of consent, did not change the fact that the Good Faith Agreement (imprecise as it was) was the only document agreed to by the two sides, and each side – not just Hammarskjold – could put a spin on it to suit its purpose if so desired.

This leaked memorandum could be viewed as expressing only Hammarskjold's private unilateral thoughts and concerns during the negotiations with Egypt and not as a final, definitive, mutually accepted interpretation of the Agreement. Having been locked up for over a decade and never entered into the public domain until it was leaked in 1967, Hammarskjold's private interpretation was never included in the formal Agreement with Egypt and had never, until then, been part of the public record.

The secret Hammarskjold memorandum, therefore, must be treated – based on the above – as a record of the negotiations and torturous legal manoeuvrings that took place *prior to* the arrival at the mutually accepted and officially sanctioned Good Faith formula, as well as the Secretary-General's wishful retrospection *after* reaching the Agreement. It could not be taken as a licence to bestow a different interpretation on the UN-Egypt agreement.

11.5   Hammarskjold Contradictions

On 9 October 1958, almost two years after concluding the Good Faith Agreement with Egypt and more than a year after Hammarskjold wrote his secret memorandum, the Secretary-General submitted a comprehensive report to the General Assembly summarizing the experience derived from the establishment and operations of UNEF (Hammarskjold 1958). Hammarskjold's Report reflected his own interpretation and was not co-authored by the Egyptian Government. This report stated "it follows from international law and the Charter" that the United Nations cannot station "units on the territory of a Member State without the *consent* of the Government concerned" (Paragraph 154). However, Paragraph 158 stated that if either side were "to act unilaterally in refusing continued presence or deciding on withdrawal...an *exchange of views* would be called for towards harmonizing the positions". An "exchange of views" is certainly different from a prior mandated and negotiated agreement *approved* by the General Assembly to authorize the withdrawal.

This exchange of views, continued Hammarskjold, "does not imply any infringement of the sovereign right of the host government". Clearly, Mr. Hammarskjold envisaged in his secret memorandum a more restrictive interpretation than he made public in his official report to the UN General Assembly. Hammarskjold's official report to the General Assembly spoke only of an *exchange of views* in case of disagreement, and no legal requirement to obtain the *General Assembly's approval* before a withdrawal of troops took place. Having formally submitted this official report confirming the Egyptian interpretation (*after* writing his secret memorandum), Hammarskjold seemed to leave no doubt as to which interpretation of the Good Faith Agreement was the valid one.

The fact was that, under the difficult circumstances of the Suez War, the Good Faith Agreement, despite its imperfections, was the only one capable of officially and publicly satisfying both sides at the time of negotiating the terms of UNEF's mandate. In hindsight, the Secretary-General could have insisted, in return for respecting Egypt's absolute right of consent in principle, on an *agreed formula* (thirty days' notice, for instance) for 'consultation'. Avoiding a contested prior agreement between the UN and Egypt before a final decision to withdraw the international troops was made, probably would have avoided embarrassing or injuring Egypt's pride and its sovereignty. Moreover, such an agreed consultation period would have provided a cooling-off period to allow for international mediation to defuse the crisis and avoid withdrawal of the international troops altogether.

The "Good Faith Agreement" would have then been transformed into the *"Face-Saving Agreement"*. Indeed, Hammarskjold had more leverage to bring to bear on Nasser as the foreign invading troops were still occupying Egyptian territory and Egypt needed international help to force them out. Yet, apparently, Hammarskjold did not press this point to his negotiating advantage, despite his assertions in the secret memorandum to the contrary.

Although Hammarskjold had been described by some as a "tightrope walker" (Miller 1961: 10), his skills in crafting the Good Faith Agreement, which at the time was considered a brilliant feat of diplomacy, were not sufficient for him to conclude his high-wire act in the way he preferred without the costly pitfall which occurred later.

11.6   U Thant's Public Response to Hammarskjold Secret Aide-mémoire

On 19 June 1967 U Thant, not surprisingly, issued a statement (Thant 1967) on the leaked Hammarskjold's secret memorandum of 5 August 1957 (leaked on 25 May 1967 on the eve of the Arab-Israeli war) in which he played down its significance. U Thant provided several arguments in response. In his introduction, Thant declared that Hammarskjold's newly uncovered contribution "could not alter the basis for the presence of UNEF on the soil" of Egypt as governed by existing public agreements and documents. Thant noted that Hammarskjold's memorandum "is not an official document", and had never been entered in the official record of the United Nations, being "of a purely private character". Thant bluntly said in his own statement that "the release of such a paper at this time would seem to raise some questions of ethics and good faith". Thant could have elaborated further in no uncertain terms on the reasons behind this suspicious 'uncovering' of this private paper, but he chose to keep his comments – angry as they were – in general terms.

U Thant also made a clear distinction between the limited scope of the Good Faith Agreement reached in *November 1956*, and the later broadening of the responsibilities of UNEF as agreed in *February 1957*. He made it clear that the earlier phase of UNEF, as governed by UN General Assembly Resolution 1000-ES-I of 5 November 1956, defined the task of UNEF "in very general terms" as being "to secure and supervise the cessation of hostilities". Once UNEF was deployed, Thant noted, hostilities ceased and withdrawal commenced; thus UNEF's "task at that time was completed". Clearly, Thant did not subscribe to the view that Egypt was obligated, contrary to the understanding of the original agreement, "to continue to accept the presence of UNEF until the task of the Force was completed" since he considered the task to have already been long completed (Who was charged with determining that the 'tasks' were completed? This point had been left vague in the original agreement). That is, U Thant believed that such a view "reads more into the 'good faith' understanding than is justified".

It was only with the second UN General Assembly Resolution 1125-XI of 2 February 1957 that UNEF's task "was broadened" to include "The scrupulous maintenance of the armistice agreement" and that UNEF was placed on the Armistice Demarcation Line between Egypt and Israel. According to U Thant, that broader task of UNEF of maintaining the Armistice Agreement of 1949 was indeed "not completed". It is important to realize that UNEF's initial role was only defined in the wake of the Suez War in 1956, and not as the original task of UNTSO in relation to the Armistice Agreement of 1949. Indeed, UNEF's role was expanded *only* in 1957 to include the maintenance of the Armistice Agreement *after* UNEF's original tasks had been completed (ceasefire and withdrawal).

But Secretary-General U Thant clearly affirmed that this expansion "was not the task envisaged or defined for UNEF when Secretary-General Hammarskjold and President Nasser reached the 'Good Faith' understanding". Also, it is equally important to realize that UNTSO was already in operation and its primary responsibility was to supervise the maintenance of the Armistice line.

A "central and decisive point" in U Thant's analysis of the decision to withdraw UNEF was related to "Israel's firm refusal to accept it on the Israeli side". Egypt alone had accepted the presence of UNEF on its side of the Armistice Demarcation Line. Israel's refusal to allow UNEF on territory under its control emanated from its declaration that the Armistice Agreement was no longer recognized by Israel after November 1956 (a declaration that seemed to give it the freedom to pursue future territorial expansion). U Thant emphasized that "UNEF's effective discharge of its buffer function" between Egypt and Israel had always depended entirely on Egypt's voluntary action of keeping its troops away from the armistice line, and giving UNEF room for its patrols, while "Israel has never observed a buffer zone…and Israel troops have always patrolled directly alongside it".

The Secretary-General finally stated that "no one could possibly question the full right" of Egypt to move its troops to the line inside its territory. Yet once Egypt began to move its troops forward and then made the request to the UN to withdraw the Force, "UNEF could no longer perform any useful function". Its continuing presence on Egyptian soil thus "lost any real significance", '*and*', he could have added '*the required host country's consent.*'

U Thant took issue with the criticism of Israel's Foreign Minister, Abba Eban, in the UN General Assembly of the Secretary-General's acceptance of Egypt's decision to withdraw its consent for the continued presence of UNEF on Egyptian soil (The Jewish Telegraphic Agency 1967). U Thant considered Eban's remarks "highly critical" and warned that they could be "very damaging to the United Nations with regard to peacekeeping functions, past and present". U Thant reminded Eban that Israel refused to extend any cooperation on UNEF to the United Nations. He added that Israel had "always and firmly refused to accept UNEF on its territory". In a sharp reminder, Thant declared that "There can be no doubt that it would have been a helpful factor of considerable importance if Israel had at any time accepted the deployment of UNEF also on its side of the line" (U Thant 1967). It became abundantly clear why Israel was so adamant against the stationing of UNEF on its territory. The plans for additional territorial expansion would have been seriously affected.

For over a decade, UNEF had indeed been successful in the task of the maintenance of ceasefire along the Egyptian-Israeli armistice line. But nobody expected this task to continue indefinitely. Conflict resolution was not part of the UNEF mandate. And that was both UNEF's Achilles' heel and the weakness of the original limited peacekeeping concept, which did not tie the end of hostilities to the beginning of a comprehensive and permanent peaceful settlement. U Thant's response to the publication of Hammarskjold's memorandum contained solid factual and logical points, but history, nevertheless, is unlikely to be kind to Thant for readily agreeing to Egypt's request (rightly or wrongly) in light of the tragic consequences of his decision.

It is hard to imagine, however, a UN Secretary-General defying and challenging a UN member state's sovereignty, outside the application of a Chapter VII Security Council resolution or a clearly stated agreement between the UN and a sovereign state, without questioning the basis of the entire international system of post-war sovereign equality and independence. However, other steps – not challenging to the state's right of consent – could have been included in the original agreement to delay and defuse the confrontation.

11.7   Contested Legal Interpretations

U Thant's report on 19 June 1967 was challenged in 1970 by Stuart Malawer in an important article criticizing the emerging "new concept of consent" for being overly broad and its interpretation as "very restrictive". Malawer viewed this new approach to consent as "detrimental to the development of a peaceful international system". Such a new approach he deemed to be actually a reaffirmation of the traditional interpretation of 'consent' based on the concept of 'obligation' prevalent in the 1920s (Malawer 1970: 170–190).

Only explicit consent of states could bind them to international obligations. Hersch Lauterpacht's 1933 study of the theory of "sovereignty of states" had stated that "the field of international law finds itself at the very start confronted with the doctrine of sovereignty [under which] the State is not bound by any rule unless it has accepted it expressly or tacitly" (Lauterpacht 1933: 82).

Lauterpacht's opinion was in line with a landmark case by the League of Nations' Permanent Court of International Justice (World Court). An established source of positivist doctrine, the *Lotus Case* (World Court 1927) became a foundational source of international law, which "identified *consent* as the basis of obligation under both conventional and customary international law". Moreover, the Court ruled in the 1927 case that "The rules of Law binding upon States therefore emanate from their free will". Later in 1958, Professor Lauterpacht, now a leading international jurist, concluded that the evolution of jurisprudence in the international legal system was moving away from the initial acceptance in the 1920s of the "principle of restrictive interpretation of obligations" (Lauterpacht 1958, 1982).

Yet the 1960s saw such moving away from restrictive interpretations of obligation in treaty law as being "arrested and reversed". State practices, including the termination of UNEF by Egypt, however, confirmed the resurgence of the traditional concept of *consent-based* obligation. As applied to peacekeeping, the withdrawal of UNEF established an international legal precedent, namely "the unilateral right of the host country to request the withdrawal of United Nations peacekeeping forces, unless explicit consent [to restrict such right] by the host state to the contrary exists in an international agreement". According to Elaraby in his 1968 study of the withdrawal of UNEF, such consent was an "extremely narrowly construed" treaty interpretation under customary international law. UNEF, according to this view, was "placed in Egypt only with the consent of the Egyptian Government" as a "temporary organ of the General Assembly with a limited mandate" (Elaraby 1968: 149–177). By 1970, Professor R. Falk concluded that "Traditional notions of obligations in international law have accorded a virtual veto to the sovereign state by making its expression of consent…an *indispensable precondition* of a legal obligation" (Falk 1970).

Moreover, Malawer in 1979 took issue with U Thant's interpretation of the 'mandate' of the Force and the 'task' to be performed by it. According to the 1979 Malawer interpretation of the Good Faith Agreement, "the force would remain until the 'task' was completed". And the 'task', as defined by the General Assembly resolutions, was to "secure and supervise the cessation of hostilities".

U Thant's interpretation of the Good Faith Agreement, which referred to Resolution 997 of 2 November 1956, and Resolution 1000 of 5 November 1956, according to Malawer, emphasized the "cessation of hostilities" and de-emphasized the supervision of the 'Armistice Agreement'.

U Thant's interpretation, Malawer believes, was "very narrow" in light of Hammarskjold's three reports to the General Assembly: in 1956 (regarding ceasefire), 1957 (regarding withdrawal of occupying forces), and 1958 (regarding compliance with the 1949 Armistice Agreement).

According to Malawer, U Thant's 'sin' was to consult the terms of the Good Faith Agreement independently and to interpret the 'task' as nothing "other than the supervision of the withdrawal" (Malawer 1970: 179–190).

Malawar's criticism is in itself too unneccesarily expansive and overreaching. It could be argued that such criticism is not accurate because UNEF was not created to supervise the 1949 Armistice Agreement. UNTSO had been in place already since 1949 to supervise this task. At the same time, UNEF was created only as a response to the invasion of the sovereign territory of Egypt in 1956, and it was established to ensure the termination of such aggression in all its forms. The supervision of the Armistice Lines can be considered ancillary to its original mandate, as UNTSO did not cease operations with the deployment of UNEF.

Moreover, the 2 February 1957 General Assembly Resolution to additionally task UNEF with the "scrupulous maintenance of the armistice agreement" was specifically adopted in view of Israel's delaying tactics in completing its withdrawal from the Gaza Strip, and in the wake of Israel's declaration that the Armistice Agreement with Egypt was dead (and buried). Supervision here should mean ensuring Israel's withdrawal in accordance with the Armistice Agreement, which was not dead and buried as far as the UN was concerned.

Another reason for the expansion of UNEF's mandate in February 1957 was to assuage Israel on the issue of Palestinian infiltrators crossing the armistice lines, as well as to reassure the Arab countries regarding Israel's devastating cross-border raids and territorial claims.

It is reasonable to argue that even if there was a firmly binding agreement tying the hands of the Egyptian Government in its ability to request a withdrawal only upon the completion of the UNEF mission, Egypt would have been able to force withdrawal. Not only was the task of UNEF completed, but it had been fully completed for over a decade after its first arrival in Egypt. The UNEF was dispatched with the mandate to enforce a ceasefire and a cessation of hostilities, the withdrawal of British and French troops from the Canal Zone, and finally the withdrawal of Israeli occupation troops from the Sinai (including the islands of Tiran and Sanafir) and the Gaza Strip to the 1949 Armistice Demarcation Lines. All these tasks were accomplished without exception by March 1957, more than ten years before the Egyptian request for UNEF's withdrawal. Moreover, it was not part of the UNEF mandate to remain on Egyptian soil indefinitely (Egypt had not forefeited its sovereignty), or to oversee peace negotiations between Egypt and Israel. If that last condition was included in the original mandate, the 1967 War would probably have never occurred.

In rejecting Hammarskjold's belated interpretation, written in 1958 after the original Good Faith Agreement was finalized in 1956, and holding that there should be an "exchange of views" between Egypt and the UN regarding 'withdrawal' of UNEF, U Thant accepted the Egyptian position completely.

Similarly, U Thant stated that "There is no official United Nations document on the basis of which any case could be made that there was any limitation on the authority of the Government of Egypt to rescind that consent at its pleasure".

This interpretation left Egypt with the right to confirm *when* UNEF's 'task' was completed; the conclusion of the UN (based on Hammarskjold's reports and their approval and adoption by the General Assembly) stressed that "When formulating UNEF, the General Assembly acknowledged that the consent of the host country was supreme and therefore the full right to request withdrawal of the UNEF is certainly a natural corollary *stemming directly from its sovereignty* as a state" (Hammarskjold 1958).

Unless forcibly occupied, no sovereign state is expected to accept the presence of foreign troops on its soil against its free will.

Agreement or no agreement, the UN could not have rejected Egypt's request for troop withdrawal. Perhaps the manner and speed of withdrawal could have been modified or altered, but not denied. Egypt was a sovereign nation and neither the UN nor any other power had the right to maintain troops on Egypt's soil without Egypt's consent, since this deployment was not a Security Council Chapter VII enforcement action. This would have been a flagrant violation of Egypt's independence and sovereignty, and contrary to the provisions of the UN Charter itself.

The international troops would have been transformed instantly from international peacekeepers to international occupiers, with all the consequences and ramifications that such action would have entailed. In other words, had Egypt's request been rejected for any reason, UNEF would have been changed from peacekeeper into the instrument of an international occupation regime.

In a speech on 22 May 1967, President Nasser made clear the position of his government on the issue of the presence of UNEF on Egyptian soil and Egypt's right to consent and to withdraw such consent: "...had UNEF ignored its basic mission...we would have regarded it as a hostile force and forcibly disarmed it". But he quickly added, "At the same time I say that the UNEF has honourably and faithfully carried out its duties" (Nasser as quoted by Rikhye 1980: 201). This position was further elaborated within Egypt in the following years.

Despite Malawer's critique, his contribution clearly asserted the preponderance of the concept of consent-based international obligation. The concept had been qualified by the post-war UN Charter, which allows the UN Security Council to initiate enforcement measures but only based on Chapter VII authorization, when the consent of the targeted nation state can be over-ridden. However, under the non-binding Chapter VI, consent-based obligation did play a major role in the deployment of UNEF in Egypt as well as in its withdrawal from the theatre of operations. From an international legal perspective, U Thant does appear to have been right to accede to Egypt's request. Politically, however, the Secretary-General did not consider other alternatives that could have preserved international peace and security, his prime responsibility as Secretary-General of the UN.

U Thant was convinced that "The assumption over the years was if the host government ever requested the withdrawal of UNEF, the request would be honoured. This assumption was never questioned". U Thant, however, acknowledged that such an assumption of an unquestioned right of the host State was peacekeeping's "basic defect". Such a 'defect', if accepted, can only be considered from a political point of view and not from a legal standpoint.

Either the state in question is sovereign or it is not. If it is sovereign, then it has the unquestioned right to exercise its sovereign consent, withhold it, or revoke it. In the case of UNEF, the basic defect was not to include in the agreement between Egypt and the UN provisions to transform the ceasefire into permanent peace, or failing that to establish an *a priori* mechanism for withdrawal accepted by both sides.

Such omission left Egypt with the incontrovertible right to force immediate withdrawal. Israel's Abba Eban self-servingly came to agree with U Thant's diagnosis, and by extension with Hammarskjold's wish list in his memorandum. Eban stated that "agreements for peacekeeping are likely to be more effective if they rely on bilateral enforcement agreement rather than on arrangements such as emergency forces which are at the mercy of the host country and which can, therefore, apparently be dismissed without notice" (Eban 1967).

Israel's refusal to accept the stationing of UNEF on its side of the border in tandem with the Egyptian deployment at the outset in 1956–57 and again when it was suggested at the end in May 1967 as a way out of the impasse did not qualify the Israeli state to criticize the deployment agreement with Egypt. Yet, as events had proven, the Israelis were only too keen to ensure the prompt withdrawal of UNEF in order to allow the launching of the Kadesh invasion plan of Egypt. U Thant, moreover, became convinced of "the necessity of formulating a withdrawal formula which would help maintain peace in the international system and which would be agreeable to host state". Elaraby additionally suggested that negotiators should "attach a standard clause to any agreement to deploy UN troops that would remedy the considerable weaknesses that were shown in the 1967 incident", referring to the right of the host state to demand withdrawal (Elaraby 1968: 149–177).

Naturally, it was easy to criticize – after the fact – the arrangement arrived at between Hammarskjold and the Egyptian Government in 1956, allowing Egypt (according to the Egyptian interpretation, at least) the absolute right to request withdrawal unilaterally and unconditionally. It was generally understood and accepted at the time of the UNEF deployment that Egypt had the undisputed right of consent for the stationing of foreign troops on its soil, a sovereign right which could be withdrawn at any time. It was clear from the negotiations between Egypt and the UN, that the Egyptian Government would not have affixed its signature on the agreement without that right. The only restriction on that right accepted by Egypt at the time (in the Good Faith Agreement) was the requirement for the implementation of the UNEF mandate to be completed in accordance with all the applicable UN resolutions. As previously noted, the UNEF completed the tasks required by the UN resolutions by March 1957.

There is no doubt that a prior agreement covering all aspects of a UN peacekeeping operation, including the right of withdrawal, would have been far more helpful in maintaining peaceful conditions than ambiguous assumptions about sovereignty and consent. But it must be remembered that the Good Faith Agreement was part of a pioneering experience occurring without previous examples or clear guidelines. Moreover, the emergency nature of the situation demanded immediate action not tied to precise legal formulations, even though they were later needed.

Unfortunately for the UN, one of the antagonists, Israel, proved a decade later to be determined to pursue a planned military course, with the acquiescence of one of the superpowers at the time, the United States. Moreover, Egypt's power struggle, combined with the absence of democratic checks and balances in the prevailing political system, sealed its fate.

The 1967 war was an event waiting to happen regardless of the pretext or the circumstances surrounding its trigger. The absence of a peaceful and just settlement of the Arab-Israeli conflict during the long presence of UNEF undoubtedly made the 1967 war easier to start, regardless of the UN's inconclusive peacekeeping efforts.

11.8   Additional Legal Arguments

To maintain troops in a country without consent, Cairo University Professor S.M. Farrajallah declared in 1969, "would be coercive and thus…illegal, if not politically unsound". Moreover, Egypt had been the victim of aggression, not an aggressor state facing international enforcement action. Farajallah concluded his examination of UNEF by affirming that:

> any UN peacekeeping operation is based on the principle of consent as to the authorization, the functioning or withdrawal of the international force. Otherwise it would turn itself into a sanctions force, appropriate only to Security Council enforcement action according to Chapter VII of the Charter (Farajallah 1970: 40–43).

In fact, this position marked a continuation of a debate that went back to the weeks following the Suez Crisis and the first deployment of UNEF.

Israel's position on consent was at first just as strong as Egypt's, at least during the deliberations to establish UNEF in 1956. The Israeli delegate to the UN General Assembly, Abba Eban, made Israel's position clear by stating that:

> The first and crucial problem which arises is that of the sovereignty of states in the context of the consent required…chiefly the consent of the states upon the territory of which it is proposed to station these forces…*the stationing of any force in a territory under Israel's jurisdiction or control is not possible in law without the Israel Government's sovereign consent*…If this question of sovereign consent were not clarified, then a precedent would be created whereby a majority of the General Assembly could decide to station forces in the territory of any State irrespective of its prior consent (Eban 1956: 83).

However, a few days later, on 23 November 1956, when discussing Egypt's right of consent in the stationing of UNEF, the Israeli delegate reversed course by stating that if Egypt was allowed the right to unilaterally request the withdrawal of UNEF from Egyptian territory, "we would reach a reduction in absurdity" (Eban 1956: 2756).

Two questions raised by Egypt at the UN – (1) "Is Egypt entitled to withdraw consent to UNEF, after having expressly approved entry of the Force on its territory?", and (2) "Is there any restriction on a host country to retract or terminate its consent unilaterally?" – were then addressed on 27 November 1956 by Egypt's Foreign Minister, Mahmoud Fawzi, who stated:

...as must be abundantly clear, this Force has gone to help Egypt, with Egypt's consent; and no one here or elsewhere can reasonably or fairly say that a fire brigade, after putting out a fire, would be entitled or expected to claim the right of deciding not to leave the house (Fawzi 1956).

Another view was expressed by Harvard Law School Professor Louis B. Sohn, who in 1958 stated that there was an "implied limitation" on Egypt's right to terminate the UN operation without UN concurrence because Egypt "accepted the Force without a specific reservation of a right to retract consent on its own" (Sohn 1958: 229–240). Contrary to Sohn's argument, the host government has the right to withdraw consent at any time, because the agreement between the two sides stated that UNEF can continue its deployment ONLY with the consent of Egypt, a fact he conveniently failed to include in his assessment.

Actually, Sohn's argument was rejected in 1960 by Farajallah when the latter stated that the host state is "the final arbiter on the continued presence of a UNEF force in its territory". He reasoned that if consent was required to 'begin' UN operations, it logically follows that consent would be required 'throughout' the tenure of the international force. This conclusion, he argued, gives the host state the "right to revoke" consent at any time unless there is an agreement, formal or tacit, to limit this right (Farajallh 1970: 40–41). In the case of the UNEF, there was – apart from the Good Faith Accord – neither formal nor implied agreement to limit the right of consent of Egypt.

Willingly accepting the presence of an international force on a sovereign territory does not place the host country under UN trusteeship or reduce its sovereign prerogatives. According to M.H. Gagnon, the lack of explicit or implicit limitations meant that "the state retains whatever rights it has *not specifically modified by agreement*" (Gagnon 1967: 825–826). This conclusion was in line with the traditional international law concept of consent-based obligation.

Despite the many legal opinions for and against Egypt's right to control consent, the 1973 War involving Egypt, Syria, and Israel, and the resulting military and political situations, according to K.P. Saksena, created new operational rules regarding consent. Following the war, a new peacekeeping operation (UNEF II) was commissioned with different ground rules from the original UNEF I (Saksena 1977: 459–481).

Ironically, it was in Egypt, the country that fought very hard to protect its right of sovereign consent, that the new situation worked to reduce – if not undermine – Egypt's insistence on the cherished principle of consent.

11.9   Egypt's Sovereign Consent Modified

Several major alterations regarding the concept of 'consent' in international peacekeeping occurred due to this new 1973 conflict:

First, the result was a diminishment in the role of the UN in conflict management, as the two superpowers were fully engaged and took direct control of the crisis.

Second, the Security Council resolution establishing the mandate for UNEF II did not mention the word 'consent' as a prerequisite of the international force's entry to the host country's territory at all. The resolution stated instead that the UN force must operate "with the full co-operation of the parties concerned". The word 'co-operation' replaced the word 'consent' used in the mandate of UNEF I.

Third, the host country's right to unilaterally demand withdrawal of the international force was annulled and placed in the hands of the UN Security Council. All matters affecting the operations of the force were to be decided by the Council. Following the Security Council's approval of the new arrangements, Egypt introduced the magical word 'consent' by declaring that the "UNEF … is on Egyptian territory with Egypt's *consent* to enable Egypt to safeguard its sovereignty and territorial integrity". However, Egypt did not dispute the US assertion that the UNEF could be withdrawn only by a decision of the UN Security Council.

Fourth, contrary to the experience of UNEF I, under the new arrangements for UNEF II, the Secretary-General had no authority to make any decision regarding the continuance or otherwise of the UN force. According to this agreement, the Secretary-General was given no right to accept the host country's request for withdrawing the forces on his own, as U Thant had done in 1967 (Saksena 1977: 459–481).

Fifth, Egypt's sovereign right of consent was further affected after the signing of the *Peace Treaty* with Israel on 26 March 1979. The UN force envisaged as part of the requirements of the Treaty was stalled and then abandoned due to the threat of a Soviet veto in the Security Council. The US, Egypt, and Israel agreed on the creation of the *Multinational Force and Observers* (MFO) on 3 August 1981. The MFO's mission was "to supervise the implementation of the security provisions of the Egyptian-Israeli Treaty of Peace and employ best efforts to prevent any violation of its terms". Egypt's acceptance of the presence of this new peacekeeping force on its soil is established as a result of a binding international treaty. It would not be easy for Egypt to demand the removal of the MFO troops without violating or abrogating the signed treaty, a very difficult task unless all the signatory countries concurred.

Sixth, these changes were not mandatory under the UN Charter, and they took place only because Egypt 'allowed' the new approach to peacekeeping operations. Once Egypt accepted the new arrangements, however, the country was bound by the altered legal foundation for the operation of an international force on its territory and, by extension, by all other future UN peacekeeping operations, unless Egypt demanded the renegotiation of the basis of operations of UNEF II or the successive MFO regime, or withdrew from the peace treaty with Israel altogether.

Seventh, although the secret 1957 memorandum of Secretary-General Dag Hammarskjold, revealed only in July 1967, caused a lot of surprised comments and speculation, its contents squared quite closely with the Secretary-General's published report of 9 October 1958.

In that report, Dag Hammarskjold had already registered his view that the *Good Faith Agreement* between the UN and Egypt implied the need for mutual and reciprocal *consultation* on all issues pertaining to the operations of UNEF on Egyptian soil. On the basis of this interpretation, if a dispute between the two sides occurred:

> an *exchange of views* would be called for towards *harmonizing* the positions...[This does] not imply an infringement of the sovereign right of the host Government...But it does mean a mutual recognition of the fact that the operation, being based on *collaboration*...should be carried on in forms natural to such collaboration, and especially so with regard to the questions of presence and maintenance (Hammarskjold 1967).

While the Secretary-General's reasoning seemed logical, the fact remained that the Egyptian Government made no undertaking in the Good Faith Agreement to restrict its decision-making regarding consent to prior consultation, collaboration, or harmonization, no matter how after-the-fact inference might lead to such a one-sided conclusion. The big question is: Why was Secretary-General Hammarskjold unable to translate his preferred version into a formal agreement? The big answer is: He was not able to secure the Egyptian Government's approval for any terms beyond the those officially agreed to in the Good Faith Agreement.

Eighth, on another contentious point relating to the issue of consent, Secretary-General Hammarskjold asserted in the same Report (A/3943) that the UN "must reserve for itself the authority to decide on the composition" [of the Force], although he admitted, "it is obvious that the host country, in giving its consent, cannot be indifferent to the composition" (Hammarskjold 1958).

Hammarskjold's formula for protecting the UN's right to choose the constituent countries in a peacekeeping operation, while respecting the host country's sovereign interests, established the principle that future UN operations would exclude "the permanent members of the Security Council", as well as other countries "having special interest in the situation which has called for the operation". It was skilful diplomacy on the part of the Secretary-General to assert the UN's right to decide on the composition of the constituent troops even though he knew that in the Good Faith Agreement Egypt never accepted such a principle for the composition of UNEF.

In fact, there was disagreement between the UN and Egypt over the countries allowed to participate in UNEF, but the problem was resolved through political negotiations, and not because of any declared or implied right of the UN to decide unilaterally regardless of the expressed wishes of the host country. It would be extremely problematic for the UN to insist on including the troops of a country not accepted by the host country. At its core, such a move would be considered a direct attack on and fundamental violation of a country's sovereignty. In a Chapter VII deployment, however, the dispute over the countries included would be a moot point.

11.10   The Position of Canada and the USA on Sovereign Consent

In 1956 Canada's position, as outlined by Lester Pearson on 23 November, was contrary to Egypt's. Pearson argued "...the Force is to remain in the area until its task is completed, and that would surely be for the determination of the United Nations itself". Pearson had indicated in his memoirs that he had a difference of opinion with Secretary-General Hammarskjold regarding the original Good Faith Agreement and the right to request withdrawal. When the Secretary-General explained that "Nasser had insisted that the UN Force should leave Egypt whenever, in the opinion of the Egyptians, their work had been accomplished", Pearson replied, "This is going to cause trouble in the future." Hammarskjold responded by noting that he had told Nasser that "that condition was quite inadmissible". Undoubtedly, however, the Secretary-General did not strike a watertight accord with the Egyptian Government to preclude an ambiguous or disputed and dangerous situation from developing in the future (Pearson 1972: 260–62).

US Secretary of State Dulles held similar views to Canada's, noting that:

> once the consent has been given, then I think a good argument can be made that the consent cannot be arbitrarily withdrawn...And we would question, certainly, whether Egypt has the right arbitrarily to alter or change a consent once given until the purpose of that consent has been accomplished (Dulles 1957).

Of course, Egypt's position in 1967 was that UNEF's task had been completed years earlier, and therefore it had the right to terminate consent. Although Egypt's decision was ill-advised, despite its sound legal basis, the Egyptian leadership was afraid – from the beginning of the crisis a decade earlier – that its absolute sovereign right of consent over the presence of foreign troops on its soil would be challenged and compromised, leading to the transformation of UNEF into a permanent occupation force replacing the invaders of 1956.

11.11   The Position of Other States on Sovereign Consent

It is interesting to note that several states which signed the Agreement of 21 June 1957 (on participation in the UNEF) with the UN did not consider UNEF to be an indefinite operation. In signing on, some states believed that they would make their own determination as to the completion of the tasks assigned to UNEF and consequently withdraw their participating troops unilaterally. Other states declared that they would automatically withdraw their contingents if Egypt requested the withdrawal of UNEF, thus revoking the host country's consent. Despite the Canadian and US positions, other states provided different interpretations:

The *Swedish Government* believed that UNEF had a limited task to perform and should not remain in the area on an open-ended basis, or pending a political solution to the overall conflict. Sweden also asserted that its troops would not be stationed in foreign territory without the consent of the host country (Swedish Ambassador 1956).

The *Indian Government* was still more explicit in its position. In its view:

a. UNEF was set up only to ensure the withdrawal of British, French and Israeli invading troops from Egypt.
b. UNEF did not constitute a successor to the invading forces, nor was it authorized to take over their functions.
c. UNEF had to obtain Egyptian consent for its establishment.
d. UNEF was a temporary Force operating on an emergency basis.
e. The composition of UNEF had to be balanced (Indian Ambassador 1956).

The *Finnish Government* stated its understanding of participation in UNEF on the basis that its troops would serve for a limited period only "determined exclusively by the needs arising out of the present conflict in the area in question" (Finnish Ambassador 1956).

Indonesia was unequivocal on the conditions of its membership of UNEF: "It was on this clear understanding of the temporary, emergency nature of the United Nations Emergency Force that my Government participated in it" (Indonesia's Representative 1957). The Indonesian Representative asserted that his Government reserved the right to "reconsider its continued participation" if the functions and the basis of UNEF were changed.

The tragedy in this controversy is that the UN troops who contributed to the absence of hostilities served as a buffer between the two sides, performing UNEF's 'peacekeeping' duties when in fact there was no peace to protect, only an absence of war. The failure of the two sides, as well as the international community, for over a decade, to put in place the ingredients of a peaceful settlement by utilizing the breathing space afforded by the presence of UNEF was directly responsible for the continuation of the conflict unabated and consequently the resumption of hostilities. Moreover, the failure to place the UN troops on both sides of the lines also contributed to the speedy eruption of warfare and the inability to continue separating the two sides. Secretary-General Hammarskjold tried to station UNEF on both sides of the confrontation lines, but without success. "The Secretary-General made several attempts to get Israel to agree to have UNEF on its side of the demarcation line", General Burns remarked. "But the Israeli Government was adamant, and never showed the least sign of agreeing" (Burns 1962).

11.12 Israel's Position on Sovereign Consent

Israel, the 1956 aggressor state, had refused UNEF entry into its own territory, citing the right of consent. The UN General Assembly in Resolution 1125 stated that after Israel's full withdrawal from Egyptian territories, "the scrupulous maintenance of the Armistice Agreement requires the placing of the United Nations Emergency Force on the Egyptian-Israel armistice demarcation line" (UN Resolution 1957). The logical intention of the resolution meant "both sides of the line", but not for Israel, which waived the consent card to avoid acceptance of UNEF. The phrasing of the resolution was deliberately vague. What does it mean for a Force to be placed on a 'Line'? This was not specified in the resolution. One option, of course, was that it meant 'both' sides.

The Secretary-General could have stated clearly in the Resolution that the Force would be placed on both sides of the Demarcation Line. However, Israel made its withdrawal conditional on the creation of UNEF, leaving deployment to the Egyptian side of the Armistice Demarcation Line. Logically, the UNEF deployment should have been made along the demarcation lines of the party which started the invasion and the war. The Secretary-General was most anxious to avoid any procedural delay over which side of the Demarcation Line the Force should be deployed that might obstruct the actual deployment of UNEF due to the contested dispute. The failure of dual deployment was detrimental to the mission of UNEF, as events in the future had proven. Hammarskjold could have stood his ground, but his political judgement at the time precluded such an option.

Indeed, Israeli Prime Minister Ben-Gurion refused all appeals by the UN Secretary-General to permit UNEF on its side of the Line, as he declared emphatically during his Knesset speech on 7 November 1956. According to Gabriella Rosner, there were two main reasons behind Israel's refusal to accept the stationing of UNEF on its side of the Armistice Line: (1) the fear that the existence of an international police force would prevent Israel's future large-scale military action against Egypt; (2) the fear of losing territory in an internationally-imposed peace settlement with reduced boundaries. The legal principle accepted by the Secretary-General in the face of Israel's refusal was: "UNEF cannot operate on a nation's territory without the latter's freely given consent." The later experience of UNEF indeed showed "The indispensability of the host state's consent in a [UN] police operation outside the framework of [Security Council] enforcement action." These comments by Hammarskjold on the indispensability of 'consent' were ignored in his later memo, in which consent was diluted or obfuscated (Rosner 1963).

11.13 Legal Obfuscation

In Resolution 1125 (XI) of 2 February 1957, the UN General Assembly accepted the Report of the Secretary-General and "considered that the situation required the implementation of the measures proposed", including not just a ceasefire, but a total withdrawal of the invading forces (UN Resolution 1957). The Palestinian territory in Gaza was thus saved from Israeli. annexation (though only until the eruption of the 1967 war, almost eleven years later). The Secretary-General's emphatic Report in 1957 confirmed the post-war rejection of military conquest and the primacy of the UN Charter. This principle was carried over during the 1967 war at the end of UNEF's role when the UN Security Council passed Resolution 242, which emphasized "the inadmissibility of the acquisition of territory by war" (UN Resolution 1967).

The UN arrangements in 1956–57 and in 1967 nonetheless feature an important difference. UN Security Council Resolution 242 also called for the "Withdrawal of Israel armed forces from '*territories*' occupied in the recent conflict". But in a feat of British diplomacy and American ingenuity, Lord Caradon, the British Ambassador to the UN and the chief drafter of the Resolution (acting with Eugene Rostow, US Under Secretary of State, and Arthur Goldberg, the US Ambassador to the UN), insisted on dropping the definite article ('*the*') from the text demanding withdrawal. So it appeared as if there was a possibility that the Israeli withdrawal would be from '*some*' territories but not from '*all*' the territories occupied.

Arab and international legal experts have pointed out that there cannot be a contradiction in the body of a UN Resolution with fundamental and accepted principles of international law. Moreover, there is both a clear reference in Resolution 242 to the 'inadmissibility' of conquest, and in the meantime a casting of doubt on Israel's obligation of 'total withdrawal' in the same resolution. The inadmissibility principle should dismiss any excuse for territorial annexation as contrary to international law. A fundamental point of international law cannot be overridden by a vague political expediency used by Israel to justify its hold on illegally conquered territories. But the latter was considered Britain's revenge for the outcome of the 1956 Suez War, and America's answer to Nasser's challenge (Lord Caradon 1976: 144–145).

It is clear now, however, that British and American designs may have downgraded Nasser's brand of secular anti-colonialism, but they simultaneously created a deadly and protracted religious-based quagmire which has engulfed the region for decades and will continue to sap the region's ability to extricate itself from this hellish snare.

Later on, Lord Caradon justified the deliberate language of the Resolution, claiming that it was chosen to avoid implying that withdrawal to the pre-existing 1949 Armistice Demarcation Lines should constitute the final borders when the final status of territorial distribution, according to the Arabs, is not totally final and cannot correspond to the Armistice lines. Yet it is tempting to surmise that Lord Caradon and his colleagues knew very well that the withdrawal Resolution was not to *permanent borders*, as they *did not exist*, but to the previously established and recognized armistice lines by agreement before the invasion. There were no such quibbles in 1956–57, when the UN demanded and obtained total withdrawal from all 'the' territories occupied by Britain, France, and Israel, and when the UN was successful in enforcing all the Suez withdrawal resolutions. The Middle East is still mired in the clutches of an Arab-Israeli conflict partly because of that missing word in the British/US-sponsored Resolution 242. Continuous Western involvement in the creation and support of Israel has precluded the achievement of any fair, balanced and just solution to the conflict in the Middle East. Britain failed in its fiduciary responsibility towards the Palestinians during the British Mandate over

Palestine. The US has helped create and maintain a mammoth Israeli military power. Both France and the US have helped Israel develop nuclear capabilities.

Moreover – as noted earlier – the US signed a Strategic Cooperation Agreement with Israel to: (1) guarantee Israeli military superiority over the Arabs, (2) pre-position US arms in Israel for use in the region, (3) ensure political support for Israel, and (4) share intelligence information. Two formal Arrangements were put in place: the Joint US-Israel Military Group; and the War Reserve Stock (Cobban 1989; The Washington Institute for Near East Policy 1986).

The Arabs' preoccupation with the Israeli threat, a threat augmented and fortified by massive Western military and economic support, partly prevented the development of the ingredients of progressive democratic governance, already embarked upon by several Arab countries. Eventually, the conflict with Israel was used to impose non-democratic and totalitarian controls in most of the Arab world. This is in no way an attempt to absolve the Arabs from any responsibility for the continuation of the conflict. But it must be recognized that the Zionist designs to occupy Palestine and the eviction of the Palestinians in 1948 are responsible for the start of this deadly and escalating incendiary cycle of violence and the deliberate paralysis in achieving an equitable settlement.

Later on, during the Camp David negotiations between Egypt and Israel with US mediation, the Prime Minister of Israel, Menachem Begin tried to justify Israel's insistence on annexation of the conquered territories. He advanced the notion that Israel's war was a 'defensive war', thus justifying annexation. Begin insisted that the reference in UN resolution 242 to the "inadmissibility of acquisition of territory by war" and its inclusion in the text of the agreement with Egypt was 'unacceptable'. The offending language, according to Begin, "applies only to wars of aggression…The war of 1967 gives Israel the right to change frontiers" (Wright 2014: 91). The Israeli position was adding insult to injury, as everyone, Begin included, knew that Israel started the 1967 war based on pre-existing plans waiting to be executed at the opportune time. The time arrived in May 1967 when Israel launched a massive attack based on the Kadesh plan. Israel's war in 1967 was indeed a 'war of aggression' precluding any territorial gains.

11.14 The Lost Decade

Although the UNEF succeeded in keeping relative calm and prevented military confrontation between Egypt and Israel for almost eleven years, both countries ultimately withdrew their support for the international Force in order to further their political and military objectives. The last UNEF Commander, General Rikhye, stated the obvious when he referred to the demise of UNEF as "the dismantling of the edifice of peace". Could the withdrawal of UNEF have been avoided, modified or postponed? Was the Egyptian request for withdrawal legal? Was Secretary-General U Thant's compliance with the request too hasty and perhaps itself illegal under the UN Charter? There is no doubt that the withdrawal request by the Egyptian Chief of Staff, General Fawzi, to the UNEF commander, General Rikhye, was *procedurally* incorrect (Rikhye 1980: 45). But Egypt's right to terminate its consent was not in doubt.

The presence of UNEF on Egyptian territory and Egyptian-controlled territory had been affected through a political-legal agreement between the highest echelon of the Egyptian Government and the UN Secretariat, which was headed by the Secretary-General himself, and endorsed by the UN General Assembly. For the Egyptian military to bypass all the political-legal channels and independently demand the withdrawal of UNEF was a violation of both the spirit and the letter of the understanding between Egypt and the UN. Egypt had every right to demand the withdrawal of UNEF, but its request to do so was not carried out in an acceptable procedural way or in an acceptable legal framework.

Nonetheless, domestic, regional, and international factors all combined to strike a fatal blow to UNEF and to the pioneering attempt by the international community to defuse a military-political conflict by relying on the notion of collective security and international legal legitimacy. The creation of UNEF was also part of the first international censure of an illegal armed invasion of the territory of a sovereign state in the new international system founded after 1945.

The ultimate failure of the UNEF's passive peacekeeping model, despite a decade of success in preventing military confrontation, therefore, was more than just the failure of a single peacekeeping operation, because it brought into question the validity of UN peacekeeping itself as a tool for defusing – and resolving – international conflicts. It also brought into focus the new structure of an international system that could make it possible for a country or a group of countries to violate the fundamentals of the system in a way similar to the violations of the totalitarian regimes of the past. Yet the Suez-UNEF experience also confirmed the demise of the world's colonial empires. Sovereignty and national independence became indispensable ingredients of the new decolonizing system of nation states. Moreover, despite the unceremonious end of UNEF, its last Commander saw something positive in the experience: "While the presence of UNEF did not use physical force to maintain peace, there was no doubt about its moral force" (Rikhye 1980).

Within a short few years of the Suez Crisis, most of the colonies of the old empires had gained their independence. A new bloc of newly-independent nation states emerged on the international scene as the pre-United Nations era came to an end.

References

Brown, Davis (1994): "The Role of the United Nations in Peacekeeping and Truce-Monitoring: What are the Applicable Norms?", in: Bruxelles: *Revue Belge de Droit International*, 1994/2 (Editions Bruylant).

Burns, E.L.M. (1962): *Between Arab and Israeli* (Toronto: Clark, Irwin & Co).

Burns, E.L.M. (1968): "The Withdrawal of UNEF and the Future of Peacekeeping", *International Journal*, 23,1 (Winter); at: https://journals.sagepub.com/doi/pdf/10.1177/002070206802300101.

Caradon, Lord (1976): "The Shape of Peace in the Middle East: An Interview with Lord Caradon", *Journal of Palestine Studies*, 5,3 & 5,4 (Spring/Summer): 144–145.

Carroll, Michael K. (2005): "From Peace (Keeping) to War: The United Nations and the Withdrawal of UNEF", *Middle East Review of International Affairs*, 9,2 (June 2005): 1–24.

Cobban, Helena (1989): "The US-Israeli Relationship in the Reagan Era", in: *Conflict Quarterly* 9, 2 (Spring).

Dulles, John F. (1957): *United States Department of State Bulletin* (11 March 1957).

Eban, Abba (1956): *Address to the UN General Assembly*, Official Records, 1st Emergency Special Session, 565th meeting (4 November 1956).

Eban, Abba (1956): *Address to the UN General Assembly*, Official Records, 592nd meeting (23 November 1956).

Eban, Abba (1967): *Statement, UN General Assembly*, A/PV 1526, 38.

Elaraby, Nabil A. (1968): "United Nations Peacekeeping by Consent: A Case Study of the Withdrawal of the United Nations Emergency Force", *Journal of International Law and Politics*, 1,2 (December 1968): 149–177.

Falk, Richard A. (1970): *The Status of Law in International Society* (Princeton: Princeton University Press).

Farajallah, Samaan B. (1970): "UN PeaceKeeping Operations", lecture delivered on 13 February 1969, at Le Caire, Société Égyptienne De Droit International, in: *Études En Droit International*, II (1970).

Fawzi, Mahmoud (1956): *Address to the UN* General Assembly, Official Records, 597th meeting (27 November 1956).

Finnish Ambassador (1956): "Letter addressed to the UN", A/3302 Add 21 (5 November 1956).

Gagnon, M.H. (1967): "Peace Forces and the Vote: The Relevance of Consent", *International Organization*, 21,4 (Autumn 1967).

Hammarskjold, Dag (1957; 1967): "Secret Aide-Memoire of the Secretary-General, dated 5 August 1957", in: *The New York Times* (19 June 1967); and in: *International Legal Materials*, 6, 3 (May-June 1967): 595–602 [Ernest A. Gross, a friend of Hammarskjold, provided a copy of the secret, unpublished and unofficial document to the *American Society of International Law* and the *New York Times*].

Hammarskjold, Dag (1958): *UNEF: Report of the Secretary-General: Summary Study of the Experience Derived from the Establishment and Operation of the Force*, A/3943 (9 October 1958).

Indian Ambassador (1956): *Letter addressed to the UN*, A/3302/Add 4/ Rev I, Addendum: 23–4 (6 November 1956).

Indonesian Government (1957): *Official Statement* – GAOR, 11th Sess, Plen Mtg 649, Vol II–III: 1,043 (1 February 1957).

James, Alan (1990): "Peacekeeping in International Politics", cited in: Brown, Davis, "The Role of the United Nations in Peacekeeping and Truce-Monitoring: What are the Applicable Norms?", *Revue Belge de Droit International*, 2 (1994): 563.

Lauterpacht, Hersch (1933): *The Function of Law in the International Community* (Oxford: Oxford University Press).

Lauterpacht, Hersch (1958; 1982): *The Development of International Law by the International Court* (Cambridge: Cambridge University Press).

Malawer, Stuart S. (1970): "The Withdrawal of UNEF and a New Notion of Consent", *Cornell International Law Journal*, 25,4: 179–190.

Miller, Richard I. (1961): *Dag Hammarskjold and Crisis Diplomacy* (New York: Oceana Publications).

Nasser, Gamal A. (1967): "Speech", cited in: Rikhye, Indar Jit (1980), *The Sinai Blunder: Withdrawal of the United Nations Emergency Force leading to the Six-Day War of June 1967* (London: Frank Cass).

Pearson, Lester B. (1972): *Mike: The Memoirs of the Right Honourable Lester B. Pearson*, Vol. 2, 1957–1968 (Toronto: Toronto University Press).

Rikhye, Indar Jit (1980): *The Sinai Blunder: Withdrawal of the United Nations Emergency Force leading to the Six-Day War of June 1967* (London: Frank Cass).

Rosner, Gabriella (1963): *The United Nations Emergency Force* (New York: Columbia University Press).

Saksena, K.P. (1977): "Not by Design: Evolution of UN Peace-Keeping Operations and its Implications for the Future", *International Studies,* 16,4: 459–481.

Sohn, Louis B. (1958): "The Authority of the United Nations to Establish and Maintain a Permanent United Nations Force", *American Journal of International Law*, 52.

Swedish Ambassador Letter (1956): *Letter addressed to the UN*, A/3302, Ann 7: 23 (5 November 1956).

Thant, U. (1967): *Report by the UN Secretary-General on UNEF*, A/6672 (12 July 1967).

Thant, U. (1967): "Report by the UN Secretary-General: The Withdrawal of the United Nations Emergency Force (UNEF)", *UN Monthly Chronicle,* IV, 7 (OPI/275-17584) (July 1967).

Thant, U. (1967): *Statement of Secretary-General U Thant on the Hammarskjold Aide-Memoire*, UN-POI (19 June 1967).

Thant, U. (1967): "UN Secretary-General Takes Issue with Eban on Withdrawal of UNEF", *The Jewish Telegraphic Agency* (21 June 1967).

The Washington Institute for Near East Policy (1986): *Policy Focus* (September 1986).

UN General Assembly (1956): 1) *The Report of the Secretary-General on the basic points for the presence and functioning in Egypt of the United Nations Emergence Force*, and 2) *The Annex of the Good Faith Agreement Aide-Memoire*, A/3375 (20 November 1956).

UN General Assembly (1956): *Approval of The Good Faith Agreement*, Resolution A/1121 (XI) (24 November 1956).

UN General Assembly (1957): *Resolution* A/1125 (XI) (2 February 1957).

UN General Assembly (1957): *Report of the Secretary-General on Arrangements Concerning the United Nations Emergency Force,* A/3526 (8 February 1957).

UN General Assembly (1957): *Approval of the Report (A/3526) of the Secretary-General on the Status of the Emergency Force*, A/1126 (XI) (22 February 1957).

UN Security Council (1967): *Resolution* S/RES/242 (22 November 1967).

Urquhart, Brian; Gordenker, Leon (interviewer) (1984): *United Nations Oral History* (15 October 1984).

World Court (1927): *S.S. Lotus Case* (Fr. V. Turk.). Permanent Court of International Justice, Ser. A. No. 10 (7 September 1927).

Chapter 12
Peacekeeping: The Assertive Years

Abstract The failure of the UNEF model of 1956 to bring a lasting peace to Egypt and Israel, and their eventual military confrontation in 1967, provided the impetus for the search for a better arrangement for conflict resolution. It was becoming increasingly obvious and acceptable that traditional peacekeeping has a useful function to perform, but has serious limitations (the Capstone Doctrine). Moreover, the increasing complexity and type of conflicts, including not just international but also intra-national confrontations and savage violations of basic human rights, have compelled the international community to search for alternative modus operandi to deal with the changing parameters of conflicts. Sovereignty, although still important, has made room for human rights considerations as an overriding value parameter for the international community. International intervention to defuse a conflict, and increasingly to protect human lives, is becoming robust and less circumspect regarding the prerogatives of the sovereignty of the national state. Increasing criticism, however, is levelled at neo-liberalism as the basis for 'liberal' peace and for framing post-conflict peacebuilding as a liberal governance project regardless of local conditions, increasing in the process conditionality and dependency.

Keywords Inadequacy of traditional peacekeeping · Imperative of conflict resolution component · Capstone Doctrine · "Peacekeeping without peacemaking" · Agenda for Peace · Brahimi Report · Responsibility to Protect · HIPPO Report · Permanent UN Peace Force · Human Rights take Centre Stage

12.1 The Changing Profile of International Peacekeeping

The traditional passive peacekeeping model utilized to stop armed conflicts between sovereign states has been gradually transformed to accommodate humanitarian disasters resulting from external and domestic conflicts. International peace operations have been armed with a robust approach based on decreasing the influence of national sovereignty while increasing international legal tools to allow international

© Springer Nature Switzerland AG 2020
H. Hilmy, *Decolonization, Sovereignty, and Peacekeeping*,
https://doi.org/10.1007/978-3-030-57624-0_12

intervention, reflecting the paramountcy of human rights protection. By the late 1960s the Fawzi/Hammarskjold 'Sword for Peace' was beginning to be deployed with a fresh mandate. Hammarskjold distrusted the role of the superpowers in the international arena, as they needed the UN to rubber-stamp their decisions, and hoped that the small and medium powers could inject meaningful international participation. Hammarskjold referred to Egypt's Foreign Minister Fawzi's speech in which he said that the "League of Nations had a book but not a sword and the United Nations must have a sword as well as a book". Following Fawzi's reasoning, the UN Secretary-General raised the question, "But how can we have a sword?" to be independent but not isolated. This could only be achieved through the support of the small powers and an active UN secretariat general (Heikal 1973: 162–163).

After the 1956–1967 Suez peacekeeping experience, the rationale for engaging in peace operations changed. The concept of peacekeeping expanded on two fronts. The first was the realization that bringing an end to fighting among foes without addressing the conflict resolution needs would only prolong and expand the conflict. Comprehensive peacebuilding is indispensable. The second was the intensification and expansion of humanitarian suffering due to ongoing conflicts. The nature of conflict was changing and expanding and the need to develop new methods of approach was pressing. The concept of absolute sovereignty – a prerequisite in international relations – is, therefore, undergoing a fundamental re-examination of its basic foundations.

Concepts for peace intervention, therefore, are being developed and improved in response to the demand for new and effective approaches to defusing international and civil strife and atrocities. 'International humanitarian law' has been, therefore, reinforced by the developing doctrine of 'international human rights law'.

An increasingly weighty concern, which was lacking during the UNEF experience, is the importance of post-conflict resolution. Important new developments emerged after the end of the Cold War, including the *Agenda for Peace* (1992), the *Supplement to the Agenda* (1995), the *Brahimi Report* (2000), the *Responsibility to Protect* (2001), and the latest report on the subject, the *HIPPO Report* initiated by Ban Ki-Moon (2015) and finalized by Antonio Guterres (2017). A Permanent UN Peace Force was additionally created (agreement in 1996 and deployment in 2000). All of these initiatives resulted in the transformation of the ethics and application of international peacekeeping.

Although the UNEF experience proved disappointing in the end, at least it partly provided – along with the increasing concern for human lives and rights – the push for alternative models for peace operations to emerge.

The end of the Bi-Polar Cold War international regime has significantly affected the nature and scope of international intervention. The international system is undergoing further changes with the emergence of new powers challenging the dominance of the prevailing basis of the international system. China, India, Brazil, the European Union bloc (and perhaps more countries in the future) are not content to let the old power configurations continue unchecked. The nature of peacekeeping undoubtedly reflects such changes.

This new post-Cold War phase assumed a post-Westphalian, post-conflict peacebuilding approach based on several foundations:

> maintaining peace in post-conflict societies requires a multi-faceted approach, with attention to a wide range of social, economic, and institutional needs. They reflect a liberal project...seeking to build peace within and between states on the basis of liberal democracy and market economics (Newman et al. 2009: 7).

The jury is still out on the efficacy of the liberal peacebuilding approach to conflict resolution.

12.2 UN Peacekeeping Credibility

Peacekeeping intervention has had its share of failures. To be fair to the efforts of the various peacekeeping forces, the nature of the expanding conflicts in many societies across the globe has complicated the ability of the peacekeepers to control the extent of the conflict, not only because conditions in the field are beyond the resources available, but also because the administration of the international peacekeeping machinery is conflicted with ideological, political, and financial constraints. The success or failure of international peacekeeping ultimately reflects the status of international relations within the international system.

UN peace operations have not always met with success, as was evident from Suez, but also from the experience in Congo, Rwanda, Yugoslavia, Darfur, and other conflict areas. The UN peacekeeping role, therefore, was challenged and was going through major changes to adapt to a new conflict-ridden world.

The adoption of a robust and active peacekeeping intervention strategy, however, received the following candid description of the outcome of peacekeeping when the *use of force* was included in its mandate:

> The use of force by UN peacekeepers has been marked by political controversy, doctrinal vacuousness, conceptual confusion and failure in the field (Chesterman 2001: 20).

These are strong words, which reflect the myriad problems occurring when peacekeeping intervention develops into armed enforcement.

In a case study (Vieira 2016: 72–73) from Sierra Leone (1998–1999 and 1999–2005), the research concluded that "the role of the UN in the field contributed to perpetuate the levels of the violence", and to "prolonging violent conflicts". The UN thus "promoted a negative peace and worsened the already existing structural violence in the country". The rules of UN engagement in the field, therefore, must be adapted to meet the conditions and nature of the prevailing conflict. UN peacekeeping in this case did not fulfil the second standard of success in peace operations (conflict resolution). On the contrary, it exacerbated the magnitude and intensity of the conflict. Other hot spots in Africa where international (or regional) peacekeeping is involved are still smouldering with occasional bouts of violent convulsions.

In Mali, the under-trained blue-helmeted peacekeeping soldiers are tiptoeing on a powder keg of violence. "The desert area is arguably more unstable now than at any time since…2013 and the deployment of UN Peacekeepers" (Smith 2017).

Another negative image attached to peacekeeping is that of sexual violence allegedly committed by the 'peacekeepers' themselves against the population under their protection. "If the UN sexual abuse crisis has an epicenter, it is Congo… despite promises of reform, the UN failed to meet many of its pledges to stop the abuse or help victims" (Larson/Dodds 2017). A former UN official "blames a bureaucratic, inefficient agency for the enduring crisis". He claims that "The UN system is essentially protecting the perpetrators of these crimes…The UN is exploiting and is complicit in the exploitation of the very people that the organization was set up to protect" (Larson/Dodds 2017).

The head of an international fact-finding mission, Jose Ramos Horta, submitted its report to the Secretary-General of the UN on the alleged sexual crimes committed by some UN peacekeepers. The report concluded that crimes are committed by isolating, inducing, and assaulting their victims, and in some cases by offering 'food-in-return-for-sex'.

The report highlighted the abuses in the Central African Republic, Liberia, and Haiti. The report also pointed to the immunity enjoyed by the peacekeepers, and said that the immunity provided to the peacekeepers does not mean a lawless license to abuse. The report recommended that the UN should name the nationalities of the peacekeepers involved in the crimes and block participation of their countries in peacekeeping missions. Finally, the report recommended that the involved countries share in the expenses of raising the children born as a result of the sexual transgressions of their soldiers (BBC 2015).

The peacekeeping experience of the former Yugoslavia forced the conclusion that the use of overwhelming force under or outside the umbrella of the UN by national government(s) produces results which the UN on its own cannot match. One of the glaring legacies of the Yugoslav conflict was that the Dutch peacekeepers allegedly failed to stop the massacre of 8,000 Muslim men in Srebrenica, a supposedly UN "safe area". It is not clear, however, what kind of constraints or failure of command the Dutch were operating under. Whatever the cause, the Srebrenica massacre will forever remain a stain on the idea of peacekeeping.

Rwanda is another human tragedy attached to peacekeeping, despite the valiant efforts of the peacekeepers operating under brutal conditions and facing international reluctance to get involved. The problem with assessing peacekeeping impact is that the subjects of conflict are not exactly willing to play by the rules. The various warring factions are not bound by lofty ideals of peace and conciliation. More often than not, the various conflicts reflect deep fissures in the fabric of society and a sad history of socio-economic, sectarian and religious strife. Moreover, some of the ethnic and territorial disputes, clashes and entrenched conflicts have been exacerbated by the colonial experience of division and exploitation.

Regardless of the preponderant stance among sovereign states of viewing 'peacekeeping' with some reservations out of fear of degrading their sovereignty, the world has changed since the Suez Crisis, and so has the rationale for engaging in peace operations.

After the horrors of genocide in the 1990s and beyond, the essence of peacekeeping has been expanded to deal with new humanitarian disasters in Europe, Africa and Asia generated by increasing domestic and cross-border strife. But whether the conflict is inter-state or intra-state, the concern of sovereign states remains the same in relation to the interaction between sovereignty and human protection. Yet, ultimately, the concept of absolute sovereignty is undergoing re-examination of its basic foundations.

12.3 New Approaches to Peace Operations (Post-Capstone Doctrine)

The experience and lessons gleaned from over sixty years of peacekeeping experience in the field were gathered and analysed in a UN document (the *Capstone Doctrine*) designed for "the benefit and guidance of planners and practitioners of United Nations peacekeeping operations" (UN 2008: 8). Over the years, realization has universally dawned that the Capstone principles are inadequate to advance and broaden a genuine peace agenda.

The Doctrine is identified as "The evolving body of institutional guidance that provides support and direction to personnel preparing for, planning and implementing UN peacekeeping operations" (Peace Operations Monitor 2008).

Putting the Doctrine into context, Cedric de Coning stated:

> The doctrine is built on the important principle that whilst UN peacekeeping operations are meant to support a peace process, it cannot deliver peace on its own. The capstone doctrine thus understands and accepts that UN peacekeeping operations are part of a larger peace process (de Coning et al. 2008).

A more supportive view of the Doctrine states:

> The Capstone has proved crucial to peacekeeping, a flexible and dynamic policy that has allowed for some of the UN's most innovative approaches to date. Subsequent efforts to evolve peacekeeping…have also reaffirmed this 'holy trinity' of peacekeeping principles. But the current portfolio of missions is stretching these principles to their limit (Hunt 2019).

With the support of the UN Secretariat, the Department of Peacekeeping Operations (DPKO) and the Department of Field Support (DFS) are continually engaged in a strategy of including some elements of peacebuilding in the overall peacekeeping efforts:

> The strategy fully recognized that 'security and development are closely interlinked' and seeks to ensure that peacekeepers contribute to this mutually reinforcing dynamic in the most efficient manner possible (DPKO/DFS 2011: 2).

Since 2018, comprehensive criticism has been asking whether peacekeeping has lost its compass and faces an existential crisis. Novosseloff (2018) points to many investigations by the UN itself which have highlighted many deficiencies in leadership, failure to protect civilians and peacekeepers, and inadequate training and equipment. The solution to this quandary is not simply going back to the 'basics' of peacekeeping, because it "is not a choice between doing nothing or continuing business as usual" (Novosseloff 2018: 1–4). The best policy, according to Novosseloff, is to accept that peacekeeping is an "inherently temporary measure" and "should no longer be stretched".

The UN Charter indicates that the maintenance of "international peace and security" is the most important task for the United Nations Organization. According to Boris Kondoch, "The rule of law is arguably the most important aspect in any peace operation" (Kondoch 2007: xxix). The provisions of the Charter specifically relevant to the maintenance of international peace and security are included in no less than twelve articles which enable the Secretary-General to put in motion measures to ensure peace. Two basic inferences may be drawn from the preoccupation of the Charter with peace and security. First, peacekeeping is an essential and inescapable task of the UN. Second, the Charter provides a basis for legal evaluations of activities in international security, as long as the relevant UN operation for the maintenance of peace and security is deemed legal.

This last stipulation is a wide-ranging assumption that needs to take into account other articles in the Charter that emphasize sovereignty and non-interference. The need to reconcile these provisions is why the latest innovations in peace operations and the invocation of international human rights law try so hard to bridge the gap between international intervention and national sovereignty.

Dag Hammarskjold referred to the peacekeeping authorization in the Charter as the 'mythical Chapter VI and a half'. Kofi Annan eloquently explained this quandary: peacekeeping is a tool that has largely been used in situations where the application of Chapter Six of the Charter was not adequate and utilization of Chapter Seven was not possible. Peacekeeping thus became, in Dag Hammarskjold's memorable phrase, 'Chapter VI and a half' (Annan 2017: 2).

A great difficulty in reconciling national sovereignty and international law is that due to the emergence of *erga omnes* (obligations owed to all) and *jus cognes* (obligations from which no derogation is ever permitted) legal provisions, the ability of the sovereign nation state to limit, curtail, or renounce human rights treaties and other international measures designed to enhance the protection of rights internationally as well as internally has been limited. Yet such protection of human rights at home and abroad requires "multilevel constitutional protection" for individuals and "multilevel constitutional restraints" on governance powers. This conflicted legal situation is a result of the move towards "multilevel constitutional pluralism" against the instinctive and intrinsic "constitutional nationalism" of many nation states (Petersmann 2006).

There is consensus, however, that the legal basis for consensual peacekeeping operations falls between UN Chapter VI and Chapter VII (because both the Security Council and the General Assembly can authorize peacekeeping operations, but only the Security Council can impose non-consensual enforcement action under Chapter VII). Moreover, UN intervention sometimes occurs in response to a particular conflict which requires only a consensual intervention under Chapter VI, only to slide into a major conflagration requiring a robust response under Chapter VII. The space between VI and VII can, therefore, get intertwined and messy.

This concern was echoed in a joint United Nations/International Peace Academy seminar, which arrived at the conclusion that "maintaining international peace and security cannot be separated from protecting individual security of civilians". Consequently, another difficulty in authorizing and conducting UN peace operations is that the Charter has not provided a "precise definition of the circumstances under which a peace-keeping activity has to be undertaken" (usually considered a credible threat to world peace), or by whose authority it can be undertaken (Security Council vs. General Assembly). This complication was emphasized by the fact that there was "no settled definition of the term peacekeeping operation" (UNDPKO/IPA 2002).

The problem of the lack of final conflict resolution in the UNEF peacekeeping mandate was raised in 1967 by Zulfiqar Ali Bhutto, later Prime Minister and President of Pakistan, who invoked the concept of international morality. Bhutto (1967: 47) believed that placing an emphasis on 'interim' measures over 'final' settlement of disputes imposed "false ethics" on international relations. This approach, according to Bhutto, encourages an "illusory view of peace." The morality established accordingly aims for "tranquillity even at the expense of justice". Bhutto concluded that the response of the UN to the challenges of reaching world peace had been "conditioned much more by power realities than by demands of peace and justice". His final concluding remark was a call for "structural changes" in the United Nations in order to streamline the peace operations of the UN. Undoubtedly, Bhutto was affected by the UN peacekeeping stalemate in Kashmir, and later by the failure of UNEF in 1967.

Relying on principles of "organization theory", Michael Lipson (2007: 5–34) queries whether peacekeeping is nothing more than "Organized Hypocrisy" because of UN's failure to act in accordance with the ideals it espouses in post-Cold War peacekeeping missions. This supposed hypocrisy is due to the failure to respond to "conflicting pressures in external environment". Such hypocrisy, according to Lipson, impedes "efforts to mitigate harmful peacekeeping externalities." But hypocrisy could, on the other hand, manage "irreconcilable pressures that might otherwise render the organization incapable of effective action". Lipson seems to apply organization theory to a fundamentally political situation where action, or lack thereof, depends a lot more on international politics and power configurations than management principles.

Echoing that sense of frustration, General Burns stated in a presentation at the University of Calgary in 1981 that "unfortunately, the interval of peaceful conditions [provided by UNEF] was not used to devise terms on which a continuing peace between Israel and her Arab neighbours could be established. We had peacekeeping without peacemaking" (Burns 1981: 5).

During the International Conference on Peacekeeping in Cairo in 2006 Paul Heinbecker, former Canadian Ambassador to the United Nations, said that 'peacebuilding' must be factored into the equation of peace operations "in recognition of its centrality to peace and to give the UN forces an exit strategy". He expressed the view that the UN is still mired in Cyprus "because peace-building *was not a priority*" (Heinbecker 2006: 9).

There is no universal or clear answer to the question "What is international peacekeeping?" The established traditional peacekeeping principles (consent; impartiality; and non-use of force) have undergone fundamental changes in view of the changing international attitudes occurring in the wake of the radical changes in international conflict profiles:

1. *'Consent'* is challenged in two ways: whether the UN operation is authorized by the Security Council or by the General Assembly; and whether the situation calling for UN intervention is triggered by humanitarian concerns as distinct from inter-state conflicts.
2. *'Impartiality'* can be overlooked if the authorized UN action is based on a binding resolution even if it is contrary to the wishes of a member state.
3. Finally, the use of *'Force'* only for self-defence becomes irrelevant if the action authorized by the UN entails the use of force in the first place.

The UNEF experience provided an invaluable template for future peacekeeping missions that followed. It also provided useful lessons based on actual performance, and highlighted the many modifications needed to deal with the changing international crisis environment and the increasing complexity of conflicts in an increasingly unstable world. It eventually became clear that conflict management and conflict resolution approaches cannot remain static.

For many, UNEF was a necessary bitter medicine required to help extricate Egypt from the consequences of the foreign invasion to which it was subjected in 1956. The presence of the international force was seen, however, as a degradation of Egypt's sovereign control. But there was also a realization that without UNEF, Egypt would have been hard pressed to get rid of the invaders on its own and restore its much-valued freedom. Eventually, the interaction and cooperation between the two sides yielded genuine appreciation and respect. The events surrounding the termination of the presence of the Force in 1967, however, cannot and should not be viewed as an indication of the whole history of UNEF in Egypt.

Following the failure of the international community's peace operations in Somalia, Rwanda, Yugoslavia, Darfur, and Congo, new approaches to international peace operations have developed into a legal self-contained regime, based on observing the rules of armed conflict, the transition from war to peace, human rights law, international humanitarian law, international criminal law, and post-conflict peacebuilding. These political and legal innovations have fundamentally striven to achieve a balance between national sovereignty and the international quest for peace, security and human protection.

The horrors experienced in Rwanda, Darfur, and the former Yugoslavia and elsewhere have induced the international community to re-examine its political and legal tools in order to confront an increasingly savage conflict conflagration, the like of which was supposed to have been checked following the end of World War II and the creation of the United Nations.

To put teeth into this new international resolve to restructure peace operations, several proposals were made to establish a permanent UN peace force. Notable among the proposals was the idea of SHIRBRIG (Standby High Readiness Brigade), a standby UN force ready to intervene without delay, which was first deployed in 2000. However, concerns for protecting national sovereignty, fear of sustaining large casualties during robust peace operations, and reluctance to commit national resources to the service of external objectives all combined to bring an end to the idea of a permanent UN peacekeeping structure.

In re-examining the relationship between sovereignty and peacekeeping, one study looks at various regional independent peacekeeping missions as components of a broader international peacekeeping regime capable of affecting state behaviour, and at how state behaviour, in turn, is able to affect the behaviour of the international regime. '*Regime theory*' is used to explain the efficacy of peacekeeping, and to assess the role and ability of international institutions in influencing state behaviour in promoting peaceful outcome to international conflicts. The study also identified the critical role of a hegemon in advancing (or hindering) the conflict resolution process by influencing the regime(s) involved in the conflict (Krasner 1983: 2).

12.4   New Peacekeeping Philosophy

During the height of the military conflict in Bosnia in 1992, Canadian Major-General Lewis MacKenzie, commanding the UN forces in the Sarajevo area (part of the UNPROFOR) in Yugoslavia, came to the conclusion that although, under the UN Chapter Six Resolution "peacekeepers should not use force unless under attack" (Stevens 2013), the Canadians were allowed to adopt aggressive tactics in order to control the situation. "There was no peace to keep…[It was] an impossible situation in which to try to adhere to the usual rules of peacekeeping", and consequently the Canadians "went beyond the rules of engagement" (Doyle 2013: 1–2).

During an interview with the Canadian Broadcasting Corporation (CBC), the Canadian General said (using Hammarskjold's earlier terminology) that he made the decision to change the rules of engagement from Chapter Six to *Chapter Six and a half* by authorizing his soldiers to fire back collectively if any of them came under fire. He considered an attack on one person in his troops an attack on the whole mission, therefore requiring a general response, not just by the affected person as per Chapter VI rules (MacKenzie/CBC 2018).

General MacKenzie went further in 2016 while testifying to the Canadian Senate (National Security Committee) by calling for the term 'peacekeeping' to be abandoned altogether in favour of emphasizing the role of 'civilian protection'. This shift also highlights the expanding nature and changing parameters of conflict itself. Echoing such a sentiment, Canada's Defence Minister, Harjit Sajjan, announced that the Canadian Government is replacing the term 'peacekeeping' with the term 'peace support'. This change in the mission of peacekeeping reflecting 'untraditional conflicts', and less involvement by state actors, should not negate the need for managing inter-state problems (Connolly 2016).

I don't believe that it would be wise to totally abandon the traditional concept of peacekeeping altogether. Inter-state conflict is always a present contingency in international relations. The ability to perform the traditional aspects of peacekeeping does still have a place in the international conflict management environment.

To accommodate newly emerging approaches to conflict resolution, the notion of *ius post bellum* (just peace) and the associated concept of *jus post bellum* (justice after war) are being developed to deal with what Tomasz Lachowski (2014) calls the "lack of sufficient legal regulations in the post-conflict situations". International law has had to improvise and consolidate the legal tools to deal with the transition from wide-ranging conflict conditions to a stricter international community involvement in maintaining peace conditions. The norms and modalities of this new approach to conflict and its aftermath are becoming, according to Lachowski, a "legal self-contained regime". Under this regime, the law is not only concerned with the rules of war or armed conflict (externally or internally), and the transition from war to peace, but with human rights law, international humanitarian law, international criminal law, and post-conflict peacebuilding as well (Lachowski 2014).

There are three major international developments in the continuing effort to intervene and moderate the nature of international and national conflicts and establish the foundations of a durable and just peace, as well as the protection of civilians through the strengthening of international human rights law.

A fourth major initiative (HIPPO Report) was added to the record in 2015 and finalized in 2017. The efforts have evolved as follows:

12.4.1 Agenda for Peace: Preventive Diplomacy, Peacemaking, and Peacekeeping (1992) and The 1995 Supplement

12.4.1.1 Agenda for Peace (1992)

On 31 January 1992 the Secretary-General of the United Nations, Boutros Boutros-Ghali, was invited by the UN Security Council, constituted at the Heads of State and Government level, to prepare for circulation by 1 July 1992 an "analysis and recommendations on ways of strengthening and making more efficient within the framework and provisions of the Charter the capacity of the United Nations for preventive diplomacy, for peacemaking and for peacekeeping" (United Nations 1992).

The Secretary-General's Report, submitted on 17 June 1992, began with an introduction on the changing international context that covered topics including increased decolonization, the fading of the Cold War, the worldwide push towards democratization, the subordination of national authorities to greater regional groupings, the intensification of ethnic and religious strife, the related spread of terrorism, the re-emergence of racial tensions, and the growing disparities between rich and poor within and among nations. The Report identified the aims of international action as: first, identifying situations of conflict in order to peacefully defuse them; second, engaging in peacemaking to resolve the issues leading to confrontation; third, preserving peace through peacekeeping; fourth, assisting in peacebuilding in all its requirements; and fifth, addressing the deepest causes of conflict within the context of international law.

The Report emphasized that the whole United Nations system is required to engage in these efforts: While assigning the primary responsibility for the maintenance of peace and security to the UN Security Council, the Report also stated that "this responsibility must be shared by the General Assembly" in an integrated approach to human security, confirming the earlier debate on the subject (Boutros-Ghali 1992).

An important aspect of this Report is that it embraces the assertion that the 'state' is a foundation stone of the international system, and that the "respect for its fundamental sovereignty" is 'crucial' to "common international progress". But, significantly, the Report states further that "The time of absolute and exclusive sovereignty...has passed", and that there is a need to find a balance in an "interdependent world". The Report also emphasizes the "commitment to human rights, and the rights of minorities". It asserts that there need be no contradiction between nationalism and globalism. Healthy globalization requires "solid identities and fundamental freedoms."

The *Agenda for Peace* report identifies the tools needed to accomplish these pressing tasks as follows:

First, 'preventive diplomacy' through diplomatic initiatives to prevent disputes from arising between parties, to prevent existing disputes from escalating into conflicts, and to limit the spread of such conflicts when they do occur;

Second, 'peacemaking', which involves action to bring hostile parties to agreement, essentially through peaceful means, as stipulated in Chapter VI of the UN Charter;

Third, 'peacekeeping' based on the deployment of a United Nations presence in the field, which had hitherto only been undertaken with the consent of all parties concerned;

Fourth, 'post-conflict peacebuilding', relying on action to identify and support structures which will tend to strengthen and solidify peace in order to avoid a relapse into conflict;

Fifth, 'early warning' through the analysis of political indicators to "assess whether a threat to peace exists", and what the UN can do "to alleviate it"; and

Sixth, 'preventive deployment', which is prescribed as a remedy for past failures when peacekeeping deployment began only "after conflict has occurred."

The *Agenda for Peace* came about to remedy the insufficiency of traditional peacekeeping operations and to confront the harrowing ethnic strife prevailing in the 1990s. Events on the ground, such as in Bosnia, certainly suggested that a renewed retooling of the UN peace arsenal was in order. However, the way to improve the situation was not always easy to imagine, owing to the myriad of political and legal considerations involved. Preventive intervention, although logical, is very difficult to enforce due to sovereignty concerns and the nature of conflict itself.

12.4.1.2 Supplement to the Agenda for Peace (1995)

In 1995, the Secretary-General (Boutros-Ghali) issued his comprehensive – and logical – *1995 Supplement to an Agenda for Peace*, in which he proposed a three-pronged strategy of '*democracy*', '*development*', and '*peace*' as constitutive of an "interdependent, mutually reinforcing" and holistic approach for the UN to contribute to a "stable and peaceful international order" (Boutros-Ghali 1995).

In a somewhat unjustified criticism of the *Agenda* (Richmond 2008: 12), the author claims that "it has been strongly influenced by idealism or utopianism, rather than reflecting a pragmatic engagement…". On the contrary, the *Agenda* identified six areas of concrete proposals (see above) to help alleviate the factors leading to a conflict, and outlined ways to push for a comprehensive resolution.

12.4.2 The Brahimi Report: Report of the Panel on United Nations Peace Operations (2000)

Because of repeated failures in the 1990s to save "succeeding generations from the scourge of war", the United Nations looked for renewed commitment, institutional change, and financial support. The United Nations Organization, through its reinvigorated peace operations, had to confront the lingering forces of war and violence in conflict zones and overcome them. Therefore, in 2000, the Secretary-General, Kofi Annan, asked the *Panel on United Nations Peace Operations*, headed by the Algerian diplomat, Lakhdar Brahimi, to "assess the shortcomings of the existing system and to make frank, specific and realistic recommendations for change".

The recommendations of the Brahimi Panel focused on political strategy and operational and organizational requirements (Brahimi 2000). UN preventive initiatives were seen to need "clear, strong and sustained political support", and a "fundamental ability to project credible force". The Panel acknowledged, however, that force alone "cannot create peace", but can only forge a "space in which peace may be built". The deployment of credible force, however, represented a change in approach by the UN, since previously force could be used for self-defence only.

The recommendations of the Panel were designed as a remedy for serious problems in strategic direction, decision-making, rapid deployment, operational planning and support, and the use of technology. A basic point made by the Panel was that peace-builders can transform a proposed peace process into a self-sustaining drive only when peacekeepers are able to secure a local non-violent environment. The Panel also questioned the principle of "sovereign consent", especially in intra-state conflicts in which human rights are at stake. One of the previous shortcomings of the UN was a reluctance to distinguish victim from aggressor in order to maintain the veneer of 'impartiality'. Although using force only in self-defence was still preferred, the new UN doctrine emphasized the need for a robust UN military response when needed. The protection of the civilian population is assumed to be a fundamental objective of any UN force.

The Panel strongly recommended the development of a "rapid and effective deployment capacity" for UN peacekeeping forces. It also recommended the expansion of the existing United Nations Standby Arrangements System (UNSAS) to include multinational brigade-size forces in order to meet the need for the deployment of robust peacekeeping forces. On-call lists of qualified military and police officers, vetted and approved by the UN Department of Peacekeeping Operations (DPKO), were recommended, as were lists of judicial and penal experts, and human rights specialists who could strengthen the rule of law in conflict situations. It noted that civilian specialists are also needed to complement the task of peace operations in post-conflict resolution. Finally, the Panel called for UN Headquarters support for peacekeeping to be treated as a "core activity" of the United Nations.

The Brahimi Report was hailed by many, but also faced its share of criticism. A Canadian study by Duane Bratt and Erin Gionet (2001) criticized the recommendations of the report for being 'banal' and an 'echo' of previous reports. In fact, Bratt and Gionet accuse the Report of repeating the same formula *ad nauseam*. They predicted, moreover, that the recommendations were unlikely to be implemented due to the unwillingness of the member states to commit to all of them. The Panel, concluded Bratt and Gionet, had neglected other more effective recommendations. Bratt and Gionet attributed the reluctance of member states to support peacekeeping reforms to three major concerns: protection of sovereignty; protecting national interest; and lack of financial commitment (Bratt/Gionet 2001).

12.4.3 The Millenium Report (2000) and The Responsibility to Protect (R2P) (2001)

In the summit of world leaders held in 2000, Secretary-General Kofi Annan issued a challenge to the world (*The Millennium Report 2000*, also known as *The Millennium Declaration*), to deal with the on-going dilemma of peace intervention (Annan 2000). Due to the lack of clear universal guidelines to justify the "infringement of sovereignty" (Abiew 1999: 16–17) in cases of violations of human lives and rights, the Secretary-General asked the important question:

> If humanitarian intervention is, indeed, an unacceptable assault on sovereignty, how should we respond to a Rwanda, to a Srebrenica – to gross and systematic violations of human rights that offend every precept of our common humanity?

In response, the Canadian government and a group of major foundations announced in September 2000 at the UN General Assembly the establishment of the *International Commission on Intervention and State Sovereignty* (ICISS), co-chaired by Gareth Evans and Mohamed Sahnoun and including ten other prominent international figures. The Commission was tasked by the UN with studying the legal, moral, operational, and political questions involved. To this end, it was to consult widely across the globe, and finally to produce a report (yet another one) to help establish a common ground for governments around the world.

The central theme of the Report, titled *Responsibility to Protect* (Evans/Sahnoun 2001: viii) and published in December 2001, was:

> the idea that sovereign states have a responsibility to protect their own citizens from avoidable catastrophe – from mass murder and rape, from starvation – but that when they are unwilling or unable to do so, that responsibility must be borne by the broader community of states.

In this vision, sovereignty entails responsibility, which resides in the first instance in the state, but if a state fails in its duties to protect its own citizens "the principle of non-intervention yields to the international responsibility to protect". Evans and Sahnoun argue that by establishing this international right to act, state sovereignty is not diluted, it only undergoes a re-characterization from "*sovereignty as control to sovereignty as responsibility*" (Evans/Sahnoun 2001: 13).

Fundamental to the Report was the idea that threats to international peace and security were expanded to include *humanitarian concerns*, as an essential justification for military intervention for human protection, according to Alex Bellamy (Bellamy 2005: 31–34).

The framework proposed for the implementation of the *Responsibility to Protect* (abbreviated as R2P) include several criteria for deployment (Hamilton 2006: 289–297):

1. *Just Cause* (defined as extraordinary level of human suffering)
2. *Right Intention* (stop human suffering)
3. *Proportional Means* (minimum necessary intervention)
4. *Last Resort* (only when non-military options are non-applicable)
5. *Reasonable Prospects* (likelihood of success)
6. *Right Authority* (Security Council authorization, General Assembly resolution, or UN-approved regional organization's intervention).

R2P was subject to a broad range of evaluations. David Malone views it as the "most comprehensive approach to humanitarian intervention ever proposed" (Malone 2003: 999–1001). Mohammed Ayoob considers it a "cover for legitimating the neo-colonialist tendencies of the major powers" (Ayoob 2004: 99–118). The latter reaction was further fuelled by calls for expansion of the R2P to include the "Duty to Prevent", as presented by L. Feinstein and A. Slaughter (2004: 136), with the aim of tackling world security disasters before they spread. Others (Daalder/Steinberg 2005) called for the concept to include the right to launch "pre-emptive strikes" against the sites of threats to peace.

Regardless of the purpose of implementing the R2P, whether for humanitarian intervention or for legitimating neo-colonialist wars, the point of the new concept was to tackle the thorny issue of state sovereignty and bring into relief the pressing need to establish a consensus on how the civilized world should deal with the continuing appalling human sufferings that were and are shielded by the concept of sovereignty. On this view, the originally 'benign' concept of sovereignty had developed to protect the genuine need for freedom and independence for identifiable nations and groups, but this came to be turned on its head in the service of dictators and war criminals. That was what the R2P Panel bravely confronted head-on.

No doubt the R2P is not a panacea for solving problems of war and peace, but it seems to be a good step in the right direction. A strong regime for the maintenance of peace and security in the world and based on justice and freedom – among and within nation states – cannot be fully realized under the current power configuration. And it is not clear that the human race can ever devise the perfect system to ensure its own security.

The misgivings and concerns about the 'contest' between sovereignty and R2P was still evident in 2009 when the UN hosted a debate on the Responsibility to Protect Doctrine (Montgomery 2009: 1–2) involving the UN Secretary-General and the President of the UN General Assembly and a host of diplomats and scholars. The debate covered the report of the UN Secretary-General, Ban Ki-moon, on "Implementing the Responsibility to Protect".

Miguel D'Escoto, the President of the UN General Assembly, expressed concerns about the "preconditions and double standards" of the implementation of the R2P, such as the politically-motivated "selective application" of the doctrine which would "ultimately unravel the UN's credibility" (D'Escoto July 2009).

As an example of this "applied selectivity", he cited the positions of some of the permanent members of the UN Security Council with the Veto power in supporting intervention in Darfur, and opposing it in Gaza. Moreover, "a few states, sometimes only one state, apply rules or benefits from treaties that carry the sanctions of law, but to which they are not subject". Referring to the Veto right, he added, "No system of justice can be legitimate that, by design, allows principles of justice to be applied differentially." Finally, he demanded that all UN member states – especially the permanent members of the Security Council – become party to the Convention of the International Criminal Court.

The then-sitting UN Secretary-General, Ban Ki-Moon, defended the R2P, emphasizing that it was a "universal and irrevocable commitment" which was "made at the highest level, without contradiction or challenge".

Undoubtedly, Mr. D'Escoto gave up any aspirations to become the UN Secretary-General. Such aspirations were diminished even further when he launched a frontal attack on the UN system during his farewell address to the Assembly at the end of his presidency in September 2009. He called for nothing short of reinventing the United Nations to deal with world inequality and poverty, and to help vulnerable countries in an unfair international system (D'Escoto September 2009).

The multitude of legal and political innovations sketched above for achieving a balance between sovereignty and human protection undoubtedly have advanced the cause of peace and increased international awareness of the individual's fundamental rights to peace and security. The political and legal developments surrounding conflict resolution over the last few decades have injected the need for the protection of human rights as a leading part in the international discourse on peace.

R2P has also offered an expansion of the original idea of peacekeeping. The concern with protecting individuals in time of strife, which has become the increasing focus of international peace operations, has brought into relief the interaction between "International Humanitarian Law" and "Human Rights Law". As in any new area of policy, as Matthew Happold observes, "Some states have resisted attempts to extend the reach of international human rights law into areas traditionally seen as governed by international humanitarian law" (Happold 2013).

Fundamentally, international humanitarian law, in contrast to human rights law, is "not based on an individual rights paradigm". But undoubtedly, the two are complementary. According to the International Red Cross, "Human Rights Laws" are enacted to "protect individuals from arbitrary behaviour by the State" (American Red Cross 2011). Although individual rights could be derogated by 'treaty' or during "public emergency", this can be done legitimately only on a temporary basis, and without affecting the 'core' rights of the individual, which in principle may never be suspended. "International Humanitarian Law", on the other hand, is concerned with conditions of armed conflicts and is designed to "protect the victims of war", and to "regulate the conduct of hostilities."

12.4.4 High-Level Independent Panel on Peace Operations (HIPPO), Ban ki-Moon (2015) and Antonio Guterres (2017)

In his second term in office, former Secretary-General Ban Ki-moon, appointed a high-powered panel (October 2014) to conduct a major review of UN peace operations (Boutellis/Novosseloff 2017: 1–42). The result was the *HIPPO Report*, released in June 2015 and 2017. In September 2015 the Secretary-General responded with a follow-up report which put forward a number of recommendations.

The 2015 Report called for four essential strategic shifts:

(1) Primacy of Politics. "Politics must drive the design and implementation of peace operations."
(2) View peace operations as a continuum. "The full spectrum of UN peace operations must be used more flexibly to respond to changing needs on the ground."
(3) Strengthening partnerships. "A stronger, more inclusive peace and security partnership is needed for the future."
(4) Focusing on the field and on people. "The UN Secretariat must become more field-focused and UN peace operations must be more people centered."

The current Secretary-General, Antonio Guterres, took office in January 2017, and inherited the unfinished reforms and recommendations. In September 2017 he informed the UN Security Council that "the HIPPO recommendations remain at the heart of my efforts to advance collective security" (Guterres 2017). In a holistic approach to reforms, Guterres presented a comprehensive set of goals and related proposals titled *Restructuring the United Nations Peace and Security Pillar* (October 2017). The Secretary-General had cautioned earlier that "Reform is necessary for the protection of the UN" itself (July 2017).

The 2017 Guterres Reforms (a combination of old and new initiatives) covered five *parallel streams*:

(1) Renewed focus on prevention and sustaining peace
(2) A new UN Office of Counter-Terrorism
(3) Reforming the UN development system
(4) Restructuring the peace and security architecture
(5) Organization-wide management reform.

The Secretary-General aimed to improve capabilities, performance, and accountability (including stamping out sexual abuse). He also advocated advancing gender parity, as well as a security agenda in peace operations. Finally, the Security Council adopted Resolution 2378 (2017), mandating "formal and comprehensive annual briefings and debate on peacekeeping reforms". This requirement followed the onset of "peacekeeping fatigue" aggravated by scandals in the field, and the push to cut the UN peacekeeping budget. Additionally, many questioned whether peace operations were "fit for purpose" to respond to different complex conflicts around the world (Boutellis/Novosseloff 2017: 2–3).

Based on the Secretary-General's *Report* (A/72/525 – adopted on 13 October 2017), the UN member states agreed on the *Peace and Security Reform Resolution* (A/72/L.33 – adopted 15 December 2017). In order to *implement such reforms*, he recommended the establishment of:

(1) Department of Political and Peacebuilding Affairs
(2) Department of Peace Operations
(3) Single Political-Operational Structure responsible for the management of all political and operational peace and securities activities
(4) A Standing Principles Group to provide unified leadership to ensure a coherent approach at Headquarters and in the field.

Although Guterres had extensively outlined his vision for the UN, "What is lacking now is an overarching vision or narrative which brings together all of the reform process" (Bernstein 2017: 4). Some critics contend that the reforms "do not go far enough, or that they have heard this all before", but the underlying notion that reforms are needed "is widely supported" (Bernstein 2017: 4).

Guterres came under criticism for not challenging the big five control over the Security Council and the key UN Departments. He was also criticized for not paying much attention to the important issue of human rights.

The *HIPPO Report* is not, and will not be, the last report on UN peacekeeping operations. Every few years, the international community feels the need to come up with a new set of recommendations to deal with the changing international environment. In reality, many of the recommendations and the studies leading to them are rehashed and reworded versions of earlier ideas presented in new forms. However, conflict environments do undergo some changes which reflect alterations in the components of national and international conflicts, and therefore some tangible adjustments both on the ground and in the documentation are required. With all these high-powered committees and glossy recommendations, one would expect the level of violence and the preponderance of conflict throughout the world to be reduced or at least lessened. The evidence does not support such a conclusion.

12.5 Peacekeeping Appreciation

In a pat on the back, the UN brass, in trying to cast a positive light on its peacekeeping record, directed its Public Information Department to commission a public information campaign highlighting the achievements and successes of peacekeeping. Undoubtedly, peacekeepers have greatly contributed to the reduction in the level of conflicts, and have helped the parties to the conflict to reach an accommodation on their own or with the help of third parties. To deny or minimize peacekeeping contributions to world peace – imperfect though they are – would undermine the world's efforts to confront conflicts threatening world peace and security (Fig. 12.1).

Successful Peace Intervention Model

A + B = C

A. Conflict Eruption: Response: *Conflict Control*:
(International or Domestic):   Passive Consent (Chap VI)
                                                     Robust without Consent (Chap VII)

B. Mediation & Negotiation: Response: *Peacemaking*:
                                                     Multi-Factorial Measures

C. Conflict Resolution   Response: *Peacekeeping*:
                                                     Maintain the peace
                                                     already achieved

---

Fig. 12.1 Peace intervention. *Source* The author

12.6   A Permanent UN Peace Force?

In 1973, the former US Secretary of State, Henry Kissinger, expressed perhaps feigned frustration with the state of peacekeeping – given the role the US plays on the international stage – by describing the record of peacekeeping as an "improvisation growing out of argument and controversy". In an address to the UN, Kissinger told the member states, "We should delay no longer. The time has come to agree on peacekeeping guidelines so that this organization can act swiftly, confidently and effectively in future crises" (Kissinger 1973).

The international community's search for the creation of an international peace force on a permanent basis – unlike UNEF – to intervene in international and domestic disputes is not new. Permanency would allow disputes to be addressed without an artificial deadline for disbanding the international force or requiring a rapid withdrawal. According to Langille and Keefe, such an international army "would be the only way to provide a reliable, rapidly deployable force capable of halting conflict". It would be a "standing UN force with no national ties" (Langille/Keefe 2003: 12).

In 1957, Canada's Lester Pearson proposed the creation of a "permanent mechanism by which units of the armed forces of member countries could be endowed with the authority of the United Nations and made available at short notice for supervisory police duties" (Pearson 1957: 401–402).

Although some commentators oppose the idea of a UN Standing Army as politically and economically unfeasible, there have been various past and ongoing efforts to achieve this goal.

The record (Koops/Varwick 2008: 7–8) shows that:

- In 1944 the creation of an "International Army" was proposed during the *Dumbarton Oaks* negotiations to establish the United Nations Organization.

- In 1945 the newly-adopted UN Charter included Article 43, which called for the establishment of military forces at the disposal of the Security Council.
- In 1948 the first Secretary-General of the UN, Trygve Lie, proposed the creation of a "United Nations Guard".
- Secretary-General Lie expanded his proposal in 1951 to suggest the creation of a permanent "UN Legion". In 1952 it was renamed a "UN Volunteer Reserve".
- Following the Suez War in 1956 and the deployment of UNEF, proposals for a "Permanent Peacekeeping Force" re-emerged without success.
- In 1964, Canadian Prime Minister Lester Pearson actually proposed the creation of a "Permanent Peacekeeping Force".
- In the same year (1964) Britain proposed the establishment of a "Commonwealth Standby Battalion", to be at the disposal of the UN.
- In 1970, the UN General Assembly recommended that the Security Council should begin a "Negotiation Process" regarding the creation of a UN Force unforeseen in Article 43.
- In 1974, eleven UN member states earmarked "units for UN Peace Operations" within their armed forces.
- In his 1992 *Agenda for Peace* UN Secretary-General Boutros Boutros-Ghali called for the utilization of Article 43 and the creation of "Peace Enforcement Units".
- In 1993 UN Under-Secretary-General Brian Urquhart proposed the creation of a "Permanent UN Volunteer Force".
- In 1994 the UN created the "UN Standby Arrangement System" (UNSAS), a database for troops and equipment of member states earmarked for peace-keeping missions.
- During the Bosnia Crisis, in 1994 the Netherlands proposed the creation of a permanent "UN Rapid Deployment Brigade".
- In his *Supplement for an Agenda for Peace* (1995), Boutros Boutros-Ghali called for the creation of a "UN Rapid Reaction Force".
- In 1995, Canada called for the creation of a "Rapidly Deployable Mission Headquarters".
- Also in 1995 Canada and the Netherlands established a body known as the "Friends of Rapid Reaction Deployment" (FORD).
- Denmark proposed the creation of a "Standby High Readiness Brigade" (SHIRBRIG) in 1995
- The "Agreement to create SHIRBRIG" was signed in 1996.
- In 1997 Secretary-General Kofi Annan officially opened the "Permanent Planning Element" for SHIRBRIG.
- The year 2000 saw SHIRBRIG's first peacekeeping deployment in Eritrea.
- The *Brahimi Report* (2000) singled out SHIRBRIG as an important role model for peacekeeping operations.

12.6.1   Early Proposals for an International Peace Force

New bases are required for a truly effective peacekeeping system. The concept of deploying peace forces in conflict situations, although sound, has run into policy and practical difficulties.

First, peacekeeping is not involved in the disputes involving the superpowers. However, conflicts among smaller nations are seldom divorced from superpower involvement. Agreeing on the terms of the deployment of an international peace force is, therefore, complicated.

Second, national sovereignty considerations cloud any mandate for peacekeeping intervention.

Third, peacekeeping deployment usually follows the outbreak of hostilities after casualties and destruction were already inflicted. Therefore, time is of the essence for international intervention.

Fourth, the peacekeeping mandate does not usually include provisions for conflict resolution, increasing the likelihood of prolonging, expanding, and intensifying the conflict.

A Proposed Global Peace Force:

(1) The international force must be a permanent structure of the UN composed from military contingents of the UN member states at large, excluding the 'permanent five' (P-5) of the Security Council. Force contribution is mandatory for all UN member states and a condition for membership in the international body. The size of each contingent depends on each country's capabilities.

(2) In case of the eruption of an armed conflict, the UN force should be dispatched immediately to the trouble spot. The force must be deployed on both sides of the lines separating the combatants. Authorization for deployment should begin in the Security Council. If the decision to deploy is blocked due to political disagreement, or the use of the 'veto' power, the General Assembly should take over without delay in order to minimize the scope of the conflict. Clearly, the UN Charter has to be amended to allow for such permanent expansion of the responsibilities of the General Assembly. This scenario applies even in the case of enforcement measure.

(3) The force deployment remains in place until the dispute is ended. Conflict resolution measures must be part and parcel of the deployment. The deployment, therefore, is not an open-ended arrangement, as the dispute must be resolved fairly and speedily. The force must respect the sovereignty of the states involved, as it does not constitute a permanent international occupation regime. In case of a failure to reach accommodation despite the efforts of the Security Council, the General Assembly, and international mediation involvement, the dispute should be referred to the International Court of Justice for a final and binding ruling (Hilmy 1971).

The idea of a UN Standing Army came to be considered an "unrealistic ideal" opposed by most UN member states "due to the fear of eroding sovereignty as well as a plethora of insurmountable legal, political and operational issues" (Mosgaard et al. 2009).

With the realization that a "permanent UN standing army" is fraught with numerous impracticalities, the only feasible alternative was the option of a "pre-pledged and pre-earmarked pool of troops on 'standby' and at a level of 'high readiness', deployable at a short notice request by the Security Council" (Koops/ Varwick 2008).

In 1995 the Secretary-General asked the UN member states to "consider how the reaction time of UN peacekeeping might be shortened" (Malik 1999: 14–17), to deal with fast-moving human catastrophes. The SHIRBRIG Brigade, as an alternative to a UN standing army, was planned basically for the dual purpose of UN-authorized rapid intervention in an armed conflict, and to protect civilians affected by the conflict. The impetus for action came from Secretary-General Boutros-Ghali in response to the UN's past failures, most notably the inability of the UN to stop the genocide in Rwanda.

The SHIRBRIG experience is considered the first serious effort to create and deploy a standby UN peacekeeping support mechanism. Based outside Copenhagen, SHIRBRIG had a strength of 4,000 to 5,000 (UNEF's numerical strength, by comparison, was around 6,000) fully trained and equipped troops ready for deployment within 15–30 days (too long in a fast-developing military confrontation) and drawing from contributions from twenty-three countries. The force became operational in January 2000.

The expansion of the mandate of SHIRBRIG from operations authorized under non-binding Chapter VI to enforcement action under Chapter VII of the UN Charter, however, discouraged many countries from participating because of the issue of sovereign consent being at risk, as well as the degree of military engagement involved. Some UN member states were averse to participation due to the fear of mandatory participation in armed conflicts if they became committed. As members they would be obligated under Chapter VII to engage in a military action which might be encroaching, in their views, on the sovereignty of other member states.

The SHIRBRIG Organizational Structure consisted of four components:

(1) A *Brigade Pool* consisting of troops and all their support requirements.
(2) A *Permanent Planning Element* of the Commander and the permanent staff of officers to prepare and plan for any required mission requested by the UN. The Planning Element worked closely with the Department of Peace Keeping Operations (DPKO) at the UN HQ in accordance with the UN Standby Arrangement System (UNSAS). The Department was also utilized to assist in the Capacity-Building process of other standby brigades modelled on the SHIRBRIG structure. Additionally, the core of the Planning Element was augmented by non-permanent staff members based in the contributing countries.

(3) A *Steering Committee*, which is the decision-making body of the multinational structure. The Committee is a 'political-military entity composed of Defence and Foreign Affairs representatives' of the SHIRBRIG member states.
(4) The *Contact Group* based in New York, which "consists of the ambassadors and military advisors" of participating countries at the UN HQ. This Group is tasked with providing a liaison and coordination mechanism between SHIRBRIG and the UN, especially the Department of Peacekeeping Operations.

SHIRBRIG was envisaged for use in *several capacities*: (1) as a complete brigade, or as force smaller than brigade size; (2) as an observer or monitoring mission; (3) as the UN peacekeeping mission Headquarters; (4) to assist the UN with the start-up of a new peacekeeping mission; and (5) to assist in capacity-building efforts for peacekeeping structures in Africa and elsewhere.

Secretary-General Kofi Annan declared enthusiastically, "SHIRBRIG is a model arrangement" that with "a small, well-trained, well-equipped force rapidly deployed with an adequate mandate and sufficient support can stop a conflict before it engulfs an entire society" (Annan 1997: 2). Annan's reference to a conflict within a society reflected the increasing UN involvement in domestic political and ethnic conflicts and strife.

SHIRBRIG's first test came in June 2000 with the Security Council resolution to establish the *United Nations Mission in Ethiopia and Eritrea* (UNMEE) to supervise the cessation of hostilities between Ethiopia and Eritrea. On 15 September 2000 SHIRBIRG was deployed in the Horn of Africa under the UNMEE mandate, and it remained there until its withdrawal in May 2001. The mission was declared a success at that time, and Secretary-General Annan lauded the effort: SHIRBRIG, he said, "has already proven its utility in the deployment of the UN mission in Ethiopia and Eritrea". Annan continued his assessment: "There, a force that had trained together and developed a high degree of coherence was able to arrive and establish itself quickly in the theatre of operation, thereby sending a message of competence and commitment" (Annan 1997: 2).

Other missions with similar mandates included the *United Nations Mission in Liberia* (UNMIL) in 2003, the *United Nations Operation in Cote d'Ivoire* (UNOCI) in 2004, the *United Nations Advance Mission in Sudan* (UNAMIS) in 2004, and the *United Nations Mission in Sudan* (UNMIS) in 2005.

12.6.2   Lessons and Conclusions Learned from SHIRBRIG

1. The majority of the missions consisted only of planning assistance and advice in the field.
2. Acting as a "rapid interim force headquarters" to start up a UN mission until a regular UN force could take over has nonetheless proven very useful and marked SHIRBRIG's real success in the field.

3. SHIRBRIG's flexibility and adaptability was demonstrated by its pragmatic adjustment of its scope and mandate when needed.
4. The concept of full brigade deployment was still ultimately unrealistic due to shortfall of commitments by the participating countries.

The *general conclusion* of the SHIRBRIG experience is as follows:

> SHIRBRIG earned a reputation for a cohesive force with the highest level of peacekeeping expertise and training standards…Yet…the organization remained well below its actual peacekeeping potential. A key problem was not only the cumbersome decision-making and force generation process, but above all, a lack of political will (Mosgaard 2009: 22).

12.6.3 Termination of the UN's First Permanent Standing International Peace Army

Despite SHIRBRIG's demonstrated successes, admittedly limited in scope, a decision was taken in November 2008 to disband this experimental force. It thus took only eight years for the contradictions and structural impediments in the international system to scuttle this pioneering experience. Concerns over protecting national sovereignty, fears of sustaining casualties during robust peace operations, and reluctance to commit national resources to international activities not related to the home front all combined to dampen any enthusiasm among UN member states for participation in a UN-sponsored permanent standing army. SHIRBRIG proved to be more adaptable to regional applications, such as support for the African Union (AU) or associated specialized groupings like the Economic Community of West African States (ECOWAS), than an international force ready to act effectively across the globe.

The international community seems to have run into a solid wall as far as harnessing and applying a credible peace operation model. In a Conference on Peacekeeping in Washington DC, Jean-Marc Coicaud stated:

> progress [in peacekeeping] has been made since the early 1990s. One has also to recognize, if one wants to be honest, that there is still a very, very, very long way to go to match words with reality (Coicaud/Myers 2007).

In an anti-climactic, but perhaps more realistic conclusion, Jocelyn Coulon (1998) states that due to the strategic calculations of the "great powers" and their "casualty-sensitive" attitude towards involvement in "peripheral conflicts", thoughts of using the UN "to reshape the world" are misplaced and outright 'mistaken'. Moreover, due to the inability to fashion a permanent UN standing army, the author proposes:

> While waiting for the member states of the UN, and in particular the great powers, to agree on a clear and coherent philosophy on military intervention and how it should be implemented, the UN must return to the great principle that governed the creation of the Blue Helmets [namely UNEF]. That is no doubt a less spectacular, less heroic mission, but

returning to it is the only way that the Blue Helmets will be able to continue to be an effective instrument of international diplomacy in the settlement of conflicts and a credible hope for thousands of people caught up in the turmoil of war (Coulon 1998: 180–181).

Yet, although the conclusion may appear to be grounded in realism, the author seems to have ignored the changing nature of international conflicts and disputes for many decades. To reach a conclusion not cognizant of the realities of the current strife-ridden world, and oblivious to the complexity and limitations of the original UN peacekeeping mission, is equally unrealistic. Moreover, to limit peacekeeping intervention to the original passive UNEF-type deployment without the injection of a conflict resolution requirement condemns the world to endure endless eruption of unresolved conflicts endangering and undermining the international system of states.

Undoubtedly, the search for mechanisms and theoretical grounding for preventing conflict and achieving peace has been and will continue to be part of the human experience, regardless of the obstacles littering the landscape.

References

Abiew, Francis K. (1999): *The Evolution of the Doctrine and Practice of Humanitarian Intervention* (The Hague: Springer Netherlands).

American Red Cross (2011): "International Humanitarian Law", in: *International Humanitarian Law and Human Rights* (April 2011).

Annan, Kofi (1993 & 2017): "The Path of Peace-Keeping: Translating Commitment into Action", in: *Harvard International Review* (Boston: Summer 1993; Summer 2017).

Annan, Kofi (1997): *UN Press Release*, SG/SM/6310 (2 September 1997).

Annan, Kofi (2000): *We the Peoples: The Role of the United Nations in the Twenty-First Century*, in: Report by the Secretary-General, A/54/2000 (27 March 2000).

Ayoob, Mohammed (2004): "Third World Perspectives on Humanitarian Intervention and International Administration", in: *Global Governance*, 10: 99–118.

BBC (2015): *UN Peacekeepers 'Barter Goods for Sex'* (11 June 2015); at: https://www.bbc.com/news/world-33089662.

Bellamy, Alex J. (2005): "Responsibility to Protect or Trojan Horse? The Crisis in Darfur and Humanitarian Intervention after Iraq", in: *Ethics and International Affairs* (Summer): 31–34.

Bellamy, Alex J.; Williams, Paul (2005): *Peace Operations and Global Order* (New York: Routledge).

Bhutto, Z.A. (1967): *Peace-keeping by the United Nations* (Karachi: Pakistan Publishing House).

Boutellis, A.; Novosseloff, A. (2017): *Road to Better UN? Peace Operations and the Reform Agenda* (New York: International Peace Institute): 1–42.

Boutros-Ghali, Boutros (1992): *An Agenda for Peace: Preventive Diplomacy, Peacemaking and Peace-Keeping)*, Report of the UN Secretary-General, A/47/277-S/2411 (17 June 1992).

Boutros-Ghali, Boutros (1995): *Supplement Report to the Agenda for Peace* by the UN Secretary-General, A/50/60-S/1995/1 (1995).

Brahimi, Lakhdar (2000): *Brahimi UN Report on Peace Operations*, A/55/305 – S/2000/809 (21 August 2000).

Bratt, Duane; Gionet, Erin (2001): "Evaluating the Brahimi Report", in: *Strategic Datalink # 96* (Toronto: The Canadian Institute of Strategic Studies) (May 2001).

Burns, E.L.M. (1981): "Canada's Role in Peacekeeping in the Middle East", Paper submitted during the *Canadian-Arab Relations Conference* (Calgary: University of Calgary, Alberta, Canada) (June 1981).

Chesterman, Simon (2001): *Just War or Just Peace?: Humanitarian Intervention and International Law* (Oxford: Oxford University Press).

Coicaud, Jean-Marc; Myers, Joanne J. (2007): *Beyond the National Interest: The Future of UN Peacekeeping and Multilateralism in an Era of US Primacy* (Washington DC: United States Institute of Peace).

Connolly, Amanda (2016): *Former General Lewis MacKenzie Lauds Lapse of Term 'Peacekeeping'*, in: *iPolitics*. (20 September); at: https://ipolitics.ca/2016/09/20/former-general-lewis-mackenzie-lauds-lapse-of-term-peacekeeping/.

Coulon, Jocelyn (1998): *Soldiers of Diplomacy: The United Nations, Peacekeeping, and the New World Order* (Toronto: University of Toronto Press).

Daalder, Ivo; Steinberg, James (2005): "Preventive War: A Useful Tool", in: *Los Angeles Times* (4 December 2005).

de Coning, Cedric; Detzel, Julian; Hojem, Petter (2008): *UN Peacekeeping Operations Capstone Doctrine: Report of the TfP Oslo Doctrine Seminar* (14–15 May 2008, Oslo, Norway) (Oslo: NUPI).

D'Escoto, Miguel (2009): *UN General Assembly Debates of the R2P* (July and September 2009).

Doyle, John (2013): "A Tale of Sarajevo", in: *The Globe and Mail* (Toronto, 9 November 2013); at: https://www.theglobeandmail.com/arts/television/a-tale-of-sarajevo-so-grim-its-must-see/article15318447/.

Evans, Gareth; Sahnoun, Mohamed (2001): *United Nations Report of the International Committee on Intervention and State Sovereignty: The Responsibility to Protect* (Ottawa: IDRC) (December 2001).

Feinstein, Lee; Slaughter, Anne-Marie (2004): "Duty to Prevent", in: *Foreign Affairs* (January/February Issue).

Guterres, Antonio (2017): *Restructuring of the United Nations Peace and Security Pillar*, Reports of the UN Secretary-General, (HIPPO), A/72/525 (13 October 2017) & UN A/72/L.33 (15 December 2017).

Hamilton, Rebecca J. (2006): "The Responsibility to Protect: From Document to Doctrine – But What of Implementation?", in: *Harvard Human Rights Journal*, 19: (289–297).

Happold, Matthew (2013): "International Humanitarian Law and Human Rights Law", in: Henderson, Christian; White, Nigel (Eds.): *Research Handbook on International Conflict and Security Law* (Cheltenham, UK: Edward Elgar Publishing).

Heinbecker, Paul (2006): "Suez Plus 50: Ten Reflections on Peacekeeping", Paper submitted at the Conference on Peacekeeping, Cairo, Egypt (27 November 2006).

Hilmy, Hanny (1971): "A Proposal for an International Peace Force", Discussion points presented during the International Peace Academy Conference in Helsinki, Finland (July 1971).

Hunt, Charles T. (2019): "Is it Time to Review the Basis for UN Peacekeeping 71 years on?", in: *The Conversation*; at: https://theconversation.com/is-it-time-to-review-the-basis-for-un-peacekeeping-71-years-on-117517.

Kissinger, Henry (1973): Address to the UN General Assembly (24 September 1973).

Kondoch, Boris (2007): *International Peacekeeping* (Essays in International law) (Farnham: Ashgate Publishing).

Koops, Joachim; Varwick, Johannes (2008): *Ten Years of SHIRBRIG: Lessons Learned, Development Prospects, and Strategic Opportunities for Germany* (Berlin: Global Public Policy Institute).

Krasner, Stephen D. (Ed.) (1983): *International Regimes* (Ithaca: Cornell University Press).

Lachowski, Tomasz (2014): *New Dimensions of International Law – The Question of 'ius post Bellum'* (Lodz: University of Lodz).

Langille, Peter; Keefe, Tania (2003): *The Future of Peacekeeping: An Experts' Discussion to Contribute to the Dialogue on Foreign Policy* (Vancouver: Liu Institute for Global Issues) (March 2003).

Larson, Krista; Dodds, Paisley (2017): "UN Peacekeepers: Congo Leads World in Sex Abuse Allegations", in: *The Associated Press* (21 September 2017); at: https://apnews.com/da1f97c260584dbca7a35cedd42efb9e/UN-Peacekeepers:-Congo-leads-world-in-sex-abuse-allegations.

Lipson, Michael (2007): "Peacekeeping: Organized Hypocrisy", in: *European Journal of International Relations*, 13,1 (2007): 5–34.

MacKenzie, Lewis (2018): "Interview" on: *As It Happens*", Canadian Broadcasting Corporation (CBC) (March 2018).

Malik, Arslan (1999): "The Beginning of a UN Army?", in: *Behind the Headlines*, 56,4 (1999): 14–17.

Malone, David M. (2003): "Recent Books on International Law, A Review", in: *American Journal of International Law*, 97: 999–1001.

Mosgaard, Kurt, *et.al.* (2009): *SHIRBRIG Lessons Learned Report* (Hovelte, Denmark) (June 2009).

Montgomery, Deidre (2009): "UN General Assembly Hosts Debate on the Responsibility to Protect Doctrine", in: *International Law Bureau* (New York: 29 July 2009): 1–2.

Newman, Edward; Paris, Roland; Richmond, Oliver (2009): "Introduction", in: *New Perspectives on Liberal Peacebuilding* (Tokyo: United Nations University Press).

Novosseloff, Alexandra (2018): "UN Peacekeeping: Back to Basics Is Not Backwards", in: *International Peace Institute*; at: https://www.theglobalobservatory.org/2018/04/peacekeeping-basics-is-not-backwards/.

Peace Operations Monitor (n.d.): *Capstone Doctrine*; at: https://www.pom.peacebuild.ca/bestpracticesCD.shtml.

Pearson, Lester (1957): "Force for UN", in: *Foreign Affairs*, XXXV (April).

Petersmann, Ernst-Ulrich (2006): *State Sovereignty, Popular Sovereignty, and Individual Sovereignty: From Constitutional Nationalism to Multilevel Constitutionalism in International Economic Law* (Florence: European University Institute, Department of Law), Paper No. 2006/45 (December 2006).

Richmond, Oliver P. (2008): *Peace in International Relations* (New York: Routledge): 1–163.

Saksena, K.P. (1977): "Not by Design: Evolution of UN Peace-Keeping Operations and its Implications for the Future", in: *International Studies*, 16,4 (October-December): 459–481.

Smith, Alex Duval (2017): *Peacekeeping Problems in Mali*, BBC documentary (20 August 2017); at: https://www.bbc.com/news/world-africa-40973432.

Stevens, Barry (2013): *Sector Sarajevo*, Canadian documentary (10 November 2013); at: https://www.imdb.com/title/tt4179986/.

UNDPKO and IPA Joint Seminar (2002): *Challenges in Peacekeeping: Past, Present and Future (Seminar Report)* New York (29 October 2002).

UNDPKO/DFS (2011): "The Contribution of United Nations Peacekeeping to Early Peacebuilding"; at: http://www.operationspaix.net/DATA/DOCUMENT/6797~v~The_Contribution_of_United_Nations_Peacekeeping_to_Early_Peacebuildinga_DPKO_DFS_Strategy_for_Peacekeepers.pdf.

United Nations (2008): *United Nations Peacekeeping Operations: Principles and Guidelines (The Capstone Doctrine)* (New York: UN Department of Peacekeeping Operations).

Vieira, Mauricio (2016): "Sierra Leone: Promoting Peace or Prolonging Violence? The Duality of the UN Peacekeeping", in: *Conflict Studies Quarterly*, 16 (July).

Chapter 13
Peace Operations in International Relations

Abstract Peace intervention has developed into a complex and sometime contested endeavour. A mere cessation of hostilities and separation of combatants does not suffice in today's international environment. The world community has grappled over the years with the proper approach to deal with conflicts, both international and domestic. The drive to achieve a 'minimalist version' of peace, has grown into an 'ideologically infused' approach to conflict resolution.

The *ad hoc* approach to peace operations is evolving into preoccupation with human rights and relations involving dominance and structural violence. The liberal and neo-liberal peace paradigm based on globalization, the pillars of liberal democracy and the free market ethos model for peacebuilding, is becoming the foundation of the international system, and the dominant internationally-supported flag bearer of peace intervention. The intensification of class division and inequality is not conducive to establishing conditions of peace in conflict-ridden societies. Moreover, across the globe, inequality is a prime ingredient in world conflict. Another problem underlying peace operations is the relationship between peacekeeping and empire. Some view peacekeeping as an embodiment of the ideological heritage of imperialism, shaping peacekeeping by necessity into a colonial mould. Peacekeeping in this view, therefore, is an imperial echo and a reverberation of empire.

Keywords Liberal peace · Liberal democracy · Free market ethos · Relations of dominance · Structural violence · Peace chain · Pecae triangle · Globalization · Imperial connection · Reverbation of empire · Imperial mould · Imperial echo

To properly situate peacekeeping – and peace operations in general – in relation to conflict management, the nature of conflict itself and the corresponding peace response must be analysed contextually.

Peace is more than the absence of violence. And it is certainly more than the dispatching of 'peacekeeping' forces to separate enemies. The situation becomes more complex when dealing with internal multi-dimensional conflict. For without fundamental conflict resolution outcome, the conflict will continue and fester

H. Hilmy, *Decolonization, Sovereignty, and Peacekeeping*,
https://doi.org/10.1007/978-3-030-57624-0_13

unabated. Moreover, conflict resolution cannot be achieved without addressing the inequality and imbalance in the conflict profile. A situation of unaddressed disparity between the antagonists can only prolong the crisis and harden attitudes.

Addressing the disparities is crucial if a genuine and just peace is to be achieved. Conflicts are the result of history-laden political, religious, and cultural flash points. Territorial claims, raw ambition, and ethnic hatred can only add to the lethal ingredients of conflict with deadly results. As if all of these components are not enough, for myriad reasons we have to factor the external input into national and international conflicts. The Arab-Israeli conflict is a prime example of external meddling preventing the development of a workable and fair solution.

Clearly, calling for a conflict resolution is easier said than done. After all, Aristotle observed that humanity may have to "make war that we may live in peace" (Richmond 2008: 23). But peaceful endeavour – as inadequate as it has been – remains the essential key to a more peaceful and just world. Tying peacekeeping intervention formally to conflict resolution measures is, therefore, indispensable because without it, all 'peacekeeping' efforts would have been squandered, leaving the original conflict in a worse state, as the attendant status quo of the UNEF experience (described as an example of 'negative' peace) has shown. It is sobering, therefore, to note that 'peace' is only a "long-term process, which is probably not achievable but is worth working towards" (Richmond 2008: 12).

Based on Hobbes, Oakeshott (2001) and Van Mill (2002), believe that the intellectual focus of peace theory has shifted, consequently, to "achieving a minimalist version of peace", which is considered a "state of non-interference in the lives of others" (Oakeshott 2001: 835–836). Moreover, for Van Mill, peace is also viewed as limited in scope and hence in duration (Van Mill 2002: 21–38). On the other hand, Hegel, as also analysed by Richmond, postulated that "war would maintain the ethical health of nations" since perpetual peace "would produce a corruption of nations" (Hegel 1996: 330–340; see also Hobbes 1651).

13.1 Peacekeeping Conceptual Framework

The proliferation of peace missions over several decades has brought to light the necessity of fashioning a new 'manual' for the new and expanding field of peacekeeping in order to establish universal and accepted ground rules for the deployment of international peace intervention.

In an effort to turn the previous UN peacekeeping *ad hoc* system into a comprehensive 'framework of intervention', A.B. Fetherston utilized Boutros-Ghali's *An Agenda for Peace* to propose a "theory of peacekeeping based on concepts of peaceful third party intervention" (Fetherston 1994: xvi). The general confusion about applying the basic tenets of peacekeeping to varied conflict situations triggered the need to explore guidelines for goal articulation and formal organization of the field of peacekeeping.

Former UN Secretary-General Perez de Cuellar was concerned about the role of peacekeeping in the effort to "build the international rule of law and a reliable system for the maintenance of international peace and security". What is needed for that task, according to de Cuellar, is to employ a "broader framework of conflict management" (de Cuellar 1989: 141–142).

Harbottle (1991) states that the concepts of mediation, negotiation, and conciliation – not the reliance on military enforcement – should be the guiding precepts in peacekeeping. Essentially, the "theoretical concept" behind peacekeeping is that the "ending of conflict and control of violence" can be achieved without "counter-violence. Towards that end, a link is needed between peacekeeping and peacebuilding. Consequently, there is a growing support for an overall linkage framework for third party peace intervention" (Harbottle 1991: 7–8).

It must be clear, however, that although peace intervention is a complex multi-layer effort, the responsibility of the peacekeeping soldier is confined to the task of interposition and not negotiation. Initial peacekeeping intervention is certainly essential in freezing the armed conflict, but the task of bringing about conflict resolution is beyond the scope of the soldiers in the field, no matter how important their contribution is. Indeed, the interposition function must be considered part of the overall peace intervention package, but it must be viewed in its proper space and responsibility.

The push for the creation of a theoretical framework for peacekeeping operations based on the totality of the peacekeeping experience is not universally accepted. Some believe that it is impossible to create a general conceptual model for peacekeeping (Bercovitch et al. 1991: 8–9). This view is based on belief in the uniqueness of each peacekeeping operation, and that conclusions emanating from one peacekeeping experience do not 'carry over' to other peacekeeping engagements.

With or without a theoretical framework, would it be far-fetched to require countries already party to a political dispute to enter into UN-supervised mediation and negotiation before the dispute reaches boiling point, hostilities break out or peacekeeping forces are deployed? Why wait until latent and growing dispute turns into military confrontation or domestic violence, and then act? If the international will to act had been present at the beginning of the Rwanda tragedy, countless lives would have been saved. Evidently, the issue of sovereignty must be evaluated in order to unshackle the ability of the UN to act decisively. Conditions on the ground and outside influence and interference remain huge obstacles for any settlement. It would be helpful, then, to enshrine mediation/negotiation as a fundamental tool for the UN when dealing with domestic or international conflicts.

In 1970, Professor Johan Galtung, a pioneer of peace research and international peacekeeping, introduced a unique theoretical framework for evaluating peace operations at the international level, one that is rooted in sociology.

Galtung differentiated between an 'elitist-individualist' approach to conflict and peace, and a 'structuralist-populist' view of the elements that shape the nature of conflict and the structure of peace. In the first approach (elitist), 'conflict' occurs over 'values', and 'peace' is defined as "the absence of direct, open violence". In the second approach (structuralist), 'conflict' is understood as a "disharmony of inter-est", while 'peace' is the "absence of structural violence" (Galtung 1970: 1–25).

According to Galtung (1970), conflicts of value lead to *direct* violence, while conflicts of interest lead to *structural* violence. Conflicts of both kinds are the root of 'non-peace'. This conflict-peace configuration operates at the domestic as well as the international level. Intrinsic to situations governing conflict and peace is the "relation of dominance" prevailing among the parties. 'Stratification' at the domestic as well as the international level is the expression of dominance affecting the degree of 'autonomy' present in the relationship. Such a relationship is not static due to the changing 'mobility' of power configurations among individuals and among nations.

Galtung (1970) rejects what he calls "*The great fallacy in liberal peace theory*", which is the idea that "peace can be equated with absence of direct violence, and can be obtained by creating a super-structure above nations of any kind so as to absorb and dampen conflicts, resolve them, or at least impede eruption of violence". For him, this super-structure itself embodies relations of dominance that "survive within international organizations", and the United Nations Organization is a prime example of such an unequal distribution of power. "The contradiction in the system can be softened", he writes, "but not resolved." In evaluating the role of 'Peace Keeping Forces' (PKF), Galtung sees value in deploying these units in order to reintroduce 'peace' which disappeared when direct violence erupted.

Liberal peace, according to this Galtungian critique, achieves the absence of violence by imposing a super-structure of dominance above the antagonists. Hence, peacekeeping is viewed by some as a colonial intervention from above to legitimize the existing world order. UNEF is seen, therefore, as more than a reverberation of empire – indeed, as a tool to maintain conditions of inequality and injustice. A new conceptual framework for peacekeeping, therefore, is needed to guarantee collec-tive security based on justice. What is needed, in fact, is a broader and funda-mentally political process of peace implementation stripped of any notion of dominance.

For Galtung (1970), violence is put to an end by using PKF to "force the parties apart by means of a third party, a peacekeeping force that is interjected between them". He argues, however, that "there can be more to peace than merely this absence of direct violence". For real success, this "absence of violence" must be effectively used "for peace-making and peace-building purposes". Galtung provides a peace triangle with three corners, each representing a stage in conflict and peace outcome. All the corners reinforce and interact with each other:

- The first corner represents '*dissociation*', which means 'peacekeeping'.
- The second corner is '*association*', which means 'peace-building'.
- The third represents '*conflict-resolution*', which is the stage of 'peace-making'.

Which stage occurs first is "very much a chicken-egg problem", according to Galtung.

One might consider that the 'chicken-egg problem' of a 'Peace Triangle' or a 'Peace Chain' could be resolved as follows:

First: *Cessation of Hostilities* through third-party intervention and the introduction of peace forces to establish and maintain a ceasefire is sought as the first step in the peace chain. Theoretically, this stage does not involve the existence of peace in a formal sense, but only a dissociation (to use Galtung's term). The mere absence of hostilities in an on-going conflict cannot be equated with peace.

Second: *Peace-Making* is the active phase when efforts are made through mediation, or international involvement, and/or direct negotiation to achieve a comprehensive settlement, or at least a long-term conflict abatement leading to an eventual agreement. At this stage, the parties are focused on achieving an end to the conflict. Galtung's association phase, if successful, will produce accommodation only at the end of this phase, because peace-making efforts could founder, as is evident from the history of international (and national) conflicts.

Third: *Peacebuilding/Peacekeeping* phase dedicated to the completion of the peace process, and – if successful – to enhance and guard the peace foundations achieved, utilizing all the tools available for reconciliation and socio-economic progress based on equity. This can be described as conflict resolution warranting a 'peacekeeping' label. Only when peace is achieved can we invoke the peacekeeping status. You cannot 'keep' something if it does not 'exist'.

The peace sequence, then, could be:

(1) Cessation of Hostilities/Peace Initiation (Dissociation).
(2) Peacemaking/Conflict Resolution (Association).
(3) Peacebuilding/Peacekeeping (Peace).

In this sequence, peacekeeping is, in fact, the last stage in the progression of conflict resolution. Therefore, to describe initial third-party intervention in an unsettled confrontation as 'peacekeeping' is perhaps overly optimistic. Ending hostilities and separating forces cannot be equated with final peace, as we have witnessed time and again.[1]

Galtung (1970) cautioned against using PKFs as instruments "to maintain the status quo" prevailing prior to the start of violence (UNEF had been a prime example of such a failing). An existing "dominance relation is not worth preserving", he declared, and it followed that "Any effort to maintain the status quo by means of PKF is an effort to preserve a dominance relation."

Thus "Preserving peace is tantamount to preserving privilege", and, therefore, a "PKF should only be used when status quo is worth preserving" (Galtung 1970). On the other hand, some form of intervention is vital, regardless of the status quo, in order to save human lives. Therefore, if the status quo is not equal, a PKF can still be used in a 'dissociative' way to keep the parties apart, giving the underdog a chance to avoid relations of dominance. Using UNEF to remove the occupation by

---

[1]I am very grateful to professor Galtung, a pioneer and a giant of peace research, for his peace triangle idea and for his influence on my research.

Britain, France and Israel achieved the 'dissociative' state. But the follow-up phase of conflict resolution was never activated. Separating two unequal parties means first preventing the stronger from persisting in attacking the weaker, and then preventing the continuation of a state of dominance.

However, PKFs would be meaningless if their deployment did not allow the weaker to build its autonomy. And if improper deployment were to happen, the PKF "becomes in itself an instrument of dominance" (Galtung 1970). Admittedly, that is the core problem of any peacekeeping force, since the PKF "cannot behave symmetrically between asymmetric parties without being asymmetric itself".

Theory aside, UNEF was not used deliberately as an instrument of dominance, regardless of the degree of symmetry or asymmetry. But its very presence indirectly allowed a situation of inequality (implying dominance) to persist. Galtung's brilliant perception of the need for both peacemaking and peacebuilding after the ending of violence has proven empirically justified along a spectrum of many conflicts, international and domestic, including the UNEF experience.

It should be remembered that the existence or non-existence of peace relations between antagonists is strongly influenced – in addition to the local ingredients of a conflict – by the position of the antagonists in the web of international alliances, ideological leanings, and geo-political interests and calculations. International conflict does not occur in a vacuum. Similarly, peace-making is a complex and involved project, with many interested parties trying to influence the process and the outcome.

13.2   Galtung's Proposals Against Direct and Structural Violence

Professor Galtung has cautioned that peacekeeping could be used to prolong violence by maintaining the status quo, leading to the persistence of conflict. Peace cannot be achieved with the existence of conditions of structural or direct violence, or the prevailing of relations of dominance. Galtung (1971) therefore offered ten proposals to fight and reduce such conditions:

(1) The creation of Regional Security Commissions under the UN Security Council to articulate and resolve international conflicts.
(2) Globalization of the *Corps Diplomatique* to transform diplomats into servants of the global community.
(3) Changing the global emphasis on economic growth to an emphasis on equality, justice, and equity. New norms of equity to be established in all international interactions.
(4) Ranking multinational corporations according to the degree of structural violence they engender.

(5) Campaigns to persuade professionals to refuse employment with nations practising structural violence, companies producing weapons of mass destruction, or laboratories developing new weapons of war.

(6) Reducing governmental monopoly over foreign policy-making by simultaneously voicing opinions and making proposals on issues at play.

(7) Campaigns against the excessive commercialisation of society.

(8) Unifying international consumers against commercial exploitation.

(9) Ending patents and commercial secrets that prolong and prevent mankind from enjoying the fruits of research and scientific developments.

(10) Re-orientation and revamping of educational programmes away from vertical division of labour. Emphasis should be placed on innovations related to human and social needs.

13.3 Evaluation and Critique of Liberal and Neo-Liberal Approaches to Peace Theory and Peacekeeping

The critique of the liberal approach by Galtung was taken up by others. Oliver Richmond (2008), in his valuable contribution to the literature and his critique of the liberal foundations for peace theory and peacekeeping, outlines what he terms the "adoption of neo-liberalism as a key framework for the liberal peace". Two World Wars and the Cold War have settled the arguments in favour of peace as a "liberal peace", which he defines as the "victor's peace". He asserts that the "liberal peace is the foil by which the world is now judged". In this critique, "Democracy, human rights, the rule of law, and marketization and development" become predatory "franchised concepts" outsourced to conflict zones regardless of the local needs. "Global peacebuilding" without a "renegotiation of norms" for achieving peace, therefore, would be ineffective (Richmond 2008: 111).

The liberal peacebuilding approach tends to "conceptualise individual freedoms as political freedoms" (Richmond 2008: 111). Freedom to vote alone – regardless of the socio-economic environment and the accompanying inequities – renders marketization, free trade and entrepreneurship the foundations of the international system. Inequity within nations and globally is a prime ingredient of world conflict. No peacekeeping measure can override the need for reform.

Richmond supports the notion that liberal peacebuilding "involves transplanting and exporting conditionality and dependency. Peace, moreover, is viewed as resulting from the establishment of the institutions necessary for the liberal governance of society, the economy and politics. The neo-liberal strategies, inserted into the liberalization process, undermine the idea of a social contract based on state-society consent and replace it with a reiterated class system" (Newman/Paris/Richmond: 15). Such a peacebuilding recipe is not conducive to establishing conditions of peace in conflict-ridden societies.

The earlier realist belief that war was part of the 'natural order' was modified by emerging enlightened and progressive views. This idealistic change, however, was dealt a catastrophic blow with the mayhem of World War II. A resurgence of realism in international relations began to take hold, relegating idealism to the status of out-of-touch dangerous naivety (Richmond 2008: 46–48).

The liberal peace concept, which is described by Richmond (2008) as "a compromise between realpolitik and idealism", is "ontologically incoherent". The "only way" for this system to work and become coherent is by becoming "hierarchical and regulative" and by being "led by hegemons" that set the political and economic priorities for the whole system. Individuals under this regime become 'subservient' to the structure itself. This neo-liberal approach undermines the local social contract because international peacemakers are imbued with liberal ideologies, political institutions and neo-liberal economic processes. This partiality disables the ability to engage with the local conflict environment, save with "local like-minded elites". Peacebuilding, therefore, has to be analysed "from the perspectives of the grass roots directly affected and not just from the perspective of states and elites" (Richmond 2008: 114–115).

In a non-liberal, "Marxist-derived orthodoxy", peace is conditional upon the "international political economy" which defines the behaviour of the key actors in the international system (Richmond 2008: 9–12). In this reading, social and economic justice or fair division of resources is the dominant focus for peace. For 'Contemporary Realists', peace is very limited, and is defined by intersecting interests. The state, in order to ensure peace, "provides security and manages equitable and transparent transnational mechanisms of exchange and communication". Realism in international relations implies that "peace is found in the state-centric balance of powers" (Richmond 2008: 9–12).

The contributions of the 'Liberal and idealist' influences led to the development of three conceptualizations of the 'liberal peace':

(1) 'constitutional peace', based on democracy and trade, which challenged the 'realist' conceptualization of peace.
(2) 'civil peace', empowering individuals through guaranteed rights and assured agency.
(3) 'institutional peace', based on international law and aiming at the construction of international legal networks (Richmond 2008: 37).

The last variation of the conception of liberal peace, 'institutional peace', was strongly supported by UN Secretary-General Boutros-Ghali (1992 and 1995), who was instrumental in defining peacekeeping as an international institution. In this reading, the UN is designed to deal comprehensively with the challenges to peace and security in the post-Cold War international regime. The highly idealistic and simultaneously practical *Agenda for Peace*, therefore, called for a multi-pronged approach to resolving conflicts and establishing peace. The *Agenda* "was an early blueprint for such a broad and ambitious project" (Richmond 2008: 107). According to Barnett (1997), the *Agenda* was controversial, as the Third World states worried that enhanced power for the UN Security Council "might threaten their sovereignty". Conversely, "the permanent members of the Security Council feared that a strengthened UN might reduce their autonomy and power". Clearly, "Boutros-Ghali's vision exceeded what member states were ready to accept" (Barnett 1997: 3–4).This reassessment of the peacekeeping role was endorsed by liberal institutionalists in academia and multi-lateralist purists.

Such a view was a repudiation of the realist school of international politics and the belief that "international stability is based on balance-of-power politics". The chief proponent of this notion of international peace based on power, John Mearsheimer, is very sceptical about the ability of international institutions, such as a UN peacekeeping regime, to independently modify state behaviour and prevent war. He came to the conclusion that international institutions "do not provide a sound basis for building a stable world", and asserted that there is "little evidence that they can alter state behaviour and cause peace" (Mearsheimer 1995: 82, 93). Until the international system can agree on a hypothetical empowered and robust international institution to force compliance across the board, a stable world is only a relative concept. Such an imagined peace is not part of the DNA of the global community.

The League of Nations' mutation into the United Nations is an example of the transformation of the 'liberal-international system' in the image of Kant's *Perpetual Peace* (1795). Kant's 'perpetual peace' offers the most comprehensive representation of a liberal and perhaps an idealistic international order. Such a peace rests on an innate and universal moral law. However, according to Richmond, this type of liberal peace did not preclude "domination, structural violence, and hegemony", as the peace was based on the image (and interests) of the states who advocated the system (Richmond 2008: 33).

Finally, Richmond (2008: 116) asserts that the three first models of peacekeeping were strongly framed in the "liberal tradition". The first model was embedded in the "Westphalian epistemological system", with its "tragic ontological assumptions". The second was constrained by rigid "official discourses" and "social engineering". Although it represented an improvement over the first, its imprint was limited. The third model aimed at implanting a liberal governance framework by transferring "liberal epistemology into conflict zones". On the other hand, a fourth model provides a "powerful critique of the liberal peace", in which peace is viewed as being "based upon emancipation" (Richmond 2008: 116).

In a concise review of 'liberal peacebuilding', Lemay-Hebert (2013: 2) posits that "the liberal peace paradigm is the dominant form of internationally-supported peacebuilding". Liberal peacebuilding, moreover, implies not just managing instability between states, but also building peace within states on the basis of liberal democracy and market economics.

Z. Tziarras (2012: 1) questions whether the model of liberal democracy (confirming the predominance of the Western ideology in the post-Cold War era) is suitable for every post-conflict state. The prescription of liberal democracy for peacebuilding in fragile countries presents the moral dilemmas of imposing liberal democracy as a form of neo-imperialism.

M. Hoffman (2009: 10) does not hesitate to state: "Not only has liberal peace-building done more harm than good, it is in reality an exercise in power that seeks to subjugate the non-West by creating dependency through chronically weak states."

Although the first peacekeeping mission was embedded in a 'Westphalian' sovereign embrace, it is questionable to label peacekeeping missions such as UNEF as 'strongly framed in the liberal tradition'. Indeed, the early UN mission was focused on 'dissociation' not 'liberalism', and there was no plan to advance beyond passive separation, into the territory of liberal global entanglement. Liberal peace can best be articulated when a peace mission enters the peacemaking/peacebuilding phase, allowing the agenda and logic of neo-liberalism and globalization to saturate the agenda, especially after the end of the Cold War.

As it is embedded in international relations theory, this critical examination of peace theory by Richmond aims to theorize a post-Westphalian peace and to render territorial sovereignty incapable of disrupting the global normative landscape. Clearly, old-fashioned territorial sovereignty stands in the way of the unchecked sweep of globalization and the trampling of the notion of independent sovereignty.

This post-structuralist theory of peace opens new 'radical' perspectives and offers new methodologies for the understanding of the relationship between 'knowledge' and 'power'. Yet in the end, post-structuralism offers neither a bal-anced *theory* nor a *concept* of 'peace'. Unless there is a major and radical trans-formation of the international system, territorial-national sovereignty cannot be dislodged easily. Indeed, globalization has played havoc with the notion of sovereignty, but the nation state is not yet ready to throw in the towel and accept a universal hegemonic system of control.

Following Nietzsche, who held that consensus would never be more than a momentary pragmatic truce, Richmond seems to take a similar approach to the development of peace theory and peacekeeping. In this post-structuralist approach, peace involves "accepting differences, rejecting all sovereignties" and making peace "without resorting to power or coercion". The solution proposed is to engage in intense interdisciplinary peace research without recourse to Marxist-orientated solutions, because, says Richmond, they have been 'discredited'. On the other hand, Richmond criticizes the US-projected contemporary neo-liberal approach that "underpins much of the peacebuilding practice around the world", and which conceptualizes individual freedoms as political freedoms, giving preference to voting over economic welfare (Richmond 2008: 152).

13.4   Criticism of the Imperial Connection in Peacekeeping

There is a wide array of criticism and positions on the nature and role of peace-keeping in the analysis of peace operations.

In a post-colonial critique of what he termed the "liberal peacekeeping project", Phillip Darby (2009: 699–716) argued that peacekeeping remains cast in "the colonial mould of intervention from above and outside". In this view, "liberal interventionism works to legitimize the existing world order".

Antony Anghie (2005: 312–315) states that "international law remains oblivious to its imperial structures, even when continuing to reproduce them". Anghie argues that the "colonial confrontation was central to the formation of international law and, in particular, its founding concept, sovereignty". According to his argument, international law has always been animated by the "civilizing mission" of the 'responsibility' of governing non-Europeans. Moreover, the "economic exploitation and cultural subordination" that resulted from the colonial encounter were "constitutively significant for the discipline" of international law. The "imperial character" of the discipline is a reflection of the "relationship between imperialism and international law" which has fundamentally affected the concept of sovereignty.

In an important contribution, Martin Jorgensen (2012: 1–23) considers the UN peacekeeping regime to be nothing more than the *continuation of imperialism by other means*. He agrees that the outline of the history of the UN is "extremely minimalist as the imperial dimensions are not included" (Weiss/Thakur 2010: 36–37).

In his study, Jorgensen (2012) points to Peer Vries' (2009: 12) work also "tying UN peacekeeping to empire" and "connecting the local and the global in UN peacekeeping". (Jorgensen 2012: 4) also comments on D. Chandler's critical work on the tragedy in Bosnia and his conclusion that the "neo-liberal paradigm" underlies peacekeeping. "Global Governance" reflects "one size fits all" prescriptions for "market liberalization", "elections", and "gender, and race biases" (Chandler 1999: 1–239).

Jorgensen (2012: 4) also criticizes Kimberly Marten's work, *Enforcing the Peace* (2004), on the comparison between peacekeeping and imperialism for its lack of historical grounding. Jorgensen notes that the lack of connectivity between peacekeeping and sensitivity to history is due to the "strong connections to the Western…and state-centric epistemologies", of Western academics (especially American and Canadian).

Jorgensen (2012) notes the criticism by Hokowhitu/Page (2011) of the study of peacekeeping and their conclusion that the missing "imperial and colonial heritage and connections in relation to the conflicts…are important". Thus, the "ideological heritage from British imperialism" in connecting the "former colonies", through peacekeeping, to "mission areas" cannot be 'ignored'.

Looking at the UNEF, Jorgensen noted that it was not a formal successor to Ottoman or British control, or what he termed "yet another imperial regime". Yet he stated: "The UNEF was nonetheless more than a reverberation of empire as the imperial past still very much shaping the present." Moreover, the "path of dependency" of the UN on British maps and initial supplies for the start of the operations of UNEF "gave the UN presence a hybrid character". The contributing countries to UNEF had relied not only on "common military cultures", but also on "national, imperial, post-imperial and post-colonial traditions". Jorgensen reminds us that some of the contributing forces to UNEF (Canada and India) were "modelled on a combination of British imperial and later military doctrine" (Jorgensen 2012: 5–7). He continued his demonstration of the interconnectedness between peacekeeping

and empire by pointing to the sport and PR events (polo games and boxing mat-
ches) of UNEF, which rely on models "promoted globally by the British Empire
over the 19th century."

Additionally, UNEF resorted to "British and American manuals for military
governments" collected during British 'imperial' or American 'overseas' experience. Jorgensen contends, therefore (based on his quotation of Darwin's (1999:
159–176) notion that "the history of the world...is an imperial history, a history of
empires"), that "The intellectual and physical heritage of empire...is hence difficult
to ignore." The Anglo-American post-war planning had British-Mandated Palestine
and Egypt as the 'centrepiece' of defence plans for the Middle East. The
British-Egyptian evacuation agreement of the Suez Canal Base (1954), and the
termination of the Palestine Mandate and the creation of Israel (1948), just a few
years before the UN operation in the Middle East (1956), provided an "almost
unbroken link".

Jorgensen notes what he terms the "imperial echo" and its "extra-territorial
legality" as manifested in the presence of UNEF on Egyptian or
Egyptian-controlled territory (the Gaza Strip) outside the purview of the Egyptian
authorities. As Jorgensen notes, "the UN troops were subject not to Egyptian law,
but the national laws of each contingent with the UN Provost or military police".
Finally, Jorgensen (2012: 4–10) applauds Phillip Darby as "the only one to have
stuck his head out and called to arms regarding a serious reflection...on the connections between peacekeeping, global governance and imperialism" (Darby 2009:
699–716).

In the spirit of the criticism of liberal peacekeeping and the call by Darby for
serious reflection, the claim that there is a strong association between peacekeeping
and imperialism – taken for granted by some – must be analysed and nuanced.
Modern peacekeeping began as an attempt by the world to avoid – or at least lessen
– the outcome of conflicts, the horrors of warfare, and, eventually, internal conflicts.
Certainly, the continuation of a colonial-imperial agenda as part of the emerging
peacekeeping regime was not the intention. As a matter of fact, it is believed that
peacekeeping was introduced to help former colonies overcome the problems
associated with decolonization and imperial aggression.

There is a long list of claims, however, which tarnish peacekeeping with the
brush of imperialism and colonialism, such as:

– Peacekeeping remains cast in the colonial mould of intervention.
– Peacekeeping is a continuation of imperialism by other means.
– UNEF is a reverberation of empire.
– Peacekeeping embodies an imperial echo.
– Ideological heritage of imperialism still shapes peacekeeping.
– Neo-liberal paradigm underlines peace operations.

These are serious accusations which perhaps infuse peacekeeping with more
ideology than is warranted.

UNEF, as the embodiment of the initiation of modern post-war peacekeeping, actually was deployed to force two old imperial powers, as well as a colonial-settler-expansionist state, to disgorge their ill-gotten booty in 1956–1957. Indeed, the international political alignments at the time made such an outcome possible.

But, on the other hand, there is ample historical evidence that peacekeeping operations do not help resolve entrenched conflicts or result in a just outcome. In this sense, peacekeeping can be considered, in Galtung's analysis, an instrument of oppression, or at least as embodying an imperial echo. Certainly, peacekeeping can be used – deliberately or not – to maitain a very harmful status quo connected to an oppressive imperial-colonial past.

In the 1948–49 Arab-Israeli war, the international community was paralysed and could not force the nascent Israeli forces to return to the 1947 Partition lines (the only legal international recognition of Israeli sovereignty, which in itself resulted from the Superpowers' pressure) because the international political calculations were different. This early version of peacekeeping was confined to observing a military situation resulting from aggression and the violation of international law.

After the 1973 War, peacekeeping forces have been used to reinforce existing ceasefire lines, and not to force the occupying army to give up its illegal territorial conquest. In this case, an accusation of peacekeeping as an echo of empire could be – and is – justified.

In other situations, however, peacekeeping was actually utilized to help a colonized territory such as East Timor to achieve independence.

In Cyprus, the entrenchment of the peacekeeping regime on the island is a sign of the failure of the antagonists and the international community alike to forge a workable peace accord. The peacekeeping forces cannot be blamed for the impasse. There are larger forces at play behind the situation in the field.

There is no doubt, however, that the label of peacekeeping has been used to facilitate military as well as political and ideological objectives not necessarily centred on achieving equitable or lasting peace and stability.

It must be argued that if peacekeeping is utilized to maintain a condition of 'dominance', as in Galtung's analysis, then peacekeeping is indeed a reverberation (or an echo) of empire. Moreover, if the resulting post-violence peace intervention is steeped into the liberal peace ideology, then the peacekeeping regime involved is indeed legitimizing the existing world order in a neo-liberal paradigm.

For his part, Doug Bland, chair of Defence Management Studies at Queen's University in Canada, believes that to continue labelling international intervention in conflict situations as 'peacekeeping' renders the definition 'mythological'. He feels that a new conceptual framework and operational rationale are needed to implement "collective security" in a changed world, in order to "better respond to global insecurity". Meanwhile, Peggy Mason, the Chair of the Canadian Peacebuilding Coordinating Committee, stated that the new UN "peace operations" doctrine embodies three components: conflict prevention, peacekeeping, and peacebuilding. In her view, the earlier primarily passive role of peacekeeping during international and local conflicts, such as that exemplified by UNEF, has evolved into a "much broader and fundamentally political process of *peace implementation*" (Bland/Mason 2010: 1–17).

For Cliff Bernath (2003: 5), the military component of UN peacekeeping is still "critically important", but it remains just one component of overall peace operations and implementation. Regardless of the changing nature of peacekeeping, the mandate to authorize peace operations is primarily 'political', and the "mission's mandate" is a "manifestation of international will", reflecting in the first place a "political rather than military reality". Bernath's position basically concerns the third traditional principle of international peacekeeping, self-defence (the other two principles being consent and impartiality). This element, too, has undergone some changes, according to Katherine Cox (1999: 239–273), over the years.

If a UN mission is not authorized as a Chapter VII enforcement measure, then peacekeepers can use force only in self-defence. Secretary-General Dag Hammarskjold stated in his Report in 1958 that "The basic element involved is clearly the prohibition against any initiative in the use of armed force" (Hammarskjold 1958). The sole exception to this rule applies in cases in which an international force was under attack or was illegally pressured to withdraw from positions it had occupied under international authorization and agreement.

In 1964 and 1973, however, two developments changed the parameters of the original concept of self-defence. The first, in 1964, was to allow the use of force when: (a) accepted agreements have been or are about to be violated, thus "risking recurrence of fighting"; or (b) attempts are made to prevent the peacekeepers "from carrying out their responsibilities" (U Thant 1964). The second development occurred in 1973, when self-defence was officially expanded by the UN to include armed action by a peacekeeping force in response to "resistance or attempts by forceful means to prevent it from discharging its duties under the mandate of the Security Council" (Waldheim 1973).

In reflecting on the role of the UN, peacekeeping, and the great powers' influence in international relations, the late UN Secretary-General, Kofi Annan (BBC 2018) said that the international institutions built after World War II are being replaced by what he termed "great-powers world" led by strong aggressive leaders. This undermining of the UN system prevents the aims of the UN Charter from being implemented.

When asked, "Has the UN failed?", he retorted, "Which UN? The ordinary membership, or the superpowers? If there is a failure, it is the failure to serve the people of the world. The Secretary-General's hands are tied. But the UN can be improved. There must be clear guidance on policy coupled with enough resources. The majority of member states are too ineffective to make a difference. It is vitally important, therefore, that civil societies must take the lead."

On peacekeeping, he said that after Rwanda, Somalia, Yugoslavia, and Congo, there is peacekeeping fatigue prevailing in the international community, as many countries are reluctant to contribute troops for fear of getting embroiled in a shooting match. If there was a peacekeeping failure, Annan emphasized that it was because the UN was not allowed to succeed. The political squabbling, leading to a failure to act in the international system, has turned the UN into a convenient scapegoat. The UN can be improved by increasing and escalating the pressure by the UN members to make changes to the UN structure to make it more responsive to the needs of the international community.

Finally, he squarely addressed the position of the United States and its newly isolationist tilt and winner-takes-all attitude, saying that America – by isolating itself – is losing the moral high ground and risking losing its world leadership position. Other powers will try to fill the resulting vacuum. As an example, he cited the nuclear agreement with Iran and said that America's position undermines international agreements (Annan 2018).

References

Anghie, Antony (2005): *Imperialism, Sovereignty, and the Making of International Law*, (Cambridge Studies in International and Comparative Law, No. 37) (New York: Cambridge University Press).

Annan, Kofi (2018): *Hard Talk*. Interview, 18 April 2018 (London: BBC).

Barnett, Michael N. (1997): "Bringing in the New World Order: Liberalism, Legitimacy, and the United Nations", in: *World Politics*, 49, 4: 526–551.

Bercovitch, J.; Anagnoson, J.T.; Willie, D.L. (1991): "Some Conceptual Issues and Empirical Trends in the Study of Successful Mediation in International Relations", in: *Journal of Peace Research*, 28,1: 7–17.

Bernath, Cliff (2003): "Contemporary and Future Challenges in UN Peacekeeping Operations", in: Langille, H.P.; Keefe, T., *The Future of Peacekeeping: An Experts' Discussion to Contribute to the Dialogue on Foreign Policy* (Vancouver: Liu Institute for Global Issues): 5.

Bland, Douglas; Mason, Peggy (2010): "Definition of Peace Operations", in: *Canada's Contributions to Peace Operations, Past, Present, and Future* (Canadian Peacebuilding Coordinating Committee) (Kingston: Queens University).

Chandler, David (1999): *Bosnia: Faking Democracy After Dayton* (London: Pluto Press): 1–239.

Cox, Katherine (1999): "Beyond Self-Defense: United Nations Peacekeeping Operations and the Use of Force", in: *Denver Journal of International Law and Policy*, 27,2: 239–273.

Darby, Phillip (2009): "Rolling Back the Frontiers of Empire: Practicing the Postcolonial", in: *International Peacekeeping*, 16,5 (November): 699–716.

Darwin John (1999): "An Undeclared Empire: The British in the Middle East, 1818–39", in: *The Journal of Imperial and Commonwealth History*, 27,2 (May): 159–176.

De Cuellar, Javier Perez (1989): "Conceptual Framework", A/44/1, cited in: Fetherston, A.B., *Towards a Theory of United Nations Peacekeeping* (New York: St. Martin's Press).

Fetherston, A.B. (1994): *Towards a Theory of United Nations Peacekeeping* (New York: St. Martin's Press).

Galtung, Johan (1970): *Peace Theory, Peace Practice and the International Peace Academy* (Oslo: International Peace Research Institute, PRIO).

Galtung Johan (1971): "Ten Proposals in the Fight Against Direct and Structural Violence", Memorandum presented during the International Peace Academy Conference, Helsinki, Finland, Summer 1971.

Hammarskjold, Dag (1958): *Report of the UN Secretary-General on UNEF*, A/3943 (8 October 1958).

Harbottle, Michael (1991): *What is Proper Soldiering?: A Study on New Perspectives for the Future Uses of Armed Forces in the 1990s* (Oxford: The Centre for International Peacebuilding): 7–8.

Hegel, G.W.F. (1996): *Philosophy of Right* (London: Prometheus).

Hobbes, Thomas (1651 & 1996): *The Leviathan* (with notes by J.C.A. Gaskin) (Oxford: Oxford University Press).

Hoffman, M. (2009): "What is Left of the 'Liberal Peace'?", in: *LSE Connect* (Winter): 11.

Hokowhito, B.; Page, T. (2011): "Postcolonial Peace", in: *Journal of Thematic Dialogue*, 14,1: 13–25.

Jorgensen, Martin Ottovay (2012): *Heaven in a Grain of Sand: The Current Paradigm of Global Governance as Understood via the Case of the United Nations Emergency Force* (Aalborg, Denmark: Aalborg University): 1–23.

Lemay-Hebert, Nicolas (2013): "Review Essay: Critical Debates on Liberal Peacebuilding", in: *Civil Wars* 15,2: 242–252.

Marten, Kimberly Zisk (2004): *Enforcing the Peace: Learning from the Imperial Past* (New York: Columbia University Press): 4.

Mearsheimer, John J. (1995): "A Realist Reply", in: *International Security*, 20,1 (Summer): 82–93.

Newman, E.; Paris, R.; Richmond, O. (2009): "Introduction", in: *New Perspectives on Liberal Peacebuilding* (Tokyo: United Nations University Press): 15.

Oakeshott, Michael (2001): 'Letter on Hobbes', in: *Political Theory*, 29, 6.

Richmond, Oliver P. (2008): *Peace in International Relations* (New York: Routledge): 1–163.

Tziarras, Zenonas (2012): "Liberal Peace and Peace-Building: Another Critique", in: *The Globalized World Post*, 1 (2 June); at: http://works.bepress.com/zenonas_tziarras/46 and http://thegwpost.files.wordpress.com/2012/06/liberal-peace-and-peace-building-zenonas-tziarras-20123.pdf.

Thant, U (1964): *Aide Mémoire of the UN Secretary-General*, S/5653 (10 April 1964).

Van Mill, David (2002): "Civil Liberty in Hobbes's Commonwealth", in: *Australian Journal of Political Science*, 37,1: 21–38.

Vries, Peer (2009): "Editorial: Global History", cited in: Jorgensen, Martin O. (2012): *Heaven in a Grain of Sand: The Current Paradigm of Global Governance as Understood via the Case of the United Nations Emergency Force* (Aalbord: Aalborg University): 1.

Waldheim, Kurt (1973): *Report of UN Secretary-General on UNEF II*, S/11052/Rev.1 (27 October 1973).

Weiss, Thomas G.; Thakur, Ramesh (2010): *Global Governance and the UN: An Unfinished Journey* (Indiana: Indiana University Press).

Chapter 14
Epilogue

Abstract The UNEF experience was the testing ground for the interaction between the new peacekeeping doctrines with the fiercely-guarded right of national sovereignty. Peace (or rather the absence of violence) was kept between Egypt and Israel for a decade. No attempt was made, however, to bring about a lasting conflict resolution. This lack of agreement is considered the major failure of the original passive peacekeeping model. The right of the independent sovereign state of Egypt to grant or withhold consent for the presence of foreign troops on Egyptian soil was pitted against the demand of the UN to dilute such a right in favour of continued international peace intervention. Since the UNEF operation was not authorized as a Chapter VII enforcement action, the legal arguments for accepting or rejecting the right of the independent state vis-à-vis the presence of foreign troops went on inconclusively for a long time. The end of the Cold War and the change in the international system resulting in increased concern for international human rights rendered the concern for national sovereignty less overriding.

Keywords Traditional peacekeeping revisited · Capstone Doctrine · Evolving peacekeeping model · New Operational Norms

14.1 The Changing International System

The 1956 Suez War ushered in a new chapter in international relations. It demonstrated beyond any doubt that the old colonial arrangements under the imperial banners were no longer valid or practical. The worldwide movement for colonial independence was unstoppable. The familiar tools of colonial control were threatened or crumbling. Meanwhile, a new and potent force, the World War II victorious United States, was becoming the *de facto* supreme Western power in the strategic Middle East. Unlike the old colonial empires, the US did not pursue formal imperial structures but opted for informal arrangements and different modus operandi to increase its political and economic penetration of the region. In the process, the US – heavily involved in the Cold War against the Soviet Bloc –

© Springer Nature Switzerland AG 2020

H. Hilmy, *Decolonization, Sovereignty, and Peacekeeping*,
https://doi.org/10.1007/978-3-030-57624-0_14

became increasingly pitted against the expanding nationalist movement in the Arab world. Thanks to increasingly generous Western military and political support, Israel became an important factor in obstructing the anti-colonial drive in this unholy confrontation.

The ensuing1956 Suez War was the result of old colonial assumptions refusing – or unable – to accept the realities of the changed geopolitical landscape. The European empires and the US, however, were determined to abort the nationalist revolt. Attempts at containment, appeasement, and half-hearted accommodation of the anti-colonial Egyptian leadership all proved unsuccessful. Events were tumbling towards a showdown.

While the old empires wanted to stop the march of history by force, the new empire was searching for new approaches to establish control. Washington was afraid that a precipitous rash action would allow the Soviets to gain strategic advantages detrimental to Western interests. In the Suez confrontation, the differences within the Western camp, in fact, were about timing and tactics and not about the ultimate objective of crushing the anti-colonial movement. The old colonial governments were losing their patience and unwisely pulled the trigger, using Israel as the bait and the theatrical justification, to wage a desperate last-stand colonial war. The historical conjunction, however, for such military action was passé.

Three crucial factors doomed the tripartite action in Suez from the beginning:

First, the anti-colonial struggle was sweeping the colonized world and gaining support worldwide. The Egyptian determination to resist despite the grievous military and civilian cost galvanized the Third World and others – including key members of the British Commonwealth – into strongly condemning the aggression. Furthermore, the establishment of the United Nations on the basis of a global Charter dedicated to freedom and equality doomed the action of the colonial powers and their collaborator during the early optimistic and idealistic days of the UN.

Second, the unique moment during the height of the Cold War that the Soviet Union and the United States came out on the same side against the tripartite invasion facilitated the task of the United Nations in dealing with the crisis, and helped to bring the confrontation to an end.

Third, the position of the US government in opposing the move by its allies as a dangerous development threatening the interest of the Western alliance. Moreover, the US wanted to demonstrate to the old colonial empires that the rules of the international game – and the leadership of the Western alliance – had changed irrevocably.

14.2   UN Pioneering Passive Peace Intervention

The United Nations intervention during the Suez War in the wake of the tripartite invasion of Egypt marked a new chapter in post-war international relations. The UN intervention was the spark that paved the way for the deployment of the peace-keeping concept in subduing or terminating international military confrontations.

The result was the introduction of a new mechanism (passive peacekeeping) for *conflict control* (but not resolution) in the shape of a UN-authorized international peace force, United Nations Emergency Force (UNEF). Basically, the UN intervention was a containment effort designed to stop the hostilities and prevent further military escalation. On the insistence of Egypt, the word 'Emergency' was inserted in the name of the force to signify that the UN action was temporary in nature, dealing with a transient crisis, precluding any long term international deployment or occupation of Egyptian sovereign territory. The emerging anti-colonial drive was confronted by a last-ditch desperate imperial military response. The formation of UNEF in the wake of the Suez War, therefore, was inextricably linked to the escalating anti-colonial struggle, and the 'end of empire' historical development which hastened the decline of the imperial powers.

The *sovereignty* of the newly-independent states – in the midst of the struggle for decolonization – became, in the process, a sacrosanct principle zealously guarded. The UN intervention in 1956, therefore, propelled the principle of sovereignty to the top of the global agenda. In confronting this dangerous escalation, UN member states bypassed the Security Council, and thus British and French veto power, and authorized the creation of the international force through a majority vote in the UN General Assembly, demonstrating the new and potential power of the emerging Third World.

The tortuous negotiations and manoeuvres to get the UNEF force formed and operational took place as the UN system was trying, in the post-World War II era, to establish its meaningful presence and effectiveness, indeed its relevance. This process was not an imposed enforcement action under Chapter VII, but a negotiated action dependent on the voluntary sovereign consent of the victim of aggression, Egypt. Naturally, Egypt was not going to oppose an international temporary action designed to end the occupation of its territory and the violation of its sovereignty. It took some wrangling and international diplomatic finesse to put the issue of national consent to rest initially and that consent was never a permanent authorization. Importantly, Egypt's sovereignty was respected, and the UN role in managing international peace and security was respected.

The termination of the UNEF mission was problematic, as it brought into focus the clash between the principle of sovereign consent and the need of the international community to ensure peace and security. Subsequent UN peace operations had to contend not only with the requirements of sovereignty, but also and increasingly with the responsibility of the international community to interfere to resolve international disputes and to ensure human rights protection regardless of the restrictions of sovereignty. Disappointingly, the UNEF operations began in order to conclude one disastrous war, and ended at the beginning of another massive war because of a failure to translate the "absence of war" into the "presence of peace".

The UNEF experience can be summed up in the words of the veteran UN hand, Ralph Bunche, who said in 1960 that "UNEF is not an end in itself … The most that can be hoped from it in this regard is to buy time" (Bunche 1960). Unfortunately, and despite maintaining 'peace' for a long time, this time was squandered by the antagonists and by the international community at large by the failure to press for a workable settlement.

Secretary-General U Thant addressed the UN Security Council on 19 May 1967, stating: "It is true to a considerable extent that UNEF has allowed us for ten years to ignore some of the hard realities of the underlying conflict" (Thant 1967: S/7896). It is often said that the result of the 1967 war was a failure of peacemaking not peacekeeping.

The experience of UNEF, therefore, warrants an extensive and detailed study of the complex political-diplomatic efforts expended (or avoided, ignored, etc.) in the period from 1956 to 1967 mainly in a futile attempt to forge an Arab-Israeli settlement. Given the lack of success in achieving an accommodation, one must examine the reasons behind such a lack of accomplishment, and whether failure was intentional.

It is a fact of international relations, however, that international conflicts occur or endure because of the structure and dimensions of the conflict itself, but also because of the nature and structure of the world distribution of power and the realities of its regional manifestations. 'Proxy' conflicts cannot be resolved without being disentangled from great power rivalries. Similarly, local conflicts are tied to political, socio-economic, and ethnic profiles and their power manifestations. It is easier to interject between warring countries through the deployment of peace-keeping forces, but it is a far more difficult proposition to address conflict-ridden societies rife with glaring socio-economic disparities and ethnic-religious fissures in an attempt to establish social peace. The pertinent question to be asked, then, is how to protect the objectives of UN peace operations from international and local variables to ensure effective outcomes.

14.3 Peacekeeping and Conflict Resolution

Canada's former Prime Minister and Secretary of State for External Affairs, Joe Clark, added his voice to the debate over the appropriate role of peacekeeping in conflict resolution in his statement:

> Peacekeeping has a new role in the new notion of security. Peacekeeping in the future must anticipate as well as react. It must deal with the causes of conflict and not just their symptoms. It must build peace, and not simply keep it (Clark 1990: DEA).

As Michael Carroll observes, "Peacemaking activities should have been part and parcel of UNEF's original mandate … The parties in conflict need to ceaselessly strive for peace, and the UN needs to have structures in place to aid with these efforts. Otherwise, the job of peacekeepers is little more than a temporary, albeit worthy, distraction" (Carroll 2005: 16).

The experience of UN peacekeeping operations in the field over the last sixty years has contributed to the growing realization that separating combatants without establishing foundations for future peaceful coexistence and political conflict resolution does not necessarily lead to peaceful and permanent solutions. This basic failure in the peacekeeping model led the late UN Secretary-General, Boutros Boutros-Ghali, to develop the concept of "post-conflict peacebuilding", defined as "action to identify and support structures which will tend to strengthen and solidify peace in order to avoid a relapse into conflict" (Boutros-Ghali 1992: 21).

As a precedent-setting peacekeeping operation, UNEF is recognized, according to Davis Brown, as having served as a guide for "future operational norms". Based on UNEF's practice in the field, the five principles developed are:

(1) consent of the host state to the presence of the force;
(2) impartiality of the force and non-intervention in the state's domestic affairs;
(3) defensive rules of engagement;
(4) UN control of the forces participating in its operations;
(5) restrictions on the constituency of UN peacekeeping forces.

The operational norm is interpreted to mean that the composition of the forces should be "international in character and that permanent members of the Security Council be excluded from participation" (Brown 1994: 561).

The stages of development in the concept and application of international "peace intervention" can now be divided into: (a) 'First Generation', missions entirely consensual based on sovereign consent; (b) 'Second Generation', missions involving more complex and wider peacekeeping based on the enforcement of peace; and (c) 'Third Generation', missions including external Governance/Administration of a territory based on what some describe as "liberal peace" schemes seeking to implement the "ideals of global liberal governance", along with the ultimate goal of realizing neo-liberal "democratization and marketization" (Arbuckle 2006: 16–24).

14.4 The Changing Peacekeeping Model

The Capstone Doctrine embodying the principles and experience of the traditional passive peacekeeping paradigm was therefore undergoing a fundamental transformation in the *raison d'être* of peace intervention. Since 1956, peace operations under UN auspices can be authorized as Chapter VI consensual arrangements, or activated as Chapter VII enforcement measures. Both the provisions of International Humanitarian Law and International Human Rights Law figure prominently in the conduct and objectives of the peace operations. By the end of the millennium, theoretical and innovative conceptual frameworks for peace operations ranged from the original UNEF model to the *Agenda for Peace* blueprint (1992) developed in response to the horrors of ethnic cleansing in the 1990s. This was then followed by the *Brahimi Report* (2000), and then the introduction of the novel concept of the *Responsibility to Protect* (2001), formulated with the objective of showing more teeth in international efforts to restore peace and protect human lives. Finally, UN

Secretary-General, Guterres, presided over the production of the recommendations of the *High-Level Independent Panel on Peace Operations* (HIPPO) in 2015 and 2017, which called for a fundamental shift in the philosophy and application of peace intervention.

Although sovereignty and sovereign consent are losing the post-war sparkle they have enjoyed in favour of more robust international intervention, independent sovereign states resist the loss of their sovereign status. The international scene is more complicated by the absence of true sovereign equality, as it is difficult, if not inconceivable, to force the big powers to submit to the same standard of conduct. No power can force the superpowers to accept any VII Security Council resolution, due to the veto power not available to the rest of the international community.

A UN international peace force was proposed and formed, but it failed to remain mobilized due to political, logistical and financial constraints. Although progress has been made, the international community has all too obviously not yet succeeded in arriving at a fail-safe formula for peace intervention. A fundamental change in international power alignments and structures would seem to be a pre-requisite for streamlining a universal collective response to peace and security issues.

Was the UNEF deployment a "controlled impasse", in the description of Sherry (1986), or is peacekeeping a "tool of the status quo" as Fetherston (1994) suggests? No doubt it was both. The components of the conflict were left festering and unresolved. Competing external actors were heavily involved, reducing the likelihood of a genuine reconciliation. The military balance was deliberately skewed in favour of one side at the expense of the other. Moreover, the expansionist-territorial objectives of one side ruled out any possibility of equitable settlement. UNEF nevertheless purchased a decade of relative peace in a volatile region. When the controlled impasse unravelled, so did the deceptive lack of warfare. Still, the failure to use UNEF (and other peace operations) as a bridge to a lasting settlement(s), constitutes one of the biggest drawbacks of peacekeeping.

14.5   The Ultimate Conclusion of the UNEF Experience

The *ultimate conclusion* for this study is provided by the answer to the following two questions:

First Question: Was the UNEF mission in the Middle East between 1956 and 1967 a success?

Undoubtedly, the qualified answer to this question is in the affirmative, but with only 'crumpled' flying colours. For over a decade, the UNEF successfully kept the ceasefire between Egypt and Israel in place. On more than one occasion during the UNEF deployment, the international force prevented serious confrontation from escalating into full-blown warfare, largely due to its presence as an interposition force, and its status as a representative of the will of the international community. UNEF fulfilled its mission in accordance with the mandate and terms of reference provided by the UN. Moreover, the international force operated within the confines of the passive peacekeeping model it followed. Such a model did not provide a stipulation for the parties to engage in a conflict resolution obligation.

The two sides of the conflict had their own priorities and calculations, which eventually led – by miscalculation or design – to the termination of the UNEF mission and the eruption of war. On the Egyptian side, the request for the withdrawal of UNEF – which Egypt was legally entitled to make – was due to domestic political pressures and regional leadership squabbles. On the other side, the Israelis never wanted the UNEF stationed on their lines of control in the first place, and refused to allow them on their side of the fence to mirror the deployment in Egypt. The presence of UNEF, therefore, was an obstacle for them which they were eager to have removed. Israel wanted to implement its long-standing plans for the invasion and annexation of Arab territories (as actual events demonstrated). The Israeli *Kadesh* invasion plan (which was prevented from fruition in 1956–57) was reactivated in 1967 and implemented beyond the wildest expectations of its planners. Egypt's request for the withdrawal of UNEF, therefore, was an opportunity not to be missed by Israel. For the record, however, Israel declared its opposition to Egypt's request for the UNEF withdrawal at the UN!

It is not accurate to portray UNEF as a failure. The only failure was the lack of a credible alternative to a protracted conflict left for years to fester. The question that must be asked, therefore, is 'How can a long-standing conflict be resolved when the antagonists display fundamental power imbalance (according to Galtung), and they are supported by external powers with their own priorities, obstructing or paralysing any chance of a fair and equitable settlement? The international community does not have a magic wand to use for conflict resolution. Principles of equality and non-aggression in international law aside, the international community in reality consists of a few powerful actors, and the rest are marginal, ineffective, or inconsequential states or institutions. At the apex of the system, the 'super' powers conduct themselves in the international arena only to serve their ideological agenda or strategic interests. Notions of justice and fairness in dealing with international conflicts do not register high in their calculations. That is why the Arab-Israeli conflict has been on the books for a long time without attempts for a fair resolution that could affect the strategic regional – and hence the international – balance, and upset their respective pecking orders.

There is, however, an undeclared suspicion that the UNEF mission was deliberately left deployed as long as it did without serious attempts at fundamental resolution of the conflict. The reason for such inaction was the inability of the two superpowers to agree the terms of a workable conflict resolution. The superpowers may have decided, moreover, that further engagement with the Middle East conflict was not worth risking military confrontation between them.

Another, perhaps a more sinister, explanation was that the delay was needed for Israel to consolidate its occupation of the Palestinian territories, illegally-occupied between 1947 and 1949, and to establish strong facts on the ground by absorbing more Jewish immigrants, to ensure the prevention of the repatriation of the Palestinian refugees in accordance with the 1948 UN resolution, and the consolidation of the institutions of the new Israeli state in accordance with Zionist aspirations. Finally, the time was needed for Israel to acquire and master more advanced weaponry (including nuclear capabilities) in order to defeat once and for all the Arab threats and complete its territorial acquisitions and regional dominance.

On the Arab side, the delay was a reprieve from a military confrontation that would inflict further defeats. However, there was the desire to increase the Arab strength substantially with the hope that this would eventually force Israel to disgorge its war booty. The Arabs were also acquiring large amounts of weaponry in preparation for their showdown with Israel. Time to train and absorb the new fighting capabilities was also needed. The continuous Arab disagreements and confrontations, however, prevented them from establishing and posing an effective and united Arab challenge. There was also the entrenched belief in the Arab mind that the West, and in particular the United States, for domestic or international reasons, would always come to Israel's defence and prevent any Israeli defeat or Arab victory. Finally, the Arabs were not rushing to war because of the fear that further defeats at the hands of the Israelis would threaten their own hold on power. Undoubtedly, the *End of Empire* in the Middle East did not happen quietly, as the region witnessed the metamorphosis of empire in the shape of an externally supported entity illegitimately consolidating territorial acquisition and population expulsion, and carrying out tasks in the colonial mould and – through the emergence of a new and extensive neo-imperial control in alliance with local oppressive regimes – obstructing the path towards genuine progressive change.

Second Question: Was the issue of sovereignty detrimental to the peacekeeping responsibilities of the international force and its relationship with the host country?

For over a decade, Egypt and the UNEF cooperated in an exemplary manner to discharge their respective duties in accordance with the agreement between the United Nations and Egypt. Early deployment frictions and several operational snags were dealt with in a spirit of cooperation and friendship. During its deployment, there is no doubt that UNEF respected Egypt's sovereignty. Egypt, in return, went out of its way to smooth the deployment and the operations of the international force. Yet at no time was there any doubt about the need for the *continued* consent of Egypt for the UNEF to enter or to remain in the country. Such a right of consent was a fundamental – and contractual – basis for UNEF's operations in Egypt.

The issue of *sovereign consent*, however, was the main legal-political bone of contention towards the end of the UNEF mandate. Egypt's exercise of its legal – and sovereign – right of consent at the end of the deployment was respected by the UN – after initial demurring. Paradoxically, the successful exercise of this right resulted in disastrous military, territorial, and political consequences affecting the entire geopolitical landscape of the Middle East, particularly Egypt, the country exercising its legitimate right of consent.

14.6   Peace Operations Evaluation

Earlier in this study I assessed the success of the UNEF deployment. Some particular conclusions and lessons were observable. In this section, I look at a general framework for evaluating peace operations in general. In an earlier work, Paul F. Diehl (1993) laid out the conditions and criteria for evaluating the success or failure of peacekeeping operations (see Chap. 4). Fundamentally, a successful outcome and the ultimate test of success require the following necessary conditions: (1) The limitation of armed conflict, and (2) resolution of the fundamental conflict.

In a follow-up study, Diehl (in collaboration with Daniel Druckman), developed the earlier concept of evaluation, and injected theoretical underpinnings for the work deemed a prerequisite for building knowledge about factors associated with success or failure and necessary for making sound policy choices. Their ambitious objective was to provide a "Decision Template" for assessing peace operations success in relation to different goals and objectives.

Traditional peacekeeping operations are difficult to compare with newer generation operations in terms of complexity, organization, and logistics. Therefore, there is a lack of consensus on the meaning of peace operation success. Hence, it is important to specify the constituents of peace operation success as a prerequisite for the overarching theoretical development of the field. For Diehl and Druckman, peace operation theory is based on a causally specified relationship that has received some empirical confirmation. Thus, bridging theory with practice is the goal of their research (Diehl/Druckman 2010: 1–6).

In another study, Diehl/Balas (2014) tackled the issue of evaluating the success or failure of peace operations by looking at the appropriate criteria needed for a valid evaluation:

(1) The target of success.
(2) Success depends on the timeframe adopted.
(3) The development of a baseline or standard of success for comparison.

A further suggestion is to relate effectiveness across multiple peace operations. Moreover, another important factor in peace operations – besides conflict abatement and conflict containment – is the crucial (and neglected) factor of the creation of an environment suitable for negotiation and conflict resolution (Diehl/Balas 2014: 141–146).

14.7   Final Reflections

Based on the UNEF experience and the results of its deployment in the midst of the 1956 Suez conflict as well as its experience on the ground for over a decade, several policy observations can be made. Simply inserting a UN force between warring parties without requiring the parties to engage in a UN-supervised conflict resolution arrangement risks wasting a historic opportunity to reach a permanent and just accommodation in the Middle East and other crisis areas.

The following is *a review and a set of discussion points* for a streamlined peace operations regime. Some of these points have been debated or under discussion nationally and internationally. The purpose here is to encapsulate the experience gained from the UNEF mission, and to re-emphasize the kind of reforms needed to implement a more efficient peace operation regime:

First, to achieve success, any peacekeeping operation authorized by the UN will ideally include, in tandem, a *mandatory conflict resolution mechanism* in accordance with the UN Charter principles, and a defined time frame for arriving at an accommodation administered by neutral UN personnel. Although the UNEF succeeded beyond all expectations in bringing an end to the initial armed conflict during the Suez War, there was a lack of ground rules for the transformation of the absence of war into a durable and stable peace. This represented a failure, not primarily of the UNEF, but of the international system and the structure of international relations, indeed of the UN itself. The main task of outside intervention, therefore, is to transform the single dimension of the mission (the end of hostilities) into a multidimensional drive to bring about a multi-faceted fundamental conflict resolution agreement addressing all the aspects of the dispute.

Lester B. Pearson, the main mover behind the UN Resolution to establish UNEF, was prescient in commenting on his 'crowning achievement' in a prophetic statement:

> There is one great omission from this resolution...It does not provide for any steps to be taken by the United Nations for a peace settlement, without which a ceasefire will be only of temporary value at best (Pearson quoted in Tucker 1973: 113).

A later Canadian Minister of External Affairs, Mitchell Sharp, echoed the sentiments of his predecessor by stating in 1972 Canada's prerequisites for participating in peacekeeping operations. Foremost among them was that a peacekeeping operation should be associated with an agreement for a *political settlement* operating under a clear mandate (Sharp 1982: 39).

The UNEF experience and other inconclusive UN interventions propelled the international community to search for a comprehensive peace approach. Several major UN initiatives emerged from the experience of the first generation peacekeeping intervention, as outlined in the relevant resulting documents: (1) *Agenda for Peace* (1992), and its 1995 *Supplement*, (2) *The Brahimi Report* (2000), (3) *The Responsibility to Protect* (2001), (4) *HIPPO* (2015; 2017). These documents represent a fundamental change in international peace intervention from preoccupation with ending hostilities to conflict resolution and, finally, human rights protection.

Second, the lack of an *agreed prior peacekeeping mission termination* mechanism, which doomed the UNEF despite its decade-long success in maintaining peace (or at least an absence of war), should not be allowed to undermine future peace operations. In future, negotiations over the introduction of UN troops into conflict zones must also embody not only an agreed-upon mechanism for setting up the international force, but certainly a clear and binding agreement on the terms of its termination, clearly linked to a successful conflict resolution regime, without being dependent on the narrow political interests of one party or the other to the conflict. The termination mentioned here is not just for the 'mission' but also for the 'conflict'. It is vital that an agreed mission termination by all parties to a conflict signals, therefore, the successful resolution of the conflict.

Third, *Respect for the sovereign rights* of the nations involved in 'interstate' conflicts is crucial for the success of any UN intervention. All the evidence suggests that Egypt would never have accepted the stationing of the UN Force on its soil against its consent. Any such unauthorized intervention risks having the deployment turned into an *international occupation regime* fraught with dangers for both the country subject to intervention and the international force. Sovereign rights, however, must never override the protection of human rights. 'Intrastate' conflicts represent a thorny problem that could undermine any intervention regime. Respect for sovereignty is not sacrosanct in civil wars, ethno-religious conflicts or genocidal atrocities in domestic disputes, as the need for urgent intervention by the international community to save human lives overrides of necessity the legalistic requirements of sovereignty, particularly when the state's central authority is crumbling, or when there are several competing factions claiming sovereignty and seeking control. The UN at the helm of the international community has been developing newer doctrines for intervention in domestic disputes. The fear of violating sovereignty is no longer an obstacle for a robust international response to crimes against humanity.

Fourth, the deployment of UN peacekeeping troops in an international conflict will ideally be *on both sides of the lines of control* separating the antagonists. The fact that Israel did not give its consent to UNEF deployment on its territory made it easier for the hostilities to break out once Egypt paradoxically demanded the withdrawal of UNEF. If UN troops had been on both sides of the ceasefire line, the ability of one side to demand the speedy termination of the peacekeeping presence would have been thwarted, or at least slowed down. In future, this measure could give the international community a breathing space to mount a concerted effort to defuse a crisis, or at least to bring about an orderly and measured withdrawal that could slow the immediate rush to reignite a conflict.

Fifth, the choice of the *commander* of the International Force from a pool of neutral and experienced personnel, as well as a competent and professional *liaison* counterpart from the host country, is of paramount importance in ensuring the successful deployment and operations of any international peacekeeping force.

Sixth, the *membership in an international peace force* not authorized by a Security Council Chapter VII enforcement resolution *must be acceptable* to the host country/ies in which it is to be deployed. Moreover, any countries engaged in a conflict with the host nation should be barred from contributing to the membership of the peace force. Respecting the sovereignty of the host nation(s) in such a case would not be impacted by a peace operation regime designed solely to defuse and resolve a serious conflict affecting international peace and security.

Seventh, any peace operation authorized by the UN should include, as a primary term of reference, the *upholding and enforcement of the applicable international human rights law* provisions aimed at protecting human lives and fundamental human rights without the constraints of the sovereign prerogatives of the member states.

Eighth, looking beyond the UNEF to current global realities, one could suggest that a permanent 25-nation expanded *UN Peace Operations Commission* (to replace the current Department of Peace Keeping Operations, DPKO) be established to oversee the standard process of 'formation', 'deployment', 'peace negotiation', and 'termination' of all UN peace operations. The Commission should be universally composed, with representation from every continent and group of nations.

Ninth, the idea of establishing a *permanent international peace force* is not new. But the experience in the field – although initially successful – has proven that such an undertaking is fraught with difficulties and complications. The magic formula for such an army has not yet been discovered.

Tenth, *long-standing 'chronic' or 'intractable' conflicts*, such as the Middle East and Cyprus conflicts, should not be allowed to continue unabated, exhausting UN peace operations capacity and resources, and posing a real danger to international peace and security. If peace is not established within a 'reasonable' time (12–24 months), a UN-sponsored international peace conference must be convened to deal with the conflict. If the parties to the conflict cannot arrive at an acceptable resolution or a workable compromise, again after a reasonable time has lapsed, then the conflict must be submitted to a binding international arbitration supervised by the International Court of Justice, thereby avoiding the crippling political factors surrounding the conflict deliberations at the UN Security Council. Naturally, such a proposed course of action – optimistic as it is – is at odds with the prevailing supremacy of the Security Council role, which, in turn, reflects the power configurations in the international arena. However, a new model for international/national conflict resolution should be developed.

Eleventh, the UNEF experience should provide a powerful incentive to *structure future peacekeeping operations* by the UN and regional organizations differently in order to provide clear and unambiguous agreements with the host nation(s) on sovereign consent and the issue of withdrawal. As well, a conflict resolution mechanism – accepted by the parties to the conflict *a priori* – should be embedded within the process.

Twelfth, international peace intervention loses its original meaning and purpose when it is *used as a cover for aggression and strategic competition* by countries on their own or under cover of UN approval.

In a succinct legal treatment of issues of war and peace, Antje Mays opines that, while sovereignty is a national prerogative, the conduct of peace operations can be blurred by international guidelines. For laws governing war and peacekeeping to be successful, "they must absolutely ensure a universal standard of conduct" (Mays 2000: 201–232). What is needed involves a new 'Vienna Congress' of sorts. This should:

- Delineate the role of the UN and regional organizations in peacekeeping
- Define the objectives and limitations of the task *a priori* when making international agreements requiring participants in peacekeeping missions.
- Facilitate appropriate measures for the international community to initiate, in the event of the complications or failure of the peace mission.

Clearly, such prescription requires a fundamental change in attitude, as well as an international agreement to put in place and facilitate the required measures. It is hoped, therefore, that the definition of peacekeeping as an "uncertain, unpredictable, and unregulated international operation" (Diehl 1994: 1) will no longer apply.

Photo 14.1 Humanity's threatened symbol of peace and justice. *Source* en.wikipedia.org

References

Arbuckle, James V. (2006): *Military Forces in 21st Century Peace Operations* (New York: Routledge).

Boutros-Ghali, Boutros (1992): *An Agenda for Peace: Preventive Diplomacy, Peacemaking and Peace-Keeping*, A/47/277, Section II.

Brown, Davis (1994): "The Role of the United Nations in Peacekeeping and Truce-Monitoring: What Are the Applicable Norms", in: *Revue Belge de Droit International*, 2 (Bruxelles).

Bunche, Ralph (1960): "Peace Prospects from the UN Perspective", Speech at the John A. Ryan Forum, New York Public Library (13 May 1960).

Carroll, Michael K. (2005): "From Peace (Keeping) to War: The United Nations and the Withdrawal of UNEF", in: *The Middle East Review of International Affairs*, 9,2, Article 5 (June 2005).

Clark, Joe (1990): "Peacekeeping and Canadian Foreign Policy", in: *Department of External Affairs*, Statement: 90/65, (Toronto, Canada) (8 November 1990).

Diehl, Paul F. (1993): *International Peacekeeping* (Baltimore: Johns Hopkins University Press).

Diehl, Paul F.; Balas, Alexandru (2014): *Peace Operations* (Cambridge: Polity Press).

Diehl, Paul F.; Druckman, Daniel (2010): *Evaluating Peace Operations* (Boulder: Lynne Rienner Publishers).

Fetherston, A.B. (1994): *Towards a Theory of United Nations Peacekeeping* (London: MacMillan Press).

Mays, Antje (2000): "War and Peace: Of Law, Lawlessness, and Sovereignty (Multinational Peacekeeping and International Law)", in: *Journal of Power and Ethics: An Interdisciplinary Review*, 1,2: 201–232.

Pearson, Lester (1973): "Canada, the UN and Peacekeeping", cited in: Tucker, Michael (1980), *Canadian Foreign Policy: Contemporary Issues and Themes* (Toronto: McGraw-Hill Reyerson).

Sharp, Mitchell (1972): quoted in John H. Sigler, (Ed.): *Carleton International Proceedings: International Peacekeeping in the Eighties: Global Outlook and Canadian Priorities* (Ottawa: Carleton University, Fall 1982).

Sherry, George L. (1986): "The United Nations, International Conflict, and American Security", in: *Political Science Quarterly*, 101,5: 753–771.

Thant, U. (1967): *UN Security Council Secretary-General Report*, S/7896, para. 15 (19 May 1967).

Appendix
Highlights from Relevant Official Documents

A. Final Communiqué of the Bandung Conference, 24 April 1955 (Highlights)

1. Afro-Asian Cooperation. The 24 countries pledged to work towards "fuller economic, cultural and political co-operation". They "recognized the urgency of promoting economic development ... to provide technical assistance to one another", recommended "the early establishment of the United Nations Fund for Economic Development" to stabilize "commodity trade" and "diversify their export trade", and, regarding "the establishment of national and regional banks", they "emphasized the particular significance of the development of nuclear energy for peaceful purposes", and they agreed on "prior consultation of participating countries in international forums".

2. The participating countries "reiterated their determination to work for closer cultural co-operation" and took note that "colonialism suppresses the national cultures of the people". The conference condemned the "denial of the fundamental rights" of the colonized peoples. In particular, the "Conference condemned racialism as a means of cultural suppression".

3. The Afro-Asian Conference "declared its full support for the fundamental principles of Human Rights", and for the "principle of self-determination".

4. The Conference declared that "colonialism in all its manifestations is an evil which should speedily be brought to an end"; the Conference agreed that the "alien subjugation of peoples is an impediment to the promotion of world peace and co-operation"; the Conference declared "its support for the cause of freedom and independence" for all peoples.

© Springer Nature Switzerland AG 2020
H. Hilmy, *Decolonization, Sovereignty, and Peacekeeping*,
https://doi.org/10.1007/978-3-030-57624-0

5. The Conference supported the "principle of equitable geographical distribution" for the UN Security Council representation. The Conference called for "disarmament and the prohibition of the production, experimentation and use of nuclear and thermo-nuclear weapons of war", and for the establishment of "effective international control" over international disarmament.

6. The Conference summarized its deliberations in a 10-point declaration of principles emphasizing respect for: fundamental human rights, sovereignty and territorial integrity, equality of all races and all nations, the right of self-defence, justice and international obligations. Finally, the declaration called for non-interference in the internal affairs of countries and for the non-participation of the big powers in collective defence, and stated its opposition to the exertion of pressure or threats of aggression or the use of force against the territorial integrity or political independence by any country.

B. The Sèvres Protocol Between Britain, France and Israel, signed in France on 24 October 1956 (Highlights)

The three governments agreed on the following course of action:

1. Israel attacks Egypt on 29 October 1956.
2. The British and French governments, in response, request, on 30 October 1956, that Egypt and Israel withdraw their troops ten miles west and east of the Suez Canal respectively.
3. Egypt is asked to accept the temporary occupation of key positions on the Canal by the Anglo-French forces.
4. Failure of Egypt to comply with the Anglo-French ultimatum would result in the commencement of Anglo-French military action against Egypt starting 31 October 1956.
5. The three governments also agree that Israel is to occupy the western shore of the Gulf of Aqaba and the Islands of Tiran and Sanafir at the entrance to the Gulf (facing Sharm El Sheikh).
6. Israel undertakes not to attack Jordan during the period of operations against Egypt, but if Jordan attacks Israel, Britain undertakes not to come to the aid of Jordan.
7. The arrangements of the present protocol must remain strictly secret.
8. Signed by David Ben-Gurion (Israel), Patrick Dean (Britain), and Christian Pineau (France).

C. The Good Faith Agreement Between Egypt and the UN – Aide-Memoire: General Assembly (A/3375) – 20 November 1956 (Highlights)

The Government of Egypt and the Secretary-General of the United Nations arrived at an understanding on the basic principles for the presence and functioning of the United Nations Emergency Force (UNEF) in Egypt as follows:

1. The Government of Egypt declares that, when exercising its sovereign rights on any matter concerning the presence and functioning of UNEF, it will be guided, in good faith, by its acceptance of General Assembly Resolution 1000 (ES-1) of 5 November 1956.
2. The United Nations takes note of this declaration of the Government of Egypt and declares that the activities of UNEF will be guided, in good faith, by the task established for the Force in the aforementioned resolutions; in particular, the United Nations, understanding this to correspond to the wishes of the Government of Egypt, reaffirms its willingness to maintain UNEF until its task is completed.

D. Status of the Force Agreement Between Egypt and the UN – General Assembly (A/1126-XI) – 22 February 1957 (Highlights)

The two sides agreed:

1. That UNEF could not stay or operate in Egypt unless Egypt continued its consent.
2. On the conditions and area of operations for UNEF.
3. That UNEF could not remain in Port Said or the Suez Canal Zone.
4. That the question of the reopening of the Suez Canal was separate from the functions of UNEF.

Bibliography

Abdallah, Nabih B. (1975): *The Evolution of the Arab Idea in Egypt* (Cairo: Egyptian Book Organization) [in Arabic].

Abiew, Francis K. (1999): *The Evolution of the Doctrine and Practice of Humanitarian Intervention* (The Hague: Springer Netherlands).

Abu-Lughod, Ibrahim (Ed.) (1971): *The Transformation of Palestine* (Evanston: Northwestern University Press).

Abu-Lughod, Ibrahim; Abu-Laban, Baha (Eds.) (1974): *Settler Regimes in Africa and the Arab World: The Illusion of Endurance* (Wilmette, Ill.: Medina University Press International).

Adas, Michael (2004): "Contested Hegemony: The Great War and the Afro-Asian Assault on the Civilizing Mission", in: Duara, Prasenjit (Ed.): *Decolonization: Perspectives from Now and Then* (New York: Routledge).

Agnew, John (2005): *Hegemony: The New Shape of Global Power* (Philadelphia: Temple University Press).

Al-Baghdadi, Abd al-Latif (1990): "Memoirs", in: Troen, S.; Shemesh, M. (Eds.): *The Suez-Sinai Crisis 1956: Retrospective and Reappraisal* (London: Frank Cass): 333–356.

Alger, Chadwick F. (2014): *Peace Research and Peacebuilding* (New York: Springer).

Al-Hakim, Tawfiq (1972/1974/1985): *The Return of Consciousness* (in Arabic and English) (Basingstoke: Macmillan).

Al-Jilby, Hassan (1970): *Principles of the United Nations and Its Organizational Classifications* (Cairo: Institute of Arab Studies, League of Arab States) [in Arabic].

Almog, Orna (2003): *Britain, Israel and the United States, 1955–1958: Beyond Suez* (London: Frank Cass).

Alpha Plan (1955): *Arab-Israeli Settlement*, PRO, FO, 371/11588.

American Journal of International Law (1947): *United Nations Documents on the Development and Codification of International Law* (Supplement 41,4).

American Red Cross (2011): "International Humanitarian Law", in: *International Humanitarian Law and Human Rights* (April).

Amery, Julian (1990): "The Suez Group: A Retrospective on Suez", in: Troen, Selwyn; Shemesh, Moshe (Eds.): *The Suez-Sinai Crisis 1956: retrospective and Reappraisal* (London: Frank Cass).

Amrallah, Borhan (1976): "The International Responsibility of the United Nations for Activities Carried Out by UN Peace-Keeping Forces", in: *Revue Egyptienne de Droit International*, 32: 57–82.

Anand, R.P. (1967): "Sovereign Equality of States in International Law – I", in: *International Studies* (India), 8,3 (January): 213–241.

Anand, R.P. (1967): "Sovereign Equality of States in International Law – II", in: *International Studies* (India), 8,4 (April): 386–421.

Anderson, Benedict (2002): *Imagined Communities: Reflections on the Origin and Spread of Nationalism* (New York: Verso).

Anghie, Antony (2005): *Imperialism, Sovereignty and the Making of International Law*, Cambridge Studies in International and Comparative Law, No. 37 (Cambridge: Cambridge University Press).

Anglo-Egyptian Treaty of Friendship and Alliance (1936): League of Nations Treaty Series, 137,6 (Geneva): 402–431.

Anglo-French Ultimatum to Egypt and Israel (1956): (30 October 1956).

Annan, Kofi (1993; 2017): "The Path of Peace-Keeping: Translating Commitment into Action", in: *Harvard International Review* (Summer 1993; Summer 2017).

Annan, Kofi (1996): *Peace Operations and the United Nations: Preparing for the Next Century* (New York: United Nations Department of Peace Keeping Operations).

Annan, Kofi (1997): *UN Press Release*. SG/SM/6310 (2 September 1997).

Annan, Kofi (1999): Speech in the UN General Assembly, 20 September 1999 (New York: UN Press Release).

Annan, Kofi (2000): *We the Peoples: The Role of the United Nations in the Twenty-First Century.* Report by the Secretary-General, A/54/2000 (27 March 2000).

Annan, Kofi (2002): "The Responsibility to Protect". Address to the International Peace Academy, February 2002 (New York: UN Press Release).

Annan, Kofi (2012): *Interventions: A Life in War and Peace* (New York: Penguin Press).

Annan, Kofi (2018): *HardTalk* Interview (London: BBC) (18 April 2018).

Arab Republic of Egypt (1982): *White Paper on the Multi-National Force and Observers* (Cairo: State Information Service).

Arbuckle, James V. (2006): *Military Forces in 21st Century Peace Operations* (New York: Routledge).

Arias, Inocencio (1999): "Humanitarian Intervention: Could the Security Council Kill the United Nations?", in: *Fordham International Law Journal*, 23,4 (Article 2): 1004–1014.

Armstrong, Hamilton Fish (1957): "The UN Experience in Gaza", *Foreign Affairs*, 35,4 (July): 600–619.

Arendt, Hannah (1973): *Totalitarianism* (New York: Harcourt Brace Javanovich).

Aspaturian, Vernon V. (1958): As quoted in: Robinson, Jacob "Metamorphosis of the United Nations", (Collected courses of the Hague Academy of International Law), in: *Recuil des Cours* (94) (Boston: Nijhoff, Leiden).

Asya, Ilan (1998): *The Question of Arab Territorial Continuity as a Cause of a Conflict in the Middle East* (Ariel, Israel: Ariel Center for Policy Research), ACPR Policy Paper 21.

Atherton, Alfred (1990): "The United States and the Suez Crisis: The Uses and Limits of Diplomacy", in: Troen, S.; Shemesh, M. (Eds.): *The Suez-Sinai Crisis 1956: Retrospective and Reappraisal* (London: Frank Cass): 266–273.

Avineri, Shlomo (2013): *Herzel's Vision: Theodor Herzel and the Foundation of the Jewish State* (New York: BlueBridge).

Avram, B. (1958): *The Evolution of the Suez Canal Statute from 1869 to 1956* (Geneva: Droz).

Axworthy, Tom (1985): "E.L.M. Burns: Intellectual Generalship", in: *Toronto Star* (22 September).

Ayoob, Mohammed (2004): "Third World Perspectives on Humanitarian Intervention and International Administration", in: *Global Governance*, 10: 99–118.

Bailey, Sydney Dawson (1960): *The General Assembly of the United Nations: A Study of Procedure and Practice* (New York: Praeger).

Bailey, Sydney Dawson (1988): *The Procedure of the UN Security Council* (Oxford: Clarendon Press).

Baker, P.J. (1923/4): "The Doctrine of Legal Equality of States", in: *British Yearbook of International Law*, 4: 1–15.

Bandung Conference Declaration (1955): "*Official Ten-Point Declaration*" (25 April).

Ban, Ki-moon (2008): "On Responsible Sovereignty: International Cooperation for a Changed World". Address by the UN Secretary-General, SG/SM/11701, Berlin, 15 July 2008.

Barker, J. Craig (2000): *International Law and International Relations* (London: Continuum).

Barnaby, Frank (Ed.) (1991): *Building a More Democratic United Nations* (New York: Routledge).

Barnett, Corelli (2006): "Suez: End of Empire", quoted by Paul Reynolds at: *BBC News Website* (24 July 2006); at: http://news.bbc.co.uk/2/hi/middle_east/5199392.stm.

Barnett, Corelli (2007): "Britain's Delusions of Grandeur". Seminar at Churchill College, Cambridge, 26 October 2007, quoted in: Reynolds, Paul: "Britain's Delusions of Grandeur" (London: BBC News Website (26 October 2007); at: http://news.bbc.co.uk/2/hi/americas/7063374.stm.

Barnett, Michael (1995): "The New United Nations Politics of Peace: From Juridical Sovereignty to Empirical Sovereignty", in: *Global Governance* 1,1: 79–97.

Barnett, Michael N. (1997): "Bringing in the New World Order: Liberalism, Legitimacy, and the United Nations", in: *World Politics*, 49,4: 526–551.

Bar-On, Mordechai (1990): "The Influence of Political Considerations on Operational Planning in the Sinai", in: Troen, Selwyn; Shemesh, Moshe (Eds.): *The Suez-Sinai Crisis 1956: Retrospective and Reappraisal* (London: Frank Cass).

Bar-On, Mordechai (1992): *The Gates of Gaza: Israel's Defence and Foreign Policy 1955–1957* (Tel Aviv: Am Oved).

BBC (2002): *Dead in the Water* (6 June 2002); at: http://www.bbc.co.uk/pressoffice/pressreleases/stories/2002/06_june/08/uss_liberty.shtml.

BBC (2002): New evidence for American cover-up of Israeli attack on US warship, 8 June 2002.

BBC (2015): *UN Peacekeepers 'Barter Goods for Sex'* (11 June 2015); at: https://www.bbc.com/news/world-33089662.

Beaufre, Andre (1969): *The Suez Expedition, 1956* (New York: Faber & Faber).

Bedjaoui, Mohammed (1996): "Preventive Diplomacy: Development, Education, and Human Rights", in: Cahill, Kevin M. (Ed.): *Preventive Diplomacy: Stopping Wars Before they Start* (New York: Basic Books): 35–60.

Begin, Menachim (1951): *The Revolt* (New York: Bell Publishing Co.).

Bell, J. Bowyer (1977): *Terror Out of Zion: Irgun Zvai Leumi, LEHI, and the Palestine Underground, 1929–1949* (New York: St. Martin's Press).

Bellamy, Alex J. (2005): "Responsibility to Protect or Trojan Horse? The Crisis in Darfur and Humanitarian Intervention after Iraq", in: *Ethics and International Affairs* (Summer): 31–34.

Bellamy, Alex J.; Williams, Paul (2005): *Peace Operations and Global Order* (New York: Routledge).

Bellamy, Alex; Williams, Paul (2004): "Conclusion: What Future for Peace Operations? Brahimi and Beyond", in: *International Peacekeeping*, 11,1 (Spring): 182–212.

Bellamy, Alex; Williams, Paul; Griffin, Stuart (2004): *Understanding Peacekeeping* (Cambridge: Polity Press).

Ben-Gurion, David (1956): "Statement to the Knesset by the Prime Minister", Vol. 1–2: 1947–1974, Israeli Ministry of Foreign Affairs (7 November 1956).

Ben-Gurion, David (1956): "Statement to the Knesset", in: "Background: Middle East – UNEF 1.

Ben-Gurion, David (1963): *Israel: Years of Challenge* (New York: Holt, Rinehart and Winston).

Bennet, A. LeRoy (1980): *International Organizations: Principles and Issues* (Englewood Cliffs, N.J.: Prentice-Hall).

Bennett, Ronan (1997): *The Catastrophist* (New York: Simon & Schuster).

Benson, Thimothy (2006): "Suez 1956", in *History Today*, 56,11: 46–47.

Benton, Barbara (Ed.) (1996): *Soldiers for Peace: Fifty Years of United Nations Peacekeeping* (New York: Facts on File).

Bercovitch, J.; Anagnoson, J.T.; Willie, D.L. (1991): "Some Conceptual Issues and Empirical Trends in the Study of Successful Mediation in International Relations", in: *Journal of Peace Research*, 28, 1: 7–17.

Bercuson, David (2010): "There's a New Peace 'Warrior' in Town: Forget Pearsonian Peacekeeping. Canada Should Get Back in the Thick of UN Operations", in: *The Globe and Mail* (2 March 2010).

Berger, Elmer (1945): *The Jewish Dilemma* (New York: Kessinger Publishing).

Berger, Elmer (1993): *Peace for Palestine* (Miami: University of Florida Press).

Bernath, Cliff (2003): "Contemporary and Future Challenges in UN Peacekeeping Operations", in: Langille, H.P.; Keefe, T. (Eds.): *The Future of Peacekeeping: An Experts' Discussion to Contribute to the Dialogue on Foreign Policy* (Vancouver: Liu Institute for Global Issues).

Betts, Raymond F. (1979): *Decolonization* (Lexington: Heath).

Betts, Raymond F. (1979): "The Retreat from Empire", in: *Europe in Retrospect: A Brief History of the Past Two Hundred Years* (London: Heath & Co.): 193–204.

Betts, Raymond F. (2012): "Decolonization: A Brief History of the Word", in Bogaerts, E.; Raben, R. (Eds.): *Beyond Empire and Nation: The Decolonization of African and Asian Societies, 1930s–1970s* (Leiden: Brill Academic Publishers): 23–38.

Bevan, Aneurin (1956): *Commentary in the British Parliament* (House of Commons). London (5 December 1956).

Bhutto, Z.A. (1967): *Peace-Keeping by the United Nations* (Karachi: Pakistan Publishing House).

Black, Edwin (2001): *The Transfer Agreement: The Dramatic Story of the Pact Between the Third Reich and Jewish Palestine* (New York: Carroll & Graf Publishers).

Black, David R.; Rolston, Susan J. (1995): *Peacemaking and Preventive Diplomacy in the New World (Dis) Order*, Centre for Foreign Policy Studies (Halifax: Dalhousie University).

Bland, Douglas; Mason, Peggy (2010): "Definition of Peace Operations", in: *Canada's Contributions to Peace Operations, Past, Present, and Future*, Canadian Peacebuilding Coordinating Committee (Kingston: Queens University).

Bligh, Alexander (2014): "The United Nations Emergency Force (UNEF), 1956–67: Past Experience, Current Lessons", in: *Middle Eastern Studies*, 50,5: 796–809.

Bloch, Brandon (2010): *Local Conflict, Global Intervention: The Origins of the United Nations Peacekeeping Force*, Penn Humanities Forum on Connections (Philadelphia: University of Pennsylvania).

Bloomfield, L.M. (1957): *Egypt, Israel and the Gulf of Aqaba in International Law* (Toronto: Carswell).

Blue, Gregory; Bunton, Martin; Croizier, Ralph (Eds.) (2002): *Colonialism and the Modern World: Selected Studies* (New York: M.E. Sharpe Inc.).

Bobal, R. Thomas (2013): "A Puppet, Even Though He Probably Doesn't Know So: Racial Identity and the Eisenhower Administration's Encounter with Gamal Abdel Nasser and the Arab Nationalist Movement", in: *The International History Review*, 35,5: 943–974; at: http://dx.doi.org/10.1080/07075332.2013.836117.

Bodin, Jean (1575/1992): "On Sovereignty", in: Four Chapters from the *Six Books of the Republic* (*The Catholic Encyclopedia*, 1576 and 1913) (Cambridge: Cambridge University Press, 1992).

Bordman, Corinne (2007): *Peacekeeping and Peace Operations in Our Time: Challenges and Opportunities for Canada* (Halifax: Canadian International Council).

Borg, Mohamed A. (1968): *Suez Canal: Its Political and Strategic Importance, and Its Effects on Anglo-Egyptian Relations, 1914–1956* [in Arabic] (Cairo: Al-Kateb Publishing).

Born, B.; Wycznski, M. (2001): *Warrior Chiefs: Perspectives on Senior Canadian Leaders* (Toronto: Dundurn Press).

Boron, Atilio A. (2005): *Empire and Imperialism: A Critical Reading of Michael Hardt and Antonio Negri* (London: Zed Books).

Boulden, Jane (1991): "Building on the Past: Future Directions for Peacekeeping", in: *Behind the Headlines*, 48,2: 1–17.

Boutellis, A.; Novosseloff, A. (2017): *Road to Better UN? Peace Operations and the Reform Agenda* (New York: International Peace Institute): 1–42.

Boutros-Ghali, Boutros (1992): *An Agenda for Peace: Preventive Diplomacy, Peacemaking and Peace-Keeping*. Report of the Secretary-General, A/47/277 – S/2411 (17 June 1992).

Boutros-Ghali, Boutros (1995): *Supplement Report to the Agenda for Peace* (An Agenda for Peace, an Agenda for Development, and an Agenda for Democratization). Report by the UN Secretary-General, A/50/60 – S/1995/1 (3 January 1995).

Boutros-Ghali, B.; Chlala, Y. (1958): *Suez Canal: 1854–1957* [in Arabic and French] (Alexandria: Egyptian Society of International Law).

Bove, Vincenzo; Ruggeri, Andrea (2019): "Peacekeeping Effectiveness and Blue Helmets' Distance from Locals", in: *Journal of Conflict Resolution*, 63,7: 1,630–1,655.

Bowett, Derek William (1964): *United Nations Forces: A Legal Study* (New York: Praeger).

Bowie, Robert R. (1989): "Eisenhower, Dulles, and the Suez Crisis", in: Louis, W.R.; Owen, Roger (Eds.): *Suez 1956: The Crisis and its Consequences* (Oxford: Clarendon Press).

Braddon, Russell (1973): *Suez: Splitting of a Nation* (London: Collins).

Brahimi, Lakhdar (2000): *Brahimi Report on Peace Operations* A/55/305 – S/2000/809 (21 August 2000).

Brahm, Eric (2004): "Sovereignty", in: Burgess, Guy; Burgess, Heidi (Eds.): *Beyond Intractability*. Conflict Information Consortium (Boulder: University of Colorado), 52,4 (September): 787–824; at: www.beyondintractability.org/essay/sovereignty.

Bratt, Duane; Gionet, Erin (2001): "Evaluating the Brahimi Report", in: *Strategic Datalink # 96* (Toronto: The Canadian Institute of Strategic Studies) (May 2001).

Brayley, Jack (1957): "Norman Swayed Nasser's Decision", in: *Montreal Gazette* (29 April 1957).

Brewer, Anthony (1960): "Theories of Imperialism in Perspective", in: Strachey, John: *The End of Empire* (New York: Random House).

Brierly, James L. (1963): *The Law of Nations: An Introduction to the International Law of Peace* (Oxford: Clarendon Press).

Briggs, Herbert W. (1952): *The Law of Nations: Cases, Documents, and Notes* (New York: Appleton-Century-Crofts).

British Cabinet Document (1956): *British Political Directive to the Allied Commander-in-Chief.* (CAB 134/1225, and CAB 134/815, D (T) C (56) 16th mtg (24 August 1956).

British Cabinet Document (1956): *Concealing the Anglo-French connection with Israel.* (CAB 134/1217, EC (56) 53 (25 September 1956).

Bromley, Anne E. (2011): "In Memoriam: Richard B. Parker", in: *UVA Today*, 7 February 2011 (University of Virginia).

Brown, Davis (1994): "The Role of the United Nations in Peacekeeping and Truce-Monitoring: What are the Applicable Norms", in: *Revue Belge de Droit International* (Brussels: Editions Bruylant), 2: 559–602.

Brown, Derek (2001): "1956: Suez and the End of Empire", in: *The Guardian*, UK (14 March 2001).

Brown, Judith M.; Louis, W. Roger (Eds.) (1999): *The Twentieth Century: Volume IV of the Oxford History of the British Empire* (Oxford: Oxford University Press).

Brown, Philip M. (1915): "The Theory of the Independence and the Equality of States in International Law", in: *American Journal of International Law*, 9: 305–335.

Brownlie, Ian (1963): *International Law and the Use of Force by States* (Oxford: Oxford University Press).

Brownlie, Ian (1979): *Principles of International Law* (Oxford: Clarendon Press).

Buchanan, Patrick J. (2006): *The Death of the Nation State*.

Bunch, Ralph (1960): "Peace Prospects from the UN Perspective", speech at the John Ryan Forum, New York (13 May 1960).

Burke, Roland (2010): *Decolonization and the Evolution of International Human Rights* (Philadelphia: University of Pennsylvania Press).

Burns, E.L.M. (1962): *Between Arab and Israeli* (Toronto: Clark, Irwin & Co.).

Burns, E.L.M. (1967): *Megamurder* (New York: Pantheon Books).

Burns, E.L.M. (1967–68): "The Withdrawal of UNEF and the Future of Peacekeeping", in: *International Journal*, 23 (Winter): 1–17.

Burns, E.L.M. (1970): *General Mud: Memoirs of Two World Wars* (Toronto: Clarke Irwin).

Burns, E.L.M. (1975): "The Third World War: Must Canada Join In?", in: *Current Comments* (Ottawa: Carleton University).

Burns, E.L.M. (1981): "Canada's Role in Peacekeeping in the Middle East", paper presented during the Canadian-Arab Relations Conference, June 1981 (Calgary: University of Calgary, Alberta, Canada).

Burns, William (1985): *Economic Aid and American Policy Toward Egypt, 1955–1981* (New York: State University of New York): 52–53.

Burrows, Bernard A.B. (1952): "Memorandum of Conversation", in: Foreign Relations of the United States, 1952–1954 (IX), US Department of State (1952).

Burrows, Mathew (1986): "*Mission civilisatrice*: French Cultural Policy in the Middle East, 1860–1914", in: *The Historical Journal*, 29,1 (March): 109–135.

Byers, Rod B.; Slack, Michael (Eds.) (1983): *Canada and Peacekeeping: Prospects for the Future* (York: York University Press).

Byroad, Henry (1956): *Diplomatic Note to Dulles*, Foreign Relations of the United States, 1955–57 (XV, 191) (14 March 1956).

Cahill, Kevin M. (Ed.) (1996): *Preventive Diplomacy: Stopping Wars Before They Start* (New York: Basic Books).

Calgary Herald (1956): "The Shameful Day That Canada Ran Out", 1 November.

Callahan, Michael (1999): "Review of Jurgen Osterhammel, *Colonialism: A Theoretical Overview*, in: H-Diplo (April); at: https://www.h-net.org/reviews/showrev.php?id=3045.

Camillieri, Joseph A.; Falk, Jim (1992): *The End of Sovereignty? The Politics of a Shrinking and Fragmented World* (Aldershot: Edward Elgar).

Campbell, John C. (1959): *Defense of the Middle East: Problems of American Policy* (The Council on Foreign Relations) (New York: Harper).

Canada (Armed Forces) (1972): *Peace-Keeping Operations: The Military Observers Handbook* (Ottawa: Armed Forces Headquarters).

Canada (Department of External Affairs) (1956): *Dispatch: London to Ottawa* (Norman Robertson) DCER, (Vol. 22, doc. 74) (27 July 1956).

Canada (Department of External Affairs) (1956): *Pearson to Robertson*, DEA-50134-40 Telegram M-1311 (30 October 1956).

Canada (Department of External Affairs) (1956): *Eden to St. Laurent*, PCO-I-60-2(a) (30 October 1956).

Canada (Department of External Affairs) (1956): *St. Laurent to Eden*, PCO-1-60-2 (a) (31 October 1956).

Canada (Department of External Affairs) (1956): *Robertson to Pearson*, DEA-50134-40 (2 November 1956).

Canada (Department of External Affairs) (1956): *Eden to St. Laurent*, PCO-I-60-2 (a) (6 November 1956).

Canada (Department of External Affairs) (1956): *Heeney to Pearson*, DEA-50134-40 (31 October 1956).

Canada (Department of External Affairs) (1967): *Department of External Affairs*, vol. 21596 (20 May 1967).

Canada (Department of External Affairs) (1970): *Foreign Policy for Canadians* (Ottawa: 1970).

Canada (Government) (1956): *Extract from Cabinet Conclusions*, PCO-105 (18 October 1956).

Canada (Government) (1956): *Extract from Cabinet Conclusions*, PCO-112 (31 October 1956).

Canada (IBID) (1943): *Officer Assessment File: Ralston Papers*, Vol. 54 (Ottawa: IBID Report).

Canada (Parliament) (1970): *Eighth Report of the House of Commons Standing Committee on External Affairs and National Defence Respecting United Nations and Peacekeeping* (Ottawa: 1970).

Canada (Parliament) (1993): *Meeting New Challenges: Canada's Response to a New Generation of Peacekeeping* (Report of the Standing Senate Committee on Foreign Affairs) (Ottawa: 1993).

Canadian Mysteries (1957a): "Suez Crisis"; at: https://www.canadianmysteries.ca/sites/norman/coldwarhotwars/suezcrisis/indexen.html.

Canadian Mysteries (1957b): "Norman on the Suez Crisis and Israel"; at: https://www.canadianmysteries.ca/sites/norman/coldwarhotwars/suezcrisis/5579en.html.

Canadian Mysteries (1957c): Death of a Diplomat: "Murder by Slander?", https://www.canadianmysteries.ca/sites/norman/archives/newspaperormagazinearticle/indexen.html

Caplan, Neil (1997): *Futile Diplomacy: The United Nations, the Great Powers, and the Middle East Peacemaking, 1948–1954* (London: Frank Cass).

Caplan, Neil (1997): *Futile Diplomacy: Operation Alpha and the Failure of Anglo-American Coercive Diplomacy in the Arab-Israeli Conflict 1954–1956, Vol. 4* (London: Frank Cass): 93.

Caradon, Lord Hugh Foot (1976): "The Shape of Peace in the Middle East: An Interview with Lord H.F. Caradon", in: *Journal of Palestine Studies*, 5,3 & 5,4 (Spring/Summer).

Caradon, Lord Hugh F. (1977): "A Tragedy for Jew and Arab", in: *The Guardian* (6 November 1977).

Carr, Robert (2004): "From Balfour to Suez: Britain's Zionist Misadventure", *History Review*, 50.

Carroll, Michael K. (2005): "From Peace (Keeping) to War: The United Nations and the Withdrawal of UNEF", in: *Middle East Review of International Affairs*, 9,2 (June).

Carroll, Michael K. (2009): *Pearson's Peacekeepers: Canada and the United Nations Emergency Force, 1956–67* (Vancouver: University of British Columbia Press).

Cassese, Antonio (Ed.) (1978): *United Nations Peace-Keeping: Legal Essays* (The Hague: Sijthoff & Noordhoff).

Cassese, Antonio (Ed.) (1986): *The Current Legal Regulation of the Use of Force* (Boston: Martinus Nijhoff).

Castro, Fidel Ruz (1995): *Address to the UN General Assembly*, UN A/50/PV.35 (22 October 1995).

Cattan, Henry (1973): *Palestine and International Law: The Legal Aspects of the Arab-Israeli Conflict* (London: Longman).

Chandler, David (1999): *Bosnia – Faking Democracy after Dayton* (London: Pluto Press).

Chandler, David (2004): "The Responsibility to Protect? Imposing the 'Liberal' Peace", in: *International Peacekeeping*, 11,1: 59–81.

Chapman, Dudley H. (1958): "International Law and the United Nations Emergency Force: Legal Status", in: *Michigan Law Review*, 57,1 (November): 56–81.

Chase, Sean (2008): "Ambush in the Desert", in: *Pembroke Daily Observer* (27 November 2008).

Chatterjee, Partha (1986): *Nationalist Thought and the Colonial World: Derivative Discourse?* (London: Zed Books).

Chesterman, Simon (2001): *Just War or Just Peace?: Humanitarian Intervention and International Law* (Oxford: Oxford University Press).

Childers, Erskine B. (1962): *The Road to Suez: A Study of Western-Arab Relations* (London: MacGibbon & Kee).

Chomsky, Noam (1999): *Fateful Triangle: The United States, Israel, and the Palestinians* (Montreal: Black Rose Books).

Choueiri, Youssef M. (2000): *Arab Nationalism: A History, Nation and State in the Arab World* (Oxford: Blackwell).

Ciechanski, Jerzy (1996): "Enforcement Measures Under Chapter VII of the UN Charter: UN Practice after the Cold Water", in: *International Peacekeeping*, 3,4 (Winter): 82–104.

Clark, Joe (1990): "Peacekeeping and Canadian Foreign Policy", in: *Department of External Affairs*, Statement 90/65 (Toronto: 8 November 1990).

Clark, Grenville; Sohn, Louis B. (1966): *World Peace Through World Law: Two Alternative Plans*, 3rd Edn (Cambridge: Harvard University Press).

Claude, Jr., Inis L. (1959): *Swords into Plowshares: The Problems and Progress of International Organization* (New York: Random House).

Cobban, Helena (1989): "The US-Israeli Relationship in the Reagan Era", in: *Conflict Quarterly* 9,2 (Spring).

Cobbett, Pitt (1909): *Cases and Opinions in International Law*, 1,3 (London): 50.

Cockburn, Andrew; Cockburn, Leslie (1991): *Dangerous Liaison: The Inside Story of the US-Israeli Covert Relationship* (New York: Harper Collins Publishers).

Cohen, Andrew (2009): *Lester B. Pearson* (Toronto: Penguin).

Cohen, Maxwell (1957): "The United Nations Emergency Force: A Preliminary View", in: *International Journal*, 21 (Spring).

Cohen, Maxwell (1967–68): "The Demise of UNEF", in: *International Journal*, 23 (Winter): 18–51.

Coicaud, Jean-Marc; Myers, Joanne J. (2007): *Beyond the National Interest: The Future of UN Peacekeeping and Multilateralism in an Era of US Primacy* (Washington: Institute of Peace).

Conetta, Carl; Knight, Charles (1995): *Vital force: A Proposal for the Overhaul of the UN Peace Operations System and for the Creation of a UN Legion* (Cambridge: Commonwealth Institute).

Connell, John (1957): *The Most Important Country: The True Story of the Suez Crisis and the Events Leading to It* (London: Cassell).

Connolly, Amanda (2016): "Former General Lewis MacKenzie Lauds Lapse of Term Peacekeeping", in: *Politics* (20 September 2016); at: https://ipolitics.ca/2016/09/20/former-general-lewis-mackenzie-lauds-lapse-of-term-peacekeeping.

Constantinople Convention (1888): *Convention Respecting the Free Navigation of the Suez Maritime Canal* (Constantinople: 29 October 1888).

Copeland, Miles (1969): *The Game of Nations: The Amorality of Power Politics* (London: Weidenfeld & Nicolson).

Cordier, Andrew C.; Foote, Wilder; Harrelson, Max (Eds.) (1973): *Public Papers of the Secretaries-General of the United Nations*, 3: Dag Hammarskjold, 1956–1957 (New York: Columbia University Press).

Coulon, Jocelyn (1998): *Soldiers of Diplomacy: The United Nations, Peacekeeping, and the New World Order* (Toronto: University of Toronto Press).

Cox, David (Ed.) (1991): *The Use of Force by the Security Council for Enforcement and Deterrent Purposes: A Conference Report* (Canadian Centre for Arms Control and Disarmament).

Cox, David (1993): *Exploring an Agenda for Peace: Issues Arising from the Report of the Secretary-General* (Ottawa: Canadian Centre for Global Security).

Cox, Katherine E. (1999): "Beyond Self-Defense: United Nations Peacekeeping Operations and the Use of Force", in: *Denver Journal of International Law and Policy*, 27 (Spring): 239–273.

Cristol, A. Jay (2002): *The Liberty Incident: The 1967 Israeli Attack on the US Navy Spy Ship* (Ann Arbor: The University of Michigan & Brassey's Inc.).

Curtis, Willie (1994): "The Inevitable Slide into Coercive Peacekeeping", in: *Defense Analysis*, 10,3: 305–321.

Daalder, Ivo; Steinberg, James (2005): "Preventive War: A Useful Tool", in: *Los Angeles Times* (4 December 2005).

Dag Hammarskjold Foundation (1999): Seminar Report, May 1999: *The United Nations and Peacekeeping: Recent Experiences and Future Challenges* (Uppsala: Dag Hammarskjold Foundation).

Dallaire, Roméo (2003): *Shake Hands with the Devil: The Failure of Humanity in Rwanda* (Toronto: Random House).

Dallaire, Romeo A. (1996): "The Changing Role of UN Peacekeeping Forces: The Relationship between UN Peacekeepers and NGOs in Rwanda", in: Whitman, Jim and Pocock, David (Eds.): *After Rwanda: The Coordination of United Nations Humanitarian Assistance* (New York: St. Martin's Press).

Darby, Phillip (2009): "Rolling Back the Frontiers of Empire: Practicing the Postcolonial", in: *International Peacekeeping*, 16,5 (November): 699–716.

Darwin, John (1999): "An Undeclared Empire: The British in the Middle East, 1818–39", in: *The Journal of Imperial and Commonwealth History*, 27,2 (May): 159–176.

Darwin, John (1981): *Britain, Egypt and the Middle East Imperial Policy in the Aftermath of War 1918–1922* (London: Macmillan).

Darwin, John (1988): *Britain and Decolonization: The Retreat from Empire in the Post-War World* (London: Macmillan).

Darwin, John (1991): *The End of the British Empire: The Historical Debate* (London: Blackwell).

Darwin, John (1999): "Decolonization and the End of Empire", in: Winks, Robin W. (Ed.): *The Oxford History of the British Empire: Historiography, Vol V* (Oxford: Oxford University Press).

Davidson, Basil (1992): *The Black Man's Burden: Africa and the Curse of the Nation-State* (New York: Random House).

Dawisha, A. I. (1976): *Egypt in the Arab World: The Elements of Foreign Policy* (New York: Macmillan).

Dayan, Moshe (1965): *Diary of the Sinai Campaign* (New York: Schocken Books).

Dayan, Moshe (1976): *Story of My Life: An Autobiography* (New York: Morrow).

de Coning, Cedric; Peter, Mateja (Eds.) (2019): *United Nations Peace Operations in a Changing Global Order* (Cham, Switzerland: Palgrave Macmillan).

de Coning, Cedric; Detzel, Julian; Hojem, Petter (2008): *UN Peacekeeping Operations Capstone Doctrine: Report of the TfP Oslo Doctrine Seminar* (14–15 May 2008, Oslo, Norway) (Oslo: NUPI).

De Cuellar, Javier Perez (1998): "Conceptual Framework", A/44/1, quoted in: Fetherston, A.B., *Towards a Theory of United Nations Peacekeeping* (New York: St. Martin's Press).

de Jouvenel, Bertrand (1957): *Sovereignty: An Inquiry into the Political Good* (Chicago: University of Chicago Press).

de Martens, Friedrich (1920): As quoted in: Dickson, E.D., *The Equality of States in International Law* (Cambridge: Harvard University Press): 25.

Delaney, Douglas E. (2005): *The Soldier's General: Bert Hoffmeister at War* (Vancouver: UBC Press).

Dershowitz, Alan (2003): *The Case for Israel* (New York: John Wiley).

D'Escoto, Miguel (2009): *UN General Assembly Debates of the R2P* (July and September 2009).

Dessouki, A. E. Hillal (1989): "Nasser and the Struggle for Independence", in: Louis, W. Roger; Owen, Roger (Eds.): *Suez 1956: The Crisis and its Consequences* (Oxford: Clarendon Press).

Dickinson, Edwin D. (1920): *The Equality of States in International Law* (Cambridge: Harvard University Press).

Diehl, Paul F. (1989): "A Permanent UN Peacekeeping Force: An Evaluation", in: *Security Dialogue*, 20,1: 27–36.

Diehl, Paul F. (1994): *International Peacekeeping* (Baltimore: Johns Hopkins University Press).

Diehl, Paul F.; Balas, Alexandru (2014): *Peace Operations* (Cambridge: Polity Press).

Diehl, Paul F.; Druckman, Daniel (2010): *Evaluating Peace Operations* (Boulder: Lynne Rienner Publishers).

Dillon, Emile Joseph (1920): *The Inside Story of the Peace Conference* (New York: Harper).

Dodd, Thomas (1963): "Is the United Nations Worth Saving?", in: Moore, Jr., Raymond (Ed.): *The United Nations Reconsidered* (Columbia: University of South Carolina Press).

Dombroski, Kenneth R. (2010 & 2007): *Peacekeeping in the Middle East as an International Regime* (New York: Routledge).

Dooley, Howard J. (1989): "Great Britain's Last Battle in the Middle East: Notes on Cabinet Planning during the Suez Crisis of 1956", in: *International History Review*, 11,3 (August): 486–517.

Doran, Michael (2016): *Ike's Gamble: America's Rise to Dominance in the Middle East* (New York: Free Press).

Doyle, John (2013): "A Tale of Sarajevo", in: *The Globe and Mail* (Toronto) (9 November 2013).

Duara, Prasenjit (Ed.) (2004): *Decolonization: Perspectives from Now and Then* (New York: Routledge).

Duara, Prasenjit (Ed.) (2004): "Introduction: The Decolonization of Asia and Africa in the Twentieth Century", in: *Decolonization: Perspectives from Now and Then* (New York: Routledge).

Duffield, Mark (2001): *Global Governance and the New Wars: The Merging of Development and Security* (London: Zed Books).

Duke, Simon (1994): "The United Nations and Intra-State Conflict", in: *International Peacekeeping*, 1,4 (Winter): 375–393.

Dulles, John Foster (1953): "Statement", in: *The New York Times* (2 June 1953).

Dulles, John Foster (1956): "Memorandum from the Secretary of State to the President", in: *Foreign Relations of the United States, 1955–57*, XV, (Washington DC: US Government) (28 March 1956).

Dulles, John Foster (1956): "Diplomatic Note to Sir Roger Makins", PRO PREM 11/1018 (30 July 1956).

Dulles, John Foster (1957): "Memo by the Secretary of State", *Foreign Relations of the United States, 1957:* 142–144.

Dulles, John Foster (1957): *US Department of State Bulletin* (11 March 1957): 392–393.

Dulles, John Foster (1957): "Statement", *US Senate Committee on Foreign Relations*, Vol. IX, 85th Congress, 1st Sess., 1957.

Dulles, John F. (1955): Alpha Speech – Council of Foreign Relations, New York City, 26 August 1955 (1)–(4) [Dulles statement on an Arab-Israeli settlement (26 August 1955)]. Foreign Relations of the United States, 1955–1957, Arab-Israeli Dispute, 1955, Volume XIV.

Durch, William J.; Holt, Victoria K.; Earle, Caroline R.; Shanahan, Moira K. (2003): *The Brahimi Report and the Future of UN Peace Operations* (Washington DC: Stimson Center).

Durkheim, Emile (1984): *The Division in Labour in Society* (New York: Free Press).

Eayrs, James (1964): *The Commonwealth and Suez: A Documentary Survey* (London: Oxford University Press).

Eban, Abba (1956): "Statement". UN General Assembly, Plenary Meeting 565. A/PV.565 (4 November 1956).

Eban, Abba (1956): "Address to the UN General Assembly", UN Official Records, 592nd Meeting (23 November 1956).

Eban, Abba (1967): "Statement". UN General Assembly, A/pv, 1526, at 38.

Eden, Anthony (1953): *Egypt: The Alternatives*, (Cabinet Memorandum). C (53) 65, CAB

Eden, Anthony (1955): *British Cabinet Minutes*, 34, 55, 8 (4 October 1955).

Eden, Anthony (1955): *Guildhall Speech on the Arab-Israeli Conflict* (the ALPHA Plan); at: https://ecf.org.il/issues/issue/4.

Eden, Anthony (1957): "Brook Papers: Eden to Brook, 16 January 1957", quoted in Kyle, Keith: "The Mandarins' Mandarin: Sir Norman Brook, Secretary of the Cabinet", in: Kelly, S.; Gorst, A. (Eds.): *Whitehall and the Suez Crisis* (London: Frank Cass).

Eden, Anthony (1960): *Full Circle: The Memoirs of Anthony Eden* (London: Houghton Mifflin).

Eden, Anthony (1965): *The Eden Memoirs: The Reckoning* (London: Cassell).

Egyptian Chronicles (1956): "Jubilation as Anglo-French Troops Leave Port Said" (16 February 1957): (7).

Eisenhower, Dwight (1956, 1988): "Letter to Prime Minister Anthony Eden", *Foreign Relations of the United States* (C), Document, 35 (31 July 1956): 69–71.

Eisenhower, Dwight (1956): "Statement". US National Security Council (9 August 1956).

Eisenhower, Dwight (1956): "Letter of Appeal to the Prime Minister of Israel Urging Withdrawal from Egyptian Territory". White House Press Release, (7 November 1956), and Department of State Release (19 November 1956): 797–798.

Eisenhower, Dwight (1957): "Address to a Joint Session of Congress", United States Department of State, United States Policy in the Middle East, Washington DC (5 January 1957).

Elaraby, Nabil (1968): "United Nations Peacekeeping by Consent: A Case Study of the Withdrawal of the United Nations Emergency Force", in: *Journal of International Law and Politics*, 1, 2.

Elaraby, Nabil A. (1983): "UN Peacekeeping: The Egyptian Experience", in: Wiseman, Henry (Ed.): *Peacekeeping: Appraisals and Proposals* (New York: Pergamon Press).

El-Bouzaidi, Imane D. (2011): "The United Nations Truce Supervision Organization (UNTSO), Does This Mark the End to the Observer Mission Model?", in: *Unmasking Illusions* (April 2012); at: http://bouzaidi.blogspot.com/2012/04/united-nations-truce-supervision.html.

Elganzoury, Abdelazim A. (1978): *Evolution of the Peacekeeping Powers of the General Assembly of the United Nations* (Cairo: General Egyptian Book Organization).

El-Hefnawy, Mostafa (1958): *The Suez Canal Story* [in Arabic] (Cairo: A. Mekheimar Books).

Eliasson, Jan (1996): "Establishing Trust in the Healer: Preventive Diplomacy and the Future of the United Nations", in: Cahill, Kevin M. (Ed.): *Preventive Diplomacy: Stopping Wars Before They Start* (New York: Basic Books): 318–343.

Elkins, Caroline (2005): *Imperial Reckoning: The Untold Story of Britain's Gulag in Kenya* (New York: Henry Holt & Co.).

Elkins, Caroline (2014): *Britain's Gulag: The Brutal End of Empire in Kenya* (New York: Vintage Publishing).

Elmessiri, Abdel Wahab (1977): *The Land of Promise: A Critique of Political Zionism* (New Brunswick, N.J.: North American, Inc.).

Evans, Gareth; Sahnoun, Mohamed (2001): *United Nations Report of the International Committee on Intervention and State Sovereignty: The Responsibility to Protect* (Ottawa: IDRC) (December 2001).

Evans, Gareth; Sahnoun, Mohamed (2002): "The Responsibility to Protect", in: *Foreign Affairs*, 81,6, (Nov/Dec 2002): 99–110.

Evans, Gareth; Stroehlein, Andrew (2007): "A Responsibility to Protect: The World's View", in: *International Crisis Group* and *Open Democracy* (April 2007).

Eveland, Wilbur C. (1980): *Ropes of Sand: America's Failure in the Middle East* (New York: W. Norton & Co.).

Everly, Steve (1996): "Truman OK'd Sabotage Plot", in: *The Kansas City Star* (Kansas City, USA), (25 February 1996): Section A-1.

Falk, Richard A. (1970): *The Status of Law in International Society* (Princeton: Princeton University Press).

Fanon, Frantz (1963): *The Wretched of the Earth* (New York: Grove Press).

Farajallah, Samaan Boutros (1969–1970): "UN Peace-Keeping Operations", Lecture delivered during the Proceedings of the Egyptian Society of International Law, Cairo, (13 February); published in: *Etudes en Droit International*, II (Cairo: Egyptian Society of International Law).

Farr, Warner D. (1999): *The Third Temple's Holy of Holies: Israel's Nuclear Weapons* (Maxwell, Alabama: USAF).

Fawcett, Eric; Newcombe, Hanna (Eds.) (1995): *United Nations Reform: Looking Ahead after Fifty Years* (Toronto: University of Toronto).

Fawzi, Mahmoud (1956): "Address to the UN General Assembly", *UN Official Records*, 597th Meeting (27 November 1956).

Fawzi, Mahmoud (1957): *Egyptian Declaration on the Suez Canal and the Arrangements for its Operations* (Letter by Egypt's Foreign Minister to the UN Security Council), A/3576 – S/3818 (24 April 1957).

Fawzi, Mahmoud (1957): *Egypt's Letter of Accession* (to the Jurisdiction of the International Court of Justice Relating to the Suez Canal Operations) (The Hague: ICJ Article 36, Para 2) (18 July 1957).

Fawzi, Mohamed (1967): "Letter to Gen. Rikhye", S/0316, Box 9, File 2, (UN-UAR Letters) (17 May 1967).

Feinstein, Lee; Slaughter, Anne-Marie (2004): "Duty to Prevent", in: *Foreign Affairs* (January/February 2004 Issue).

Ferencz, Benjamin B. (1982): "The Future of Human Rights in International Jurisprudence: An Optimistic Appraisal", in: *Hofstra Law Review*, 10,2.

Ferris, Jesse (2012): *Nasser's Gamble: How Intervention in Yemen Caused the Six-Day War and the Decline of Egyptian Power* (Princeton: Princeton University Press).

Fetherston, A.B. (1994): *Towards a Theory of United Nations Peacekeeping* (New York: St. Martin's Press).

Fetherston, A.B. (2000): "Peacekeeping, Conflict Resolution and Peacebuilding: A Reconsideration of Theoretical Frameworks", in: *International Peacekeeping*, 7,1 (Spring): 190–218.

Fieldhouse, D.K. (1976): "Imperialism and the Periphery", in: Wright, Harrison M. (Ed.): *The New Imperialism: Analysis of Late-Nineteenth-Century Expansion* (Toronto: Heath Publications).

Figgis, John Neville (1907/1916): *Studies of Political Thought from Gerson to Grotius, 1414–1625* (Cambridge: Cambridge University Press).

Findlay, Trevor (2002): *The Use of Force in UN Peace Operations* (Stockholm and Oxford: Stockholm International Peace Research Institute [SIPRI] and Oxford University Press).

Finkelstein, Norman (1995): *Image and Reality of the Israeli-Palestine Conflict* (London: Verso).

Finkelstein, Norman (2005): *Beyond Chutzpah: On the Misuse of Anti-Semitism and the Abuse of History* (Berkley: University of California Press).

Finkelstein, Norman G. (2000): *The Holocaust Industry: Reflections on the Exploitation of Jewish Suffering* (London: Verso).

Finnish Ambassador (1956): Letter: "Official Position addressed to the UN Secretary-General", A/3302/Add 21 (13 November 1956).

Fisher, Roger (1967): "Editorial Opinion", in: *New York Times* (9 June 1967).

Foote, Wilder (Ed.) (1962): *Servant of the Peace: A Selection of the Speeches and Statements of Dag Hammarskjold, Secretary-General of the United Nations, 1953–1961* (New York: Harper & Row).

Foreign Relations of the United States, 1952, US Department of State. Memorandum of Conversation (by Frank Ortiz – MEDO). Participants: B.A.B. Burrows (British Embassy), J. Jernegan, and F. Ortiz (State Department), Vol. IX, Part 1, Document 106, (two parts) Circular 780.5/11-1052 (Washington: Government Printing Office, 10 November 1952).

Foreign Relations of the United States, 1952–1954, US National Security Council, The Near and Middle East, Statement of Policy, "Removal and Destruction of Oil Facilities, Equipment and Supplies in the Middle East", Volume IX, Part 1, Document 219 (Washington: Government Printing Office, 23 July 1954).

Foreign Relations of the United States, 1953, US Department of State, Statement by Secretary Dulles, Volume IX, 1952–1954, 831–835 (Washington: Government Printing Office).

Foreign Relations of the United States, 1954, US National Security Council, The Near and Middle East, Middle East Policy Paper, Document 5428 (Washington: Government Printing Office, 23 July 1954).

Foreign Relations of the United States, 1955–1957, US Department of State, Near East., Volumes XII, XIII, XV, XVI, XV11, Documents 187, 164, 241, 590, 143, 225, 229, 234, and 298 (Washington: Government Printing Office).

Foreign Relations of the United States, 1956, US Department of State, Memorandum of Conversation between Prime Minister Eden and Secretary of State Dulles in Washington, 31 January 1956, Document 54 (Washington: Government Printing Office, 1988).

Foreign Relations of the United States, 1956, US Department of State, Memorandum of Conversation between British Prime Minister Anthony Eden and US Secretary of State John Dulles, 10 Downing Street, London, 1 August 1956, 12:45 p.m., Document 42: 98–99. (Washington: Government Printing Office, 1988).

Foreign Relations of the United States, 1957, US Department of State, Memorandum of Conversation: US Secretary of State John Dulles, Israeli Ambassador Abba Eban, and Israeli Minister Reuven Shiloah, Washington, 3:30 p.m. (Washington: Government Printing Office), (24 February 1957).

Freiberger, Steven Z. (1982): *Dawn over Suez: The Rise of American Power in the Middle East, 1953–1957* (Chicago: Ivan Dee).

Frohlich, Manuel (2005): "Dag Hammarskjold Revisited: International Law and Institutions in a Constitutional Perspective", in: *Report of the Dag Hammarskjold Symposium on Respecting International Law and International Institutions* (Uppsala: Uppsala University).

Frohlich, Manuel (2008): *Political Ethics and the United Nations: Dag Hammarskjold as Secretary-General* (Routledge: New York).

Frye, William R. (Ed.) (1957): *A United Nations Peace Force* (New York: Oceana).

Fulbright, J. William (1963): "A Concert of Free Nations", in: *International Organization*, 17,3 (Summer): 787–803.

Furedi, Frank (1994): *Colonial Wars and the Politics of Third World Nationalism* (London: Tauris).

Gallagher, John (1982): "The Decline, Revival and Fall of the British Empire", in: Seal, Anil (Ed.) *The Ford Lectures* (Cambridge: Cambridge University Press).

Gallagher, John; Robinson, Ronald (1953): "The Imperialism of Free Trade", in: *Economic History Review, Second Series*, 6,1: 1–15.

Galtung, Ingrid; Galtung, Johan (1966): "Some Factors Affecting Local Acceptance of a UN Force: A Pilot Project Report from Gaza", in: *International Peace Research Institute* Publication No. 17-1, PRIO, Oslo, (1966): 1–25.

Galtung, Johan (1970): *Peace Theory, Peace Practice and the International Peace Academy* (Oslo: International Peace Research Institute, PRIO).

Galtung Johan (1972): "Three Approaches to Peace: Peacekeeping, Peacemaking and Peacebuilding", in: *The True World: A Transnational Perspective* (Oslo: International Peace Research Institute).

Galtung, Johan (2014): "Needed: Regime Change in Israel", in: *Palestine Israel Journal*, 19,3 (2014).

Gagnon, Mona H. (1967): "Peace Forces and the Veto: The Relevance of Consent", in: *International Organization*, 21,4 (Autumn).

Gandhi, Mahatma (2015): *The Collected Works of Mahatma Gandhi* (New Delhi: Government of India Ministry of Information and Broadcasting).

Garvey, Jack I. (1970): "United Nations Peacekeeping and Host State Consent", in: *The American Journal of International Law*, 64,2 (April): 241–269.

Gaubatz, Kurt Taylor (2012): *Democratic States and the Sovereign Equality Norm* (Stanford: Stanford University Press): 1–36.

Gerges, Fawaz Z. (2001): "Egypt and the 1948 War: Internal Conflict and Regional Ambition", in: Rogan, E.; Shlaim, A. (Eds.): *The War for Palestine: Rewriting the History of 1948* (Cambridge: Cambridge University Press).

Ghaleb, Morad (2001): Excerpts from: *The Memoirs of Dr Morad Ghaleb* [in Arabic]), (Cairo: Al-Ahram).

Ghali, Mona (1993): "United Nations Truce Supervision Organization", in: Durch, W.J. (Ed.): *The Evolution of UN Peacekeeping: Case Studies and Comparative Analysis* (New York: St. Martin's Press).

Ghilan, Maxim (1974): *How Israel Lost its Soul* (Middlesex: Penguin Books).

Gibbs, David N. (1997): "Is Peacekeeping a New Form of Imperialism?", in: *International Peacekeeping*, 4,1 (Spring).

Gilmour, David (1986): "Eden and Suez", in: *London Review of Books*, 8,22 (18 December 1986).

Gizewski, Peter (Ed.) (1998): *Non-Proliferation, Arms Control and Disarmament: Enhancing Existing Regimes and Exploring New Dimensions* (Toronto: York University Press).

Globe and Mail (1959): "3 Canadians, Israeli Girls, Held in Gaza", 21 January 1959 (Toronto).

Goodman, Major Charles E. (2014): *Conversations with the Author*, 28 December 2014 (Victoria, BC, Canada).

Goodrich, L.M.; Rosner, G. (1957): "The United Nations Emergency Force", *International Organization*, XI, 3 (Summer).

Gordon, J. King (1985): "A Soldier for Peace: A Tribute in Memory of General E.L.M. Burns", in: *The Citizen* (Ottawa) (24 September).

Gorst, Anthoy; Johnman, Lewis (1997): "Introduction", in: *The Suez Crisis* (London: Routledge).

Gray, Christine (2004): *International Law and the Use of Force: Foundations of Public International Law* (New York: Oxford University Press).

Green, Stephen J. (1984): *Taking Sides: America's Secret Relations with Militant Israel* (New York: William Morrow & Co).

Grimal, Henri (1978): *Decolonization: The British, French, Dutch, and Belgian Empires, 1919–1963* (London: Routledge).

Gross, Leo (1948): "The Peace of Westphalia 1648–1948", in: *American Journal of International Law*, 42,1: 20–41.

Grove, Eric; Rohan, Sally (2000): "The Limits of Opposition: Admiral Earl Mountbatten of Burma, First Sea Lord and Chief of Naval Staff", in: Kelly, Saul; Gorst, Anthony (Eds.): *Whitehall and the Suez Crisis* (London: Frank Cass): 98–116.

Guéhenno, Jean-Marie (2000): *The End of the Nation-State* (Minneapolis: University of Minnesota Press).

Guéhenno, Jean-Marie (2004): *Challenges in UN Peacekeeping Operations* (New York: Carnegie Council).

Guterres, Antonio (2017): *Restructuring the United Nations Peace and Security Pillar*. (The HIPPO Report). Reports of the Secretary-General A/72/525 (13 October 2017) & A/72/L.33 (15 December 2017).

Gwertzman, Bernard (1981): "US and Israel Sign Strategic Accord to Counter Soviet", in: *New York Times* (1 December 1981); at: https://www.nytimes.com/1981/12/01/world/us-israel-sign-strategic-accord-counter-soviet-text-memorandum-page-a14.html.

Hahn, Peter L. (1991): *The United States, Great Britain, and Egypt, 1945–1956: Strategy and Diplomacy in the Early Cold War* (Chapel Hill, N.C.: University of North Carolina Press).

Hahn, Peter L. (2004): *Caught in the Middle East: US Policy Toward the Arab-Israeli Conflict* (Raleigh, N.C.: University of North Carolina Press).

Haig, Alexander M. Jr. (1966): *Military Intervention: A Case Study of Britain's Use of Force in the 1956 Suez Crisis* (Carlisle Barracks, PA: US Army War College).

Halderman, John W. (1968): "The Middle East Crisis: Test of International Law", in: *Law and Contemporary Problems*, 33,1 (Winter).

Halkin, Hillel (2014): *Jabotinsky: A Life* (New Haven: Yale University Press).

Hall, Ian (2011): "The Revolt Against the West: Decolonization and Its Repercussions in British International Thought, 1945–75", in: *International History Review*, 33,1: 43–64.

Hamilton, Rebecca J. (2006): "The Responsibility to Protect: From Document to Doctrine – But What of Implementation?", in: *Harvard Human Rights Journal*, 19: 289–297.

Hammarskjold, Dag (1954): *Statement to the Press*, quoted in Annan, Kofi (2012): *Intervention: A Life in War and Peace* (New York: The Penguin Press).

Hammarskjold, Dag (1956): *Declaration of Conscience*: Address to the UN Security Council, 11th year, 751st Meeting. New York; UN Official Records (31 October 1956).

Hammarskjold, Dag (1956–1957): Reports of the UN Secretary-General concerning the Suez Crisis:

1. "First Report", A/3267 (3 November 1956).
2. "Second Report", A/3284 (4 November 1956).
3. "Final Second Report" (First Report on the Creation of an Emergency International Force), A/3289 (4 November 1956).
4. "Third Report, On Cease-Fire Developments", A/3296 (5 November 1956).
5. "Final Report" (Second Report on the International Force), A/3302 & Adds 1–6 (6 November 1956).

6. "Good Faith Agreement" (Report on the Presence and Functioning of UNEF), A/3375 (20 November 1956).
7. "Clearing the Suez Canal", First Report, A/3376 (20 November 1956).
8. "Clearing the Suez Canal", Second Report, A/3492 (10 January 1957).
9. "Report on Restoring the Status Quo" A/3512 (24 January 1957).
10. "Status of Forces Agreement", A/3526 (8 February 1957).
11. "Report on the Experience Derived from UNEF", A/3943 (9 October 1957).

Hammarskjold, Dag (1957): *UN Response to the Egyptian Declaration on the Suez Canal* (S/3819).

Hammarskjold, Dag (1957, 1967): *Secret Aide-Memoire of the Secretary-General* (originally dated 5 August 1957), in: *New York Times*, 19 June 1967, and *International Legal Materials*, 6,3 (May–June 1967): 595–602.

Hannum, Hurst (1990): *Autonomy, Sovereignty, and Self-determination: The Accommodation of Conflicting Rights* (Philadelphia: University of Pennsylvania Press).

Hansen, Wibke; Ramsbotham, Oliver; Woodhouse, Tom (2004): *Hawks and Doves: Peacekeeping and Conflict Resolution* (Berlin: Berghof Research Centre for Constructive Conflict Management).

Happold, Matthew (2013): "International Humanitarian Law and Human Rights Law", in: Henderson, Christian; White, Nigel (Eds.): *Research Handbook on International Conflict and Security Law* (Cheltenham, UK: Edward Elgar Publishing).

Harbi, Mohamed (1975): "The Movement of Arab Unity", in: Wallerstein, Immanuel (Ed.): *World Inequality: Origins and Perspectives on the World System* (Montreal: Black Rose Books): 129–138.

Harbottle, Michael (1991): *What is Proper Soldiering?: A Study on New Perspectives for the Future Uses of Armed Forces in the 1990s* (Oxford: The Centre for International Peacebuilding).

Harbottle, Michael N. (1970): *The Impartial Soldier* (Oxford: Oxford University Press).

Harbottle, Michael N. (1971): *The Blue Berets: A Study of UN Peacekeeping Operations* (London: Leo Cooper).

Harootunian, Harry (2004): *The Empire's New Clothes: Paradigm Lost, and Regained* (Chicago: Prickly Paradigm Press).

Harvard Policy Brief (2007): "From Legal Theory to Policy Tools: International Humanitarian Law and International Human Rights Law in the Occupied Palestinian Territory", Policy Brief (May 2007), in: *Program on Humanitarian Policy and Conflict Research* (Boston: Harvard University).

Harvey, David (2003): *The New Imperialism* (Oxford: Oxford University Press).

Hashmi, Sohail H. (Ed.) (1997): *State Sovereignty: Change and Persistence in International Relations* (University Park: Pennsylvania State University Press).

Hass, Ernst (1964): *Beyond the Nation-State: Functionalism and International Organization* (Stanford: Stanford University Press).

Hazboun, Norma N.M. (1994): The Resettlement of the Palestinian Refugees of the Gaza Strip (Leeds: The University of Leeds).

Hazen, Jennifer M. (2007): "Can Peacekeepers Be Peacebuilders?", in: *International Peacekeeping*, 14,3 (June 2007): 323–338.

Heiberg, Marianne (1991): "Peacekeepers and Local Populations: Some Comments on UNIFIL", in: Rikhye, I.; Skjelsbaek, K. (Eds.): *The United Nations and Peacekeeping: Results, Limitations and Prospects* (New York: International Peace Academy and Palgrave Macmillan): 147–169.

Hegel, G.W.F. (1996): *Philosophy of Rights* (London: Prometheus).

Heikal, Mohamed H. (1973): *The Cairo Documents* (New York: Doubleday).

Heikal, Mohamed H. (1986): *Cutting the Lion's Tail: Suez through Egyptian Eyes* (London: Andre Deutsch).

Heikal, Mohamed H. (1990): *1967: Al-Infijar [The Explosion]* [in Arabic] (Cairo: Al-Ahram).

Heikal, Mohamed H. (2004): *The Thirty-Year War: The Suez Files* [in Arabic] (Cairo: Al-Shorouq).

Heikal, Mohamed H. (2009–2010): "Life Experience" [*Tagrobat Hayat*, in Arabic], on: Al-Jazira (Arabic TV Network).

Heinbecker, Paul (2006): "*Suez Plus 50: Ten Reflections on Peacekeeping*", Paper presented at the Conference on Peacekeeping, Cairo, Egypt (27 November 2006).

Heinlein, Frank (2002): *British Government Policy and Decolonization 1945–1963: Scrutinizing the Official Mind* (London: Frank Cass).

Held, David (2003): "The Changing Structure of International Law: Sovereignty Transformed", in: Held, David; McGrew, Anthony (Eds.): *The Global Transformation* (Cambridge: Polity Press).

Helms, Jesse (2000): "A Statement to the UN Security Council", quoted in: Urquhart, Brian (2000): *Between Sovereignty and Globalization: Where Does the United Nations Fit In?* (Uppsala, Sweden: Dag Hammarskjold Foundation).

Henkin, Yagil (2015): *The 1956 Suez War and the New World Order in the Middle East: Exodus in Reverse* (Lanham: Lexington Books).

Hennessy, Peter (1987): "No End of an Argument: How Whitehall Tried and Failed to Suppress Sir Anthony Nutting's Suez Memoir", in: *Contemporary British History*, 1,1.

Hershey, Burnet (1961): *Dag Hammarskjold: Soldier of Peace* (London: Britannica Press).

Herzel, Theodor (1896, 1917): *A Jewish State: Proposal of a Modern Solution for the Jewish Question* (Leipzig – Vienna: Verlags-Buchhandlung).

Hewedy, Amin, 1989: "Nasser and the Crisis of 1956", in: Louis, W.R.; Owen, R., (Eds.): *Suez 1956: The Crisis and Its Consequences* (Oxford: Clarendon Press): 161–172.

Hicks, Frederick C. (1908): "The Equality of States and the Hague Conference", in: *The American Journal of International Law*, 2,3 (July): 530–561.

Higgins Rosalyn (1963): *International Law and the United Nations* (London: Oxford University Press).

High-Level Meeting (1959): UN and Egyptian Officials, Cairo, January 1959 (unpublished document).

Hilmy II, Amin (n.d.): *Unpublished Memoirs*.

Hilmy, Hanny (1971): *A Proposal for a Permanent International Peace Force*, International Peace Academy Seminar (Helsinki, Finland).

Hilmy, Hanny (1972): "Re-Partition of Palestine: Toward a Peaceful Solution in the Middle East", in: *Journal of Peace Research*, 2.

Hilmy, Hanny (2001): Interview with General Indar Jit Rikhye, Victoria, BC, Canada.

Hilmy, Hanny (2014): Discussions with Major Charles Goodman (Retired), Victoria, BC, Canada.

Hilmy, Hanny (2015): "Sovereignty, Peacekeeping, and the United Nations Emergency Force (UNEF), Suez 1956–1967: Insiders' Perspectives" (Ph.D. thesis, University of Victoria, British Columbia, Canada).

Hinnebusch, Raymond (2005): "The Politics of Identity in Middle East International Relations", in: Fawcett, L. (Ed.): *International Relations of the Middle East* (Oxford: Oxford University Press).

Hobbes, Thomas (1651, 1968): *Leviathan* (London: Penguin).

Hobsbawm, Eric (1987): *The Age of Empire: 1875–1914* (London: Abacus).

Hobson, John A. (1965): *Imperialism: A Study* (Ann Arbor: University of Michigan Press).

Hobson, John A. (1902, 1978): *Imperialism* (London: Cosimo).

Hod, Mordechai (1967): "Interview", in: *The Sunday Times* (London) (16 July 1967): 7.

Hoffman, M. (2009): "What is Left of the 'Liberal Peace'?", in: LSE (London) *Connect* (Winter).

Hogg, Garry (1969): *Suez Canal: A Link Between Two Seas* (London: Hutchinson Books).

Hokowhito, B.; Page, T., (2011): "Postcolonial Peace", in: *Journal of Thematic Dialogue*, 14,1: 13–25.

Holland, R.F. (1985): *European Decolonization 1918–1981: An Introductory Survey* (London: Macmillan).

Holland, Robert (2012): *Blue-Water Empire: The British in the Mediterranean Since 1800* (London: Allen Lane-Penguin).

Horn, Carl von (1966): *Soldiering for Peace* (London: Cassell).

Horne, Alistair (1977): *A Savage War of Peace: Algeria 1954–1962* (Harmondsworth: Penguin).

Horowitz, Irving L. (1982): "Socializing Without Politicization: Emile Durkheim's Theory of the Modern State", in: *Political Theory* 10,3 (August 1982): 353–377.

Huang, Thomas T.F. (1957): "Some International and Legal Aspects of the Suez Canal Problem", in: *American Journal of International Law*, 51,2 (April): 277–307.

Hunt, Charles T. (2019): "Is it Time to Review the Basis for UN Peacekeeping 71 years on?", in: *The Conversation*; at: https://theconversation.com/is-it-time-to-review-the-basis-for-un-peacekeeping-71-years-on-117517.

Hurewitz, J.C. (1965): "The UN and Disimperialism in the Middle East", in: *International Organization*, 19,3: 749–763.

Hurewitz, J.C. (1989): "The Historical Context", in: Louis, W.R.; Owen, R. (Eds.): *Suez 1956: The Crisis and its Consequences* (Oxford: Clarendon Press).

International Development Research Centre (IDRC) (2001): *Report of the International Commission on Intervention and State Sovereignty* (Ottawa: IDRC).

Igartua, Jose E. (2005): "Ready, Aye, Ready No More? Canada, Britain and the Suez Crisis in the Canadian Press", in: Buckber, Phillip (Ed.): *Canada and the End of Empire* (Vancouver: UBC): 60.

Ignatieff, Michael (2002): "Intervention and State Failure", in: Mills, Nicolaus; Brunner, Kira (Eds.): *The New Killing Fields: Massacre and the Politics of Intervention* (New York: Basic Books): 229–244.

Ikenberry, G. John (2006): *Liberal Order and Liberal Ambition: Essays on American Power and World Politics* (Cambridge: Polity Press).

Indian Ambassador (1956): Letter: *Official Position addressed to the UN Secretary-General*, A/3302/Add 4/ Rev I, Addendum: 23–24 (6 November 1956).

Indonesian Position (1957): *Conditions for Continued Participation in UNEF*. GAOR, 11th Sess., Plen. Mtg. 649, VOL. II-III (1 February 1957): 1,043.

International Coalition for the Responsibility to Protect (ICRP) (2009): *Report on the General Assembly Plenary Debate on the Responsibility to Protect*, New York: ICRP (15 September 2009).

International Court of Justice (1962): *Reports* (The Hague: The International Court of Justice).

International Court of Justice (1962): *UNEF Expenses Opinion*, (Advisory Opinion) (The Hague, The Netherlands).

International Court of Justice (1988): "Taba Award – Egypt/Israel Dispute Concerning Certain Boundary Pillars", in: *International Law Reports*, 80 (29 September 1988): 224–691.

International Court of Justice (2004): *Legal Consequences of the Construction of a Wall in the Occupied Palestinian Territory*, Advisory Opinion (9 July 2004).

International Peace Institute (2007): *The Middle East: Fragility, Crisis, and New Challenges for Peace Operations*, Vienna Seminar (New York: I.P.I.).

International Review Service (1957): *The Suez Canal: Nationalization, Invasion, International Action*, (III, 30) (February 1957).

International Review Service (1957): *The United Nations Emergency Force (UNEF): Precedents, Creation, Evolution*, III, 33 (May 1957).

Institute for Palestine Studies (1968): *Death of a Mediator* (London: Newman Neame).

Ismail, Tareq Y. (1973): "Canada and the Middle East", *Behind the Headlines*, XXXII (December).

Israeli Government (1981): "Memorandum on US-Israel Strategic Cooperation", signed on 30 November 1981.

James, Alan (1990): "*Peacekeeping in International Politics*", cited in: Brown, Davis. "The Role of the United Nations in Peacekeeping and Truce-Monitoring: What are the Applicable Norms?", *Revue Belge de Droit International*, 2 (1994).

Jakobsen, P.V. (2003): "Reflections on the Peacekeeping Doctrine", in: *International Peacekeeping*, 7.

Jackson, Robert (2007): *Sovereignty: Evolution of an Idea* (Cambridge: Polity Press).

Jackson, Robert H. (2004): "The Evolution of International Society", in: Baylis, J.; Smith, S. (Eds.): *The Globalization of World Politics: An Introduction to International Relations* (Oxford: Oxford University Press): 112.

Jernegan, John D. (1952): "*Memorandum of Conversation*", in: US Department of State (1952), Foreign Relations of the United States, 1952–1954, IX.

Jennings, Ivor (1959): *The Law and the Constitution* (London: University of London Press).

Johnson, Lyndon B. (1967): "Remarks by President Johnson on the Near East Situation", (23 May 1967), LBJ, NSF, NSC, History, in: *Middle East Crisis*, Vol. 1, Tabs 11–20 (12 May–19 June 1967).

Johnson, Paul (1957): *The Suez War* (London: MacGibbon & Kee).

Jones, Bruce et al. (2009): *Robust Peacekeeping: The Politics of Force* (New York: New York University).

Jorgensen, Martin Ottovay (2012): *Heaven in a Grain of Sand: The Current Paradigm of Global Governance as Understood via the Case of the United Nations Emergency Force* (Aalborg: Aalborg University, Denmark).

Judd, Denis (1997): "The Suez Crisis of 1956", in: *Empire: The British Imperial Experience from 1765 to the Present* (London: Fontana Press).

Kantorowicz, Ernst H. (1957, 1998): *The King's Two Bodies: A Study in Mediaeval Political Theology* (Princeton: Princeton University Press).

Kay, David (1967): "The Politics of Decolonization", in: *International Organization*, 21 (Autumn): 786–811.

Kedourie, Elie (1998): *Nationalism* (Oxford: Blackwell).

Kelly, Saul (2000): "Transatlantic Diplomat: Sir Roger Makins, Ambassador to Washington and Joint Permanent Secretary to the Treasury", in: Kelly, Saul; Gorst, Anthony (Eds.): *Whitehall and the Suez Crisis* (London: Frank Cass): 157–177.

Kelly, Saul; Gorst, Anthony (Eds.) (2000): *Whitehall and the Suez Crisis* (London: Frank Cass).

Kelsen, Hans (1951): *The Law of the United Nations* (London: Institute of World Affairs): 51.

Keohane, Robert (2003): "Political Authority after Intervention: Gradations of Sovereignty", in: Holzgrefe, J.L.; Keohane, Robert (Eds.): *Humanitarian Intervention: Ethical, Legal and Political Dilemmas* (Cambridge: Cambridge University Press): 275–298.

Khalidi, Rashid (1989): "Consequences of the Suez Crisis in the Arab World", in: Louis, W.R.; Owen, R. (Eds.) *Suez 1956: The Crisis and its Consequences* (Oxford: Clarendon Press): 377–392.

Khalidi, Rashid (1997): *Palestinian Identity: The Construction of Modern National Consciousness* (New York: Columbia University Press).

Khalidi, Rashid (2004): *Resurrecting Empire: Western Footprints and America's Perilous Path in the Middle East* (Boston: Beacon Press).

Khalidi, Rashid (2007): *The Iron Cage: The Story of the Palestinian Struggle for Statehood* (Boston: Beacon Press).

Khalidi, Walid (1971): *From Haven to Conquest: Readings in Zionism and the Palestine Problem until 1948* (Beirut: Institute for Palestine Studies).

Khalidi, Walid (1988): "Plan Dalet: Master Plan for the Conquest of Palestine", in: *Journal of Palestine Studies*, 18,1 (Autumn): 4–33.

Kingdom of Egypt (1936): Anglo-Egyptian Treaty of Friendship and Alliance (1936), *League of Nations Treaty Series*, 137, 6 (Article 9): 402–431.

Kingseed, Christian (1995): *Eisenhower and the Suez Crisis of 1956* (Baton Rouge: Louisiana State University Press).

Kingston, Paul W.T. (1996): *Britain and the Politics of Modernization in the Middle East 1945–1958* (Cambridge: Cambridge University Press).

Kinloch, Stephen P. (1996): "Utopian or Pragmatic? A UN Permanent Military Volunteer Force", in: *International Peacekeeping*, 3,4 (Winter): 166–190.

Kissinger, Henry (1973): Address to the UN General Assembly, 24 September 1973.

Kohl, Uta (2018): "Territoriality and Globalization", in: Allen, S., et al. (Eds.): *Oxford Handbook on Jurisdiction in International Law* (Oxford: Oxford University Press).

Kohn, Hans (1944): *The Idea of Nationalism: A Study of Its Origins and Background* (New York: Macmillan).

Knoops, G.J. Alexander (2004): *The Prosecution and Defense of Peacekeepers under International Criminal Law* (Ardsley, NY: Transnational Publishers).

Kondoch, Boris (2007): *International Peacekeeping* (Essays in International Law), (Farnham: Ashgate Publishing).

Koops, Joachim; Varwick, Johannes (2008): *Ten Years of SHIRBRIG: Lessons Learned, Development Prospects, and Strategic Opportunities for Germany* (Berlin: Global Public Policy Institute).

Korman, Sharon (1996): *The Right of Conquest: The Acquisition of Territory by Force in International Law and Practice* (Oxford: Oxford University Press).

Krasner, Stephen D. (Ed.) (1983): *International Regimes* (Ithaca: Cornell University Press).

Krasner, Stephen D. (1996): "Compromising Westphalia", *International Security*, 20,3: 115–151.

Krasner, Stephen D. (1999): *Sovereignty: Organized Hypocrisy* (Princeton: Princeton University Press).

Krasner, Stephen D. (2004): "Sharing Sovereignty: New Institutions for Collapsed and Failing States", in: *International Security*, 29,2 (Fall): 85–120.

Kreisler, Harry (1996): "A Life in Peace and War: Conversation with Sir Brian Urquhart", in: *Critical Currents*, 5 (March 1996).

Kyle, Keith (1989): "Britain and the Crisis, 1955–1956", in: Louis, W.R.; Owen, Roger (Eds.): *Suez 1956: The Crisis and its Consequences* (Oxford: Clarendon Press): 103–130.

Kyle, Keith (1991): *Suez* (New York: St. Marten's Press).

Kyle, Keith (1992): *Suez: Britain's End of Empire in the Middle East* (London: Weidenfeld & Nicolson).

Kyle, Keith (2000): "The Mandarin's Mandarin: Sir Norman Brook, Secretary of the Cabinet", in: Kelly, Saul; Gorst, Anthony (Eds.): *Whitehall and the Suez Crisis* (London: Frank Cass): 64–78.

Kyle, Keith (2006): "The Ghosts of Suez", in: *The Guardian* (13 July 2006).

Lachowski, Tomasz (2014): *New Dimensions of International Law – The Question of 'ius post Bellum'* (Lodz, Poland: University of Lodz).

Lake, D.A. (2002): *The New Sovereignty in International Relations* (Boston: The American Political Science Association).

Lal, Nand (1974): "India and the Withdrawal of the United Nations Emergency Force, 1967", in: *International Studies* (New Delhi), 13,2 (April–June).

Lal, Nand (1975): *From Collective Security to Peacekeeping: A Study of India's Contribution to the United Nations Emergency Force, 1956–67* (Calcutta: Minerva Associates).

Lall, Arthur (1968): *The UN in the Middle East Crisis, 1967* (New York: Columbia University Press).

Lall, Arthur (1971): "A Note on UN Peacekeeping Operations", Meeting of the International Peace Academy Conference, Helsinki, Finland (July 1971).

Lall, Arthur (1971): "Negotiating Theory", (Meeting of the International Peace Academy) (Helsinki, Finland. July 1971).

Landes, David S. (1979): *Bankers and Pashas: International Finance and Economic Imperialism in Egypt* (Boston: Harvard University Press).

Langille, Peter (2000): "Conflict Prevention: Options for Rapid Deployment and UN Standing Forces", in: *International Peacekeeping*, 7,1 (Spring): 219–253.

Langille, Peter (2000): *SHIRBRIG: A Promising Step Towards a United Nations that Can Prevent Deadly Conflict* (London, Ontario: Global Human Security).

Langille, Peter; Keefe, Tania (2003): *The Future of Peacekeeping: An Experts' Discussion to Contribute to the Dialogue on Foreign Policy* (Vancouver: Liu Institute for Global Issues, University of British Columbia and the University of Victoria).

Lansing, Robert (1921): *The Peace Negotiations: A Personal Narrative* (Boston: Houghton Mifflin).

Lash, Joseph P. (1961): *Dag Hammarskjold: Custodian of the Brushfire Peace* (London: Doubleday).

Lash, Joseph P. (1962): *Dag Hammarskjold: A Biography* (London: Cassell).

Lauterpacht, Hersch (1933): *The Function of Law in the International Community* (Oxford: Oxford University Press).

Lauterpacht, Hersch (1958, 1982): *The Development of International Law by the International Court* (Cambridge: Cambridge University Press).

Leach, Norman S. (2005): *Canadian Peacekeepers* (Edmonton: Folklore Publishing).

League of Nations (1936): The Montevideo Convention on the Rights and Duties of States, signed on 26 December 1933 (Geneva: League of Nations Treaty Series), 165: 20–43.

Lee, Thomas H. (2004): "International Law, International Relations Theory, and Preemptive War: The Vitality of Sovereign Equality Today", in: *Law and Contemporary Problems*, 67 (Autumn): 147–167.

Legault, Albert; Cox, David (Eds.) (1995): *UN Rapid Reaction Capabilities* (Toronto: Canadian Peacekeeping Press).

Lemay-Hebert, Nicolas (2013): "Review Essay: Critical Debates on Liberal Peacebuilding", in: *Civil Wars*, 15,2: 242–252.

Lesch, Ann Mosely (1979): *Arab Politics in Palestine, 1917–1939: The Frustration of a Nationalist Movement* (Ithaca: Cornell University Press).

Lesch, David W. (2012): "Syria: Playing with Fire", in: Shlaim, A.; Roger, W. (Eds.): *The 1967 Arab-Israeli War: Origins and Consequences* (Cambridge: Cambridge University Press).

Leslie, E. (1981): "The Position and Role of the Military in Peacekeeping", Extracts from article CDQ, 7, 3 (1978), in: *The Vienna Peacekeeping Seminar* (Vienna: International Peace Academy).

Le Suer, James D. (Ed.) (2003): *The Decolonization Reader* (London: Routledge).

Lilienthal, Alfred M. (1953): *What Price Israel?* (Washington DC: Henry Regency Company).

Lilienthal, Alfred M. (1983, 1978): *The Zionist Connection: What Price Peace? I & II* (Vancouver: Veritas Publishing).

Lipsey, Roger (2013): *Hammarskjold: A Life* (Ann Arbor: University of Michigan Press).

Lipson, Michael (2007): "Peacekeeping: Organized Hypocrisy", in: *European Journal of International Relations*, 13,1 (2007): 5–34.

Lister, Matthew (2011): "The Legitimating Role of Consent", in: *Chicago Journal of International Law*, 11,2 (Winter): 1–29.

Logan, Donald (1986): "Narrative of Suez Meetings at Severs, 22–25 October 1956", Selwyn Lloyd Papers (SELO), Churchill College, Cambridge University, 6/202, (24 October 1986), in: Gorst, A.; Johnmann, L. (Eds.): *The Suez Crisis* (New York: Routledge).

Loomba, Anita (1998): *Colonialism/Post-Colonialism* (London: Routledge).

Lopez, Ralph (2014): *Jerusalem Post Confirms Israel Knew USS Liberty was American*; at: http://www.digitaljournal.com/news/world/jerusalem-post-confirms-israel-knew-usslibertywas american/article/413296#ixzz5b6WZ68H0.

Louis, W.R. (1999): "The Dissolution of the British Empire", in: Brown, J.M.; Louis, W.R. (Eds.) *The Oxford History of the British Empire, Vol. IV, the Twentieth Century* (Oxford: Oxford University Press): 329–356.

Louis, W.R. (2006): *The End of British Imperialism: The Scramble for Empire, Suez and Decolonization* (London: MacMillan).

Louis, W.R.; Owen, Roger (Eds.) (1989): *Suez 1956: The Crisis and Its Consequences* (Oxford: Clarendon Press).

Louis, W.R.; Robinson, Ron (1994): "The Imperialism of Decolonization", in: *Journal of Imperial and Commonwealth History*, 22,3.

Love, Kennett (1969): *Suez: The Twice-Fought War* (New York: McGraw-Hill).

Lucas, Scott (1990): "Redefining the Suez Collusion", in: *Middle Eastern Studies*, 26,1 (January).

Lundstrom, Aage (1968): *Death of a Mediator [Bernadotte]* (Beirut: Newman Neame Ltd).

Lyon, Peyton V.; Tomlin, Brian W. (1979): *Canada as an International Actor* (Toronto: Macmillan).

MacFarlane, John (2007): "Sovereignty and Standby: The 1964 Conference on UN Peacekeeping Forces", in: *International Peacekeeping*, 14,5 (November): 599–612.

MacKenzie, Lewis (1994): *Peacekeeper: The Road to Sarajevo* (Toronto: Harper Collins).

MacKenzie, Lewis (2018): "Interview", on: *As It Happens*" Canadian Broadcasting Corporation (CBC) (March 2018).

MacMillan, Margaret (2001): *Paris 1919: Six Months that Changed the World* (New York: Random House).

Magdoff, Harry (2003): *Imperialism without Colonies* (New York: Monthly Review Press).

Malanczuk, Peter (1987): *Akehurst's Modern Introduction to International Law* (New York: Routledge).

Malawer, Stuart S. (1970): "The Withdrawal of UNEF and a New Notion of Consent", in: *Cornell International Law Journal*, 25,4: 179–190.

Malawar, Stuart S. (1974): "Israeli Foreign Policy and International Legal Issues, 1948–1971", in: *The Changing International Community* (Boussannt ed.): 269–282.

Malik, Arslan (1999): "The Beginning of a UN Army?", in: *Behind the Headlines*, 56,4.

Malone, David M. (2003): "Recent Books on International Law, A Review", in: *American Journal of International Law*, 97.

Maloney, Sean M. (2006): "The Forgotten: Lt Gen E.L.M. 'Tommy' Burns and UN Peacekeeping in the Middle East", in: *Canadian Army Journal*, 9,2 (Summer).

Mamdani, Mahmood (1996): *Citizen and Subject: Contemporary Africa and the Legacy of Late Colonialism* (Princeton: Princeton University Press).

Mankell, Henning (1990): *The Eye of the Leopard* (London: Harvill Secker).

Maritain, Jacques (1951): *Man and the State* (Chicago: Chicago University Press).

Marlowe, John (1961): *Arab Nationalism and British Imperialism: A Study in Power Politics* (London: Cresset Press).

Marshall, J., Chief Justice (1825): *Supreme Court of the United States* (23 US 66 1825 US Lexis 219).

Marten, Kimberly Zisk (2004): *Enforcing the Peace: Learning from the Imperial Past* (New York: Columbia University Press).

Martin Sr., Paul (1965): *Peace-Keeping, Non-Proliferation, and Disarmament* (Geneva: World Veterans Foundation) (May 1965).

Martin Sr., Paul (1967): *Canada and the Quest for Peace* (New York: Columbia University Press).

Mattar, Gamil (1970): *The Decision of the UAR Government to Request the Redeployment of UNEF, May 16, 1967: Background to Decision* (Montreal: McGill University).

Matumbi, Paul Bruno (2016): *Peacekeeping through the Court: The ICC and UN Security Council* (Saarbrücken, Germany: LAP LAMBERT Academic Publishing).

Mayer, Thomas (1983): *Egypt and the Palestine Question: 1936–1945* (Berlin: Klaus Schwarz Verlag).

Mayer, Thomas (1986): "Arab Unity of Action and the Palestine Question, 1945–48", in: *Journal of Middle Eastern Studies*, 22,3: 331–349.

Mays, Antjie (2000): "War and Peace: Of Law, Lawlessness, and Sovereignty (Multinational Peacekeeping and International Law)", in: *Journal of Power and Ethics: An Interdisciplinary Review*, 1,2: 201–232.

McCullough, Colin (2016): *Creating Canada's Peacekeeping Past* (Vancouver: UBC Press).

McDermott, A.; Skjelsbeck, K. (Eds.) (1991): *The Multinational Force in Beirut, 1982–1984* (Miami: Florida International University Press).

McIlwain, Charles Howard (1932): *The Growth of Political Thought in the West: From the Greeks to the End of the Middle Ages* (New York: The Macmillan Company).

McIntyre Jr., John D. (1985): *The Boycott of the Milner Mission: A Study in Egyptian Nationalism* (Bern: Peter Lang).

McNamara, Robert (2003): *Britain, Nasser and the Balance of Power in the Middle East 1952– 1967: From the Egyptian Revolution to the Six Day War* (London: Frank Cass).

Mearsheimer, John J. (1995): "A Realist Reply", in: *International Security*, Summer, 21,1: 82–93.

Mearsheimer, John J.; Walt, Stephen M. (2007): *The Israel Lobby and US Foreign Policy* (Toronto: Viking Canada).

Melady, John (2006): *Pearson's Prize: Canada and the Suez Crisis* (Toronto: Dundurn).

Meir, Golda (1957): *Address to the General assembly* of the United Nations, New York: (1 March, 1957).

Melman, Yossi (2006): "The IDF Archive Reveals Secret Files from Operation Kadesh", in: *Haaretz* (Israel) (8 October 2006).

Memmi, Albert (1974): *The Colonizer and the Colonized* (London: Souvenir Press).

Mendes-Flohr, Paul R. (1983): *A Land of Two Peoples: Martin Buber on Jews and Arabs* (Oxford: Oxford University Press).

Menuhin, Moshe (1969): *Not By Might, Nor by Power: The Zionist Betrayal of Judaism* (New York: Open Road).

Menuhin, Yehudi (1988): "Violinist Menuhin Sees Nazi Illness in Israel", in: *Chicago Tribune* (22 January 1998).

Mehuhin, Yehudi (1997): *Unfinished Journey: Twenty Years Later* (New York: Fromm International).

Mezerik, A.G. (Ed.) (1969): *The United Nations Emergency Force (UNEF): 1956–1967; Creation, Evolution, End of Mission* (New York: International Review Services).

Mezerik, A.G. (Ed.) (1969): *The Suez Canal 1956 Crisis-1967 War* (New York: International Review Services).

Miller, D.H. (1924): *My Diary at the Peace Conference of Paris* (New York: Appeal Printing).

Miller, D.H. (1928): *The Drafting of the Covenant* (New York: Pullman).

Miller, Richard I. (1961): *Dag Hammarskjold and Crisis Diplomacy* (Washington DC: Oceana Publications).

Mills, Nicolaus; Brunner, Kira (Eds.) (2001): *The New Killing Fields: Massacre and the Politics of Intervention* (New York: Basic Books).

Mingst, Karen A.; Karns, Margaret P. (2012): *The United Nations in the 21st Century* (Boulder: Westview Press).

Mohamed, Saira (2005): "From Keeping Peace to Building Peace: A Proposal for a Revitalized United Nations Trusteeship Council", in: *Columbia Law Review*, 105,3 (April): 809–840.

Mommsen, Wolfgang J. (1960): "The End of Empire and the Continuity of Imperialism", in: Strachey, John, *The End of Empire* (New York: Random House).

Mommsen, Wolfgang; Osterhammel, Jürgen (Eds.) (1986): *Imperialism and After: Continuities and Discontinuities* (London: Allen and Unwin).

Montgomery, Deirdre (2009): "'The Responsibility to Protect Doctrine': Analysis of the press release of UN General Assembly President, Miguel D'Escoto, on R2P", in: *International Criminal Law Bureau* (July).

Montreal Gazette (1956): "Editorial: Painful Departure", 28 November: 8.

Morris, Benny (2008): *1948: A History of the First Arab-Israeli War* (New Haven: Yale University Press).

Morris, Benny (1993): *Israel's Border Wars, 1949–1956: Arab Infiltration, Israeli Retaliation and the Countdown to the Suez War* (Oxford: Clarendon Press).

Morris, Benny (2001): *Righteous Victims: A History of the Zionist-Arab Conflict, 1881–2001* (New York: Vintage Books).

Morsy, Laila Amin (1993): "The Role of the United States in the Anglo-Egyptian Agreement of 1954", in: *Middle Eastern Studies*, 29,3: 526–558.

Mosgaard, Kurt et al. (2009): *SHIRBRIG Lessons Learned Report* (Hovelte, Denmark).

Mountbatten, Lord Louis (2013): *War History Facts* (27 February 2013).

Mullerliele, Andreas (2016): "What is Preventive Diplomacy?", in: *European Institute of Peace Publications* (Brussels: EIP).

Murray, Geoffrey (1973/74): "Glimpses of Suez 1956", in: *International Journal*, XXIX, 1 (Winter).

Mutawi, Samir (1987): *Jordan in the 1967 War* (Cambridge: Cambridge University Press).

Nasser, Gamal Abdel (1955): *The Philosophy of the Revolution* (Cairo: Dar al-Maaref; Washington: Public Affairs Press).

Nandy, Ashis (1988): *The Intimate Enemy: Loss and Recovery of Self Under Colonialism* (Oxford: Oxford University Press).

Nasu, Hitoshi (2012): "The Place of Human Security in Collective Security", in: *Journal of Conflict & Security Law* (Oxford): 1–35.

Neff, Donald (1966): "1949 Lausanne Conference Seals Fate of Palestine", in: *Washington Report on Middle East Affairs* (April).

Nelson, Richard, W. (1985): "Multinational Peacekeeping in the Middle East and the United Nations Model", in: *International Affairs*, 61,1 (Winter): 67–89.

Newman, E.; Paris, R.; Richmond, O. (2009): "Introduction", in: *New Perspectives on Liberal Peacebuilding* (Tokyo: United Nations University Press).

Nicholas, David A. (2011): *Eisenhower 1956* (New York: Simon & Schuster).

Norman, the Estate of Howard and Gwen (1957): "*Norman on the Suez Crisis: Private Papers*", donated to the Special Collections Library University of British Columbia, Vancouver, Canada (Box 1, File 1–2) (4 March).

Normand, Roger; Zaidi, Sarah (2008): *Human Rights at the UN: The Political History of Universal Justice* (Bloomington: Indiana University Press).

Norton, William (2004): *Air War on the Edge – A History of the Israel Air Force and Its Aircraft since 1947* (Milbank: Midland Publishing).

Novosseloff, Alexandra (2018): "UN Peacekeeping: Back to Basics Is Not Backwards", in: *International Peace Institute*; at: https://www.theglobalobservatory.org/2018/04/.

Nutting, Anthony (1958): *I Saw for Myself: The Aftermath of Suez* (London: Hollis & Carter).

Nutting, Anthony (1967): *No End of a Lesson: The Story of Suez* (London: Constable).

Nutting, Anthony (1972): *Nasser* (London: Constable).

Oatley, Keith (2010): *Therefore Choose* (Fredericton, N.B.: Goose Lane Editions).

Obieta, Joseph A. (1970): *The International Status of the Suez Canal* (The Hague: Martinus Nijhoff).

O'Brien, William (1967): "International Law and the Outbreak of War in the Middle East, 1967", *ORBIS*, XI, 3 (Fall).

Ohmae, K. (1995): *The End of the Nation State* (New York: Free Press).

Oakeshott, Michael (2001): "Letters on Hobbes", in: *Political Theory*, 29,6.

Olonisakin, Funmi (2000): *Reinventing Peacekeeping in Africa: Conceptual and Legal Issues in ECOMOG Operations* (The Hague; Boston: Kluwer Law International).

Onozawa, Toru (2005): "Formation of American Regional Policy for the Middle East, 1950–1952: The Middle East Command Concept and its Legacy", in: *Diplomatic History*, 29,1.

Oppenheim, Lassa (1912): *International Law: A Treatise* (London: Longmans and Green).

Oppenheim, Lassa (1928, 1955): *International Law* (London: McNeir).

Oppenheim, Lassa F.E. (1905): *International Law* (London: Longmans).

Orakhelashvili, Alexander (2003): "The Legal Basis of the United Nations Peace-Keeping Operations", in: *Virginia Journal of International Law*, 43: 485–524.

Orakhelashvili, Alexander (2008): "The Interaction between Human Rights and Humanitarian Law: Fragmentation, Conflict, Parallelism, or Convergence?", in: *European Journal of International Law*, 19,1: 161–182.

Oren Michael B. (1990): "Secret Egypt-Israel Peace Initiatives Prior to the Suez Campaign", in: *Middle Eastern Studies*, 26,3 (July): 351–370.

Oren, Michael B. (2002): *Six Days of War: June 1967 and the Making of the Modern Middle East* (New York: Oxford University Press).

Oren, Michael B. (2003a): *Six Days of War: June 1967 and the Making of the Modern Middle East* (New York: Ballantine Books).

Oren, Michael B. (2003b): "Levi Eshkol, Forgotten Hero", in: *Azure*, 14 (Winter): 5,763; at: http://azure.org.il/article.php?id=248.

Orford, Anne (2011): *International Authority and the Responsibility to Protect* (Cambridge: Cambridge University Press).

Orwell, George (1945). "Notes on Nationalism", in: *Polemic*, 1 (October 1945).

Orwell, George (1945): *As I Please: The Collected Essays, Journalism & Letters*, Vol. 3, (Boston: Harcourt, Brace & World Inc.): 363.

Osiander, Andreas (2001): "Sovereignty, International Relations, and the Westphalian Myth", in: *International Organization*, 55,2: 251–287.

Osterhammel, J. (1977): *Colonialism: A Theoretical Overview* (Princeton: Markus Weiner Publishers).

Ostrower, Garry B. (1996): *The League of Nations: From 1919 to 1929* (New York: Avery Publishing).

O'Sullivan, Arieh (2004): "Liberty Revisited: The Attack", in: *Jerusalem Post* (4 June 2004): 20.

Otunnu, Olara A.; Doyle, Michael W. (Eds.) (1998): *Peacemaking and Peacekeeping for the New Century* (Lanham: Rowman & Littlefield Publishers).

Pappe, Ilan (2004): *A History of Modern Palestine: One Land, Two Peoples* (Cambridge: Cambridge University Press).

Pappe, Ilan (2006, 2007): *The Ethnic Cleansing of Palestine* (Oxford: Oneworld Publications).

Pappe, Illan (2015): *The Idea of Israel: A History of Power and Knowledge* (London & New York: Verso).

Paris, Roland (1997): "Peacebuilding and the Limits of Liberal Internationalism", in: *International Security*, 22,2 (Fall): 54–89.

Paris, Roland (2002): "International Peacebuilding and the 'Mission Civilisatrice'", in: *Review of International Studies*, 28,4 (October): 637–656.

Paris, Roland (2003): "Peacekeeping and the Constraints of Global Culture", in: *European Journal of International Relations*, 9,3: 441–473.

Parker, Richard B. (1993): *The Politics of Miscalculation in the Middle East* (Indiana; Indiana University Press).

Parker, Richard B. (Ed.) (1996): *The Six-Day War: A Retrospective* (Gainsville: University Press of Florida).

Parker, Richard B. (1997): "USAF in the Sinai in the 1967 War: Fact or Fiction?", in *Journal of Palestine Studies*, 27,1 (Autumn): 67–75.

Parry, Marc (2016): "The Long Road: Uncovering the Brutal Truth About the British Empire", in: *The Guardian* (London: 16 August 2016).

Patai, Raphael (1973): *The Arab Mind* (Tucson: Recovery Resources Press).

Patnaik, Prabhat (2019): "Nationalism Without Other", in: *Indian Express* (5 October).

Paton, Paul D. (1995): "International Law as a Language for International Relations: Legal Reform and the United Nations", in: Fawcett, Eric; Newcombe, Hanna (Eds.): *United Nations Reform: Looking Ahead After Fifty Years* (Toronto: Science for Peace Series, University of Toronto): 270–286.

Pavel, Carmen E. (2015): *Divided Sovereignty: International Institutions and the Limits of State Authority* (Oxford: Oxford University Press).

Peace Operations Monitor (n.d.): *Capstone Doctrine*; at: https://www.pom.peacebuild.ca/
bestpracticesCD.shtml.

Pearson, Anthony (1978): *Conspiracy of Silence: The Attack on the USS Liberty* (London: Quartet
Books).

Pearson, Geoffrey (1993): *Seize the Day: Lester B. Pearson and Crisis Diplomacy* (Ottawa:
Carleton University Press).

Pearson, Geoffrey (1995): "Peacekeeping and Canadian Policy", in Fawcett, Eric; Newcombe,
Hanna (Eds.): *United Nations Reform: Looking Ahead After Fifty Years* (Toronto: Science for
Peace Series, University of Toronto): 112–120.

Pearson, Lester B. (1957): "Force for U.N.", in: *Foreign Affairs*, 35 (April): 395–404.

Pearson, Lester B. (1957): "Address to the UN General Assembly", in: *The Crisis in the Middle
East: January-March 1957* (Ottawa: Parliament of Canada/The Queen's Printer).

Pearson, Lester B. (1972): *Mike: The Memoirs of the Right Honourable Lester B. Pearson*, 2
(1957–1968) (Toronto: Toronto University Press).

Pearson, Lester B. (1973): Comments on Peacekeeping, quoted in: Tucker, Michael (1980):
Canadian Foreign Policy: Contemporary Issues and Themes (Toronto: McGraw-Hill
Reyerson).

Pearson, Lester B. (1980): Comments quoted in: Tucker, Michael (1980): *Canadian Foreign
Policy: Contemporary Issues and Themes* (Toronto: McGraw-Hill Ryerson).

Peled, Miko (2016): *The General's Son: Journey of an Israeli in Palestine* (Charlottesville,
Virginia: Just World Books).

Peretz, Don (1993): *Palestinians, Refugees, and the Middle East Peace Process* (Washington DC:
United States Institute of Peace Press).

Petersen, Tore T. (Ed.) (2010): *Challenging Retrenchment: The United States, Great Brutan and
the Middle East, 1950–1980* (Trondheim, Norway: Tapir Academic Press).

Petersmann, Ernst-Ulrich (2006): *State Sovereignty, Popular Sovereignty, and Individual
Sovereignty: From Constitutional Nationalism to Multilevel Constitutionalism in
International Economic Law* (Florence: European University Institute, Department of Law),
Paper No. 2006/45 (December 2006).

Piel, Jean (1975): "The Current Role of the Nation-State", in: Wallerstein, Immanuel (Ed.): *World
Inequality: Origins and Perspectives on the World System* (Montreal: Black Rose Books): 98–
111.

Picco, Giandomenico (1994): "The UN and the Use of Force", in: *Foreign Affairs*,
(September/October).

Polanyi, John C. (1995): "From Peacekeeping to Peace Making", in Fawcett, Eric; Newcombe,
Hanna (Eds.): *United Nations Reform: Looking Ahead After Fifty Years* (Toronto: Science for
Peace Series, University of Toronto): 121–130.

Policy Brief (2007): *From Legal Theory to Policy Tools: International Humanitarian Law and
International Human Rights Law in the Occupied Palestinian Territory* (Cambridge, Mass:
Harvard University).

Possony, Stefan T. (1946): "Peace Enforcement", in: *Yale Law Journal*, 55,5 (August): 910–949.

Power, Samantha (2002): "Raising the Cost of Genocide", in: Mills, Nicolaus; Brunner, Kira
(Eds.) *The New Killing Fields: Massacres and the Politics of Intervention* (New York: Basic
Books): 245–264.

Pruen, John B.; Selim, Mohamed (1955): *Survey Report: Northwest Sinai Project: An Agreement
between UNRWA and Egypt* (Cairo: Republic of Egypt).

Pufendorf, Samuel (1674, 1992): *On the Duties of Man and Citizen According to Natural Law,*
edited by Tully, J. and translated by Silverthorne, M., (Cambridge: Cambridge University
Press).

Pugh, Michael (2005): "Peacekeeping and Critical Theory", in: Bellamy, Alex J.; Williams, Paul
(Eds.): *Peace Operations and Global Order* (New York: Routledge): 39–58.

Pugh, Michael (2003): "Peacekeeping and International Relations Theory: Phantom of the
Opera?", in: *International Peacekeeping*, 10,4 (December 2003): 104–112.

Quigley, John (2012): *The Six-Day War and Israeli Self-Defence: Questioning the Legal Basis for Preventive War* (Cambridge: Cambridge University Press).

Raafat, Samir (1997): "Death in Dokki", in: *Egyptian Mail* (31 May).

Rabin, Itzhak (1966): "Report to the Israeli Knesset", in: *The Rabin Memoirs* (Berkley: University of California Press).

Rabin, Itzhak; Avineri, Shlomo (1990): "The Sinai Campaign and the Limits of Power", in: Troen, Selwyn; Shemesh, Moshe: *The Suez-Sinai Crisis 1956: Retrospective and Reappraisal* (London: Frank Cass): 238–247.

Rai, Saurav Kumar (2017): "Nation and Nationalism: Revisiting Gandhi and Tagore", *Gandhi Marg*, 39, 2 and 3 (July–September and October-December): 205–216; at: https://www.academia.edu/36441992/NationandNationalismRevisitingGandhiandTagore

Ralston Papers (1943): *Officer Assessment File*, 54 (Ottawa: IBID Report).

Ramadan, Abdel-Azim (2000): *The Historical Facts About the Decision to Nationalize the Suez Canal Company* [in Arabic] (Cairo: The Egyptian Society for Books).

Raman, K. Venkata (1995): "Law, Politics and United Nations Enforcement of Peace", in: Fawcett, Eric; Newcombe, Hanna (Eds.): *United Nations Reform: Looking Ahead After Fifty Years* (Toronto: Science for Peace Series, University of Toronto): 158–166.

Ramsbotham, David (1995): *The Changing Nature of Intervention: The Role of UN Peacekeeping* (London: Research Institute for the Study of Conflict and Terrorism).

Renan, Ernest (1882): *Qu'est-ce qu'une Nation?*, Paper at the Sorbonne, Paris.

Renan, Ernest (1996): "What is a Nation?", in: Eley, Geoff; Suny, Ronald (Eds.): *Becoming National: A Reader* (New York and Oxford: Oxford University Press): 41–55.

Republic of Egypt (1954): *Anglo-Egyptian Agreement on the Suez Canal Base* (19 October 1954).

Republic of Egypt (1956): *White Paper: On the Nationalization of the Suez Canal Maritime Canal Company* (Cairo: Government Press) (12 August 1956).

Republic of Egypt (1956): *The Nationalization of the Universal Suez Maritime Canal Company*, Decree Law No. 285, 26 July 1956 (Cairo: Government Press).

Republic of Egypt (1956): Statement by the Egyptian Government on the Anglo-French-Israeli Aggression, 20 November 1956 (Cairo: Egyptian State Information Department).

Republic of Egypt (1957): *Declaration on the Suez Canal: Official Egyptian Position*, S/3818 (24 April 1957).

Reynolds, Paul (2006): "Suez: End of Empire", BBC News, 24 July 2006; at: http://news.bbc.co.uk/2/hi/middle_east/5199392.stm.

Reynolds, Paul (2007): "Britain's Delusion of Grandeur", BBC News, 26 October 2007; at: http://news.bbc.co.uk/2/hi/americas/7063374.stm.

Riad, Mahmoud (1967): "Letter to U Thant", S-464-373, file 3017. UN-UAR. Letters (18 May 1967).

Riad, Mahmoud (1981): *The Struggle for Peace in the Middle East* (London: Quartet Books).

Riches, D.H.M. (1957): "Minutes", TNA, FO 371/126910/EA 10345/1", UK Foreign Office (25 January 1957), quoted in: Smith, Simon C. (2010): "Anglo-American Relations and the End of Empire in the Far East the Persian Gulf", in: Petersen, Tore T. (Ed.): *Challenging Retrenchment: The United States, Great Britain and the Middle East, 1950–1980* (Trondheim, Norway: Tapir Academic Press).

Riches, D.H.M. (1957): "Letter from Riches to Burrows", TNA, FO 371/126910/EA 10345/1, UK Foreign Office (8 February 1957), quoted in: Smith, Simon C. (2010): "Anglo-American Relations and the End of Empire in the Far East the Persian Gulf", in: Petersen, Tore T. (Ed.): *Challenging Retrenchment: The United States, Great Britain and the Middle East, 1950–1980* (Trondheim, Norway: Tapir Academic Press).

Richmond, Oliver P. (2008): *Peace in International Relations* (New York: Routledge).

Rikhye, Indar Jit (1964): *Preparation and Training of UN Peacekeeping Forces* (London: Institute of Strategic Studies).

Rikhye, Indar Jit (1967): *United Nations Peacekeeping Operations: Higher Conduct* (Paris: International Information Center on Peacekeeping Operations).

Rikhye, Indar Jit (1970): *Training for Peacekeeping* (The Hague: Vredesvraagstikken Institute).

Rikhye, Indar Jit (1970): *Report from Vienna* (New York: International Peace Academy).

Rikhye, Indar Jit (1971): *Cooperation for Peacekeeping: Narrowing Great Power Differences* (New York: International Peace Academy).

Rikhye, Indar Jit (1971): *Consent, Good Offices and the Future of Peacekeeping: A Special Report on the Vienna Pilot Project in Peacekeeping Training* (New York: International Peace Academy).

Rikhye, Indar Jit (1974): *Vienna and Tokyo: Seminar Evaluations and Reports* (New York: International Peace Academy).

Rikhye, Indar Jit (1980): *The Sinai Blunder – The Withdrawal of the United Nations Emergency Force Leading to the Six-Day War, June 1967* (London: Frank Cass).

Rikhye, Indar Jit (1981): "The Problems of International Peacekeeping", Lecture originally given on 29 September 1976, in: *The Vienna Peacekeeping Seminar* (Vienna: International Peace Academy).

Rikhye, Indar Jit (1984): *The Theory and Practice of Peacekeeping* (London: Hurst & Co.).

Rikhye, Indar Jit (1989): *The Future of Peacekeeping* (New York: International Peace Academy).

Rikhye, Indar Jit (1992): *Strengthening UN Peacekeeping: New Challenges and Proposals* (Washington DC: United States Institute of Peace).

Rikhye, Indar Jit (1992): *The United Nations of the 1990s and International Peacekeeping Operations* (Southampton: Mountbatten Centre for International Studies).

Rikhye, Indar Jit (1993): *Military Adviser to the Secretary-General* (New York: St. Martin's Press).

Rikhye, Indar Jit (2002): *Trumpets and Tumults: The Memoirs of A Peacekeeper* (New Delhi: Manohar Publishers).

Rikhye, Indar Jit; Skjelsbaek, Kjell (Eds.) (1990): *The United Nations and Peacekeeping: Results, Limitations and Prospects: The Lessons of 40 Years of Experience*, Paper presented in Oslo in 1988 (Basingstoke: Macmillan in association with the International Peace Academy).

Rikhye, Indar Jit; Harbottle, Michael N.; Egge, Bjorn (1974): *The Thin Blue Line: International Peace-Keeping and Its Future* (New Haven: Yale University Press).

Roberts, Andrew (2006): "Suez: The Betrayal of Eden", BBC News (30 October 2006); at: http://news.bbc.co.uk/2/hi/middle_east/6085264.stm.

Robertson, Terence (1964): *Crisis: The Inside Story of the Suez Conspiracy* (Toronto: McClelland & Stewart).

Robinson, Jacob (1958): "Metamorphosis of the United Nations", in: *Recueil des Cours*, The Hague Academy of International Law, 94 (Boston: Nijhoff, Leiden).

Robinson, Shira (2013): *Citizen Strangers: Palestinians and the Birth of Israel's Liberal Settler State* (Stanford: Stanford University Press).

Rodinson, Maxime (1973): *Israel: A Colonial-Settler State?* (New York: Pathfinder).

Rogan, Eugene L.; Shlaim, Avi (Eds.) (2001): *The War for Palestine: Rewriting the History of 1948* (Cambridge: Cambridge University Press).

Rogers, C.M. Ann (1988): *Murder By Slander? A Re-examination of the E.H. Norman Case*, (MA thesis, University of British Columbia, Vancouver, Canada).

Roosevelt, Theodore (1897): "Address to the Naval War College", in: *The Roosevelts*, PBS documentary, 14 September 2014; at: https://www.theodorerooseveltcenter.org/Research/Digital-Library/Record?libID=o284490.

Rosner, Gabriella (1963): *The United Nations Emergency Force* (New York: Columbia University Press).

Rostgaard, Marianne; Jorgensen, Martin Ottovay (2012): "Academic History and the Future of the Past", in: *Academic Minutes*: 33.

Rostow, Walt (1967): *Memo to the President*. LBJ, National Security File, Country File, Middle East – UAR (box 16), 14 February 1967.

Rountree, William (1956): "Memorandum from the Under-Secretary of State to Secretary Dulles", Eisenhower Library, Memorandum Series, Box # 4 (23 May 1956): 658–667.

Rousseau, Jean-Jacques (1762, 1968): *The Social Contract* (London: Penguin Classics).

Russett, Bruce (1997): "A Review of: *An Agenda for Peace*; *An Agenda for Development*; and *An Agenda for Democratization*, by Boutros Boutros-Ghali", in: *The American Political Science Review*, 91,2 (June): 494–496.

Sa'di, Ahmed H.; Abu-Lughod, Lila (2007): *NAKBA: Palestine, 1948, and the Claims of Memory* (New York: Columbia University Press).

Safi, Michael (2019): "Churchill's Policies Contributed to 1943 Bengal Famine", in: *The Guardian* (29 March).

Sagi, Nana (2009): "The Sinai Campaign: The Political Struggle October 1956–March 1957", in: *Documents on the Foreign Policy of Israel* (Jerusalem: Israel State Archives).

Said, Edward W. (1979): *Orientalism* (New York: Vintage Books).

Said, Edward W. (1980): *The Question of Palestine* (New York: Vintage Books).

Said, Edward W. (1993): *Culture and Imperialism* (New York: Vintage Books).

Said, Edward W. (2001): "Imperial Perspectives", in: *Al-Ahram Weekly* (11 March).

Said, Edward W. (2001): *The End of the Peace Process: Oslo and After* (New York: Vintage Books).

Said, Mohamed Kadry (2007): *Egypt's Evolving Role in Peacekeeping: Capabilities and Cooperation Prospects within the EMP* (Cairo: Al-Ahram Center for Political and Strategic Studies).

Saksena, K.P. (1977): "Not by Design: Evolution of UN Peace-Keeping Operations and its Implications for the Future", in: *International Studies*, 16,4 (October–December): 459–481.

Saoud, Abdel-Hamid (1960): Dispatch from the Egyptian Ambassador in Ottawa to the Ministry of Foreign Affairs in Cairo, 13 July 1960.

Sarigiannidis, Miltiadis (2007): "Legal Discourse on Peacemaking/Peacekeeping/ Peacebuilding: International Law as a New Topography for Human Security", in: *International Journal*, 62,3 (June): 519–538.

Sayyid, Afaf Lutfi (1968): *Egypt and Cromer: A Study in Anglo-Egyptian Relations* (London: Murray).

Sayyid-Marsot, Afaf Lutfi (1985): *A Short History of Egypt* (Cambridge: Cambridge University Press).

Schachter, Oscar (1964): "The Use of Law in International Peace-Keeping", in: *Virginia Law Review*, 50,6: 1,096–1,114.

Schmemann, Serge (1997): "General's Words Shed Light on the Golan", in: *The New York Times* (11 May 1997).

Schoenbaum, David (1966): "Review of Guéhenno, Jean-Marie: *The End of the Nation State*".

Schoenman, Ralph (1988): *The Hidden History of Zionism* (Santa Barbara: Veritas Press).

Schulzinger, Robert D. (1990): "The Impact of Suez on United States Middle East Policy, 1957–1958", in: Troen, S.; Shemesh, M. (Eds.): *The Suez-Sinai Crisis 1956: Retrospective and Reappraisal* (London: Frank Cass): 251–265.

Schwartz, Stephen (2006): *Is it Good for the Jews? The Crisis of America's Israel Lobby* (New York: Doubleday).

Scott, James (2009): *The Attack on the Liberty: The Untold Story of Israel's Deadly 1967 Assault on a US Spy Ship* (New York: Simon & Schuster).

Segev, Tom (2007): *1967: Israel, the War, and the Year that Transformed the Middle East* (New York: Metropolitan Books – Henry Holt).

Sellers, J.A. (1990): "Military Lessons: The British Perspectives", in: Troen, Selwyn; Shemesh, Moshe (Eds.): *The Suez-Sinai Crisis 1956: Prospective and Reappraisal* (London: Frank Cass): 17–53.

Sevareid, Eric (c. 1968–69): *Commentary* (New York: CBS News).

Shahak, Israel (1994): *Jewish History, Jewish Religion: The Weight of Three Thousand Years* (London: Pluto Press).

Shahak, Israel; Mezvinski, Norton (2004): *Jewish Fundamentalism* (London: Pluto Press).

Shapira, Anita (2014): *Ben-Gurion: Father of Modern Israel* (New Haven: Yale University Press).

Shlaim, Avi (1994): "Israel's Dirty War", A Review of Benny Morris' Book (Oxford 1993) Israel's Border Wars: 1949–1956, in: *London Review of Books*, 16,16 (8 August 1994), at: https://www.lrb.co.uk/the-paper/v16/n16/avi-shlaim/israel-s-dirty-war and https://www.users.ox.ac.uk/-ssfc0005/IsraelsDirtyWar.html.

Shlaim, Avi (1995): *War and Peace in the Middle East* (New York: Penguin Books).

Shlaim, Avi (2001): *The Iron Wall: Israel and the Arab World* (New York: Morton & Company).

Shalabi, E.A. (2011): "NATO, the Right to Protect in Libya", in: *Al-Ahram Weekly*.

Shalev, Aryeh (1993): *The Israeli-Syrian Armistice Regime: 1949–1955* (Boulder: Westview Press).

Shamir, Shimon (1989): "The Collapse of Project Alpha", in: Louis, W.R; Owen, Roger (Eds.): *Suez 1956: The Crisis and its Consequences* (Oxford: Clarendon Press).

Shapiro, T. Rees (2011): "Richard B. Parker, Ambassador and Middle East Expert, Dies at 87", in: *The Washington Post* (4 February 2011).

Sharp, Mitchell (1972): 'General Prerequisites for Canadian Participation in Peacekeeping Operations', quoted in: Sigler, John H. (Ed.): *International Peacekeeping in the Eighties: Global Outlook and Canadian Priorities* (Fall 1982) (Ottawa: Carleton University).

Shemesh, Moshe (1990): "Egypt: From Military Defeat to Political Victory", in Troen, Selwyn; Shemesh, Moshe (Eds.): *The Suez-Sinai Crisis 1956: Retrospective and Reappraisal* (London: Frank Cass): 150–161.

Sherry, George L. (1986): "The United Nations, International Conflict, and American Security", in: *Political Science Quarterly*, 101,5: 753–771.

Shipler, David K. (1979): "Israel Bars Rabin From Relating '48 Eviction of Arabs", in: *The New York Times* (23 October 1979).

Shlaim, Avi (2001): *The Iron Wall: Israel and the Arab World* (New York: Norton).

Shlaim, Avi (1995): *War and Peace in the Middle East: A Concise History* (New York: Penguin Books).

Shuckburgh, Evelyn (1986): *Descent to Suez: Foreign Office Diaries, 1951–56* (London: Weidenfeld & Nicolson).

Shuckburgh, Evelyn (1987): *Descent to Suez: Foreign Office Diaries 1951–1956* (London: Norton & Co.).

Sigler, John H. (Ed.) (1982): *International Peacekeeping in the Eighties: Global Outlook and Canadian Priorities* (Fall 1982) (Ottawa: Careleton University).

Simoni, Arnold (1995): "A United Nations Peace Force", in: Fawcett, Eric; Newcombe, Hanna (Eds.): *United Nations Reform: Looking Ahead After Fifty Years* (Toronto: Science for Peace Series, University of Toronto): 155–157.

Sinclair, Ian (1984): *The Vienna Convention on the Law of Treaties* (Manchester: Manchester University Press): 185–202.

Slonim, Shlomo (1987): "Origins of the Tripartite Declaration on the Middle East", in: *Middle Eastern Studies, 23,2: 135–149.

Smith, Adrian (2013): "Resignation of a First Sea Lord: Mountbatten and the 1956 Suez Crisis", in: *History*, 98,329: 105–134.

Smith, Alex Duval (2017): *Peacekeeping Problems in Mali*, BBC documentary (20 August 2017); at: https://www.bbc.com/news/world-africa-40973432.

Smith, Charles D. (2001): *Palestine and the Arab-Israeli Conflict* (Boston: Bedford/St. Martin's).

Smith, Courtney B. (2006): *Politics and Process at the United Nations: The Global Dance* (Boulder: Lynne Rienner).

Smith, Gary V. (Ed.) (1974): *Zionism: The Dream and the Reality* (London: David & Charles).

Smith, Simon C. (2010): "Anglo-American Relations and the End of Empire in the Far East and the Persian Gulf, 1948–1971", in: Petersen, Tore T. (Ed.): *Challenging Retrenchment: The United States, Great Britain and the Middle East, 1950–1980* (Trondheim, Norway: Tapir Academic Press).

Sohn, Louis B. (1958): "The Authority of the United Nations to Establish and Maintain a Permanent United Nations Force", in: *American Journal of International Law*, 52,2: 229–240.

Southerland, Daniel (1984): "Ex-Pilot Says US Jets Spied for Israel in '67", *The Christian Science Monitor* (15 March 1984).

Spiegel, Steven L. (1985): *The Other Arab-Israeli Conflict: Making America's Mideast Policy from Truman to Reagan* (Chicago: University of Chicago Press).

Spieker, Heike (2000): "Changing Peacekeeping in the New Millennium? The Recommendations of the Panel on United Nations Peace Operations of August 2000", in: *International Peacekeeping*, 6: 144–152.

Springhall, John (2001): *Decolonization Since 1945: The Collapse of European Overseas Empires* (New York: Palgrave).

Spruyt, Hendrik (1994): *The Sovereign State and Its Competitors: An Analysis of Systems Change* (Princeton: Princeton University Press).

Spruyt, Hendrik (2005): *Ending Empire: Contested Sovereignty and Territorial Partition* (Ithaca: Cornell University Press).

Stacy, Helen (2003): "Relational Sovereignty", in: *Stanford Law Review*, 55,5 (May): 2029–2059.

Stanford Encyclopedia of Philosophy (2009): "*Sovereignty: The Rise of the Sovereign State, Theory and Practice*".

Stanford Encyclopedia of Philosophy (2009): *The Social Contract – Book II, Chapter III* (Stanford: Stanford University).

Steger, Manfred B. (2000): "Mahatma Gandhi on Indian Self-rule: A Nonviolent Nationalism?", in: *Strategies: Journal of Theory, Culture and Politics*, 13,2: 247–263; at: https://www.tandfonline.com/doi/abs/10.1080/104021300750022634?journalCode=cstj20.

Stein, Janice G. (1985): "Detection and Defection: Security 'Regimes' and the Management of International Conflict", in: *International Journal*, 40,4 (Autumn): 599–627.

Stephens, Robert (1971): *Nasser: A Political Biography* (New York: Allen Lane).

Stevens, Barry (2013): *Sector Sarajevo*. Canadian documentary (10 November 2013); at: https://discovery.ucl.ac.uk/id/eprint/1426984/.

Stevenson, William (1957): "Norman Seen Victim of US Witch Hunters", in: *Toronto Daily Star* (4 April 1957).

Stewart, Desmond (1958): *Young Egypt* (London: Allan Wingate).

St. John, Robert (1960): *The Boss: The Story of Gamal Abdel Nasser* (New York: McGraw-Hill).

Stoessinger, John G. (1967): *The United Nations and the Superpowers* (New York: Random House).

Stoessinger, John G. (1967): "The Suez Crisis and the United Nations Emergency Force", in: *The United Nations and the Superpowers* (New York: Random House): 61–75.

Stone-Lee, Ollie (2006): "Eden: A Man Under Strain", on: BBC News Website (21 July 2006); at: http://news.bbc.co.uk/2/hi/uk_news/politics/5193202.stm, US Liberty also available: https://www.rallypoint.com/deployments/israel/shared-links/uss-liberty-dead-in-the-water-bbc-documentary-2002-4?loc=similar_main&pos=4&type=qrc.

Suez Canal Authority (1956): The Suez Canal Company – Nationalization Law, Government of Egypt, Decree Law No. 285 (July 1956).

Suter, Keith (1991): "The United Nations and Non-Governmental Organizations", in: Barnaby, Frank (Ed.): *Building a More Democratic United Nations* (New York: Routledge).

Swedenburg, Ted (2003): *Memoris of Revolt: The 1936–1939 Rebellion and the Palestinian National Past* (Fayetteville: University of Arkansaa Press).

Swedish Ambassador Letter (1956): *Official Position addressed to the UN Secretary-General*, (A/3302, Ann 7): 23. (5 November 1956).

Swettenham, J.A. (R.C.E), Capt. (1958/1959): "*Some Impressions of the UNEF, 1957 to 1958*", Report No. 78, Appendix A, Historical Section (G.S.), Canadian Army Headquarters, Ottawa (signed on 17 December 1958; compiled on 2 January 1959).

Tal, David (Ed.) (2001): *The 1956 War: Collusion and Rivalry in the Middle East* (London: Frank Cass).

Tardy, Thierry (2011): "A Critique of Robust Peacekeeping in Contemporary Peace Operations", in: *International Peacekeeping*, 18,2: 152–167.

Taylor, Alastair M. (1983): "Peacekeeping: A Component of World Order", in: Wiseman, Henry (Ed.): *Peacekeeping: Appraisals & Proposals* (New York: Pergamon Press).

Taylor, John (1920): quoted in Dickson, Edwin D., *The Equality of States in International Law* (Cambridge: Harvard University Press).

Taylor, Hannis (1901): *A Treatise on International Public Law* (Chicago: Callaghan & Co.).

The Economist (2016): "The New Nationalism", in *The Economist* (17 November 2016).

Teveth, Shabtai (1989): "The Evolution of "Transfer", in *Zionist Thinking* (Tel Aviv: Tel Aviv University).

Teveth, Shabtai (1996): *Ben-Gurion's Spy: The Story of the Political Scandal that Shaped Modern Israel* (New York: Columbia University Press).

Thakur, Ramesh C. (2006): *The United Nations, Peace, and Security: From Collective Security to the Responsibility to Protect* (Cambridge: Cambridge University Press).

Thakur, Ramesh; Schnabel, Albrecht (Eds.) (2001): *United Nations Peacekeeping Operations: Ad Hoc Missions, Permanent Engagement* (Tokyo: United Nations University Press).

Thant, U. (1963): *United Nations Use of Peacekeeping Forces in the Middle East, the Congo, and Cyprus*. Address to the Harvard Alumni Association, Boston (13 June 1963).

Thant, U. (1964): *Note by the UN Secretary-General*, S/5653 (11 April 1964).

Thant, U. (1967): Reports of the UN Secretary-General on the 1967 Middle East Crisis:

(1) *Report of the UN Secretary-General to the General Assembly on the Situation in the Middle East*, A/6669 (18 May 1967).

(2) *Report of the UN Secretary-General to the Security Council on the Situation in the Middle East*, S/7896 (19 May 1967).

(3) *Report of the UN Secretary-General on the Situation in the Middle East to the Security Council*, S/7906 (26 May 1967).

(4) *Reports of the UN Secretary-General to the General Assembly and the Security Council*, A/6730 and Add. 1–3, on 17 and 18 May (26 June 1967).

(5) *Report of the UN Secretary-General to the General Assembly on the Situation in the Middle East*, A/6672 (12 July 1967).

Thant, U. (1967): *Statement of Secretary-General U Thant on the Hammarskjold Aide-Memoire*. POI (19 June 1967).

Thant, U. (1967): *Statement by Secretary-General U Thant, supra note 38*, A/PV 1527 at 5 (1967).

Thant, U. (1967): "UN Secretary-General Takes Issue with Eban on Withdrawal of UNEF", in: *The Jewish Telegraphic Agency* (21 June 1967).

Thant, U. (1967): "The Withdrawal of the United Nations Emergency Force (UNEF)", in: *UN Monthly Chronicle* (OPI/275-17584), IV, 7 (July 1967).

Thant, U. (1978): *View from the UN: The Memoirs of U Thant* (New York: Doubleday).

The Washington Institute for Near East Policy (1986): *Policy Focus* (September).

Theobald, Andrew G. (2014): "The United Nations Truce Supervision Organization (UNTSO)", in: *The Oxford Handbook of United Nations Peacekeeping Operations*.

Thomas, Hugh (1967): *Suez* (London: Weidenfeld & Nicolson).

Thomas, Hugh (1986): *The Suez Affair* (Littlehampton Book Service).

Thomson, Janice E. (1995): "State Sovereignty in International Relations: Bridging the Gap Between Theory and Empirical Research", in: *International Studies Quarterly*, 39,2: 213–233.

Thornhill, Michael (2002): "Resistance at all Costs", in: *Al-Ahram Weekly* (25 January 2002).

Thornhill, Michael T. (2000): "Alternatives to Nasser: Humphrey Trevelyan, Ambassador to Egypt", in: Kelly, Saul; Gorst, Anthony (Eds.): *Whitehall and the Suez Crisis* (London: Frank Cass): 11–28.

Thornhill, Michael T. (2006): *Road to Suez: The Battle of the Canal Zone* (London: Sutton).

Thorpe, D.R. (2004): *Eden: The Life and Times of Anthony Eden First Earl of Avon, 1897–1977* (London: Pimlico).

Tignor, Robert L. (1998): *Capitalism and Nationalism at the End of Empire: State and Business in Decolonizing Egypt, Nigeria, and Kenya, 1945–1962* (Princeton: Princeton University Press).

Tolly, Jr., Howard (1987): *The UN Commission on Human Rights* (Boulder: Westview Press).

Troen, Selwyn; Shemesh, Moshe (Eds.) (1989): *The Suez-Sinai Crisis 1956: Retrospective and Reappraisal* (London: Frank Cass).

Tsiddon-Chatto, Yoash (1995): *By Day, By Night, Through Haze and Fog* (Tel Aviv: Ma'ariv Books).

Tucker, Michael (1980): *Canadian Foreign Policy: Contemporary Issues and Themes* (Toronto: McGraw-Hill).

Tully, J. (Ed.), transl. M. Silverthorne (1991/2000); *On the Duty of Man and Citizen According to Natural Law* (Cambridge: Cambridge University Press).

Turner, Barry (2006): *Suez 1956: The Inside Story of the First Oil War* (London: Hodder & Stoughton).

Tvedt, Terje (2004): *The River Nile in the Age of the British: Political Ecology and the Quest for Economic Power* (London: Tauris).

Tyler, Patrick (2012): *Fortress Israel: The Inside Story of the Military Elite Who Run the Country – and Why They Can't Make Peace* (New York: Farrar, Straus and Girouz).

Tziarras, Zenonas (2012): "Liberal Peace and Peace-Building: Another Critique", in: *The Globalized World Post* (2 June 2012).

University of British Columbia, Rare Books and Special Collections (BC2-124-145, January 1957).

University of British Columbia, Rare Books and Special Collections (BC2-124-246, September 1956).

UK Foreign Office (1955): *Detailed Alpha Plan* (371/115866) (February 1955).

UK Parliament (1954): "Suez Canal Base (Anglo-Egyptian Agreement)", House of Commons debate (28 July 1954), in: *Hansard*, vol. 531, cc. 495-7; at: https://api.parliament.uk/historic-hansard/commons/1954/jul/28/suez-canal-zone-base-anglo-egyptian-1.

UK Parliament (1954): Agreement Between the Government of the United Kingdom and Northern Island and the Egyptian Government Regarding the Suez Canal Case, Cmd. 9298 (19 October 1954).

UK Public Record Office (1956): *Conclusions: Cabinet Minutes* (19th), 128/30 (6 March 1956).

UNDPKO/DFS (2011): *The Contribution of United Nations Peacekeeping to Early Peacebuilding*; at: http://www.operationspaix.net/Data/Document/6797 ~ v ~ The_Contribution_of_United_Nations_Peacekeeping_to_Early_Peacebuilding___a_DPKO_DFS_Strategy_for_Peacekeepers. pdf.

UNDPKO/IPA (2002): "Challenges in Peacekeeping: Past, Present and Future". Report of joint UNDKPO and IPA seminar, 29 October 2002 (New York: UNDPKO/IPA).

United Nations: Middle East–UNEF I (Background): Summary of the 1956 Crisis.

United Nations (1945): *Charter of the United Nations and Statute of the International Court Of Justice* (New York: UN Office of Public Information – 1967).

United Nations (1945): *United Nations Charter, Article 2, 33, and 36* (San Francisco & New York: UN Office of Public Information).

United Nations (1945): *UN Conference on International Organizations (UNICO)*, Vol. 6. (San Francisco: April-June 1945).

United Nations (1961): *Exchange of Letters between the UN and the Government of the UAR*, UN Treaty Series No. 5575 (13 February 1961).

United Nations (1967): *The Arab-Israeli Armistice Agreements: February–July 1949, Texts and Annexes* (Beirut: Institute for Palestine Studies).

United Nations (1970): *Rules of Procedure of the General Assembly*, A/520/Rev.10 (New York: United Nations Publications).

United Nations (1987): *Basic Facts about the United Nations* (New York: UN Department of Public Information).

United Nations (2005): *The Humanitarian Impact of the West Bank Barrier on Palestinian Communities*. (New York: Office for Coordination of Humanitarian Affairs, OCHA) (5 March 2005).

United Nations (2008): *United Nations Peacekeeping Operations: Principles and Guidelines* (The Capstone Doctrine) (New York: UN Department of Peacekeeping Operations).

UN-Egypt (1959): *"Report on the Meeting between UN and Egyptian Officials"* (Classified & Unpublished) Cairo, Egypt (6 January 1959).

United Nations General Assembly (1956): *First Emergency Session*, Plenary Meeting 561, 562, 565, Item 5 (1, 2 & 4 November 1956).

United Nations General Assembly Resolutions on the Suez Crisis and UNEF:

    UN General Assembly Resolution 997 (ES-I), (1 November 1956)

    UN General Assembly Resolution 998 (ES-I), (4 November 1956)

    UN General Assembly Resolution 999 (ES-I), (4 November 1956)

    UN General Assembly Resolution 1000 (ES-I), (5 November 1956)

    UN Resolution General Assembly 1001 (ES-I), (7 November 1956)

    UN General Assembly Resolution 1002 (ES-I), (7 November 1956)

    UN General Assembly Resolution 1003 (ES-I), (10 November 1956)

    UN General Assembly Resolution 1121 (ES-I), (24 November 1956)

    UN General Assembly Resolution 1122 (ES-I), 26 November 1956

    UN General Assembly Resolution 1124 (ES-I), (2 February 1957)

    UN General Assembly Resolution 1125 (ES-I), (2 February 1957)

    UN General Assembly Resolution 1126 (XI), (22 February 1957).

UN General Assembly (1956): 1: *The Report: The Secretary-General on the basic points for the presence and functioning in Egypt of the United Nations Emergence Force*; 2: *The Annex: The Good Faith Agreement Aide-Memoire*, A/3375 (20 November 1956).

UN General Assembly (1956): *Approval of The Good Faith Agreement*, Resolution 1121 (XI), (24 November 1956).

UN General Assembly (1957): *UN Demand for Israeli Withdrawal and Observance of the Armistice Agreement*, A/1125 (XI) (2 February 1957).

UN General Assembly (1957): *Report of the Secretary-General on Arrangements Concerning the United Nations Emergency Force*, A/3526 (8 February 1957).

UN General Assembly (1957): *Approval of the Report (A/3526) of the Secretary-General on the Status of the Emergency Force*, A/1126 (XI) (22 February 1957).

United Nations Juridical Yearbook (1964): A/AC. 119/SR. 30, 7 (2 October 1964).

United Nations/International Peace Academy (2002): Seminar Report: *Challenges in Peacekeeping: Past, Present and Future* (New York: United Nations/International Peace Academy).

United Nations Office of Public Information (1967): "The Withdrawal of the United Nations Emergency Force (UNEF): Report of the Secretary-General", in: *UN Monthly Chronicle*, IV, 7 (July 1967).

United Nations Resolution (1949): *Essentials of Peace*, A/290, IV (1 December 1949).

United Nations Resolution (1950): *Uniting for Peace*, A/377, V (3 November 1950).

UN Security Council Resolution (1951): *Freedom of Passage in the Suez Canal*, S/RES/2322 (1 Sept 1951).

UN Security Council Resolution (1956): *The Suez Question*, S/RES/118/3675 (13 October 1956).

UN Security Council (1956): *US Vetoed Draft Resolution (The Immediate Cessation of the Military Action of Israel in Egypt)*, S/3710 (30 October 1956).

UN Security Council Resolution (1973): Arab-Israeli War, S/RES/ 340 (25 October 1973).

UN Security Council Resolution (1973): Arab-Israeli War, S/RES/ 339 (23 October 1973).

UN Security Council Resolution (1973): Arab-Israeli War, S/RES/ 338 (22 October 1973).
UN Security Council Resolution (1967): Arab-Israeli War, S/RES/242 (22 November 1967).
United States National Security Council Report (1948): "Removal and Demolition of Oil
    Facilities, Equipment and Supplies in the Middle East", NSC **26/1**, Top Secret (Washington: 19
    August 1948).
United States National Security Council Report (1948): "Removal and Demolition of Oil
    Facilities, Equipment and Supplies in the Middle East", NSC **26/2**, Top Secret (Washington: 30
    December 1948).
United States Congress (1973): *United Nations Peacekeeping in the Middle East*. Hearing before
    the House of Representatives Subcommittee on International Organizations and Movements,
    and the Subcommittee on the Near East and South Asia, December 1973 (Washington DC: US
    Congress).
United States Department of State (1954): US National Security Council – Middle East Policy
    Paper No. 5428 (23 July 1954).
United States Department of State (1981): "Israel-United States: Memorandum of Understanding
    on Strategic Cooperation", in: *International Legal Materials, Cambridge University*, 20,6
    (November): 1,420–1,423; at: https://www.jstor.org/stable/20692373?seq=1.
United States Senate (1993): *Reform of United Nations Peacekeeping Operations: A Mandate for
    Change*. Report to the Senate Committee on Foreign Relations (Washington DC: US
    Congress).
Urquhart, Brian (1963): "United Nations Peace Forces and the Changing United Nations: An
    Institutional Perspective", in: *International Organization*, 17,2 (Spring): 338–354.
Urquhart, Brian (1989): *Decolonization and World Peace* (Houston: University of Texas Press).
Urquhart, Brian (1972): *Hammarskjold* (New York: Alfred Knopf).
Urquhart, Brian (1984): *United Nations Oral History*. Interviewed by Leon Gordenker (15 October
    1984).
Urquhart, Brian (1987): "International Leadership: The Legacy of Dag Hammarskjold", in:
    Development Dialogue, 1: 6–16. Originally delivered in Uppsala, Sweden, 18 September 1986,
    sponsored by the Dag Hammarskjold Foundation.
Urquhart, Brian (1987): *A Life in Peace and War* (New York: Harper Collins).
Urquhart, Brian (1990): "Peacemaking, Peacekeeping and the Future", John W. Holmes Memorial
    Lecture (Toronto: Éditions du GREF).
Urquhart, Brian (1991): *Hammarskjold: The Diplomacy of Crisis* (New York: Knopf).
Urquhart, Brian (1992): "Forward", in: Liu, F.T. (Ed.): *United Nations Peacekeeping and the
    Non-Use of Force* (Boulder: Lynne Rienner).
Urquhart, Brian (1993): "For a UN Volunteer Military Force", in: *New York Review of Books* (10
    June 1993).
Urquhart, Brian (1994): "The UN and International Security After the Cold War", in: Roberts, A.;
    Kingsbury, B. (Eds.): *United Nations, Divided World: The UN Role in International Relations*
    (New York: Clarendon Press).
Urquhart, Brian (2000): *Between Sovereignty and Globalization: Where Does the United Nations
    Fit In?* The Second Dag Hammarskjold Lecture (Uppsala: Dag Hammarskjold Foundation).
Van Mill, David (2002): "Civil Liberty in Hobbes's Commonwealth", in: *Australian Journal of
    Political Science*, 37,1: 21–38.
Van Vollenhoven, C. (Ed.) (1915): *War Obviated: By an International Police* (The Hague:
    Martinus Nijhof): 145–157.
Varble, Derek (2003): *The Suez Crisis 1956* (London: Osprey).
Vatikiotis, P.J. (1971): *Conflict in the Middle East* (London: George Allen & Unwin Ltd.).
Verrier, Anthony (1981): *International Peacekeeping: United Nations Forces in a Troubled World*
    (New York: Penguin).
Vienna Pilot Program (1971): *Consent, Good Offices and the Future of Peacekeeping* (New York:
    International Peace Academy).

Vieira, Mauricio (2016): "Sierra Leone: Promoting Peace or Prolonging Violence? The Duality of the UN Peacekeeping", in: *Conflict Studies Quarterly*, 16 (July 2016).

Vokes, Christopher (1958): *My Story* (Toronto: Gallery Publishing).

Vries, Peer, (2009): "Editorial: Global History", in: *Osterreiichische Zeitschrift fur Geschictswissenschaten*, 2.

Waines, David (1977): *A Sentence in Exile: The Palestine/Israeli Conflict, 1897–1977* (Wilmett, IL. : The Medina Press).

Waldheim, Kurt (1973): *Report of the UN Secretary-General on UNEF II*, S/11052/Rev.1 (27 October 1973).

Walker, H.B. (1996): "The United Nations: Peacekeeping and the Middle East", *Asian Affairs*, 27,1 (March): 13–19.

Walker, Robert B.J. (1998): "Both Globalization and Sovereignty: Reimagining the Political". Lecture delivered at the Universities of Wales, Oslo, and Western Washington; policy brief at the Centre for Global Studies, University of Victoria, Canada.

Wallerstein, Immanuel (Ed.) (1975): *World Inequality: Origins and Perspectives on the World System* (Montreal: Black Rose Books): 129–138.

Walzer, Michael (1977): *Just and Unjust Wars: A Moral Argument with Historical Illustrations*, 2nd Edition (New York: Basic Books).

Walzer, Michael (2002): "Arguing for Humanitarian Intervention", in: Mills, Nicolaus; Brunner, Kira (Eds.): *The New Killing Fields: Massacre and the Politics of Intervention* (New York: Basic Books): 19–35.

Weber, Max (1948): "The Nation", cited in: Gerth, H.; Mills, W. (Eds.) (1991): *From Max Weber: Essays in Sociology* (Oxford: Routledge).

Wehberg, Hans (1935): *The Theory and Practice of International Policing* (London: Constable & Co).

Weiss, Thomas G.; Thakur, Ramesh (2010): *Global Governance and the UN: An Unfinished Journey* (Indiana: Indiana University Press).

Weiss, Thomas George (Ed.) (1993): *Collective Security in a Changing World* (Boulder: Lynne Rienner).

Weiss, Thomas George (1995): *The United Nations and Civil Wars* (Boulder: Lynne Rienner).

Westlake, John (1910): *International Law*, I (Cambridge: Cambridge University Press).

Wheeler, Nicholas J. (2000): *Saving Strangers: Humanitarian Intervention in International Society* (New York: Oxford University Press).

Wheeler, Nicholas J. (2001): "Humanitarian Intervention after Kosovo", in: *International Affairs*, 77,1: 113–128.

White, Michael (2006): "How Suez Debacle Proved the Tipping Point in Final Retreat From Empire", in: *The Guardian* (12 July); at: https://www.theguardian.com/uk/2006/jul/12/egypt.past.

White, Nigel D. (1996): "The UN Charter and Peacekeeping Forces: Constitutional Issues", in: *International Peacekeeping*, 3,4 (Winter): 43–63.

Whitton, D. (1954): "Anglo-Egyptian Relations", in: *Australian Outlook*, 8,4: 213–224.

Wilford, Hugh (2013): *America's Great Game: The CIA's Secret Arabists and the Shaping of the Modern Middle East* (New York: Basic Books).

Wills, Siobhan (2006): "The Responsibility to Protect by Peace Support Forces under International Human Rights Law", in: *International Peacekeeping*, 13,4 (December): 477–488.

Wilson, Woodrow (1918): "Fourteen Points Declaration (War Aims and Peace Terms)". Address to the US Congress, Washington DC (8 January 1918).

Wippman, David (1996): "Military Intervention, Regional Organizations, and Host-State Consent", in: *Duke Journal of Comparative and International Law*, 7: 209–239.

Wiseman, Henry (Ed.) (1983): *Peace-Keeping: Appraisals and Proposals* (New York: Pergamon Press).

Wiseman, Henry (1974): "UNEF II: New Chance to Set Firm Peacekeeping Guidelines", in: *International Perspectives* (March/April).

Wiseman, Henry (1995): "Commentary: Peace and Security", in: Fawcett, Eric; Newcombe, Hanna (Eds.): *United Nations Reform: Looking Ahead After Fifty Years* (Toronto: Science for Peace Series, University of Toronto): 110–111.

Wolf, Robert Paul (1970): *In Defence of Anarchism* (New York: Harper Row).

Woodhouse, Tom; Ramsbotham, Oliver (2006): *Peacekeeping and Conflict Resolution* (London: Frank Cass Publishers).

World Court (1927): *S.S. Lotus Case* (Fr. V. Turk.). Permanent Court of International Justice, Ser. A. No. 10 (7 September 1927).

Wright, Harrison M. (Ed.) (1976): *The New Imperialism: Analysis of Late-Nineteenth-Century Expansion* (Toronto: Heath).

Wright, Lawrence (2014): *Thirteen Days in September: Carter, Begin and Sadat at Camp David* (New York: Alfred A. Knopf).

Yost, Charles W. (1968): "The Arab-Israeli War: How It began", in: *Foreign Affairs*, 46.

Young, Robert J.C. (2001): *Post-Colonialism: An Historical Introduction* (Oxford: Blackwell Publishing).

Zartman, I. William; Rasmussen, J. Lewis (Eds.) (1997): *Peacemaking in International Conflict: Methods and Techniques* (Washington DC: United States Institute of Peace Press).

Zeidan, Abdel-Latif M. (1976): *The United Nations Emergency Force, 1956–1967* (Stockholm: Almqvist and Wiksell International).

Zelikow, Philip; May, Ernest R. (2018): *Suez Deconstructed: An Interactive Study in Crisis, War, and Peacemaking* (Washington DC: The Brookings Institution).

Zisser, Eyal (2002): "June 1967: Israel's Capture of the Golan Heights", in: *Israel Studies*, 7,1: 168–194.

About the Author

Dr. Hanny Hilmy completed his undergraduate work in Cairo, Egypt. He obtained a Master's degree in International Relations at the University of Pennsylvania in the USA, and a Master's Degree in Economics at the University of Ottawa, Canada. His Interdisciplinary Ph.D. degree in History, Political Science, and International Law was completed at the University of Victoria in Canada.

Dr. Hilmy worked for the Egyptian Government and for the League of Arab States at home and abroad, where he was a senior advisor on political and legal matters. He attended many sessions of the UN General Assembly in New York. He worked as a Visiting Research Fellow at the International Peace Research Institute in Oslo, Norway, and the School of International Studies, New Delhi, India. Later he became an Associate Fellow at the International Peace Academy in New York, USA, and participated in the Academy's Conference in Helsinki, Finland. Dr. Hilmy was a member of the United Nations Association in Canada, and the Society for International Development in Rome, Italy. He has taught courses on the Arab-Israeli Conflict, Political Islam, Nationalism, International Relations, Conflict Resolution, Peacekeeping, and International Law. He has attended numerous national and international conferences and seminars in Canada and abroad. His research interests include Decolonization, Democratic Governance, Foreign Aid, and Frontier Development. Currently, Dr. Hilmy is an Associate Fellow at the Centre for Global Studies, and Coordinator of the Middle East Discussion Group, both at the University of Victoria in Canada. Dr. Hilmy has extensive experience of research, teaching, consulting, government, publishing, and giving public lectures. His interdisciplinary approach and his wide-ranging research have produced many contributions in a variety of fields:

© Springer Nature Switzerland AG 2020
H. Hilmy, *Decolonization, Sovereignty, and Peacekeeping*,
https://doi.org/10.1007/978-3-030-57624-0

- "Repartition of Palestine: Toward a Peaceful Solution in the Middle East", in: *Journal of Peace Research* (Oslo, Norway)
- "Sovereignty, Peacekeeping, and the United Nations Emergency Force (UNEF), Suez 1956–67: Insiders' Perspectives" (Ph.D. thesis, University of Victoria)
- A Proposal for a Permanent International Peace Force. International Peace Academy Seminar (Helsinki, Finland)
- International Peacekeeping and Conflict Resolution (University of Victoria)
- Theoretical Foundations of the International Balance of Power (University of Pennsylvania)
- Intellectual Roots of Islamic Fundamentalism & Political Thought
- The Muslim Brothers and the Trials of Political Islam
- Political Islam: Democracy vs. Theocracy
- The Erosion of Secular Values in the Muslim World
- Tango with a Tiger: Flirting with Islamic Radicalism (University of Victoria)
- Arab Nationalism & Islamic Fundamentalism: The Radical Transformation
- A Review of Communist Ideology in the Arab East
- Soviet Policy in the Middle East in the 1960s
- The Arab Spring and the Binary Division Between Islamists and Liberals
- The Arab Spring: Opportunity or a Mirage?
- Egypt's Military and the Political Process: A Saviour or a Curse?
- Nationalism: A Manifest Destiny or a Murderous Dogma?
- Conference of the Canadian Professors for Peace, University of Toronto
- Canada's International Development Aid: CIDA's Role in the Policy-Making Process
- The Political Economy of Frontier Expansion in the Brazilian Amazon
- Land Settlement and Growth Centres in New Developing Regions
- Frontier Expansion in Peripheral Regional Planning
- The Origins and Development of Arab Nationalism
- The Role of the Military in Middle Eastern Governance
- Canadian-Arab Relations Conference. University of Calgary
- Colonial Nationalism and the End of Empire. University of Victoria
- The Arab-Israeli Conflict and the Rights of the Palestinian People
- Rapporteur, North-South Rountable Conference, S.I.D., Department of External Affairs. Ottawa
- Recycling of Oil Revenue Surpluses & International Resource Transfers
- Arab League Position Paper to the External Affairs Committee, Parliament of Canada
- The Intellectual and Ideological Schools within the Egyptian Nationalist Movement
- Planning and Distribution in India's Development
- The Multinational Corporations and the Third World (University of Ottawa)
- Foreign Aid: Economic and Moral Dependency? (Carleton University)
- American Foreign Policy during the Suez War, (University of Pennsylvania)
- Muslims in the West: The Difficult Legal & Cultural Consequences
- Foreign Refugees and Migrants: Integration, Diversity, and Political Correctness

- The Need for Electoral Reforms in Canada
- The Canadian Charter should protect Canadians Against Criminal Cultural Practices
- Conference on The Muslim World and the West (University of Victoria)
- The Role of Parliament in the Foreign Policy formulation in Canada
- Israeli-Palestinian Peace: Illusion or Delusion? (University of Victoria)
- Visiting Research Fellow: International Peace Research Institute (PRIO), Oslo, Norway (Summer 1971);
- Associate Fellow, Centre for Global Studies, University of Victoria, British Columbia, Canada;
- Coordinator, Middle East Discussion Group, University of Victoria, Canada.

Hanny Hilmy was born in Cairo, Egypt. He is married to Marjukka Hilmy (née Välimaa), born in Helsinki, Finland. He is the father of Nadine and Nora, both born in Ottawa, Canada. Currently, he lives with his wife in Victoria, British Columbia in Canada.

Address: Dr. Hanny Hilmy, Centre for Global Studies, University of Victoria, PO Box 1700 STN CSC, Victoria, British Columbia (BC), V8W 2Y2, Canada. *Email*: hilmyh@uvic.ca.

Index

© Springer Nature Switzerland AG 2020
H. Hilmy, *Decolonization, Sovereignty, and Peacekeeping*,
https://doi.org/10.1007/978-3-030-57624-0